Great Issues of International Politics

Great Issues of

The
International
System and
National
Policy

International Politics

Edited
by
Morton A. Kaplan   *The University of Chicago*

Aldine Publishing Company   *Chicago*

D
843
.K337

First published 1970 by
Aldine Publishing Company
529 South Wabash Avenue
Chicago, Illinois 60605
Second Printing 1970

Library of Congress Catalog Card Number 70–113084
SBN *202-24022*
Printed in the United States of America

88775

ACKNOWLEDGMENTS

"International Law and the International System" by Morton A. Kaplan is reprinted from "Constitutional Structures and Processes in the International Arena." From *The Future of the International Legal Order*, Vol. 1, *Trends and Patterns*, eds. Cyril E. Black and Richard A. Falk, Center of International Studies, Princeton University (Copyright © 1969 by Princeton University Press), pp. 155–182. Reprinted by permission.

"The Beirut Raid and the International Law of Retaliation" by Richard A. Falk is reproduced by permission of the author and the American Society of International Law from *American Journal of International Law*, 63:415–443, 1969. Copyright © 1969 by the American Society of International Law.

"Sisyphus and the Avalanche: The United Nations, Egypt, and Hungary" by Stanley Hoffmann is reprinted by permission of the author and the publisher from *International Organization*, 10(3):446–469, Summer 1957.

Excerpts from "Obstinate or Obsolete? The Fate of the Nation-State and the Case of Western Europe" by Stanley Hoffmann are reprinted by permission of the author and the publisher from *Daedalus*, Journal of the American Academy of Arts and Sciences (Boston, Massachusetts), 95(3), Summer 1966.

"NATO in the International System of the 1970s" by Morton A. Kaplan is reprinted by permission from *ORBIS*, Spring 1969. Copyright by the Trustees of the University of Pennsylvania.

"Preventing Nuclear Proliferation through the Legal Control of China's Bomb" by Seymour C. Yuter is reprinted by permission of the author and the publisher from *ORBIS*, Winter 1969, pp. 1018–1041. Copyright by the Trustees of the University of Pennsylvania.

Contributors

Sanford Aranoff is a physicist and staff member, Hudson Institute.

Edward S. Boylan is Associate Professor of Mathematics, Rutgers University, and consultant to the Hudson Institute.

McGeorge Bundy, president of the Ford Foundation, was formerly dean of Harvard University and an assistant to Presidents Kennedy and Johnson on national security policy.

Frank Church is a U.S. Senator from Idaho and a member of the Senate Foreign Relations Committee.

Alan Dowty is an instructor at Hebrew University.

Richard Falk is Milbank Professor of International Law, Princeton University.

J. William Fulbright is a U.S. Senator from Arkansas and chairman of the Senate Foreign Relations Committee.

Charles M. Herzfeld, a physicist, is technical director of the Defense Space Group of IT&T and former director of the Advanced Research Projects Agency of the Department of Defense.

Stanley Hoffmann is professor of government, Harvard University.

Morton A. Kaplan is professor of political science, The University of Chicago.

William R. Kintner is director of the Foreign Policy Research Institute, University of Pennsylvania.

Henry A. Kissinger is professor of government, Harvard University, and President Nixon's assistant for national security policy.

Hedrick Smith is a leading writer for *The New York Times*.

Albert Wohlstetter is University Professor, The University of Chicago, and a former member of the Rand Corporation and consultant to the Department of Defense.

Herbert F. York, a physicist, is Provost of the University of California at Los Angeles and former director of Defense Research and Engineering of the Department of Defense.

Seymour C. Yuter is a well-known patent lawyer and a writer on international law.

Contents

Preface

THERE ARE a number of good textbooks in the areas of international politics and foreign policy. Unfortunately, these textbooks usually fail to perform one very important function from a teaching standpoint. They do not make the subject matter of either international politics or foreign policy relevant to policy questions in ways that a student can comprehend or that stimulate him to think about policy questions or relate them to the broader international framework within which state behavior manifests itself.

The demands by students for relevance can be misleading if they are yielded to in ways that deter him from the academic understanding of the subject of international relations and foreign policy. However, unless the academics of international politics can be brought to life for the student—something that can be accomplished by policy questions—failure of interest will lead to mechanical memorization or to an insistence on a puerile kind of relevance that impedes rather than facilitates understanding of international system constraints on state action.

This book of readings is divided into three sections: great issues of international order, great issues of foreign policy, and great issues of military policy. The section on international order is an attempt to delineate the character of the international system within which state policy is determined. The selections adopted for this book, unlike most texts, relate this important subject matter to policy considerations. They are meant to bridge the gap between theory and practice. For the most part they do so in styles that are lively and entertaining and without any impairment—indeed with a heightening—of academic relevance. As in the other sections, the principle of selection has not been comprehensiveness but incisiveness. If we can influence the student to think seriously about a few of the great issues, we will have trained him in how to pursue the other issues on his own. It is important not to appear to present an entirely closed system that overwhelms with the completeness of its systematic conclusions and leads the student, impressionistically perhaps, to believe he cannot make any contribution of his own. A proper selection of readings will stimulate the student to ask for more; it will not satiate him and lead him to believe that the last word has been said.

The issues raised in the section on international order are among the most important of the entire book, and they are highly controversial. Yet the introduction is shorter than in the other two sections because I deal directly with these controversies in my own article.

The subject matters of the other two sections—foreign policy and military policy—need little comment here. With these sections, we have moved from direct concern with the character of the international system or of regional organizations within it to the "gut" issues of national policy.

The selections in this reader focus attention on the adversary issues of international relations. This emphasis is not intended to slight the importance of issues dealing with population growth, economic and political development, or the control of technology. However, the adversary issues and the aspects of international order related to them constitute the "gut" issues of international politics. Unless these issues can be controlled in ways permitting the growth of a more durable international order, then the other issues that pit man against nature or the developed nations against the underdeveloped—a subject touched upon in several of the essays of the first part of the book—are unlikely to be resolved in a manner consistent with reasonable values.

Although many of the articles are obviously timely, an effort has been made to select issues that have a recurrent focus. Thus, although one hopes that American involvement in Viet Nam will be resolved shortly, the issues raised include problems of bargaining with Communists, of coalition government involving Communists, of fighting counter-guerrilla wars, of fighting limited wars for limited objectives. We tend, for instance, to forget that in 1952 the Korean War was almost as unpopular as the Vietnamese War is today, although the froth of extreme protest was absent, and that the Eisenhower administration decided against intervention in Viet Nam in 1954 only after General Ridgeway said that ground troops would be required. The details of American overextension are different in the 1960's from those of the 1950's, and the 1970's will pose still new problems. Still the problem of the overextension of American resources remains central. These issues are discussed both in general and in specific in several of the readings.

Two selections on the Middle East are in the part of the book dealing with international order. Although they deal with the 1956 Suez crisis and with the Israeli reprisal against Lebanon in 1969, they raise the recurrent issues significant to that unhappy area of the world and the problems of international order associated with them. The Dowty article in the subsequent section of the book considers this area of the world from the standpoint of American interests. The arms race is also a recurrent issue. The part of the book dealing with military policy is focussed on the specific features of the ballistic missile debate and projected features of the arms race through the 1970's. It is this concentration on recurrent problems that I hope will permit the teacher to use the reader to train students to think analytically about and to raise the most important and useful questions concerning the central issues of politics in international life.

I have not made an effort to be neutral in the introductions. The articles in this book explore the great issues and I take a stand on them and indicate that stand in my critique of the articles in the section introductions. Yet, if I have not attempted to be neutral, I have attempted to be fair in the light of my opinions.

MORTON A. KAPLAN

Great Issues of International Politics

PART ONE
Great Issues in International Order

Introduction

THE FIRST THREE PIECES in this section on great issues in international order pose important questions concerning the extent to which justice, order, and law can be reconciled. They raise the issue of whether justice means the same thing for small states and for large states and even to what extent justice and law are desirable. Even if the United Nations' action in the Suez crisis of 1956 was distinctly limited, it is possible to compare its control over that situation with its approach to the border clash in 1962 between China and India, the Russian invasions of Hungary in 1956 and of Czechoslovakia in 1968, the Cuban missile crisis, and the American intervention in the Dominican Republic. It is because the questions are genuinely difficult that the easy answers often provided by advocates of world order cannot provide control or moderation to events.

In the first article, which is on international law and the international system, I relate the normative framework of international law to the general political structure to which it is adapted and at the same time distinguish the kinds of hard choices states must make between national security, international order, and international law. In the article on the Beirut raid Richard Falk presents a much more detailed analysis of the kinds of choices facing states when they must engage in self-help and the relationship of such choices to a normative legal structure. He attempts to set forth criteria that permit reasoned criticism of state action, to indicate the conditions under which law-observing behavior cannot be expected, to indicate the criteria to which norms must conform in cases of retaliation if they aspire to govern behavior, and to show the limitations of the United Nations' organs as law-proposing and law-imposing organizations.

The first article by Stanley Hoffmann is an investigation of the 1956 Suez crisis within the framework of the United Nations' peacekeeping activities. He examines the conditions under which order can be imposed by an international organization. He shows the limitations as well as the capabilities of the organization as a peace-keeping organization.

The nation state as a tenacious survival in the modern world and the role of General de Gaulle in retarding European unity are the subjects of the following article. Hoffmann shows that despite the immense personal power of the general, he used resistances that were inherent within the present European system. Yet, the European idea has shown enormous resilience despite the wrecking activities of the general.

It is difficult to say whether the delays imposed by de Gaulle and the waning of the enthusiasm of European youth will have caused important impediments to the future of a united Europe. Two things seem certain: the roles of France as leader of a united Europe and of Paris as its capital have been gravely damaged by the activities of the general and his attempts at *grandeur* have ultimately failed. The Russian invasion of Czechoslovakia revealed the impotence of French military resources. The collapse of the franc revealed basic weaknesses in the French economy. To anyone but General de Gaulle it might have been almost self-evident that Europe could play an independent role in the world both diplomatically and militarily only to the extent that its population and economic skills were used in a relatively united Europe. Divided, Europe can only be a dependency of the United States or Russia; united, it has the capacity to play a major role in the world.

My article on NATO in the international system of the 1970's is an attempt to explore the possible alternative futures that may face a NATO organization that appeared moribund during the height of General de Gaulle's power. In the mid-nineteen fifties, I invented the concept of a joint NATO-nuclear force to avoid the difficulties inherent in the American nuclear guarantee to NATO (despite official American assurances) and to maintain the potential political unity of the organization.

The proposal for MLF that grew out of my original suggestion but violated its intent, had by the early 1960's destroyed whatever potential there was for a joint NATO force. In addition, the Kennedy administration, which lied to its own negotiators to increase their confidence concerning the characteristics of the proposed MLF fleet, did grave injury to American credence in this respect. As a consequence I then proposed what appeared the most viable remaining alternative—a European nuclear force. The article on NATO explores some of the circumstances in which a European nuclear force might still prove a feasible and useful alternative and not entirely inconsistent with the maintenance of NATO.

A united Europe that could play a major ro'e in the world and that had its own formidable conventional and nuclear forces could pave the way for an American withdrawal from Europe. Although this would not be an unmixed blessing, it could permit a European security treaty that would not be a likely Trojan horse. It might permit the withdrawal of Soviet forces behind Soviet borders, renunciation of the Soviet doctrine on intervention, and a favorable reorganization of world politics including a mitigation of the arms race. Alternatively, if the Soviet forces are not withdrawn, the heavy hand of Soviet imperialism might be revealed more clearly and the Soviet Union placed on the defensive politically.

The debate between Dr. Yuter and myself over the nuclear non-proliferation treaty also considers some of the problems of NATO and, in particular, of Germany. Although most thoughtful individuals would prefer a world in which nuclear proliferation was minimized, very serious questions are raised by the treaty regarding the nature of international politics, political justice, and the future prospects of international law. One of the virtues of the article by Dr. Yuter is that it makes clear that the treaty has reasonable prospects for success only if drastic actions are taken against China. The Chinese are not entirely wrong when they refer to the treaty as an effort to establish an American-Soviet condominium. Seen from this perspective, it is likely that at least some popular misperceptions concerning the treaty might be corrected.

1. International Law and the International System

MORTON A. KAPLAN

It is generally accepted that the social structure of international politics places constraints upon the possible variations in international norms. This assertion implies neither that law can be derived from social structure—for if that were true one could adopt or propose norms consistent with that structure regardless of whether these new norms fit into either the body of existing norms or a framework of legal reasoning—nor that there is a strict determinism between a systematic substructure and a normative superstructure, in which case one would expect the political and social structure to generate the norms of international law almost automatically. The first alternative would make law too much a matter of preference and dependent largely upon the perceived advantages accruing to the actors in adjusting or failing to adjust the law to actual or desired social structures. The second alternative would make law too little a matter of preference; it would derive the law from the political and social structure and divorce it from the values and choices by means of which we interact with the present to create the future.

International law, we can agree, is not a disembodied essence concocted from covenants, treaties, or customs, and unrelated to the social institutions that permit its observance. In the absence of central legislative organs, creative action by the member actors changes the international normative structure. If solemn treaty obligations enunciate intentions based upon rea-

6

sonable expectation, that fact is a significant element for the process of juridical reasoning. Even when a norm is violated, referral to signs embodied in treaties of the existence of a norm may be important for later restorative actions that help to keep the norm alive and to maintain other important values as well. Sometimes, however, solemnly enunciated norms are based upon expectations that, although reasonable when first formed, are invalidated by later developments. The Charter of the United Nations, for instance, insists upon the outlawry of resort to arms except in self-defense. Yet some might—and I would—argue that the present structure of world politics is as far out of line with such a norm as current state practice would seem to indicate. In such a case—if I have correctly interpreted the situation—the attempt to avow the norm despite repeated and insistent violations may serve only to cast doubt upon the structure of international law generally. Too rigid an insistence upon an absolute ban on force may do a disservice to efforts to regulate the use of force and to maintain other norms that sustain important national and international values, including peace and security. Even within American domestic law judges make law; if wise, their creative efforts will be subsumed within a chain of legal reasoning that establishes a reasonable relationship with existing norms. There is perhaps even more reason in international law not to lose sight of legal logic; it is at least equally important not to become a prisoner of disembodied legal logic. Creative statesmanship that takes into account the (flexible) limits that the international system places on possible international norms retains the likelihood of developing norms constructively—and thus of enhancing important values, including that of a law-abiding international community—even while acquiescing in the demise of a solemnly agreed-to norm, at least in its pure and unrealistic wording.

The present international system seems to be evolving away from the loose bipolar system as we have known it. This will probably provide a number of opportunities for wise political leadership to help "legislate" the direction of change in the international political order and in the international legal order. Before turning to the future and the alternatives it may hold for us, it may be useful to return briefly to the past and to sketch some plausible relationships between the international social and political order and the international legal order. This may serve as a comparative foundation for our speculations concerning the future. To accomplish this purpose we will describe models of the "balance of power" international system and of the loose bipolar system to show the consequences they plausibly have for the international normative order. These models are not intended to be descriptive of reality. They are primarily analytic devices that permit one to test for internal consistency and for logical clarity. These models are abstracted from a much more complex world. This raises questions concerning the application of derivations from the models to the world that cannot be considered here.

However, if appropriate caution is used, models such as these may provide illuminating insights.

"Balance of Power" Model

The "balance of power" model has the following characteristics.

1. The only actors in it are nation-states and thus there is no role differentiation in the model. This is a somewhat counterfactual assumption for there were other organizational forms such as the Danube Authority and the League of Nations during the historical "balance of power."

2. The goals of the major nations of the system are oriented toward the optimization of security. By this we mean that major nations will prefer a high probability for survival as major nations, even though this excludes the possibility of hegemony, to a moderate probability for hegemony combined with a moderate probability for elimination as a major actor. Most analysts would argue that Napoleon and Hitler did not operate according to this assumption. It is possible, although far from obvious, that the model would function differently were the assumption relaxed. There is sufficient factual validity to the assumption for large and interesting periods of history, however, to more than justify its use as a first-order approximation.

3. The weaponry in the system is not nuclear.

4. There are stochastic and unpredictable increases in productivity which, in time, unless compensated for, might destabilize the system. Therefore each actor seeks a margin of security above its proportionate share of the capabilities of the system.

5. There must be at least five major nations in the system. A two-nation system would be unstable. If either of the two nations gained a clear margin of superiority, it would be tempted to eliminate the other in order to guarantee that the other would not eliminate it, if, through some combination of circumstances, the ratio of capabilities was reversed. In a three-nation system, if there were a war of two nations against one, the probably victorious coalition would have some incentive to limit its demands upon the defeated nation. To eliminate the defeated nation would throw the victors into an unstable two-nation system. Under our assumptions, this would be undesirable, unless one nation could gain such an advantage from the elimination of the third that it could eliminate the second nation. But this would also give the second nation an incentive to combine with the third against the first unless it misunderstood its own interests. On the other hand, if the first nation refrains from sacrificing the third nation, that nation may later combine against it with the second nation in a subsequent war. And, if one of the victorious nations in this subsequent war sees some advantage in eliminating the first nation, it is dependent upon the ability of the only remaining nation to recognize that its own interests require it to oppose this. The reasoning here is inconclusive; therefore three is not a clear lower bound for stability.

However, if there are at least five nations, it seems plausible that the argument for limitation in war would hold.

6. Each state, even though of great nation status, is likely to require allies to obtain its objectives. Thus it desires to maintain the existence of potential future alliance partners.

The assumptions specified give rise to the following essential rules of conduct:

1. Act to increase capabilities but negotiate rather than fight.
2. Fight rather than pass up an opportunity to increase capabilities.
3. Stop fighting rather than eliminate an essential national actor.
4. Act to oppose any coalition or single actor that tends to assume a position of predominance with respect to the rest of the system.
5. Act to constrain actors who subscribe to supranational organizing principles.
6. Permit defeated or constrained essential national actors to reenter the system as acceptable role partners or act to bring some previously inessential actor within the essential actor classification. Treat all essential actors as acceptable role partners.

The first two rules follow from the need for a margin of security in a world in which capabilities change stochastically. The third rule is essential for maintaining the availability of future coalition partners. The fourth and fifth rules recognize that deviant actors may destabilize the system by their actions or by the actions of their followers or cohorts within other nations. The sixth rule is also related to the need for potential alliance partners and warns against restricting one's own choices unnecessarily.

These rules are not descriptive rules. They are prescriptive rules. That is, under the governing assumptions, these are rules that states would follow in order to optimize their own security. Thus there is motivation to observe the rules, abstracting from other considerations, but no requirement to do so.

If the major nations follow the specified rules under the specified system conditions, there will be a number of consequences, some of which are obvious and others of which are not so obvious. Alliances will tend to be specific, of short duration, and to shift according to advantage, not according to ideologies (even without war). Wars will tend to be limited in objectives and the rules of war and the doctrine of nonintervention will tend to be observed.

Alliances will tend to be of short duration because permanent alliances would tend to undermine the "balancing" characteristics necessary for the security of the member states. Thus alliances will tend to be for specific objectives as determined by short-term interests. And to use a phrase current in the eighteenth and nineteenth centuries, nations will be disposed to act in terms of interest rather than in terms of sentiment. In short, there is, in this system, a general, although not necessarily consistent, identity between short-term and long-term interests.

The limitation of war in the "balance of power" system requires no further discussion.

We will not go into detail on the expected norms of international law except in a few specifics. One would expect belligerents to behave in ways consistent with maintaining the essential rules of the system since they are required for the security of all essential nations, including belligerents. For instance, behavior during the war or in occupation of territory that infuriated the population of an enemy state would probably preclude the possibility that such a state would be a potential future ally. Although this might not be the only constraint operating to enforce the rules of war, nonetheless it is an important factor tending in that direction.

The rule against intervention in the domestic affairs of another state—a rule violated on a number of occasions—also tends to be sustained under conditions of the model. If the intervention—for instance, in favor of rebels—were successful, there might be a permanent alliance between the states or a tutelage of one over the other. This would injure all other states in the system and thus would tend to draw their active opposition. For this reason the intervention would probably be unwise or unsuccessful. And if, for any reason, the intervention were unsuccessful, the state in which the intervention took place would probably have a serious revulsion for the interventionary state that would tend to make it a permanent enemy of that state. Even if the intervention is successful, the new government may oppose the aiding state to demonstrate its independence. Although these reasons are not absolutely compelling, they are strong enough to make likely rather general observance of the rule of nonintervention in the "balance of power" system.

It should be noted that other states by and large did not tend to intervene on the side of the government in the historic system; rather they merely maintained normal state relations and trade with the government. If the rebels grew strong enough, then the rules of belligerency would apply and other states would behave neutrally toward the belligerents, at least with respect to shipments of the articles of war or the goods of trade. These reasons are not dissimilar to those given above; intervention would have had potentially destabilizing consequences for the system and would have tended to be opposed by the other members of the system.

Recognition, whether of new governments or of new states, tended to follow universal norms in the "balance of power" system. Was there a definite territory? Did the government control the territory? Was there reasonable support on the part of the population or at least the absence of strong overt opposition? If these questions were answered affirmatively, then the government or state would tend to be recognized regardless of the form of internal government or regardless of its friendship or antipathy toward particular states. Although the act of recognition itself was a political act, so that the facts of the case did not absolutely require the act of recognition, nonetheless, with notable exceptions, there was fair concordance between rule and practice. Moreover, since nonrecognition was a political act, its consequences for international law were less than massive, the nonrecognized state merely being denied access to the privileges stemming from comity. Failure to recognize did not remove the duties and obligations under international law that nonrecognizing states had toward the nonrecognized state as a state. Even before the facts were clear that established the legitimacy of a government or a state, this did not imply a reign of anarchy with respect to the non-recognized government or state. Intervention in its affairs would have been contrary to the rules of the system. Recognition may have been a political act and a negotiating tool in getting the new government or state to recognize its obligations under the rules of the international community, but it was not a weapon in a cold war designed to undercut its existence.

The Loose Bipolar Model

A second model—one that has some relevance to present-day international politics—is that of the loose bipolar system. This model contains two blocs, each of which is led by a leading bloc actor. There is role differentiation in this model; in addition to blocs and bloc members, there are nations not joined to blocs and universal organizations as, for instance, the United Nations. The weaponry in this model is nuclear. In an age of efficient logistics and great organizational capacity, this latter feature is an essential element of the system; for, unless factors of scale precluded it, one would expect one of the blocs to overwhelm the other unless deterred by a weapons system such as a nuclear one.

This system operates according to the following simplified set of essential rules:

1. Blocs strive to increase their relative capabilities.
2. Blocs tend to be willing to run at least some risks to eliminate rival blocs.
3. Blocs tend to engage in major war rather than to permit rival blocs to attain predominance.
4. Blocs tend to subordinate objectives of the universal actor to objectives of the bloc but to subordinate objectives of the rival bloc to the universal actor.
5. Non-bloc actors tend to support the universal actor generally and specifically against the contrary objectives of the blocs.
6. Non-bloc actors tend to act to reduce the danger of war between blocs.
7. Non-bloc actors tend to be neutral between blocs except where important objectives of the universal actor are involved.
8. Blocs attempt to extend membership but tend to tolerate the status of non-bloc actors.

The first three rules reflect the uncertainties of the bipolar system and the need for at least a margin of security. Rule 4 is related to the need within the system for mediatory functions. Particularly in the nuclear age, mediatory activities help to coordinate conflicting blocs and to achieve an agreement short of nuclear war. This is similar to other types of bargaining situations in which optimal solutions for both conflicting parties are aided by the mediatory process. On the other hand, although these processes should be supported by the blocs, each bloc should nonetheless attempt to take advantage of any favorable opportunities to obtain better than a "fair" outcome. That is, maneuvering will take place and it will be related to situational advantages. Moreover, it is advantageous, even apart from the concept of mediatory functions, to subordinate the goals of one's opponents to those of the universal organization and to subordinate the goals of the organization to those of the bloc, provided this can be done with minimal inconsistency.

Universal organizations are major supports for the interests of actors not belonging to blocs—the greatest protection for them—insofar as they can be protected by universally applicable rules of conduct. Therefore non-bloc members have an interest in subordinating both blocs to the universal actors. This would become difficult, and probably impossible, in the event of major war; and minor wars might escalate into major wars. Hence, according to Rule 6, non-bloc actors are to reduce the danger of war between blocs. The non-bloc actors cannot properly fulfill these functions unless they remain neutral between the blocs; lack of neutrality would impede their mediatory functions and their support for the universal actor. On the other hand, a neutrality that threatened to undercut the universal actor would injure their interest. Thus Rule 7. Rule 8 emphasizes the fact that although extension of bloc membership is important to the bloc, the mediatory role is sufficiently important to the blocs to tolerate it and even possibly, under appropriate conditions, to support it.

The consequences of the rules are straightforward and for the most part have already been stated. Consequences: Alliances are long-term, are based on permanent and not shifting interests, and have ideological components; wars, except for the fear of nuclear weapons, tend to be unlimited; however, the fear of nuclear war has a strong dampening effect on war; the universal organization tends to support mediatory and war-dampening activities; with respect to international law, there are few restrictions on intervention and these arise mainly out of the fear of escalation.

Some of the reasons for these consequences may now be stated. Alliances tend to be long-term and based on permanent interest; in other words, there is a tendency in the system for bloc members to support the leading member of the bloc even on issues where there is a temporary divergence of short-term interests between them. Moreover, there is a tendency for ideological congruity within the blocs; for the kind of close association involved either requires organizational uniformity, as in the Communist bloc, or the kind of public support and cultural similarity which helped at one time to support NATO. If one bloc were organized according to long-term interests, and other nations were not, the bloc might well gain its way on most issues by splitting the opposition issue by issue.

There would be a tendency in this system for wars to be unlimited; neither bloc would regard the other as a potential coalition partner. The greatest inhibitor of a central confrontation lies in the nuclear component and also perhaps in certain factors of scale that would make administration of the world an extremely difficult, if not impossible, task.

As for the rule of intervention in international law, at least some of the constraint present in the "balance of power" system would not be operative in the loose bipolar system. The opposition to intervention would come from the other bloc and would not have the same massive quality as in the "balance of power" system where most major actors could be expected to oppose it; fear of confrontation and escalation nonetheless would inhibit intervention to some extent. In areas where one bloc had easy access and the other did not, intervention would not be unlikely. Where both blocs had relatively similar access, they might agree to insulate the area from bloc competition or alternatively they might decide to compete for it. The decision would depend upon the specifics of the situation; the model could not be expected to give rise to a specific prediction on this point. One factor inhibiting intervention would be the fear that the erosion of this particular rule of law might tend to undermine the general system of law. Although this fear might be a factor in decisions concerning intervention, the consequence feared is not so direct or so massive that it would be likely to prove overriding; moreover, most interventions would be indirect and covert.

One would expect the use of force to be permissible in this system; the same factors that permit intervention also operate to permit the use of force, the Charter of the United Nations to the contrary notwithstanding. Historically, Palestine, the Congo, Cyprus, Greece, Korea, Vietnam, Suez, Hungary, and various other episodes firmly illustrate the erosion of the so-called rule of law enunciated in the Charter. The bipolarity of the system tends to focus competition between the blocs and to produce a resort to force in those circumstances where one of the blocs has a clear preponderance of capabilities. The rule can to some extent be enforced against non-leading nations, as in the Suez case, or even in the Pakistan-Indian case. But it runs into greater difficulties in cases such as the Indian-Chinese case.

To some extent this stems from the fact that the bloc leaders have no desire for the continuance of a war that neither supports, especially since any armed conflict might lead to a central confrontation even if with low probability; the bloc leaders see no reason to risk even the lowest probabilities of a nuclear war if there is some convenient way of avoiding it and if there is no clear gain for the bloc leaders to be got from the use of force. Where the universal organization tends to dampen the armed confrontations and to mediate quarrels among non-leading nations, it therefore tends to reinforce the interests of the bloc leaders.

Recognition of states or of governments is based not on the criterion of control with reasonable support from the people within a region but is based upon the consequences of the act of recognition for bloc policy. Thus nonrecognition of East Germany, North Korea, or Communist China was, during the height of bipolarity, part of a program of political warfare designed to erode the position of these governments. This does not mean that nonrecognized states or governments are entirely without rights within the system or that unprovoked major acts of military warfare against them are permitted. However, whereas in the "balance of power" system the objective of nonrecognition is to secure the compliance of the nonrecognized state or government with the norms of the system, in the loose bipolar system the objective of nonrecognition is to weaken the international position of the nonrecognized state or government, and under favorable circumstances, to contribute to its demise.

Factors Making for a Change

A number of features of the existing world make for greater divergence from the model of loose bipolarism than would perhaps permit retention of the model in its present form. First, however, mention will be made of those divergences of model from reality that have always been present but that do not clearly invalidate the model. In the model, uncommitted nations are not distinguished from bloc members by internal characteristics. In the real world, most of the uncommitted states are ex-colonies of the members of the NATO bloc. Their historical memories are conditioned by the fight against colonialism and by their fear of a reimposed colonialism, even if in the form of so-called neocolonialism. Their search for identity leads them to distinguish themselves from the former patron state and, even more specifically, from the leader of the NATO bloc, even though the United States has not historically been an imperialist power.

Most of the uncommitted states are also "colored." Although this characteristic should be irrelevant in countries that have values that are universalistic and achievement-oriented, historically this has not been the case. This creates resentment on the part of the uncommitted states against the members of NATO. In their fight against colonialism, most of the uncommitted nations have adopted some form of socialist or Marxist ideology. Although most of the uncommitted countries are not socialist in meaningful applications of that term, they nonetheless accept a number of intellectual corollaries of the socialist or Marxist position. Thus, it is widely believed among them—and even believed by many Western intellectuals—that capitalism is responsible for both colonialism and war.

The uncommitted countries are also by and large underdeveloped. Whereas in the nineteenth century, the newly developing countries, such as Japan, turned to Western Europe or to the United States for their models of development, there has been until recently a tendency among the contemporary developing nations to view either Russia or China as acceptable, or at least as partly acceptable, models.

One consequence of this set of conditions has been the emphasis of the uncommitted nations upon exterminating the remnants of colonialism, mostly through moral pressure or United Nations resolutions, and upon opposing so-called neocolonialist government among the uncommitted states. Thus a government in an uncommitted state that was relatively conservative, bound to NATO nations by treaty, or more concerned with its internal problems than with the export of revolution tended to find itself opposed by the more revolutionary uncommitted states, which at times even intervened in its internal affairs. Rather than lending support to the old rules of nonintervention, which necessarily suffer attrition as a consequence of the shift from the "balance of power" to bipolarity, the uncommitted states have tended to reinforce the shift away from this rule of law and even more narrowly to circumscribe its applicability. Although they have often attempted to distinguish between colonialist intervention and revolutionary intervention—a distinction the Soviet Union has also tried to maintain—and have not been entirely unsuccessful in this effort, nonetheless there has been a further weakening of the rule. These interventions sometimes threatened the stability of the bipolar system and the interests of NATO. A largely revolutionary world would probably be as inimical to American interests as a largely fascist world would have been. Such a world, even apart from conceptions of monolithicity, would confront the United States with strategic military problems and also, and perhaps even more importantly, with political problems that might affect both its systems of alliances and its internal institutional forms.

The above factors, however, would not by themselves necessarily produce instability or invalidate the model. Other factors may, however, invalidate the applicability of the model, although this is not completely clear.

Among the features eroding the loose bipolar system is the recovery, both political and economic, of Western Europe. Until 1948, the Communist parties of Italy and France seemed to pose a possible threat of violent revolution. The national economies of the occupied but liberated nations were slowly recovering from the havoc of war. Without the infusion of massive aid from the United States, social and political upheaval might easily have occurred. With more than six million men in its armies, the Soviet Union seemed to pose a threat of an immediate military nature. Although this threat never objectively existed in the form in which it was visualized, in the absence of the organized Western bloc that developed, Italy, France, or West Germany might have collapsed as Czechoslovakia did. Now that these nations are once again economically vigorous and politically stable and now that the threat of Soviet military action is visualized as only residual, national pride tends to counsel some degree of independent action. Moreover, the failure of Great Britain to join the Common Market upon its formation, the fear that a vigorous Germany might dominate a united Europe without Britain, and the specific policies followed by General de Gaulle that derive at least as much from his own ideology and view of the world as they do from external circumstances, seriously threaten the existence of NATO as an organized bloc and the Common Market as a supranational agency.

If the threat of Soviet military attack seems to have lessened, the likelihood of an American nuclear response to an actual attack by the Soviet Union also seems to have lessened. Before the Soviet Union acquired nuclear weapons, or even while its nuclear force was highly vulnerable to an American first strike, American nuclear retaliation for a Soviet attack was extremely credible. No doubt a massive Soviet attack out of the blue, that is, without provocation—and in the absence of a suitable conventional response—would still in all likelihood incur an American nuclear response. If, however, war were to develop in ambiguous circumstances, in which the Soviet Union suffered a plausible provocation, and after a prelude that gave much time for Americans to consider the potential damage to their own cities in the nuclear exchange, then although an American nuclear response is by no means precluded, neither does it appear quite so credible as it did in the early 1950's. Regardless of the motives that led General de Gaulle to emphasize the development of an independent French nuclear force, the fact that he has seen fit to call attention to the possibility that the United States would not use its nuclear force in defense of Europe is an indication that he felt the argument at least had some merit in securing support for his decisions. The failure of the Western allies to find some solution to this difficulty that satisfied jointly the needs of the United States and of the European nations no doubt has played a role in the weakening of NATO and hence in the growing instability of the loose bipolar system.

Problems of nuclear control may also have played a role, although it is difficult to say how large a role, in the rupture between China and the Soviet Union. Economic aid, personality conflicts, and conflicting national interests in border quarrels, may also have played important roles in this development. The quarrel between them has provided the other satellite parties with alternate founts of authority. The Communist bloc will not soon recover from the demonstration of the extent to which opposition between Socialist states can occur or from the shattering of the myth of the infallible leadership that resulted from Khrushchev's secret speech on Stalin in 1956.

The independence shown by China has had multifarious consequences within the Communist camp. Hungary and Rumania, for example, have been able to resist political pressures from Moscow and to develop at least partly independent policies that increase their support at home and that stabilize their regimes. These developments have increased the appeal of Communism by demonstrating that Communism can be at least in part an indigenous phenomenon and not merely a Moscovite plot. At the same time the world Communist movement has been weakened both by the fact that division exists and by the fact that the two leading Communist actors—Russia and China—must now expend much of their energies on the contest for the leadership of the bloc or, alternatively, in a contest to attract or to neutralize members of the other's bloc. Consequently they must turn much of their management capacity away from problems of international politics; this reinforces the reduction in their external opportunities that has resulted as a consequence of greater political and economic stability in the world. Thus the Communist bloc is no longer seen as a monolithic conspiratorial apparatus—an image that characterized much of the postwar debate.

If the Communist bloc is not seen as an imminent threat and if many believe that further liberalization will occur within the nations of that bloc, the world then will respond to a psychological détente, the logic of which may further reinforce the breakup of bipolarity. The assumption will be that an era of "good feelings" may promote international agreements and help to turn the world from a policy of blocs to one of independent states operating according to a flexible system of alignments.

The belief that détente helps to fragment bloc structure is not entirely wrong. Although the great breaks in the Soviet bloc—those of Yugoslavia, China, Albania, and temporarily of Hungary—did occur during periods of great international tension, the increases in autonomy and collegiality within the bloc are not entirely unrelated to the amelioration of world conflict. To some extent, similar processes are occurring within NATO, although both processes are much more complicated than generalizations concerning the détente imply. Moreover, even if the generalizations concerning the consequences of détente for internal bloc structure have some—but only some—validity, the relationship between détente and international agreement may radically overstate the importance of the psychological variable. The test ban agreement, after all, was reached subsequent to the Cuban missile crisis—a period of great tension in which restrained threat and counter-threat dominated the international scene. To the extent that détente implies moderate external policies and the likelihood of international agreement, the atmosphere of goodwill that is so highly valued in many circles may play only a minor role.

Some would argue—and I believe correctly—that the psychology of the détente mistakes the epiphenomena of international politics for the phenomena. Just as the popular images of the cold war were in part a response to the frustrated hopes of international cooperation that were held during the war period, the psychology of the détente is in part a reaction to the exaggerated fears of the cold war period. According to this view, Stalin's so-called aggressive policies were more likely responses to the opportunities and dangers that the immediate postwar period provided than they were to a generalized policy of expansion. It is also unlikely that Stalin's policies were the product of the uncontrolled nature of his power within the Soviet governmental system. On the other hand, Khrushchev's seemingly more passive policies—it must be remembered that Khrushchev initiated the Cuban missile crisis and sent troops into Hungary although Stalin only threatened Yugoslavia—responded more to lack of opportunity than to a generalized policy of agreement or to the benignity of a more moderate form of internal rule. If this is a correct interpretation, then expressions of goodwill and the amelioration of the internal Soviet regime, no matter how desirable the latter may be on humanitarian grounds, play little role in achieving international agreement. However, even if this view is correct, it is too subtle for the public. Subjective feelings, at least in the West, concerning the alleged fragility of the détente will probably continue to play a role in the formation of international policy and in the erosion of bipolarity.

Thus, the fact that confronts us is the possible, and even probable, erosion of bipolarity. If the loose bipolar system is becoming unstable, perhaps the model of loose bipolarity no longer functions very effectively as a representation of the world. We will, therefore, consider alternative models that, depending upon circumstances, might represent the alternative worlds that might evolve out of the present world. These systems may give us some insights into the kinds of international law that might accompany them.

Unit Veto System

We present here the model of an equilibrium system that conceivably could develop out of the existing international system. The unit veto system is a system in which each nation possesses a nuclear force capable of surviving a first strike by an enemy and of imposing unacceptable damage upon him. We consider this system before considering some more realistic alternatives because these more realistic alternatives do not constitute equilibrium models and because one or more of them are more closely related to the unit veto system than to the loose bipolar system.

Military alliances would be relatively meaningless in this world. Nuclear deterrence would be credible and effective. Conceivably minor military skirmishes would occur within a quite limited framework; presumably a strategy of limited strategic retaliation might be employed where the conventional forces of one side are too limited to halt successfully the armies of an opponent. Catalytic and anonymous wars would lack plausible motivation.

Nonmilitary, that is, political, interventions, would occur with relative frequency in this world. Such interventions could not easily be deterred by nuclear systems; the gap between penalty and transgression would be too huge to bear the burden of credibility; neither aggressor nor victim would likely be convinced by the argument for this kind of response. The universal organization, however, might well be employed by the other nations of the system to dampen such occurrences because of the danger, even if remote, of escalation. Yet, this will be an isolationist world in which the functions of the universal organization are largely underdeveloped. If the revolutionary ambitions of Russia and China, for instance, are likely to be dampened by lack of opportunity, the development of common interests is also likely to play a minimal role in this system. Neither law nor international organization will burgeon in this system. The citizens of the nation-states are likely to be suspicious of foreign nations, uninterested in the morals of quarrels or the morals of other regimes, and lacking in the assurance required for an articulated foreign policy. The dangers in this system may lie in the political deviancy that begins to develop within nations and in the withdrawal of affect from the external world. This will be a system with superficially low entropy that may suddenly flare up.

The systems presented below are not equilibrium models. They are neither highly analytical nor highly theoretical. However, by suitable adjustments at the parameters one might derive them either from the loose bipolar or unit veto models. Although some writers believe that future systems may be variants of a "balance of power" model, I do not agree; in my opinion the introduction of nuclear weapons and changes in scale make variations based on that model less probable than those adumbrated below. These nonequilibrium systems presumably would develop as the consequence of one or more parameter changes inconsistent with the equilibrium models discussed above. If these nonequilibrium systems are not exceptionally stable in their nature, they may nonetheless be maintained by favorable concatenations of circumstances. Most importantly, one can see how any of them could develop out of the present loose bipolar system as a consequence of changes in the parameters of this system. Thus they are useful intellectual tools for considering possible ranges of variation in international norms; we need to think not merely of the desirability of specific norms but also of the ways in which norms interact with international systems. Norms that are desirable when considered independently may either move us toward international systems the other aspects of which are undesirable or turn out to be unenforceable unless still other changes are made in the international system. Alternatively norms that are less desirable when considered independently may (or may not) help to promote international systems more in accord with our values. Perhaps even more important than the possible inconsistencies between specific norms and the development of alternative international systems will be the problem of relating national policy choices to either or both of these problems. We will not—and perhaps cannot—say much that is significant about these problems in one chapter. The systems described below, however, will be useful if they provide a framework within which the relevant policy choices can be discussed. Whether one thinks likely or unlikely the variations discussed, the style of thinking that underlies them may still prove useful.

DÉTENTE SYSTEM

The détente system is one in which the United States and the Soviet Union are the two strongest nations in the system although they are confronted by other national challenges greater than those confronting them in the loose bipolar system. They are still highly competitive but are reasonably relaxed about their competition. The United States no longer finds it necessary to suspect Communist plots in revolutionary movements while the Soviet Union has learned that many of these distant revolutionary movements are so difficult to control and so alien in cultural background that they are not worth more than merely minor risks. China has alienated many of the uncommitted states, such as Indonesia, Algeria, and Cuba. Moreover, she is in her second generation of revolutionary leadership and is becoming more conservative. Nuclear diffusion has not extended beyond the United States, the Soviet Union, Great Britain, France, and China. The test ban has been extended to underground tests. France and China also have become signatories to this pact. Neither the United States nor the Soviet Union is capable of a credible first strike, and as a consequence either they refrain from increasing the size of their nuclear forces or they decrease them somewhat. France has withdrawn its armed forces from integrated NATO control; the pro-French faction in Germany has won a signal victory within German politics. As a consequence NATO becomes, as General de Gaulle demands, a loose alliance without integrative mechanisms. Rumania develops alternate ties to France to counterbalance its dependence upon the Soviet Union. Other signs of increased independence occur in the Communist bloc.

The anticolonial revolution has been carried to completion. The rule of nonintervention has been reestablished in international politics with support from both the United States and the Soviet Union. With both American and Soviet support, the United Nations Security Council condemns efforts by uncommitted nations to interfere in each other's activities. The rule on compensation in cases of expropriation is relaxed. The United Nations begins to play a strong role in the governance of space, celestial bodies, and polar regions. It also sets up a regime for the development of the mineral resources of the seas.

Breaches of the peace—or even wars—occasionally occur in this system but they do not directly involve any of the major nations. These wars are quickly regulated by the United Nations organization; observer teams are sent to prevent continuation of the fighting. A tradition develops of arbitration of major disputes. National courts increasingly apply international law. There are fewer restrictions on this process by either constitutional or legislative requirements within the national systems.

Recognition, as in the "balance of power" system, is based upon universalistic criteria. Recognition policy is no longer part of the arsenal of political warfare as in the loose bipolar system. However, the motivations that uphold recognition policy—as well as those that uphold noninterventionary norms—differ from those of the "balance of power" system. In the détente system these norms are desirable because they reduce those challenges to the existence of a regime or state that could involve the resort to force and increase the dangers of escalation. The mellowing of the Soviet Union—and to some extent of China—reduces the dangers of nonintervention and of universalistic treatment of new regimes and new states. The lack of cohesion of the blocs has similar consequences and also increases the difficulty of gaining support from one's own bloc for interventionary efforts. The rise of major nations either that are not in blocs or that pursue independent foreign policies reduces the pressure on the bloc leaders to assume that security depends upon their initiative in responding to revolutionary change in the world. Small changes no longer seem to threaten cumulative change as seemed to be the case in the loose bipolar system, viz., the case of Korea.

FOUR BLOC SYSTEM

NATO has been dissolved. Western European nations including England have put together a nuclear force with a substantial second strike capability. This force has been integrated in a new organization based on the Common Market and including the Court of Human Rights. Constitutional democratic processes are guaranteed for all the European nations. The United States takes a special responsibility for Latin America and certain areas of Asia. It utilizes the OAS to intervene in Latin America to maintain constitutional processes within that region. It no longer intervenes globally; Europe now also has a capacity in, for instance, the Middle East or Africa comparable to that of the United States in Latin America. Therefore responsibility does not fall inescapably on the United States. The attractiveness of the Western European alternative has reduced the consensus supporting the governments of the Communist satellites in Europe. Consequently for the protection of their own regimes, they are forced to depend more on the Soviet Union. Thus Russian hegemony within the Eastern European bloc is reestablished. Southeast Asia has been neutralized. Communist China has entered the United Nations and has regularized its relationship with the United States. The rule of nonintervention applies in those areas that are not defined as bloc areas. Thus Japan, Africa, India, and certain portions of Southeast Asia fall within this rule. As none of the blocs aspires to control the world and as all now recognize the difficulty of controlling revolutions in developing nations, this rule is reasonably well-enforced.

There are many similarities to the détente system. Space, the Arctic regions, and the seas come under the control of the United Nations, except that the rules according to which this is done are established primarily by bargaining among the four blocs. The rule of expropriation also has been changed to give greater latitude to expropriating states. Some degree of compensation is demanded but not necessarily that amount that corresponds to the market values of the seized assets.

Recognition is usually based upon the criteria of control of territory and support, or at least lack of opposition, by a substantial part of the population. In areas of special sensitivity to the blocs, however, this rule is not followed. Thus, in Latin America, for instance, only republican forms of government are recognized. Those governments that do not provide for political competition have sanctions applied against them by the Organization of American States.

Resorts to force are regulated by a United Nations organ. Ad-hoc control, advisory, or observer groups are employed to separate the combatants. If these disputes are mediated or arbitrated, the blocs intervene to assure themselves that the principles of settlement are principles not discordant with their interests.

The influence of the uncommitted states is considerably smaller in this system than in either the loose bipolar or the détente system. Even in the détente system, the competition between the United States and the Soviet Union for the support of uncommitted states is likely to give such states considerable leverage. In the four bloc system, on the other hand, the existence of a number of alternatives reduces the pressure on any particular bloc to seek the support of any uncommitted state. As this holds for each of the blocs, the price to be paid for support is significantly lowered. Although in order to keep the Organization of American States viable the United States is quite likely to establish sets of economic arrangements that guard against violent fluctuations for the single-commodity countries, the global extension of rationalized procedures is less likely than in a bipolar system.

A variant of the four bloc system deserves consideration. The removal of the United States from Europe and the development of a united Europe exerts a major attraction upon the Soviet bloc. Instead, however, of clinging to the Soviet Union for support, the governments of at least some of the East European states begin to bring into the government only nominally Communist elements in order to foster consensus in the immediate period and association with the economically more vigorous European community in the future. As part of this process, they increase their treaty ties with one or more of the European nations and even enter into what might be regarded as alliances with them. In some of the Eastern European nations, these transitions take place smoothly. In others regime crises occur, as old guard Communist elements either rebel against these regimes, while calling on the Soviet Union for support, or take control of the government legally, while provoking revolutions against themselves in the process.

Developments past this point depend upon a context that has not been sketched here and that is obviously contingent in terms of prediction. Some of the potentialities are, however, obvious. The Soviet Union may also go through a regime crisis and may either intervene or not intervene with the consequences these decisions may have for the outbreak of war or the norms involving the use of force or intervention. Appeals may be made to a united Europe by either the governments or the revolutionaries, and the decisions made by Europe will also affect this set of norms. Attempts may be made to invoke United Nations procedures to pacify the situation. These may succeed, in which case there may be a major enhancement of international organization and world law. Alternatively the intervention by the United Nations may be so ineffective that the organization is discredited, its mediatory activities paralyzed, and the extension of its control over such areas as space and the seas inhibited. A situation parallel to that of the cold war may develop except that four blocs rather than two play major roles. Great instability may result.

UNSTABLE BLOC SYSTEM

The unstable bloc system is one in which the two major blocs have either begun to fragment or are well along in the process of fragmentation. Arms control agreements are minimal. Third area conflicts are extensive. Local outbreaks of violence are frequent. National liberation movements and internal revolt are rampant in the uncommitted areas. Qualitative aspects of the so-called arms race have made nuclear weapons cheaper and easier to acquire.

Although perhaps ten or fifteen nations have nuclear weapons systems in the unstable bloc system, the United States and the Soviet Union are the only nations with technologically advanced systems. The systems acquired by the United States and the Soviet Union have greatly increased accuracy in delivery, much greater efficiency in the use of warhead materials, and multiple warheads. Although increased mobility of missiles and extensive use of the seas have lowered the vulnerability to first strike of the US and USSR that otherwise would be present in the system in the absence of *these* qualitative improvements, other qualitative improvements, e.g., improved search techniques and increased delivery accuracy, make first strikes much less infeasible than they are at present. The increased instability in the relationships between the Soviet Union and the United States produces further fragmentation of the bloc structure, as the credibility of deterrence has been lessened.

The minor nuclear powers have systems that are good for minimum deterrence only. Their systems are highly vulnerable to first strike. They cannot do serious damage to the nuclear systems of the two major nuclear powers, and they are subject to rapid obsolescence. Alternatively, West Germany and Japan may develop large and sophisticated nuclear systems, while China may utilize its vast territory and large population to offset other deficiencies of its nuclear threat.

This is a system in which the leaders of the two blocs have a strong incentive to insulate themselves from quarrels that might escalate into nuclear war, even at the expense of deserting alliances of which they may be members. Growing recognition of this fact will tend to discredit the value of alliances and will also tend to free the more adventurous nations from the restraints that have previously characterized their behavior. Thus, for instance, a nation such as Rumania might seek support from France as well as from the Soviet Union. Inversely Hungary might turn to the protection of a nuclear-armed West Germany. West Germany, cut off from the support of both the United States and France, might reduce its pressure on East Germany, even to the extent, for instance, of giving tacit support to East German demands on Poland for ex-German territory. This nationalistic West Germany might make a deal with Communist China, in which it uses Chinese territory for nuclear experiments and, in exchange, provides technical aid. This might place great pressure on the Soviet Union, which then might turn either to the United States, or to a deal with either or both Germanies at Polish expense.

This system will be characterized by nuclear blackmail and unstable political coalitions. Although the need to avoid such a potentially unstable system would provide an incentive for the states of Europe to unite within the framework of a supranational organization and for the United States to provide them with the know-how to produce a stable nuclear system, by hypothesis, that alternative has been bypassed. As a consequence, resort to violence is widespread in this system. The United Nations is reduced to a debating body. Arms control agreements are minimal or nonexistent. Outer space, the seas, and the Arctic regions are not governed internationally but are sources of conflict. Recognition is used as a political weapon, and intervention in the affairs of other states is common. The uncommitted states will not be aided by other states to any considerable extent in their development efforts. There will be a general retrogression of international law.

One other variation of the unstable bloc system can be considered. This is a version in which the first strike potentiality of the United States and the Soviet Union is minimal, either because of improvement in antiballistic missile programs or because of failures in search procedures for sea-or-land-based mobile missiles. In this case, alliances would be possible between major and minor nuclear powers or among minor nuclear powers. But the former type of alliance would be inhibited by the small state's possession of nuclear arms. Possession would be a sign of independence and distrust. Moreover the large nuclear state would fear commitment (triggering) by the small nuclear power's use of the weapon. It would desire to insulate itself from a chain of actions that it could not control. And although a general alliance among most of the small states possessing nuclear forces might create a sizable nuclear force, unless there were exceptional political or cultural circumstances, the alliances would be susceptible to nuclear blackmail and splitting tactics.

Wars in this system would tend to be limited but the possibility of escalation would be greater than in the others. Limited direct confrontations between the United States and the Soviet Union might occur in non-European areas. A central confrontation might also occur. But as the danger of escalation beyond the limited war category would be very great, there would be strong pressure to avoid it.

The foreign policies of the United States and the Soviet Union would tend to be interventionist. American policy would tend toward conservatism, that is, toward the support of status quo, conservative regimes. Although one could argue that to retain the support of its own intellectuals, the United States would do better by supporting progressive regimes, American behavior will more likely support regimes opposed to change. There will be a consequent alienation of a considerable portion of the intellectual elite both within the United States and in other NATO states. Soviet policies will support to some extent national liberation movements but in a very cautious way. Additional "Hungaries" may occur that serve to disillusion Soviet intellectuals. Russia will also be torn between a desire to maintain solidarity with China and a fear of the strategic threat and organizational challenge that China presents to the Soviet Union. This will lead to inconsistencies in Soviet policy that conceivably could lead to the fragmentation of the satellite system. This again might produce East German pressure on Poland, depending upon a number of parameters that are too complicated to specify here.

The role of the United Nations will be primarily mediatory and adapted to dampening the consequences of outbreaks of violence. Although each bloc will support political changes contrary to the interests of the opposing bloc, the efforts to secure a constitutional majority in the United Nations will generally prove ineffective. It is not likely that in this system the United Nations will acquire authority over outer space, celestial bodies, or arms control measures. The United Nations will prove ineffective in dampening local outbreaks of violence. Ad-hoc United Nations forces will become difficult to establish. Intervention and recognition policy will not be based on universalistic criteria but will not be used for purposes of political warfare quite as much as in the other variation of the unstable bloc system, as the blocs will introduce some small amount of constraint.

DEVELOPMENT WORLD

The model sketched here goes much further in its optimistic reading of world possibilities than any other of the models. It ignores the failures of development in so many nations, and the even more disheartening apparent failures in nation-building, as in the case of Nigeria, and instead adumbrates the outline of a world in which most of the more optimistic projections from the current world materialize.

In the development world, we would expect that a large number of successful regional groupings would enhance cooperation among the members of the region on both economic and political matters. Success in nation-building has stabilized the national political units. The internal social systems of the nations have developed sufficient infrastructure to provide satisfactory alternatives for those who lose out in political contests and thus to reduce the need for and the frequency of coercive politics. Increased internal political pluralism reduces the costs of political failure, provides alternative career lines and the potentiality for come-backs, and invests amalgamative activities with additional desirable alternative opportunities. Thus Africa and Latin America, for example, would form common markets and would establish the kinds of transportation and communication networks that they presently lack. There is now more intercommunication with Europe and the United States respectively than within the two geographical areas.

We assume that the Common Market flourishes, that with the demise of a general the Seven join the Market, and that the supranational features of the market are emphasized. The Commission on Human Rights becomes a full-fledged court of final constitutional review that sustains political liberalism as well as individual freedom. Although supranational features are less emphasized in Eastern Europe what had been known as the Soviet bloc develops self-regulating agencies in functional areas; these agencies operate either through COMECON or through more specialized and separate arrangements. Although the governments in Eastern Europe do not become democratic and remain, with a few exceptions, one-party systems, individual rights are much more regularized than had been the case in the past; and the freedom to move either within or outside the bloc becomes almost general.

The regime in China has meliorated. Although China has good relations with Korea and Vietnam, and is developing successfully, these nations do not enter into a regional grouping. Japan, which has emerged as the second most industrialized nation on earth, and which is pressing the United States strongly for world leadership, has a very strong aid program toward Southeast Asia. Most nations of this area have entered their own regional association through which Japanese aid and leadership is funnelled. Supranational characteristics of this association are weak, although there are a substantial number of regional cooperative arrangements.

The United States has retreated from global interventionism, although it has become the only "world" power with the incorporation of Australia, New Zealand, and the Philippines as American states. Israel has also joined this new grouping. With the death of the Israeli hope that the Arab states would make peace eventually and with the withdrawal of American protection to foreign states, except under United Nations auspices, incorporation of Israel into the American union remained the only solution for both nations. Cuba has also joined the American nation after a successful democratic revolution, as have the Dominican Republic, Haiti, and the former English West Indies.

The Arab states have formed their own regional association although development is retarded as a consequence of the replacement of oil by other energy sources. Some instability exists in the Arab Middle East as a consequence of internal instability and political extremism. United Nations controls, however, manage to dampen these instabilities.

The United Nations has assumed administration of outer space and the resources of the seas and, in particular, assures that all nations have equitable access to these resources. The United Nations also carries out arms control activities. A United Nations force also has nuclear weapons—to be used only under command of a Standing Committee and upon the authorization from the political organs of the United Nations. England has abandoned her independent nuclear force, as has France, although the European organization possesses a small nuclear force. Only the United States, the Soviet Union, and China possess individual national nuclear forces; and these are far smaller than presently existing forces. Moreover, there has been a widespread distribution of effective ABM systems to other nations and to regional organizations.

In case of civil war, the theories of neutrality and of intervention only in behalf of existing regimes have been discarded in favor of collective intervention organized by or under the terms of resolutions passed by the political organs of the United Nations and consonant with a universally agreed-upon set of standards. Thus interventions against existing governments would be permissible when these governments discriminated among their nationals according to race or religion (or some other unreasonable standard) with respect to their political rights; or when human or essential political rights were denied; or when access to information or freedom of movement was denied. The universal organization, however, would not authorize action prior to the outbreak of organized violence in the absence of a demonstration of widespread support for the demands of those in revolt, or except in circumstances that indicated that change could be brought about according to some reasonable schedule of human costs. When the revolutionaries sought to deny any of the specified values, the universal organization would authorize intervention in support of the existing government. Where the values were unclear or contested, the universal organization would authorize intervention on the side of those who would permit international supervision during a transitional period to help to enforce the stated values. Under these standards intervention under international authorization occurred in South Africa in favor of the blacks, in Kenya in favor of the whites, and in Cuba in favor of the democrats (prior to accession to the United States). In all these cases intervention was against the existing regime. In the cases of Uruguay and Venezuela, intervention occurred in favor of the existing governments.

Where possible, these interventions were organized by appropriate regional groupings whose findings of fact were subject to approval and whose decisions to act were subject to authorization by the universal organization, as in the Kenyan case. Occasionally, the actions were collective actions by the entire universal organization, as in the South African case, and occasionally by one or a few states, as when the United States, Mexico, and Brazil organized the action against Cuba. The case of Hungary was the only instance in which the United Nations authorized intervention against both the existing government and the findings of the appropriate regional body. In this case action was organized by the Western European organization when the Eastern European unit supported the Hungarian government in its repressive measures.

DISCUSSION

These models obviously are not exhaustive of the alternatives that the future may provide. Also even within the models, depending upon variations in the parameters, there are multiple complications we have not even begun to sketch. As mentioned earlier, these are not equilibrium models. They are intended merely to permit discussion of the range of variation potentially inherent in the existing world situation. Despite these deficiencies in the models and in the discussion necessarily based upon them, it should nonetheless be apparent that national decisions seemingly unrelated to normative consequences may have extremely important side effects with respect to these normative consequences. For instance, present American policy designed to prevent nuclear diffusion may perhaps permit maintenance of a bipolar world with the prospects for world order inherent in that bipolarism. It may alternatively fail to prevent diffusion and also fail to encourage such alternatives as a European system, thus bypassing either a stabilized bipolarity or a four bloc system for a nonstable bloc system in which the restraints of international law are poorly developed. Even though bipolarity may provide a less stable legal structure than a "balance of power" system there are not improbable alternatives even less favorable for the development of international law than loose bipolarity. Even the détente, which is commonly regarded as one of the foundations of an expanded world legal order, may have the opposite consequences. It may help destabilize bipolarity at a time when the possible alternatives are worse from the standpoint of world order.

There are possible conflicts between the policies best designed to secure law-abiding behavior and those best designed to maintain the strategic interests of the United States. For instance, every time the United States engages in a Bay of Pigs, a Guatemalan coup, or even in bombing north of the seventeenth parallel in Vietnam, it weakens the already loosened fabric of international law. The failure to engage in such actions may injure American strategic interests. Yet American strategic interests, although not identical with the prospects for world order, are not unrelated to them. Sacrifice of these strategic interests may impede the development either of any kind of universalistic system of norms or of one consonant—or at least not inconsistent—with our values and interests. Questions of this kind are always difficult to assess; they involve choices at the margin, large uncertainties, and competing values. None is susceptible to dogmatic or facile answer such that one can assert "policy A builds law and policy B tears law apart," even with respect to the particular norm at issue. The argument that the best way to build law is to act lawfully, although not entirely incorrect, obviously rests on a form of legal determinism that will not withstand serious analysis. Moreover, there are interests and values other than those that flow from the development of a system of international law.

Thus the truism that the United States has an interest in upholding, maintaining, and enlarging the area of international law obscures as much as it clarifies. There can be little doubt that if the United States could choose that world of all possible worlds in which it wished to participate as a nation, it would be a world organized according to strong principles of international law. It would be a world that maintained freedom of political choice for the peoples of the various nations; access to supranational tribunals in cases of violations of human rights by national governments; noninterference in the affairs of individual nations except perhaps in pursuit of an international bill of rights; the outlawry of the use of force except in the pursuit of recognized common interests; objective standards for recognition; international governance of space, the seas, and Arctic regions; international control of violent fluctuations of the commodity markets; and developed supranational law in those geographic regions and functional areas where a common framework of customs, values, and economic development permit a highly developed set of common legal rules. Yet it defies at least this writer's imagination to project an institutional development that would support this kind of body of law. In a world in which we must choose from among a set of bad alternatives the least bad, we will continue to be confronted with hard and ambiguous choices. Some policies may seem best adapted to supporting the development of international institutions, others to implementing one or another international norm (perhaps at the expense of still some other international norm), others to promoting American strategic interests or political values. Some policies may seem to provide the greatest opportunity for the development of world order if they succeed. These may possibly create the greatest risks for maintaining even that minimal degree of world order we presently have should they fail.

No discussion at this level of generality could hope to provide any hard answers to such questions. The choices that will face our statesmen will be choices defined by the actual sets of circumstances that confront them—circumstances that are at best only vaguely predictable now. A discussion at this level of generality, however, may reveal some of the reasons why the choices are hard, what alternatives may compete for our attention, and what factors may play a role in our decision. It may also provide a framework within which our thoughts about the matter can be organized in advance, so that the choices may be perceived in terms of their intermediate as well as of their immediate contexts and consequences.

We have recently passed through an episode in which the United States sought to have the United Nations punish the Soviet Union for refusing to contribute toward the support of institutional measures that were incompatible with perceived Soviet interests. Suspension of Soviet membership obviously would have been incompatible with the functioning of the United Nations in a bipolar world. Yet in the absence of a genuine world consensus on institutions and values, was it not perhaps unreasonable to expect the Soviet Union to use its scarce resources to support measures designed to bring about a world community not in accord with Soviet values? Was not Soviet recalcitrance at least in part the consequence of an effort to shift the burden of intervention from the United States and its allies to an international organization whose useful functions in the international system were different from those which we attempted to impose on it? No doubt from the standpoint of the values of the United States wanted to implement, United Nations ventures in the Congo, among others, were perceived as helpful. No doubt American and Western European intervention in the Congo was made easier by reason of United Nations cover. Perhaps failure to act would have produced chaos in the Congo and the disintegration of the Congolese state. Perhaps alternatively, though not surely, UN intervention prevented successful revolution by a radical Congolese grouping that would have squandered the resources of the Congo and that would have fettered the Congolese people with a bloodthirsty and inefficient tyranny. Surely, however, the actions taken were not designed to secure Soviet support for the peace-keeping activities of the United Nations, or for the role of the Secretary-General; nor were they even designed to demonstrate to the Asian and African nations the development of "objective" and impartial enforcement procedures by the United Nations.

The UN has recently taken measures against the Rhodesians. It has yet to take measures against the Soviet bloc or other authoritarian nations for violations of human rights within national territory. Should action against Rhodesia be opposed on the ground either that it is a violation of domestic jurisdiction or that the Asian and African states will not support actions against violations of human rights when these involve the rights of white people? Alternatively should such actions be supported because they are politically expedient, because they constitute a first step toward widespread UN jurisdiction in the area of the violation of human rights, or because any good that can be supported constitutes an appropriate basis for action? How do such decisions affect the structural processes of international law and interact with other decisions to promote one or another of the alternative possible international systems?

We have not begun to discuss these questions; yet clearly they deserve systematic discussion. Generally laymen and also scholars have argued in terms of simplistic notions and of projections of existing lines of development. If scientific answers to these important questions cannot be obtained and if intuition will prove more important than quantification, symbolic logic, and sustained argument, yet systematic discussion is likely to reveal interconnections, turning points, and unconsidered alternatives that are essential to informed intuition and to selected empirical investigations that are related to these informed intuitions.

We have adumbrated the truism that law and international organization, if pursued too single-mindedly, may undercut the development of both law and organization. We can all agree that it would be unwise either to overstress the impact of the social and political structure of world politics on the normative structure of the international system or to fail to recognize the relationship between the two. We know that placing our ambitions too low forsakes the possibility of progress and that placing our ambitions too high may assure retrogression. What we lack is a sense of ordered relationship between national policy, international organization, international norm, and international system. In short, we are ignorant where we need knowledge and full of abstract generalization where we require articulated theory.

2. The Beirut Raid and the International Law of Retaliation

RICHARD A. FALK*

I

ON THE NIGHT of December 28, 1968, eight Israeli helicopters took part in an attack on the Beirut International Airport. Israeli commandos descended from six of the helicopters (the other two hovered above) that had landed either on runways or at the hangers of the airport. All commercial aircraft belonging to Arab airlines were destroyed by explosives being placed in the nose-wheel well and in the undercarriage well of each plane. The attack resulted in the destruction of 13 planes whose worth has been estimated to be $43.8 million.[1] Additional damage has been reported done to hangars and other airport installations. Lebanese sources report that two Israeli commandos were injured by gunfire from airport guards. There was no loss of life.

The Beirut raid was defended by the Israeli Government as a retaliation for an attack by two Arabs two days earlier, on December 26, upon an El Al

*Work on this article was completed during my period (1968–69) as a Fellow at the Center for Advanced Study in the Behavioral Sciences at Stanford, California. The atmosphere and facilities of the Center are a great encouragement to this sort of scholarly speculation. William W. Bishop, Jr., Gidon Gottlieb, Leon Lipson, Nadav Safran, Oscar Schachter, and Louis B. Sohn, without in any way endorsing my approach to these difficult issues, gave me the benefit of critical comments of an earlier version.

Semantic choices inevitably imply political values in relation to situations of violent international conflict. This issue of characterization is particularly acute in relation to the para-military violence of irregular forces seeking to overthrow the formal government of a passenger plane at the Athens Airport. The Athens attack was the work of two men, Mohmand Mohammed Issa and Maher Hussein Suleiman, who belonged to the Popular Front for the Liberation of Palestine.[2] The terrorists used gasoline bombs and submachine guns to attack the El Al Boeing 707 as it was preparing to take off with 41 passengers and a crew of 10 on a flight bound for New York City. One passenger, an Israeli engineer named Leon Shirdan, was killed by machine gun bullets that penetrated his plane window. Israeli reports suggest 86 piercing of the fuselage from the cockpit to the tail, with many of the bullet holes through windows at seat level.[3] Greek authorities have charged the two Arabs before a magistrate with first-degree murder, a crime subject to the death penalty in Greece. The Greek magistrate, Nikolas Stylianikis, disclosed that the defendants said, despite the character of their attack, that they had been under orders from a Popular Front official in Beirut to destroy the El Al plane but not to kill any of the passengers.[4] The two

---

foreign country. It is precisely this kind of problem that faces the analyst of Arab-Israeli violence since the end of the June war of 1967. Those who favor Israel's position refer to these para-military endeavors as "terror" or as "guerrilla activity," whereas those who take the Arab side use terms like "liberation movement" and "freedom fighters." There is no very adequate, non-cumbersome neutral terminology available for the analysis of these relationships. I have tried to balance my characterization of this para-military activity by using both sets of descriptive terms.

1. According to the New York Times, Jan. 5, 1969, Sec. 4, p. 1, the owners of the airlines whose planes were destroyed were not only the Arab governments. Middle East Airlines, which lost eight aircraft, is owned 30 percent by Air France, 5 percent by Lebanese individuals, and 65 percent by Intra Company, an inter-governmental corporation constituted by the Kuwaiti, Qatari, Lebanese, and United States governments. The United States is evidently represented by the Commodity Credit Corporation, which is owed money for wheat sales by Intrabank, a predecessor of Intra Company. Lebanese International Airways, which lost three planes, is 58 percent American-owned. Trans-Mediterranean Airways, which lost two planes, is owned by private Lebanese interests. Early reports indicated that British insurance underwriters had agreed to accept $18 million in claims, rejecting claims from policies that did not cover war risks. Note that, aside from Lebanon, none of the interests affected by the Beirut raid involved principal Arab countries. For a detailed inventory of the damage done in the raid, including damage to terminal facilities, see letter of Jan. 14, 1969, from Assad Kotaite, the Lebanese Representative on the Council of the International Civil Aviation Organization, to the Secretary General of I.C.A.O., WP/4945, Jan. 1, 1969.

2. There are several "liberation" groups constituted by Palestinian refugees. The most important group is the Palestine Liberation Organization now presided over by Yasr Arafat. Arafat earned his reputation, and remains, as the leader of Al Fatah, which is the military commando section of Al Asifa. Then there is a group called the Popular Liberation Corps, with anonymous leadership, and associated with the Palestinian branch of the Baath party. Finally, there is the Popular Front for the Liberation of Palestine headed by Dr. George Habbash. It is the Popular Front, a relatively secondary liberation group, that has claimed credit for the attacks on El Al planes. This Popular Front has been weakened by an internal split which led 600 of its estimated 2,000 members to join the Marxist-Leninist Popular Democratic Front for the Liberation of Palestine in late 1968 and early 1969. See note 16.

3. Cf. Ambassador Shabtai Rosenne of Israel, International Civil Aviation Organization, Minutes of Third Meeting of the Extraordinary Session of the Council, Jan. 23, 1969, p. 5.

4. This account of the arraignment proceedings is based on an article in the New York Times, Dec. 31, 1968, p. 3. This contention must be set off against some of the elements

Arabs had traveled from Beirut on Lebanese travel documents provided stateless persons. The Popular Front for the Liberation of Palestine has been operating in Lebanon rather openly since the June war of 1967, with the knowledge and apparent acquiescence of the Government.

On December 29 Lebanon requested an emergency session of the Security Council to consider its charge that Israel has committed a "wanton and pre-meditated attack" upon the Beirut International Airport. Israel also requested an urgent meeting of the Security Council to consider its counter-charge that Lebanon was "assisting and abetting acts of warfare, violence, and terror by irregular forces and organizations" against Israel.[5] On December 31, after a considerable period of debate, the Security Council, by a vote of 15–0, unanimously adopted a resolution censuring Israel for the Beirut raid.[6] The preliminary language of the resolution emphasized that the attack was "pre-meditated and of a large scale and carefully planned nature." There were four operative paragraphs in the resolution indicating that the Security Council:

1. Condemns Israel for its premeditated military action in violation of its obligations under the Charter and the cease-fire resolutions;
2. Considers that such premeditated acts of violence endanger the main-tenance of the peace;
3. Issues a solemn warning to Israel that if such acts were to be repeated, the Council would have to consider further steps to give effect to its decisions;
4. Considers that Lebanon is entitled to appropriate redress for the de-struction it suffered, responsibility for which has been acknowledged by Israel.[7]

On the evening of December 31 a rocket bombardment of Kiryat Shmona, an Israeli town close to the Lebanese border, was presumed to be the work of the Popular Front, in effect a counter-retaliatory use of force. The attack killed two Israeli civilians; a third inhabitant died from a heart attack that appeared to have been provoked by the raid. The rocket bombardment evi-

---

of the attack itself. The assailants evidently could have proceeded more easily to destroy the plane when it was empty and yet chose to wait until it was loaded for take-off. In fact, the semi-official Egyptian newspaper, Al Ahram, praised the members of the liberation group for their willingness to wait at the airport at risk to themselves until their attack would have maximum effect, and exaggerated the damage done by falsely reporting that the El Al plane was destroyed by fire. Al Ahram, Dec. 27, 1968, p. 1.

5. For the text of the two letters, both dated Dec. 29, 1968, requesting an urgent meeting of the Security Council, see S/8945, S/8946.

6. S/Res/262 (1968). For the reactions of various delegations to this resolution, see S/PV. 1462, Dec. 31, 1968, pp. 7–88. The factual circumstances surrounding the Beirut raid, as well as their divergent interpretations, are well stated by the representatives of Lebanon and Israel in their presentations to the Security Council. See S/PV. 1460, Dec. 29, 1968, pp. 6–27, S/PV. 1461, Dec. 30, 1968, pp. 11–20, 43–62.

7. For full text see S/PV. 1462, p. 6; 6 U. N. Monthly Chronicle 19 (January, 1969); also reprinted below, p. 681.

dently originated from Lebanese territory and the nature of the rockets suggested that it was an act of irregular forces. Israel has not brought this attack to the attention of the Security Council. There have been a series of minor incidents along the frontier between Israel and Lebanon, both before and since the Beirut raid, leading to what has been described by both governments as a deteriorating border situation. Shortly after December 28 Lebanon also complained to the U.N. Mixed Armistice Commission about Israeli reconnaissance flights over Lebanese territory, especially those associated with the inspection of the damage done to the airport.

These basic facts surrounding the Beirut raid are, by and large, not in dispute. The relevant context is, of course, both intricate and indefinite, and might be enlarged by either side in contradictory ways. It seems helpful to consider several additional features of the context. The first is an antecedent one. On July 23, 1968, an El Al plane was hijacked by three Arab guerrillas while the plane was subject to Rome air traffic control and, possibly, still in Italian airspace en route from Rome to Tel Aviv. The plane was forced to land in Algiers. The non-Israeli passengers were released, but the Israeli male passengers and crew were held until August 31, when they were released in exchange for some Arab common law criminals imprisoned in Israel, in a transfer arranged under the auspices of the Red Cross.[8]

The second event, a consequence of the Beirut raid, was the formation of a new government in Lebanon that has indicated its intention to join more actively in the struggle against Israel. At the time of the Beirut raid the Lebanese Premier was Abdullah Yaffi, a moderate on Arab-Israeli relations and the leader who assumed responsibility for keeping Lebanon out of the June war of 1967. Yaffi has now been replaced by Rashid Karami, who has a reputation of favoring a somewhat greater Lebanese effort to achieve military preparedness, as well as the acceptance of a more active rôle in opposing Israel.[9] In June, 1967, Mr. Karami was Prime Minister of Lebanon and ordered the army to advance on Israel, but the army refused to obey.

The third event involved the execution of 14 men by the Iraqi Government in punishment for allegedly spying on behalf of Israel. Eleven of these men were put on public display in Baghdad on January 27, 1968, in a very provocative fashion, involving mass demonstrations to celebrate these hangings and intense public displays of anti-Israeli feelings. This gruesome event was accompanied by reports of Israeli concern about the welfare of 3,000 or so

8. Ambassador Rosenne's initial statement in the Security Council specifically invoked this earlier interference with an international flight of El Al Airlines as a part of the context which conditioned the decision to make the Beirut reprisal raid, *cf.* debate of December 29, 1968, in the Security Council, S/PV. 1460, p. 23. Note that Lebanon was not the sole target; all Arab-owned aircraft at the airport were destroyed. See note 1 for specification. As was made clear at various points by Mr. Rosenne and later by Mr. Tekoah, the Beirut raid was intended as a warning directed at all Arab governments.

9. For statistics on comparative arms expenditures in the Middle East, see Nadav Safran, From War to War: The Arab-Israeli Confrontation, 1948–1967, pp. 433–434 (New York: Pegasus, 1969).

Jews living in Iraq and intimations from the Iraqi Government that additional spy trials were going to be held. Nine of the men hanged were Jews and so, too, were many of those (reported to be about 60) being held for subsequent trial as Israeli spies.[10]

Israel, although very explicitly disturbed by these events in Iraq, refrained from any action in retaliation. The reason given was that Israel does not engage in reprisals as a punishment for what is past, but only as a warning about what is to come.[11] Such an explanation of Israeli restraint is not altogether convincing on these grounds because of the prospect of future trials and executions. More convincing as an explanation, however, was the apparently influential diplomatic protests received by Iraq from many parts of the world, including the Pope, the dissociation of other Arab countries from the Iraqi action, and the fear that retaliation might jeopardize further the welfare of the Jews still living in Iraq. Despite these considerations, there was speculation that Israel might launch an air attack against Iraqi military units stationed in Jordan.[12] It may be that one further pressure against retaliation was the adverse reaction of the international community to the Beirut raid. This pressure could not be openly acknowledged by Israeli officials without tending to give weight to the deliberations of U.N. organs that have been growing increasingly hostile to Israel's position in the over-all Arab-Israeli dispute.

A fourth event of some significance is the attack on February 18, 1969, also by four members of the Popular Front for the Liberation of Palestine (apparently operating out of the group's headquarters in Jordan) on an El Al plane as it was about to take off from the Zurich airport. Six persons on board were injured and one of the assailants was killed by an Israeli security guard who was on board the plane. Israel refrained from any specific retaliation; its officials blamed the Zurich incident on "the climate of forgiveness" within international society in relation to Arab governmental responsibility for the Athens attack. The Zurich attack was condemned by U Thant, who stressed the seriousness of this new occurrence, especially its terroristic impact on innocent travelers, and appealed to Israel to refrain from retaliation. Both the repetition of the Athens incident after such a short lapse of time and the recollection of the very strong Israeli act of retaliation at Beirut led to much

10. For an account of the Iraqi hangings see The Economist, Feb. 1, 1969, p. 20. Eight more persons, all Moslems, were reportedly executed for similar crimes on Feb. 20, 1969. A further report indicates that in a third Iraqi spy trial seven more persons have been condemned to death, including two or three Jews and a former Premier of Iraq, Dr. Abdel Rahman Al-Bazzaz. New York Times, March 1, 1969, p. 9.

11. "There is still little talk here of an Israeli military reaction to the hangings, in part because this would contradict the Israeli policy of using raids as warnings rather than reprisals, and also because this might do more harm than good." James Feron, "Israeli Consulting on Ways to Assist the Jews of Iraq," New York Times, Jan. 30, 1969, pp. 1–2, at p. 2.

12. See article by James Feron, "Israel Ponders Issue of Reprisal," *ibid.*, Feb. 2, 1969, Sec. 4, p. 1.

greater attention being given to the Zurich incident than had been earlier given to the Athens incident. Israel used its posture of restraint after Zurich to appeal for world support to secure better protection for its international aviation flights. A formal statement attributed to the Swiss Cabinet indicated that the attack at Zurich was viewed by Switzerland as an act of armed intervention for which Arab governments would be held responsible if investigations disclose governmental links with the attack at Zurich;[13] and, in fact, on February 28 the Swiss Government delivered formal notes of protest to Jordan, Syria, and Lebanon in which the attack at Zurich was condemned and in which each of the three governments were urged to take steps "to prevent any new violations of Swiss territory."[14]

A further event occurred on February 24, 1969, when an Israeli air strike was carried out against two major guerrilla camps of Hama and Maisalun located close to the city of Damascus in Syria. There was unofficial speculation in Israel, as a result of the timing, that these camps were attacked in partial retaliation for the Zurich incident; other motivating circumstances were a bombing of a Jerusalem supermarket a few days earlier that had resulted in the death of two Israeli students and an upsurge of Arab commando activity in the vicinity of the Golan Heights.[15] To attack Al Fatah bases in retaliation for activities of its rival organization, the Popular Front, appears at first to be rather surprising, especially as Al Fatah had not been responsible for any of the attacks on El Al and had indicated its determination, in differentiation from the Popular Front, to focus its use of violent means upon military targets.[16] If Israel, however, regards itself as confronted at this point by an adversary relying primarily on a multifaceted liberation strategy employing a variety of terrorist tactics, then responses would seem rational that weaken this over-all para-military capability or that emphasize the collective responsibility of all liberation groups for any acts-of-terror kinds of responses. Also, far less adverse international reaction seems to arise if retaliatory uses of force by Israel are directed at Arab military and para-military targets. Evidently, for instance, the attacks on the Syrian bases resulted in fairly large Arab casualties and yet failed to provoke any sense of international opposition to the Israeli action. An attack of this kind on bases seems well assimilated, unlike the Beirut raid, into the structure of international expectations about tolerable levels of Arab-Israeli violence, given current levels and forms of conflict and hostility.

13. For various accounts of the Zurich attack and reactions to it, see New York Times, Feb. 19, 1969, pp. 1, 2, 3; Feb. 20, 1969, pp. 1, 3.

14. *Ibid.*, March 1, 1969, pp. 1, 14.

15. See James Feron, "New Israeli Strategy Seen in Raid Near Damascus," *ibid.*, Feb. 25, 1969, p. 3.

16. For some discussion of the differences between the activities of these Arab guerrilla groups, see Dana Adams Schmidt, "An Arab Guerrilla Chief Emerges," New York Times, March 4, 1969, p. 6. On the different ideas of tactics between the two main Arab organizations, Al Fatah and the Popular Front, see another report by Schmidt, *ibid.*, Feb. 20, 1969, p. 2.

II. Certain Special Contentions

Both Lebanon and Israel have advanced very special claims in relation to their conduct.

Lebanese officials have denied any specific responsibility whatsoever for the Athens attack, although the work of the Popular Front, including these specific acts, received praise from Lebanese leaders.[17] The Popular Front has freedom of movement in Lebanon and has been allowed officially to recruit members and support in the Lebanese refugee camps containing some 140,000 Palestinians, and to disseminate propaganda throughout the country. Since the June war this activity has been stepped up and the Popular Front has been allowed to carry on its full program, including the planning of commando raids such as the one that took place at Athens. Premier Yaffi described the work of the Arabs who participated in the Athens attack as "legal and sacred."[18]

Both sides have been very displeased with the outcome within the Security Council. The Lebanese had sought more definite action, including a commitment to Chapter VII sanctions that would assure action against Israel, and not just words of censure.[19] The Arab countries and their supporters have argued that Israel has been found guilty of many Charter violations by the Security Council, but that nothing has been done as yet to secure Israeli compliance with the directives of the U.N. organ.

Israel, in contrast, argued that Security Council condemnation is without any significance because the organ is so one-sided in its composition and its

17. Mr. Boutros, the Lebanese representative who appeared before the Security Council, offered a categorical denial of any governmental responsibility for the Athens incident in the following principal language: ". . . Lebanon cannot be held responsible for acts which were committed by Palestinian refugees outside its territory and of course without its knowledge, and which were committed by Palestinian refugees whose intentions were not known to Lebanon." Furthermore, ". . . If Israel really felt that Lebanon was responsible for the incident at Athens, [why] did it not immediately file a complaint against Lebanon in the Council." S/PV. 1461, Dec. 30, 1968, p. 12.

18. See New York Times, Jan. 5, 1969, Sec. IV, p. 1; for further documentation of Lebanese praise for the work of the Popular Front (and other liberation efforts), see release of Israel's Information Office, "The Israeli Action at the Beirut Airport," Dec. 28, 1968. This document included the following quotation attributed to Mr. Yaffi, the Lebanese Prime Minister, on Nov. 2, 1968: "Fedayeen action is legitimate, and no one can condemn the fedayeen for what they are doing. Their aim is to retrieve their homeland and their plundered rights. . . . Thus, I say, fedayeen action is legal." Israeli sources have also quoted specific Lebanese praise for the perpetrators of the Athens incident. See Mr. Tekoah's statement before the Security Council (S/PV. 1461, pp. 52–55), especially the following excerpt: "The attention of the Lebanese Government has been drawn on numerous occasions to the activities of the terror organizations within its borders. The Lebanese Government, however, has not only continued to condone these activities, but has publicly identified itself with them. Prime Minister Al-Yafi has announced several times that his Government supports terror operations against Israel." S/PV. 1461, p. 52.

19. Mr. Boutros indicated that he had "reservations" about the action of the Security Council because "it did not draw the conclusions to which the findings should have led and it hesitated to order the application of Chapter VII of the Charter to Israel." S/PV. 1462, p. 81.

assessment of responsibility.[20] Israeli spokesmen have pointed to the failure of the Security Council resolution even to refer to the earlier Athens raid or to the general Lebanese rôle in tolerating, at the very least, the active use of its territory to mount terroristic activities against Israel.[21]

From the perspective of international law three very important sets of issues are raised by the Beirut raid and its interrelations with the principal contentions advanced by the adversary states:

1. The quality of governmental accountability for terroristic acts that have some link with territory and the rights of response enjoyed by the state that is the target of such terror; this problem is accentuated in the special case where the locus of terror is within a third state and the tactic is to disrupt the security of commercial airline service;
2. The legal status of action by organs of the United Nations in a situation wherein the decisional process is politically one-sided and voting behavior appears less concerned with the specific merits of the disputes;
3. The residual competence of an aggrieved state to use force against a state that persistently refuses to adhere to the recommendations and decisions of the United Nations.

These areas of concern are central to the realization of security and justice in the contemporary world. In particular, in the Middle East the principal antagonists hold sharply contradictory conceptions of the nature of a just outcome. These conceptions govern the perception of any particular sequence of events, such as those surrounding the Beirut raid.[22] Such events provide a rather clear "case" that helps focus an inquiry into the relationship between law and behavior in the Middle East.

Often particular situations, such as the dispute arising out of the Beirut raid, are instances of more general problems of conflict that may arise in several quite distinct settings throughout international society that call for somewhat distinct treatment. The conflict between "territorial sovereignty" and "liberation" is one such contemporary problem that takes several distinct

20. Mr. Tekoah, in reacting to the adverse judgment of the Security Council, said: "Let no one make the mistake of thinking that the people of Israel might be swayed by inequitable pronouncements." Further, ". . . not Security Council resolutions, but the attitude and actions of the Governments in the area will determine the destiny of the Middle East." S/PV. 1462, p. 52.

21. A somewhat more balanced debate took place at I.C.A.O., Minutes of the First, Second, Third, and Fourth Meetings of the Extraordinary Session of the Council, Jan. 20, 21, 23, 31, 1969.

22. For over-all legal perspective, with representative statements by adversary analysts, see the symposium published under the title "The Middle East Crisis: Test of International Law," 32 Law and Contemporary Problems 1–193 (Winter, 1968); W. V. O'Brien, "International Law and the Outbreak of War in the Middle East," 11 Orbis 692, 723 (1967). For general background see Nadav Safran, From War to War. The Arab-Israeli Confrontation, 1948–1967 (New York: Pegasus, 1969); Fred J. Khouri, The Arab-Israeli Dilemma (Syracuse University Press, 1968). On problems of biased and incompatible perception of identical circumstances in relation to international conflict, see Ralph K. White, Nobody Wanted War: Misperception in Vietnam and Other Wars (Garden City, N. Y.: Doubleday, 1968).

forms in different parts of the world. These distinct settings should be borne in mind whenever a legal analysis is made. Otherwise particularities of fact and policy preference may distort the search for more general principles of assessment.

In a legal system as consensual as international law it is especially important to regard particular cases as instances of general problems. For this reason it seems appropriate to mention some of the other settings wherein the broad policy issues at stake in the Beirut raid are presented.[23]

(1) TERROR, LIBERATION MOVEMENTS, AND THE PROCESSES OF SOCIAL CHANGE

In any social system in which strong claims for change are advanced, the threat or use of force is likely to play a major rôle. International society lacks any effective legislative process that might facilitate peaceful adjustment to changes in value and power structures. The idea of national sovereignty, the sanctity of domestic jurisdiction, and the absence of central sanctioning procedures work against the non-violent implementation of the will of the international community on matters of social and political justice. The modern state often enjoys a great technological advantage over its population in a struggle for political control, especially if the struggle assumes a military form.[24] To overcome this disadvantage, social forces favoring change have used techniques of coercion that give a maximum rôle to their distinctive capabilities. Recourse to terror and random violence has been a principal tactic of the dispossessed, insurgent, revolutionary faction seeking to gain control over the machinery of government of a state. The rise of Communism, the rapid collapse of colonialism, the formation of "liberation" movements to deal with racism and residual colonialism in southern Africa, and the predominance of the Afro-Asian outlook in the General Assembly are among the factors that have given prominence to terror as an instrument of political change and as a "legitimate" tactic of military struggle.[25]

23. There are problems of characterization arising from contradictory interpretation of the *facts* (*e.g.*, extent of knowledge by Lebanese officials of the activities of the Popular Front), of the *legal duties* (*e.g.*, extent of obligation to regulate activity of liberation activities within territory), and of *policy issues* (*e.g.*, conflict between security of territory and recourse to retaliatory force).

24. Although variations of terrain, tradition, and political milieu make certain societies very susceptible to internal opposition of an insurgent character; also, of course, in many parts of Asia, Africa, and Latin America the central government is not able to exert its control over the entire expanse of national territory. Of course the logic of governmental control involves the capacity to control liberation activity as well as the incentive to engage in it.

25. There is also absent any consensus as to the character of political legitimacy in international society. The presence of such a consensus induces moderation in the choice of means and ends of political conflict; its absence induces extremist tactics and strategy, making compromises difficult to specify, and giving a prominent rôle to violence and warfare. See Henry A. Kissinger, "Central Issues of American Foreign Policy," in Kermit Gordon (ed.), Agenda for the Nation 585–614, esp. 585–589 (Washington: Brookings Institution, 1968). The sharpest global cleavage related to political legitimacy is concerned with the status of radical socialism as the basis for organizing a sovereign state. The

The use of an external base to mount an insurgent campaign also enjoys a recent tradition of respect in the West. It is relevant to recall the rôle and status of "governments-in-exile" during World War II and the generally heroic imagery used to describe anti-Nazi terrorism in German-occupied Europe. The idea of "liberation" was very strongly endorsed by conservative governments generally committed to the *status quo* in international society, including the leading colonial Powers. And even in more recent times the United States has given "aid and comfort" to anti-Castro exiles who have proposed to liberate their country by violent means, most spectacularly at the Bay of Pigs in April, 1961.[26]

The principal point is that the politics of terror and the use of exile sanctuaries to disrupt "the enemy" society enjoys an ambiguous status in recent international experience. All principal states in the world have in some situations at least, given their support to such practices. Therefore, the approval given to the liberation movements and their tactics of terror by the Arab governments is quite consistent with the behavior of other governments seeking a revision of the jural *status quo*, but unwilling or unable to make an orthodox military challenge or to negotiate a satisfactory diplomatic compromise.

The status of "liberation" movements and their practices has not been dealt with in any systematic and non-polemical fashion by either diplomats or experts in international law.[27] Governments that have been among the most enthusiastic sponsors of recent liberation activity have also been among the most ardent advocates of adherence to the principle of nonintervention in the affairs of sovereign states.[28] Such an apparent contradiction arises from

---

Arab-Israeli conflict that can be expressed in several distinct fashions, perhaps most fundamentally in terms of the status of Zionist claims, is one in which there is almost no consensus as to legitimacy. There is not even a willingness to accept as settled the right of Israel to exist as a distinct sovereign state.

26. One might also mention the psychological support given exile groups from East Europe by the official Congressional celebration of "Captive Nations' Week" each year. For legal critique see Q. Wright, "Subversive Intervention," 54 A.J.I.L. 521 (1960). In Sec. 101 of the Mutual Security Act of 1951 (in similar legislative enactments of several subsequent years) the U. S. Congress appropriated and earmarked 100 million dollars for escapees from Eastern Europe for a Liberation Legion for Eastern Europe, specifically "to form such persons into elements of the military forces supporting the North Atlantic Organization or for other purposes." 46 A.J.I.L. Supp. 14 (1952). For citations see 2 American Foreign Policy, 1950–1955, Basic Documents 3060, 3119.

27. There is some polemical treatment of these issues in relation to the controversy over the legal status of support for various kinds of "wars of national liberation." But there has been no effort to deal with the generality of claims in light of some consistent body of doctrine.

28. In this regard see the Declaration on Inadmissibility of Intervention, adopted as Resolution 2131 (XX) of the General Assembly on Dec. 21, 1965; 60 A.J.I.L. 662 (1966). In recounting the grave concern of the membership with "the increasing threat to universal peace due to armed intervention and other direct or indirect forms of interference," the Declaration "solemnly declares" in its second numbered paragraph that: ". . . Also, no State shall organize, assist, foment, finance, incite or tolerate subversive, terrorist or armed activities directed towards the violent overthrow of the régime of another State,

simultaneously seeking national autonomy for their own society and the drastic revision of certain foreign societies. The pursuit of such a combination of goals tends to undermine the status of rules of restraint, as well as to diminish the force of legislative claims. One or the other priority would be consistent with legal authority, but not both, manipulated to suit specific preferences of a particular government.

(2) REPRISALS, DEFENSE AGAINST TERROR, AND THE
   MAINTENANCE OF MINIMUM ORDER

The kind of sporadic violence associated with liberation movements presents difficult choices to the target government, especially if its general orientation is unpopular within the regional and world community. For one thing, the terroristic acts are rarely of sufficient salience to command widespread attention from world public opinion. For another, there is normally a partially successful effort to dissociate the liberation movement from the government of the territory wherein exist facilities for training, financing, sanctuary, and guidance. The sponsoring government attempts to minimize its accountability for the conduct of violent operations by the liberation movements, and there does exist a wide range of variation as to the extent and character of control (or even knowledge) possessed by the territorial government over the conduct of specific guerrilla operations and the formation of more general liberation strategy.[29] Finally, the organized international community at the regional and the world level may endorse the objectives of the liberation movement to such an extent as to make censure, much less opposition, impossible for the target state to obtain. The use of terror as an instrument of change is given a certain legitimacy, then, to the extent that its use receives the endorsement of international institutions.[30]

These problems of response are even greater in a situation in which the terrorists' activity involves attacks upon commercial aircraft carried out in a third country. The Palestinian perpetrators of the Athens incident expected, presumably, to be apprehended and punished under Greek law for the common law crimes that they had committed. But this hardly offsets the damage done, by way of real loss of life and inconvenience to passengers; but even more, by way of making people everywhere quite hesitant to fly on airlines

---

or interfere in civil strife in another State." Such a contradiction between Assembly assertion and liberation practice helps discredit the guidance rôle of international norms and to give comfort for those who would dismiss restraints upon violence as "legalisms."

29. Compare Security Council statements of Mr. Boutros and Mr. Tekoah on the issue of responsibility. S/PV. 1461, pp. 12–20, 46–56.

30. A consensus within the General Assembly is strongly supportive of anti-colonial and anti-racist liberation movements. This attitude of support has assumed a quasi-legislative status because of the law-creating rôle of the Organization. See, generally, Falk, The Status of Law in International Society, Ch. VI (Princeton University Press, 1969).

that are likely to be endangered en route. What is the victim government to do? It hardly makes sense to hold the Greek Government accountable in any way, provided it carries out the provisions of its criminal law and, perhaps, issues a protest to the governments giving sanctuary to a liberation movement. The only effective target of response would involve inflicting unacceptable damage upon those governments that can impose limits upon the tactics used by the liberation movements. In the Arab setting, at least since June, 1967, it is not even clear that the Arab governments have much leverage over the activities of the principal liberation groups within their territory. These groups currently enjoy such strong popular backing that some Arab governments (most obviously Jordan) would risk their stability and jeopardize their popular backing if deliberate and over measures to control a liberation movement were undertaken as official policy.[31]

The government of the target state is presented, then, with a difficult choice among options in trying to devise an effective response against terror of this externally-based variety. Its defensive options are much more likely to be limited to regular sorts of military operations. The extremist commitment of terrorist groups means that their leaders are virtually undeterrable by any kind of responsive violence. In fact, responsive violence of an intergovernmental kind, such as the Beirut raid, may actually prove of positive benefit to the liberation movement, inducing the territorial government to declare openly its support. The most generally effective defensive maneuver is to seek and destroy guerrilla training camps and bases. The only other kind of effective defensive measure is one that inflicts injury upon the foreign government such that it will be induced to suppress or curtail the activities of the liberation movement. In both instances, the target state tends to appear to be making a disproportionate response, the scale is large, and the form of operation is overt. In addition, such military action is undertaken by the regular military forces of the government against a foreign state; as such, the *prima facie* indication of a Charter violation seems much more clearly established, and especially so if the state pursues a domestic or international course that is widely unpopular to begin with. Without centralized impartial fact-finding procedures, the state that acts overtly and on a large scale is much more likely to be regarded as the one that has endangered peace and

31. The statement in the text is a very crude generalization. The effect of exerting governmental control of varying degrees over different categories of liberation group activity varies from country to country in the Arab world and through time in each country. In general, Jordan has been most vulnerable to a takeover from the liberation movement as a result of the strong Palestinian influence within the Jordanian armed forces. The Governments of Syria and the United Arab Republic enjoy greater freedom of action, although within each government élite there is a faction strongly committed to the liberation cause that would be deeply alienated by any interference with the freedom of action of the guerrilla group. The same comment also seems true for Lebanon. In all Arab countries the liberation movement seems popular with the masses, and governmental regulation or suppression would be regarded as a very unpopular policy.

initiated "aggression."[32] In effect, traditional legal criteria create a certain asymmetry in favor of the use of more covert and irregular forms of violence across international frontiers. Of course, this asymmetry should be balanced against the central bias of international law in favor of the incumbent government and the absoluteness of its authority over the territory under its control. Such a government can resist with legal "impunity" claims for change, however widely and deeply supported as just and reasonable.

In such a situation there is hardly an alternative to violence for the advocates of change and jural revision. Similarly, a state that is the target of persistent terror has virtually no effective response, in the event that the foreign government is unable or unwilling to suppress the terroristic tactics of a liberation movement, other than recourse to what is traditionally regarded as "aggressive" war. Israel in 1956, and again in 1967, was "provoked," in effect, by its inability to maintain its national security, given its vulnerability to penetration and harassment by externally based terrorists. In the last analysis, protection may involve conquest of the territory from which the terrorism emanates. The logic of self-help which continues to underlie the search for security in a world of sovereign states may encourage this sort of border-crossing military operation, although the provocation does not constitute "an armed attack" and the response is difficult to classify as an instance of "self-defense." The paradoxical relationship between the status of violence and the procedures of social change is a central deficiency of the present structure of international legal order, especially evident at a time of emergent claims for social and political justice.

(3) THE LIMITS OF U.N. AUTHORITY, TRADITIONAL GREAT POWER
DIPLOMACY, AND NUCLEAR PROLIFERATION

The general problem of curbing this kind of disruptive pattern is accentuated, as has already been suggested, by the character of the United Nations.[33] The United Nations is capable neither of implementing the justice demands of those groups that seek objectives approved by the world community nor of policing compliance with its prohibition upon recourse to violence. The geopolitical and ideological splits in international society generally prevent any kind of operative consensus arising out of U.N. activity. As a consequence, nineteenth-century patterns of alliance diplomacy assume great prominence in the effort to moderate the course of conflicts carried on at the regional

32. For a profound inquiry into these problems, see Myres S. McDougal and Florentino P. Feliciano, Law and Minimum World Public Order 97–260 (New Haven: Yale University Press, 1961). *Cf.* also the French explanation of their refusal to supply arms to Israel, initially as a consequence of Israel's initiation of force in June, 1967, and recently in reaction to Israel's action at the Beirut Airport. New York Times, Jan. 8, 1969, pp. 1, 19.

33. This assertion rests on several considerations: (1) the inability of the U.N. to implement its decisions; (2) the political factors that act to shape such a decision. The problems of control are particularly severe in the Middle East because of the rivalry between the United States and the Soviet Union for influence within the region.

level. Patterns of Great Power competition and co-ordination provide the fuel for arms races, the incentive for compromise and settlement, and the basis of uneasy forms of temporary equilibrium. The prospect of easy access by secondary states to nuclear weapons technology may even mean that a state unwilling to risk the sacrifice of its interests by a Great Power ally will seek to develop its own nuclear deterrent.[34]

International society is vulnerable to a series of disruptive conflicts that involve various kinds of externally-based insurgent operations challenging the control of an incumbent regime. These conflicts are particularly resistant to settlement because the stakes of conflict are perceived by participants in such contradictory terms. Quite often the issue is nothing less than the political identity of the state. Resentments are so deep and bases of power so divided that reconciliation appears virtually impossible. Victory, defeat, stalemate, or a temporary truce are the only plausible outcomes.

International law is conditioned in its operation by this international setting. The remainder of this article seeks to clarify the legal situation by examining two topics: (1) to present briefly the traditional rule-oriented static analysis of respective rights and duties of parties to such a conflict and to point out the inadequacies of this approach for these sorts of problems, and (2) to offer a more process-oriented legal analysis that works toward a multidimensional conception or test of relative legality.

The Beirut raid will be used as "the case" that illuminates broader issues of legal approach and disposition. The approach urged is one that could be adopted either by an official advising a government on the legal implications of a proposed course of conduct or by a diplomat, civil servant, or expert seeking to pass judgment on adversary appeals to international law.

III. Traditional Legal Perspectives

ANALYSIS AND APPRAISAL

My purpose is to illustrate the traditional mode of analysis with sufficient clarity and fairness to provide an adequate background for the proposal of an alternative mode of legal analysis.

There are several kinds of legal issues that are raised by the Beirut raid:

(1) What is the legal status of a reprisal claim? Under the U.N. Charter? Under customary international law? What is the relationship between Charter law and customary international law?

---

34. *Cf.* speculation to this effect as part of the Israeli reaction to censure by the Security Council and imposition of an arms embargo by France, New York Times, Jan. 12, 1969, pp. 1, 9. A state such as Israel might also seek to avoid inter-regional trade-offs at her expense if the settlement bargain is achieved by super-Power consensus (*e.g.*, in simplistic terms, the Soviet position on Middle Eastern problems is accepted in exchange for Soviet acceptance of the U. S. position on South Asian problems).

(2) Does the Beirut raid constitute a reasonable exercise of the right of reprisal?

(3) Does the Security Council resolution of December 31, 1968, constitute a definitive legal assessment of the conflicting contentions of Israel and Lebanon?

THE LEGAL STATUS OF REPRISALS

The prevailing expert view is stated clearly by Ian Brownlie:

> The provisions of the Charter relating to the peaceful settlement of disputes- and non-resort to the use of force are universally regarded as prohibiting reprisals which involve the use of force.[35]

It does seem appropriate to conclude that the U.N. Charter prohibits all forms of forcible self-help other than the exercise of self-defense within the meaning of Article 51.[36] The Security Council clearly confirmed this view of the legal status of reprisals under the Charter when it acted to censure Great Britain for carrying out a reprisal against the Yemeni town of Harib on March 28, 1964, in retaliation for alleged Yemeni support of the anti-colonial struggle in Aden. The resolution passed by a vote of 9–0, with two abstentions, and had as its initial operative clause the Council conclusion that it "*Condemns* reprisals as incompatible with the purposes and principles of the United Nations."[37] Israel has not even claimed that the Beirut attack was an exercise of the right of self-defense, but rather has rested her case on the right to retaliate against Lebanon in view of its alleged connection with "the Athens incident." The Israeli Chief of Staff, General Yetzhak Bar Lev,

35. Ian Brownlie, International Law and the Use of Force by States 281 (and sources cited therein) (Oxford University Press, 1963). Brownlie's statement is supported with additional citations and discussions in R. Higgins, The Development of International Law Through the Political Organs of the United Nations 217–218 (Oxford University Press, 1963). For a general background, see Evelyn Speyer Colbert, Retaliation in International Law (New York: King's Crown Press, 1948).

36. But for more flexible views of what is permitted under the Charter in the name of self-defense, see McDougal and Feliciano, cited note 32, pp. 1–260; see also pp. 679–689; Julius Stone, Aggression and World Order (Berkeley: University of California Press, 1958); D. W. Bowett, Self-Defense in International Law (New York: Praeger, 1958).

37. S/RES/188 (1964). The next clause of the resolution "*deplores* the British military action at Harib on 28 March 1964." And the Charter basis of the condemnation is suggested by language in the preambular section "*Recalling* Article 2, paragraphs 3 and 4 of the Charter of the United Nations." The Security Council resolution here, unlike the one condemning Israel for the Beirut raid, does widen the context and establish some kind of reciprocal obligation on the part of Yemen. For instance, the fourth operative paragraph "Calls upon the Yemen Arab Republic and the United Kingdom to exercise the maximum restraint in order to avoid further incidents and to restore peace to the area." And in the last paragraph, the Secretary General is called upon to use his "good offices to settle outstanding issues, in agreement with the two parties." Thus, although the United Kingdom is censured, the sense of mutual responsibility is stressed in a way that it is not in the December 31 resolution. See also I. F. Stone, "International Law and the Tonkin Bay Incidents," in Marcus G. Raskin and Bernard B. Fall (eds.), The Viet-Nam Reader (New York: Vintage, 1965).

has been quoted as saying that the Beirut raid was a reprisal the purpose of which "is to make clear to the other side that the price they must pay for terrorist activities can be very high."[38]

It seems clear that on the doctrinal level Israel is not entitled to exercise a right of reprisal in modern international law. Such clarity, however, serves mainly to discredit doctrinal approaches to legal analysis. International society is not sufficiently organized to eliminate forcible self-help in either its sanctioning or deterrent rôles. Therefore, each reprisal claim needs to be appraised by reference to these two rôles. Israel contended that the Beirut raid was a sanction imposed as a consequence of Lebanese responsibility for the Athens incident. Assessing the reasonableness of these claims involves a complex inquiry into the over-all factual context. The legal rules of prohibition isolated from context offer very little guidance for the conduct of such an inquiry, except to the uncertain extent that they embody various policies

38. See New York Times, Jan. 5, 1969, Sec. 4, p. 1; General Bar Lev said that "the large-scale operation" against the fedayeen bases of Karameh and Es-Salt in Jordan during 1968 "were not reprisals." He went on to say that "these were actions intended to strike directly at the heart of the terrorists." As an earlier example of a reprisal General Bar Lev cited the Israeli commando attack upon Egyptian bridges and upon a transformer station serving the Aswan Valley, the destruction taking place in the Nag Hamadi area. This reprisal was in retaliation for alleged Egyptian violations of the cease-fire along the Suez Canal. For a summary of the meetings of the Security Council devoted to this question on November 1 and 4, 1968, see 5 U.N. Monthly Chronicle 3–16 (November, 1968). Another prominent Israeli reprisal action occurred in October, 1967, after Eyptian rockets sank an Israeli destroyer, *Elath*, leading to the death of most of the crew. Israel alleged that the *Elath*, the largest ship in the Israeli Navy, was on "a routine patrol" and sailing in international waters, more than twelve miles from the Egyptian shore. Egypt contended that the *Elath* was only ten miles from shore and heading for Port Said in a "provocative" manner. The *Elath* was sunk on October 21 and the Israelis retaliated three days later with a heavy artillery barrage directed at the City of Suez situated near the cease-fire line. One result of the barrage was to destroy or badly damage the two most important oil refineries in Egypt that supplied 80 percent of the country's gasoline and cooking fuel. The *Elath* reprisal contrasts with the Beirut raid because the provocative action—sinking the ship—was clearly governmental in character. Hence, there was no issue as to whether Egypt was responsible, if in fact it was "illegal" to sink the *Elath*, itself a complicated issue of both fact and law. A resolution in the Security Council condemned both acts of violence as violations of the cease-fire and called for strict adherence by all governments in the future. Account of the *Elath* incident is based on Khouri, note 22 above, p. 279.

The principal purpose of retaliatory uses of force by Israel is to influence decision-making by Arab governments, especially with respect to their encouragement of terroristic tactics on the part of liberation groups located on their territory. Mr. Tekoah's conclusion of his final statement in the Security Council makes the centrality of this objective very clear. He says: "Israel's action in Beirut, taken in defense of its rights, should bring the Arab Governments to understand the full depth of Israel's determination to ensure its right to peace and security. When the Arab States realize that determination, become persuaded by its tenacity and draw the appropriate conclusions, there will be peace in the Middle East." S/PV. 1462, p. 52. Arab spokesmen, in contrast, refused to treat the Beirut raid as raising any issue that was broader than the permissibility of such an attack by the Israeli Government, given the absence of any prior governmental act of provocation on the part of Lebanon. Both the Beirut and the *Elath* reprisal raids seemed to include an element of punitive action, a policy of inflicting losses on Arab governments that exceed those inflicted upon Israel by prior action.

about the minimization of violence in the adjustment of international disputes.

THE RIGHT OF REPRISAL IN CUSTOMARY INTERNATIONAL LAW

In view of the inadequacy of Charter doctrines either to provide authoritative guidance or to give insight into the comparative merits of legal positions in the Beirut context, it would seem appropriate to consider the question by reference to pre-Charter legal conceptions contained in customary international law on the subject of reprisals.[39] For a valid exercise of the customary right of reprisal it is necessary to satisfy three main requirements:

1. That the target of the reprisal be guilty of the commission of a prior illegal act directed against the claimant state;
2. That the claimant state make an effort to obtain redress from the target state;
3. That the damage inflicted in retaliation be roughly proportional to the damage initially inflicted.[40]

In relation to the controversy over the Beirut raid it is difficult to apply these standards. It is especially difficult to determine whether the Lebanese Government should be properly held responsible for the commando acts of the Popular Front at Athens. Does the Lebanese failure to take reasonable steps to suppress the activity of the Popular Front on its territory establish a sufficient link to make it responsible for the specific acts of the organization?[41] Can the failure of the Lebanese Government to disavow the terrorist

39. As a technical matter, Charter law is properly accorded priority over inconsistent rules of customary international law. Therefore, the clear rejection of the right of reprisal in U.N. practice seems to establish the general authority of this conclusion in positive international law. However, the inability of the United Nations to impose its views of legal limitation upon states leads to a kind of second-order level of legal inquiry that is guided by the more permissive attitudes toward the use of force to uphold national interests that is contained in customary international law. This point has considerable jurisprudential importance, as it suggests the usefulness of a method of successive legal approximations. If the Charter status of reprisals exhausted legal inquiry, then there would be no prospect of moderating force in retaliatory settings wherein the Charter approach was ineffectual. Specifically, in the Arab-Israeli setting it appears useful to maintain second-order levels of legal inquiry so as to retain criteria of reasonableness in a situation that threatens at many points to deteriorate into intense and limitless forms of violent conflict. The customary international law of reprisal is a very important illustration of such second-order legality. Note, especially, that this kind of inquiry is associated with the contention of Israel that the purpose of a reprisal is not to inflict a punishment, but to communicate a claim with respect to future behavior. Even second-order legal inquiry may be ill-adapted to the kind of retaliatory claim being made by Israel, see above, Sec. II, and a third-order legal inquiry involving the specification of considerations bearing on the relative legal status of a particular retaliatory claim, see below, Sec. IV.

40. A useful short discussion of the background and character of the right of reprisal is given by Gerhard von Glahn (ed.), Law Among Nations 498–501 (New York: Macmillan, 1965).

41. Many international documents that formulate governmental duties of conduct include the responsibility to prevent the use of territory as a base for liberation activities

acts or warn the Popular Front to cease such acts be used to constitute a post-facto ratification that establishes the link? The need to make this kind of demonstration would appear strong in view of Lebanon's especial effort, unlike that of any other Arab state,[42] to remain at peace with Israel.[43] Israel's reprisal claim seems to fall short of satisfying the test for the first legal requirement.

Israel did not protest to Lebanon in any public forum about its responsibility for the Athens incident, nor did it demand redress prior to its raid on the Beirut airport.[44] There is no indication that the Israeli Government

---

against a foreign state. For example, the Declaration on Inadmissibility of Intervention, Resolution 2131 (XX) of the General Assembly, Dec. 21, 1965 (see note 28), declares that "no State shall . . . tolerate subversive, terrorist, or armed activities." See also citations in note 69 below, especially Garcia-Mora and Lauterpacht.

42. Note that Israeli representatives in the Security Council indicated that Arab countries other than Lebanon were also intended as targets of the Beirut raid. All Arab aircraft were destroyed, and not only those associated with Lebanese interests. Also the context was defined by Israel to include (1) the Athens incident, (2) the diversion of an El Al plane to Algiers in July, 1968, and (3) the over-all Arab policy of supporting the activities on their territory of the liberation groups. As Mr. Rosenne suggested to the Security Council: "Without in any way belittling the gravity of this terrorist warfare being conducted against Israel's civil aircraft, wherever they might be, the complaint that we are discussing must also be seen in the broader context of the continuation by the Arab States, including Lebanon, of active belligerency and warfare against Israel through the instrumentality of irregular forces and organizations armed, trained and financed by the Arab Governments, including the Government of Lebanon." S/PV. 1460, pp. 24–25.

43. On the comparatively low level of Lebanese hostility toward Israel, see Khouri, cited note 22, pp. 191, 230–231; Safran, cited note 9, pp. 182–185, 245–247. On its more recent increase, however, see "The Israeli Action at the Beirut Airport," Israeli Information Office, undated release, and the statement by Prime Minister Eshkol in Jerusalem on December 29, 1968, bearing the title, "Lebanon Cannot Disclaim Responsibility for Terrorism."

44. The Arab governments, but even more pointedly the Soviet Union, took the position that the Athens incident was a matter for Greek internal criminal law, and of no relevance at all to the debate on the Beirut raid. As Mr. Ghorra of Lebanon said, "In our view, that incident which took place at the Athens airport is a matter of common law, and the Greek courts have sole jurisdiction in the matter." S/PV. 1460, p. 61. Mr. Malik of the Soviet Union put his view as to the territorial, non-governmental character of the Athens incident very forcefully:

"This incident, which took place in Athens, relates to the sovereignty and competence of Greek authorities; it occurred on Greek territory. According to the press reports, the competent authorities of that country are dealing with this matter; they are studying it, and apparently they have taken some measures. They have executive as well as judiciary authorities there. How is this matter at all related to the Security Council? As I have already pointed out in my observations following the adoption of the agenda, if the Security Council were to begin to consider all the terrorist acts which are being perpetrated, no matter where, including even this country [the United States], then the Security Council would simply cease to be a Security Council. . . . The representative of Israel is dragging the Security Council into the consideration of events which took place on the territory of a sovereign power which is certainly entitled to deal with this matter . . . and that country has not appealed to the Security Council." S/PV. 1460, p. 13.

And later on the last day of the debate Mr. Malik reiterated his position in more succinct form:

"It must be stressed that the attack against the Israeli airplane was indeed carried out by citizens of a third State on the territory of yet another State; and, in accordance with

issued a public warning to Lebanese officials that they must take steps to curtail the operations of the Popular Front.[45] The record suggests that the Israeli decision to raid the Beirut airport was not preceded by any reasonable effort to obtain pacific redress. Thus the Israeli claim also appears to fall short of the second reprisal requirement.

It is difficult to apply the test of proportionality to specific factual circumstances. How does one weigh the loss of an Israeli life at Athens or the harassment of El Al operations against the destruction of civil aircraft and other equipment valued at more than $43.8 million or the blatant military incursion upon Lebanese territory? In terms of international salience the Beirut raid seems to have been disproportionately greater than the Athens provocation.[46] It was a larger, necessarily spectacular military operation carried out on an inter-governmental basis.[47] It is fair to ask, however, "Proportional to what?" If the Israeli raid is understood as a reprisal for the willingness of the Lebanese Government to tolerate operations by the Popular Front on its territory, then the Beirut raid might be regarded as proportional to inducing greater government control (although probably ineffective to achieve it). The application of this third requirement, and to some extent the first as well, depends on whether the delinquency of the Lebanon Government is regarded as its complicity in the Athens incident or its toleration of the activity of the Popular Front on its territory. Israel did not clearly communicate the character of its claim, although it seemed spe-

---

international law, a State can be held responsible only for acts of its own organs, such as its armed forces or its citizens, on the territory of that given State." S/PV. 1462, p. 22.

Mr. Wiggins, the representative of the United States, did take the position that "Israel was rightly aroused and legitimately concerned about the attack upon an Israeli aircraft in Athens on 26 December" but, nevertheless, he concluded that "[N]othing that we have heard has convinced us that the Government of Lebanon is responsible for the occurrence in Athens." S/PV. 1460, pp. 28–30.

45. Mr. Rosenne did tell the Security Council that "[A]ll through 1968 Lebanon, turning a deaf ear to Israel's appeals has been playing an ever increasing role in the overall Arab belligerency against Israel." S/PV. 1460, p. 21. There is no indication of any specific Israeli effort to persuade the Lebanese Government to exercise stronger control over the Popular Front in view of the Athens incident. Israel's justifications for focusing the attack upon Lebanon rested on allegations involving (1) the departure of the Arab perpetrators from Beirut; (2) the Lebanese toleration of increasing activity by the Popular Front on its territory; and (3) official and semi-official Lebanese endorsement of the use of terroristic methods by the perpetrators of the Athens incident.

46. Mr. Wiggins, the United States representative in the Security Council, made this point forcefully when he said that the Beirut raid was "an unacceptable form of international behavior. In magnitude it is entirely disproportionate to the act that preceded it. It is disproportionate in two ways: first, on the degree of destruction involved; and secondly, in a more fundamental way, in the difference between the acts of two individual terrorists and those of a sizable military force operating openly and directly under governmental orders." S/PV. 1460, pp. 28–30.

47. The visibility of the two occurrences can be gauged by comparing their treatment in newspapers around the world. The Athens incident was reported as a relatively minor terroristic act, whereas the Beirut raid received headlines and the damage done was shown in large photographs.

cifically related to safeguarding the operations of El Al rather than punishing Lebanon or inducing the over-all suppression of the Lebanese activities of the Popular Front.

The reprisal argument turns out to be weak if the events that are appraised concern only the Athens incident and the Beirut raid. The reprisal argument is far stronger, however, if based upon the connection between a Lebanese-based liberation movement operating with government knowledge and approval and the Beirut attack calculated to influence the leaders of the Government to alter this course of policy. The fact that the raid may have produced the opposite effect, moving the Lebanese Government into a position of more overt support for the liberation efforts of the Popular Front, is of no legal consequence; such an effect bears, if at all, on the political perspicacity of Israeli policy-makers. Such a consideration is also of reduced significance if the Beirut raid was directed toward warning all Arab governments, not only Lebanon, that the security of Arab airlines would be disrupted if these governments failed to prevent terroristic acts against El Al Airline. The effectiveness of the Beirut raid in communicating this claim can only be judged after the lapse of a period of time and by evidence of whether the Arab governments do take measures to discourage liberation groups from disrupting El Al.

The customary international law of reprisal does direct inquiry at more specific features of the context than does a mere assessment of the compatibility between the Beirut raid and Charter norms. At the same time, the inquiry is necessarily inconclusive because there is no agreed way to frame the basic issue as to the relationship between liberation activity and the target of a reprisal claim.[48] Furthermore, traditional inquiry relies on far too restrictive ideas about how to assess a particular claim. There is a need to assess a claim by reference to what constitutes reasonable behavior under all of the relevant circumstances.[49] Among the relevant circumstances is the inability to secure territory against terrorism if a neighboring country provides support, or even merely a sympathetic sanctuary.[50]

48. There are underlying the specific allegations of terror and counter-terror the more general allegations about bringing the conflict to an end either by "disintegrating" Israel and replacing it with the secular state of Palestine or by carrying out the provisions of Security Council Resolution 242 of Nov. 22, 1967, or by working out an agreed solution through the good offices of Gunnar V. Jarring, the special representative of the Secretary General, or by accepting a solution for the area that is worked out by guarantor Powers such as the United States, the Soviet Union, France, and the United Kingdom.
49. As pointed out already, Israel, in particular, objected throughout to the effort to restrict the scope of inquiry to the Beirut raid. See note 8.
50. The problem is fully depicted from an Israeli viewpoint in an article: Amnon Rubinstein, " 'Damn Everybody' Sums up the Angry Mood of Israel," New York Times Magazine, Feb. 9, 1969, pp. 24–27, 93, 96–99. See especially p. 98, on which there is a discussion of why Israel does not engage in counter-terror against Arab interests by organizing irregular military forces of its own, thereby cutting the overt link between retaliation and the Israeli Government. A senior officer is quoted as saying " '[t]error for terror is the only solution,' " but Mr. Rubinstein writes, "This solution is unacceptable in

A special situation exists, however, when a series of terroristic incidents is undertaken by adversary states to disrupt the security of national society. It becomes somewhat more artificial in such a situation to assess the legal status of a retaliatory act in isolation from this ongoing and cumulative process of incitement through liberation activity. The situation in the Middle East is one of quasi-belligerency in which there is an agreed cease-fire and a *de facto* situation of hostility that frequently results in intergovernmental violence.

We need to evolve a legal framework that is able to deal with a situation of prolonged quasi-belligerency. Such a framework would at least have the advantage of overcoming the dichotomy between war and peace, and would be more sensitive to the continuities of terroristic provocation and retaliatory response such as are evident in the Middle East.[51]

THE STATUS OF THE RESOLUTION OF THE U.N. SECURITY COUNCIL

The Security Council resolution of December 31, 1968, (1) confines the context to the facts of the Beirut raid, and (2) holds Israel responsible for the damage done. The resolution was unanimous after debate by both sides. States normally friendly toward Israel, including the United States, joined in voting with the majority. The resolution is a formal act of the international institution most competent to consider such questions and an authoritative determination of the respective merits of the adversary contentions.[52] There appears to be no valid legal basis for Israel's evident refusal to accept the formal conclusion of the Security Council as entitled to respect by its government.[53]

---

the Israeli Government." He advances three arguments: (1) "The whole philosophy" of Israeli resistance "runs contrary to any suggestion of counter-terror." (2) Recourse to irregular forces would weaken Israel's contention that Arab incitement of irregular forces is a violation of the cease-fire agreement reached at the end of the June war; this reasoning is attributed to Moshe Dayan. (3) Regular troops can be militarily protected in the course of their mission in a way that irregular forces cannot; this view is attributed to General Bar Lev.

51. For somewhat similar suggestions in different circumstances of conflict, see Philip C. Jessup, "Should International Law Recognize an Intermediate Status between Peace and War?" 48 A.J.I.L. 98 (1954); Myres S. McDougal and Florentino P. Feliciano, Law and Minimum World Public Order 97–120 (New Haven: Yale University Press, 1962).

52. The duty of respect arises from the obligation of a Member of the United Nations to accord respect to acts of the Security Council when that organ is acting, as it was here, within its sphere of competence. As the Council was acting under Chapter VI, not VII, its resolution was formally a "recommendation" rather than a "decision." On this point see further discussion in note 59 below.

53. There were extended discussions of the legal consequences of the Beirut raid in the I.C.A.O. These discussions resulted from a Lebanese complaint that the Israeli action was a violation of the Chicago Convention on Air Transport and that Israel should be condemned and made to pay for the damage done. Although questions about the competence of I.C.A.O. to deal with a complaint of this character dominated the debate, the issues were discussed generally in a manner more favorable to the Israeli position than was the case in the Security Council. The outcome of these discussions was a decision *sine die,* which is quite a contrast with the result within the U.N. forum.

The Foreign Minister of Israel, Abba Eban, has suggested that "The UN does not express the idea [of international order] with any effectiveness in its present composition."[54] But one can hardly imagine any alternative composition of the Security Council that would have given a much more favorable review to the claims of Israel. Since the end of the June war of 1967 Israel has been increasingly in an isolated diplomatic position. This isolation is partly a consequence of an Israeli insistence upon securing certain territorial and economic advantages from its military victory in 1967.[55] The attitudes that dominate world community procedures have been oriented against Israel as a consequence of this underlying feature of the conflict, and this orientation shapes the approach of U.N. organs toward specific issues or "events."[56] The failure of the Security Council resolution to widen the ambit of its concern (1) to include the condemnation of Arab terrorism, such as the Athens raid, and (2) to encompass the responsibility of the Lebanese Government for the control of terrorist activity emanating from its territory is probably properly understood as part of the wider judgment that has been passed against Israel by the Security Council.

Under these circumstances, it is to be expected that Israel will contend that the United Nations is not prepared to deal fairly with specific instances of Arab-Israeli charges and countercharges.[57] On another level of response, it is not surprising that spokesmen for Israel point out that some states joining in the resolution of censure have been completely unmoved by U.N. censure of their own conduct. A most obvious and prominent recent example con-

54. An interview published in Time, Jan. 10, 1969, p. 28.

55. In violation of the Nov. 22, 1967, resolution of the Security Council and of the stated objectives of all states other than Israel, there does not seem to be any serious disposition by the Israeli Government to re-establish the *status quo ante* June 5, 1967. In particular, the retention of administrative control over Jerusalem, of the Golan Heights, a strip of Sinai needed to assure control over the Straits of Tiran, and of a portion of the West Bank of the Jordan and of the Gaza Strip seems to be insisted upon by Israel. There is, then, on the Arab side an unwillingness to accept the existence of the state of Israel and on the Israeli side an insistence upon expansion through conquest. For an assessment of Israel's intention to retain conquered Arab lands, see interview with Levi Eshkol published in Newsweek, Feb. 17, 1969, pp. 49–56; see also analysis of these claims by James Feron, "Eshkol Mentions the Unmentionable," New York Times, Feb. 16, 1969, Sec. 4, p. 2. Israel's claims are a mixture of security demands of a defensive nature and of territorial demands of an expansionist nature.

56. The position of Israel before the political organs of the United Nations is coming to resemble that of South Africa in certain critical respects, especially with regard to the degree of its diplomatic isolation. Israel does continue to enjoy some diplomatic support from the United States and from some countries in Western Europe, but, since the end of the 1967 war, even these governments have grown increasingly critical of Israel's expanding demands and exercise of prerogatives.

57. *E.g.*, Julius Stone, "No Peace—No War in the Middle East" (Sydney, Maitland, 1969), especially pp. 4–5. Professor Stone writes on p. 4: "Everyone knows that too many present Security Council Members are committed to voting on the Arab side, for pro-Israel resolutions to be adopted, no less than five of these Members refusing even to maintain diplomatic relations with her."

cerns the failure of the Security Council to censure by formal resolution the Soviet military occupation of Czechoslovakia in August of 1968.[58]

The conclusion seems evident:

1. The Security Council resolution, despite its technical character as a recommendation, is an authoritative pronouncement on the legal status of the Beirut raid;
2. The quality of authority exercised, however, is diluted by the extent to which "the event" was approached with a disposition against Israel arising from the over-all political setting of the Arab-Israeli dispute;
3. The "duty" of Israel to comply with the terms of the resolution is qualified by its status as a recommendation (rather than a decision) and is impaired by the extent to which other states, including Members of the Security Council, have themselves recently acted in defiance of U.N. directives.[59] There is no established tradition of governmental respect for adverse U.N. determinations.[60] Quite the contrary.

It seems proper to conclude, then, that the United Nations has passed judgment against Israel but that this judgment does not mean very much, given the structure and prevailing habits of international society.

IV. Appraising the Beirut Raid: the Search for a Legal Method

Earlier sections of the paper have tried to demonstrate that:

1. the legal rules and standards embodied in international law do not come to grips with the underlying policy setting provided by the Arab-Israeli conflict;
2. the determinations of the Security Council are authoritative, but are nevertheless not very likely to engender respect.

58. Abba S. Eban, Foreign Minister of Israel, suggested that anti-Jewish discrimination is embodied in the recent diplomatic attacks upon Israel: "I have no other explanation for the fact that the Soviet Union, which invaded Czechoslovakia, can condemn alleged Israeli 'aggression' at the UN without the public gallery bursting into laughter." Interview, Time, January 10, 1969, p. 28.

59. There is a certain legal ambiguity created by the status of various actions taken by the Security Council. In a formal sense, the judgments of the Security Council have the status of "recommendations" unless they are made under Chapter VII of the Charter. Except for "decisions" relating to the observation of the cease-fire, the Security Council has relied upon its "recommendatory" powers under Chapter VI. The resolution censuring Israel after the Beirut raid was a "recommendation." As such, it can be argued that Israel has no formal obligation to obey it. On the other hand, a resolution of censure involves an authoritative act of community review that constitutes strong evidence as to the respective rights and duties of parties to an international controversy.

60. Countries that have been the targets of U.N. directives have almost invariably refused to comply. In fact, when an international conflict gets to the point where the U.N. takes sides, it is almost assured that "the losing side" will not voluntarily obey the will of the Organization.

At the same time, it is important to sustain some framework of constraint in circumstances of conflict such as exist in the Middle East. There is, in particular, a need to establish indicators of reasonableness that can be applied to appraise specific flash-points in a setting of continuous conflict. These indicators can influence, above all else, national decision-making processes to adopt a course of conduct that tends to appear reasonable from an objective or third-party point of view. The structuring of expectations, those of the adversary and of the community, are normally the principal purpose of retaliatory uses of force.[61] More specifically, the chief Israeli purpose (presumed and disclosed) in attacking Arab aircraft at the Beirut Airport on December 28, 1968, was to communicate a message about the disruption of Israeli civil aviation to Lebanese government leaders, secondarily to other Arab governments giving support to liberation movements, and thirdly, to other governments concerned with the Middle East.[62] In such a context of conflict, world public opinion can become influential should it crystallize in favor of one party in a dispute; this influence can affect what the parties regard as a reasonable basis of settlement, and hence, the shape and prospects for a negotiated settlement. In this sense, the censure by Pope Paul VI, the imposition of an arms embargo on Israel by France, the replacement of the Yaffi regime by the Karami regime, when added to the unanimous censure of the Security Council, make the Beirut raid a costly act from Israel's point of view. In brief, the reasons why it is costly are as follows:

1. It worsens Israel's diplomatic position within the international community, alienating friendly and more neutral governments and hardening the attitude of more hostile governments.
2. It gives the impression, created by the evidence of censure at the international level, that Israel is relying upon excessive force to impose its will on weaker countries; such an impression creates, in turn, greater toleration for counter-violence, including Arab terrorism.
3. It seems to work against the diplomatic effort to secure a negotiated or agreed-upon settlement of the underlying conflict.
4. It leads Israel to assume a militarily defensive posture in response to international censure, thereby putting itself into an adversary relationship toward the rest of the international community, according greater strength to more militaristic perspectives within its own élite, thereby

61. That is, in strategic parlance, the objective is one of *deterrence* rather than *defense*. The primary effort is to influence decision-making in the target state's government rather than to diminish its capabilities for action. The Beirut raid aimed at shaping the policies of Arab governments with respect, in particular, to terroristic activities directed at the operations of El Al Airlines by liberation movements based within their territory. There was no intention to deprive Arab countries of commercial aircraft, which were obviously replaceable at relatively little cost.

62. Ambassador Tekoah's statements to the Security Council confirm the conclusion that the Israeli Government sought, above all else, to induce Arab governments to prohibit liberation movements operating within their territory from interfering with El Al flights.

inclining the Government to even greater reliance on force (rather than persuasion) in future instance.[63] There is, in other words, a dangerously escalatory cycle generated by any use of force that has been perceived as excessive in third-party contexts.

The principal point is that a retaliatory use of force that is perceived as excessive tends to engender a variety of bad consequences, including some that may be detrimental to the user. The further point is that rules of international law, as traditionally conceived, are too rigidly formulated to give appropriate insight into the factors that shape a decisional process of government and thus does not, in a realistic way, help officials or observers identify when a use of force is "excessive." The excessiveness of a particular use of force depends upon a combination of objective and subjective (value and ideological outlooks) factors, including the effort at justification made by the claimant state.[64] A more useful conception of international law than the specification of categorical rules would be the enumeration of objective factors likely to shape authoritative judgment and expert commentary. Such an enumeration would be useful for legal advisers to the adversary governments and to those passing judgment on contested behavior.

A rule of conduct isolated from context is often too abstract to guide choice and action. The more significant the connection between the overall context that conditions the action and the particular choice and act, the more difficult it is to make beneficial use of rule-guidance. The situation is subject to such a variety of relevant considerations that a generalized rule is unable to offer much guidance for those entrusted with the responsibility of specific governmental policy. A list of policy considerations can be used by the claimant government to shape its course of conduct to assure the achievement of its own ends. These considerations are only part of the input that enters the decisional process. At times, for instance, conduct that appears highly "illegal" by reference to past appraisals might be deemed essential to sustain the security of the state. But if it is demonstrably essential, then the policies supporting defensive force would tend to mitigate or even overcome any perception of "illegality."[65]

63. *Cf.* New York Times, January 12, 1969, pp. 1, 9; see, especially, article by Rubinstein cited in note 50 above. However, the Israeli response to the Zurich incident (see above, pp. 419–420) casts some doubt on the generality of the statement in the text.

64. The objective factors are those that can be formulated in general terms, whereas the subjective factors are those that involve the perceptual framework of the participants in the situation and are subject to wide variation depending on personality, cultural, and ideological considerations.

65. This tendency would be strengthened if the claimant state executed its operation in such a way as to minimize the injury to innocent civilians and third-party interests. The United States claiming pattern in the Cuban missile crisis is a model for this contention. A novel claim by the United States to use force on the high seas was made to appear so reasonable in assertion and execution that critical reaction, even though the Soviet Union was the target of the claim, was kept to a minimum. For two legal arguments by government officials in support of the United States claim, see Leonard C.

The principal objective reasons why the Beirut raid seems illegal are as follows:

1. It involved a governmental use of force by Israel in retaliation against non-governmental provocation.
2. It involved holding the Lebanese responsible for the Athens incident without the production of sufficient evidence establishing a direct link between the Beirut Government and the Arab terrorists.
3. It involved recourse to force without any prior recourse to diplomatic remedies in a situation where no necessity for immediate recourse to retaliation was demonstrated to exist.
4. It involved the destruction of what appeared to involve an excessive amount of property in an unusually spectacular and inflammatory fashion, thereby constituting an affront to the dignity and security of Lebanon.[66]

These elements of the Beirut raid seem to underlie the objective side of the international judgment, explaining, for instance, the hostile reaction of Pope Paul VI and the United States Government to the Israeli conduct.[67] A greater sensitivity to these factors might have shaped the Israeli action in a manner that would have been both more effective to attain the end in view and less at variance with community perceptions of lawful conduct. In the paragraphs that follow, some effort is made to suggest a suitable framework for claims to use force in retaliation against prior terroristic acts.[68] This framework embodies certain general policies concerning the use of force in periods of peace:[69]

Meeker, "Defensive Quarantine and the Law," 57 A.J.I.L. 515 (1963); Abram Chayes, "The Legal Case for U.S. Action on Cuba," 47 Dept. of State Bulletin 763 (1962).

66. I have elsewhere analyzed the reactions of African countries to the so-called Stanleyville operation of December, 1964, in these terms. Falk, Legal Order in a Violent World 324–335 (Princeton University Press, 1968).

67. There are certain other factors that explain censure from third-party sources: (1) prior uses by Israel of excessive force in response to terroristic provocation; (2) the selection of Lebanon as the target of retaliation, given the long period of non-involvement by the Lebanese Government in the Arab-Israeli conflict; (3) the growing realization that Israel was insisting upon retaining some of the territorial fruits of the 1967 war; (4) the timing of the Beirut raid seemed to be damaging prospects for either a Great Power or U.N. initiative to bring some measure of stability, if not real peace, to the Middle East.

68. A subsequent article will attempt to evolve a suitable framework for the assessment of acts of violence relied upon by liberation groups to achieve their political ends. Such a framework would involve, necessarily, some assessment of the compatibility between the aims of these groups and appraisal of these aims by regional and global institutions and their conformity with norms of international law. In addition, the choice of means used to pursue such aims requires an innovative legal analysis that reconsiders para-military violence as an instrument of political change. Eventually the two frameworks of legal appraisal will need to be integrated into a single coherent approach to the relevance of international law to this species of international conflict that has assumed such great importance in world affairs.

69. For some relevant legal background see Fritz Grob, The Relativity of War and Peace (New Haven: Yale University Press, 1949); Albert E. Hindmarsh, Force in Peace:

1. That the burden of persuasion is upon the government that initiates an official use of force across international boundaries;
2. That the governmental user of force will demonstrate its defensive character convincingly by connecting the use of force to the protection of territorial integrity, national security, or political independence;
3. That a genuine and substantial link exists between the prior commission of provocative acts and the resultant claim to be acting in retaliation;
4. That a diligent effort be made to obtain satisfaction by persuasion and pacific means over a reasonable period of time, including recourse to international organizations;
5. That the use of force is proportional to the provocation and calculated to avoid its repetition in the future, and that every precaution be taken to avoid excessive damage and unnecessary loss of life, especially with respect to innocent civilians;[70]
6. That the retaliatory force is directed primarily against military and para-military targets and against military personnel;[71]
7. That the user of force make a prompt and serious explanation of its

---

Force Short of War in International Relations (Cambridge: Harvard University Press, 1933); M. R. Garcia-Mora, International Responsibility for Hostile Acts of Private Persons against Foreign States (The Hague: Nijhoff, 1962); Hersch Lauterpacht, "Revolutionary Activities by Private Persons against Foreign States," 22 A.J.I.L. 105, 130 (1928). For some specification of support given terroristic groups in Egypt and Jordan since the June war, see Stone, note 57 above, pp. 4–6. According to Israeli sources there have been 1,288 acts of sabotage and border incidents between June 6, 1967, and December 31, 1968. 920 of these acts occurred in the Jordanian-Israeli sector, 166 in the Egyptian sector, 37 in the Syrian, 35 in the Lebanese, and 130 in the Gaza Strip sectors. Israeli losses have been put at 234 soldiers and 47 civilians killed and 765 soldiers and 330 civilians wounded. Arab losses are reported by Israel as considerably greater than these figures. See New York Times, Feb. 13, 1969, pp. 1, 4. There are indications of a rising Israeli concern about the growing capacity of the guerrilla groups to impair Israel's security, including especially the character of its administration of occupied territories inhabited largely by Arabs. See James Feron, "Israel Concerned over Guerrillas," *ibid.*, March 9, 1969, Sec. 1, p. 12.

70. Israeli statements before the Security Council emphasized the effort to carry out the Beirut raid without inflicting casualties upon Lebanese citizens. See, *e.g.*, S/PV. 1460, p. 23. And in the official release of the Israeli Information Office in New York, the following language appears: "At great risk to themselves, Israeli troops at the Airport exercised the strictest precautions to prevent civilian casualties. The planes were emptied of passengers and ground crews, and people in the vicinity were led away to safety. Loudspeakers were employed to issue instructions in Arabic and English. The only shots fired were warning shots in the air." Release dated Dec. 28, 1968.

71. Israeli attacks against Arab para-military bases associated with guerrilla activities have occasioned little adverse reaction, especially if "provoked" by an upsurge in miscellaneous incidents of terrorism within Israel. See paragraphs on the air strike against Syrian bases of Al Fatah on Feb. 24, 1969, above, p. 420. To some extent the governmental character of a retaliation against non-governmental provocation is neutralized if the targets are military. This is especially true if the victims of the terrorism were civilians and damage done to non-military targets. The choice of a non-military target for Israeli retaliation after the Athens incident seems to be a very significant element in explaining the strong adverse international reaction to the Beirut raid.

conduct before the relevant organ(s) of community review and seek vindication therefrom of its course of action;

8. That the use of force amounts to a clear message of communication to the target government so that the contours of what constituted the unacceptable provocation are clearly conveyed;

9. That the user of force cannot achieve its retaliatory purposes by acting within its own territorial domain and thus cannot avoid interference with the sovereign prerogatives of a foreign state;

10. That the user of force seek a pacific settlement to the underlying dispute on terms that appear to be just and sensitive to the interests of its adversary;

11. That the pattern of conduct of which the retaliatory use of force is an instance exhibits deference to considerations 1–10, and that a disposition to accord respect to the will of the international community be evident;

12. That the appraisal of the retaliatory use of force take account of the duration and quality of support, if any, that the target government has given to terroristic enterprises.

V. Conclusion

There are several parts of the approach to the kind of legal analysis recommended in this article: (1) a depiction of the central policy issues embodied in the underlying conflict; (2) a check-list of objective considerations relevant to the assertion and appraisal of a claim by a state to make a retaliatory use of force.

The Beirut raid was an event situated in an unusually complicated politico-military setting. Its assessment as a legal act is not a dichotomous "either/or" judgment, nor should its legal appraisal be isolated from antecedent or subsequent conduct. The essential problem confronting Israel is the design of a response against provocative terror carried out by liberation movements enjoying varying degrees of tacit and overt support from various Arab governments. This single problem is related to the over-all search for a resolution or stabilization of the conflict in the Middle East, a conflict that is dangerous to both regional and global stability, containing even some threat of igniting a world war fought with nuclear weapons.[72]

The rôle of legal analysis is to facilitate the process of shaping and judging action: specifically, to promote constructive effects to the actor and to the community. The assumption underlying such an approach is that the primary rôle of international law is to help governments plan *how* to act, rather than to permit some third-party judge to determine whether contested action is legal or not. In fact the function of the third-party judge can be performed

72. *Cf.* analysis of Safran, cited note 22 above, at pp. xii–xv, 21–142, in terms of the levels: (1) Arab-Israeli; (2) inter-Arab; (3) U.S.–U.S.S.R.

properly only by attempting to assess *in what respects* and *to what extent* the governmental actor "violated" community norms of a prescriptive nature. Given the present character of international legal order, the essence of law consists of an interactive process of communication among governments and between governments and international institutions as to the character of acceptable behavior. The more this communication is premised upon a consensus as to relevant considerations and the more it reflects the dominance of objective over subjective factors, the more plausible it becomes to say that international law is playing a significant rôle.[73]

The Beirut raid exhibits a failure of the appropriate legal considerations to guide the Israeli Government's claim to use force in retaliation against terroristic provocation. This failure is important because of its bearing on world attitudes toward the relevant merits of the adversary positions of Israel and the Arab states on the underlying issues, including a peaceful settlement on mutually acceptable terms, as well as attitudes toward the whole matter of the existence of the state of Israel. It is also important because retaliation across frontiers against terroristic activity has significance in several other world contexts: Southern Africa, Latin America, and Southern Asia. It is, finally, important because the claim to be acting in a retaliatory capacity is one that involves recourse to self-help that is generally only available to the strong against the weak. As such, the ethics of retaliation is related to the rôle of military superiority in shaping the resolution of international conflict. However, the vulnerability of some states to an externally-based and supported liberation movement points up the artificiality of territorial boundaries. It is arguable that in certain situations actions against terror in the form of striking at the camps and sanctuaries amounts to extraterritorial police enforcement.[74] A reprisal, such as the Beirut raid, seeks to influence the target government to suppress or regulate terrorist activity within its territorial limits; it can be understood as a demand for co-operative law enforcement. If this demand is refused, then the state that is a target of the activity is confronted by a difficult choice. It can either tolerate the foreign sanctuary or it can violate the international boundary. If it does the former, then its enemies often grow stronger and its security diminishes, whereas if it does the latter, then it often puts itself in the position of appearing to be

73. The significance of this rôle, it should be noted, depends on a conception of international law that is wider than one concerned with rules of behavior. Neither the Charter norms nor the norms of customary international law delimiting the right of reprisal, come to grips with the kind of choice that confronts a government that needs to design responses to persistent terrorism directed at the security of its national territory. In such circumstances, the exigencies of response cannot be cast aside by the invocation of legal rules. At the same time, retaliatory claims can be asserted in accordance with a framework of restraint that is designed to minimize disruption, to maximize the clarity of the message conveyed, and to solicit the sympathy of the organized world community.

74. *Cp.* problems associated with the effort by the United States to extend its antitrust regulation to govern the foreign operations of business firms that have an anti-competitive impact on the U.S. economy.

the violator of international peace, the initiator of aggression; in time such a state risks becoming an international pariah. Israel's dilemma in the Middle East is of this sort. The best way out of this dilemma is for Israel to achieve greater sensitivity to world order considerations, especially on matters bearing on the basis for permanent reconciliation. There is a need for reciprocity and mutuality in the course of clarifying the line of ultimate solution, as well as in maintaining a tolerable degree of domestic security during the difficult interim period.

International lawyers can contribute greatly to the quality of world order by working out a systematic framework for the assessment of claims to use retaliatory force. This article is a first step in this direction taken within a limited policy and factual setting.

3. Sisyphus and the Avalanche: The United Nations, Egypt, and Hungary

STANLEY HOFFMANN

THE GODS HAD CONDEMNED Sisyphus to push a rock up the top of a mountain, from which the rock kept rolling down. International organization seems to be a modern illustration of an old myth. After each crisis, new attempts are made to push the rock of peace up again, and no crisis has revealed the frustrating task of international organization more sharply than the recent shock of the Middle Eastern and Hungarian explosions.

First, the crisis has revealed that, in spite of multiple efforts, the mechanisms which the United Nations had established for the prevention and repression of threats to peace did not work well enough to save the organization from having once again to improvise in an emergency. Secondly the crisis has shown that in its policies also, the United Nations was limited to a Sisyphus-like role; the United Nations could not prevent a return to the *status quo* of Soviet control of Hungary, and in the Middle East the strenuous efforts of the organization have not been able to achieve much more than a restoration of a slightly amended but still unsatisfactory *status quo*. Thirdly, the crisis has thrown a strong light over some of the deeper reasons for these procedural and political shortcomings. Fourthly, the split among the leading western powers over the Middle East and the embarrassment provoked in the west by the simultaneity of the Middle Eastern and Hungarian affairs have shown the need for a political strategy common to the western nations (the United States as well as western Europe) for their relations with the United Nations in matters concerning peace and security.

The present article is an attempt to examine briefly the four aspects of the crisis of last fall.

Institutional Weaknesses

Just as after each disappointment the horse in Orwell's *Animal Farm* thought that the happy days would come at last if it only did more work, so after each major incident the statesmen of the world have deplored the chinks in the armor of international organization and have striven for more and better institutional engineering. Thus, the "Uniting for Peace" resolution tried to institutionalize the Korean miracle so that despite the big powers' split, future threats to peace or aggressions would again be handled effectively by the United Nations. The resolution created an impressive series of procedures and organs for preventive and repressive purposes. A more limited but complementary system of alarm bells had been established in such dangerous parts of the world as the Middle East and Kashmir. In last year's crisis, most of these mechanisms proved useless—either because they were simply not used by the very nations that had created them, or because they had been allowed to decay, or because they were not adapted to the circumstances of last fall.

1. Let us look first at the preventive arsenal. The "Uniting for Peace" resolution had established a Peace Observation Commission to "observe and report on the situation in any area where there exists international tension the continuance of which is likely to endanger the maintenance of international peace and security." This Commission has been singularly neglected. It has been used only with reference to the Balkans, where a subcommission was appointed in 1951 by the General Assembly to succeed the United Nations Special Committee which was being discontinued. The subcommission, which submitted no reports of its own—as indeed, there was no need for any, since Greece was now a quiet NATO member. Since 1954, the Peace Observation Commission has been totally lethargic. Thailand requested a subcommission shortly before the end of the Indochina war, but no decision was taken. The Commission was not used in the crisis over the nationalization of the Suez Canal Company. The Security Council, when it discussed the matter in October 1956, was politically in no position to do so. The Egyptian complaint against English and French threats of force and mobilization measures was put on the agenda but never taken up, and Egypt, whose consent or invitation was required under the terms of the 1950 resolution, never asked for a subcommission to be sent into its territory. Indeed, since the threats came from across the sea, a system patterned after Korea was somewhat inappropriate. Thus, only the Anglo-French complaint against Egypt

was discussed, and it was dealt with as an ordinary dispute. The whole emphasis was put on diplomacy and conciliation, not on alarm and prevention.

The Peace Observation Commission was not used in connection with the Arab-Israel dispute either. And why should it have been? Was not this dispute taken care of by an elaborate international machinery? The trouble is that this machinery was in pitiful condition. The Palestine Conciliation Commission was left without instructions ever since the General Assembly, at its seventh session, failed to agree on any resolution. The Commission has long ago acknowledged the impossibility of reconciling the various parties on the fundamental issues (borders, refugees, and Jerusalem) with which it had been asked to deal in those earlier days when the young international organization was setting its hopes very high indeed. The Commission had turned to more modest tasks: the question of Arab accounts blocked in Israeli banks and compensation for abandoned Arab lands in Israel. Such efforts were sure neither to stir nor to calm the troubled waters of Arab-Israel relations.

With no prospect of global settlement, the whole burden of preserving peace in the area fell upon the Truce Supervision Organization (UNTSO). But no mechanism of observers and mixed armistice commissions could forever bear the weight that was put on the UNTSO by the failure to achieve a lasting settlement. Inevitably, a system whose organs could pass judgments on armistice violations but whose condemnations and proposals were ineffective if the parties did not want to accept them was bound to wear down. The strain was increased by a frequently used and complicated circuit. The more important violations were sent by their victims before the Security Council, which in turn called for the Chief of Staff (or his deputies, the chairmen of particular armistice commissions) to report or to appear in person; then after "condemning," "taking note" or "endorsing," the Council dumped the whole matter back into the commanders' laps.

Even more striking, however, was the extraordinary fragility of the mechanism itself, and the passivity of the members of the United Nations who were presiding over its decay. There were so few observers—at one point only five for the whole Israel-Jordan border—that they could intervene only *after* the incidents, waste their energies in post-mortems, and merely maintain a score-board. Ever since the days of the much more numerous truce observers of 1948 the grievances of United Nations representatives in the field have been the same: "the uncooperative attitude" displayed by local authorities, the huge number of complaints by both sides, the violation of the armistice provisions which called for reciprocal reduction and withdrawal of forces, the attempts at limiting the freedom of movement of the observers. Year after year, the Security Council resolutions and the reports of the Chiefs of Staff have monotonously referred to the same sore spots.

The deterioration of the mechanism accelerated in 1955 and 1956. After the Israeli raid into the Gaza Strip in February 1955, General Burns restated a previous proposal for joint patrols, a barbed wire fence, and the manning of outposts by regulars; the Security Council endorsed his suggestions, but no agreement was reached. A new incident occurred in August; the Chief of Staff asked again for an effective physical barrier along the demarcation line. Once more the Security Council backed him. What followed was a series of incidents on the eastern front of Israel. Sisyphus went to work anew; in April 1956, the Security Council asked the Secretary-General to go to the Middle East. Mr. Hammarskjold, when he returned one month later, seemed to believe that he had consolidated the truce mechanism. He had formulated the doctrine of absolute, unconditional observance of each provision referring to the armistice lines; he had obtained an agreement (limited to October 31 by Israel) for the stationing of observers on both sides of the Gaza Strip, and he had hopes for a prompt agreement on the separation of forces, the erection of physical obstacles, and a clearer delimitation of the line. However, he noted that "there is not in all cases an adequate functioning machinery for resolving disputes" over the armistice agreements, and that "no procedure has been established for the handling of conflicts covered by the *general* clauses of the armistice agreements," conflicts over which the mixed commissions had no jurisdiction and which were not usually referred by the parties to the Security Council. He emphasized both the need for such procedures and the impossibility of making any proposals acceptable to the parties. In spite of a new endorsement by the Security Council, which nodded itself back to sleep, the machinery was not repaired and storm signals accumulated.

The hopes of the spring did not materialize, as General Burns reported early in September. Twice the mixed commissions broke down. Mr. Hammarskjold issued a warning to all Middle Eastern states—and not only to them. He stressed that there were limits to what the United Nations could do if the governments concerned did not want to cooperate, and with the same discretion as in his May report he added that "these matters . . . can in no way excuse the United Nations from resolutely pursuing its efforts." The United Nations did not do anything about it, and when the crisis came, the alarm bell was out of order: the Truce Supervision Organization was prevented from investigating the incidents that preceded Israel's attack, and Israel's mobilization and invasion of Egypt came before the United Nations could wake up.

In the weeks that separated Mr. Hammarskjold's warning from Israel's move, and especially after Israel's statement on the Suez Canal blockade, Mr. Ben Gurion's denunciation of Colonel Nasser and Mr. Eban's statements in the Security Council during the discussion of the Jordanian complaint on October 25, the United Nations still had at its disposal one big preventive weapon which could theoretically have been used for the first time: Part A of the "Uniting for Peace" resolution, which provided for an emergency session of the Assembly when "there appears to be a threat to peace," and when the Security Council is paralyzed. But this provision was not used for the same obvious reason which accounts for the failure of Mr. Hammarskjold's warning; the states were either not listening, or they did not want to listen. If a resolution asking for emergency measures had been brought before the Council, an Anglo-French (or French) veto might well have paralyzed the Council, and thus created the conditions for a resort to the 1950 procedure. But no such resolution was introduced or contemplated; on the 25th of October, further debate in the Council was postponed to the 30th.

Thus, the preventive mechanisms had failed. The arsenal was, on the whole, rich enough; but both its exploitation and the repair of those of its weapons that were in bad shape depended on the will and alertness of the United Nations Members. No foolproof set of procedures could ever automatically oblige states to take measures once a certain danger point is reached; and no system would have alerted either the Council or an emergency session of the Assembly about the gravity of the Suez crisis just before the Anglo-French intervention. The Anglo-French ultimatum came at a moment when the dispute apparently had entered a cooler period of bargaining and compromises under the auspices of the Secretary-General. The preventive parts of the "Uniting for Peace" resolution, modelled on the Korean example, can only be operative in cases where the tension is building up gradually and where no party succeeds in concealing its plan to use force. For similar reasons, there was no mechanism which could have prevented the Hungarian crisis.

2. Let us turn next to the repressive equipment of the United Nations. What we find here, paradoxically, is both a poorer and a more useful arsenal. The weapon which was used with great speed and efficiency, contrary to the expectations of the British and the French, was that very Part A of the "Uniting for Peace" resolution which had not been invoked preventively. At the request of the Security Council, two emergency sessions of the Assembly were summoned.

Now, Part C of the 1950 resolution had asked states to take certain initiatives which would facilitate the resort to "collective measures" (including armed force once peace has been broken); and it had established a Collective Measures Committee to study methods of maintaining and strengthening peace. After the failure of the system of Chapter VII, after the watering-down of Mr. Trygve Lie's proposal for "an internationally recruited police force," Sisyphus had been trying again. But this time the rock did not get pushed very high. The states did not react very enthusiastically to the requests of the 1950 resolution, nor to those of the resolution of January 1952 which embodied some suggestions of the Collective Measures Committee's first report. Indeed, the way in which these suggestions were emasculated by the Sixth Assembly was remarkable enough: imperative exhortations for advance preparation (including if necessary legislative changes) were turned into soft recommendations studded with reassuring grants of liberty. The key idea of getting Members to earmark certain elements of their armed forces for service as United Nations units quietly got lost.

The Committee itself based its work on two principles which were probably unavoidable and certainly unfortunate from the point of view of last fall's crisis. First, entrusted with what amounted to a general study of collective security, and realizing that advance commitments to "particular procedures or specific contributions" were unlikely, it tried to design measures that could fit as many circumstances as possible. One of the requirements of collective security is anonymity, but the price one has to pay is vagueness. It is therefore not too astonishing that the efforts of the Committee "were sterile." Secondly, what made them still more surely useless for the Assembly in 1956, even as a mere guide, was the way in which the Committee, just like the "Uniting for Peace" resolution itself, had taken the Korean case as a model—both in order, no doubt, to have at least one island of reference in an ocean of generalities, and because of the permanent tendency of statesmen and generals to prepare meticulously for the previous crisis. This principle had two consequences. The whole effort of the Committee was oriented toward collective enforcement against a transgressor. The Committee thus neglected the cases in which there would be a need for a supervisory force but not for a shooting one, and of course all its efforts were superfluous for a case such as Hungary where what was going to be decided was collective blame without enforcement. Also, the work of the Committee, almost from the first page of its first report, as based on the hypothesis of a clear-cut case of aggression; the other hypothesis (a "breach of peace" which is not a clear-cut aggression) got lost. Now, in the fall of 1956, the United Nations was faced with two baffling situations. One was an armed intervention in a civil war, opposed by one revolutionary government, but called for by the previous cabinet. The other case was a breach of peace composed of two separate invasions. About each of them one could argue endlessly as to whether it constituted a naked aggression, a partly provoked aggression, or a use of force devoid of "aggressive intention" which a well-known international lawyer once stated to be a necessary part of any definition of aggression and then refused to define abstractly. Indeed, the flaw of the Commission's decision to study the suppression of acts of aggression is well indicated by the failure of a host of international bodies to agree on any legally or politically satisfactory definition of aggression. Surely the apex of confusion is reached when a group as serious as the International Law Commission decides that all acts of aggression are crimes against mankind, after having failed to define aggression. Politico-legal concepts should not be defined by lawyers and cannot be adequately defined by politicians either.

At any rate, when the challenge came, the Members of the United Nations had once again to improvise a response in the heat of the moment. Nations condemned to improvisation are rarely willing to go beyond what is immediately needed to save peace, except perhaps for vague promises to think about more stable structures once the danger has receded. Indeed, the history of international organizations is like a graveyard of specialized commissions, or *ad hoc* representatives, who have been more or less gracefully allowed to fade away after finishing their temporary job.

The Policies Followed

We turn now to a brief discussion of the way in which the United Nations used its freedom last fall.

Ever since 1945, the organization has been faced with a series of disputes which were not the traditional quarrels of a stabilized period—quarrels of limited scope which do not challenge the international *status quo* or the internal regimes of states. The United Nations has had to deal with the explosions of a revolutionary period—disputes tainted by violence or at least accompanied by threats of violence. In such circumstances, the neat categories provided for by the Charter ("disputes," "situations," "aggression") often make little sense, and the United Nations has felt free to discard them and to select its course empirically. Last fall the Assembly decided to take a middle road between the two following extremes. On the one hand there is the policy which we might call "pure coercion"; it tries through injunctions, threats or collective enforcement to oblige the transgressors to give up any gains obtained through violations of the Charter; it refuses to subordinate a return to law to concessions asked or conditions raised by the transgressors. On the other hand, there is what might be called a policy of "pure conciliation"; it treats all parties to a dispute as equals and tries to reach a compromise through accommodation without any pressure being put on either side. Of course these two extremes are ideal types, but they have at times been realized. Thus, "pure coercion" was the United Nations policy in Korea, and "pure conciliation" was used during much of the Palestine crisis of 1948, during the first Indonesian conflict (1947–1948), and in the Kashmir stalemate. Now in the case of the Suez crisis, the middle road taken by the Assembly proved to be an increasingly narrow path, and in the case of Hungary, the road soon led to a dead end.

1. In the Middle Eastern crisis, there were excellent reasons for eliminating the two extremes. First, any policy that aimed merely at coercing France, England and Israel back into compliance with the Charter, even if it was not initially accompanied by collective enforcement measures, was risky. If the violators did not choose to obey the injunctions of the United Nations any more than the north Koreans had observed the provisions of the resolution of June 25, 1950, the United Nations would have either to lose face or to turn to sanctions, just as it had on June 27, 1950. Sanctions were both dangerous and questionable. The draft resolution introduced by the United States in the

Security Council after the beginning of the Israeli attack was almost a replica of the resolution of June 25, 1950; England and France were right in pointing out the differences between the cases of north Korea and Israel. After the English and French intervention, any attempt at treating the crisis as a new Korea disappeared. No one was called an aggressor. Consequently, the United Nations on the one hand refused to take up the Soviet appeal for an international mandate to an American-Russian expedition against the invaders—an appeal made, significantly enough, not to the Assembly, where it might have been well received, but to the Security Council, where it was sure to die fast. On the other hand, the United Nations also decided to offer to the parties an instrument that belongs not to the coercive but to the conciliatory arsenal of international organization: the United Nations Emergency Force (UNEF). UNEF is the sort of procedural guarantee which has in previous cases led belligerents to accept a cease-fire. States unwilling to lose face by obeying purely and simply a United Nations call because they do not want to appear to give in to their enemy in the field have often proved more ready to bow to an international mechanism. Seen in this light, UNEF has been playing a role comparable to the role of United Nations commissions and truce organizations in Palestine, Kashmir and Indonesia.

Secondly, however, there were good reasons for discarding a policy of mere conciliation. An organization committed to the defense and illustration of certain principles of international behavior could not accept as *faits accomplis* a series of moves which, however explainable by previous failures of the United Nations itself to redress certain wrongs, nevertheless violated the ban on the use of force against the territorial integrity or political independence of states. Israel had a strong case. The situation that existed before October 29, when Egypt claimed to be still at war with its neighbor but wanted to be protected against it ("unilateral belligerence") was indeed absurd. The need for Israel to defend itself, even through retaliation, against armed Egyptian attacks and against Colonel Nasser's plans for encirclement cannot be dismissed lightly either. But there remain enough arguments on the other side, such as the perils of preventive war, the well established principle that retaliation should not be disproportionate, and the idea that violations of the Charter presented as justified by the opponent's own breaches of treaties can only lead to international anarchy. Mr. Hammarskjold's firm decision to refuse to "condone a change of the *status juris* resulting from military action contrary to the provisions of the Charter" cannot be seriously challenged. Furthermore, in previous cases of disputes in which one side had resorted to military action and which the United Nations had tried to solve through purely conciliatory techniques, the organization had come close to failure; it had been able to remain in control of events only by coming around to Mr. Hammarskjold's doctrine. Consequently, the Assembly aimed some sharp recommendations at the invaders of Egypt; the resolution of November 2 called for their prompt withdrawal. This call had few precedents in the history of the United Nations, outside of the plain collective security case of Korea.

Now, once the two extreme policies had been eliminated, there remained a very broad range of possible "middle roads." Coercion and conciliation can be combined in infinitely varying doses. The crucial question is whether the mixture used after the resolution of November 2 was the best one. The course followed by the Assembly became rather like collective security, with moral and negative political sanctions (the denial of certain claims) substituted for the positive political, economic or military sanctions envisaged by the Collective Measures Committee. In other words, the Assembly and the Secretary-General moved further and further from the pole of "pure conciliation" and closer and closer to the pole of "pure coercion." Instead of achieving both an elimination of illegally obtained advantages and a peaceful settlement of the problems that had led to a violation of the law, the United Nations allowed the first aspect to obliterate the second. In the first place, the issue of "cease-fire and withdrawal" was separated from the underlying substantive issues; consideration of the Suez nationalization problem and of an over-all Arab-Israel settlement was postponed until after the first issue had been disposed of. The two United States draft resolutions which aimed at removing the fundamental causes of tension were shelved. Now, neither during the second Indonesian conflict nor when the Security Council invoked Chapter VII against the Arabs in the summer of 1948 had a policy of strong pressure against one side ruled out consideration of the deeper political issues which explained the breach of peace. In the second place, the elimination of the breach of peace and the restoration or quasi-restoration of the *status quo* became synonymous; Mr. Hammarskjold refused to permit Israel's withdrawal to be accompanied by guarantees over what one might call the "intermediate" issues—issues half way between the return to the *status quo* and a general political negotiation: Gaza, the Gulf of Aqaba, and passage of Israeli ships through the Suez Canal. These two decisions really condemned the United Nations to play the role of Sisyphus; for the crisis had its origins in the precariousness of a *status quo* which was never supposed to last eight years, at least as much as in the bad will of the parties.

Mr. Hammarskjold stated that his proposals tended to restore not the *status quo,* but the *status juris.* But the distinction is a fragile one: indeed, what *is* the *status juris?* The parties disagree, and this disagreement itself explains in part the collapse of the armistice agreements. For the Israelis, the law includes not only the end of border raids, or the scrupulous observance of articles VII and VIII of the Israel-Egypt armistice agreement, dealing with the armistice lines, but also the end of the blockade of the Suez Canal and of the Gulf of Aqaba. For the Egyptians, this is not the case, and in his report of January 24 the Secretary-General (who has constantly refused to answer Israel's questions concerning Egypt's policy of belligerency) was only able to say about the Gulf of Aqaba that "any possible claims of belligerent rights . . .

if asserted, should be limited to clearly non-controversial situations." In his report of January 24, he defined the return to the *status juris* as "a withdrawal of troops, and . . . the relinquishment or nullification of rights asserted in territories covered by the military action and depending upon it." The *status juris* is a return to the *status quo* accompanied by hopes that the parties would in the future respect the law.

A policy should be judged by its results. Mr. Hammarskjold's policy led to an impasse. The Assembly resolution of February 2—the last document adopted by the United Nations—merely endorsed his report of January 24. It asked, as he had done, for a stationing of UNEF "on" the armistice lines—with no length of time suggested. It also called for "the implementation of other measures as proposed in the Secretary-General's report with due regard to the considerations set out therein with a view to assist in achieving situations conducive to the maintenance of peaceful conditions in the area." "It seems very pretty," said Alice in Wonderland after she had read the poem "Jabberwocky," "but it is *rather* hard to understand." If one goes back to Mr. Hammarskjold's report, what one finds is the hope that the parties will let UNEF take over the functions of the Truce Supervision Organization and the familiar wish that the parties will accept at long last "such supporting measures as would guarantee a return to the state of affairs envisaged in the armistice agreement and avoidance of the state of affairs into which conditions, due to a lack of compliance with the agreement, progressively deteriorated." This year's hope for a mined fence replaces last year's hope for a barbed wire one. Sisyphus trusted that the rock would stop rolling down the next time. The Secretary-General, in answer to Israel's request, also stated in his report that "if it is recognized that there is such a need for such an arrangement," UNEF units could be stationed at the entrance of the Gulf of Aqaba. If this was a hint for specific Assembly endorsement, the Assembly, by its wholesale endorsement of Mr. Hammarskjold's "other measures," did not in turn do much more than hint back that it did not mind Mr. Hammarskjold's own hint. It was a tie. It became a deadlock when Israel persisted in asking for more, and Mr. Hammarskjold refused because "adherence to principle and law must be given priority and cannot be conditioned"—an admirable statement that would be even more perfect if the meaning of the law were clear and if Egypt had not, in one instance, defied successfully a principle affirmed by the Security Council.

Therefore, the United States, which until then had left the Secretary-General in charge of all the discussions with Egypt and Israel, had to intervene and to take the matter, in effect, out of the Secretary-General's hands. But it could not, at that stage, contradict him too vigorously. Hence the twists and turns of an "unconditional withdrawal" nevertheless subordinated not to conditions, but to "assumptions," to "hopes and conditions that are not unreasonable." Both because these "assumptions" went a little beyond Mr. Hammarskjold's doctrine, and because they had to be so obscure in order not to clash with it, they became controversial enough to make impossible the drafting of any resolution that would embody them.

It is instructive to establish a sort of balance sheet. By way of documents, we have only the United Nations resolution of February 2, the Secretary-General's report to which it refers, and the "assumptions" of Israel as qualified by the United States and interpreted by Mr. Hammarskjold. (*a*) On the Egyptian side of the former armistice line the United Nations has a police force tolerated by Egypt, but whose mission has not been clearly spelled out. The appeal for a stationing "on" the line, still unheeded by Israel, gives Egypt a most useful political weapon, in addition to Egypt's legal right to ask the Force to leave. (*b*) In the Gaza Strip, Israel's expectations (which Mr. Hammarskjold never encouraged) have proved in great part wrong. The temporary period of United Nations civilian control has been short indeed. Egyptian troops have not returned but they have the legal right to do so. (*c*) At the entrance of the Gulf of Aqaba, a UNEF unit has been stationed. But its duration is shaky, its mission most obscure, and the only solid guarantee seems to be Israel's solemn warning that any interference with free navigation will be considered as an attack giving rise to the right of self-defense. (*d*) As to passage through the Suez Canal, Egypt has not renounced its belligerency. (*e*) Nothing new, except more hatred, has happened with reference to a general settlement between Israel and its neighbors. (*f*) The Suez Canal Company issue has been handled after the Anglo-French withdrawal, and has ended in a *de facto* acceptance of a unilateral Egyptian declaration—with no United Nations pronouncement of any kind.

An abundance of texts calling for a cease-fire and withdrawal had been succeeded by a stunning dearth of authoritative documents covering the present and the future. The interplay between public international debates and secret diplomacy has produced a series of stop-gap agreements differently interpreted by the parties. Some of the multilateral gobbledygook which has replaced the elegant obscurity of nineteenth century diplomacy is still with us—but not much of the authority attached to previous United Nations pronouncements, an authority which has often offset their obscurity. The course followed through the United Nations seems to have led to little more than a temporary reinforcement of the truce system at the Israel-Egypt border. Egypt's present informal acceptance of UNEF can hardly be seen as a big concession. UNEF might prevent new raids, but it also protects Egypt from Israel; and Egypt made sure that the Force would be absolutely weightless in the political balance of power in the Middle East; UNEF is not, as Egypt had feared, an "occupation force," it had served far more, as Egypt wished, as a "fire brigade" called to the rescue of Egypt. Indeed, in an area where all issues *are* linked, the elimination of the breach of peace does not merely restore Egypt's position in the supposed "next phase" (the discussion of the underlying issues). The position has improved. Egypt's right of veto over UNEF provides Colonel Nasser with an instrument of blackmail against any attempt at a solution that he would dislike. We must therefore ask whether another "middle road," a different combination of coercion and conciliation, might not have been *tried* (this is not to say that it would have *succeeded*). For it is one thing to condone violations of the Charter, but it is quite another to refuse to follow a course that makes new violations timely.

It seems that there remained a choice between the Secretary-General's policy of proceeding step-by-step, so that no new issue would be considered before the previous one had been disposed of, and the policy outlined by Mr. Pearson. The Canadian foreign minister wanted to continue the tradition, often used with success, of having the political organs of the United Nations take without delay a stand on all issues involved in the crisis, i.e. suggest procedures for settlement of the deeper underlying problems and define a policy concerning the "intermediate" issues. This would still have upheld the principle that gains obtained by force should not be kept. But it would also have taken into account the fact that the issues raised by Israel's, France's and the United Kingdom's action were linked. After all, the trouble in the Middle East did not begin on October 29, 1956.

It might be argued on legal and on political grounds that Mr. Pearson's "middle course" was not realistic, and that Mr. Hammarskjold's line was the only possible one—except for appeasement or collective enforcement. The legal objections do not seem decisive. One could argue that under international law Egypt's consent was needed at every stage. But Mr. Pearson's proposals did not overlook this requirement. They merely invited the United Nations *first* to define a line of policy and *then* promote negotiations with the parties to get this line adopted. Maybe Egypt's consent would have been hard to get; but Egypt, which had been rescued by the United Nations, which was still partly occupied by a victorious enemy, and which was economically as badly shaken as its opponents, was in no strong position to resist pressure, had it come. One could also object that the resolutions of the Assembly did not leave much leeway to the Secretary-General. Nevertheless, we can observe that Israel did not withdraw "forthwith." Furthermore, the key resolution of November 2 mentioned the problem of raids and the need for observance of "the armistice agreements"—terms which left the door open for arrangements over the "intermediate" issues, as, for instance, Egypt's claiming of belligerency rights, which the Security Council had declared to be in contradiction to the armistice agreements.

In fact, both legal objections do raise far more serious political problems. How could the Secretary-General *himself* exert pressure on Egypt? How much *political* leeway did he have in interpreting the resolutions? It is not enough to state that he probably had much to say in the drafting of the instructions he received from the Assembly, and that the Assembly was unlikely to overrule him if he decided to follow Mr. Pearson's course, at a time when American policy was to praise, paraphrase, and propose whatever Mr. Hammarskjold suggested. For even if he had obtained from the Assembly directives in accordance with Mr. Pearson's program, the success of such a policy depended on one major criterion, which was missing: the willingness of the United States to exert pressure on Egypt in order to gain Egyptian consent. Pressure by the Assembly in the form of resolutions, recommending certain measures was not enough. It had to be accompanied by pressure outside of the United Nations. It was the combination of United Nations and United States pressure which obliged the Dutch to give in in Indonesia—and the Israelis to evacuate Egypt. When it came to the second aspect of the Middle Eastern crisis (the settlement of the deeper and "intermediate" issues) the United States was willing to support the Secretary-General in the Assembly, but Mr. Hammarskjold, had he selected a more vigorous course, would have needed the United States in front of him, in Cairo, so to speak, and not merely behind him in New York.

This objection cannot be dismissed. The decisions of the Assembly and the silence of the United States did condemn the Secretary-General to the following dilemma. He had to take political initiatives that belong to an independent executive rather than to an official with little political power. Or else he had to zigzag between the question marks of ambiguous resolutions. However, it seems to this writer that Mr. Hammarskjold resigned himself to the latter course with such skill, caution and good grace that the dangers of the dilemma were too easily overlooked; the members of the Assembly were encouraged to travel a road which has justly been called a "reversion to the abnormal." Finally, if Mr. Hammarskjold's policy was the inevitable product of the Assembly's feelings and of United States inaction, it becomes necessary to transfer the blame, but not to whitewash the policy.

2. One can argue whether it is Egypt or the United Nations which has been the master in the Middle Eastern crisis. No argument, alas, is possible in the Hungarian one. The road which the Assembly tried to travel was different from the Middle Eastern one; it amounted to an attempt at pure coercion through mere dictation. No collective measures were undertaken, but Soviet military action was condemned far more severely and directly than the Israeli, French and British operation. The call to desist "forthwith" and to withdraw "without any further delay" was not accompanied by the offer of a face-saving international mechanism such as a truce or "nonshooting" police force, or by the offer of a conciliatory device such as a commission of mediation between Hungary and the Soviet Union (such as, for instance, the Balkan Commission). The United Nations merely offered its Secretary-General and observers designated by him, not as peacemakers or mediators, but as investigators, and soon thereafter decided that free elections should be held under United Nations auspices. Conciliation was ruled out. However, when dictation failed, as had all previous attempts in similar circumstances (in the Balkans, in Korea before June 1950, and in Berlin during the United Nations phase of the dispute), the United Nations had to reconsider its policy and to face the dilemma: retreat or toughness. Some Members would have

liked the United Nations to introduce a certain dose of conciliation, by offering its services and by avoiding unilateral definitions of policy. Hence India protested against the call for free elections, and appealed for negotiations with the Soviet and Hungarian governments the sort of discussion of underlying political issues that was being avoided in the Middle East because it seemed to some that such a negotiation would be a reward for aggression! However, the United Nations remained consistent and did not follow Mr. Menon; but it did not change the nature of the pressure exerted on the Soviet Union either. No sanctions of any kind were decided; even one rather mild sort of collective measure that had been suggested was not taken up: the appointment as observers of diplomatic representatives serving in Hungary. The United Nations margin of action was thus quite small. The United Nations could solemnly condemn the violation of the Charter, try to post observers outside of the iron curtain and create an investigation committee which by necessity operated outside of Hungary, but these measures amount to solemn protests, and the formal condemnation has more in common with the Stimson doctrine than with the branding of Red China as an aggressor, which was accompanied by sanctions.

Thus, in effect, the *status quo* was restored everywhere, but it was the Hungarian revolution which was contained, and the Israelis who were rolled back. This apparently paradoxical balance sheet carries with it some important lessons.

Political Limitations of the United Nations

1. The first lesson seems to be that the assumptions of the drafters of the Charter have been vindicated: international organization can operate with maximum effectiveness, i.e. both preserve the political independence and territorial integrity of its members and settle international disputes, only if big power unity is preserved and if the claims to be reconciled do not involve the existence of states or the nature of regimes.

The first of these assumptions was contradicted by the "Uniting for Peace" resolution, which was based on the thought that the organization should not be paralyzed by the cold war and that collective security could be organized even against big powers. Now, it is to a large extent the breakdown of the negative Russian-American concert in the Middle East which led to last year's explosion; between 1947 and the death of Stalin, neither the Soviet Union nor the United States was actively involved in Middle Eastern politics. The Soviets had not intervened in the Iranian oil crisis, and a long series of Security Council resolutions from 1948 to 1953 proved that the two great powers were not on opposite sides of the fence in matters concerning the "Palestine problem." The first Soviet veto came in January 1954—at a time when the British were trying to convince Colonel Nasser to join a Middle Eastern defense organization. What followed is familiar enough: the Bagh-

dad Pact, the Egyptian arms deal, the Aswan Dam affair, and the Soviet veto
of the second part of the western resolution over Suez submitted to the Security Council in October. Inversely, it is to a large extent the temporary
return to a big power concert which explains the success of the United Nations in getting a Middle Eastern cease-fire and withdrawal without resort
to sanctions. The carrot of UNEF was accompanied by the stick of combined
(although antagonistic) Soviet and American pressure. Soviet threats of resort
to "collective measures" increased in effect the weight of American pressure.
Finally, it is of course the existence of a "bi-polar" world which explains the
failure of the United Nations to achieve any comparable result in Hungary.

The "Uniting for Peace" resolution provided only a procedure for acting in
an emergency such as the Hungarian one. The success of the Korean experiment in collective action was misleading; there, the Russian armed forces
were not *directly* involved, and the Chinese were not a military power of the
first magnitude. It has been said quite rightly that the "Uniting for Peace"
resolution, to be effective, supposes that the world is "divided for war" and
ready to fight. To fight north Korea, indeed; far less ready to fight Red China
and not at all to fight the Soviets. On the one hand, in 1950 and again in 1956
certain small or medium-size Members of the United Nations have been most
unwilling to go beyond the original Charter and to envisage any form of
coercion (even purely verbal) against a great power. On the other hand, the
United States itself adopted toward the Soviet Union a policy which in effect does not have much use for the United Nations. The doctrine of massive
retaliation "by means and at places of our own choosing" implies that when
the United States decides to strike at the Soviet Union, the main American
action will take place outside of the United Nations, which is too slow, militarily unprepared, and anyhow heavily compelled by its own principles to
fight on the field chosen by the enemy. The doctrine also means that, when
the United States decides that there is no point in striking back, as it did last
October, the United Nations can only hurl rhetorical thunderbolts at the
Soviets.

As for the other original assumption of the Charter, it seems that the very
inability of the United Nations to do much more than restore the *status quo*
in the Middle East shows the limitations of the policy of collective assertion,
parliamentary debates and majority votes with which the United Nations has
tried to tackle the problem of change and the anticolonial revolution. Various
factors contribute to the deadlock. In the first place, if the majority tries to
accelerate the process, the nation whose sovereignty is infringed by United
Nations policies still has the legal power to resist—as the Union of South
Africa has shown and as Israel shows now in connection with the stationing
of UNEF. In the second place, if, on the contrary, nations adversely affected
by the nationalist revolutions try to reverse the trend, the states that owe
their existence to these revolutions, those that stand to gain by encouraging
the trend and those that are afraid of resisting it are numerous enough in the

Assembly to prevent any such move. The new nations of Asia and Africa can therefore save the territorial *status quo* of any one of them, when it is threatened from the outside. They tend to favor or accept a measure such as the nationalization of the Suez Canal Company because it is presented politically as a victory over colonialism and legally as the mere exercise of territorial sovereignty. (Far less concern is shown over matters involving persons.) Thus, the "new United Nations" can operate as a boomerang against countries like England, France or Israel—a western bridgehead in the Arab world.

Thirdly, there is a deeper reason which explains why it is so difficult for international organization to provide peaceful change in a revolutionary world. Most of the causes of trouble and change are completely beyond the reach of the United Nations. The United Nations in this respect is both restricted and anachronistic. It approaches dynamic forces such as pan-Arabism or communism with nineteenth century concepts such as the duty of non-intervention of states. It approaches the crucial problem posed by the different behavior of different regimes—dictatorships, totalitarian governments, democracies—with the old liberal concept according to which the type of government has to be discounted in international affairs, as if ideologies and national politics really did stop at each border or at "the water's edge." It ignores the submerged part of the iceberg of world politics, such as the techniques of subversion or the struggle for control of raw materials and sources of energy. By its occasional attempts at concentrating on the technical aspects of a dispute so as to make it less explosive, the United Nations can be led to underestimate such imponderable elements as those without which the Suez crisis can hardly be understood: the issue of national prestige, the fear of humiliation, the defensive nationalism of France and England (a reaction to the triumphant nationalism of Asia and Africa) the Anglo-French instinctive Munich reaction in the summer of 1956, or the fear of colonialism which explains why Asian countries reacted more violently to Suez than to Budapest. The United Nations tries to play Hamlet with Fortinbras alone.

2. Even though the original assumptions of the Charter have been vindicated, the United Nations has to operate in a world in which those assumptions simply do not apply. Hence there has appeared in the debates and policies of the United Nations a number of inequities and discrepancies which the last crises have put into clear focus and which weaken the influence of the organization. There is first of all the problem of the use of force. The ban of the Charter seems either too rigid or too narrow; it has led in practice to a different treatment of *faits accomplis* without armed violence, or of the subtler forms of pressure or subversion, and of "coups" accomplished by armies. Now, if the first category is tolerated, the ban on the second cannot be interpreted as an absolute. The Charter was an attempt at providing states with a better alternative to the solution of international disputes. If this alternative does not work, if states' claims of great emotional or political importance are either not taken into account by international mechanisms or

are merely dragged or gradually compromised away from one conference to the next, we will have more Suez expeditions. The alternative to collective adjustment is certainly not collective sainthood and it cannot be individual suicide. The successful suppression by the United Nations of a big scale attempt at solving disputes by armed force in the Middle East might merely encourage states caught in such a dilemma to resort to all kinds of force except armed force, or to attack anything (through subversion, blockade, embargoes, etc.) as long as it is not someone's territory. Even the resort to armed force has often been successful. It has been unpunished when it was decided by the Soviet Union within its zone of influence; it has also been unpunished when the dose of force used each time has been small although it was administered frequently, such as in armistice line violations, or when the theater of operations was not a vital one in world politics (such as in the case of Hyderabad and to some extent Kashmir), or when the plea of domestic jurisdiction still has some authority (as in Algeria).

Inconsistencies in United Nations attitudes have also been criticized with reference to the power of the states which the United Nations has challenged. Messrs. Pineau, Lloyd and Spaak have complained about the differences between the United Nations' "kindness" toward the Soviets and harshness toward England, France and Israel. Here some distinctions must be made. If one looks at the documents, this accusation is quite unfair. It is not the United Nations which has treated the transgressors differently; it is the transgressors who have reacted differently to United Nations resolutions; to whitewash violations of the Charter in one part of the world because they cannot be remedied elsewhere is a policy of chaos. Similarly, if one looks at the problem from the point of view of the preservation of world peace, it could be argued that the failure of the United Nations in Hungary and its success in Egypt contributed equally to the safeguarding of peace. Those who would have liked the United Nations to send a UNEF to Hungary forget among other things that UNEF was sent to Egypt with the consent of all parties and that any other kind of force would be not a supervisory unit but an international fighting army. As for non-military sanctions (economic reprisals or the suspension or expulsion of Mr. Kadar's United Nations delegates), they would merely have assuaged the nerves of United Nations members—and further demonstrated the lack of effective United Nations power in that area. However, if one looks at the problem from the point of view of "justice" rather than of "peace," and if one considers the actual amount of pressure that was put respectively on the Soviets and on Britain, France, and Israel, rather than the texts voted upon, Messrs. Pineau, Lloyd, and Spaak do have a very real point. The contrast in the amount of pressure, however justified by power considerations, is shocking precisely because the principles of the Charter are supposed to apply equally to all. "Two wrongs don't make one right," said Mr. Eisenhower. In a way, this is true; but in another way, one wrong (the Soviet refusal to budge) and one right (Israel's unconditional withdrawal) do finally make two wrongs: the Soviet immunity and the difference in pressure. Through some perverse law, it also seems that the more a state resists the United Nations, the more this state gets away with: the Soviets, and Egypt on the issue of the Suez blockade, have emerged scot free; Israel has finally saved a bit more than England and France, which agreed faster to withdraw.

A final discrepancy was alluded to by Barbara Ward, when she defined international agencies as "mechanisms for making other nations do what one would not do oneself." There have been admirable examples of this during the recent crises. The Israelis have insisted that UNEF should not be stationed on Israeli soil or on any territory controlled by Israel, but at the same time they have protested against the Secretary-General's reminder that all the requests made by Israel concerning Gaza or UNEF required the consent of Egypt. Yugoslavia refused to accept United Nations observers who would investigate about Hungary because this would be "a dangerous precedent," whereas for years similar investigations were conducted about the Union of South Africa's *apartheid* policies. India protested against mere "propaganda" resolutions condemning the Soviets, but she also wanted to see maximum pressure put on Israel, as though blame became propaganda only when the recipient was not easily influenced by outside pressure. The states which have used the United Nations most effectively as an instrument for the advancement of their cause are the ones which have insisted most constantly upon the limited and temporary role of UNEF. The main common bond among the members of the United Nations is the defense rather than the moderation of their sovereignty; that there should be growing cynicism or skepticism as a result is not surprising.

The West and the United Nations

Nevertheless, the United Nations is here to stay, and western powers should adopt a policy or strategy toward the United Nations. The Soviets have one; so do the new nations. We have just mentioned some inconsistencies; we could add here the example of the United States, which last summer showed no enthusiasm whatsoever toward bringing the Suez Canal issue to the United Nations, and which after October 30 emphasized vehemently its reliance on the United Nations in all Middle Eastern problems except the fight against "international communism."

1. An obvious starting point would be the fact that the western nations cannot put the United Nations at the center of their foreign policies. This is as true with reference to the competition for the "uncommitted" world as it is in relation to straight east-west issues. The predominance of small states in the Assembly and the sort of "bloc veto" or diluting power of the African-Asian nations when they are allied with the Soviet group have somewhat tarnished Mr. Morganthau's vision of "new United Nations" as a field in

which the United States could multilateralize its national interest. On the contrary, given the rules of the Assembly, the interests of the Africans and Asians (and, at times, through the intermediary of these nations, the interests of the Soviet group) might receive American naturalization. When the weight of multilateral restraint on American or western interests is such that these interests emerge quite unrecognizable, how acceptable is such a restraint, and how useful the mechanism in which this alchemical process takes place. In certain cases, a tail constituted by a few small states, whose support is needed, can wag the American dog.

But there is a second and equally obvious starting point. The west has a tremendous interest in keeping the United Nations alive and in good health—even in political matters. The United Nations provides the west with an indispensable, although too lofty, set of ideals and with a necessary, although too narrow, set of procedures. It is not merely because the United Nations has defended the national sovereignty of non-western countries that so many of the latter have applauded the American attitude in the crisis of last fall. It is also, as Hugh Gaitskell has recognized, because the Charter constitutes the only hopeful international ideal for most nations of the present world, as well as a code of behavior which represents the maximum that anyone has a right to expect. The way in which the Soviets have in turn exploited this ideal and this code in the Middle Eastern crisis should be a warning.

The crisis of last fall demonstrated that the United Nations plays a legitimizing role of increasing importance—at least negatively. The United Nations does not quite have the strength to *initiate*, but it has the authority to prevent certain things and to stop others, and it has enough moral force to legitimize what it endorses. Consequently, actions (other than the construction of regional or functional organizations, or action aimed directly at the Soviet bloc) which are undertaken outside and without the *imprimatur* of the United Nations risk losing part of their value. The two London conferences over Suez last summer suffered somewhat from that risk. It is easy to show how shaky this international legitimacy is and to denounce "international majoritarianism." But every state today, however grudgingly, gropes for the former and wants the benefits of the latter. It was a majority which England and France were trying to get behind their (and Mr. Dulles') scheme at the first London conference. When Mr. Dulles stated that "it is one thing for a nation to defy one or two nations but it is quite another thing to defy the sober and considered judgment of many nations," England and France approved, since the defiant nation, then, was Egypt. The Menzies mission did its best to impress Colonel Nasser with the importance of majority rule. In September and October, when England and France first began to lose that majority, then decided to go it alone, the fact that an overwhelming number of nations decided against them did influence their policy. The legitimacy of the United Nations is bound to be fragile, given the political limitations and inconsistencies imposed by a revolutionary period, as well as such structural defects as the right of veto and the egalitarian voting formula. But any kind of legitimacy in such a period is a blessing and a guide for future stabilization.

No western nation can afford to define the national interest so narrowly that such an asset would be left to others. Nor can any western nation afford deliberately to put the United Nations to a test which the organization will lose, so as to use this failure as a pretext for Charter violations; for if this nation's bold attempt should go wrong, it will be only too happy if there is an international mechanism available to rescue it from the mess. "In an inflammable world, it is no mean achievement of international organization to serve as a candle snuffer so as to minimize the necessity for relying upon an unreliable fire department." If there were no United Nations that could offer a United Nations Emergency Force to a suspicious Egypt, the alternative would be a clash between Soviet "volunteers" and Anglo-French "policemen." The nations' almost hysterical emphasis on sovereignty explains both why the candle snuffer can do so little and why only an international organization can be the candle snuffer. Anything else would smell of "intervention," neo-colonialism, or gunboat diplomacy.

2. With these two opposed starting points, we can at least suggest certain lines of policy. No doubt, it is uncomfortable for the west to have to live in two rather conflicting eras at the same time: The traditional era of "power politics," sovereignty, and unilateral action, which is still with us, and the emergent era of the "rule of law," symbolized more by ideals than by acts. The Soviets have the advantage of living almost exclusively in the first. The underdeveloped nations are carried by a "wave of the future" or "stream of history" which allows them to use quite naturally the principles and purposes of the Charter as a tool of national policy. The west has done the same thing in the cold war but finds it far more difficult with respect to the anti-colonial revolution; nevertheless, a way must be found to bridge the gap between the two eras.

A first precept would be to avoid any head-on clash with the ideals which the west professes (and profits from). This involves, first of all, in cases where attempts at conciliation or peaceful change have failed, the duty to defend one's interests by methods which are not internationally regressive. The use of armed force, except for collective security, in self-defense and perhaps in circumstances as tragic as Israel's position after years of encirclement and insecurity, is to be avoided. Israel itself has not brought lasting peace any nearer either by its former massive retaliatory raids or by last fall's war. The case of England and France is even clearer. It could be shown quite persuasively that Colonel Nasser's nationalization of an international public service accompanied by statements which expressed a will to use this service for national purposes and which presented the move as an act of retaliation was going against the direction which international society is bound to take if complete disintegration is to be avoided. Thus, England and France had a number of perfectly "progressive" arguments. Legally, Egypt could exploit the letter of international law and invoke the narrowest interpretation of rather ambiguous provisions, but the western powers could resort to an interpretation in which the spirit and purposes of the law rather than the textual arguments served as criteria. In fact, a number of Asian and African nations did agree with the western reasoning in the first London conference. If a special session of the United Nations Assembly had been summoned at the time instead of the Conference, as the British Labor Party had suggested, the west might have obtained the legitimizing seal of the United Nations. However, this "progressive" case was destroyed by the use of military force in circumstances that seemed to combine the perils of a plot and the imprudence of an improvization. Such a move immediately provoked a clear opposition by Asia and Africa against the invaders—the very kind of alignment that threatens to wreck both the United Nations and the international politics of the west, and that had been miraculously avoided in the Suez crisis until then. The only justification is that the wavering of Mr. Dulles seemed to shut out all the more subtle forms of pressure on Egypt. But perhaps Mr. Dulles would have been less anxious to stress "peace" so absolutely if there had been fewer war noises in Paris and London. The arsenal of coercion is rich enough for western states to find in it other weapons than bombers and tanks.

Our precept also involves the duty to prevent situations in which a head-on clash between the Charter and western nations seems like a lesser evil. Whenever the United Nations is unable to provide adequate procedures of peaceful adjustment, or whenever the only possible decisions of the United Nations would conflict with western interests, other mechanisms must be tried. The United Nations as a set of procedures is not necessarily the best means toward the ideals for which these procedures stand. In such cases to avoid the United Nations altogether is far more respectable than the tactic which consists in finally bringing to the United Nations disputes which many previous attempts have failed to solve and which have reached such a temperature that they can only explode in the faces of the United Nations Members. The United Nations should be a hospital, not a morgue. Nor can western policymakers let it become a force which would weaken or increase the weaknesses of the west in world affairs. A second precept would be to use the United Nations in such a way that United Nations ideals and western interests would be brought together without too much strain. This involves, first of all, the need to strengthen as much as possible those very alarm bells and mechanisms whose weaknesses we have deplored in the beginning. The more fragile the *status quo* and the smaller the chance of peaceful adjustment, the more necessary it becomes to repair the institutional deficiencies described last year by the Secretary-General and to equip the Assembly with devices which will allow it, should the crisis recur, to react more smoothly instead of staggering "from crisis to crisis improvising in haste."

Our precept involves, secondly, the need at least to try to find ways in which the United Nations could play a more active role in efforts toward peaceful change. The hope is dim, as recent failures in Kashmir have confirmed. However, attempts at substituting small negotiating bodies for unruly parliamentary debates or at restoring the League of Nations system of rapporteurs might be fruitful. As the Assembly works now, it is far more capable of creating subsidiary organs than of providing conciliation, and it would be good to use more of the former in order to gain more of the latter.

Our precept also requires a thorough effort at leadership by western nations in the United Nations in order to obtain the necessary two-thirds majority for proposals which are in the interest of the west. The crisis of last fall has shown that only such political leadership can produce results. For a great power such as the United States to "leave to the United Nations" matters of great concern to itself or to its allies is a mistake, whenever it means that this great power has no policy of its own to propose to the United Nations. Abandoned without such leadership to the free play of voting blocs, the Assembly will inevitably tend to pass the buck to the Secretary-General, and no civil servant, national or international, however subtle and dedicated, will ever tend to take bold initiatives in a political vacuum. Mr. Acheson has wisely reminded us that in the minds of the authors of the "Uniting for Peace" resolution, the Assembly was supposed to execute, not to frame, policy. Such leadership should imply a will to refuse excessive dilution of vital proposals for the sake of getting a text on the books, and a readiness to take matters out of the United Nations if necessary (as last February). The alternative to a "bloc veto" in the Assembly does not have to be a weak compromise where important interests are lost and only sponsors gained. Western nations have enough voting power of their own to block any proposals that would conflict with their policies; chess can be played by more than one group. In the long run no non-communist member of the United Nations has anything to gain either by refusing institutional improvements or by opposing efforts at coping with the problem of change in areas where the *status juris* has all the marks of a powder keg.

Our precept means, finally, that such leadership must not only be exerted within the United Nations but must also be extended outside of the United Nations. Precisely because many factors in world affairs are beyond the control of the organization, and because it is not a world government with an executive branch entrusted to the Secretary-General (even though the Assembly tries to act as a legislature), the Members of the United Nations have the duty to supplement and not just to echo the calls of the United Nations for peaceful adjustment. This is another major lesson of the crisis.

To sum up, the tragic events of Hungary have confirmed the powerlessness of the United Nations in the zone under Soviet control; there, a change of the *status quo* cannot be obtained by the United Nations and it is anyhow hard to see how other mechanisms can obtain it at a price acceptable to the west.

In the Middle East a general settlement satisfactory to all parties was and still is probably impossible either in or outside the United Nations; but no efforts were made at all. A considerable "intermediary" improvement was probably far less impossible; but it was not achieved. Diplomatic efforts that might have been aimed at a settlement will have to be devoted instead to a consolidation and improvement of the *status quo*. Because of the very limitations and inequities revealed by the crisis it is not possible to expect the United Nations itself to contribute much in the future to a settlement of the more explosive Middle Eastern issues. This imposes upon the statesmen of the west the triple duty to see that such a settlement be attempted within or outside the United Nations by all means compatible with the Charter; to avoid moves and maneuvers that imperil the principles upon which the United Nations rests; and to strengthen those United Nations techniques whose purpose it is to postpone or to limit explosions until a deeper settlement has been achieved.

Already the Middle East in the United Nations has become disturbingly similar to the Turkish question in the Concert of Europe. There too, the main powers of the world had for years agreed only on the maintenance of the *status quo* and on the need to prevent the peoples of the area from disturbing peace by trying to settle their own fate violently. When the hands-off policy of the big powers disappeared and when the nationalities so long contained began to lift the lid and to exploit their guardians' rivalries, the first world war put an end to the game. The Concert was institutionally and politically too weak to prevent the catastrophe. A war temporarily averted or repressed is not a world restored—it might simply mean a bigger blast prepared.

Thus Sisyphus has survived the avalanche. He will have to stay on the job. To be sure, if other mortals do not come to help him, his rock will never remain on top of the mountain and the next landslide might crush him. But if he does not try again, however clumsily, with their help, the gods of war and want will have won a remarkable victory.

4. Obstinate or Obsolete? The Fate of the Nation-State and the Case of Western Europe

STANLEY HOFFMANN

I

THE CRITICAL ISSUE for every student of world order is the fate of the nation-state. In the nuclear age, the fragmentation of the world into countless units, each of which has a claim to independence, is obviously dangerous for peace and illogical for welfare. The dynamism which animates those units, when they are not merely city-states of limited expanse or dynastic states manipulated by the Prince's calculations, but nation-states that pour into their foreign policy the collective pride, ambitions, fears, prejudices, and images of large masses of people, is particularly formidable.[1] An abstract theorist could argue that any system of autonomous units follows the same basic rules, whatever the nature of those units. But in practice, that is, in history, their substance matters as much as their form; the story of world affairs since the French Revolution is not merely one more sequence in the ballet of sovereign states; it is the story of the fires and upheavals propagated by nationalism. A claim to sovereignty based on historical tradition and dynastic legitimacy alone has never had the fervor, the self-righteous assertiveness which a similar claim based on the idea and feelings of nationhood presents: in world politics, the dynastic function of nationalism is the constitution of nation-states by amalgamation or by splintering, and its emotional function

1. See Pierre Renouvin et Jean-Baptiste Duroselle, *Introduction a l'histoire des relations internationales* (Paris, 1964).

is the supplying of a formidable good conscience to leaders who see their task as the achievement of nationhood, the defense of the nation, or the expansion of a national mission.[2]

This is where the drama lies. The nation-state is at the same time a form of social organization and—in practice if not in every brand of theory—a factor of international non-integration; but those who argue in favor of a more integrated world, either under more centralized power or through various networks of regional or functional agencies, tend to forget Auguste Comte's old maxim that *on ne détruit que ce qu'on remplace:* the new "formula" will have to provide not only world order, but also the kind of social organization in which leaders, élites, and citizens feel at home. There is currently no agreement on what such a formula will be;[3] as a result, nation-states —often inchoate, economically absurd, administratively ramshackle, and impotent yet dangerous in international politics—remain the basic units in spite of all the remonstrations and exhortations. They go on *faute de mieux* despite their alleged obsolescence; indeed, not only do they profit from man's incapacity to bring about a better order, but their very existence is a formidable obstacle to their replacement.

If there was one part of the world in which men of good will thought that the nation-state could be superseded, it was Western Europe. One of France's most subtle commentators on international politics has recently reminded us of E. H. Carr's bold prediction of 1945: "we shall not see again a Europe of twenty, and a world of more than sixty independent sovereign states."[4] Statesmen have invented original schemes for moving Western Europe "beyond the nation-state,"[5] and political scientists have studied their efforts with a care from which emotional involvement was not missing. The conditions seemed ideal. On the one hand, nationalism seemed at its lowest ebb; on the other, an adequate formula and method for building a substitute had apparently been devised. Twenty years after the end of World War II—a period as long as the whole interwar era—observers have had to revise their judgments. The most optimistic put their hope in the chances the future may still harbor, rather than in the propelling power of the present; the less optimistic ones, like myself, try simply to understand what went wrong.

My own conclusion is sad and simple. The nation-state is still here, and the new Jerusalem has been postponed because the nations in Western Europe have not been able to stop time and to fragment space. Political unification could have succeeded if, on the one hand, these nations had not been caught

2. In a way, the weaker are the foundations on which the nation rests, the shriller the assertions become.

3. On this point, see Rupert Emerson, *From Empire to Nation* (Cambridge, Mass., 1962), Ch. XIX; and Raymond Aron, *Paix et Guerre entre les Nations* (Paris, 1962), Ch. XI.

4. E. H. Carr, *Nationalism and After* (London, 1965), p. 51. Quoted in Pierre Hassner, "Nationalisme et relations internationales," *Revue française de science politique,* Vol. XV, No. 3 (June 1965), pp. 499–528.

5. See Ernst B. Haas' book by this title (Stanford, Calif., 1964).

in the whirlpool of different concerns, as a result both of profoundly different internal circumstances and of outside legacies, and if, on the other hand, they had been able or obliged to concentrate on "community-building" to the exclusion of all problems situated either outside their area or within each one of them. Domestic differences and different world views obviously mean diverging foreign policies; the involvement of the policy-makers in issues among which "community-building" is merely one has meant a deepening, not a decrease, of those divergences. The reasons follow: the unification movement has been the victim, and the survival of nation-states the outcome, of three factors, one of which characterizes every international system, and the other two only the present system. Every international system owes its inner logic and its unfolding to the *diversity* of domestic determinants, geohistorical situations, and outside aims among its units; any international system based on fragmentation tends, through the dynamics of unevenness (so well understood, if applied only to economic unevenness, by Lenin) to reproduce diversity. However, there is no inherent reason that the model of the fragmented international system should rule out by itself two developments in which the critics of the nation-state have put their bets or their hopes. Why must it be a diversity of nations? Could it not be a diversity of regions, of "federating" blocs, superseding the nation-state just as the dynastic state had replaced the feudal puzzle? Or else, why does the very logic of conflagrations fed by hostility not lead to the kind of catastrophic unification of exhausted yet interdependent nations, sketched out by Kant? Let us remember that the unity movement in Europe was precisely an attempt at creating a regional entity, and that its origins and its springs resembled, on the reduced scale of a half-continent, the process dreamed up by Kant in his *Idea of Universal History*.[6]

The answers are not entirely provided by the two factors that come to mind immediately. One is the legitimacy of national self-determination, the only principle which transcends all blocs and ideologies, since all pay lip service to it, and provides the foundation for the only "universal actor" of the international system: the United Nations. The other is the newness of many of the states, which have wrested their independence by a nationalist upsurge and are therefore unlikely to throw or give away what they have obtained only too recently. However, the legitimacy of the nation-state does not by itself guarantee the nation-state's survival in the international state of nature, and the appeal of nationalism as an emancipating passion does not assure that the nation-state must everywhere remain the basic form of social organization, in a world in which many nations are old and settled and the shortcomings of the nation-state are obvious. The real answers are provided by two unique features of the present international system. One, it is the first truly *global* international system: the regional subsystems have only a re-

6. See on this point my essay "Rousseau on War and Peace," in *The State of War* (New York, 1965).

duced autonomy; the "relationships of major tension" blanket the whole planet, the domestic polities are dominated not so much by the region's problems as by purely local and purely global ones, which conspire to divert the region's members from the internal affairs of their area, and indeed would make an isolated treatment of those affairs impossible. As a result, each nation, new or old, finds itself placed in an orbit of its own, from which it is quite difficult to move away: for the attraction of the regional forces is offset by the pull of all the other forces. Or, to change the metaphor, those nations that coexist in the same apparently separate "home" of a geographical region find themselves both exposed to the smells and noises that come from outside through all their windows and doors, and looking at the outlying houses from which the interference issues. Coming from diverse pasts, moved by diverse tempers, living in different parts of the house, inescapably yet differently subjected and attracted to the outside world, those cohabitants react unevenly to their exposure and calculate conflictingly how they could either reduce the disturbance or affect in turn all those who live elsewhere. The adjustment of their own relations within the house becomes subordinated to their divergencies about the outside world; the "regional subsystem" becomes a stake in the rivalry of its members about the system as a whole.

However, the coziness of the common home could still prevail if the inhabitants were forced to come to terms, either by one of them, or by the fear of a threatening neighbor. This is precisely where the second unique feature of the present situation intervenes. What tends to perpetuate the nation-states decisively in a system whose universality seems to sharpen rather than shrink their diversity is the new set of conditions that govern and restrict the rule of force: Damocles' sword has become a boomerang, the ideological legitimacy of the nation-state is protected by the relative and forced tameness of the world jungle. Force in the nuclear age is still the "midwife of societies" insofar as revolutionary war either breeds new nations or shapes regimes in existing nations; but the use of force along traditional lines, for conquest and expansion—the very use that made the "permeable" feudal units not only obsolete but collapse and replaced them with modern states often built on "blood and iron"—has become too dangerous. The legitimacy of the feudal unit could be undermined in two ways: brutally, by the rule of force—the big fish swallowing small fish by national might; subtly or legitimately, so to speak, through self-undermining—the logic of dynastic weddings or acquisitions that consolidated larger units. A system based on national self-determination rules out the latter; a system in which nations, once established, find force a much blunted weapon rules out the former. Thus agglomeration by conquest or out of a fear of conquest fails to take place. The new conditions of violence tend even to pay to national borders the tribute of vice to virtue: violence which dons the cloak of revolution rather than of interstate wars, or persists in the form of such wars only when they accompany revolutions or conflicts in divided countries, perversely respects borders by infiltrating under them rather than by crossing them overtly. Thus all that is left for unification is what one might call "national self-abdication" or self-abnegation, the eventual willingness of nations to try something else; but precisely global involvement hinders rather than helps, and the atrophy of war removes the most pressing incentive. What a nation-state cannot provide alone—in economics, or defense—it can still provide through means far less drastic than hara-kiri.

These two features give its solidity to the principle of national self-determination, as well as its resilience to the U.N. They also give its present, and quite unique, shape to the "relationship of major tension": the conflict between East and West. This conflict is both muted and universal—and both aspects contribute to the survival of the nation-state. As the superpowers find that what makes their power overwhelming also makes it less usable, or rather usable only to deter one another and to deny each other gains, the lesser states discover under the umbrella of the nuclear stalemate that they are not condemned to death, and that indeed their nuisance power is impressive—especially when the kind of violence that prevails in present circumstances favors the porcupine over the elephant. The superpowers experience in their own camps the backlash of a rebellion against domination that enjoys broad impunity, and cannot easily coax or coerce third parties into agglomeration under their tutelage. Yet they retain the means to prevent other powers from agglomerating away from their clutches. Thus, as the superpowers compete, with filed nails, all over the globe, the nation-state becomes the universal point of salience, to use the new language of strategy—the lowest common denominator in the competition.

Other international systems were merely conservative of diversity; the present system is profoundly conservative of the diversity of nation-states, despite all its revolutionary features. The dream of Rousseau, concerned both about the prevalence of the general will—that is, the nation-state—and about peace, was the creation of communities insulated from one another. In history, where "the essence and drama of nationalism is not to be alone in the world,"[7] the clash of non-insulated states has tended to breed both nation-states and wars. Today, Rousseau's ideals come closer to reality, but in the most un-Rousseauan way: the nation-states prevail in peace, they remain unsuperseded because a fragile peace keeps the Kantian doctor away, they are unreplaced because their very involvement in the world, their very inability to insulate themselves from one another, preserves their separateness. The "new Europe" dreamed by the Europeans could not be established by force. Left to the wills and calculations of its members, the new formula has not jelled because they could not agree on its role in the world. The failure (so far) of an experiment tried in apparently ideal conditions tells us a great deal about contemporary world politics, about the chances of unification movements elsewhere, and about the functional approach to unification.

7. P. Hassner, *op. cit.*, p. 523.

For it shows that the movement can fail not only when there is a surge of nationalism in one important part, but also when there are differences in assessments of the national interest that rule out agreement on the shape and on the world role of the new, supranational whole.

The word nationalism is notoriously slippery. What I suggest is the following threefold distinction, which may be helpful in analyzing the interaction between the nation-state and the international system:

1. There is *national consciousness* (what the French call *sentiment national*)—a sense of "cohesion and distinctiveness,"[8] which sets one off from other groups. My point is that this sense, which tends to have important effects on international relations as long as it is shared by people who have not achieved statehood, is rather "neutral" once the nation and the state coincide: that is, the existence of national consciousness does not dictate foreign policy, does not indicate whether the people's "image" of foreigners will be friendly or unfriendly (they will be seen as different—nothing else is implied), nor does it indicate whether or not the leaders will be willing to accept sacrifices of sovereignty. One cannot even posit that a strong national consciousness will be an obstacle for movements of unification, for it is perfectly conceivable that a nation convinces itself that its "cohesion and distinctiveness" will be best preserved in a larger entity. Here, we must turn to the second category.

2. For lack of a better phrase, I shall call it the *national situation*. Any nation-state, whether pulsing with a strong "national consciousness" or not—indeed, any state, whether a true nation-state or a disparate collection of unintegrated groups—is, to borrow Sartre's language, thrown into the world; its situation is made up altogether of its internal features—what, in an individual, would be called heredity and character—and of its position in the world. The state of national consciousness in the nation is one, but only one, of the elements of the situation. It is a composite of objective data (inside: social structure and political system; outside: geography, formal commitments) and subjective factors (inside: values, prejudices, opinions, reflexes; outside: one's own traditions and assessments of others, and the other's attitudes and approaches toward oneself); some of its components are intractable, others flexible and changeable. Any statesman, whether he is a fervent patriot or not, must define the nation's foreign policy by taking that situation into account; even if he is convinced of the obsolescence of *the* nation-state (or of *his* nation-state), the steps he will be able and willing to take in order to overcome it will be shaped by the fact that he speaks—to borrow de Gaulle's language this time—for the nation as it is in the world as it is. He cannot act as if his nation-state did not exist, however sorry its shape may be, or as if the world were other than it is. The national situation may facilitate unification moves, even when national consciousness is strong. It may prove a

8. Karl Deutsch, *Nationalism and Social Communication* (Cambridge, Mass., 1953), p. 147.

formidable obstacle, even when national consciousness is weak. The point is that even when the policy-maker tries to move "beyond the nation-state" he can do it only by taking along the nation with its baggage of memories and problems—with its situation. I do not want to suggest that the situation is a "given" that dictates policy; but it sets complicated limits that affect freedom of choice.[9]

3. I will reserve the term *"nationalism"* for a specific meaning: it is one of the numerous ways in which political leaders and élites can interpret the dictates, or rather the suggestions, of the national situation, one of the ways of using the margin it leaves. Whereas national consciousness is a feeling, and the national situation a condition, nationalism is a doctrine or (if one uses a broad definition) an ideology—the doctrine or ideology that gives to the nation in world affairs absolute value and top priority. The consequences of such a preference may vary immensely: nationalism may imply expansion (that is, the attempt at establishing the supremacy of one's nation over others) or merely defense; it may entail the notion of a universal mission or, on the contrary, insulation. It may be peaceful or pugnacious.[10] It is less an imperative determinant of choice than a criterion of choice and an attitude which shapes the choices made. But whatever its manifestations, its varying content, it always follows one rule common to all the former, it always pours the latter into one mold: the preservation of the nation as the highest good. Nationalism thus affects, *at least* negatively, the way in which the freedom of choice left by the national situation will be used; indeed, it may collide with, and try to disregard or overcome, the limits which the situation sets.

The relation between nationalism and the two other factors is complicated. Nationalism (in the sense of the will to establish a nation-state) is triggered by, and in turn activates, national consciousness in oppressed nationalities; but nationalism, in colonial areas as well as in mature nation-states, can also be a substitute for a still weak or for a fading national consciousness. In nation-states that are going concerns, national consciousness breeds nationalism only in certain kinds of national situations. The national situation may be assessed by a nationalist leader exactly in the same way as by a non-nationalist one; however, nationalism may lead the former to promote policies the latter would have rejected and to oppose moves the former would have undertaken. That bane of international relations theory, the national interest, could be defined as follows:

9. A more systematic and exhaustive analysis would have to discriminate rigorously among the various components of the national situation; if the purpose of the analysis is to help one understand the relations between the nation-state and the international system, it would be particularly necessary to assess (1) the degree to which each of these components is an unchangeable given (or a given unchangeable over a long period of time) or on the contrary an element that can be transformed by will and action; (2) the hierarchy of importance and the order of urgency that political élites and decision-makers establish among the components.

10. See Raoul Girardet, "Antour de l'ideologie nationaliste," *Revue française de science politique, op. cit.,* pp. 423–45; and P. Hassner, *op. cit.,* pp. 516–19.

N.I. = National situation × outlook of the foreign policy-makers.

It is obvious that the same situation can result in different policies, depending in particular on whether or not there is a nationalist policy-maker. It is obvious also that national interests of different nations will not be defined in easily compatible terms if those respective outlooks are nationalist, even when the situations are not so different. But the same incompatibility may obtain, even if the outlooks are not nationalistic, when the situations are indeed very different.[11]

II

Let us now look at the fate of the nation-states in the part of Europe occupied by the so-called Six, that is, the continental part of Western Europe, first by examining the basic features of their national situations, then by commenting upon the process of unification, later by discussing its results, and finally by drawing some lessons.

Western Europe in the postwar years has been characterized by three features which have affected all of its nations. But each of those features has nevertheless affected each of the six nations in a different way because of the deep differences that have continued to divide the Six.

1. The first feature—the most hopeful one from the viewpoint of the unifiers—was the temporary demise of nationalism. In the defeated countries—Germany and Italy—nationalism had become associated with the regimes that had led the nations into war, defeat, and destruction. The collapse of two national ideologies that had been bellicose, aggressive, and imperialistic brought about an almost total discredit for nationalism is every guise. Among the nations of Western Europe that were on the Allied side, the most remarkable thing was that the terrible years of occupation and resistance had not resulted in a resurgence of chauvinism. Amusingly enough, it was the Communist Party of France that gave the most nationalistic tone to its propaganda; on the whole, the platforms of the Resistance movements show an acute awareness of the dangers of nationalist celebrations and national fragmentation in Western Europe. The Resistance itself had had a kind of supranational dimension; none of the national resistance movements could have survived without outside support; the nations whose honor they had saved had been liberated rather than victorious. All this prevented the upsurge of the kind of cramped chauvinism that had followed the victory of World War I, just as the completeness of the disaster and the impossibility of putting the blame on any traitors crushed any potential revival in Germany of the smoldering nationalism of resentment that had undermined the Weimar Republic. There was, in other words, above and beyond the differ-

11. As will be stated more explicitly in part V, what matters is not the "objective" difference detected by scholars or outsiders, but the "felt" difference experienced by political élites and decision-makers.

ences in national situations between indubitable losers and dubious winners, the general feeling of a common defeat, and also the hope of a common future: for the Resistance platforms often put their emphasis on the need for a union or federation of Western Europe.

However, the demise of nationalism affected differently the various nations of the half-continent. On the one hand, there were significant differences in national consciousness. If nationalism was low, patriotic sentiment was extremely high in liberated France. The circumstances in which the hated Nazis were expelled and the domestic collaborators purged amounted to what I have called elsewhere a rediscovery of the French political community by the French:[12] the nation seemed to have redeemed its "cohesion and distinctiveness." On the contrary, in Germany especially, the destruction of nationalism seemed to have been accompanied by a drop in national consciousness as well: what was distinctive was guilt and shame; what had been only too cohesive was being torn apart not by internal political cleavages, but by partition, zones of occupation, regional parochialisms blessed by the victors. The French national backbone had been straightened by the ordeal, although the pain had been too strong to tempt the French to flex nationalistic muscles; the German national backbone appeared to have been broken along with the strutting jaw and clenched fist of Nazi nationalism. Italy was in slightly better shape than Germany, in part because of its Resistance movements, but its story was closer to the German than to the French.

However, there were other elements in the national situation, besides patriotic consciousness, that also affected differently the various nations' inclination to nationalism. The defeated nations—Germany in particular—were in the position of patients on whom drastic surgery had been performed, and who were lying prostrate, dependent for their every movement on the surgeons and nurses. Even if one had wanted to restore the nation to the pinnacle of values and objectives, one could not have succeeded except with the help and consent of one's guardians—who were not likely to give support to such a drive; in other words, the situation itself set the strictest limits to the possibility of any kind of nationalism, expansive or insulating. The lost territories were beyond recuperation; a healing period of "*repli*" comparable to that which had marked the early foreign policy of the Third Republic was not conceivable either. One could not get anything alone, and anything others could provide, while limited, would be something to be grateful for.

On the other hand, France and, to a lesser extent (because of their much smaller size), Belgium and Holland were not so well inoculated. For, although the prevalence of the nation meant little in the immediate European context, it meant a great deal in the imperial one: if the circumstances of the Liberation kept national consciousness from veering into nationalism in one realm, the same circumstances tended to encourage such a turn with

12. See "Paradoxes of the French Political Community," in S. Hoffmann, *et al.*, *In Search of France* (Cambridge, Mass., 1963).

respect to the colonies. Cut down to size in Europe, these nations were bound to act as if they could call upon their overseas possessions to redress the balance; accustomed, through their association of nationalism with Nazi and Fascist imperialism, to equate chauvinism only with expansion, they would not be so easily discouraged from a nationalism of defense, aimed at preserving the "national mission" overseas. The Dutch lost most of their empire early enough to find themselves, in this respect, not so different from the German and Italian amputees; the Belgians remained serene long enough not to have nationalistic fevers about the huge member that seemed to give them no trouble until the day when it broke off—brutally, painfully, but irremediably. The French, however, suffered almost at once from dis-imperial dyspepsia, and the long, losing battle they fought gave rise continuously to nationalist tantrums of frustration and rage. Moreover, the French inclination to nationalism was higher because of an internal component of the national situation as well: there was in France one political force that was clearly nationalist, that had indeed presided over the Liberation, given whatever unity they had to the Resistance movements, and achieved in the most impressive way a highly original convergence of Jacobin universalist nationalism and of "traditionalist," right-wing, defensive nationalism—the force of General de Gaulle. His resignation had meant, as Alfred Grosser suggests,[13] the defeat of a doctrine that put not only a priority mark on foreign affairs but also a priority claim on *Notre Dame la France*. The incident that had led to his departure—a conflict over the military budget—had been symbolic enough of the demise of nationalism referred to above. But his durability, first as a political leader, later as a "capital that belongs to all and to none," reflected a lasting nostalgia for nationalism; and it was equally symbolic that the crisis which returned him to power was a crisis over Algeria.

2. The second feature common to all the West European national situations, yet affecting them differently, was the "political collapse of Europe." Europe did not merely lose power and wealth: such losses can be repaired, as the aftermath of World War I had shown. Europe, previously the heart of the international system, the locus of the world organization, the fount of international law, fell under what de Gaulle has called "the two hegemonies." The phrase is, obviously, inaccurate and insulting: one of those hegemonies took a highly imperial form, and thus discouraged and prevented the creation in Eastern Europe of any regional entity capable of overcoming the prewar national rivalries. Nothing is to be gained, however, by denying that U.S. hegemony has been a basic fact of life. American domination has indeed had the kinds of "domination effects" any hegemony produces: the transfer of decision-making in vital matters from the dominated to the dominator breeds a kind of paternalism in the latter, and irresponsibility (either in the form of abdication or in the form of scapegoatism) in the former. But the consequences of hegemony vary according to its nature. The peculiar nature of this

13. *La politique extérieure de la V République* (Paris, 1965), p. 12.

domination has also had unique consequences—better and worse than in the classical cases. One may dominate because one wants to and can; but one may also dominate because one must and does: by one's weight and under the pressures of a compelling situation. This has been America's experience: its hegemony was "situational," not deliberate.

The effects have been better than usual, insofar as such hegemony restricted itself to areas in which European nations had become either impotent or incapable of recovery by self-reliance. It left the dominated with a considerable freedom of maneuver, and indeed prodded them into recovery, power recuperation, and regional unity; it favored both individual and collective emancipation. But the effects have been worse precisely because this laxity meant that each party could react to *this* common feature of the national situations (that is, American hegemony) according to the distinctive *other* features of his national situation, features left intact by the weight and acts of the U.S., by contrast with the U.S.S.R. American domination was only one part of the picture. Hence the following paradox: both America's prodding and the individual and collective impotence of Western European nations, now reduced to the condition of clients and stakes, ought logically to have pushed them into unity-for-emancipation—the kind of process Soviet policy discouraged in the other half of Europe. But the very margin of autonomy left to each West European nation by the U.S. gave it an array of choices: between accepting and rejecting dependence, between unity as a weapon for emancipation and unity as merely a way to make dependence more comfortable. It would have been a miracle if all the nations had made the same choice; the diversity of national situations has ultimately prevailed. To define one's position toward the U.S. was the common imperative, but each one has defined it in his own way.

At first, this diversity of domestic outlooks and external positions did not appear to be an obstacle to the unification movement. As Ernst Haas has shown,[14] the movement grew on ambiguity, and those who accepted American hegemony as a lasting fact of European life as well as those who did not could submerge their disagreement in the construction of a regional entity that could be seen, by the former, as the most effective way for continuing to receive American protection and contributing to America's mission and, by the latter, as the most effective way to challenge American predominance. However, there are limits to the credit of ambiguity. The split could not be concealed once the new entity was asked to tackle matters of "high politics"— that is, go beyond the purely internal economic problems of little impact or dependence on the external relationship to the U.S.[15] It is therefore no sur-

14. *The Uniting of Europe* (Stanford, Calif., 1958).
15. See my discussion in "The European process of Atlantic cross-purposes," *Journal of Common Market Studies* (February 1965), pp. 85–101. The very success of internal economic integration raised those external issues far earlier than many expected. (Cf. Britain's application for membership, the problem of external commercial policy.)

prise that this split should have disrupted unification at two moments—in 1953–54, when the problem of German rearmament was raised; and in 1962–65, when de Gaulle's challenge of the U.S. became global.[16]

This is how the diversity of national situations operated. First, it produced (and produces) the basic split between those I would call the resigned ones, and those I would call the resisters. The resigned ones were, on the one hand, the smaller nations, aware of their weaknesses, realizing that the Soviet threat could not be met by Europeans alone, accustomed to dependence on external protectors, grateful to America for the unique features of its protection, and looking forward to an important role for Europe but not in the realm of high politics. Italy had, in the past, tried to act as a great power without protectors; yet not only were those days over, but also the acceptance of American hegemony provided the creaky Italian political system with a kind of double cushion—against the threat of Communism, but also against the need to spend too much energy and money on Italian rearmament. For the smaller states as well as for Italy, the acceptance of U.S. hegemony was like an insurance policy, which protected them against having to give priority to foreign affairs. On the other hand, Germany accepted dependence on the U.S. not merely as a comfort, but as a necessity as vital as breathing. West Germany's geographical position had turned it into the front line, its partition has contributed to imposing security as the supreme goal, the staunch anti-Communism of its leadership had ruled out any search for security along the lines of neutrality. There followed not only the acceptance of U.S. leadership but also the need to do everything possible in order to tie the United States to Western Europe. Moreover, in West Germany's helpless position, the recovery of equality was another vital goal, and it could be reached only through cooperation with the most powerful of the occupying forces. Defeat, division, and danger conspired to making West Germany switch almost abruptly from its imperialistic nationalism of the Nazi era to a dependence which was apparently submissive, yet also productive (of security and status gains) under Adenauer.

As for the resisters, they, like the West Germans, gave priority to foreign affairs—only not in the same perspective. The French reading of geography and history was different.[17] To be sure, the present need for security against the Soviet Union was felt. But there were two reasons that the "tyranny of the cold war" operated differently in France. One, French feelings of hostility

16. The latter case is self-evident; the first, less so, since the crisis over E.D.C. was primarily an 'intra-European" split, between the French and the Germans over the return of the latter to arms and soldiery. However, there was more to it than this: E.D.C. was accepted mostly by those who thought that Europe could and should not refuse to do what the U.S. had demanded—that is, rearm in order to share the defense of the half-continent with the U.S., and to incite the U.S. to remain its primary defender; E.D.C. was rejected by those who feared that the Defense Community would freeze existing power relationships forever.

17. There was, however, in France, a minority of "resigned ones," like Paul Reynaud.

toward Russia were much lower than in Germany, and, although it may be too strong to speak of a nostalgia for the wartime grand alliance, it is not false to say that the hope of an ultimate détente allowing for European reunification, for a return of the Soviets to moderation, and for an emancipation of the continent from its "two hegemonies" never died. The French time perspective has been consistently different from, say, the German: the urgency of the threat never overshadowed the desire for, and belief in, the advent of a less tense international system. This may have been due not only to France's location, but also to other elements in France's national situation. Whereas Germany's continuity with its past was both wrecked and repudiated, France (like England) looked back to the days when Europe held the center of the stage and forward to the time when Europe would again be an actor, not a stake: the anomaly was the present, not the past. Also, on colonial matters, France (more than England) often found little to distinguish America's reprobation from Soviet hostility. Two, France continued to worry not only about possible Soviet thrusts but also about Germany's potential threats: the suspicion of a reborn German national consciousness and nationalism has marked all French leaders. An additional reason for fearing the perpetuation of American hegemony and the freezing of the cold war, for hoping for a détente that would help Europe reunite, was thus provided by the fear that any other course would make Germany the main beneficiary of America's favors. Germany looked East with some terror, but there was only one foe there; when the French looked East, they saw two nations to fear; each could be used as an ally against the other—but for the time being the Soviet danger was the greater, and, should Germany be built up too much against the Soviets, the security gained by France in one respect would be compromised in another.[18]

There was a second way in which the diversity of national situations operated. As I have suggested, situations limit and affect but do not command choices. A general desire for overcoming the cold war and American hegemony did not mean a general agreement on how to do so. What I have called "the resistance" was split, and it is this split that has become decisive for an analysis of the obstacles to European unification. Had all the resisters calculated that the best way to reach France's objectives was the construction of a powerful West European entity, which could rival America's might, turn the bipolar contest into a triangle, and wrest advantages from both extra-European giants, the "ambiguity" of a movement led by resigned as well as resisting forces might not have damaged the enterprise until much later. However, there was a sharp division over methods between those who reasoned along the lines just described—like Jean Monnet—and those who feared

18. There is an impressive continuity in French efforts to preserve the difference between France's position and Germany's: from the préalables and protocols to E.D.C., to Mendès-France's Brussels proposals, to de Gaulle's opposition to any nuclear role for Germany.

that the sacrifice of national sovereignty to supranational institutions might entail a loss of control over the direction of the undertaking. The latter consisted of two kinds of people: on the one hand, the nationalists who, as indicated above, were still very much around, exasperated by the colonial battles, anxious to preserve all the resources of French diplomacy and strategy in order, in the present, to concentrate on the fronts overseas and, later, to promote whatever policies would be required, rather than let a foreign body decide; on the other hand, men like Mendès-France, who were not nationalists in the sense of this paper, but who thought that the continental European construction was not France's best way of coping with her situation—they thought that priority ought to go to more urgent tasks such as the search for a détente, the liberalization of the Empire, the reform of the economy.[19]

The success of the European movement required, first, that the "resisters" suspicious of European integration remain a minority—not only throughout the six but in the leadership of every one of the six, not only in Parliament but above all in the Executive, the prime decision-making force in every state: a requirement which was met in 1950–53 and in 1955–58, but not in the crucial months for E.D.C. in 1953–54, and no longer after 1958. The movement proceeded after 1958 because of the dialectic of ambiguity; however, there was a second requirement for success: that the "minute of truth"—when the European elites would have to ask themselves questions about the ultimate political direction of their community—be postponed as long as possible; that is, that the cold war remain sufficiently intense to impose even on the "resisters" a priority for the kind of security that implied U.S. protection—a priority for the *urgent* over the *long-term important* as they saw it. This is precisely what was already, if temporarily, shaken by the brief period of nervous demobilization that followed Stalin's death, in 1953–54, and then gradually undermined by the third basic feature of Europe's postwar situation. But before we turn to it, one remark must be made: in French foreign policy, "resistance by European integration" prevailed over "resistance by self-reliance" only as long as France was bogged down in colonial wars; it was this important and purely French element in France's national situation whose ups and downs affected quite decisively the method of "resistance."[20]

---

19. France's "integrationist resisters," like Jean Monnet himself, often chose not to stress the "resistance" aspect of their long-term vision, but nevertheless aimed ultimately at establishing in Western Europe not a junior partner of the U.S. but a "second force" in the West. Mendès-France's political vision never put the nation on top of the hierarchy of values; however, in 1954 (especially in his ill-fated demands for a revision of E.D.C. at the Brussels meeting in August) as well as in 1957 (when he voted against the Common Market), his actual policies did put a priority on national reform over external entanglements.

20. It is no coincidence if E.D.C. was rejected six weeks after the end of the war in Indochina, if the Common Market was signed while war raged in Algeria, if de Gaulle's sharpest attack on the "Monnet method" followed the Evian agreements. The weight of the situation affected and inflected the course of even as nationalist a leader as de Gaulle,

3. The divisions and contradictions described above were sharpened by the third common feature, which emerged in the mid-1950's and whose effects have developed progressively since: the nuclear stalemate between the superpowers. The impact of the "balance of terror" on the Western alliance has been analyzed so often and well[21] that nothing needs to be added here; but what is needed is a brief explanation of how the two splits already discussed have been worsened by Europe's gradual discovery of the uncertainties of America's nuclear protection (now that the U.S. could be devastated too), and how some new splits appeared. For to the extent to which the stalemate has loosened up a previously very tight situation—tight because of the threat from the East and the ties to the U.S.—it has altogether sharpened previous differences in national situations *and* increased the number of alternatives made available to élites and statesmen. Greater indeterminacy has meant greater confusion.

First, the split between French "resistance" and German "resignation" has become deeper. The dominant political élites in Germany have interpreted the new national situation created by the balance of terror as merely adding urgency to their previous calculation of interest. The nuclear stalemate was, given Germany's position, deemed to increase the danger for the West: the U.S. was relatively less strong, the Soviet Union stronger, that is, more of a threat. Indeed, the Socialists switched from their increasingly more furtive glances at neutrality to an outright endorsement of the Christian Democratic interpretation. If America's monopoly was broken, if America's guarantee was weakened thereby, what was needed—in a world that was not willing to let Germany rearm with nuclear weapons, in a continent that could not really develop a nuclear force of its own capable of replacing America's and of matching Russia's—was a German policy so respectful of America's main concerns, and also so vigilant with respect to the Soviet Union, that the U.S. would both feel obligated to keep its mantle of protection over Germany and not be tempted into negotiating a détente at Germany's expense. German docility would be the condition for, and counterpart of, American entanglement. The German reaction to a development that could, if General Gallois' logic were followed, lead to the prevalence of "polycentrism" at bipolarity's expense was the search for ways of exorcising the former and preserving the latter. On the whole, the smaller nations and Italy, while not at all fearful

---

between 1958 and 1962. Even he went along with the "Monnet method," however grudgingly, right until the end of the Algerian War. It is not a coincidence either if the French leaders most suspicious of the imprisoning effects of the community of the Six from France were the ones who labored hardest at improving the national situation by removing the colonial burdens (Mendès-France, de Gaulle)—and if those French rulers who followed Monnet and tried to place the pride of a nation with a sharp but wounded patriotic sense in its leadership of a united Europe were the men who failed to improve the national situation overseas (the M.R.P., Mollet). The one French politician who sought both European integration and imperial "disengagement" was Antoine Pinay.

21. Especially by Henry Kissinger in *The Troubled Partnership* (New York, 1965).

about the consequences of polycentrism (on the contrary), were nevertheless not shaken out of their "resignation"; the mere appearance of parity of nuclear peril was not enough to make them anxious to give, or to make them domestically capable of giving, priority to an active foreign policy.

In France, on the contrary, the balance of terror reinforced the attitude of resistance: what had always been a goal—emancipation—but had in fact been no more than a hope, given the thickness of the iron curtain, the simple rigidity of the superpowers' policies in the days of Mr. Dulles, and Europe's inability to affect the course of events, now became a possibility; for the giants' stalemate meant increased security for the less great (however much they might complain about the decrease of American protection and use it as a pretext, their lament coexisted with a heightened feeling of protection against war in general). What the Germans saw as a liability was an opportunity to the French. Germany's situation, its low national consciousness, incited most German leaders to choose what might be called a "minimizing" interpretation of the new situation; France's situation, its high national consciousness and, after 1958, the doctrine of its leader, incited French political élites to choose a "maximizing" interpretation. The increasing costs of the use of force made this use by the superpowers less likely, American protection less certain but also less essential, Europe's recovery of not merely wealth but power more desirable and possible—possible since the quest for power could be pushed without excessive risk of sanctions by the two giants, desirable since power, while transformed, remains the moving force and *ultima ratio* of world politics. This recovery of power would help bring about the much desired prevalence of polycentrism over bipolarity.[22]

Secondly, as this feud shows, the balance of terror heightened the split over method among the "resisters." On the one hand, it provided new arguments for those who thought that emancipation could be achieved only through the uniting of Western Europe: individual national efforts would remain too ridiculously weak to amount to anything but a waste in resources; a collective effort, however, could exploit the new situation, make Western Europe a true partner of the U.S., and not merely an economic partner and a military aide-de-camp. On the other hand, those who feared that the "united way" could become a frustrating deviation reasoned that the theory of graduated deterrence justified the acquisition of nuclear weapons by a middle-sized power with limited resources and that this acquisition would increase considerably the political influence as well as the prestige of the nation. The increased costs of force ruled out, in any case, what had in the

22. One should not forget that the original decisions that led to the French force de frappe were taken before de Gaulle, or that the French opposition to a national deterrent came from men who did not at all object to his argument about the need for Europe as a whole to stop being a client of the U.S., and who thought that, indeed, America's nuclear monopoly in the alliance was obsolete.

past been the most disastrous effort of the mushrooming of sovereign states—a warlike, expansionist nationalism—but they simultaneously refloated the value of small or middle-sized nations, no longer condemned by the cold, bipolar war to look for bigger protectors or to agglomerate in order to assure their security. Moreover, the "united way" would be a dead-end, since some, and not exactly the least significant, of the associates had no desire for collective European power at the possible expense of American protection. Not the least significant reason for the prevalence of the second line of thought over the first has been one important element of the national situation—the army: almost destroyed by its Algerian experience, it had to be "reconverted." In the circumstances of 1962, this meant inevitably a conversion to French atomic concerns. Its success builds up in turn a vested interest in the preservation of the new establishment—and increases the difference in national situations between France and a non-nuclear Germany.

Thirdly, the new situation affected European unification negatively not only by sharpening those splits but in two other ways as well. On the one hand, until then, opposition to a supranational entity had come only from a fraction of the "resisters"; in the early 1950's the U.S. had strongly—too strongly—urged the establishment of a European defense system which was not considered likely to challenge America's own predominance in the military area. In the 1960's, the U.S. no longer urged the West Europeans to build such a system. American leadership has developed a deep concern for maintaining centralized control over the forces of the alliance, that is, for preserving bipolarity, and a growing realization that Europe's appetite would not stop short of nuclear weapons. As a result, some of the "resigned ones," instead of endorsing European integration as unreservedly as when the situation of a dependent Europe in a cold-war-dominated world did not allow Europeans to entertain thoughts of genuine military "partnership" with the U.S., now for the first time showed themselves of two minds—they were willing to pursue integration in economic and social fields, but much less so in matters of defense, lest NATO be weakened. It is significant that the Dutch resisted de Gaulle's efforts, in 1960–62, to include defense in his confederal scheme and that the German leaders, in their quest for security, put their hopes in the MLF—a scheme that ties European nations one by one to the U.S.—rather than in a revised and revived E.D.C. Inevitably, such mental reservations of those who had been among the champions of supranationality could only confirm the suspicions of those "resisters" who had distrusted the "Monnet method" since the beginning. Thus, the national situation of Germany in particular—a situation in which America's own policy of reliance on Germany as the anchor of U.S. influence on the continent plays a large role—damaged the European movement: the German leaders were largely successful in their drive to entangle the U.S., but found that the price they had to pay was a decreasing ability to push for European integration. European integration and dependence on the U.S. were no longer automatically compatible.[23]

On the other hand, even that minority of German leaders who began to read Germany's national interest differently did not really compensate for the weakening of the majority's integrating ardor. Increasingly, in 1963 to 1965, suspicions about the value of the policy of docility-for-entanglement were voiced by a group of Christian Democrats, led by Adenauer and Strauss. They still read the German situation in terms of security first; but their faith in America's aptitude to provide it was shaken, and they saw that Germany had sufficiently gained from America's support not to have to behave as a minor any longer. Their nickname of German Gaullists is however totally unsuitable. To be sure, these men are "resisters" in the sense of turning away from America; they are close to the French "integrationist resisters," insofar as they propose a European defense effort and a joint European nuclear policy (rather than a purely German one). Nevertheless, their foreign policy goals are quite different from those of all the French resisters, integrationist or nationalist. The national situation of France made most French leaders agree on a common *vision,* described above, that can be summed up as the end of the cold war and a continent reunited with a Germany placed under certain wraps. That common vision coexists with the split on *policies* already discussed—the "European" policy (in which the wraps are organic, that is, the net and bonds of integration) *vs.* the "national" policy (in which the wraps are contractual). The national situation of Germany has made most German leaders, after the Social Democratic switch,[24] agree on a common *vision* deeply different from the French—a perpetuation of the cold war, hostility to the Soviet Union, the hope for a reunification tantamount not merely to the thawing of the Eastern "camp" but to its disintegration, and with as few concessions as possible. Since 1963, this vision has coexisted with two different *policies:* the majority policy of reliance on the U.S., the minority policy of substituting a strong, tough Europe for an increasingly less reliable, increasingly détente-happy U.S. At present, "resisters" are thus split not only on methods (French integrationists *vs.* French anti-integrationists) but also on objectives (French *vs.* German).

This long discussion of the different responses to common situations has been necessary in reaction to the dominant approach to European integration which has focused on process. The self-propelling power of the process is severely constrained by the associates' views and splits on ends and means. In order to go "beyond the nation-state," one will have to do more than set up procedures in adequate "background" and "process conditions." For a procedure is not a purpose, a process is not a policy.

---

23. Hence the rather vague or embarrassed formulas used by Jean Monnet's Action Committee for the United States of Europe with regard to defense in the past two years.
24. The case of Erich Mende's Free Democrats is more complicated.

III

However, since it is the process of European integration that is its most original feature, we must examine it also.[25] We have been witnessing a kind of race, between the logic of integration set up by Monnet and analyzed by Haas, and the logic of diversity, analyzed above. According to the former, the double pressure of necessity (the interdependence of the social fabric, which will oblige statesmen to integrate even sectors originally left uncoordinated) and of men (the action of the supranational agents) will gradually restrict the freedom of movement of the national governments by turning the national situations into one of total enmeshing. In such a milieu, nationalism will be a futile exercise in anachronism, and the national consciousness itself will, so to speak, be impregnated by an awareness of the higher interest in union. The logic of diversity, by contrast, sets limits to the degree to which the "spill-over" process can limit the freedom of action of the governments; it restricts the domain in which the logic of functional integration operates to the area of welfare; indeed, to the extent that discrepancies over the other areas begin to prevail over the laborious harmonization in welfare, even issues belonging to the latter sphere may become infected by the disharmony which reigns in those other areas. The logic of integration is that of a blender which crunches the most diverse products, overcomes their different tastes and perfumes, and replaces them with one, presumably delicious, juice. One lets each item be ground because one expects a finer synthesis: that is, ambiguity helps rather than hinders because each "ingredient" can hope that its taste will prevail at the end. The logic of diversity is the opposite: it suggests that, in areas of key importance to the national interest, nations prefer the certainty, or the self-controlled uncertainty, of national self-reliance, to the uncontrolled uncertainty of the untested blender; ambiguity carries one only a part of the way. The logic of integration assumes that it is possible to fool each one of the associates some of the time because his over-all gain will still exceed his occasional losses, even if his calculations turn out wrong here or there. The logic of diversity implies that, on a vital issue, losses are not compensated by gains on other (and especially not on other less vital) issues: nobody wants to be fooled. The logic of integration deems the uncertainties of the supranational function process creative; the logic of diversity sees them as destructive past a certain threshold: Russian roulette is fine only as long as the gun is filled with blanks. Ambiguity lures and lulls the national consciousness into integration as long as the benefits are high, the costs low, the expectations considerable. Ambiguity may arouse and stiffen national consciousness into nationalism if the benefits are slow, the losses high, the hopes dashed or deferred. Functional integration's gamble could be won

25. See my previous discussion in "Discord in Community," in F. Wilcox and H. F. Haviland, Jr. (eds.), *The Atlantic Community* (New York, 1963), pp. 3–31; "Europe's Identity Crisis," *Dædalus* (Fall 1964), pp. 1244–97, and the article listed in reference 15.

only if the method had sufficient potency to promise a permanent excess of gains over losses, and of hopes over frustrations. Theoretically, this may be true of economic integration. It is not true of political integration (in the sense of "high politics").

The success of the approach symbolized by Jean Monnet depended, and depends still, on his winning a triple gamble: on goals, on methods, on results. As for goals, it is a gamble on the possibility of substituting motion as an end in itself, for agreement on ends. It is a fact that the trans-national integrationist élites did not agree on whether the object of the community-building enterprise ought to be the construction of a new super-state—that is, a federal potential nation, *à la* U.S.A., more able because of its size and resources to play the traditional game of power than the dwarfed nations of Western Europe—or whether the object was to demonstrate that power politics could be overcome through cooperation and compromise, to build the first example of a radically new kind of unit, to achieve a change in the nature and not merely in the scale of the game. Monnet himself has been ambiguous on this score; Hallstein has been leaning in the first direction, many of Monnet's public relations men in the second.[26] Nor did the integrationists agree on whether the main goal was the creation of a regional "security community,"[27] that is, the pacification of a former hotbed of wars, or whether the main goal was the creation of an entity whose position and might could decisively affect the course of the cold war in particular, of international relations in general. Now, it is perfectly possible for a movement to feed on its harboring continental nationalists as well as anti-power idealists, inward-looking politicians and outward-looking politicians —but only as long as there is no need to make a choice. Decisions on tariffs did not require such choices. Decisions on agriculture already raise basic problems of orientation. Decisions on foreign policy and membership and defense cannot be reached unless the goals are clarified. One cannot be all things to all people all of the time.

As for methods, there was a gamble on the irresistible rise of supranational functionalism. It assumed, first, that national sovereignty, already devalued by events, could be chewed up leaf by leaf like an artichoke. It assumed, second, that the dilemma of governments having to choose between pursuing an integration that ties their hands and stopping a movement that benefits their people could be exploited in favor of integration by men representing the common good, endowed with the advantages of superior expertise, initiating proposals, propped against a set of deadlines, and using for their cause the technique of package deals. Finally, it was assumed that this approach would both take into account the interests of the greater powers

26. See, for instance, Max Kohnstamm's "The European Tide," in Stephen R. Graubard (ed.), *A New Europe?* (Boston, 1964), pp. 140–73.
27. See K. W. Deutsch, *et al., Political Community and the North Atlantic Area* (Princeton, N.J., 1937).

and prevent the crushing of the smaller ones. The troubles with this gamble have been numerous. One, even an artichoke has a heart, which remains intact after the leaves have been eaten. It is of course true that a successful economic and social integration would considerably limit the freedom governments would still enjoy in theory for their diplomacy and strategy; but why should one assume that they would not be aware of it? As the artichoke's heart gets more and more denuded, the governments' vigilance gets more and more alerted. To be sure, the second assumption implies that the logic of the movement would prevent them from doing anything about it: they would be powerless to save the heart. But, two, this would be true only if governments never put what they consider essential interests of the nation above the particular interests of certain categories of nationals, if superior expertise were always either the Commission's monopoly or the solution of the issue at hand, if package deals were effective in every argument, and, above all, if the governments' representatives were always determined to behave as a "community organ" rather than as the agents of states that are not willing to accept a community under any conditions. Finally, functional integration may indeed give lasting satisfaction to the smaller powers, precisely because it is for them that the ratio of "welfare politics" to high politics is highest, and that the chance of gaining benefits through intergovernmental methods that reflect rather than correct the power differential between the big and the small is poorest; but this is also why the method is not likely *à la longue* to satisfy the bigger powers as much: facing them, the supranational civil servants, for all their skill and legal powers, are a bit like Jonases trying to turn whales into jellyfish. Of course, the idea—ultimately—is to move from an essentially administrative procedure in which supranational civil servants enter a dialogue with national ministers, to a truly federal one in which a federal cabinet is responsible to a federal parliament; but what is thus presented as a linear progress may turn out to be a vicious circle, since the ministers hold the key to the transformation, and may refuse it unless the goals are defined and the results already achieved are satisfactory.

There was a gamble about results as well. The experience of integration would entail net benefits for all, and bring about clear progress toward community formation. Such progress could be measured by the following yardsticks: in the realm of interstate relations, an increasing transfer of power to the new common agencies, and the prevalence of solutions "upgrading the common interest" over other kinds of compromises; in the realm of transnational society, an increasing flow of communications; in the area of national consciousness—which is important both for interstate relations, because (as seen above) it may set limits to the statesmen's discretion, and for transnational society, because it affects the scope and meaning of the communication flows—progress would be measured by increasing compatibility of views about external issues. The results achieved so far are mixed; negative on the last count (see below), limited on the second, and marked on the first by features that the enthusiasts of integration did not expect. On the one hand, there has been some strengthening of the authority of the Commission, and in various areas there has been some "upgrading of common interests." On the other hand, the Commission's unfortunate attempt to consolidate those gains at de Gaulle's expense, in the spring of 1965, has brought about a startling setback for the whole enterprise; moreover, in their negotiations, the members have conspicuously failed to find a common interest in some vital areas (energy, England's entry), and sometimes succeeded in reaching apparently "integrating" decisions only after the most ungainly, traditional kind of bargaining, in which such uncommunity-like methods as threats, ultimatums, and retaliatory moves were used. In other words, either the ideal was not reached, or it was reached in a way that was both the opposite of the ideal and ultimately its destroyer. If we look at the institutions of the Common Market as an incipient political system for Europe, we find that its authority remains limited, its structure weak, its popular base restricted and distant.[28]

It is therefore not surprising if the uncertainty about results already achieved contributes to uncertainty about future prospects. For the very divisions among the partisans of integration make it hard to predict where the "Monnet method" would lead, if the process were to continue along the lines so fondly planned by the French "inspirator." Would the enterprise become an effective federation, gradually turning the many into one, or would it lead to a mere façade behind which all the divergences and rivalries would continue to be played out? It is at least remarkable that Gaullist and American fears should converge in one respect: de Gaulle has consistently warned that the application of the supranational method to the area of high politics would lead not to a strong European entity, but to a dilution of national responsibility whose only beneficiary would be the U.S.; incapable of defining a coherent policy, the "technocrats" would leave the decisions in vital areas to the U.S., at least by default. On the contrary, many Americans have come to believe, on the basis of some of E.E.C.'s actions in the realm of tariffs and trade, that a united Europe would be able to challenge U.S. leadership much more effectively than the separate European states ever could. The truth of the matter is that nobody knows: a method is not a policy, a process is not a direction; the results achieved so far are too specialized, and the way in which they have been reached is too bumpy, to allow one to extrapolate and project safely. The face of a united Europe has not begun to emerge; there are just a few lines, but one does not know whether the supranational technique would finally give to Western Europe the features of a going concern, or those of a Fourth Republic writ large—the ambitions of a world power, or the complacency of parochialism. The range of possibilities is so broad, the alternatives are so extreme, that the more the Six move into the

28. Under authority, I include three distinct notions: autonomy (the capacity to act independently of the governments, and particularly the financial capacity), power (control over acts of others), and legitimacy (being accepted as the "rightful" center of action).

stormy waters of high politics, the less not only they but also the outside powers, such as the U.S., which may be affected by their acts are willing to extend the credit of hope and to make new wagers: neither Gaullist France nor the present U.S. leadership is willing to risk a major loss of control. Contrary to the French proverb, in the process of functional integration, only the first steps do not cost much.

There are two important general lessons one can draw from a study of the process of integration. The first concerns the limits of the functional method: its very (if relative) success in the relatively painless area in which it works relatively well lifts the participants to the level of issues to which it does not apply well any more—like swimmers whose skill at moving quickly away from the shore suddenly brings them to the point where the waters are stormiest and deepest, at a time when fatigue is setting in, and none of the questions about ultimate goal, direction, and length of swim has been answered. The functional process was used in order to "make Europe"; once Europe began being made, the process collided with the question; "making Europe, what for?" The process is like a grinding machine that can work only if someone keeps giving it something to grind. When the users start quarreling and stop providing, the machine stops. For a while, the machine worked because the governments poured into it a common determination to integrate their economies in order to maximize wealth; but with their wealth increasing, the question of what to do with it was going to arise: a technique capable of supplying means does not *ipso facto* provide the ends, and it is about those ends that quarrels have broken out. They might have been avoided if the situation had been more compelling—if the Six had been so cooped up that each one's horizon would have been nothing other than his five partners. But this has never been their outlook, nor is it any more their necessity. Each one is willing to live with the others, but not on terms too different from his own; and the Six are not in the position of the three miserable prisoners of *No Exit*. Transforming a dependent "subsystem" proved to be one thing; defining its relations to all other subsystems and to the international system in general has turned out to be quite another—indeed, so formidable a matter as to keep the transformation of the subsystem in abeyance until those relations can be defined.

The model of functional integration, a substitute for the kind of instant federation which governments had not been prepared to accept, shows its origins in important respects. One, it is essentially an administrative model, which relies on bureaucratic expertise for the promotion of a policy defined by the political authorities, and for the definition of a policy that political decision-makers are technically incapable of shaping—something like French planning under the Fourth Republic. The hope was that in the interstices of political bickering the administrators could build up a consensus; but the mistake was to believe that a formula that works well within certain limits is a panacea—and that even within the limits of "welfare politics" administrative skill can always overcome the disastrous effects of political paralysis or mis-management (cf. the impact of inflation, or balance of payment troubles, on planning). Two, the model assumes that the basic political decisions, to be prepared and pursued by the civil servants but formally made by the govern-ments, would be reached through the process of short-term bargaining, by politicians whose mode of operation is empirical muddling through, of the kind that puts immediate advantages above long-term pursuits: this model corresponds well to the nature of parliamentary politics with a weak Execu-tive, for example, the politics of the Fourth Republic, but the mistake was to believe that all political regimes would conform to this rather sorry image, and also to ignore the disastrous results which the original example produced whenever conflicts over values and fundamental choices made mere empiri-cal groping useless or worse than useless (cf. decolonization).[29]

The second lesson is even more discouraging for the advocates of func-tionalism. To revert to the analogy of the grinder, what has happened is that the machine, piqued by the slowing down of supply, suddenly suggested to its users that in the future the supplying of grinding material be taken out of their hands and left to the machine. The institutional machinery tends to become an actor with a stake in its own survival and expansion. The same thing happens often enough within a state whose political system is ineffec-tive. But here we deal not with one but with six political systems, and the reason for the ineffectiveness of the Council of Ministers of the Six may be the excessive toughness, not the weakness, of the national political systems involved. In other words, by trying to be a force, the bureaucracy here, in-evitably, makes itself even more of a stake that the nations try to control or at least to affect. A new complication is thus added to all the substantive issues that divide the participants—one that provides them with a whole trunkful of screens and masks. Thus, the agricultural problem is one that could have been solved "technically," since the governments had previously reached basic compromises, and more or less agreed on the relations between Common Market and outside agriculture. But the way in which these accords had been reached left scars, and the nature of the agreement meant a victory for one state (France) over another (Germany). The whole issue has been reopened, due not to the states' but to the Commission's initiative. In the crisis of 1965, the Commission's overly bold proposal of a common agricul-tural policy (along pro-French lines) cum supranationality (against French determination) has, on the one hand, allowed some of the Six, hostile in fact to the substantive proposals, to endorse the Commission's plan and stand up as champions of supranationality, while knowing that the French would block the scheme; the French have been able to use the Commission's rashness as a pretext for trying to kill supranationality altogether; a German government not too kindly disposed toward a Commission whose initiatives and economic

29. Along similar lines, see Francis Rosenstiel, *Le principe de "Supranationalité"* (Paris, 1962).

inspiration were hardly in line with Mr. Erhard's views has found itself defending the Commission, whose head, now under French attack, is a German; a French government anxious to get its partners committed to a protected agricultural market has preferred to postpone the realization of this goal rather than let the Commission's autonomy grow. The states have found something more to disagree about, and the Commission, in an attempt to push the car out of the bog, has stopped the motor for months. To be sure, the Commission's dilemma had become acute: either its members resigned themselves to being merely patient brokers to their quarreling clients, and letting them set the pace; or else they tried to behave both according to the ideal-type of the Monnet method, and as if a genuine community had already been established; but if prudence meant sluggishness, anticipation has meant delay. In the immediate future, the settlement of the various substantive issues—"the uniting of Europe, what for?"—is likely to be postponed while the Six try to repair the damaged machinery; in a way, haggling about the kind of grinder one wants is a polite method for appearing to want to keep grinding together, while really disagreeing completely on what one wants to put in and get out.

IV

We must come now to the balance sheet of the "European experiment." The most visible aspect is the survival of the nations. To be sure, they survive transformed: first, swept by the advent of the "age of mass consumption," caught in an apparently inexorable process of industrialization, urbanization, and democratization, they become more alike in social structure, in economic and social policies, even in physical appearance; there is a spectacular break between a past which so many monuments bring to constant memory, and a rationalized future that puts these nations closer to the problems of America's industrial society than to the issues of their own history. Second, these similarities are promoted by the Common Market itself: it is of no mean consequence that the prospect of a collapse of the Market should have brought anguish to various interest groups, some of which had fought its establishment: the transnational linkages of businessmen and farmers are part of the transformation. Third, none of the Western European nations is a world power any longer in the traditional sense, that is, in the sense either of having physical establishments backed by military might in various parts of the globe, or of possessing in Europe armed forces superior to those of any non-European power.

And yet they survive as nations. Let us go back to the criteria of integration listed above. On foreign and defense policies, not only has no power been transferred to common European organs, but France has actually taken power away from NATO, and, as shown in part two, differences in the calculations of the national interest have, if anything, broadened ever since the advent of the balance of terror. As for intra-European communications, re-search shows that the indubitably solid economic network of E.E.C. has not been complemented by a network of social and cultural communications;[30] the links between some of those societies and the U.S. are stronger than the links among them. Indeed, even in the realm of economic relations, the Common Market for goods has not been completed by a system of pan-West European enterprises: enterprises that find themselves unable to compete with rivals within E.E.C. often associate themselves with American firms rather than merge with such rivals. Finally, views about external issues, far from becoming more compatible, appear to reflect as well as to support the divergent definitions of the national interest by the statesmen. French élite opinion puts Europe ahead of the North Atlantic partnership, deems bipo-larity obsolete, is overwhelmingly indifferent or even hostile to the U.S., and is still highly suspicious of Germany; only a minority comes out in favor of a genuine political federation of Western Europe and thinks that U.S. and French interests coincide. German élite opinion puts the North Atlantic entente ahead of Europe, believes that the world is still bipolar, is over-whelmingly favorable to the U.S., deems U.S. and German interests in agreement, is either favorably inclined toward France or at least not hostile, and shows a majority in favor of a European federation. There is no common European outlook. Nor is there a common "project," a common conception of either Europe's role in world affairs or Europe's possible contribution to the solution of the problems characteristic of all industrial societies.

It is important to understand where the obstacles lie. To some extent, they lie in the present condition of national consciousness. I mentioned earlier that there were at the start considerable differences from country to country. In two respects, similarities have emerged in recent years. There has been a rebirth of German national consciousness, largely because the bold attempt at fastening Germany's shattered consciousness directly to a new European one did not succeed: the existence of a German national situation has gradu-ally reawakened a German national awareness, and thus reduced the gap between Germany and France in this area. Moreover, all the national con-sciences in Western Europe are alike in one sense: they are not like Rousseau's general will, a combination of mores and moves that define with a large degree of intellectual clarity and emotional involvement the pur-poses of the national community. Today's national consciousness in Europe is negative rather than positive. There is still, in each nation, a "vouloir-vivre collectif." But it is not a "daily plebiscite" *for* something. It is, in some parts, a daily routine, a community based on habit rather than on common tasks, an identity that is received rather than shaped. Thus Germany's sense of "cohesion and distinctiveness" is the inevitable result of the survival and recovery of a West German state in a world of nations, rather than a specific

30. I am using here unpublished studies done under Karl Deutsch, especially by Donald J. Puchala.

willed set of imperatives. In other parts, national consciousness is a daily refusal rather than a daily creation, a desire to preserve a certain heritage (however waning, and less because it is meaningful today than because it is one's own) rather than a determination to define a common destiny, an identity that is hollow rather than full and marked more by bad humor toward foreign influences than by any positive contribution.

To be sure, the negative or hollow character of national consciousness need not be a liability for the champions of integration: general wills *a la* Rousseau could be formidable obstacles to any fusion of sovereignty. However, the obstacle resides partly in the common nature of the present state of national consciousness, partly in the remaining differences. A patriotic consciousness that survives in a kind of nonpurposive complacency may not be a barrier to efforts at transcending it, but it is a drag: it does not carry forward or push statesmen in the way in which an intense and positive "general will" prods leaders who act on behalf of national goals, or in the way in which European federalists have sometimes hoped that enlightened national patriotisms would propel Europe's national leaders into building a new European community, into which those enlightened patriotisms would converge and merge. Moreover, two of the "national consciences" have raised obstacles: the French one because it remains too strong, the German one because it remains too weak. The French may not have a sense of national purpose, but, precisely because their patriotism has been tested so often and so long, because the pressures of the outside world have continued throughout the postwar era to batter their concerns and their conceits, and because modernization, now accepted and even desired, also undermines traditional values still cherished and traditional authority patterns still enforced, French national consciousness opposes considerable resistance to any suggestion of abdication, resignation, *repli*—so much so that the "Europeans" themselves have had to present integration as an opportunity for getting French views shared by others instead of stressing the "community" side of the enterprise.[31] Germany's national consciousness, on the other hand, remains marked by a genuine distaste for or timidity toward what might be called the power activities of a national community on the world stage; hence a tendency to shy away from the problems of "high politics" which a united Europe would have to face and whose avoidance only delays the advent of unity; a tendency to refuse to make policy choices and to pretend (to oneself and to others) that no such choices are required, that there is no incompatibility between a "European Europe" and an Atlantic partnership. In one case, a defensive excess of self-confidence makes unity on terms other than one's own difficult, and obliges integrationist leaders to use cunning and flattery and deceit (with often lamentable results—like the E.D.C. crisis); in the other case, an equally defensive lack of self-confidence projects itself

31. On this point, see Raymond Aron and Daniel Lerner (eds.), *France Defeats EDC* (New York, 1957).

into the external undertakings of the nation and weakens the foundations of the common European enterprise.

And yet, if the "national consciousness" of the European nations could be isolated from all other elements of the national situation, one would, I think, conclude that the main reasons for the resistance of the nation-state lie elsewhere.

They lie, first of all, in the differences in national situations, exacerbated by the interaction between each of the Six and the present international system. Earlier, we have looked at concrete instances of such differences; let us return to them in a more analytic way. One part of each national situation is the purely *domestic* component. In a modern nation-state, the very importance of the political system, in the triple sense of functional scope, authority, and popular basis, is already a formidable obstacle to integration. It is comparatively easier to overcome the parochialism of a political system which, being of the night-watchman variety, has only a slender administrative structure, whose power consists of punishing, rather than rewarding, with the help of a tiny budget, and whose transmission belts to the mass of the people are few and narrow, than it is to dismantle the fortress of a political system which rests on "socially mobilized" and mobilizing parties and pressure groups, and handles an enormous variety of social and economic services with a huge bureaucracy. To be sure, it was the hope and tactic of Monnet to dismantle the fortress by redirecting the allegiance of parties and pressure groups toward the new central institutions, by endowing the latter with the ability to compete with the national governments in the setting up of social services. In other words, the authority of the new European political system would deepen as its scope broadened and its popular basis expanded. The success of this attempt at drying up the national ponds by diverting their waters into a new, supranational pool depended on three prerequisites which have not been met: with respect to popular basis, the prevalence of parties and pressure groups over Executives; with respect to scope, the self-sustaining and expanding capacity of the new central bureaucracy; with respect to both scope and popular basis, the development of transnational political issues of interest to all political forces and publics across boundary lines. The modern Executive establishment has one remarkable feature: it owes much of its legitimacy and its might to the support of popularly based parties and pressure groups, but it also enjoys a degree of autonomy that allows it to resist pressures, to manipulate opposition, to manufacture support. Even the weak Fourth Republic has evaded pressure toward "transnationalism" and diluted the dose of "bargaining politics" along supranational lines. The civil servants' careers are still made and unmade in the national capitals. Above all, each nation's political life continues to be dominated by "parochial" issues: each political system is like a thermos bottle that keeps warm, or lukewarm, the liquid inside. The European political process has never come close to resembling that of any Western European democracy because it has been starved of common and distinctive European issues. It is as if, for the myth-ical common man, the nation-state were still the most satisfying—indeed the most rewarding—form of social organization in existence.[32] As for what it can no longer provide him with by itself, the state can still provide it without committing suicide, through cooperation, or the citizens can go and find it across borders, without any need to transfer their allegiance—or else there is, in any event, no guarantee that any form of social organization other than a still utopian world state could provide it. If we look at the issues that have dominated European politics, we find two distinct blocs. One is the bloc of problems peculiar to each nation—Italy's battle of Reds *vs.* Blacks, or its concern for the Mezzogiorno; Belgium's linguistic clashes; Germany's "social economy" and liquidation of the past; France's constitutional troubles and miraculously preserved party splintering. Here, whatever the transnational party and interest group alignments in Luxembourg, the dominant motifs have been purely national. The other bloc of issues are the international ones (including European unity). But here is where the *external* component of the national situation has thwarted the emergence of a common European polit-ical system comparable to that of each nation.

It is here that the weight of geography and of history—a history of nations —has kept the nation-states in their watertight compartments. It is no accident if France, the initiator of the process, has also been its chief trouble-maker: for in those two respects France's position differed from everyone else's in the community, and was actually closer to England's. Historically first: for Germany, integration meant a leap from opprobrium and impotence, to respectability and equal rights; for the smaller powers, it meant exchang-ing a very modest dose of autonomy for participation in a potentially strong and rich grouping. France could not help being much more ambivalent, for integration meant on the one hand an avenue for leadership and the shaping of a powerful bloc, but it also meant on the other the acceptance of perma-nent restrictions to an autonomy that was indeed quite theoretical in the late 1940's, but whose loss could not be deemed definitive. For a once-great power, whose national history is long, and therefore used to rise and fall, inherits from its past a whole set of habits and reflexes which make it conduct its policy as if it were still or could again become a great power (unless those habits and reflexes have been smashed, at least for a while, as completely and compellingly as were Germany's); for this once-great power showed, as described above, a still vigilant national consciousness, often the more viru-lent for all its negativism; for the international system itself seemed to open vistas of increased freedom of action to middle-sized states. In other words, integration meant an almost certain improvement in the national situation of the other five, but for France it could be a deterioration or an adventure.[33]

32. See Rupert Emerson, *op. cit.*, Ch. XIX.

33. England's refusal to join European integration, before 1961, could not fail to in-crease French reticence, for integration thus meant equality with Germany, and a clear-cut

There is no better example than the nuclear problem: integration here meant, for France, giving up the possibility of having a force of her own, perhaps never even being certain that a united Europe (with no agreement on strategy and diplomacy in sight) would create a common deterrent, at best contributing to a European force which would put Germany in the same position as France; but the French decision to pursue the logic of diversity, while giving her her own force, has also made a European nuclear solution more difficult and increased France's distance from Germany. Moreover, a geographical difference has corroborated the historical one: France had lasting colonial involvements. Not only did they, on the whole, intensify national consciousness; they also contributed to France's ambivalence toward European ently tried to tie their partners to the prevalence of France's overseas plight became, the more integration was preached as a kind of compensatory mechanism. But, on the other hand, this meant that integration had to be given a "national" rather than a "supranational" color, to be presented as a new career rather than as a common leap; it meant that the French consistently tried to tie their partners to the prevalence of France's overseas concerns, much against these partners' better judgment; above all, it meant that there was a competition for public attention and for official energies, between the "load" of integration and the burden of the overseas mission. The great power reflex and the colonial legacy combine today in the policy of cooperation with the former imperial possessions, despite its costs: cooperation is presented as a transfiguration of the legacy, and a manifestation of the reflex.[34]

Thus, the national situations have multiplied the effects of differences between the shapes of the various national consciences. But the resistance of the nation-state is not due only to the kind of loan of life that its inevitable entanglement in international affairs and the idle motion left by its past provide even to nations with a low national consciousness. It is due also to the impact of the revival of nationalism in France. Even without de Gaulle the differences analyzed above would have slowed down integration and kept some fire in the nation's stoves. But the personal contribution of de Gaulle to the crisis of integration has been enormous. Not only has he raised questions that were inescapable in the long run, earlier and more pungently than they would have been otherwise, but he has also provided and tried to impose his own answers. His impact is due to his style as well as to his policies. The

difference between France's position and England's, that is, a reversal of French aspirations and traditions. England has on the whole rejected the "resignation-resistance" dilemma—and as a result, both the aspects of its foreign policy that appeared like resignation to U.S. predominance and the aspects that implied resistance to decline have contributed to the crisis of European integration: for France's veto in January 1963 meant a French refusal to let into Europe a power that had just confirmed its military ties to the U.S., but Britain's previous desire to play a world role and aversion to "fading into Europe" encouraged France's own misgivings about integration.

34. See Alfred Grosser, *op. cit.,* Ch. IV.

meaning of de Gaulle has been a change in French policy from ambivalence toward supranational integration to outright hostility; from a reluctance to force one's partners to dispel the ambiguities of "united Europe" to an almost gleeful determination to bring differences out into the open; from a tendency to interpret the national situation as oppressively difficult to a herculean effort at improving all its components in order to push back limits and maximize opportunities. The meaning of de Gaulle has also been a change in the national situations of the others, leading to a sharpening of antagonisms and to a kind of cumulative retreat from integration. Each one of those meanings must be briefly examined.

Insofar as France is concerned, the key is provided by de Gaulle's concept of grandeur.[35] Greatness is a mixture of pride and ambition—the nation shall not at any point leave the control of its destiny to others (which does not mean that he does not acknowledge the existence of irresistible waves with which the ship of state must roll, lest, precisely, it fall in the hands of others who would rush to a predatory rescue or to a plunder of the wreck). The nation must try at any point to play as full a role in the world as its means allow. The consequences are clear: First, the kind of supranational integration which would leave decisions on vital issues to majority votes or to executive organs independent of the states is out of the question; even if the interests and policies of France should happen to prevail for a while (as indeed they did as long as the Commission, in its drive for economic integration, remained very close to French ideas), there would be no assurance against a sudden and disastrous reversal. Second, extensive cooperation is not at all ruled out: on the contrary, such cooperation will benefit all participants as long as it corresponds to and enhances mutual interests. Third, however, it is part of the very ambition of grandeur that in such schemes of cooperation which aim not merely at exchanges of *services* but at the definition of common *policies,* France will try to exert her leadership and carry out her views: the degree of French cooperativeness will be measured by the degree of responsiveness of the others.

It is true that the General is an empiricist, and that his analysis of the European situation is to a large extent irrefutable. What could be more starting from what exists—the nation-state—refusing to act as if what does not yet exist—a united Europe—had already been established, and refusing to forget that each of the European nations is willy-nilly engaged in an international competition that entails a fight for rank and power? But pragmatism is always at the service of ends, explicit or not (the definition of a bad foreign policy could be: that which uses rigid means at the service of explicit ends, as well as that whose flexible means are not serving clearly-thought-out ends). De Gaulle's empiricism is a superb display of skill, but on behalf of a thoroughly non-empirical doctrine. It is obvious that his distrust of supra-

35. For a more detailed analysis of this concept, see my article: "De Gaulle's Memoirs: The Hero as History," *World Politics,* Vol. XIII, No. 1 (October 1960), pp. 140–155.

national integration, which, within Europe, could submit French interests to the dictates of others, and could expose Europe to the dictates of the "hegemonists," while it is perfectly comprehensible as a starting point, nevertheless results in a kind of freezing of integration and perpetuation of the nation-state. If his chief foreign policy objective were the creation of a European entity acting as a world power, his "empirical" *starting point* would be a most unrealistic *method*. But the fact is that such a creation is not his supreme objective, and Europe not his supreme value.

His supreme value remains the nation-state; his supreme political objective is the creation of a world in which the "two hegemonies" will have been replaced by a multipolar international system, whose "first floor" would be the numerous nations, endowed with and entitled to political integrity and independence, and whose "second floor" would be inhabited by the nuclear powers, in a role comparable to that of the late European concert. Again, the implications are clear: de Gaulle's doctrine is a "universalist nationalism," that is, he sees France's mission as world-wide, not local and defensive, but this means that Europe is just one corner of the tapestry; Europe is a means, not an end. "Things being what they are," it is better to have separate nation-states (whose margin of freedom is undoubtedly smaller than when the use of force was not so costly, whose capacity to shape history is also undoubtedly limited if their size, population, and resources are mediocre, but whose ability to behave as self-determined actors on the stage is enhanced precisely by the blunting of force and by the opportunities opened to other instruments of power and influence) than it is to have a larger entity, undoubtedly more able to act as a forceful competitor in the world's contests should it be coherent, but more likely to be incoherent, given the divisions of its members and the leverage interested outsiders possess over some of the insiders. The size of the unit is less important than its "cohesion and distinctiveness," for its effectiveness is not merely a function of its material resources: if the unit has no capacity to turn these to action, because of internal cleavages and strains, the only beneficiaries would be its rivals. In a contest with giants, a confident David is better than a disturbed Goliath. This is a choice that reflects a doctrine; the refusal to gamble on European unity goes along with a willingness to gamble on the continuing potency of the French nation-state; the determination to accept only the kind of Europe that would be France writ large[36] corresponds to a conviction that French policies could be made to prevail whether Europe contributes its support or not: "with Europe if they follow, without Europe if they do not," Europe is just a card in a global game. Schumpeter had defined imperialism as an objectless quest; de Gaulle's nationalism is a kind of permanent quest with varying content but never any other cause than itself.

As I suggested above, a nationalist leader is one whose reading of the

---

36. Grosser, *op. cit.*, pp. 112–113, draws attention to Prime Minister Pompidou's statement: "France is condemned by geography and history to play the role of Europe."

national situation is likely to be quite different from the reading other leaders would give. De Gaulle's brand of nationalism being what it is—universalist, aimed at overcoming the "two hegemonies," exploiting both of the somewhat contradictory trends that dominate the present world (the conservation of the nation as its basic unit, the concentration of what one might call "final power" among the nuclear states)—it is not surprising that he has altogether liquidated a colonial burden that kept France away from every one of the routes he wanted to travel, and replaced it with an ambitious policy of cooperation with the "Third World." In a way, it is true, as some critics have charged, that this policy is a kind of self-consolation prize for the failure of his European policy; but in another sense it conforms deeply to his most vital designs and to his most constant habit of never relying on one line of policy only: In the first place, cooperation manifests France's universal destiny; in the second, it aims at consolidating a system of independent, if cooperating, nations; in the third, it tries to use the prestige thus gained as an elevator to the floor of the "big five," to which access has been denied so far by the "big two." It is clear that the first two missions rule out a concentration on Europe alone, that the second prevents in any case his putting any passion into overcoming the nation-state in Europe, that the third is precisely a substitute for the "elevator" Europe has failed to provide. As a result, all that has made France's historical heritage and geographic position distinctive has been strengthened.

Every great leader has his built-in flaw, since this is a world in which roses have thorns. De Gaulle's is the self-fulfilling prophecy. Distrustful of any Europe but his own, his acts have made Europe anything but his. Here we must turn to the impact of his policy on France's partners. First of all, there is a matter of style: wanting cooperation not integration, de Gaulle has refused to treat the Community organs as Community organs; but, wanting to force his views about cooperation on partners still attached to integration, and attempting to impose his views about a "European Europe" on associates who might have settled for cooperation but only on behalf of another policy, de Gaulle has paradoxically had to try to achieve cooperation for a common policy in a way that smacked of conflict not cooperation, of unilateralism not compromise. Thus we have witnessed not just a retreat from the Monnet method to, say, the kind of intergovernmental cooperation that marks O.E.C.D., but to a kind of grand strategy of nonmilitary conflict, a kind of political cold war of maneuver and "chicken." With compromises wrested by ultimatums, concessions obtained not through package deals but under the threat of boycotts, it is not surprising if even the Commission ended by playing the General's game instead of turning whatever other cheek was left; its spring 1965 agricultural plan was as outright a challenge to de Gaulle as de Gaulle's veto of January 1963 had been an affront to the Community spirit. Just as de Gaulle had tried to force Germany to sacrifice her farmers to the idea of a European entity, the Commission tried to call de Gaulle's bluff by

forcing him to choose between French farmers' interests and the French national interest in a "European Europe" for agriculture, on the one hand, and
his own hostility to supranationality and the French national interest (as seen
by him) in the free use of French resources, on the other. Playing his game,
the Commission also played into his hands, allowing him to apply the Schelling tactic of "if you do not do what I ask, I will blow up my brains on your
new suit," and in the end buying his return at the price of a sacrifice of integration.[37] In other words, he has forced each member to treat the Community
no longer as an end in itself; and he has driven even its constituted bodies,
which still insist it is that, into bringing grist to his mill.

Second, his impact on his partners is a matter of policy as well. Here we
must examine Franco-German relations. As long as he hoped that Germany
would follow his guidance and provide the basis for the "European Europe"
of his design, his attitude toward West Germany was one of total support of
her intransigence toward the Communists. As soon as the increasing clarity
of his own policy (half-veiled until the end of the Algerian ordeal and his
triumph in the constitutional battle of October-November 1962) provoked
German suspicion and reticence, as soon as the U.S., in response to his challenge, consolidated its ties with a still loyal Germany and even promised her
substantial rewards for her loyalty, he applied to Germany the shock tactics
so effectively used on Britain and the U.S. during World War II: he made his
own opening to the East and gradually shifted away from the kind of celebration of a "new Germany" (heir to her greatness in her past but now willing to
take her place as France's aide in the new "European Europe"), so characteristic of his German visit in the fall of 1962. He now resorts to carefully worded
reminders to the Germans of their past misdeeds, of the risk which their
loyalty to the U.S. entails for their reunification, and of the interest France
and the Eastern states (including Russia) share in keeping Germany under
permanent restrictions. Had Germany been willing to follow France, he
would have given priority to the construction of a "half-Europe" that would
thereafter have been a magnet (as well as a guarantee of German harmless-
ness) to the East. Germany's refusal leads him to put the gradual emergence
of a "Europe from the Atlantic to the Urals"—indeed from the British Isles to
the Urals[38]—if not ahead of at least on the same plane as the development of
the "European Europe" in the West; for the containment of Germany, no
longer assured in a disunited Western Europe of the Six, may still be obtained
in a much larger framework. The implications are important. First, there is a
considerable change in Germany's national situation. On the one hand, its external component has been transformed. Whereas for more than fifteen years
both the U.S. and France carried out tacitly Robert Schuman's recommendation—"never leave Germany to herself"—the Franco-American competition
for German support, the Gaullist refusal to tie Germany to France in a federal

---

37. See Thomas Schelling's *Strategy of Conflict* (Cambridge, Mass., 1960).
38. See de Gaulle's reference to England in his press conference of September 9, 1965.

Europe so to speak for the knot's sake (that is, unless Germany follows France), America's disastrous emulation of the sorcerer's apprentice in titil-lating Germany's interest in nuclear strategy or weapons-sharing, in the belief, or under the pretext, of anticipating her appetite, all of these factors have contributed to loosen the bonds between Germany and the West: to the European part of the West, because of the slump in integration, and even to the U.S., because of America's failure to follow up after raising in Germany hopes that should not have been raised, but which, once raised and frus-trated, are unlikely to fade. On the other hand, and consequently, the domestic component of Germany's national situation has also been affected: Still concerned with security as well as with reunification, but less and less capable of believing that loyalty to their allies will deliver any goods, the German leaders and élites may well come to feel less dependent and less con-strained. Of course, objectively, the external constraints remain compelling: a policy of self-assertion may not lead anywhere; an attempt at bypassing the nuclear restrictions of the Paris agreements is not likely to make the East Europeans and the Soviets any more willing to let East Germany go; and the price the Soviets may want to exact for reunification is not likely to increase German security. But the fact that Germany's ties to Western powers are weakening means at least potentially that the capacity to test those con-straints by unilateral action may well be used. To be in a cell with a chain around one's ankles and the hope of being liberated by one's jailers is one kind of situation. To be in that cell without such a chain and with such hopes gone is another situation, although the cell has not changed.

In other words, although the impact of de Gaulle on Germany so far has not been a rebirth of German nationalism, it has been a transformation of the situation that gives to nationalism some chances—chances if not of ex-ternal success, given the nature of the cell, then of being at least "tried." The temptation to use one's economic power and potential military might in order to reach one's goals and the example of one's allies competing for accommo-dation with one's foe are not resistible forever, especially if one's past is full of precedents. To be sure, a nationalist Germany may well find itself as unable to shake the walls or to escape through the bars as Gaullist France is unable to forge the "European Europe." But the paradox of a revisionist France, trying to change the international system to her advantage despite her complete lack of "traditional" grievances (lost territories, military dis-crimination, and so forth), next to a Germany full of such grievances, yet behaving in fact like a *status quo* power, may not last eternally. Of course, a less aggressively ambitious France might not have prevented Germany from trying to follow her own path one day: the possibility of someone else's imitative *hubris* is no reason for one's own *effacement;* but precisely because the "essence and drama" of nationalism are the meeting with others, the risk of contagion—a risk that is part of de Gaulle's gamble—cannot be discarded.

Thus the nation-state survives, preserved by the formidable autonomy of politics, as manifested in the resilience of political systems, the interaction between separate states and a single international system, the role of leaders who believe both in the primacy of "high politics" over the kind of managerial politics susceptible to functionalism, and in the primacy of the nation, struggling in the world of today, over any new form, whose painful establishment might require one's lasting withdrawal from the pressing and exalting daily contest.

V

This long balance sheet leaves us with two sets of questions: What are the prospects in Western Europe? What generalizations can one draw from the whole experience? As for the prospects, what precedes reads perhaps too much like a post-mortem. Is there no chance for the European Community? Is it condemned to be, at best, a success in the economic realm but a fiasco in "high politics," something like a hydra with one single body but a multitude of heads?

It would be presumptuous indeed to read hope out of court. One of the decisive elements in the movement's "spillback," de Gaulle's nationalism, may not outlive him. His successors may have a less sweeping vision and may make exactly the opposite gamble from his—that is, prefer the risks of the common enterprise, whose rewards might be high if it works, to the dividends of national action; they could indeed attempt to revive the Monnet concept of Europe, and even to overcome the deficiencies of functionalism by a leap into more genuinely federal institutions. Moreover, whereas de Gaulle has had the backing of a parliamentary majority hostile to supranational integration and has exerted the kind of rule that parties and pressure groups do not affect much anyhow, his successors may depend for domestic support and survival precisely on those parties and pressure groups which had started to weave a transnational fabric. Should this be the case, the "Europe of the Six," instead of being as close as it now is to the traditional model of interstate relations, might move again toward the other ideal-tpye, that of political community-building, so well described by Ernst Haas, who sees in it the wave of the future.[39]

Whereas in the case of a revival of German nationalism, the prospect of failure may not be enough to deter an attempt, here I would maintain that an attempt would not be tantamount to success. In the first place, while nothing (not even the Common Market) is irreversible, no important event leaves the world unmarked, and after the event one can never pick up the pieces as if nothing had happened: this, which is true of the Common Market, is true also of General de Gaulle. It will not be easy to sweep under the rug the curls of dust he has willfully placed in the sunlight; it will not be easy to ignore

39. See his essay "Technocracy, Pluralism and the New Europe," in Stephen R. Graubard (ed.), *op. cit.*, pp. 62–88.

the kinds of questions he has asked, even if his answers are rejected, precisely because they are the questions any European enterprise would have faced sooner or later. Second, even the passing of his nationalism might not transform the national situations of the European nation-states so deeply that all the cleavages discussed here would suddenly disappear. For, even if all the political leaders of Western Europe had once again the same non-nationalist approach, the differences in the national situations would still lead to divergent definitions of the national interests. In particular, the problem of nuclear weapons control and command in a grouping divided between nuclear "have-nots" and nuclear "haves" may prove to be as intractable, and to raise as much of an obstacle to community-formation among Western Europeans, as in the Atlantic alliance. The ideal conditions not merely for the resumption but for the success of a forward march would be a transformation of Germany's external situation and of France's domestic one. If the search for a détente should lead the U.S. to put a rapprochement with the U.S.S.R. ahead of its bonds to West Germany, and if it became clear in West Germany, as a result, both that security is neither the most urgent problem nor entirely provided any more by the U.S., and that reunification cannot be obtained from and through the U.S.; if, in addition, such disappointment with the U.S. does not encourage West German leadership to follow a nationalist path, or if an attempt by West Germany to obtain for itself from Moscow what its allies had failed to provide for her should end in frustration, then—at last—West Germany might be willing to accept a foreign policy close to de Gaulle's "European Europe" with its indifference to regimes and ideologies, its repudiation of the cold war outlook, its opening to the East, and its cautious promise of eventual reunification at the cost of border limitations and arms restrictions. In other words, on the German side, what would be required would be a "polycentric," yet non-nationalist, reading of the external situation. This would be likely to happen if at the same time France had given up her nationalist interpretation of "polycentrism," and become again more humble, more willing to trust the Community organs, more in need of adopting European integration as a goal in itself. Such a possibility would exist if, domestically, the impervious stability of de Gaulle's regime were to be replaced not merely with a political system whose Executive would lean on an "integrationist" party majority, but with the kind of instability that both prevents political leaders from acting on the world stage as if they were its managers and pressures them into seeking a European solution, or alibi, for their difficulties. Europe as Germany's least frustrating framework, Europe as the best compensation for France's domestic troubles, a Europe following Monnet's approach toward de Gaulle's objectives:[40] it may appear like a

40. As Grosser points out in his book and the presidential election campaign of 1965 confirmed, even the opposition to de Gaulle's foreign policy accepts his notion of a "European Europe" and rejects American "hegemony" (with the exception of a very few men like Reynaud or perhaps Lecanuet). There is disagreement about methods and style rather than on objectives.

dream; it cannot be dismissed. But whether it has a chance depends essentially on *when* the General's nationalism will pass from the scene, on *what* degree of cooperation among the nations of Western Europe there will be at that time, on *whether* a new attempt by Britain to join the Community would introduce additional complications, on *what* the U.S. policy in Europe will be; the chance depends on the timely convergence of too many variables to be counted on.

5. NATO in the International System of the 1970's

MORTON A. KAPLAN

SINCE WE CAN only surmise what the international system of the 1970's will be like, we cannot say with confidence what place NATO will occupy in it. For policy purposes, projections extending through the next several years are less hazardous but also less significant.

The world in 1970 or 1971 is not likely to differ greatly from the world of 1969. If the policies of the Nixon Administration are shaped by the expectation that the world will not radically change after 1972, however, it risks adopting military and diplomatic postures that will be grossly inadequate for the problems of the mid-1970's. The long lead time for the development of weapons systems or for the institutionalization of structural changes in international instruments invalidates the expectation that postures adopted for foreseeable problems will be adequate to the surprises almost sure to confront us. On the other hand, the surprises may be so diverse in nature that policies adapted to any particular segment of the possible range could be even more inadequate than policies based on the expectation that things will continue as they are.

Are we then led into a cul-de-sac from which there is no exit? Or can we take prudential measures that will optimize the flexibility of succeeding administrations? Perhaps no firm answer can be given to such questions. However, we shall be in a better position to respond if we examine briefly the reasons for the formation of NATO; the changes in the international system that have compounded NATO's difficulties; the structural features of the international system that are not likely to change greatly over the next five to ten years, and the range of surprising developments that might either enhance our security prospects or confront us with a threatening crisis.

I

NATO was both a cause and a consequence of developing international bipolarity. The institutional reforms NATO undertook during the Korean War established an American ground presence in Europe that, during a period when the Soviet nuclear arsenal was small and ineffective, constituted a tripwire for our nuclear force. The members of NATO were bound together by long-term interests in a way that protected them against the organizational and military capabilities of the Soviet bloc. It was NATO and not the United Nations that assumed the chief responsibility for guarding the world against the outbreak of major war in Europe. NATO protected the individual nations of Western Europe against the divide-and-conquer tactics that Josef Stalin utilized in his treatment of the satellites and of party and government factions in the Soviet Union.

The reasons for the weakening of NATO are several. The perception of an imminent Soviet military attack against Western Europe diminished as the Cold War receded. Eventually, most Western interpreters of Soviet foreign policy came to believe that such fears had always been nourished by misconceptions about Soviet goals in Europe and elsewhere in the world. The nations of Western Europe recovered economically from the war and, in most cases, went forward to new and unprecedented prosperity. As a consequence, their dependence upon the United States declined, and their irritation over American dominance in NATO correspondingly increased. The peculiar but definite perceptions of the world and of the nation-state held by General de Gaulle further weakened NATO. The incomplete but effective military rupture of France from NATO made the conventional defense of Western Europe more difficult. As NATO became increasingly dependent on the U.S. nuclear deterrent the unreliability of this safeguard came to the fore.

Although the United States officially insisted upon the reliability of its nuclear protection of Europe, its attempts to delineate the differences between a deterrence posture and a war-fighting posture seemed to many Europeans to call into question American willingness to use nuclear weapons. Moreover, Europeans were aware that a prolonged crisis in Europe would provide the United States with the opportunity to consider in vivid detail the vulnerability of American cities to nuclear weapons. If the equities of the crisis were not absolutely clear—and they were not likely to be if the Soviet Union developed the crisis intelligently—the United States would, in all likelihood, exert pressure on the most threatened European nation to make concessions contrary to its interests.

The alliance-splitting potential of a crisis would operate even more gravely against European members of NATO which were not at the center of the controversy. Such countries, lacking the second-strike nuclear capabilities of the United States, would be subject to greater pressure than the United States and would be more prone to press for concessions, or to leave NATO at the height of a crisis. It is no accident that West Germany, which would probably absorb the initial blow of any Soviet move in Western Europe, has been the Western ally most willing to coordinate its policies with the United States. Although the artificial division of Germany also plays a role in its alliance with the United States, West Germany, unless it makes a deal with the Soviet Union, is the West European nation least able to divorce itself from crisis in the heart of the continent.

The failure of the United States to provide either a joint-NATO nuclear force or a European nuclear force—either of which would minimize the alliance-splitting potential of a Soviet-inspired crisis or nuclear blackmail—is one of the major causes of the crisis in NATO. The search of the United States for détente with the Soviet Union is another. There are few, if any, accommodations with the Soviet Union that the United States is capable of making that would not threaten some existing West European interest. The nuclear Nonproliferation Treaty is a specific case in point.

It may appear paradoxical to some that West Europeans, who were disturbed by the reputed American Cold War psychology and who demanded changes in the American perspective, are now frightened by the change in perspective they appeared to ask for. Apart from inconsistencies in human personalities, motivations and reasonings, the answer to this seeming paradox is not particularly difficult. As long as the Cold War continued, many Europeans feared that American differences with the Soviet Union might thrust Western Europe into the maelstrom of nuclear conflict. They were fearful that what they regarded as American intransigence would provoke war. As the United States began to accommodate its objectives to those of the Soviet Union, they began to perceive another and a larger danger: the compromise of their interests that might result from détente. They now discount the possibility of war and see as increased the possibility of a settlement at their expense.

Other concerns influenced their reactions to American war-fighting strategies. Deterrence in the view of many Europeans avoided war. They did not like to ask what would happen if war actually occurred. War-fighting strategies raised the specter of actual war—a war that would be fought on their territories. Discussion of tactical nuclear war, an enterprise that is quite dubious in my opinion, further enhanced these perceptions.

A similar explanation may be given for their misperception of the problem of ballistic missile defense. Although BMD increases the likelihood that the

United States would actually live up to its commitments in Western Europe by reducing the Soviet threat to the continental United States, it brings home to West Europeans the possibility of an actual nuclear war—one in which the United States would have some protection and in which they would not.

II

What are the structural features of the international situation most directly relevant to NATO that are not likely to change surprisingly in the next five to ten years? Only the United States and the Soviet Union will possess major stable nuclear forces. Only the United States and the Soviet Union will possess secondstrike capabilities, although the introduction of MIRV (Multiple Independent Re-entry Vehicles) might raise the possibility that one or the other superpower might gain a credible first-strike capability. BMD installations in the United States and the Soviet Union might deprive those West European nations which possess unstable nuclear forces of posing even the threat of a penetration capability against the Soviet Union or the United States.

It is likely that Great Britain and France will continue to deploy unstable and provocative nuclear forces. By the end of the 1970's West Germany may have an unstable nuclear force. Developments in ASW (anti-submarine warfare) and in orbital weapons may further increase the first-strike potential of the United States or the Soviet Union.

Increasing prosperity in the developed nations may reduce the incentive for external adventure. Improvements in logistics, large increases in world trading combines, and increased economic interdependence among all developed nations, and between the United States and the Soviet bloc, will create a disincentive for external adventure.

The Soviet Union will retain an authoritarian regime. Decision-making will be centralized in a small body of men who in turn will be dependent only upon a technocratic class that will be relatively uninterested in acquiring political power and that will be less shocked by Soviet external adventure than were the emerging humanistic and technological groupings of the mid-1950's.

These last two considerations are not contradictory, although they lead to inconsistent consequences. Economic interdependence reflects a characteristic of economy and technology in a world that is becoming smaller. The attitudes of particular elites toward particular kinds of actions reflect the development of a social consciousness within a particular milieu that creates certain kinds of rewards and incentives. Thus the difference between Soviet intellectual reactions to Czechoslovakia in 1968 and to Hungary in 1956 is striking. Part of the difference may result from dissimilarities between generations and the increasing accommodation of the intellectual class to the post-Stalinist regime. Part of it may lie in the fact that Hungary was the first case of such intervention and thus was much more shocking than the second occasion to the susceptibilities of certain kinds of Marxists. Perhaps this last factor should not be placed among the structural features, for, should the Soviet Union fail in Czechoslovakia, there may be another reshaping of attitudes toward such events.

III

We will now briefly consider the wide range of possible surprises the next decade might bring and then sketch the possible relevance of these for NATO. We will finally adumbrate a few of the measures that might improve the operations of NATO in the existing world and in the expected world of the 1970's and that might be adaptable to some of the consequences of the surprising, although not entirely unexpected, worlds.

Consider a world in which the Soviet pressure on China is successful, in which tight Soviet control over Rumania is restored, and in which Yugoslavia is occupied or otherwise brought back within the confines of the Soviet bloc. Despite the prosperity prevailing in Western Europe, this world would have a much more frightening aspect for Western Europe than did the situation after the close of the Second World War or even at the height of bipolarity. A conventional defense of Western Europe would not seem feasible. The credibility of the U.S. nuclear guarantee would be subject to serious doubts. Moreover, it is unlikely that Soviet pressure, under the sponsorship of a younger and more confident leadership, would be used in ways that would confront the United States with a situation clearly justifying the use of its nuclear deterrent. The Russians could be expected to employ the processes of "chemical dissolution" so powerfully applied by Adolf Hitler against the Czechoslovak Republic in 1938. Local communist parties would be used as fronts to create incidents giving rise to plausible grounds for Soviet intervention. Threats would be employed that would not be fully explicit. Members of NATO, other than the one directly threatened, would be reassured of Soviet good intentions toward them. Only if the members of NATO were bound indissolubly or if the threatened member had a credible deterrent of its own would the prospects for organizational survival and the successful blunting of Soviet demands be reasonably high.

Consider a world in which China and the Soviet Union are reconciled after the death of Mao and Lin Piao. In this world it is likely that the pressures against Japan and India would be increased, thus diverting American attention from Europe. By maintaining a passive policy against Western Europe, the Soviet Union could play upon the fears of West European nations that, in the Orient, the United States might drag them into adventures contrary to their security interests. Moreover, despite the absence of Soviet threats or overt pressures, the existence of a unified communist bloc would be likely to stir in Europe fears of a military nature stemming from entanglements with the United States and doubts concerning the long-term viability of democratic systems. The temptation to move in a socialist direction and to multiply entanglements with the Soviet bloc would increase. In this case, the prospects for NATO would be high only if Europe had an independent military capability. Thus a European nuclear force or developments leading to the beginnings of an Atlantic Union would minimize, but far from eliminate, the dangerous consequences of this particular surprise.

Consider a world in which the Russians decide to settle accounts with the Chinese. They bomb the Chinese nuclear installations and allow volunteer groups to invade Mongolia and Sinkiang in support of dissident nationalist forces in those areas. In this circumstance, a number of requirements would confront American policymakers. The United States ought not to be so tightly bound to NATO that any action it takes elsewhere in the world would appear to involve its allies. Unless Washington loosened the integration of NATO, there might be enormous and perhaps successful pressures from our allies to halt American activities in the Asian theater. Given the demonstrated Russian willingness to take extreme measures, the United States might deem it a prudent move to place its fleet between Taiwan and the mainland and thus prevent the Nationalists from intervening counterproductively, inasmuch as they have little or no remaining support on the mainland. Whether the United States would wish to send supplies to the Communist Chinese government or to act in a manner that severely limited Russian objectives would depend upon the circumstances. If we were too eager, our aid might be accepted but at the cost of great suspicion. Yet the opportunities for intervention which could produce a more favorable world environment for the United States would probably be present. If any important faction of the Chinese Communist Party or military decided to cast its lot with the Russians, then a much more threatening situation would arise for the United States; it would increase the incentives for direct intervention, but limit the opportunities.

Consider a world in which there is a left-wing socialist revolution in Japan and in which Southeast Asia goes communist. Even if the communist nations remain disunited, the establishment of what would appear to be a "wave of the future" would increase the pressures against Western Europe enormously. The more closely Western Europe was integrated in NATO and aligned with the United States, the more secure American security interests would be.

Consider a world in which one of several events occurs. There is a revolt in East Germany that arouses sympathy in, and possibly intervention by, West Germany. Alternatively, in an effort to build consensus behind a shaky East German government, there is an East German invasion of either Poland or West Germany. A revolt in East Germany that appears to invite West German responses would engender great pressure from France, Britain and the small members of NATO to prevent Bonn's intervention or, alternatively, to loosen the bonds of NATO. Measures that maintained centralized control of NATO military forces would, in this case, reduce the centrifugal forces of the alliance. In the case of an East German invasion of West Germany, such centralized measures would increase the likelihood of the cohesion of the alliance in resisting the invasion. In the case of an East German invasion of Poland, German integration in NATO and, more particularly, in a united Europe would diminish the chances that nationalistic pressures could force West Germany to support the East German move and thus threaten the stability of the existing Bonn regime and of its alignment with the West.

Consider a world in which the West Germans regard a solution for the problem of German reunification out of the question as long as they maintain cordial relations with the West. In this world the Germans would feel betrayed by both the French and the Americans. They might feel discriminated against because they lacked nuclear weapons, although in other respects they would have great power status. In an effort to resolve their problems and to demonstrate their independence as a great power, the West Germans make a deal with the Soviet Union at the expense of East Germany. In this world, France is likely to return to NATO. However, the rational grounds for conventional defense, weak though they may previously have been, are now despairingly inadequate. Nuclear defense or deterrence must be relied upon, but this is likely to work only if the plan for its use approaches automaticity. Thus it is likely that the conditions for the use of nuclear weapons must be spelled out and vetoes removed from the hands of political leaders.

Consider a world in which France, alarmed by German resurgence, makes an alliance with the Soviet Union. A ground defense for the remaining NATO nations would hardly be feasible, and a collective nuclear defense might be difficult to implement. The existence of a stable independent nuclear deterrent in German hands might in this case be the only plausible alternative for U.S. policy.

Consider a world in which there is a major revolutionary upheaval in Latin America. American attention would naturally shift to the south. If NATO had not yet become a more viable instrument, armed with procedures for consultation and integrated militarily, it might easily be allowed in these circumstances to wither away, thus opening up Europe to Soviet pressures. In all likelihood, the existence of a European nuclear force would serve to protect important American security interests. If NATO remained intact, the existence of such a force would enable the Europeans to assume an increasingly important role in it while the United States turned its attention to the Western Hemisphere. Given such a force, NATO might remain viable even in the absence of forceful American leadership.

Consider a world in which a minor nation uses a nuclear weapon against another minor nation. Although this occurrence need not directly involve either the Soviet Union or the United States, it would constitute a precedent threatening to both. Yet unilateral intervention by either might appear dangerous to both. In such a world, there woud be major incentives for the United States and the Soviet Union to establish a condominium, at least with respect to the nuclear weapons issue and probably with respect to quarrels that grew so intense that a danger of nuclear escalation arose. If such a condominium were instituted, it would introduce severe strains between the United States and its Western allies—unless NATO were so organized that various consultative measures could reduce the fears of the West European nations that important interests of theirs would be sacrificed to the requirements of the American-Soviet détente. It would probably be important in this circumstance to exclude Europe from the condominium and to support the creation of a European nuclear system.

Consider a world in which China becomes a substantial nuclear power, and Japan and West Germany acquire nuclear weapons. These weapons systems are likely to be unstable. The Soviet Union would probably be deterred from overt military action and its power of blackmail would be greatly reduced, even though the nuclear weapons systems were not enormously effective against the defenses of the Soviet Union. In this world, NATO would not be important, although its absence might lead to political instability. The possibility of provocation in such a world is reasonably high. The Eurasian land mass would constitute a zone of extreme danger. It is most unlikely that the United States would desire to be bound to it by stringent security treaties. One way to avoid this contingency would be to have previously prepared the way for a European nuclear system or for viable national nuclear forces through the transfer of know-how or perhaps through the actual transfer of weapons.

Consider a world in which the Czechoslovak invasion of 1968 was a last gasp by the Soviet hardliners. Increasingly, Soviet domestic policy is moderated and Soviet controls over the bloc are lifted. Although a Europe from the Atlantic to the Urals still seems a figment of the imagination, the prospects for favorable political developments would be eased by a loosening of the bonds between the United States and Europe. The greater the extent to which Europe could transfer its attention from West to East, the greater the likelihood that developments of this type would strengthen American security. If there were, in addition, a democratic revolution or nationality uprisings in the Soviet Union, the quick dissolution of NATO might enhance favorable prospects.

IV

It is obvious that we cannot protect ourselves against all the contingencies considered above by the same measures—at least not equally effectively. In some cases, NATO becomes a liability for American security and interests. Nonetheless, certain minimal requirements common to most of the surprising worlds stand out. It seems that NATO cannot remain viable either in existing circumstances or in our "most surprising worlds" unless its decision-making machinery becomes more consultative and less dominated by the United States. Although the United States should not permit NATO to be in a position to circumscribe American actions over the entire globe, it must find some way to insulate the consequences of these extra-European actions from the European sphere. A more or less united Europe facing the United States within NATO as a relative equal would both increase European bargaining power in a desirable fashion and facilitate distinctions of spheres of activity, thus to some extent insulating Europe from the consequences of American actions elsewhere in the world. This means that Europe would not be expected to come to the aid of the United States in such cases, a reasonable price to pay to secure the compensating advantages.

Possession of an independent nuclear capability by a united Europe would permit a degree of disengagement between U.S. strategic forces and NATO strategic forces. Although the insulation of the two forces from each other would not be automatic and complete, the distinction could legitimately be made. It may well be in the interest of an enemy of the United States to recognize the distinction and to observe it. Nuclear escalation by the United States in Asia would not automatically invoke the involvement of the West Europeans. This would decrease European fears of America's extra-European ventures. Although Europeans would still be likely to pressure the United States to disengage itself from Asia, these pressures would be greatly diminished by Europe's possession of an independent nuclear force and by the strength resulting from unity.

Even in the absence of West European unity, a European nuclear force with appropriate control machinery would have many of the same desirable advantages. If the European nuclear force were programmed in advance for use either if the Russians first used nuclear weapons or if they invaded Western Europe and failed to withdraw within a stated period of time, then the demands for a political veto on use of the force would be diminished. This doctrine of nuclear control would be further improved if it were linked to the doctrine of limited strategic retaliation. The establishment of relatively autonomous command and control procedures not subject to veto before crisis would diminish the blackmail capabilities of an enemy state. The European nuclear force, used under these two circumstances, would appear to be adequate to meet most of the various contingencies posed earlier. For the United States, the existence of such a force would reduce the nuclear risks of involvement in the alliance. But it would eliminate neither the risks nor the rationale for American membership.

If a European nuclear force should be infeasible for political reasons, then one possible alternative would be to aid West European nations to acquire national nuclear systems with second-strike capabilities and adequate command and control systems. Although such a solution would satisfy fewer of the contingencies considered, it would be responsive to a number of them.

It would reduce the dangers of American involvement in the NATO system that would result from the acquisition by West European nations of unstable and provocative nuclear systems. Stable independent national nuclear systems would probably deter the Soviet Union—even if, later, NATO were to be loosened or dissolved.

If this alternative is politically infeasible, then a last fallback position might rest on American development of a capacity that would permit the transfer of nuclear weapons to a threatened ally at the inception of a crisis. Polaris-type submarines may prove to be the only satisfactory way to achieve a quick transfer capacity; the effectiveness of such a capacity would depend on the prior training of crews from the relevant nations. None of these measures would be inconsistent with the dissolution of NATO in those cases in which the communist bloc breaks up and the internal Soviet system "mellows." However, the acquisition of independent national nuclear systems would transfer to Western Europe the capabilities that would be useful in deterring the Kremlin if further "surprises" revived a Soviet threat to Europe.

In the absence of appropriate European nuclear capabilities, it is likely that increased consultative arrangements for the West Europeans, as proposed by some, would serve primarily as a brake upon U.S. actions elsewhere in the world. Moreover, in the absence of a unified Europe, such increased power for the European allies of the United States would probably inhibit rather than enhance military support for a threatened member of the alliance. Thus, there is some reason to believe that West Germany would be exposed rather than protected by a decrease in American dominance within the alliance; this, in addition to other factors, might tend to move the West Germans toward a deal with the Soviet Union.

In political organizations political power and military weakness only rarely constitute desirable coordinate attributes. NATO is unlikely to be an exception to this rule. Reforms of NATO that increase consultation and collective control instead of strengthening the organization may bring to a focus conflicts of interest and different perceptions of the situation. Such reforms are more likely to enhance the complexity of organizational charts than the activities of the alliance.

NATO is far gone on the road to extinction. Yet unified American direction and military policy still preserve some organizational potential. The defects of American dominance give rise to the tribulations of the alliance, but it is far from clear that coordinate control will remedy NATO's ills in the absence of coordinate military capabilities. If it is true that under present circumstances—as contrasted with those of the immediate postwar period —NATO requires political as well as military goals, it still does not follow that political goals can be implemented in advance of the solution of the security problem.

A joint-NATO nuclear system would enhance the unity of the organization at the expense of the ability of the United States to act in Asia. A European nuclear force attenuates the relationship between the United States and Europe, but it enhances the prospects for a viable European response while increasing the potential of the United States for extra-European intervention. The dependence of Europe upon American know-how and transfer capabilities provides a rationale for NATO and leaves open the prospect of large areas of mutual political interest not directly involving a war in Europe. Independent national nuclear forces greatly increase the risk of the fragmentation of NATO. However, they also decrease the likelihood of military pressure and therefore diminish the prospect of crises that would accelerate the centrifugal tendencies in the alliance. Thus, this prospect permits, although it does not facilitate, the development of joint political goals.

A quick transfer capacity is perhaps the least promising but the politically most feasible of the alternatives. Furthermore, the knowledge that such a quick transfer capacity exists diminishes the likelihood of a deliberate escalation of a crisis by an enemy state. In addition to the deterrence provided by the American SAC, the actual transfer of nuclear weapons to a West European state will be undesirable from the standpoint of that enemy state. Thus, there will be an effort to avoid triggering the transfer. This, in turn, is likely to damp political crises and preserve the prospect that NATO members will be able to attain common political goals.

A failure to find even a "jerry-built" solution to NATO's security problems is hardly likely to facilitate the attainment of joint political goals. At the same time, an increase in consultation and joint control in the absence of appropriate military measures is likely to be counterproductive.

6. Preventing Nuclear Proliferation through the Legal Control of China's Bomb

DR. SEYMOUR C. YUTER

THE SPREAD of nuclear weapons poses a serious threat to the survival of mankind. If proliferation is not halted, the probability of their eventual use will increase through a variety of incalculable contingencies: mistakes in predicting the response of an enemy to a limited war or blackmail; failure to exercise effective control over nuclear arsenals and their operators, increasing the chance that these weapons will fall into unauthorized and irresponsible hands; errors in tracing the source of a nuclear attack, leading to an inappropriate response; an attack launched by a country whose leaders are ignorant of, or unconcerned with, the consequences of their action. One can imagine other equally tragic scenarios.

Fortunately, the two nuclear-armed superpowers seem to be convinced that further proliferation would work against their best interests. They must now demonstrate that their concern is matched by the will to cooperate in establishing and enforcing meaningful arms control measures. This raises the possibility of a Washington-Moscow global condominium, a prospect that does not upset historian Arnold Toynbee:

> . . . I believe that peace and affluence are what most people desire, and we cannot have these without order in the age of mechanization. I therefore believe that the human race would submit to a Russo-American . . . dictatorship if it believed that, at this price, it could have affluence and

peace. . . . Of course, if nuclear weapons were limited to Russia and America, there wouldn't be democratic government of the world. A Russo-American world government would probably be very authoritarian, but it would at least ensure the survival of the human race—and that is the first consideration, to my mind.[1]

Raymond Aron agrees that the two nuclear giants must collaborate for their own safety, but dismisses the possibility of joint authoritarian rule:

The governing idea by which I interpreted the diplomatic situation was that of the solidarity of the two great powers—the warring brothers—against a total war of which they would be the first victims. Inevitably enemies by position and by the incompatibility of their ideologies, the United States and the Soviet Union have a common interest not in ruling together over the world (of which they would be quite incapable), but in not destroying each other.[2]

Even if the United States and the Soviet Union agree to arms control and nonproliferation measures, they cannot damp the arms race unless these measures can be made universally binding. Above all else, the superpowers must support arms control arrangements that can effectively freeze Communist China's nuclear development program; otherwise, Chinese progress will probably drive India, Japan and eventually West Germany into the nuclear club. While it is unlikely that West Germany would be the sixth nuclear power, she might well follow India and Japan in "going nuclear."

China's nuclear capability could be stunted by a universally-binding test ban which is either observed voluntarily by China or forced on her by both superpowers or by one superpower with at least the tacit support of the other. However, in the absence of a traumatic event, such as an accidental nuclear exchange, universal arms control measures do not appear to be feasible. In this case, the nuclear club will be expanded to admit, among others, West Germany, a development foreseen by Professor Morton A. Kaplan:

Although the United States and the Soviet Union do have a common interest in not destroying each other, the Soviet Union has not learned to be satisfied with its present resources and influences. A nuclear-armed Federal Republic is in the best interests of the United States as a buffer against the Soviet Union; in any event nuclear proliferation to West Germany and other states is most likely regardless of U.S. policies. When the U.S.S.R. first learns that West Germany is acquiring nuclear weapons, the U.S. will deter the Soviet Union from forcibly disarming the West Ger-

1. Interview with Arnold Toynbee, *Playboy*, April 1967, pp. 68, 70; confirmed in a private memorandum received by the author on August 16, 1967. Also see Arnold Toynbee, *Change and Habit: The Challenge of Our Time* (New York: Oxford University Press, 1966), p. 157.

2. Raymond Aron, *Peace and War: A Theory of International Relations* (New York: Doubleday, 1966), p. xi.

mans. After West Germany has an operational nuclear arsenal which poses at least a minimal threat to the major Soviet cities, reunification with East Germany will not improbably follow. A reunited nuclear-armed Germany would in that case play a leading role in Europe and would provide an effective buffer to Soviet expansion and influence. The Soviet Union would then be sandwiched between a reunited nuclear-armed Germany and a nuclear-armed mainland China. Even if nuclear proliferation to West Germany and other states leads to small nuclear wars, the world will survive. The remaining practicable alternatives to this world are worse.[3]

II

The perils of proliferation which we will examine in this article lead me to conclude that the United States is currently faced with three difficult alternatives: (1) accepting a nuclear-proliferating world, in which a confrontation with the Soviet Union over a nuclear-arming West Germany could easily lead to general nuclear war; (2) attempting, with at least the tacit support of the Soviet Union, to prevent further nuclear proliferation by freezing or destroying the Chinese nuclear program, which might lead to a nuclear exchange in the Far East; or (3) withdrawing in isolation behind a heavy anti-ballistic missile system, leaving the rest of the world to be dominated by the Soviet Union and China—a policy that could lead to U.S. surrender or a nuclear war if and when the noose got too tight.

My analysis also leads to the conclusion that the Soviet Union is faced with three similar and difficult choices: (1) accepting a nuclear-proliferating world in which a confrontation with the United States over a nuclear-arming West Germany could easily lead to nuclear war; (2) attempting, with at least the tacit support of the United States, to prevent further nuclear proliferation (particularly to West Germany) by freezing or destroying the Chinese nuclear program; or (3) withdrawing in isolation behind a heavy anti-ballistic missile system, leaving the rest of the world to be dominated by the United States, China and Western Europe (probably led by a nuclear-armed and unified Germany), with the likelihood of having to relinquish former German territory to the Germans and former Chinese territory to the Chinese.

If Professor Kaplan is correct, the Soviets will back down in the confrontation with the United States over the nuclear arming of West Germany; and later, in a second crisis with the United States over the attempts of a nuclear-armed West Germany to force reunification, the USSR will back down again. The ultimate result will be a truncated "fortress Russia." But if Kaplan is wrong and the Soviets resist, the danger of an escalating crisis leading to general nuclear war is real. The Soviet invasion of Czechoslovakia, partly to counter a perceived military threat from West Germany, evidences strong Soviet resolve to prevent a nuclear-armed West Germany; and U.S. policy in

3. Morton A. Kaplan, private memorandum, received by the author June 15, 1967.

Viet Nam (at least prior to President Nixon's inauguration) seems to indicate that the United States would not risk nuclear war over the right of West Germany to go nuclear.

The least undesirable of the alternatives listed above is a joint attempt by the United States and the Soviet Union to prevent further nuclear proliferation by attempting to freeze or destroy the Chinese nuclear program. Such a plan is worth exploring if one agrees with Toynbee that the human race would submit to a "Russo-American dictatorship" in order to have affluence and peace. Nor is a Russo-American condominium, designed to minimize the threat of nuclear war, inconsistent with Aron's view. Such a condominium might take the form of an international organization to administer a universally-binding nuclear test ban law, i.e., an international nuclear peacekeeping law recognized by a large majority of states, including the United States and the USSR, and expressing an intent to bind nonassenting states.

India advocated a universal test ban during the UN disarmament debate in November 1965,[4] presumably to control the Chinese nuclear threat. The Nonproliferation Treaty not only fails to deal with the Chinese nuclear threat, but probably encourages the Chinese to consider giving nuclear weapons to "socialist" countries, which could include Syria and the UAR. On the other hand, a universal test ban could result in the removal *under law* of the Chinese nuclear threat and thus prevent further nuclear proliferation.

III

Kaplan's prognosis that in all likelihood West Germany will go nuclear and then reunite with East Germany, notwithstanding the resistance of the Soviet Union, might produce one, or perhaps two, dangerous crises: the first, when the Soviet Union learns about the Federal Republic's plans to go nuclear (the transition crisis), and a second, if and when a nuclear-armed West Germany attempts to force reunification from a position of nuclear strength (the reunification crisis). In the transition crisis, the Soviets will have an option to conduct a preemptive or disarming strike against the embryonic nuclear-weapon manufacturing capability of the West Germans, whether located in West Germany or elsewhere. Less dangerous Soviet responses would include blocking Western access to West Berlin, seizing West Berlin, or giving nuclear weapons to the East European allies, perhaps Poland and East Germany.

Washington could react to such Soviet moves by temporizing and taking no substantive action, meeting the escalating crisis by effectively countering each Soviet move, or leaving West Germany and therefore Europe to their fate and withdrawing behind an anti-ballistic missile system. Kaplan believes the United States could not afford to adopt an isolationist posture and permit

4. General Assembly, Official Records, Twentieth Session, First Committee, pp. 169–170 (November 24, 1965).

the Soviets to dominate Europe; therefore, Washington will counter each Soviet move, preventing the Soviets from disarming the West Germans—i.e., Moscow will back down. The U.S. government would have little choice but to oppose Soviet moves, since the alternatives would lead to a substantial change in the world balance of power against the United States, with a consequent threat of nuclear conflict when Soviet pressure became intolerable.

Under almost any conceivable circumstance the transition crisis presents a serious threat of a nuclear holocaust, since a confrontation between the United States and the USSR is likely to occur. In light of the strong Soviet resolve shown in the invasion of Czechoslovakia and the lack of comparable U.S. resolve in Viet Nam, the United States might not succeed in forcing the Soviets to back down over the German problem, and instead might leave Europe to Soviet domination rather than risk nuclear war over the right of the West Germans to go nuclear. Therefore, Washington might well prefer to take action to avoid a transition crisis that could lead to nuclear war or an adverse change in the world balance of power.

A reunification crisis could also lead to a confrontation between the United States and the Soviet Union, since a move by a nuclear-armed West Germany to force reunification against the will of the USSR is likely to be countered by the Soviets and any threat by the Soviets against the West Germans will probably be countered by the United States. This pessimistic prediction is based on the reasonable assumption that the Soviets oppose a reunited Germany as inimicable to their interests; therefore, reunification will not be achieved by peaceful means in the foreseeable future. A forced reunification could result from an uprising in East Germany against the Soviet overlords, whether or not sponsored by the West Germans, or even by a national liberation war, directly or indirectly supported by the Federal Republic, to free the "Soviet-occupied zone of Germany" (the jungles and mountains of the communist-style liberation war being replaced by nighttime sabotage and terrorism against Soviet installations, personnel and sympathizers).

The people of a nuclear-armed West Germany, after many years of unsuccessful attempts to reunify peacefully, and in a state of increasing frustration, might elect a neo-Nazi or other radical nationalist government dedicated to reunification by force if necessary. These radical leaders might engage in an escalating crisis with the Soviets in the belief that a smaller West German nuclear capability could neutralize Soviet nuclear strength and force the Soviets ultimately to back down. While the outcome of such a crisis is difficult to foresee, it seems likely that if the United States remained a power in Europe, it would have to back the West Germans, thus setting up a second U.S.-USSR confrontation and threat of nuclear war.

There appears also to be a direct connection between a nuclear-arming mainland China and a U.S.-USSR confrontation leading to nuclear war. A plausible scenario can be constructed along the following lines:

(1) India continues to refuse to sign the Nonproliferation Treaty because of the Chinese nuclear threat and the failure of the superpowers to give credible guarantees to defend her against that threat. At an opportune moment, India goes nuclear,[5] on the pretext of developing an anti-ballistic missile system for protection against mainland China. However, such a defensive nuclear program would probably initially pass through a stage where the Indians would mount offensive missiles as a deterrent against Chinese nuclear blackmail. A nuclear missile program would probably have to be pursued in a joint venture with either West Germany or Japan.

(2) Japan, also because of the Chinese nuclear threat, either reserves the option to go nuclear by refusing to sign the Nonproliferation Treaty, or signs and later opts out for substantially the same reasons as the Indians. Japan could join with India to develop a ballistic missile defense system, the Indians providing the nuclear warheads and the Japanese the missile vehicles.[6] The Japanese have a sophisticated electronics capability and have had valuable experience in designing and manufacturing high-altitude rockets. Their rocket technology could probably be supplemented with the electronic guidance system necessary to develop a ballistic missile with sufficient range to threaten most of the major Chinese cities from either Japan or India, and ultimately to develop an ABM system. The Indian civilian nuclear capability could easily be converted to military purposes to produce the nuclear warheads.

(3) When India and Japan acquire nuclear weapons for defense, it will be difficult to deter such countries as Israel and Sweden from going nuclear, again nominally in order to deploy an anti-ballistic missile system against potential nuclear threats. Pakistan and the UAR are quite likely to go nuclear shopping in Peking in order to counter threats from India and Israel, respectively.

(4) Increasing nuclear proliferation and the threat from Soviet missiles targeted on West Germany will certainly force the Bonn government to acquire nuclear weapons, previous commitments notwithstanding. After all, why should the Federal Republic be discriminated against when Great Britain, France, India and Japan have found it necessary to defend themselves against nuclear threats and blackmail?

Paradoxically, the USSR is making it easier for the West Germans to go nuclear because of its deployment of an ABM system. This action offers India and Japan a good excuse to acquire ABM systems and will most probably

5. In the UN debate in May 1968 concerning the Nonproliferation Treaty, India explicitly stated that it could not subscribe to it. (UN Document A/C.1/PV. 1567 [May 14, 1968], p. 82.) By 1966 India was in a position to produce about two atomic bombs a year; additional facilities were being constructed to provide an increased atomic bomb capability.

6. As of February 1969, Japan, India and West Germany had not yet signed the Nonproliferation Treaty.

encourage the West Germans to do the same. After all, would the Soviets deploy a system which was not effective against a Chinese nuclear attack? While the answer to this question might well be yes (since an ABM cannot be fully tested today, its effectiveness even under light nuclear attacks cannot be proved), how could the Indians and Japanese be persuaded, in light of the Soviet deployment, that ABM systems are not worthwhile? Ironically, then, the Soviets may be deploying an *ineffective* ABM system, yet indirectly encouraging the West Germans to go nuclear, and thus defeating one of the most important goals of Soviet foreign policy.

The failure of the two superpowers to deal effectively with the developing Chinese nuclear threat, coupled with the Soviet deployment of an anti-ballistic missile system probably chiefly deployed against the threat from the East, seems likely to result in the further proliferation of nuclear weapons, eventually to West Germany. Kaplan believes the resulting containment of the Soviet Union between a nuclear-armed West Germany and a nuclear-armed mainland China is in the best interests of the United States—even though small nuclear wars may occur. He sees no better practicable alternatives. However, for those of us who hope that he is wrong about practicable alternatives, a *limited* U.S.-USSR condominium aimed at containing the Chinese nuclear threat and preventing further nuclear proliferation (particularly to West Germany) must be explored as a feasible alternative to a nuclear confrontation between the two superpowers.

Such a condominium is unlikely to be abused to the detriment of the nonnuclear-weapon states, given the fundamental ideological and power dispute between the superpowers. It would work only when vital selfish interests coincide, as is the case with the superpowers' common desire to prevent further nuclear proliferation. Understandably, some have asked what gives the United States and the USSR the right to set up a condominium, no matter how limited. The clearest answer is that the American and Soviet peoples have the most to lose in a nuclear war stemming from nuclear proliferation.

IV

Aron's view of the two superpowers' mutuality of interests in preventing a total war in which they would be the major victims was supported by the circumstances surrounding the Arab-Israeli war of June 1967. Notwithstanding what appeared to be its firm support of Israel's right of passage through the Straits of Tiran and of Israel's claim that the Aqaba Gulf was an international waterway which could not legally be blockaded by the United Arab Republic, the United States temporized in fear of a possible confrontation with the Soviet Union. On the other side, the Arabs thought they had a firm promise on the part of the Soviets to provide effective support for them against "Israeli aggression." Yet, in the face of an overwhelming Israeli military victory, Moscow joined with Washington in calling for a cease-fire which effectively confirmed the new territorial status quo, with Israel occupying vast sections and strategic areas of former Arab territory. As soon as it appeared to Soviet leaders that they might be heading for a possible confrontation with the United States, they got on the hot line to Washington to assure President Johnson that they had no intention of meddling in the Middle East war if he would give similar assurances, which he quickly did. Thus, the United States and the USSR appeared ready to sacrifice what most observers thought were firm guarantees to their "client" states in order to avoid a possible confrontation with each other.

The Arab-Israeli war demonstrated that both superpowers would go to great lengths to avoid a face-to-face encounter, providing vital interests were not involved. On the other hand, the Cuban missile crisis of 1962 proved that dangerous confrontations are possible when vital interests *are* involved—in that case the vital interests of the United States. Similarly, it is surely against the essential interests of the Soviet Union to have a nuclear-armed "revanchist" West Germany on its western flank or to have a strong reunified Germany in Europe. If there is a potential crisis which could produce a U.S.-USSR confrontation and lead to nuclear war, it would be a West German decision to go nuclear or a West German decision to force reunification against the will of the Soviet Union. It was not surprising then that, despite continued U.S. bombing of the socialist state of North Viet Nam, the Soviets continued to negotiate with the U.S. government in an attempt to obtain a nonproliferation treaty that would hinder what the Soviets perceive to be West German nuclear ambitions. The Soviets fear that some West German leaders want to acquire nuclear arms one way or another, and there is fairly persuasive support for their fears:

> Former Chancellor Adenauer expressed dissatisfaction late in 1965 with the prospect that Germany's NATO allies, Great Britain and the United States, as part of a "select club" of nuclear powers, might negotiate at Geneva an agreement deleterious to German interests. This prospect led Adenauer to announce he could not commit himself "forever" to German nonacquisition of nuclear weapons. Similarly, Franz-Josef Strauss has warned that "a new Fuhrer-type" who "would promise and probably also acquire nuclear weapons" might emerge if Germany were subjected to continued nuclear discrimination within the Atlantic Alliance.
>
> .   .   .   .
>
> The renunciation by the Federal Republic of the production of atomic weapons on its territory would not necessarily preclude German participation in an Atlantic or European nuclear force.[7]

A foreign policy adviser to Franz-Josef Strauss, one of the most influential

7. Diane A. Kressler, "Germany, NATO and Europe," ORBIS, Spring 1966, p. 234.

members of the current West German coalition government, made the following statement:

> The Federal Republic will only gain its national independence and full political sovereignty if it abandons the demand for the creation of a larger national . . . entity in favor of promoting the reunification of the German people *within the process of European integration.* . . . A West European confederation would have every right in law and ethics to state and to pursue its purpose, namely, to end the division of Europe and to create a European community extending from the Atlantic to the present borders of the Soviet Union.[8]

Some influential German politicians appear to believe that German reunification should be pursued from a position of strength provided by a European nuclear force. Despite the evidence that the vast majority of the West German people and their political leaders have no present desire to acquire a national nuclear force,[9] a future West German government, whether or not led by a "Fuhrer-type," may decide to go nuclear in the face of fading hopes for a European nuclear force and continued frustration caused by the division of the German people. Nuclear proliferation to states such as India and Japan could readily provide the excuse for Bonn officials to take this step.

V

What is the likelihood that India would change its policy and sign the Nonproliferation Treaty and forego nuclear arms? Mason Willrich has summarized India's conditions:

> Would a guarantee against nuclear blackmail help India decide to forgo the chance of developing a nuclear capability? Since Communist China began setting off nuclear blasts, India has raised its price for making an unequivocal renunciation; it indicates that it wants considerably more than a simple guarantee. An undertaking "through the United Nations" to safeguard the security of nonnuclear nations is only part of its demand. Also included are an agreement by the nuclear powers not to transfer nuclear weapons to other powers, a comprehensive nuclear test ban and a freeze on further production of nuclear weapons and delivery systems, coupled with substantial reductions in existing inventories. Moreover, India had not excluded Communist China from the list of required subscribers to a nonproliferation agreement. It seems clear that a "paper" guarantee other than one by the United Nations, or conceivably one given

8. Klaus Bloemer, "Germany and a 'European Europe'," Orbis, Spring 1966, pp. 245–246.

9. Karl Deutsch, *Arms Control and the Atlantic Alliance* (New York: John Wiley, 1967), p. 52.

jointly by the United States and the Soviet Union, would be unacceptable as contrary to India's commitment to nonalignment.[10]

Any guarantee to defend India against Chinese nuclear blackmail and attack would probably be unsatisfactory to India since it would have to depend on joint U.S.-USSR action, which could be undermined by a credible Chinese nuclear threat to the superpowers or their allies, or even by a Moscow-Peking realignment after the passing of Mao from the Chinese scene. In any case, India was not satisfied by the Security Council Resolution of June 17, 1968, jointly sponsored by the United States, the Soviet Union and Britain, which recognized "that aggression with nuclear weapons or the threat of such aggression against a nonnuclear-weapon state would create a situation in which the Security Council, and above all its nuclear-weapon state permanent members, would have to act immediately in accordance with their obligations under the United Nations Charter."

Therefore, if India is to remain nonaligned, New Delhi must deal sooner or later with the Chinese nuclear threat, unless it is removed by one or both of the superpowers or by some unforeseen upheaval in China itself. The Chinese nuclear threat could be minimized by an effective anti-ballistic missile system supplied to India by either or both of the superpowers, or independently developed in cooperation with Japan or perhaps West Germany. However, since an ABM system, to be effective, most likely requires nuclear warheads, and since these and the system as a whole have not been proven and probably cannot be proven under the restrictions of the Test Ban Treaty, a more likely option is an independent Indian nuclear deterrent. Either option is incompatible with an Indian signature on the Nonproliferation Treaty.

Unless the Chinese nuclear threat is removed by a disarming strike, or is otherwise dealt with to the satisfaction of India, a voluntary Indian signature seems unlikely. Of course, India may bow to joint pressure by the superpowers, particularly from a U.S. threat to terminate grain shipments. But such an involuntary signature is unlikely to be meaningful after the first good Indian harvest, and the consequent long-term damage to U.S.-Indian relations should hopefully deter the U.S. government from using such tactics to obtain an Indian signature.

There is the slight possibility that a Chinese misstep in connection with the Vietnamese conflict may provide the Pentagon with sufficient reason to preempt the Chinese nuclear capability, but the Chinese are no doubt aware of this possibility and have been careful not to give the United States such an excuse. The past policy of both superpowers has obviously been not to launch a preemptive strike even under severe provocation, and it seems unlikely that this policy will change. Further, Soviet deployment of an ABM system, prob-

10. Mason Willrich, "Guarantees to Non-Nuclear Nations," *Foreign Affairs,* July 1966, pp. 689–690.

ably aimed chiefly at China, supports the belief that Moscow has decided to live with the Chinese nuclear threat.

Unless the Chinese threat can otherwise be dealt with to the satisfaction of India, or India gives up its nonaligned status and moves under the American nuclear umbrella (a very remote possibility), it is likely that New Delhi will not sign the Nonproliferation Treaty and will eventually go nuclear.[11] If West Germany follows the Indian example, as it well might, a U.S.-Soviet confrontation is almost inevitable and a nuclear exchange cannot be ruled out. The prospect of continuing enmity in the Middle East coupled with nuclear proliferation to Israel and the United Arab Republic (not to mention India and Pakistan), could set off small and disastrous nuclear wars. While all evidence seems to indicate that the superpowers will not become involved in minor nuclear wars, every effort should be made to avoid them, notwithstanding Professor Kaplan's suggestion that there are no better practicable world alternatives.

Even if India and other nonnuclear-weapon states do not sign the treaty, this does not mean that it would not be beneficial—at least to the Soviet Union. From the Soviet view, a treaty bearing American and West German signatures is desirable, since such a commitment might hinder the United States in coming to the aid of the West Germans if they decide to abrogate the treaty and acquire nuclear weapons, and are then confronted by determined Soviet opposition, including the possibility of a disarming strike. A U.S. decision to counter Soviet threats might not be popular with the American people, who believe treaties should be observed and who still have residual fears of German militarism. But if the alternative is to allow Europe to be dominated by the Soviet Union, as it probably would be, then a dangerous superpower confrontation would be likely. In this light, it is not surprising that many West German leaders resisted signing the treaty, while the Soviets promoted the treaty—despite Peking's accusations of U.S.-Soviet collaboration, the irritations caused by the war in Viet Nam, and the expressed opposition of India and other nuclear club candidates.

Several other complications connected with the treaty should be noted briefly. It has been stated on high authority that the treaty will prevent the spread of nuclear weapons because mainland China, although denouncing the treaty, is not able to offer its weapons for export.[12] China's position, in reality, is that the more socialist countries with nuclear weapons the better,[13] and Syria or the UAR might meet the ideological qualifications. A Chinese

11. A 1968 report by India's government-sponsored Institute of Defense Studies and Analyses made the case for India's ability to afford the bomb by noting that she has the tenth largest gross national product in the world, and argued that India should "develop its nuclear option." *New York Times*, September 8, 1968, p. 34. An Indian ambassador put it to the author more simply, saying: "If China can afford the bomb, so can India."

12. Former U.S. Ambassador to the UN, Arthur J. Goldberg, *New York Times*, October 5, 1968, p. 34.

13. Morton Halperin, *China and the Bomb* (New York: Praeger, 1965), p. 47.

transfer of even a few nuclear weapons to Syria or the UAR could instantly and radically change the balance of power in the Middle East, and a U.S. treaty obligation not to transfer nuclear weapons to Israel to redress the balance actually encourages such Chinese action. Further, should Washington attempt to pressure Bonn to sign the treaty, many top West German political leaders will be alienated, and the same is probably true with respect to the Japanese. Also, some U.S. allies, not likely to go nuclear in any case, will want additional guarantees of nuclear security, thus increasing U.S. obligations.

Thus, the treaty hardly seems worth ratifying if it does not deal effectively with the principal cause of proliferation, namely, mainland China. And the treaty may not survive its first five years if the superpowers continue to escalate the nuclear arms race. Atmospheric or space testing of anti-ballistic missiles by the superpowers would kill the Nonproliferation Treaty and the Test Ban Treaty.

VI

Is there an international arms control alternative which might deal with the Chinese nuclear threat to the satisfaction of India and thus lead to a voluntary Indian signature on the Nonproliferation Treaty? In September 1965, I proposed that the Partial Nuclear Test Ban Treaty, agreed to by the United States, the United Kingdom and the Soviet Union in Moscow in 1963 and later signed or acceded to by the vast majority of states (with the notable exceptions of mainland China and France), be made universally binding. This proposal was set forth in a privately circulated memorandum to U.S. and foreign arms control specialists, including Ambassador V. C. Trivedi, the Indian delegate to the Eighteen Nation Disarmament Committee. I later discussed it in detail with Ambassador Trivedi, and on November 24, 1965, during the disarmament debate in the First Committee of the UN General Assembly, the Ambassador, referring to Chinese atmospheric tests, stated that:

The first priority is the task of making the Moscow Test Ban Treaty universally binding. We have requested and we have urged, we have deplored and we have condemned; but neither our displeasure nor our appeals have borne any fruit. The international community cannot, I submit, continue to remain helpless and impotent in the teeth of such defiance and will be obliged to examine what it can do to ensure that the health of humanity is not periodically attacked by the death-dealing debris of radioactive fallout.[14]

14. General Assembly, Official Records, Twentieth Session, First Committee (November 24, 1965), pp. 169–170.

On February 15, 1966, Ambassador Trivedi told the Eighteen Nation Disarmament Committee:

> As the Indian delegation said in New York during the last session of the General Assembly, the first priority in this field is thus to be accorded to the task of making the Moscow Test Ban Treaty universally binding. This is not a treaty which is subscribed to by a few powers with vested interests and their allies; it is a treaty which the non-aligned and nonnuclear nations have urged from the beginning and have signed in overwhelming number.[15]

Again, on June 30, 1966, he said:

> When we talk of nuclear weapons tests, therefore, it is essential that we talk comprehensively of all nuclear weapon tests, that we talk of tests in all environments and that we remember the terms of United Nations resolution 2032 (XX) of the last session, namely, "arrangements to ban effectively all nuclear weapon tests in all environments". . . .
>
> In working out those arrangements, the first priority should logically and coherently be given to the task of making the Moscow Test Ban Treaty universally applicable.[16]

However, in October 1966 China exploded on target a nuclear weapon carried by a guided missile; on December 28 China conducted another explosion; and on June 17, 1967 she successfully detonated her first hydrogen bomb. Apparently the disruptions of the Cultural Revolution had not slowed the Chinese nuclear weapon development program.

After the Chinese guided-missile test of October 1966, some observers thought India had lost interest in a universally-binding test ban and had turned her attention to acquiring an ABM system, presumably from one or both of the superpowers—an action that would have been incompatible with an Indian signature on the nonproliferation treaty. If this was New Delhi's intention, it may have been based on a belief that it was too late to freeze Chinese nuclear development, or on the U.S. failure to respond to India's suggestions for a universally-binding test ban. The United States presumably believed that it was not politically feasible to force compliance with arms control agreements, particularly on mainland China and possibly on France, the only states that have not signed or acceded to the 1963 Test Ban Treaty and continue to conduct atmospheric tests.

It is highly unlikely that France would risk a confrontation with the superpowers if they decided to support and enforce a universal test ban, but it must be assumed that China would challenge the ban. If that conclusion is correct, then we are face-to-face with a tragic dilemma: If the Chinese

15. Conference of the Eighteen-Nation Committee on Disarmament, Document ENDC/PV.240 (February 15, 1966), pp. 9–10.
16. *Ibid.*, Document ENDC/PV.269 (June 30, 1966), p. 12.

nuclear threat is not checked or removed, the likely result is a dangerous superpower confrontation over a West German decision to go nuclear, which could lead to general nuclear war. On the other hand, if an attempt is made by one or both of the superpowers to check or remove the Chinese nuclear threat, then a dangerous confrontation with China is likely—one that could lead to Chinese nuclear threats, and possibly nuclear and conventional attacks on neighboring areas, such as Japan, India, South Viet Nam, South Korea, Taiwan and Siberia. The danger of such attacks depends on whether the Chinese have an operational nuclear capability at the time of the confrontation; in view of Chinese nuclear progress, such a capability might be achieved in a few years. While China may even now have a small number of atomic bombs, she does not have long-range bombers. Chinese leaders seem to be counting on mating a hydrogen warhead to an intercontinental missile delivery system. But there is some danger that in a confrontation in the near future, China might be able to deliver atomic bombs by aircraft, triggering a nuclear response by one or both of the superpowers or even by a missile-supplied Taiwan.

Because of China's nuclear progress, Washington decided to deploy a "thin" anti-ballistic missile system originally estimated to cost about four to five billion dollars. A similar system will probably have to be supplied to Japan, Taiwan and other U.S. allies at comparable costs. It would be difficult to turn down an Indian request for a similar system. Thus, the initial cost of deploying extensive "thin" ABM systems would be in the order of tens of billions of dollars, and such "thin" systems would have to be periodically "thickened" to keep up with increasing Chinese nuclear capabilities. Eventually, "heavy" ABM systems would exist in many areas of the world at a cost reaching into the hundreds of billions of dollars. Under such circumstances we would have little money left for the global war on poverty.

But even a worldwide ABM deployment would not prevent the foreseeable superpower confrontation over West Germany. Indeed, it may even increase the chances for a confrontation since the United States and the Soviet Union may believe the danger of mass destruction has been lessened by their ABM systems. The resulting arms race would be catastrophic in cost and potential danger, for advances in ABM systems would force the superpowers simultaneously to deploy more advanced offensive missile systems. The effect would be to render arms control measures completely meaningless.

It is the author's view that—to paraphrase Gresham's Law that bad money drives out good money—arms race measures drive out arms control measures. In their syndicated column ("Inside Washington") of December 9, 1966, Robert S. Allen and Paul Scott reported:

U.S. authorities are gravely concerned by an authoritative warning that Russia may use Red China's next atomic test as the pretext to withdraw from the [nuclear test ban] treaty. The State Department has been informed that this alarming possibility was clearly intimated by Deputy Foreign Minister Vasily Kuznetsov during a long talk with UN Secretary-General U Thant last week.

Kuznetsov, the highest ranking Soviet official to visit the UN in two years, observed that abrogation of the 1963 test ban pact may become necessary because of the growing threat to Russia's security from Peking's unrestricted development of nuclear weapons.

If a way isn't found soon to curb China's atomic activity, Kuznetsov maintained, the Soviet would have no other recourse but to resume atmospheric testing.

Significantly, Goldberg was directed by President Johnson to find out whether the Russians or U Thant have recommendations on how the Chinese nuclear program could be curbed without triggering a war.

This report may still have validity for today. The probable reason for a Soviet abrogation of the 1963 Test Ban Treaty would be to test the ABM system it is deploying. This would require atmospheric nuclear explosions. It is unlikely that the Soviets would spend tens of billions of rubles on an untested ABM system. Thus, the 1963 treaty is likely to become a casualty of Chinese nuclear developments, in much the same way as the Nonproliferation Treaty will become a casualty if some of the leading candidates for the nuclear club go nuclear in response to the Chinese threat.

Given these dismal prospects, the political feasibility of a universally-binding test ban, designed to freeze or permit the destruction of the Chinese nuclear capability, seems worth serious consideration. Such a universal test ban should be comprehensive, that is, include all types of nuclear tests, especially underground tests. Otherwise, the Chinese could continue their development program by testing underground. But nuclear weapons specialists in both the United States and the USSR may be counting on underground shots to perfect and test warheads for anti-ballistic missiles, even though extensive underground tests already conducted by both superpowers may have solved most of the foreseeable problems. In any case, determined and probably successful opposition from the military and their supporters in both countries against a universal comprehensive test ban is reasonably predictable.

It should be remembered, however, that the primary reason for deploying a "thin" ABM system is to defend against a Chinese attack. If a universal comprehensive test ban is successful in halting or eliminating the Chinese nuclear development program, a "thin" ABM system would not be required, and the Soviets might readily agree to remove their probably unproven ABM system in order to avoid an expensive arms race escalation with the United States—particularly if there was little likelihood that the West Germans would go nuclear. One would certainly hope that underground testing could be safely suspended until the effectiveness of a universal ban was determined; this would not require a long period of time, because as the Chinese nuclear arsenal becomes more and more advanced, the likelihood that an attempt would be made to enforce a universal test ban decreases.

VII

The following feasibility analysis assumes that a universal test ban rider has been attached to the Nonproliferation Treaty with U.S. and Soviet approval to induce India and possibly other nuclear club candidates to sign. The rider would prohibit all nuclear tests by a party or a nonparty, and would obligate all parties, particularly the nuclear states that signed the treaty, to exert appropriate efforts, consistent with the UN Charter, to prevent any banned activities by a nonparty.[17]

(1) *France would probably not challenge the rider.* A major obstacle to U.S. acceptance of a universal test ban rider is the possibility that it could further strain U.S.-French relations. However, France would probably avoid a confrontation with the United States and would either await challenge of the rider by mainland China or would accept the Nonproliferation Treaty with the rider, for the following reasons: (a) France continues to rely on the U.S. nuclear umbrella, which could be removed as a consequence of a U.S.-French confrontation over effective arms control measures. (b) The French *force de frappe* is so far only a political device to help France achieve world power status; it could be politically neutralized by a Soviet anti-ballistic missile system deployed primarily against a Chinese nuclear threat. (c) Continued testing would probably not significantly improve the sophistication of the French nuclear arsenal or enhance French prestige and status as a world power. Thus, France does not really need to conduct a lengthy series of tests and may be ready to sign the treaty with a rider. (d) French tests could be prevented by blockading their Pacific test islands or by surrounding the islands with ships of many states. (e) The treaty and rider would require the establishment of an organization to administer and enforce the test ban, and France could be given equal world status with the United States and the USSR in the organization's peacekeeping activities.[18] (f) Washington could offer other concessions to France to induce her to sign a treaty with a rider.

17. Such a rider would be similar to Article X of the Antarctic Treaty which provides that "Each of the Contracting Parties undertakes to exert appropriate efforts, consistent with the Charter of the United Nations, to the end that no one engages in any activity contrary to the principles or purposes of the Present Treaty." Paragraph 1 of Article V specifically prohibits any nuclear explosions in Antarctica. December 1, 1959 [1961], 12 U.S.T. 794; T.I.A.S., No. 4780; 402 U.N.T.S. 71 (effective June 23, 1961).

18. According to a leading French nuclear strategist, "It is a pretty safe bet that at the latest when ['democratization' of the nuclear weapon] happens, the nuclear powers will close their ranks in face of this common danger and will be forced to conclude between themselves a control agreement which they will not hesitate to enforce, more or less politely, on the rest of the world." André Beaufre, *Deterrence and Strategy* (New York: Praeger, 1966), p. 99.

(2) *Mainland China would probably challenge the rider.* A universal test ban rider would probably be challenged by mainland China for the following reasons: (a) Continued testing is essential if China is to develop a credible nuclear weapons arsenal. (b) Testing produces important political gains, both domestically and abroad. (c) The rider would be a precedent for other universal arms control measures likely to be opposed by mainland China, such as a universal nonproliferation treaty. Therefore, a Chinese challenge of the rider and a confrontation with the international community is probable, although a prudent government in Peking could postpone such a confrontation for a long time and might even terminate its expensive nuclear weapons development program.

(3) *Probable U.S. position.* If the U.S. government believes that the rider is acceptable to the USSR and that France is willing to cooperate by signing or at least by postponing additional tests until the Chinese have challenged the rider, then it could be acceptable to Washington. If France postponed testing to await the Chinese challenge, and the international community then failed to compel Peking to abide by the rider, France could safely resume her testing program. In any case, French cooperation is probably attainable, particularly if the French are led to believe that the United States will accept the rider and attempt to enforce it against the French if challenged. In view of the long series of anti-American actions taken by France, particularly with respect to NATO, Viet Nam and the Middle East, it should not be difficult to convince her leaders that the United States would actively help to enforce such a test ban against her. If mainland China postponed testing or terminated its nuclear weapons development program, France would almost certainly follow suit.

(4) *Probable USSR position.* The Soviet Union would sign the Nonproliferation Treaty with a universal test ban rider for the following reasons: (a) An overriding Soviet goal is to prevent the Federal Republic of Germany from acquiring nuclear weapons, and this goal would be closer if the United States and West Germany signed the Nonproliferation Treaty. (b) If India and Japan refused to sign the treaty without a universal test ban rider, then the Federal Republic might not sign; even if Bonn did sign, it is likely that it would eventually opt out rather than suffer discrimination. (c) There is reason to believe that India would sign the Nonproliferation Treaty with a rider, and would opt out only if the rider were not successfully enforced against the Chinese. (d) Another Soviet goal is to prevent the proliferation of nuclear weapons generally; if India refused to sign the Nonproliferation Treaty, or signs and then opts out at a convenient time, that goal would be unattained. (e) The Soviets would like to diminish the severe worldwide criticism of their invasion of Czechoslovakia. (f) The Soviet Union seems to have many reasons to freeze or reduce the Chinese nuclear weapon capability. Since the Soviet inva-

sion of Czechoslovakia, a fellow socialist state, was probably motivated by a strong Soviet resolve to prevent a West German military threat, the Kremlin in all likelihood is prepared to take even more direct action, if necessary, against the more immediate and more dangerous threat from a nuclear-armed China. Maoist China will probably soon be formally ejected from the socialist camp, thus reducing the political cost of Soviet action against China.

(5) *Both the United States and the USSR might accept the rider.* In the face of New Delhi's insistence on the rider, the USSR might accept it in order to obtain India's signature and to freeze or reverse the Chinese nuclear development program. Washington might accept the rider for substantially the same reasons. Certainly, neither superpower would agree to the rider without acceptance by the other, but the possibility of mutual agreement could be secretly explored prior to their taking public positions on it.[19]

(6) *Probable consequences of a rider.* If the United States, Great Britain, the Soviet Union and a large number of other states agreed to adding the universal test ban rider to the Nonproliferation Treaty, the burden would fall on the United States (with the help of the Taiwan Chinese) and the USSR to enforce it against any mainland Chinese challenge, preferably before an international enforcement organization was established in order to avoid unnecessary delay and additional political obstacles. It seems unlikely that the superpowers would accept the rider unless both were prepared at least tacitly to support its enforcement. Each superpower would probably maneuver to place the enforcement burden on the other. However, it is likely that both superpowers would at least tacitly support Taiwan in enforcing the test ban against the mainland Chinese (for example, by enabling Taiwan to destroy Chinese nuclear facilities), or both would accept substantially equal responsibility for enforcing the test ban *in the name of the law* with the help of other volunteers, such as the Taiwan government.[20] While Peking's short-term reaction would obviously be one of great anger and bitterness, the Chinese are unlikely to respond with offensive thrusts and risk nuclear attack on their major cities. The long-

---

19. Paradoxically, the chances for meaningful arms control agreements have probably increased as a result of the Soviet invasion of Czechoslovakia and the election of Richard Nixon. The invasion symbolized Soviet interest in maintaining the global status quo and generated a Soviet need to lessen the adverse reaction by agreeing to further arms control agreements. President Nixon probably has a freer hand to negotiate than Johnson had because he need not fear attack from the right; and "hard-liners" in Washington and Moscow will probably be able to do business together on the basis of coinciding selfish interests (with respect to mainland China, for example), since to some extent they think alike.

20. Such an enforcement action might be carried out successfully through conventional bombing, but some ground action, similar to the British commando action against the Nazi heavy water plant in Norway during World War II, might also be required. If the mainland Chinese were to rebuild their nuclear weapon facilities, enforcement action would have to be repeated if they resumed nuclear tests.

term Chinese reaction might also be one of revanchism; yet it should be kept in mind that, although the United States dropped atomic bombs on Japanese cities and fire-bombed German cities, within a few years the Japanese and Germans were among America's best allies.

(7) *Universal observance or enforcement of the rider could lead to world peace through law.* If the rider were universally observed or successfully enforced, *nuclear* peace could probably be maintained through law as long as the superpowers cooperated; in view of the alternatives, this might be for a long time. In any event, the danger of a nuclear war would be minimized and a giant step taken toward the goal of attaining peace through law.

Whether or not there is any logic in this feasibility analysis, the ineluctable fact remains that neither superpower is likely to support arms control measures that might require enforcement against noncomplying states—even though the long-term alternative may be a nuclear war over West German acquisition of nuclear weapons. Only an extremely dangerous crisis which thoroughly alarms the world, such as an accidental nuclear missile exchange, might alter the nuclear powers' outlook. Therefore, the Chinese quite likely will be able to create an operational nuclear missile arsenal which will eventually pose a credible threat to the United States, the USSR and other countries resisting Chinese political objectives. A Chinese announcement of June 1967 looked forward to the day when the superpowers' nuclear blackmail tactics would no longer be effective:

> The success of China's hydrogen bomb test has further broken the nuclear monopoly of United States imperialism and Soviet revisionism and dealt a telling blow at their policy of nuclear blackmail.
>
> It is a very great encouragement and support to the Vietnamese people in their heroic war against United States aggression and for national salvation, to the Arab people in their resistance to aggression by the United States and British imperialists and their tool, Israel, and to the revolutionary people of the whole world.[21]

A major purpose of China's nuclear arsenal is to neutralize the nuclear advantage of the superpowers, leaving her mass army free to accomplish its goals. These goals are, at the very least, the ejection of U.S. influence from the Western Pacific, Southeast Asia and Japan, the acquisition of Taiwan, and the recovery of former Chinese territory in Siberia. Additionally, China wants to dictate formation of pro-Peking governments in New Delhi and the capitals of Southeast Asia, and to gain recognition as a superpower, with the expectation that her views would have to be taken into account in connection with the settlement of all international disputes and the allocation of resources. Last, but not least, Peking wants to be free to lend active sup-

21. *New York Times,* June 18, 1967, p. 3.

port to revolutionary peoples throughout the world so they may be liberated from "Western imperialism" and "Soviet revisionism."

The envisioned failure to deal with the Chinese nuclear threat is likely to produce a threat of nuclear conflict over a nuclear-arming West Germany, small nuclear wars between countries such as India and Pakistan and Israel and the UAR, and the expenditure of many tens, even hundreds, of billions of dollars in ABM systems at the expense of the world war against poverty. Additionally, both the United States and the USSR can expect to be involved in escalating crises caused by what China believes to be legitimate complaints—Taiwan, U.S. military bases, and former Chinese territories in Siberia. Considering the commitment of present Chinese rulers to violence, revolution and turmoil, Peking's acquisition of a sizeable nuclear arsenal before the end of the 1970's threatens to create instability over large portions of the globe—and possibly nuclear conflict. It is not hard to envision the Chinese winning "nuclear chicken" games and thus acquiring Taiwan and bordering Soviet territories; they may also influence establishment of pro-Peking governments in New Delhi and Tokyo, Seoul and Saigon. The Chinese would probably be emboldened to support "wars of national liberation" in Venezuela and even Mexico, and the developing countries of Africa and Asia. It is not comforting to envision Vietnamese-type "liberation wars" in our own backyard. Many undeveloped countries have masses of discontents, potential "revolutionary patriots" whom the Chinese might actively support by supplying arms and by neutralizing "imperialist nuclear blackmail." Also, China, mischievously or in an effort to replace Soviet influence, might give nuclear weapons to countries such as the UAR, thus instantly creating a dangerous situation likely to involve the two superpowers. China could no doubt find many ways to trigger a nuclear war between the superpowers.

It has been argued that her increasing affluence might diminish China's present revolutionary fervor—along the lines of the Soviet experience—so that these dismal predictions might not come true. But there is a fundamental difference between China and the Soviet Union. The Soviet Union is reasonably satisfied with the territorial status quo, at least to the extent that her leaders are unwilling to take grave risks. China is not willing to settle for the status quo.[22]

The prospects for the Soviet Union are not much better. If, as predicted by Kaplan, the Soviets cannot prevent China and West Germany from gaining access to nuclear arms, they may not be able to stop these two states from reacquiring their former territories in Siberia and Central Europe. A some-

22. The Soviet invasion of Czechoslovakia, which upset nearly all communist parties in the West and many nonaligned states, is evidence of the Soviet desire to maintain the status quo of the "Socialist Commonwealth" at the expense of extending its control to other states. It will be more difficult now, for example, to persuade the people of France and Italy to elect a communist party to power and thus put their country into the communist bloc.

what truncated Russia surrounded by unfriendly nuclear-armed powers might be forced into isolationism and a "fortress" mentality.

VIII

Arms control measures cannot be effective if they are binding only on those states which assent to be bound. This is particularly true with respect to nuclear arms. Chinese nuclear arms progress apparently has forced the Soviet Union to deploy an anti-ballistic missile system, and it is unlikely that the Soviets will expend the vast sums needed to complete the system until they are sure of its effectiveness. Since an anti-ballistic missile will almost certainly use a nuclear warhead, the testing of the system will require atmospheric and space test explosions which will force the Soviet Union to withdraw from the 1963 Nuclear Test Ban Treaty. Further, Chinese nuclear arms progress is likely to prevent the attainment of an *effective* nuclear nonproliferation treaty.

Arms control measures can prevent arms race measures only when they are universally binding, i.e., by virtue of being accepted by assenting states and imposed on nonassenting states. A universally-binding nuclear test ban in all environments which had enforcement credibility could be effective in preventing further Chinese work on nuclear weapons if Peking observed the ban or if it were forced on the Chinese by a threat to destroy, or the actual destruction of, their capability.[23] The failure to freeze or terminate the Chinese nuclear program is likely to lead to a superpower confrontation with its danger of a general nuclear war, to small nuclear wars, and to the expenditure of vast sums of money on ABM systems of questionable effectiveness.

But is there a legal basis for binding nonassenting states against their will? In my view, *generally-recognized* international peacekeeping laws can be relied on to bind nonassenting states because they are recognized by a large majority of the states. These laws are limited to international peacekeeping purposes, express an intent to bind nonassenting states, and are adhered to by a large majority of the states, specifically including the United States and the Soviet Union. They can be relied on to bind nonassenting states because the international community says they are universally binding.

The UN Charter is the principal example of a generally-recognized international peacekeeping law. Article 2(6) of the Charter makes its peacekeeping provisions applicable to nonparties against their will. The UN action in repelling the North Korean invasion of South Korea is just one example of UN actions against nonparties deemed to have violated the Charter.[24]

23. A universally-binding *partial* nuclear test ban (forbidding tests in the atmosphere, in outer space and under water, as the present ban does) might be a more feasible first step. It would also be a precedent for a universally-binding test ban in all environments, as well as other universal arms control measures such as a universal nuclear nonproliferation treaty, and could bring a halt to the Chinese nuclear arms development program.

24. For an excellent survey of the precedents for binding nonassenting states, see Louis B. Sohn, "Enforcement of Disarmament Controls with Respect to States which have

If enforcement measures are to be carried out by volunteering states, then generally-recognized international peacekeeping laws will have enforcement credibility to the extent that a nonassenting state, desiring to conduct the activity banned by the law, believes that at least one volunteering state with adequate capability would punish it. For example, if the Nationalist Chinese had an enforcement capability, such as a fleet of long-range bombers, the mainland Chinese might believe that Taiwan would volunteer to punish them for conducting the banned activity.

An organization established to administer these peacekeeping laws could be controlled by a small number of responsible powers and develop into an "upper house" to the United Nations, particularly if the government of mainland China is admitted to the world body and takes the Chinese seat in the Security Council.

It is the task of the political leaders of the United States, the Soviet Union, the United Kingdom, and other states to determine whether, as a practical matter, universal nuclear arms control laws can be enforced against non-assenting states. If they conclude that it is feasible to enforce compliance of these laws, a significant step toward the goal of maintaining nuclear peace through law may be taken. If enforced compliance is not feasible, arms control agreements such as the Nuclear Test Ban and the Nonproliferation Treaty will inevitably be "driven out" by arms race measures such as a Chinese missile deployment, ABM defenses and ABM-penetrating offensive missile systems.[25] To put it plainly, if the Chinese are able to deploy an effective nuclear missile system, there will be no effective nuclear arms control measures.

---

not Ratified a Disarmament or Arms Control Treaty," in Donald G. Brennan and Robert Maxwell, editors, *Arms Control and Disarmament* (Oxford: Pergamon Press, 1968), p. 99. It should be noted that most states, including the United States and the USSR, also agree that both customary law and peace treaties settling wars can bind states against their will. Based on my discussions with some Soviet international law experts in August 1968, a universal test ban, if politically acceptable, would present no legal problems to the Soviets with respect to binding nonassenting states. The U.S. position on this legal issue is not publicly known.

25. This view is supported by the result of the London Naval Agreement, signed on March 25, 1936 by Great Britain, France and the United States, which provided for restrictions on the size of certain types of naval vessels and the caliber of guns of the signatories. The treaty also had an "escalator clause" allowing signatories to exceed the restrictions in the event of competitive building by another state. Within two years, the United States and Great Britain announced that they were resuming competitive building due to the accelerated naval construction of Japan, a nonsignatory. Historical Evaluation and Research Organization, *Responses to Violations of Arms Control and Disarmament Agreements* (Washington: HERO, April 1964), p. 152, and in the Annex, Volume II, p. A-161. This report was prepared for the Arms Control and Disarmament Agency under ACDA Contract GC-17, March 29, 1963, and is on file in the ACDA library in Washington.

7. The Nuclear Non-Proliferation Treaty: Its Rationale, Prospects, and Possible Impact on International Law

MORTON A. KAPLAN

I. Introduction

THE TREATY on the Non-Proliferation of Nuclear Weapons, proposed at the twenty-second session of the United Nations General Assembly, was signed by sixty two nations on July 1, 1968. The treaty essentially prohibits each nuclear-weapon State, defined as one which had manufactured and exploded a nuclear weapon or other nuclear explosive device prior to January 1, 1967, from transferring any nuclear weapons or nuclear devices to any other nation, and it commits any non-nuclear weapon State to a policy of not accepting or producing these weapons or devices. Additional provisions seek to establish safeguards through international inspection of the non-nuclear weapon States by the International Atomic Energy Agency based on agreements to be negotiated with that Agency. The treaty is clearly intended not to affect the rights of the parties to the treaty to continue research and development in the production and use of nuclear energy for peaceful purposes, and it provides that the benefit of peaceful applications of nuclear energy which one party derives are to be made available to the other parties. The Preamble declares that it is the intention of the parties to the treaty to achieve at the earliest possible date the cessation of the nuclear arms race and eventual nuclear disarmament. Yet the only provision in the treaty for accomplishing such a goal is the agreement of the parties to pursue negotiations in the future, and only the non-nuclear weapon States are subject to the safeguards in the treaty.

While history will be the ultimate judge of the success or failure of the treaty, it is both possible and justifiable at this time to evaluate the effectiveness of this attempt at international cooperation in reaching certain international goals.

II. Rationale

Interest in a non-proliferation treaty represents part of a larger interest in the subject of nuclear arms control. The history of arms control and disarmament conferences extends back for more than two thousand years and the control and banning of certain weapons has received much international attention in the last one hundred years, but the development of nuclear weapons has greatly intensified the concern with this problem. The reasons for this increased concern are fairly obvious. In the first place, nuclear weapons can be used to destroy modern civilization with a speed and efficiency that was unknown to any previous weapons system. Although Douhet's theory of air warfare[1] presented a similar view on the advent of military aircraft which was criticized by his contemporaries, the realization now by governments and heads of state that weapons systems exist which actually can be used to end life on earth (but not as easily as many believe) has had an enormous impact upon state behavior. This growing concern with the problem of nuclear weapons properly manifests an urgency that earlier weapons systems did not justify.

Another reason for concern lies in some conceptions concerning the nuclear arms race. Although it has been asserted incorrectly that arms races produce wars—a conclusion for which there is little empirical or theoretical justification—the nuclear arms race is still believed to increase the dangers of proliferation and of destruction.[2] Actually, this conception of the problem is much oversimplified. The early stages of the nuclear arms race were highly dangerous, but also contained some stabilizing elements. The early nuclear weapons carriers—airplanes and liquid-fuelled missiles—were slow reacting and highly vulnerable to surprise attack. A nuclear accident, an unauthorized attack, or misinterpreted radar indications under such conditions of vulnerability increased the probability of a preemptive strike during times of crisis to a greater level than prudent statesmen found acceptable. While the danger of such preemptive strike was clearly a reality, this does not necessarily imply

1. See G. DOUHET, THE COMMAND OF THE AIR (D. Ferrari transl. 1942). General Giulio Douhet was an Italian strategist who argued that military aircraft were weapons designed for offensive action of incomparable destructive potential, against which no effective defense could be foreseen. Any nation which attained command of the air could then proceed to shatter the enemy's military potential and will to wage war by direct aerial bombing.

2. For a good discussion of the nuclear arms race and its accompanying dangers, see Kahn, *The Arms Race and Some of its Hazards*, in 1 THE STRATEGY OF WORLD ORDER 17 (R. Falk & S. Mendlovitz eds. 1966). *See also* Boulding, *The Prevention of World War III*, 38 VA. Q. REV. 1 (1962).

that the probability of its occurrence was very high. On two occasions, for example, radar "blips" were recorded which, if indicative of enemy action, would have led to the initial deployment of Strategic Air Command (SAC) forces to the positive control point to await presidential authorization for a strike under the "failsafe" procedure. In both instances, however, the forces were not activated. SAC leaders had decided that it was extremely unlikely that the radar indications represented a possible Russian attack since there was no present international crisis. Thus, the early dangers of a preemptive strike were apparently stabilized by the hesitancy of nuclear powers to respond prematurely under such conditions in the absence of a full-blown international crisis. Nevertheless, the dangers still existed and the possibility that misinterpreted blips might occur during an actual crisis could not be ruled out.

A second stabilizing factor in the early stages lay in the peculiar mathematics of a missile arms race itself. Depending upon the specific characteristics of the weapons systems, a larger number of missiles possessed by a defending nation requires a greater proportional superiority on the part of an enemy in order to launch an effective first strike. This consequently makes it more difficult for the enemy to acquire the necessary striking superiority, makes it more difficult to maintain secrecy in the attempt to achieve superiority, and makes it easier to respond successfully to the effort to reach such superiority. Thus, although increases in the nuclear arsenals of the major nations increased the potential amount of damage that each side could do to the other, the resultant danger was at the same time stabilized by these very increases, and the likelihood became less that the large-scale use of nuclear forces would be made. As systems were improved both quantitatively and qualitatively with the introduction of solid-fuelled, quick-reacting missiles with hardened bases, it became even more likely that a prudent and responsible national leadership could maintain a militarily non-responsive posture, even in times of crisis.

It is, however, no longer true that the qualitative arms race is mutually stabilizing. Multiple Independent Re-entry Vehicles (MIRV), Fractional Orbital Ballistic Systems (FOBS), orbital weapons, and the early stages of the deployment of Ballistic Missile Defenses (BMD) are reintroducing some of the dangers of the early stages of the arms race, such as the possibility of preemptive strikes, without any of the corresponding stabilizing elements. While the Nuclear Non-Proliferation Treaty does not meet this new problem directly, it is intended, at least in part, to prevent an unstable arms race from multiplying in intensity as even increasing numbers of nations attempt to acquire nuclear forces.[3]

The nuclear systems now being developed by nations other than the United States and the Soviet Union have many of the hazardous characteris-

3. G.A., Res. 2373, 22 U.N. GAOR____, U.N. Doc. A/7016/Add. 1 (1968).

tics of the early qualitative stages of the arms race. The French *force de frappe* is an example of such a force. This system is based on the *Mirage,* a very effective plane which, because it does possess the capability of reaching Moscow or Leningrad, except insofar as the Russians improve their low altitude radar control from overhead sources, is sufficiently provocative to raise a serious possibility of a Russian preemptive strike during an intense crisis. Indeed, the force is sufficiently provocative to act as a self-deterrent for the French. They probably would not actually dare to use it in a first strike, for, although they might destroy Moscow or Leningrad, all of France could be obliterated in retaliation. On the other hand, possession of the force during an escalating crisis, with the possibility of its irrational use, might tempt the Russians to strike first in order to protect their own national security. Therefore, possession of the force would seem to weaken, rather than strengthen, the resolve of a prudent French leadership during a time of crisis.

If this type of force is so provocative and inherently dangerous, why should France or any other country wish to have such a system? One possible explanation is national pride and grandeur. A more sound reason, however, lies in the lack of the credibility of the United States' nuclear commitment to NATO. The United States has never given an ironclad nuclear "guarantee" to Western Europe.[4] America's persistent and wise declaratory war policy which delays the application of an immediate nuclear response to an attack on Western Europe has raised serious, even if not entirely justified, questions in the minds of many Europeans concerning the credibility of the American nuclear guarantee. If Russia were to strike without provocation, the United States in all likelihood would respond nuclearly. A crisis that developed over a period of time, however, and in which the equities were not clear would provide the United States with alternatives to the use of nuclear weapons. Under these circumstances, the United States would have an opportunity to consider the potential damage to American cities from a nuclear exchange and would probably pressure European nations to make concessions which they would view as inconsistent with their interests and security. If the Europeans did not yield to these pressures, they would be left defenseless. Although the American nuclear guarantee would not entirely lack credibility in this situation, that credibility would be limited and political costs would be involved. From this standpoint, then, it is not difficult to see why European countries would consider possession of an independent nuclear system to be an essential part of their national defense and security.

Moreover, the Russian invasion of Czechoslovakia has taught those Europeans who did not previously understand this issue that one important function of nuclear weapons is to deter conventional attack and that conven-

---

4. *See generally* Agreement Between the Parties to the North Atlantic Treaty for Cooperation Regarding Atomic Information, June 18, 1964, art. I, [1965] 1 U.S.T. 109, 111, T.I.A.S. No. 5768; North Atlantic Treaty with Other Governments, April 4, 1949, art. 5, 63 Stat. 2241, 2244 (1949), T.I.A.S. No. 1964.

tional rather than nuclear attack might well be the danger they face. Many Europeans are asking themselves whether the Soviet Union would have invaded Czechoslovakia if that nation had had in its possession even the most primitive nuclear weapons and delivery systems. In order to allay the fears of non-nuclear weapon States, the United States, Great Britain and the Soviet Union offered identical security guarantees pertaining to attacks on signatory nations.[5] The guarantees are, of course, not self-enforcing and, apart from the reliability or unreliability of the pledgers, will no doubt prove subject to interpretation depending upon the conditions of particular cases. In any event, however, Czechoslovakia demonstrated that it is not merely nuclear strikes but also conventional attacks that must be deterred.

These thoughts may appear inconsistent with the arguments concerning the self-deterrent quality of unstable nuclear forces. This will not be the case, however, if a distinction is made between a crisis that escalates out of control and a crisis in which a deliberate decision is made to escalate its intensity. In the first case, the possessor of the unstable nuclear system will likely suffer a failure of resolve. In the second case, the aggressor State will more likely decide that the risks of escalation are not worth the potential gains.

One might ask whether nuclear proliferation might not have advantages that compensate for its defects. If the proliferation of nuclear systems reduces the likelihood of deliberate aggression across national borders, then perhaps the increased risk of inadvertent, unauthorized or accidental war might be sufficiently compensated for. Yet this is not simply the case. The sheer proliferation of the number of unstable nuclear systems intuitively seems to increase the risks beyond reasonable limits. There is, however, an additional and even more basic reason for mistrusting the extensive spread of nuclear weapons. Both the United States and the Soviet Union, as well as China, Japan, West Germany, France, Great Britain and other developed nations, have decision-making systems that ensure bureaucratic delays, the rational and systematic calculation of alternatives, and the adjustment of military means to responsible, even if conflicting, national goals. In the hands of countries with governmental decision-making processes such as this, the presence of nuclear weapons does not immediately raise the threat of irrational deployment. But the possession of nuclear systems by nations that are subject to intense and recurrent regime crises, that regard themselves as being in such bad situations that they would have nothing to lose by becoming involved in a nuclear conflict, or that have romantic notions of the world and their role in it, is less than reassuring. The leader of such a country might

5. S.C. Res. 255, 23 U.N. SCOR, 1433d meeting____, U.N. Doc. S/8631 (1968). The text of the resolution adopted by the Security Council may also be found in 7 INT'L LEGAL MATERIALS 895 (1968). While not included as a part of the treaty, these guarantees were designed to win adherence to its provisions by assuring non-nuclear States that, although they would not be able to acquire their own systems, they could rely on the response of the guarantors, through the United Nations, in the event of attack.

not hesitate to use nuclear-weaponry in a crisis, and while he would probably not be able to destroy the world, he could still inflict considerable material, moral and political damage. The idea of the proliferation of nuclear systems to nations of that kind is distinctly frightening. One does not have to believe that these nations would necessarily use nuclear weapons in an irresponsible way, but the probability that they might is still too large for comfort and causes concern about the unchecked spread of nuclear arms.

It is not difficult to see where further pressures for nuclear proliferation will come from in the future. Although many Japanese are still bitterly opposed to a nuclear system in their country, they must sooner or later end their nuclear reliance upon the United States. As the second leading industrial power in the non-Communist world, Japan must eventually acquire a military and political authority commensurate with her economic power. The Japanese are known for their one hundred eighty degree turns in policy, so it is quite possible that their views on the nuclear issue will change. They must also cope with the Chinese problem and someday their feelings of guilt toward China may turn to resentment. India also faces a problem of potential aggression from China and the pressures within India for the development of nuclear forces are constantly increasing. West Germany is presently fearful of acquiring nuclear weapons, but the invasion of Czechoslovakia by the Soviet Union has made it clear to many Germans that they may soon face a greater danger if they do not acquire a nuclear system. These and other nations can be expected to press for nuclear arms with any increase in cold war tensions and conflicts.

III. Prospects

Prior to promulgation of the treaty, there had been a number of occasions when nuclear proliferation might have been halted, or at least slowed, by the use of military measures.[6] Since such steps would have been diplomatically and politically infeasible,[7] the adoption of a multilateral instrument designed to impede the expansion of nuclear arms appears to be the only effective means of reaching this desired result. The question must remain, however, whether or not such a treaty will indeed be effective. The Nuclear Non-Proliferation Treaty, assuming it is signed by the requisite number of States, will depend for its effectiveness upon several factors. To begin with, the

6. In 1946, for example, the United States could have delivered an ultimatum to the Soviet Union that a single testing of a nuclear weapon would lead to a strike against Soviet nuclear facilities. In the 1960's, similar measures might have been taken by the Soviet Union against China or by the United States against France.

7. The attempted establishment of an American world dictatorship, even though rigidly limited to restricting the possession of nuclear weapons, would have been misunderstood by the American public and bitterly resented by Russia and the West European nations. The almost certain attempts to evade this dictatorship could only have resulted in the United States taking increasingly more onerous and unpopular measures to preserve its role as a nuclear policeman.

Chinese threat to Japan and India must be minimized before these nations can be expected to acquiesce in the provisions of the treaty. It is difficult to see how this might be done short of removing China's nuclear capability. At this point in time, such a step seems extremely difficult, if not impossible. Like Japan and India, other nations on the threshold of nuclear arm acquisition may also resist the treaty on the grounds that it constitutes a danger to their national integrity and security. Without the acceptance of the treaty by those countries with the capability of developing nuclear weapons, it "will become little more than a pious declaration of intention."[8] Furthermore, the success of the treaty will depend upon the Soviet Union, the United States and France maintaining constant pressure upon West Germany not to acquire nuclear weapons. Neither the removal of China's force nor the prevention of West Germany's acquisition of nuclear arms seems likely. The Chinese system cannot be neutralized and West Germany cannot be impeded in its effort to obtain nuclear forces in the absence of an United States—Soviet Union condominium that extends at least to the nuclear weapons issue. It is quite difficult to believe that the coincidence of American and Soviet interests is sufficiently great so as to enable them to maintain the requisite joint pressure over a significant period of time. The Russian invasion of Czechoslovakia is only one illustration of how the conflict of interests between the United States and the Soviet Union could interfere with the efforts of the two countries to act jointly in a manner to prevent proliferation. In fact, the two nations have been unwilling to coordinate, let alone to collaborate, on other measures against China that would be necessary in order to maintain the effectiveness of the treaty. In addition, such a condominium would raise serious moral issues. It would impose upon the other nations of the world a Soviet-American leadership that would not be justified by diplomatic skill, culture, economic power or any other reasonable criterion. Moreover, one might always ask the question that if the United States and the Soviet Union can be trusted to control nuclear weapons, why cannot Japan, India, Italy or any other country be trusted? If the success of the Nuclear Non-Proliferation Treaty must depend upon extended Soviet-American cooperation, then its effectiveness will be severely limited.

I am grateful to Dr. Yuter (see his article in this issue of ORBIS) for making intellectually clear one of the most significant conditions necessary for success of a nuclear nondiffusion treaty: a universal nuclear test ban. Politicians or statesmen obfuscate the conditions requisite for a successful treaty in an effort to secure support for the NPT by hiding its weaknesses; they dissemble its blemishes, its dangers and its immoralities. Three major conditions requisite for the treaty's success are a universal test ban, as Yuter notes; a condominium between the United States and the Soviet Union; and a guarantee by the nuclear powers to nonnuclear powers against aggression by countries possessing nuclear weapons.

8. 114 CONG. REC. S. 11785 (daily ed. Oct. 1, 1968).

It is important not to ignore one of the purposes of the universal test ban that Yuter advocates. Although a universally binding test ban would operate to prevent any nation from testing nuclear weapons, one of the main purposes of such a ban is to legitimate an attack on China's nuclear facilities if China continues to develop her nuclear arsenal. Peking is well aware that the Geneva negotiations on nuclear diffusion, although addressed to the general problem of the spread of nuclear weapons, were also directed against China and West Germany. The failure to include an explicit universal test ban in the treaty—largely the result of a failure of nerve on the part of the United States and the Soviet Union—or alternatively to provide India with ironclad guarantees against aggression, accounts for stubborn Indian resistance to the NPT. Unless the Indians can be induced to sign, the prospect that the treaty will hold for the twenty-five years of its life is slight.

Of course, unexpected changes in world politics leading to the peaceful settlement of disputes, the reduction of issues among nations, and enormous increases in international cooperation and international governance might confound this prediction. Yet, it is doubtful whether even supporters of the treaty, at least those in official positions, would expect such developments.

IV. The China Problem

Consider the enormity of a decision to destroy China's nuclear facilities. The United States refrained from carrying out a similar attack on the Soviet Union at a time when to do so would have maintained the American nuclear monopoly. That monopoly cannot be restored by destroying the fledgling Chinese arsenal. If many regard the war in Viet Nam as a racist war, a conclusion from which this writer vigorously dissents, an attack on Chinese nuclear facilities would seem to most of the world to be unmistakably of that character. Such an attack, even if it succeeded, and this cannot be assumed, would not end China's nuclear ambitions. The resentment accumulated within that sleeping giant would likely produce both political and military disturbances and eventually a resumption of nuclear production. The shock generated by the initial attack would more likely deter those who undertook it than those who suffered from it. Moreover, the message conveyed to other nations in Asia, regardless of whether they thought they wished to see the Chinese facilities destroyed, would be that the United States or the Soviet Union can intervene in Asia affairs without provocation—hardly a reassuring message or one the United States should desire to convey. Even those who believe, mistakenly in my opinion, that we are morally capable of carrying out such an attack on China would not be able easily to contemplate a similar attack on a nuclear-armed India or a nuclear-armed Japan—an outcome an attack on China would do more to promote than forestall.

Furthermore, unless the attack were carried out by the United States and the Soviet Union in concert, which would not be easy to manage considering how difficult it is to secure cooperation on much less momentous issues, the single nation mounting it might drive China into the arms of the other. Only the most reckless of American administrators would entertain the prospect of thus reunifying the communist world, for, even though the Soviet Union might wish and might secretly encourage a U.S. attack on Chinese facilities, Moscow would denounce us for it with the utmost vehemence. We would be foolish to do otherwise were circumstances reversed.

One can discount the possibility that such an attack could be carried out by an international administration. The attempt to bring an international body to such a decision, by means of sophisticated arguments concerning the binding quality of a treaty on a nonsignator nation, would stir up so much horror in contemplating the act that the consensus necessary for carrying it out could not be achieved. A decision to attack China's nuclear facilities requires secrecy, stealth and guile. The nature of this decision-making process leading to an attack would help to discredit it. In any event, such secrecy is not genuinely possible for an international administration under contemporary circumstances.

Since it is most improbable at this late stage of China's program that purely conventional military operations would suffice, the attack on the Chinese facilities would have to be nuclear. It would thus constitute the first use of nuclear weapons since the Second World War. The resort to nuclear weapons toward the end of that war did not sociologically or psychologically set a precedent for the post-World War II period. To employ them now in the absence of a cause for war, other than nuclear testing by China, would demonstrate the shocking uses to which nuclear weapons could be put in the world; it would instruct nations in their utility in a way not favored by the present leaders of the United States or by any intelligent leaders who might later take office. It would at the same time legitimize the use of nuclear weapons. The impact on the structure of world politics would be one I would contemplate with the greatest concern.

V.   A Russo-American Condominium

That an effective nuclear nonproliferation treaty would require a Soviet-American condominium appears beyond question. The process of securing passage of the treaty in the General Assembly of the United Nations demonstrated the power of such a condominium, as threats, promises and pressures were employed against reluctant nations in a way not seen since Stalin's ham-handed rule of the Soviet satellites—except for Moscow's attempt to halt the liberalization process in Czechoslovakia in 1968. Although U.S. pressures and threats were less harsh and more veiled behind superficial politeness than those used by the Soviet Union, the episode is a shameful chapter in recent history, falling far short of the quality of behavior we have a right to expect between supposedly friendly and nearly equal nations.

But whence comes the warrant for such a condominium? Where is the moral authority for it? What right does either the United States or the Soviet Union have to such a role, apart from the present possession of massive nuclear systems, that would not pertain equally to Great Britain, France, West Germany, India, Japan or Communist China? At the very time when the Soviet and American blocs are breaking up and when the superiority of these two nations over the other nations of the world is diminishing, what reason is there to believe that their military ascendancy will be accepted for the next twenty-five years? What warrant is there for believing that this condominium will not be resisted, revolted against, subverted and challenged in ways that might prove even more destabilizing than the diffusion of nuclear weapons? Are we prepared to maintain this condominium by such brutalities that we would interfere with the independent political life going on in the various nations of the world? Are we ready and willing to take on the enormous responsibilities entailed? And are such responsibilities really in our own interest?

What is there in the nature of Soviet-American relations in the past twenty-five years, in the social and political systems of the two nations, in their goals in the world, in the means they use to achieve these goals, that leads us to believe they could maintain this harmony of interest in face of the unexpected problems virtually sure to arise in the near and intermediate future? Upon what basis can we believe that the national regimes in the two countries will find such harmony consistent not merely with external interests but with their interests in winning elections or maintaining regime continuity? What reason is there to believe that maintenance of such a condominium will so overshadow all other values, beliefs and commitments that the governments of both nations will maintain it with single-minded purpose? And, even were all these other doubts to be overcome, what reason is there to believe that the two regimes could overcome problems of bargaining among themselves in such a way that agreement upon spoils and responsibilities would continue to be reached over so long a time?

The condominium, in effect, did not even survive the process of negotiating the treaty, for the terms of the treaty failed to meet the minimum requirements for effective implementation over the intermediate period. Thus, faith that such a condominium could be established and maintained for a quarter-century constitutes a touching reaffirmation of the simplistic nature of politics, to wit, that the most complicated events can be manipulated from the right vantage points. This is a charming notion, but it gives more credit to social engineering than is warranted and ignores the complexities, ambiguities, absurdities and novelties that help to make up the historical process. The treaty represents a flight from reality.

VI. The Nuclear Guarantee

The third item required for the success of a nonproliferation treaty is a guarantee by the United States and/or the Soviet Union to defend the victims of aggression. This guarantee must be not merely against nuclear attack but also against conventional attack, for one virtue of a nuclear arsenal is its deterrent effect against attack by a conventionally superior foe. The United States and the Soviet Union have restricted their guarantees to other nations to cases of nuclear attack, but even these guarantees are less than automatic. India asks for a guarantee going far beyond anything we have extended to our NATO allies. And our NATO allies interpret the American "pause" strategy as a retreat from the restricted nuclear guarantee we have offered them.

The guarantee issue has been buried beneath a web of deceptive verbiage. At this point in time nuclear attacks are unlikely and, with few exceptions, wars designed to exterminate another nation are almost equally unlikely. For most situations that could arise either the U.S. or Soviet nuclear force would constitute a sufficient deterrent, apart from any question of guarantee. As long as our image of the threat is one of criminals huddling behind closed doors, plotting conquest, and preparing their massive attack in secrecy and without provocation, we will misunderstand the nature of the problem. If such a threat ever existed, and it is doubtful whether this image correctly describes even the Nazi aggressions or the Japanese attack on Pearl Harbor, then the guarantees being offered by the Soviet Union and the United States should suffice; for, although it is not clear that the guarantees would be honored in all cases, the risk that they would be honored would seem to outrun any conceivable gain "criminal" aggressors might achieve in their strikes out of the blue.

It is the unanticipated crisis, in which the equities are mixed or unclear and in which regimes or international interests arise in a not entirely controllable manner, that lies at the root of the concern of other nations. Such crises develop slowly, although they may accelerate rapidly toward the end, and provide opportunity for the guaranteeing powers to conclude that their guarantees were not meant to be extended under the prevailing conditions. This would place the guaranteed power under enormous pressure to make concessions to which it might object for legitimate national reasons, as in the case of Czechoslovakia during the Munich crisis. Otherwise the guaranteeing power would in all likelihood attempt to withdraw from its commitment in consideration of the damage that might occur to its major cities as a result of action in support of a state not vital to its interests, a regime of which it might not entirely approve, or a bargaining sequence it had come to believe, under pressure of events, was stubborn, unintelligent or unrealistic.

Surely the United States does not desire to give a blank check to other states for nuclear wars. Blank checks almost invariably work out poorly, as the Kaiser learned during the First World War and as Britain learned after its blank check to Poland in 1939. They may increase rather than decrease the prospect of war, improper political demands, and risks that no reasonable U.S. government would desire to subject the American population to. Yet, in the absence of a blank check, a conditional and vague guarantee of the sort being offered to other states by the United States and the Soviet Union may only constitute a source of pressure against the victimized or weaker state, as at Munich. Torn by our ambivalence over the concept of the guarantee, we make a weak guarantee that entails the worst of the possible political prospects. We are led into deceit, as we were when we proposed the MLF. Such deceit is not often a sound basis for policy.

It is ironic that this particular form of guarantee, deceitful though it may be, is being offered at a time when the American public is threatening to return to a new version of its prewar isolationism. The 1967 Middle East war demonstrated the extent to which the events in Viet Nam have produced a cautious response in our highest official circles with respect to crises elsewhere. The slogan of reducing U.S. commitments has gained great popularity, and most of our leading political figures vie in proclaiming their adherence to that slogan. Yet we ask the rest of the world to believe that we are making the most momentous, and grave, and risk-bearing, form of commitment, that will cover circumstances we cannot begin to visualize. We fool only ourselves, for our self-deception is transparent to most other nations of the world; the latter temporarily cooperate with our policy and with that of the Soviet Union only because of the enormous pressures we have brought to bear against them.

Worst of all, we are attempting to force vigorous countries, with proud histories and dignified cultures, to accept the position of international wards. Were they to accept such an ignoble role, there would doubtless be unfortunate domestic political repercussions. Were they to resist the role, international problems might be worsened by the very existence of the treaty we are forcing upon them. At a time when important political pressure is being applied to lower the voting age to eighteen in the United States, and when university students are demonstrating in favor of increasing autonomy in control of their institutions, we are trying to force proud nations led by civilized and intelligent adults into the role of international juveniles. Does anyone really believe that such a solution could be maintained for long?

VII.   The German Problem

The treaty involves the additional danger that it will not halt the spread of nuclear weapons but will only force the spread to occur under the worst possible auspices. The Germans endorsed the MLF not because they thought it a viable military force but because they thought agreement to the plan was the most practicable method for maintaining U.S. support and because they hoped it would evolve so as to give them a potential finger on the American nuclear trigger. They have since come to fear that German interests are being sacrificed by the United States to the concept of American-Soviet détente. This may (or may not) be a reasonable policy for the United States to follow but at least the decision concerning it should be made with a view to the potential consequences. Eventually it will become clear to the Germans that the French as well as the Americans have been playing games with German interests, and that the French are also opposed to German reunification.

It is now twenty-four years since the end of the Second World War. Germans who were fifteen years old at the conclusion of the war in 1945 are now thirty-nine. In five years all Germans under age forty-four will have been fifteen years old or less when the war ended. These Germans rightly feel no guilt for the crimes of the Nazis, and, to the extent that they may recognize the complicity of older German citizens, a complicity that is somewhat less than crystal clear, they do not recognize that any of this bears upon themselves. Although the NPT superficially applies to all nonnuclear states, Germans as well as Chinese are aware that it is particularly directed against them. They are sure to resent this unequal treatment of their great nations.

Granted that such speculations are hazardous, I would not expect the pressure for German nuclearization to become severe before 1975. The change of generations both in Germany and in her neighbors, as well as the changes in international circumstances, will by then allow what is now only latent to become manifest. In this respect it is interesting to note that resistance to Germany's signature on the NPT includes such distinguished crusaders for peace as Carl von Weizsacker, ostensibly because the treaty would interfere with Germany's peaceful uses of nuclear energy. Yet this reason, cited by many Germans, seems so weak intellectually that we must suspect latent motivations perhaps not understood by those who advance it.

If the present generation of responsible and democratic German leaders is forced to accept the onus for Germany's signature on the nuclear nonproliferation treaty, as now appears likely, the nationalistic reaction of betrayed German youths toward the nations that have treated Germany as an inferior and toward the democratic politicians who have accepted such a role could inspire a movement leading to the development of a German nuclear force under the direction of a radical regime. Acquisition of the force would not be difficult, for Germany will in the near future have the capability of producing several hundred nuclear weapons a year. Were it to be acquired during a period that is fairly quiet on the international scene, I do not believe Moscow would do more than bluster. Moreover, were the Soviets to attack in an effort to destroy Germany's nuclear force, the impact upon world politics would be shattering and the prognosis for the future less than sanguine. Neither of these projected outcomes would be consonant with American national interests, and a Soviet attack would be particularly threatening.

VIII.   Thoughts on Czechoslovakia, 1968

The preceding sections of this article were written just before the invasion of Czechoslovakia by the Soviet Union, Poland, East Germany, Hungary and Bulgaria. It would have been possible to revise the entire article to remove inconsistencies between the statements made here and those made in the body of the article, but this would indicate a degree of prescience that is not warranted. I had stated several times during the crisis that, were I a dedicated communist and a member of the Soviet Politburo, I would vote for the invasion of Czechoslovakia, but that I thought the Soviet leadership was sufficiently conservative to make that course of action less than a 50/50 contingency. The events of August 1968 showed that the Kremlin leaders were able to mobilize their courage for a vicious assault upon the freedom of the Czechoslovakian people.

Although the bloc is far from monolithic and was less than monolithic even under Stalin, the unity of the five invading powers has been forged anew. Rumania remains defiant and recalcitrant, but shows no signs of defecting. China pursues its lonely path, but, when Mao dies, it is not inconceivable that Chinese military leaders may turn to the USSR as the only power capable of supplying them with modern arms, and attempt to repair the rupture between the two countries and diminish the distance between their policies. If the Soviet Union can hold to this new tough course, it is possible that even Rumania and Yugoslavia may be brought into line. This is speculative, however, and much depends upon the events of the near future.

The situation in Czechoslovakia remains uncertain. The Soviet Union has been unable to find the kind of "stooge" government it was able to set up in Hungary under Janos Kadar. It cannot administer and run Czechoslovakia without aid from at least some remnants of the Communist Party. The truce between the Dubcek Government and Moscow is uneasy, but the prospects for Czechoslovak freedom and independence are dim. As to the reaction of the United States to the Soviet intervention, the story dispatched from Warsaw by Jonathan Randal to the *New York Times* on August 21 remains pertinent.

Eastern Europeans find it difficult to understand why the Johnson administration chose to negotiate a number of important deals with the Soviet Union during the height of the Czechoslovak crisis. Many Eastern Europeans feel that the United States is more interested in fostering its relations with the Soviet Union than in exerting influence in the area of Europe that since 1956 the United States has accepted as a Soviet sphere of influence. "The inaugural flights between New York and Moscow, the signing of the treaty to halt proliferation of nuclear weapons, and the bilateral cultural exchanges may have led the Soviet Union to intervene militarily," an

Eastern European diplomat said recently, "because the Kremlin calculated that the United States was not even morally concerned with Czechoslovakia."

Comments of this kind manifest how some East Europeans engaged in the art of international politics interpret the significance of American behavior. The Soviets by analogy may reason in the same way. Moreover, since these diplomats have many contacts with their Soviet colleagues, their observations may possibly represent some of the expressed opinions of highly placed Soviet personnel. It is not inconceivable that their advice on how to bargain with the Soviets is preferable to the generalizations about projection and the theories about mirror images that Senator Fulbright obtains from his consulting psychiatrists.

The quotation from the Randal news story confirms what intelligent observers already knew: that it was not the example of the Viet Nam conflict that led to Soviet action in Czechoslovakia, but rather the combination of the danger of internal liberalization in the Soviet Union and the threat to the bloc, particularly to East Germany. These serious problems motivated the Soviet Union to act at a time when the United States was showing an indecent desire for détente with the USSR. For the past several years, and particularly during the crisis, Washington has displayed enthusiasm for measures that are of more importance to the Soviet Union than to the United States. The nuclear nonproliferation treaty is a prime example. After having made the mistake of agreeing to the NPT, the United States might have deterred the invasion of Czechoslovakia by informing the Soviet Union privately that such an invasion would lead to the immediate cancellation of the pact and the possible nuclear armament of West Germany. That intelligent and sensible step was not taken because the Johnson Administration was in fact, despite the attacks upon it by the doves, inclined to the same sort of flabby sentimental enthusiasm for détente that motivates such people as Senators Fulbright and McCarthy.

The present sequence of events dims the prospects for the continued gradual dissolution of the Soviet bloc, although this possibility still cannot be ruled out despite the vigorous action taken against Czechoslovakia. We cannot exclude the possibility that the Soviet Union might some day attack West Germany. Although this probability is not very great, no doubt many Germans today feel less secure, as indeed they should, than they did before the Czech crisis. The fact that West Germany is a member of NATO and Czechoslovakia is a member of the Warsaw Pact does not entirely invalidate the conclusion some Germans might draw that the U.S. guarantee, either under NATO or under the nuclear nondiffusion pact, is somewhat less than certain. The innocent expressions in Washington that there is, after all, nothing we can do but accept a *fait accompli*, undercut seriously the value of both guarantees. Few Germans will miss this point, and those Germans who have been particularly associated with the concept of détente and with acceptance of the nuclear nondiffusion treaty, such as Willy Brandt of the Social Democratic Party, will be seriously injured in their political prospects because of it. The changing German viewpoint increases greatly the likelihood that Germany will some day seek nuclear weapons and that if the democratic politicians do not lead this move, radical nationalists will. Let us hope that Washington will understand this message.

One cannot draw the conclusion that the Germans will be deterred from acquiring nuclear weapons by fear that the United States will desert them during an acquisition crisis. If assurance concerning the U.S. guarantee in a political crisis is not strong enough for Germans to rely on it firmly, still their acquisition of nuclear weapons in time of tranquillity, particularly if Japan or India has already taken similar action, would hardly justify a resort to force by the USSR—except in a way threatening to the United States and world stability and therefore invoking the possibility of an American nuclear response. This probability need not be high to deter the Soviets. Their hesitancy about Czechoslovakia before the decision to invade was obvious enough that they might have been deterred by expressions of American opposition or even by indications of a Czechoslovak willingness to fight.

Thus we are confronted by the apparent (but not genuine) paradox that a U.S. guarantee which is not fully credible for a political crisis might nonetheless be sufficient to dissuade the Soviets from creating a crisis over the German acquisition of nuclear weapons. This need not be the case and much will depend upon circumstances. Included in such circumstances will be the speed with which Germany acquires at least some nuclear weapons, either through clandestine production—she will have the fissionable materials required to produce several hundred bombs a year in the 1970's—or through collusion with another nation. German possession of only a few bombs, even if they do not constitute an otherwise viable nuclear force, would probably be adequate to deter the Soviets, apart from the American deterrent. Would the Soviets have invaded Czechoslovakia if that nation had possessed a few bombs and even the most primitive kind of delivery capability? Germans are likely at some time in the future to ask themselves this question.

Assuming any initial resistance is overcome and the treaty is signed by the requisite number of States, will this automatically insure its success? Although signatures on a treaty do constitute some kind of moral obligation and thus give rise to the possibility of treaty success, the probability that the treaty will fail still remains substantial.

If the Nuclear Non-Proliferation Treaty fails to accomplish its objectives, does this necessarily imply that there were no measures against proliferation which might have been successful? On the contrary, there were alternatives. One such alternative was a joint NATO nuclear system, the nuclear force of which could have been used by the military command under, for example, two criteria: a nuclear attack by the Soviet Union or a Soviet conventional invasion and failure to withdraw after a stated interval upon demand. The proposed Multi-Lateral Force was a hypocritical substitute for such a measure and fooled no one in Europe, since the system was ineffective when compared with SAC and would have been subjected to six vetoes, including the American veto that exists with respect to the American nuclear force. As a second alternative to the treaty, the United States could have helped to build a joint European nuclear force to which it would not have been a party. Such a force might have satisfied the legitimate security needs of western European nations, and neither it nor a NATO system would have served as an incentive for smaller countries to acquire nuclear weapons. By supplying "know how" to Europe, Japan and perhaps even India, the United States would have established the lesson that nuclear forces are very difficult and expensive to acquire and depend for their acquisition upon the cooperation of one of the nuclear superpowers.

Although future qualitative developments in nuclear systems may produce nuclear proliferation anyway, even with the existence of alternatives to the treaty, one of these proposals might have delayed or possibly halted nuclear proliferation. The Nuclear Non-Proliferation Treaty, however, is being adopted too late in the process of nuclear expansion to have an even chance of success. It attempts to exclude too many nations from the acquisition of nuclear weapons, a decision that will make it even more difficult to halt proliferation because it is more likely to produce an early violation of the treaty. Moreover, the treaty negotiations themselves have forced other nations to consider nuclear policy much more systematically than they have before, and have also whetted the appetites of many other nations concerning nuclear weapons in a way that likely would not have occurred in the absence of negotiations. This increased awareness of nuclear arms and development can only make enforcement of the treaty among signatories more difficult. A further obstacle to complete acceptance of treaty obligations can be found in the certain degree of hypocrisy present in the positions of both the United States and the Soviet Union by their rejection of the demands of other nations to link specific nuclear disarmament measures with non-proliferation provisions.

If the treaty fails, its demise will lead to a number of results. It will provide an example that arms control treaties in the present world situation are ineffective. It will induce a system crisis by leading to proliferation under circumstances that involve violations of the spirit, if not the letter, of the treaty. A failure can, in all probability, induce a law-enforcement crisis.

IX.   Impact on International Law

The Nuclear Non-Proliferation Treaty raises several problems concerning the enforcement of its provisions on an international level. Each signatory to the treaty, for example, has the right to withdraw from its coverage on three months notice upon a unilateral finding and statement that extraordinary events related to the subject matter of the treaty have jeopardized the supreme interests of its country,[9] but there are no procedures in the treaty for validating this claim or for asserting a counterclaim. Suppose that a State were to withdraw on grounds that appeared to others as not related to extraordinary events or failed to give the three month notice before withdrawing because it wished to avoid counter-pressures that might produce security dangers. Some States would no doubt view such technical violations as requiring some type of enforcement action, even though none is provided for in the treaty. Suppose a non-signatory State acquired nuclear weapons. This act could well lead to demands for enforcement action under the tenuous claim that the treaty, like customary international law, binds nonsignatory as well as signatory States.[10] Yet if non-signatory States are really not covered by the treaty or any enforcement measures pertaining to it, the acquisition of nuclear weapons by non-signatories would only further emphasize the unreasonable inferiority of non-nuclear signatory States.

Consider the problem of enforcement under ambiguous circumstances. Could such enforcement take place through the United Nations? If there were a formal sanction for treaty violations, it might prove difficult to pass such a measure through the Security Council without a veto. Moreover, since many nations might not wish to establish a precedent that might be directed against them in the future, it is conceivable that two-thirds of the states in the General Assembly would not support an enforcement action. If the ultimate decision were defeated by the General Assembly, would this improve general attitudes toward the effectiveness of international law?

Suppose claimed treaty violations were not brought before the United Nations but were enforced by the United States and the Soviet Union, acting either individually or in concert. Would this be a good example for the world? Would an invasion by either nation designed to destroy nuclear facilities increase confidence in international law or would it constitute instead a lesson that the nuclear super-powers intended to maintain their monopoly? In the absence of a political and military crisis, would the threat of using nuclear force merely to prevent the acquisition of nuclear weapons by another State— on the unilateral claim that its behavior is contrary to the treaty and despite the fact that a number of other States with no superior right except prior possession are exempted—induce respect for the law? This type of enforcement procedure would appear to be unjustified and only an exercise of naked power. Either an invasion or the use of nuclear power as a means of enforcement would constitute an incredibly powerful lesson concerning the

9. Treaty on the Non-Proliferation of Nuclear Weapons, *opened for signature* July 1, 1968, art. 10, [1968]____ U.S.T. ____, T.I.A.S. No. ____, ____ U.N.T.S. ____.
10. *See* Sohn, *Enforcement of Disarmament Controls with Respect to States Which Have Not Ratified a Disarmament or Arms Control Treaty,* in 1 ARMS CONTROL AND DISARMAMENT 99 (M. Miller ed. 1968).

advantages of acquiring a nuclear system, provided this could be done under circumstances that did not invite attack. Even if the treaty violation were unambiguous and if the treaty had an enforcement clause, would not either enforcement method present a shock to the entire political and social fabric of the world?

Are non-enforceable treaties that conflict with the clear interest of major States really good ideas? Perhaps the no-strike clause in labor contracts—a much less sensitive area of law—provides a valid precedent for the Nuclear Non-Proliferation Treaty. The treaty does not contain—and the United States and the Soviet Union were unable to write into it over the resistance of the other negotiating States—the definite enforcement procedures contained in some no-strike clauses. Instead, the treaty merely emphasizes the unequal positions of the signatories. Its effectiveness thus rests in part upon its morally compelling character, although the distinctions between signatory States do not conform to any reasonable system of classification. It is inherently capricious and arbitrary; in this respect, as in others, it sets a bad precedent for international law.

The probable failure of the treaty can only induce disrespect for international law by those who do not appreciate either that the treaty may not have been violated in a precise technical sense or that it was not meant to be enforceable. While in operation, it will undermine respect for the law because of its arbitrary system of classification. Contrary to delaying proliferation, the treaty may only hasten this result. Moreover, if the treaty eases the path of radical nationalists into government office, these regimes are likely to become disruptive elements to the stability of international law. If the treaty is simply used as a pretext to forcibly prevent other nations from acquiring nuclear weapons, still further damage to the bases of international law can be expected. In an era of nuclear development, a stable international legal system is needed. Some method of checking the spread of nuclear arms must be found which will, at the same time, preserve the integrity of the international system. The Nuclear Non-Proliferation Treaty appears to be misconceived for both these purposes and actually presents a threat to the prospects for a successful system of international law.

PART TWO
Great Issues in Foreign Policy

Introduction

THE FIRST ARTICLE in this section is concerned with changes in American perspectives on the Soviet Union and détente. In it I attempt to show how views held by the public and even by an educated élite tend to be overreactions to the demonstrated inadequacies of past beliefs. Although written in 1964 and published in 1965, there is little that would have to be changed in it.

It is a balanced view of Soviet objectives. Interestingly, as one can see in the excerpts from the article on the nuclear nonproliferation treaty (in the previous section), even I gave credence to wishful thinking during the crisis before the Czechoslovak coup of 1968 despite my own statements to the effect that Soviet interests dictated their intervention. Although I had been aware of, and had pointed out to interlocutors, the parallel to 1956 in Hungary when Russian troops withdrew only to re-enter that unhappy country again, I desired so much to believe that Soviet policy had meliorated and that the cold war and the arms race would end that against my better judgment I expected Soviet nonintervention. Although it is true that I was not dogmatic in this forecast, it indicates the extent to which even a relatively objective analyst can succumb to hope.

I wrote the second article, "United States Foreign Policy in a Revolutionary Age," in 1961. It represents a liberal interventionist point of view, but there are at least some places in this article that do not entirely stand the test of time. The comments on the danger in Berlin or the danger posed by Communist Cuba have not been validated by subsequent developments. Whether I merely overestimated the threat or the watershed of the Cuban missile crisis defused the Berlin situation and, at least for a significant period of time, undercut the credibility of the Castro regime in Latin America is a subject that can be hotly debated and about which different perspectives may legitimately be held. However, the argument for removing American bases from Japan still seems valid. Despite the obvious military utility of the bases in Japan and, in particular, of American control of Okinawa, the political penalty which is being imposed on the present Japanese regime seems excessive. Moreover, the American presence is a constant irritant in Japanese politics and prevents the Japanese from assuming their legitimate role in the Asian sphere. There are times when some security risks must be run for valid political purposes. The suggestion on U.S. investments in Latin America seems very pertinent.

The two selections by Senators Fulbright and Church represent the new isolationism. Fulbright's arguments are treated later in my review of his book from which the selection is taken. A few comments may be made about the article by Senator Church. The senator writes, "How we can demonstrate faithfulness to our commitments by honoring dubious promises to the Saigon generals while blatantly violating our treaty commitments in the Western Hemisphere—as we did in the covert intervention against the Arbenz government in Guatemala in 1954, the Bay of Pigs in 1961, the Dominican Republic in 1965—is beyond my understanding."

The Senator's understanding obviously is not far reaching. What concerns other countries is whether the United States will support them if they are subjected to an internal war abetted by external attack. The interventions in the Western hemisphere have nothing to do with American credibility in that respect. In any event, the senator distorts the record of American policy and oversimplifies the problems.

Although John F. Kennedy's use of the American fleet off the Dominican Republic prevented the maintenance of a Trujillo-type regime on that island, the military coup in Peru taught him how difficult it was consistently to oppose military and authoritarian regimes effectively. Indeed his attempts to use pressure in cases of that type usually only stirred up nationalistic resistance in Latin America. Although I would not defend complacency in support of corrupt or authoritarian regimes, Senator Church's generalizations do little to illuminate policy issues.

If the outcome of the Vietnamese war is very bad for the United States and if we are unable to provide assurances to the nations of Southeast Asia, the senator may be right in a subsidiary contention. We might at least give the impression of both an inability to intervene effectively and a lack of will to do so. Yet the senator assumes too much when he argues that "All we have proved in four years of bitter, inconclusive warfare is that, even with an army of over 500,000 Americans, we cannot win a victory for an unpopular and incompetent regime against a disciplined, nationalist insurrectionary force." Similar comments were made about the Greek regime in 1947, and yet the Communist insurrection there was defeated. The British succeeded in Malaya even within a colonial framework. The Huc revolution was defeated in the Philippines within the context of a corrupt political system (although there was a popular and effective president). Despite all the mistakes that have been made in Vietnam, we are achieving a military victory that may be lost for reasons of domestic politics.

What bothers me about the senator's point of view is not that he is necessarily wrong about the intervention. Conceivably a bad decision was made. I dislike, however, the degree to which the senator finds totalitarian regimes acceptable for Asians and the unconscious paternalism that underlies this attitude. Even if we agree that the conditions for western-style democracy do not fully exist in Southeast Asia, there is much to be said, at least comparatively, for moderately corrupt and authoritarian regimes which are incapable of suppressing political dissent or local autonomy as alternatives to totalitarian regimes.

Although our abilities to predict the future must always be held in at least mild contempt, the paternalistic argument that totalitarian regimes are necessary for development has little empirical evidence to support it. According to the senator, "With our support, repressive governments in Brazil and Greece and a conservative government in the Dominican Republic, to cite but a few examples, have successfully held down popular aspirations for social and economic change." Surely it is a cross to bear for any honest liberal that the United States is not in a situation where it can freely oppose repressive governments such as the present one in Greece. However, I would like to know on the basis of what evidence the senator argues that the governments in Brazil and Greece "have successfully held down popular aspirations for social and economic change." There is some evidence, at least in the case of Brazil, that the previous government was doing less in the way of development and economic reform. Moreover, in what sense was the Goulart regime in Brazil a reforming regime? In what sense did Ho Chi Minh represent progress?

I wonder whether, for instance, Senator Church would like to compare the economic development rate in Communist Cuba, despite the reported $400,000,000 of yearly aid by Russia, with the now self-sustaining economic growth rate in Taiwan or even in South Korea, despite the military pressure and the disruption from North Korea. To cite two cases which are perhaps even more comparable, I wonder if Senator Church would like to compare the economic growth rate in western-allied Iran with the growth rate in revolutionary Iraq. I do not believe that the evidence would sustain the senator's thesis that such revolutionary regimes as Iraq and Cuba release the desires of the masses of people for social change and economic progress. The article by Albert Wohlstetter is a consideration both of immediate problems with respect to Vietnam and the general problem of bureaucracy and intervention in revolutionary wars. As Wohlstetter points out, there was a great discrepancy between our objectives and our means in Vietnam. The case of Vietnam points up one of the difficulties of foreign policy decision-making in a democracy. In 1962, I went to Washington to argue to people in the Kennedy administration that they either had to withdraw from Vietnam while their commitments were small or to engage in a major political reorganization and reform in Vietnam and a major escalation at once. This advice was ignored for strong political reasons. If Kennedy had agreed to withdraw, he would have been accused of appeasement and would almost surely have lost the 1964 election. A massive escalation before the demonstrated failure of the then current American intervention would have been very difficult to explain to the American public. Instead he pursued the one policy that I argued was sure to fail—a policy of continual small escalations to which the North Vietnamese would find it easy to respond. When the United States did intervene in force, it fought a conventional rather than a counter-guerrilla war. In addition, the practice of rotating personnel insured that field grade officers would be shifted as soon as they learned their jobs. Consequently, what is remarkable is not that the United States has not won a military victory before now but that it has achieved an impending military victory that apparently it cannot consummate for political reasons.

The Vietnam situation has demonstrated, as did that of Korea, that the American public has no patience for a long, drawn-out war being fought for moderate objectives. As was true after the Korean War when we refused to intervene in Vietnam in 1954, the Vietnamese venture may very well, in the absence of creative statesmanship, lead to an American retreat from support for threatened regimes and that policy may eventually be followed by another shift in opinion under new circumstances. It is difficult for us to remember that the boost in the 1947 defense budget from 11 to 13 billion dollars was viewed as a move toward a preventive war budget. The climate of those times has been forgotten, as we have also conveniently forgotten the climate immediately after the Korean war. As Santayana has said, "Those who do not understand history are condemned to repeat it."

Why, if the Communist world is not monolithic, must the United States organize to oppose the advances of Communism? Because there is no certain or clever answer to this question we enter the realm of the ambiguous. Before the Second World War, the interventionists argued that if Hitler conquered Europe, he would then conquer Africa, the rim of which approached the bulge of South America, which he would then invade and conquer, finally to move up toward the North American continent. Intelligent isolationists such as Herbert Hoover pointed out the absurdity of this thesis, given the then existing technologies. However, if Hitler had conquered Europe, Fascism which was then viewed as the wave of the future, would have spread through Latin America. There were also large numbers of hopeful Fascist movements in the United States supported by respectable people such as the wife of Colonel Lindbergh. The texture of American politics would have changed in a way extremely bad for American values. The security of the United States in a hostile world would have been diminished. Let me suggest, although I cannot prove and cannot even take the space to state in detail, that in the absence of creative statesmanship an American defeat in Vietnam may have very broad consequences for the texture of future world politics. The impact of an American retreat will not be lost on India or Japan. Even those Europeans who demand that the Americans get out of South Vietnam will accuse us of unreliability and lack of credibility if we do so.

Perhaps what stability has returned to Southeast Asia is at least partly the consequence of the American escalation in Vietnam in 1965. One might ask whether Indonesian army resistance to the attempted Communist coup in 1965 would have been effective (whether as many officers would have rallied to the non-Communist cause and whether those who did so would have had as much hope) in the absence of political expectations related to the American escalation in Vietnam or whether political leaderships in Thailand and Malaysia would not already have been making accommodations with the Communist forces in Asia in its absence. Again, these are not questions to which definite answers can be given, for the evidence to "prove" such propositions does not exist; but they surely raise interesting and important issues.

If Southeast Asia falls, the Soviet shadow will incline more heavily on Europe. One of the most significant events in recent political history was the Soviet invasion of Czechoslovakia in 1968. The shock throughout the Western world was strong; the event undercut the basis of General de Gaulle's foreign policy; and many Western liberals viewed the event as demonstrating the bankruptcy of Russian policy. These liberals pointed to the effects in the Italian and French Communist parties and disavowals by the latter of the Soviet invasion. It seems to me that many of the immediate effects were mistakenly perceived. The French Communist Party found a strong pro-Soviet backlash among its own supporters. The Russian public, and apparently great sections of the intelligentsia, unlike in the Hungarian crisis of 1956, gave at least passive assent and in many cases active support to Soviet policy (a situation asymmetric with the American). The invasion itself, unlike the American venture in Vietnam, at least met quick military success. Although the result is not yet certain, the "salami" tactics of the Russians—the taking of large objectives in successive small slices—have been reestablishing hardline control within the Czechoslovak Communist Party. The masses of ordinary Czechoslovaks, however, apparently remain revolutionized, with large numbers tuning in on the rebroadcast of Chinese programs from Albania. Whether these effects will continue for a long time, thus creating enormous difficulties for the Soviet Union and the new pliant Czech leadership, is difficult to say. The "salami" tactics now being applied to the party leadership may fail with the public or may merely take longer. However, the dismay in the West has quickly been dissipated. The liberals have overlooked their own predictions in their eagerness to reach arms control agreements with the Soviet Union. Moreover, the Soviet Union, beset by troubles with the Chinese on their mutual border, has been making overtures to the West and even to the West Germans.

Yet either success in the Czechoslovak venture or a failure that creates internal regime problems eventually may impel the Soviet Union toward more expansive ventures in Europe. This might be particularly true if a younger and more vigorous leadership comes into office. Developments of this kind are not genuinely predictable and they depend upon a number of contingencies which can hardly be spelled out in advance. There is a major problem, however, with the complacency of the West, with its willingness to accept the view that Soviet ambitions are not limited only immediately but in the long term view as well. Much depends upon how we respond to Soviet ventures, how we press upon their weaknesses, how we build up our own strength, and upon how we maintain our strategic position (a subject which will be considered in the next section of the book).

There are obviously dangers to be avoided as well as opportunities to be seized. As usual, however, Western policy is largely responsive; it avoids attempts, some of which are suggested in my paper on "U.S. Foreign Policy in a Revolutionary Age," to reshape the world according to our own desires.

It would be wrong to object to attempts to reach agreements with the Soviet Union. Many agreements, particularly in arms control, if reachable, would be highly desirable. There is, however, a curious unwillingness to regard ourselves to be in a competitive position, a fear that pursuit of our own ideals may close the door to agreements that are reachable. This involves an underestimate of the Soviet Union and a mistaken perception of its view of the world.

Soviet policy in the past has never operated on mere sentiment. It is unlikely to do so in the future. As Maxim Litvinov stated, "We Marxists are the last who can be reproached with allowing sentiment to prevail over policy." Or, as another spokesman put it, "Our security does not depend upon paper documents . . . ." After the Munich settlement in the autumn of 1938, Potemkin, the undersecretary of the Foreign Office, said to Coulandre, the French ambassador to Moscow, "This means the fourth partition of Poland." The Russians obviously were not put off by the Anti-Comintern Pact or by the vicious vituperation—for instance, calling them inhuman beasts—that was put out by the Berlin radio. We underestimate the Russians gravely when we act like school boys on good behavior. As Sir William Hayter pointed out, bargaining with the Russians is like putting a coin in a slot machine. Sometimes something comes out and sometimes not. It sometimes helps to kick or bang on the machine but it never helps to argue with it. Although this is obviously a metaphor not to be taken literally, there is much wisdom in the observation.

If the world becomes hostile to American values and American influence and security, even if the growth of Communist influence and values is not monolithic, I do not think that American reactions to this would be liberal (at least in the sense in which I use that word) or that our military expenditures in the long run would diminish as a consequence; on the contrary, I think they would increase greatly. This would be even more true if the Soviet Union preempts the Chinese nuclear force and establishes greater control over local Communisms. The threat of living in such a world would bring to the surface less generous American characteristics and suppress the more generous. Although many liberals are right to point out the damage that the Vietnamese war has done to the texture of American politics, they overlook the damage defeat may do. The efforts of the American administration to find an honorable solution rather than a surrender appears essential.

In an article in *Foreign Affairs*, Clark Clifford refers to the unwillingness of many Southeast Asian countries to send additional forces or combat forces to South Vietnam. He cites this as evidence that they do not accept the domino theory. His selection of information appears inspired to support the partisan political position he assumed in his article. The evidence he presents shows only the extent of domestic political opposition to involvement in Vietnam; it is not evidence of the importance that the leaders attach to the area. It is only natural that they wish the United States to assume the political risks. There is, indeed, as Mr. Clifford must know, much evidence in the form of private political statements to prove that the leaders of the countries he cites do regard the American presence in Vietnam as extremely important. If the domino theory is not accepted in the mechanical sense, there is much evidence to suggest that the leaders in the area do accept it as a major and dangerous tendency if the United States is defeated. Even Premier Sihanouk of Cambodia, who reacts so violently to American policies in Vietnam, has stated privately that it is extremely important that the United States not withdraw entirely from Southeast Asia.

If the manner of settlement of the Vietnamese War is important, what are the major issues connected with it? Is it possible to transform the military strife of a civil war into the political strife of a constitutional system as Averill Harriman apparently argues in the interview by Hedrick Smith. The mission of General Marshall to China after the end of the Second World War foundered on this problem. An attempt was made to impose a coalition government on two contending forces both of which were organized according to the principles of democratic centralism. The agreements of both sides to abide by a cease fire were intended to prevent either American withdrawal of support from the Nationalists or American intervention against the Communists. Neither side, however, thought (and in my opinion rightly so) that a stable coalition was possible. Thus the cease fire was continually violated because each side sought advantages within the limitations necessitated by their efforts to maintain the viability of the Marshall mission at least for a time.

Ambassador Harriman speaks of the experience with coalition governments in France and in Italy, where large Communist parties coexist in a constitutional framework. He does not mention that these parties have not carved out military enclaves of their own which they control. The Communist parties of France and Italy survive in part at least because of the relatively democratic structure of the constitutional systems in the two countries and of the democratic methods of the governmental parties. The democratic parties survive because the Communists never controlled the armed forces and the interior ministries.

The analogy which comes closer to the situation of Vietnam is that of Laos. The coalition government which functioned briefly gave the Communist forces some influence over policy in all of Laos, but the areas controlled by the Pathet Lao were not permeable to government writ. The situation would probably be similar in South Vietnam if the suggestions of Ambassador Harriman were followed. If the agreement, unlike the case in Laos, is effective, the Communists would have influence over the government of all of South Vietnam but the government would have no influence in the areas controlled by the Viet Cong. Thus, Communist or pro-Communist forces would be allowed to organize politically in the areas controlled by the government but the areas controlled by Viet Cong would remain under the monolithic control of the Viet Cong. No political opposition would be allowed there, a process of *Gleichschaltung* which occurred in North Vietnam after the 1954 settlement, despite agreements to the contrary.

Perhaps, even so, this is a risk that ought to be run and can conceivably be overcome, considering the awful costs of the war and the obvious political needs of the United States for termination. If so, the composition of the non-Communist elements of the government and the degree of influence of the Viet Cong within the national government become crucial issues, for if the influence is sufficiently strong they may be able to disrupt activities generally while merely waiting two or three years for complete American withdrawal to start the war over again or to disrupt the government from within. If the United States is interested not merely in saving face but in responding with some degree of honor and concern for its interests, it has an obligation not to gloss over these questions as Ambassador Harriman has, but to insist upon a settlement that provides the South Vietnamese government with some opportunity to maintain a non-totalitarian system in South Vietnam.

It is somewhat relevant to remember that the Laotian settlement negotiated by Ambassador Harriman had many of the same defects as the kind of settlement he is recommending for South Vietnam. Many trained observers believe that North Vietnamese military pressure on Laos has been relatively mild only because of the direction of North Vietnamese attention to South Vietnam. As the fighting diminishes to some extent in the south and as the North Vietnamese turn their attention to Laos again, perhaps as a bargaining lever for revising the earlier agreement, the defects of the settlement are becoming even clearer.

Yet it is important to limit American involvement in the war. The previous overinvolvement of the United States in the conduct of the war not only removed from the South Vienamese government any incentive to clean up its own house but increased the difficulties of doing so. The clear intention of the United States to transfer to the South Vietnamese a major share of the job of solving their own problems is an extremely desirable decision. The extent to which the South Vietnamese government should be broadened requires careful political analysis. Unless the government is sufficiently cohesive and strong, its political processes will be disrupted when faced by an almost monolithic Viet Cong. Whether broadening the political base of the government will permit greater unity or create greater disunity is not a question I feel capable of answering. But I doubt that this question has been raised in any serious way by Ambassador Harriman.

The Nixon administration, some of whose policy decisions appear foreshadowed in the Kissinger article, has apparently decided that it prefers to continue unilateral withdrawals to arriving at a political settlement which undercuts the political chances of the South Vietnamese regime. I believe that this decision is in better accord with the practicalities and the moral issues involved than the suggestions made by Ambassador Harriman. If the North Vietnamese are not prepared to arrive at a political settlement which gives the Saigon regime a reasonable chance of surviving while providing the Viet Cong an opportunity to engage in political activity in the new regime, then it seems preferable to thrust upon the South Vietnamese the major responsibility for determining their own fate than to force them into a *cul de sac*.

Although a political settlement would appeal to the American sense of politics, it rests on a kind of abstract legalism. There are other ways of settling issues. The guerrilla war in Malaya simply died out. The Greek civil war dribbled to a stop. It is not inconceivable, although it is far from certain, that the same thing can happen in South Vietnam. The outstanding political—not military—requirement for the United States consists of a major reduction of the American military commitment. There would not likely be great public opposition, and there might even be substantial public support, for some military and economic aid to the Saigon regime, even including some military advisors and special military units. The abstract desire for an agreement *per se* might force the United States into an unnecessary defeat. A political settlement based on an agreement is desirable only if the terms are desirable and only if there is a not unreasonable prospect for maintaining them.

One last issue to be discussed is values. Much of the current polemic is based on the assumption that interventionism is a conservative or establishment policy. Yet it was the Kennedy administration, with its involvement in the overthrow of President Diem to more readily prosecute the war, that committed the United States. This policy of concern for the political autonomy of other areas of the world is not illiberal, even when the motivation is mixed (there are strategic interests also). The fact that many of these areas are colored does not mean that any kind of regime is good enough for them or that we should be entirely unconcerned about them (although there are obvious limits to our ability to intervene effectively or to the price we can be expected to pay). I find it strange that a racist senator, such as Fulbright, whose Republican opponent publicly stated in the last campaign that he would have voted for civil rights legislation the senator opposed, has been able to seize the mantle of liberalism on this issue.

I do not accept the judgment of arrogance. There are surely some arrogant people who favor interventionist policies. Yet the arrogance for the most part lies in the eyes of the beholders. Consider, for instance, the arrogance of Senator Fulbright in arguing that President Marcos of the Philippines was paid off for his support of American policy in Vietnam, although the senator is well aware that most leaders of Southeast Asian countries do not want the United States to get out. Senator Fulbright more recently accused George Meany, president of the American Federation of Labor and Congress of Industrial Organizations, of accepting a "pay-off" for its support of the Vietnamese policies of the Kennedy-Johnson administrations. Meany has for long been a well-known supporter of the Vietnamese war. The payments to which the senator refers were made by the Agency for International Development under contracts with the American Institute for Free Labor Development in Latin America, the African-American Labor Center and the Asian-American Free Labor Institute, all subsidiaries of the AFL-CIO. These organizations support the development of free labor unions in other areas of the world, a policy Meany supported before he received any government funds and which the United States independently supports. Yet, when this was pointed out, Senator Fulbright said that "perhaps the term pay-off was too strong and I'll withdraw it if it is—although I think it amounts to the same thing." In short, all who disagree with the senator receive pay-offs. The only people acting for good or true motives are those who support the senator. If this is not arrogance, then I find it difficult to know what is.

8. Changes in United States Perspectives on the Soviet Union and Détente

MORTON A. KAPLAN

Nature of the Détente

What is meant by *détente*—a term generally used in an exceedingly obscure and ideological fashion? In what ways may the détente affect the normative structure of the world? My conclusion, which I now anticipate, will be that the term implies too great a disjunction with the immediate past, at least in terms of objective conditions, if not of attitudes toward these conditions, and that, although conditions have changed, our attitudes toward them have changed even more, and perhaps in some misleading ways.

The term *détente* is, of course, contrasted with the term *cold war*. No doubt if one reads newspaper editorials, public speeches by our political leaders, and memoirs these contrasts have real meaning. Use of these terms, however, has obscured certain kinds of fundamental political processes and has confused short-term system needs, which produced consonant policies on the part of the blocs, with longer-range national motivations which would be extremely difficult to substantiate.

The American cold war image of the Soviet Union was that of a conspiratorial octopus engaged in a program of world-wide revolutionary activity and preparing for ultimate world conquest by military means. No doubt the objective of military conquest was not entirely excluded by Stalin. He is quoted by Djilas as saying, "The war will soon be over. We shall recover in 15 or

20 years, and then we'll have another go at it."[1] Although a nation can prepare for an event 15 or 20 years in the future and although this quotation tells us something of Stalin's mentality, there is an enormous gap between that kind of long-term objective and the meaningful decisions of foreign policy in a short-range time scale. Indeed, if anything, the quotation helps to discredit the notion widely held in the West in the late 1940's to the effect that an unprovoked Soviet military attack was imminent or, if deterred, was deterred by the American nuclear monopoly. The evidence would seem overwhelming that Stalin had no such short-term objectives, that despite the superiority of Soviet conventional forces, Stalin's main immediate objectives were rebuilding the Soviet Union and re-establishing Russian spheres of influence in zones bordering on the Soviet Union. Stalin strongly resisted Yugoslav demands for Soviet support on the question of Trieste. The Communist parties in France and Italy cooperated in holding down demands for wage increases to rebuild both countries until after the Trotskyite-inspired Renault strike in France. Only after Communist expulsion from the cabinet in both countries (following Marshall Plan proposals) did Communist Party behavior in both countries become consistently disruptive for the economy. The Greek civil war was largely supported by Yugoslavia and Bulgaria and, to the extent that we can trust Yugoslav accounts, was resisted to some extent by Stalin. The Soviet Union gave little aid to the Chinese Communists.[2] In 1949, the Russian embassy was the only major embassy to follow the Kuomintang nationalists from Peking to Canton, while the American and British embassies remained in Peking. Even during the retreat, the Soviet Union was carrying on complicated diplomatic negotiations with the Kuomintang régime.

This is a picture which runs counter to the cold war images of the 1950's. The alternate picture—the one generally accepted in the United States—cites the Soviet presence in Iran in the postwar period and support for the Tudeh party, the civil war in Greece, the economic disruption that occurred after late 1947 in France and Italy, the formation of the Cominform in the fall of 1947, the Communist take-overs in eastern European countries in 1947 and 1948, the coup in Czechoslovakia in 1948, the spy trials, the Berlin blockade, and finally, the Korean war of 1950. All of these moves fit in with the conspiratorial hypothesis, as do the revolutionary efforts, including the coup attempt in Indonesia, in Southeast Asia beginning in 1948.

The Communists, of course, present a different picture. They point to the shutting off of lend-lease by the United States before the end of the Second

1. Milovan Djilas, *Conversations with Stalin*, New York, Harcourt, Brace & World, Inc., 1962, pp. 114–115.
2. They did permit the Chinese Communists to seize the Japanese arms piles in Manchuria. It is quite conceivable that Stalin simply remembered the fiasco of Shanghai in 1927, when the Comintern ordered the Chinese Communists to bury their weapons and the Kuomintang took advantage of the situation to execute as many of the Communist leaders as they could capture.

World War, to the exclusion of the Russians from the Japanese occupation,[3] to our recalcitrance on the problem of Poland, to the Marshall Plan and the consequent elimination of the Communists from the governments of Italy and France, to the rehabilitation of the German economy and Bizonia, to the Truman Doctrine, and, finally, to the Brussels pact and NATO to which, in their account, the Cominform and the Warsaw Pact were mere responses.

Both these pictures—and indeed the current picture of détente—overlook the situational components of policy. The immediate postwar period left Europe in a state of rapid flux, without social, political, or economic stability. This fluidity created risks and also provided opportunities for both the United States and the Soviet Union. Rapid shifts—too rapid—in the constellation of political forces were possible. The instability of the external environment required reactive and interventionary policies.

That interventions or reactions were required by the situation lest too drastic a shift in the required constellation of forces occur does not imply that every action which was taken can be fully accounted for by this need. The situation provides a constraint on policy; it does not preclude alternative decisions or consonant decisions taken for different reasons. Nonetheless, even if this gross constraint cannot fully account for the policies followed and the positions taken, it is true that no explanation eliminating this factor can begin to explain the history of the postwar period. One could thus view the 1945–1950 period as one in which situational factors created opportunities for bloc formation and bloc consolidation. The period 1945–1950 was the period of the growth of structure of the emerging international system.

The period 1945–1950 was also the period in which the wartime images of the world and, in particular, of the Soviet Union had to be readjusted. The main wartime image was an image in which the victorious and "democratic" allies would reconstruct a new world while holding down the vicious fascist states. This simple-minded picture could not survive the end of the war, for, at the end of the war, the United States and the Soviet Union discovered a fact that could no longer be ignored. Each was the greatest potential threat to the other, to its image of the world, and to its own internal stability. And each faced a highly unstructured world which was susceptible to rapid change if either nation did not quickly counter the moves of the other. Thus the hopes for postwar cooperation of the victorious allies were frustrated. Frustrated hopes rarely find their expression in realistic analysis. If the cooperative image of the world had to be rejected, then a villain had to be discovered. And it was not sufficient to discover a real villain—that is, a nation with a totalitarian political system—but a villain whose every move represented an unprovoked step in a cynical and aggressive plan to conquer the world.

3. These, of course, countered what the Russians did in late 1944 and 1945 in the occupied eastern European nations.

Seen more realistically, two processes were going on. One was a process of bloc development and consolidation which was necessitated by the structure of the postwar period; accompanying it was the new structure of belief that to some extent functioned not as a representational picture of the world as it was, but as an explanation or rationalization of the frustrated hopes of the war period.

There was a third process that helps to place the other two in better perspective. This is accounted for by the internal structure and organization of the Soviet Union. If the image of the Soviet Union in the late 1940's as a nation striving for world conquest through subversion and military war is a caricature, there are, nonetheless, aspects of the Soviet Union that give some credence to a more moderate version of this analysis. The goals pursued by any actor function both with external opportunity and with internal resources. The average citizen, for instance, does not attempt to buy the world's leading newspaper, but if he possessed enough money he might develop this ambition. It is a well-known phenomenon, and one that really should not require further explanation (were it not for the crudity of the literature on the subject) that latent or even entirely unanticipated goals rise to the level of consciousness and attempted implementation upon the concatenation of favorable opportunity and internal potentiality.

In the 1940's the Soviet Union possessed a party apparatus that permitted a genuine degree of international direction. No doubt if a Deminform were possible, the United States might find itself giving directions to satellite parties in uncommitted areas of the world. This means is not available to us and we must proceed, where we desire to influence events, through other instrumentalities. That kind of instrumentality—the party instrumentality—was open to the Soviet Union; it does not require any devil theory of history to infer that upon suitable opportunities it was used. It is one thing, however, to acknowledge the existence and even the use of such instrumentalities, and it is quite a second thing to derive the conspiracies that occurred merely from the existence of that apparatus.[4] We are always faced with the question of why an event occurred when it did.

For instance, why did the Czech coup take place in 1948 and not in 1945, even though the Soviet Union could have maintained military control in 1945? Obviously, motivations other than merely the motivation to create a Communist state in Czechoslovakia operated upon the Soviet leadership. In cases of complex motivation, where perhaps no single motive is sufficient to produce the event that occurred, historical evaluation and explanation is more difficult. One thing does seem plausible though: the explanation that these events had long been planned in advance is not good enough. That

4. See Morton A. Kaplan, *The Communist Coup in Czechoslovakia*, Research Monograph No. 5, Center of International Studies, Princeton University, January 4, 1960, for an analysis of the way in which external circumstances and opportunity possibly combined to bring about the Czech coup in 1948.

Soviet ideology and Communist organization might create certain kinds of latencies toward activities of this kind may be accepted, but latency is not manifestation. The thesis being argued here is that the disorganization of the world system moved these latent objectives into the manifest area. The frustrated hopes of the war years gave rise to the overinterpretation of this behavior. If this explanation is plausible, it would then follow that although the democratic centralist nature of Communism played a major role in the kinds of disvalued activities in which the Soviet Union participated, Stalinism or terror as such, even though an internal component of the Soviet régime, did not. If this is so, one runs the risk of deriving from putative ameliorations of Soviet internal politics an amelioration of foreign policy that may be unrelated, at least in a direct way.

There are two qualifications that I would like to make. The first is that although the change, or the seeming change, in Soviet foreign policy was not to any great extent a direct product of evolution in the internal structure of the government, an internal crisis which produced a hardening of the régime might produce a temporary hardening of Soviet foreign policy. This would be difficult to predict, however, for the very opposite might occur. The new Soviet régime might need increased détente to secure internal public support, particularly with respect to the hardening of internal practices. Although the example is no precedent because Beria appeared to have been committed to internal liberalization in terms of the apparent drift of his policy, Beria—perhaps because of his bad reputation—apparently was prepared to go farther toward a solution of the German problem that would have been acceptable and even desirable to the West than was any subsequent Soviet leader.

The other qualification involves the relationship between latent and manifest goals. The order in which Hitler's conquests were carried out, and even to some extent the fact that they were carried out at all, depended upon circumstances. However, his goals were well articulated and he was actively searching for and attempting to create circumstances which enabled him to execute his expansionist objectives. This does not imply that he wanted the world war he got. He much preferred to pick and choose among his adversaries, to eliminate them one at a time, and to achieve his objectives systematically. He may even have been sincere in promising to protect the British Empire after Germany's territorial and colonial objectives were satisfied, although this would have meant not a genuinely independent Britain but a satellite Britain. Still, even if Hitler's plans for war were not those of immediate world war, they were of a nature which perhaps did call for world war as a defensive reaction by the other powers. Again, when the Arab states look at Israel, they recognize that they are in no position to launch a military attack against Israel today. They would be beaten. However, by maintaining a state of formal war and of armed incidents and tension, by refusing to regularize relationships, and by keeping their own people stirred up, they are keeping high the probability that should, in the future, circumstances arise which strengthen them or weaken Israel, they will be able to seize the opportunity to attack.

Therefore, the question arises, apart from the favorable character of circumstances, what the nature of the latency in Soviet objectives was. Under Stalin one could argue that extreme conservatism and caution prevailed. Despite the reputation of the Soviet Union for disruptive external activities, the Soviet Union, unlike Nazi Germany, was not engaged in a campaign of chemical dissolution and disruption of adjacent areas. Its conspiratorial apparatus seized opportunities in those areas where disruption and chaos already existed and where the alternatives would have been dangerous to the security of the Soviet Union. Stalin's objectives were long-term objectives. He did not attempt to force fate. His system, no doubt, was different from and more dangerous than the bourgeois state apparatus, for a conspiratorial apparatus was indeed an intrinsic part of the system. But it was used cautiously. Even his talk of another go in 15 or 20 years involves a timetable that was a generation distant. The operational consequences for current policy were extremely peripheral. Even the one apparent gamble he took—and this toward the close of his life—the Korean War, may be put into perspective. The operation was carried out by a third team, the North Koreans. It was an area the United States had apparently written off; American forces had been withdrawn and the area had been placed outside our defense perimeter. Congress had voted against arms aid to Korea and had overridden this vote by a margin of a single vote only after a plea from both President Truman and Secretary of State Acheson. Moreover, the operation took place when the United States was virtually disarmed. The Soviet Union apparently was so surprised by the American reaction that it was not able to attend Security Council meetings of the United Nations before the crucial votes were taken. The Soviet Union clearly had no scruples about taking over independent nations and transforming them into satellites, as the case of Czechoslovakia indicates. But its political strategy was a slow-motion strategy adjusted to its philosophy of conservatism and the limitation of its ambitions to "ripe" situations.

To state that Stalin was cautious, however, and had no intention of engaging in a frontal military assault does not mean that the situation lacked danger. Economic turmoil, political disillusionment, and lack of American military commitment would have had profound effects upon the politics of Western Europe. Those who viewed Communism as the wave of the future would have begun to make their compromises with it. And the local Communist parties and the Soviet Union likely would have begun to put brutal pressure on the Western European nations—one at a time, and after real or manufactured provocations. The Truman Doctrine, the Marshall Plan, and NATO were inspired and necessary responses to a weakness in Western organization without which Western Europe might have been lost to Communist pressure. The beliefs as to the nature of the Soviet threat, however, were awry. The Czechoslovak coup of 1948 was likely the better metaphor. Even Hitler had not intended a bold massive assault against the west, although he had contemplated war with more readiness than did Stalin.

It is important to consider some of the changes in the Soviet system that have occurred since Stalin's death and the ways in which these may affect the nature of the détente and of the processes of conflict resolution and norm formulation in the contemporary world. Before doing so it is well to state that the theme of coexistence—a theme that does imply active political conflict—was Stalin's theme, that Stalin declared that war between the Soviet and capitalist states was not inevitable, and that the Soviet Union as early as 1949 was sponsoring world-wide peace movements. Moreover, under both Lenin and Stalin, the Soviet Union had supported bourgeois nationalist revolutions, for instance, in Turkey and in China. The changes in Soviet policy to which I refer, therefore, do not affect these elements as such. They refer to the internal structure of the Communist world as it affects the implementation of foreign policy goals. I can only adumbrate these changes.

Just as the partners of the United States in the West recovered from their postwar states of destitution, so in the Soviet zone the states recovered from the ravages of war and the régimes began to gain a modicum of consent, if only in the sense that the régimes were viewed by the local population as not so bad as some of the probable alternatives. Moreover, to meet production goals, in view of the resentment of the Soviet Union by the populaces of a number of the satellite nations, some degree of nationalism and independence was required. The secret speech by Khrushchev at the 20th party congress denouncing Stalin shattered for many of the committed intellectuals of the Communist parties the myth of the infallibility of the leadership, just as the demotion of Khrushchev later further helped undermine this myth.

The consequences of the shattering of this myth have been overstated in some quarters and insufficient differentiation has been made as to which groups both in the populations and in the leaderships were affected by disillusionment, for not all were. Moreover, the degree of subsequent polycentrism can also be overstated. China always was for practical purposes a genuinely independent member of the bloc. China was further irritated by Russian refusal to give China substantial economic aid, by Russia's reneging on its pledge to aid China's nuclear development, and by other Russian activities within the bloc that ran against Chinese interests. This resulted in the split between China and Russia and helped to increase polycentrism and independence within the bloc itself. The consequences of this have not been entirely bad from the standpoint of world Communism, for the demonstration that a nation can be Communist and not completely subservient to the Soviet Union undoubtedly reduces the resistance to involvement with the Communist nations and with local Communist parties by a number of elites in underdeveloped and uncommitted nations. This same development undoubtedly increases the problems of the Soviet Union in using the bloc as a mere instrument of Soviet foreign policy. However, because the only kind of appeal China can make to the other members of the bloc is in terms of ideological dogma and revolutionary Communism—despite the extremely conservative nature of China's own foreign policy—the Soviet Union is almost required by the nature of this conflict to adhere to a more revolutionary policy than it otherwise might, even though the bloc is no longer in some ways the effective instrument of Soviet foreign policy that it once had been.

Furthermore, at least under Khrushchev, the actions of the Soviet Union were influenced by the non-conservative personality of the ruling figure in the régime. The installation of Soviet missiles in Cuba, for instance, created both a political and military threat for the United States. It threatened actively to create opportunities for revolution and intervention to Latin America, both through positive action and symbolically through the demonstration of American inability to counter this move. This action was much closer to Hitler's style of policy than to Stalin's. Unlike the situation at Munich in 1938, however, the leadership of the democratic countries still retained military superiority and also had the will to exercise the superiority. Khrushchev's gambit did not work any more than his earlier attempted nuclear blackmail in Europe. In this sense, Khrushchev's policy was even more radical and reckless than any of Hitler's between the Rhineland reoccupation of 1936 and the outbreak of war in 1939. The military occupation of Hungary in 1956 also contrasted strongly with Stalin's inaction with respect to Yugoslavia in 1948.

Thus, the Soviet Union is pictured as a nation whose bloc structure no longer created the opportunities for external intervention which existed in the immediate postwar period and whose environment also dampened these possibilities. It nonetheless behaved in a more radical way than Stalin had ever behaved. However, this attempt by Khrushchevite Russia to follow this provocative course was frustrated by American resistance. And the possibilities for aggressive foreign policy were reduced both by lack of external opportunity and by a decline in the utility of the Communist apparatus. Much Russian attention necessarily was given to rivalry with China and the struggle over control of the world Communist movement. Thus, the immediate likelihood of direct conflict between the Soviet Union and the United States was greatly diminished. The so-called détente was to a considerable extent a consequence of these factors. This does not mean that the potentialities for cooperation in some areas cannot be developed or are insignificant any more than an assessment of Soviet motivation in the late 1940's, different from the then current one, would have implied that conflict was unreal or unimportant. Yet in each case reactive public—and occasionally governmental—images have misrepresented the situation and have produced mis-estimates of the dangers, opportunities, and probable outcomes that the situation presents.

It could be argued that a similar and perhaps even more stable détente was in fact beginning to develop under Stalin's régime, despite Korea. The détente was created largely by the nature of the changes in the world, that is, by the stabilization of nations other than the Soviet Union and the United States, the reduced opportunities for external intervention in these stable areas, and the changes in the nature of the two blocs. Attitudes were changing too. It is a generation since the close of the Second World War. We no longer remember the hopes we had and the ways in which they were frustrated. Therefore, there is a tendency—almost surely wrong—to interpret the present change as a radical change. As a consequence we may tend to overestimate the nature of the change and to underestimate the potentiality for continued indirect clashes in the underdeveloped areas of the world and elsewhere.

9. United States Foreign Policy in a Revolutionary Age

MORTON A. KAPLAN

I Introduction

The following essay is necessarily oversimplified. In the first place, it attempts to deal briefly with many broad-ranging topics of foreign policy. The complexities of the problems involved in American foreign policy can barely be adumbrated. In the second place, the general line of policy recommended represents a striking departure in many respects from general postwar policy as practiced under both the Truman and Eisenhower administrations. The effort to outline the nature of the policy and to relate it to the structural features of contemporary world politics can best be carried out if the policy is presented in its most stark and simple form.

Of course, no policy can be implemented in this simple fashion, for it is not possible to obtain sufficient domestic or allied agreement. In addition, particular features of individual situations almost always require qualification of generalized prescriptions, regardless of the nature of the prescriptions, unless they are so general as to be meaningless or inapplicable. General formulations are better for establishing frameworks of attitudinal responses than for deriving detailed policy. This essay is intended primarily to indicate the changes in attitudes toward foreign policy that are desirable in today's revolutionary world.

There are many difficulties with the pursuit of American foreign policy, and it is, of course, much easier to criticize than to undertake the responsibility for formulating and executing national policy. If I were to single out, however, two general criticisms, they would be: (1) that the policy of the recent past has been more appropriate to a "balance of power" system than to a bipolar system; and (2) that policy has been more appropriate to an era in which society is static than to one in which there is rapid and revolutionary social change.

II Bipolarity and Revolutionary Change

With respect to the first criticism, that past policy has been more appropriate to a "balance of power" system, several brief observations may be made. The "balance of power" system operates on the basis of short-term alignments of a flexible nature. It is a system in which alignment preferences are based on specific and limited interests. Thus, the enemy of today may be the ally of tomorrow. The nature of regimes and of internal social conditions are indifferent to alignment decisions. And, hence, morality or sentiment, as contrasted with "interest," plays a subordinate role in the decision process. Although the system can tolerate neutrals, neutrals as such do not play an essential role in the system. Indeed, if important states essayed such a role as permanent, their decision might be quite inconsistent with the stability of the system and with their own long-range interests.

The loose bipolar system, on the other hand, depends upon the formation of blocs based upon considerations of long-term interest. The closer the value patterns of the bloc members, the easier it is to maintain the solidarity of the bloc. Clearly democratic nations could not easily function as members of the Soviet bloc. Although the converse proposition has less force, it still has some validity. NATO solidarity is strong because there are many shared values and institutional practices among most members of the organization. In addition, in the bipolar system it is not desirable to have all nations within the bloc structures. The uncommitted nations play a stabilizing role that, in a nuclear age, is of value to the blocs. The United Nations may also play a mediating role that, within limits, merits the support of the blocs.

For the reasons just enumerated, the policy of building blocs has definite limits in a bipolar age. Also, the distinction between "interest" and "sentiment" is not as compelling as in the "balance of power" age. The kinds of nations one aligns with, and the policies one pursues internationally, ought to be more closely oriented to value—or moral—considerations than was the case in the past.

If we take into consideration that the present age is also a revolutionary one in which change sweeps from nation to nation, sometimes without respect to alignment pattern, the preceding conclusion is strengthened. Blocs cannot obtain generalized support from uncommitted nations, and specific support may very well depend upon what values the bloc stands for and attempts to propagate. The solidarity of the bloc and the willingness of the populace within a nation to take those risks necessary for long-term stability in a nuclear age may depend upon the pursuit of policies that accord with basic ideals.

If we move from the confines of the model of international politics, this conclusion becomes even more compelling. The West, in particular, the United States, is on the defensive. We have become modern Canutes, attempting to hold back the tides, unresponsive to the currents of our time. In an age when new nations have been proliferating and old nations undergoing revolutionary changes, the United States has been implementing a policy designed in general to discourage radical change and to aid governments in power, regardless of the nature of their regimes, provided they are avowedly anti-Communist. The two aspects of the policy, of course, are related, for often the most anti-Communist governments are those which fear radical change at home and which are willing to join American military alliances to receive support that may bolster them against the forces making for internal change. As a consequence, in many areas of the world, the United States seems to represent reaction and a barrier to the hopes and aspirations of large masses of people. It seems to stand for corruption, inefficiency, and maintenance of the status quo. And, at least to many, the alliances it espouses raise the danger of local war for causes not understandable to large masses of the local populations.

The United States has so defined the issues that, for many revolutionary social movements, to pursue what they desire both nationally and internationally is to oppose the United States. This, of course, gives the Soviet Union great leverage. This also makes the bipolar system even more unstable than it otherwise would be. Since, in addition, many Westerners are opposed to the policies that produce these results, it weakens the ability of the United States to counter the Soviet offensive. Coalition problems increase and elements within the United States become disaffected.

The Soviet Union is an active and disturbing foe. Supported by its belief in the historic inevitably of Communism, it challenges the present structure of world politics. It is little inhibited by domestic opinion or by bloc dissidence. It is not associated with colonialism by the new nations and it can support, almost without qualification, actions designed to change the status quo radically. It holds forth the threat of nuclear war and, because it seems impervious to change or to influence, drives those who fear war to put pressure upon the West to make concessions. Along with the threat of war, it advocates disarmament under conditions that are not genuinely acceptable to the West.

Under pressure from the Soviet and Chinese threats, and faced by revolutionary changes in the world, the West retreats. Its alliances become fragile. Compromise and temporization are the order of the day. And, even in the United States, there is difficulty in mobilizing domestic opinion behind policies involving risks. The effort to halt Communism hardly seems worth the risk of nuclear war to many, particularly if a stand must be made in a remote and seemingly unimportant area of the world. It is much easier to postpone risks and to enjoy the luxuries of contemporary American life or to seek scapegoats either on the left or right of the political spectrum. After all, the hard choices can also be avoided by blaming our problems on Communist subversives or on warmongering generals. The witch hunt and the peace march are both symptoms of the breakdown and rejection of political life. They are both symptoms of an essential malaise in the West—of the absence of a unifying political ideal.

Western societies are no longer politically vigorous. Large segments of the public are complacent and desire to preserve what they have rather than to lead crusades that will transform the world. Their attitudes are largely defensive and even the protests against these attitudes are fed more by a gnawing discontent or by impotent anger than by a vision of the future. The bright hopes of the past are transformed into disillusion and bitterness.

There was a day—not too far in the history of the world—when political democratization held forth to most the hopes of redress of past grievances. It was thought that democracy shattered the chains of tradition, made man master of his fate, vanquished ignorance and poverty, and permitted a race of Prometheans to rule the world. Vain hope! It is not that democracy is worse than other forms of government. However futile the hope of self-government and thus of individual dignity, democracy comes closer to reaching these goals than any other form of government. It is consistent with economic vigor, with a standard of living and health higher than any the world has ever known, and with the freedom of man to pursue his own future as he wills rather than as the state dictates. The disillusion does not lie in the comparative lack of achievement of democracy as contrasted with other forms of government. The disillusion stems from the gap between the ideals of the democratic creed and the performance of democratic government.

We have explored the possibilities of democracy and we know that there are limitations on its ability to transform the world. It takes tremendous self-discipline to recognize these limitations as inherent in human organization and to work for limited but possible improvements. For most people, there is a tendency to become complacent about the achievements of democracy and to value personal satisfactions. Such people do not want to sacrifice in the name of an ideal that cannot be achieved. Others find their mission in fighting injustice in some abstract sense. These fasten onto the past and present "sins" of democracy; and, in their desire to punish democracy for its shortcomings, they ignore the immensely larger evils of a creed that still promises abstract justice at some future time if only it can conquer the world.

The essential difficulty of the democratic position is that it seems to deny to many, in democratic nations as well as to those elsewhere, goods that are legitimized by the democratic creed. Any political system must suffer defects. No system can be consistently true to its own ideals. Democracy is challenged in the present age in terms of its own ideals. Its inability to satisfy this challenge by present performance—and sometimes its indifference to real and pressing injustices—creates an internal opposition which cannot be suppressed consistently with the institutions and values it espouses.

Thus, within the democratic nations, there are articulate groups, with some political effectiveness, that are essentially disaffected and that are motivated to inhibit effective political action designed to maintain the security of the NATO bloc. These groups are at basis recriminatory, they are more inclined to view Western policy with suspicion because of its "sins" than they are to view Soviet policy with suspicion. They have a mistrust of capital, which they feel has alienated and exploited man, of military leaders whom they suspect of warlike aims, and of politicians who they believe desire to suppress movements for national freedom and independence. Because many of the articulate intelligentsia belong to these movements, they have a political effect disproportionate to their numerical strength. And, because they are citizens of democracies, their arguments convince many in other nations of the injustice of the democratic nations.

To describe what is necessary to rejuvenate American political life may be beyond the powers of any individual. That subject certainly cannot be considered within the scope of this paper. A few aspects of the problem as it affects the conduct of foreign policy can, however, be mentioned. The goals of American foreign policy must be derived from the basic ideals of the nation if they are to obtain sufficient support for a chance of effective implementation. The United States must begin to think not in terms of specific deals or outcomes but in terms of the kind of world in which American democracy can survive. *Realpolitik* and cynicism may once have been effective techniques for the conduct of foreign policy. If they are resorted to today at the highest levels of policy-making, they will corrode the political faith required for an effective American policy and, if necessary, for the resort to force in support of that policy.

If we enunciate policies merely to gain support and not because we are convinced of their rightness, we encourage others to raise the price of their support. If we assume a posture of strength in support of policies we are not really willing to run risks to implement, the Soviet Union is likely soon to call our bluff and expose our irresolution. If we are to act with hope of success, we must find a source of strength not merely in weapons, but also in our values and ideals.

The United States can no longer afford to be a conservative nation. Conservatism is appropriate when change threatens desirable values *and* when these values can be defended best by defensive measures. There must be an ability to weather the storm. It made sense for Franklin Roosevelt to replace "Dr. New Deal" with "Dr. Win the War." But we are no longer faced with a military conflict of relatively short duration. We are confronted with a revolution of world-wide dimensions, a revolution that cannot be halted by military measures or by temporary defeats. The United States cannot—and should not attempt to—halt this revolution. It can attempt to influence the direction this revolution takes and the values that flourish as it progresses.

Although the "Free World-Communist" dichotomy is grossly oversimplified—witness the authoritarian satrapies of the United States, such as Spain—it points to an essential truth about the present world struggle. Imbedded in the American tradition as it has developed is a belief in the right of each individual to find his own truth, provided only that he respect the rights of others to find their truths. Just as the American political process encourages the enunciation and pursuit of any political goal compatible with the maintenance of a political system permitting such a pursuit for all, the American intellectual system permits an experimental attitude toward beliefs—permits the individual to pursue his thought as best he can. There is no official dogma that circumscribes this process, that must be accepted, that cannot be tested or denied. There is a distaste for official or governmental indoctrination, and a belief that the only dignified beliefs worthy of free men are those that can withstand free and public challenge. There is the belief that the proper goal of society is the mature, free man—and that it is the object of society to provide, or at least to permit, the conditions under which such men can flourish.

The democratic system is one that institutionalizes dissent and that encourages criticism, as long as it does not attack the fundamental principle that others also, even if members of a minority, possess this right. These ideals are imbedded, even if imperfectly, in American institutions. But they are not otherwise related to class, race, religion, or nationality. If we believe in these values, we must believe in them for others as well. And, if we are moral people, within the limits of prudence, we shall not hold to these beliefs passively, but we shall encourage and support those who also subscribe to these values in other lands.

Before examining specific problems, we can summarize the three kinds of major problems facing the United States:

1. The uncommitted states are alienated and act in ways that increase the instability of the bipolar age.

2. The West has no positive set of ideals to generate a confident set of foreign policies. NATO is beset by divisions and fears. The individual member nations complacently desire to protect what they have but lack an image of a world they desire that will induce bold and purposeful programs and policies.

3. The Soviet Union and the Communist bloc constitute an active set of foes. They take advantage of the divisions in the West, and of the fears and complacencies of individual Western nations, to increase the pressure on the West and to force concessions disadvantageous to it. The Communist leaders know the kind of world they want to build and are willing to take risks to achieve their goals. Despite some internal quarrels, they achieve rea-

sonable cooperation and are able to induce reasonable domestic support. The United States must learn how to deal with the Soviet challenge and, to the extent possible, increase the problems facing the Soviet bloc both internally and externally.

There are no complete or easy solutions for these problems. But the United States must learn to cope with them in an adequate way if it is to preserve the values that underlie the American experiment.

III   The Uncommitted States and United States Policy

The passion for self-rule, for independence, applies both to groups and to individuals. Colonial existence, no matter how necessary it may seem at some times to promote still further development, is incompatible with human dignity. And although rule by a local dictatorship is far removed from the ideal, it at least extends to the group that which should also be extended to the individual. It is a necessary, if not a sufficient, condition for human dignity, and Americans ought not to be indifferent to the desire for independence, whether that desire be of the black man in Africa, the white man in Eastern Europe, or the yellow man in Asia.

ALLIANCES WITH THE UNCOMMITTED STATES

Most of the new nations are weak and backward. Their leaders remember a period of colonial subjection. They are fearful that their new independence may be compromised and are dedicated to modernizing. The problems of these new nations are enormous, and their leaders desire to insulate them from quarrels they do not recognize as their own. Moreover, they have a genuine interest in attempting to shift the burden of defense against Soviet aggression to others. They will resent any effort to commit them to objectives that divert them from modernizing or that threaten to move them toward the center of the Cold War.

The United States has, fortunately, given up the idea of creating extensive chains of military alliances that depended on the adherence of uncommitted states. This attempt frightened the leaders of many of the new nations. It brought their nations to the center of the Cold War and subjected them to Soviet political attack. The leaders did not desire this—except where internal problems or national divisions, as in Korea or Viet Nam, seemed to necessitate it. Where the populace knew of the commitment, it often misunderstood it. Counterelites opposed to the governments often used the commitments as weapons, as in Iraq. Those who thought the first problem of their nation was development viewed such alliances as a diversion of resources and effort. They much preferred an anticipated insulation from the Cold War and the opportunity to play the East and West off against each other both politically and in terms of access to investment funds.

Where conservative regimes desired alliances to support internal policies, the alliances identified the United States with the policies of these regimes. Where nationalist regimes existed, the attempt to induce them into alliances against their resistance appeared as a threat to their goals, as in Egypt.

In addition, the idea behind these alliances was unsound from the very start. Such nations had little to add in a military sense, although some of them were able to provide bases that temporarily were important. The military aid often unbalanced the economies of these states. In addition, the real and undervalued mediatory role these nations could play when uncommitted was neglected. Where they might have been bulwarks in upholding desirable principles of international law as uncommitted nations, they were instead weak, vulnerable, and temporary members of a Western alliance.

With few exceptions in the present period, military alliances with the new and largely uncommitted states will serve neither their interests nor ours. Alliances or even strong political coalitions are unlikely to work out well. We shall do best if we attempt to commit these nations to the support of universalistic principles of international law or norms of international behavior rather than to specific American interests. Economic aid and the political problems arising therefrom also will constitute an important problem area for American relations with the new and uncommitted nations. This last problem will now be considered.

ECONOMIC DOMINANCE OVER THE UNCOMMITTED STATES

Many of the uncommitted nations believe that the United States, because of its economic power, represents an economic threat to their independence. This fear undoubtedly is greatly exaggerated, but it exists even in our Canadian neighbor to the North. Whatever the economic arguments to the contrary, it would probably make good political sense to encourage at least some other countries, particularly in Latin America, to purchase controlling interests in large local corporations controlled from or owned abroad, especially those which dominate important natural resources such as oil. The United States government should attempt to facilitate the transfer of ownership and control by underwriting it to some extent.[1] This would help to circumvent extremist demands which might force nationalization under conditions that would cause political strains between particular foreign nations and the United States and that would lead to local irrational economic decisions inconsistent with American efforts to support modernization and political liberalism. Moreover, transfers of ownership and control, freely

1. John Kaplan of the Hudson Institute has suggested that this might be accomplished by eliminating tax credits for entirely owned foreign subsidiaries of United States corporations doing business in underdeveloped countries. Although this might possibly have too extensive an effect, it might well be investigated. American business ought to consider such arrangements voluntarily, as well as those in which their interests could be liquidated after a fixed period of years. Business may be deterred from such arrangements more by ideological than economic considerations.

204 : *Great Issues in Foreign Policy*

offered, might do much to dampen the entire issue and to forestall extensions of the nationalization principle that would be economically harmful or that would interfere with needed access by developing nations to the American capital market.

SOVIET AID TO THE UNCOMMITTED STATES
The United States has tended to view Soviet aid to uncommitted nations as a calamity, inconsistent with their independence and with American attempts to entice them into political or military alliances or ententes. This has reinforced the auction aspects of American relations with the uncommitted nations and it has debased American generosity. Instead, the United States should welcome Soviet aid as a substitute or complement for American aid even where we may consider the specific forms of aid undesirable. The receiving nations should be depended upon to insist on conditions that preclude major political gains by the Soviet Union. The United States should be prepared to cooperate with such efforts on the part of the uncommitted states. We should insist that the major burden of maintaining independence rest with the uncommitted states; it should not permit these nations to exploit American fears that they might not want to maintain their independence.

American aid offered merely as an alternative to Soviet aid necessarily leads to an auction that cannot be won. The Soviet Union can pick and choose its aid targets. It was always able to breech the wall of aid containment, even at a time when it was relatively weak economically, and was able to force the United States to utilize its aid in ways that were not economically rational. As the Soviet Union grows stronger economically, the problem worsens. If the United States welcomes Soviet aid as an alternative and offers it own aid without regard to securing allies, this vicious cycle can be broken.

PRINCIPLES OF AMERICAN AID—GENERAL
We can now inquire into the principles that ought to govern the extension of American aid to the uncommitted nations. Although the United States may properly give preference to nations that cooperate with it politically and deliberately bail these nations out of political difficulties, it should not attempt to buy outright support and should even discourage such support on the part of those nations where there is no popular local basis for it. In these last cases, failure to follow the suggested principle makes the regimes vulnerable to criticism for forfeiting independence and drives the opposition into an anti-American position. In general, aid should be given because we desire to live in a world where people can look forward to better lives, not because we expect political support, or even because we believe that better conditions will make Communism less likely. Indeed there is little evidence that aid will accomplish these latter objectives.

The United States and the uncommitted states do not have the same community of values or institutions that the United States and Europe have. Except where there are quite specific and compelling common interests—as in the case of South Korea, for instance—we cannot expect the uncommitted states to share our foreign-policy burdens, whatever some abstract ethical system might seem to imply. It would be foolish, therefore, to use aid as a weapon in an attempt to gain foreign-policy support. Within broad limits, aid ought not to be dependent on the external policies of the aided state— unless, of course, that state goes so far as to become a member of the Communist bloc or unless that state acts in a manner consistently disruptive of desirable principles of international order rather than merely in a manner opposed to specific American interests. Attempts to condition aid on foreign-policy support confuse the purpose of the aid, injure the national pride of the aided nations, and eventually undercut the purposes of the aid either by identifying local regimes with the United States in ways that alienate them from their bases of local support, or by driving such regimes into anti-American positions.

However, we should attempt to convince the uncommitted nations that independence and lack of commitment does not imply that they attempt to compromise the differences whenever the United States and the Soviet Union differ. If they really essayed such a role, then it would be strategically advisable for the United States and the Soviet Union to exaggerate their demands and differences; otherwise, the suggested compromises would be disadvantageous to them. And if either failed, or was unable to do this, the other would gain a strategic advantage that might destabilize the international system. The uncommitted nations must be persuaded—but not coerced by aid policy—to the extent possible, to support universalistic normative rules of behavior consistent with the kind of international system in which their own best interests will be protected. It can be argued that opposition to some specific American objectives might be a small price to pay if the uncommitted states could be committed to certain stabilizing norms of international behavior.

In applying its aid, the United States should be concerned with building the kind of world it desires to live in. Modernization, regional cooperation, and democracy undoubtedly are features of the world the United States desires for the future.

SPECIFIC PRINCIPLES OF AID—MODERNIZATION

The leaders of the new nations—in particular the educated elites—desire modernization and independence. These two goals are viewed as inseparable, for it is thought that independence cannot be maintained without modernization and that modernization can be carried out only by independent governments. The existence of dependent colonial areas or of non-modernizing independent states is viewed as a threat to the modernizing regimes.

American exhortations to act moderately, responsibly, or democratically seem, to many modernizing leaders, so irrelevant to their difficult tasks that some believe them to be hypocritical.

The disorder in the Congo and the authoritarian regimes in some of the uncommitted states shock American susceptibilities. But we may be judging these nations by the wrong standards. The historical plays of Shakespeare depict situations no better than those of the Congo; Tudor England was hardly democratic; the Spanish women treated Napoleon's soldiers more cruelly than the *Force Publique* behaved in the Congo; and the Nazi and Ustachi villainies are barely two decades old.

The nations of Europe were not built without bloodshed, corruption, villainy, and misery. But at least these nations did not have modern neighbors to set spectacular expectations for them. They could accept slow progress not only in economic development, but also in the development of a national consciousness and of a state apparatus. Their independence was not seemingly threatened by more developed and more powerful states. In the new nations national consciousness does not exist, except perhaps in inchoate form. There is no state in the European sense. Tribal ties, illiteracy, low levels of resources, production, and skills are inconsistent with the entry into the modern world that their educated elites demand. Even though considerable assistance is available to them, their task is much harder than was the task of the European nations.

Most of the European nations had considerable governmental intervention when entering the modern world. Even in England, Tudor intervention preceded Manchesterian capitalism. Many of the new nations believe they require—and in fact they may be correct—more governmental intervention in the economy than seems proper to us. But we must remember that their economic development is dependent upon political and social revolutions that can be carried out only against the resistance of powerful vested interests. In some of these states, territorial loyalties must replace tribal loyalties. In some, land reform is required. In all, agricultural techniques must be modernized. In many, there is no entrepreneurial class and, even if there were, it could not be expected to take the huge risks required to establish industry, transportation, and communication—without which no contemporary state is viewed as modern. In most, the moneyed interests—where such exist—refuse to use their money productively. Education is essential, but only the state can insure an adequate educational program. These considerations could be multiplied, but that would not be profitable. It is necessary only to point out that these new nations cannot repeat the experience of the United States. If they are to succeed in modernizing at all[2]—and this may be in doubt—there must be considerable intervention in the economy by the state.

2. When and if the modernizing elites of some of these countries discover that the attempts to modernize must fail, there may be far-reaching consequences. They may lapse into sloth and corruption. Or, in desperation, they may resort to the most radical of measures.

Morton A. Kaplan : 207

Economic aid should be related to the ability of the aided area to modernize, to solve its economic problems, and to build a viable and independent nation or areal grouping.

In many of the countries where American aid may be wanted, modernization cannot be carried out without radical social change. This does not mean that existing regimes are always opposed to modernization, any more than were the Shogunate in pre-Meiji Japan or the Nuri as-Said regime in Iraq. But these last two—perhaps unlike the present Thai regime, which is not based on a large landholding class—were unable to carry modernization through without undercutting their bases of political support. In these cases, political revolution was probably a necessary if not sufficient condition for modernization. In some of the Latin American nations the requirements for radical social reform by existing regimes are not so formidable but may still be sufficient to deter the regimes from taking political risks in order to modernize.[3] Where this is the case, American aid is likely to be used ineffectively, and the extension of large-scale aid may even identify the United States with anti-modernist goals.

Intervention in internal affairs to induce modernization is a risky business that may well fail or backfire. Intervention should not be resorted to blithely. On the other hand, the failure of existing regimes to modernize may only insure radical and pro-Soviet revolutions. No specific answers to this problem can be attempted here. There will be cases where intervention may work and others where the risks are too great. But the United States must avoid association with anti-modernist goals. It must display sympathy with modernizing regimes even where specific American economic interests may be affected adversely.

SPECIFIC PRINCIPLES OF AID—REGIONAL COOPERATION

Modernization and cultural independence may be aided by regional cooperation or even by regional integration. The Mahgreb, for instance, is possibly an area where cooperation crossing national boundaries may be feasible and desirable from the standpoint of building a new world order consistent with American principles. Oil-pooling in the Arab Middle East might also be encouraged. Although the Iraq claim to Kuwait could hardly be conceded, the defense of the sovereignty of what is essentially a non-viable political unit demonstrated lack of political foresight.[4]

---

3. This is an exceptionally serious problem for which no clear solutions are in sight. Few ruling groups are sufficiently disinterested to reform themselves out of power, particularly if the reforms are not guaranteed to be workable. Perhaps some of these groups should be bought out or ways discovered to force others to get out or to cooperate.

4. The British were undoubtedly concerned to protect their oil interests. But the present situation is quite unstable. Too much of the Middle East is impoverished and there are too many small oil oases disposing of immense riches. Eventually this situation will change, and the change may be preferable if anticipated and encouraged than if opposed.

The American government presently proposes to set up regional groups in Latin America and Africa with which aid negotiations would be carried on. Little study, however, has been made of the consequences of such a scheme for Africa, in particular, where the question of which states to include would have profound political effects both within the continent and elsewhere. It is at least worth asking whether the political consequences of region-wide economic planning would moderate the policies of the more forward African states, inflame the more moderate states, increase continental harmony, or make worse continental frictions. The inclusion of the United Arab Republic would, of course, have other consequences for American foreign policy.

The commitment of the United States to the OAS leaves little choice except to encourage some kind of regional cooperation in the use of American aid to Latin America. Yet, the program of the Kennedy administration is tied to land reform and to other social and economic reforms. It is doubtful that many of the existing regimes in these countries will, in fact, carry through reforms of a needed radical nature. For this reason, even within the OAS framework, the United States should consider concentrating its aid to those countries that have the desire and ability to modernize themselves. Brazil, Venezuela, Mexico, and Argentina may fall within this category. By committing the major portion of its aid to areas that do modernize economically and socially, the United States would identify itself with such progress. The nations so aided might serve as examples to still others that they need not go the way of the Castro regime in Cuba. On the other hand, by not entirely denying aid to other Latin American countries, the framework of hemispheric solidarity is maintained and American sympathy for the peoples of the hemisphere affirmed. Within this framework, smaller, specific aid programs oriented to other and shorter-term needs could be formulated and carried out. The case for picking and choosing may be even stronger in Africa where the United States lacks historic ties that demand continental solidarity and cooperation. In all cases, major American aid should be conditioned on efforts by the nations involved to help themselves.

The United States should make clear to all that the major purpose of its aid is to help other countries to enter the modern world. Thus, in general, the United States should not commit itself to outworn social or political systems that cannot satisfy aspirations with which it, in terms of its own national values, must strongly sympathize.

SPECIFIC PRINCIPLES OF AID—INTERNAL POLITICS

For reasons specified previously, new nations, in the effort to modernize, must engage in considerable governmental intervention. Efforts to overcome tribalism or to carry through social revolutions necessary for modernization may lead to considerable authoritarianism. The democratic and humane values destroyed in the process may not be properly appreciated by the leaders of the new nations. Many may lack the sophistication of Attaturk, who used authoritarian forms in an effort to create the conditions under which democracy can maintain itself.

Moreover, many of the leaders of the new nations unfortunately have accepted Marxist myths concerning capitalism. Although in fact the socialism of the new states is more pragmatic and accommodates more capitalism than some Americans believe, there is a real danger that the new states may either stifle or fail quickly to create the middle class that stood as a bulwark against governmental despotism in the West (but that took more than a century to develop). Moreover, much of the human misery of the European economic revolution was the consequence of an impersonal market mechanism rather than of a conscious governmental decision. The governments of the new nations, however, largely take responsibility for economic decisions. Resentment, therefore, may crystallize against these governments for the real or seeming failures of governmental policies. And, in their efforts to modernize rapidly and to maintain control of the situation until this is done, the governments may institutionalize repressive mechanisms resistant to change from below although possibly subject to *coup*.

The United States should leave no doubt concerning its sympathy for the efforts of the elites in the new nations to modernize, of its desire to aid them, and of its recognition that modernization cannot be carried through painlessly or according to its own model. On the other hand, we should not be indifferent to the internal politics of the countries that receive economic aid or assistance from it.[5] The effects on American institutions and values, if the United States becomes an isolated island in a totalitarian—even if non-Communist—world, are too complicated to describe here and in any event are moot. But surely Americans prefer not to live in a totalitarian world and even more surely they do not desire to permit their aid to modernizing nations to be diverted toward the maintenance of a totalitarian police state. (Even if the funds are not used directly for this purpose, they permit the diversion of other funds.) If the United States cannot police the world to maintain democracy everywhere—indeed even if it must recognize that the conditions for democracy are not everywhere present or that in some places democracy may be incompatible with modernization—it does not have to close its eyes to the human drama and to resolve political issues in favor of totalitarianism either through a failure of will, or in a fit of absent-mindedness.

In applying a criterion related to the nature of the regime, an effort must be made to make decisions in context rather than in the abstract. Thus, for instance, a distinction can be made between an area where the conditions for some degree of political liberalism are present but repressed by the government and an area where such conditions are not present. For instance, given

5. Unfortunately, until recently the United States did little to support modernizing democracies, particularly when important economic interests objected to their policies. Venezuela under Betancourt was until recently an unfortunate example of this national myopia.

the cultural and social background of Cuba, it is dubious that most of the totalitarian measures of the Castro regime are necessary for—or even consistent with—rapid modernization, although a mere return to the old constitution might have forfeited the possibilities for social revolution.

The situation is quite different in Ghana and Guinea—which, in any event, are authoritarian and not totalitarian—where tribalism must be overcome to create a national state where one did not properly exist previously. A distinction must also be drawn between a Guinea which has had little experience in government and little time to create liberal institutions and a Spain which has made no effort to create such institutions and which seems determined to maintain a rigidly authoritarian regime indefinitely. Moreover, although Guinea or Ghana may be given the benefit of the doubt, because of their brief existence, it is possible to distinguish between those two cases and Nigeria, which seems more inclined, at present, to develop representative institutions.

African single-party systems which seem to permit debate and consent within the single-party structure must also be differentiated from Communist-type single-party systems which prevent national debate or dissent and which restrict debate to centralized and hierarchical party structures. Thus, whether a nation such as Yugoslavia is aided might be made to depend on whether the party structure is sufficiently loosened to permit genuine and general debate and political alternatives not decided on in advance by the party leadership.

Even if the only two criteria for aid were those previously discussed—modernization and regime character—the applications would be subject to some debate. Spain would clearly be excluded, for it is not modernizing, and it is committed to the maintenance of an authoritarian regime. Cuba would not receive aid because, although it is attempting to modernize, it is now doing so within the framework of a totalitarian regime, which applies terroristic methods in case of dissent. Nigeria and some of the French African states are modernizing, but not rapidly, in an effort to avoid harsh political methods. Even so, many of those French African states are one-party states. At this stage of their development they should probably be given the benefit of the doubt on both counts. Ghana and Guinea are attempting to modernize rapidly, are following foreign policies that are unpalatable to the United States, are probably on balance pro-Soviet, and are employing quite harsh political methods. Even so, they are not totalitarian and, within the framework of African political experience, do permit political alternatives. They should probably receive the present benefit of doubt, but the decision might well be re-evaluated after a reasonable period of time. So also should the Jagan regime in Guiana receive the benefit of the doubt unless it shows signs of becoming totalitarian or of entering the Soviet bloc.

The difficult questions will involve the choice between the rapidly modernizing and less liberal and the more slowly modernizing and more liberal

African regimes. No single criterion can be applied here, for policy decisions must rest on prognostications concerning the probable future course of development of these nations. If the judgment is that the more slowly modernizing nations have a reasonable chance to succeed in modernizing with external support, while maintaining relatively liberal institutions, preference should be given to them where emphasis in allocation is made. If, on the other hand, one comes to the conclusion that modern nationhood in any of these areas rests on rapid and forced evolution from tribalized relations to national solidarity or that political demands on the part of the younger educated elite permit no good alternative, then despite dissatisfactions with their external policies and fears concerning their future political development, aid to the more radically modernizing African nations might have higher priority than would otherwise seem desirable.

In any event, although the United States may prefer a particular set of choices for developing nations, based on its own values and prognostications, and may legitimately allocate aid on the basis of these choices, the decisions on modernization affect it only indirectly. Advice may be offered. Attempts to encourage desirable values can and should be made. But in the last analysis, the developing nations must make their own independent choices, for it is their fate that is directly involved. Where the choice that is made involves a destruction of human dignity that offends our most important values and degrades the human beings so manipulated, as in the case of Cuba, we have an obligation to make our opposition clear. But where the differences are based upon tolerable differences in basic values or prognostications concerning the consequences of particular policies, sympathetic understanding would be more appropriate than harsh rejection.

It is inevitable that particular American decisions, even within the framework of clear policy principles, will be misunderstood by some and resented by others. We do not always properly understand or appreciate the actions or intentions of other nations. The new nations require radical change, and the rich United States is not likely to be viewed sympathetically by the harassed leaders and uneducated masses of these nations. Their values, their goals, and their interpretations of policies differ from ours. Popularity is not to be expected. If, however, there is a posture of disinterested support for modernization, social reform, and political liberalism, if American policy is not tied merely to anti-Communism or to attempts to build systems of alliances, there is some hope that American policy will command respect and that it will invite support when it accords with the most important interests of the uncommitted developing nations.

It must be clear that the United States does not seek *direct* political benefits from its aid. Unlike Communism, which, despite its talk of many roads, has a relatively narrow doctrinal content and organizational form, American favoritism for democracy implies little with respect to the content of legislation—apart from support for modernization—and party and governmental structure. It implies support only for organizational forms that permit the institutionalization of dissent and the relatively free play of ideas. Indeed, the democracies do not possess political means by which control can be exercised over other countries, and, as long as the United States does not attempt to force uncommitted nations into pacts for which they are not prepared, it presents no political threat to their independence.

MODE OF AID

The question of whether aid should be given bilaterally or multilaterally is a difficult one to answer. However, proposals to siphon aid through the United Nations according to its normal constitutional procedures would almost surely be unfortunate. As long as the amount of aid handled through the United Nations is small, the temptation to assert the kind of political control that would be inconsistent with the objectives of the aid will be minimal. As soon, however, as large-scale contributions of aid money to be spent by the organization come to be viewed as a tax to be contributed regularly by the richer nations, the kinds of pork-barrel decisions that are often made in the United States Congress will be made in an even more exaggerated form in the United Nations General Assembly. Since economically irrational decisions are also likely to be made at the national level, this compounding of irrationality would be thoroughly inconsistent with the aims of the aid. Multilateral aid, however, might insulate the United States from criticism in the choice of aid recipients. It is true that the history of bilateral aid leaves little room for optimism. But it is at least easier to reform United States aid programs than to reform international political processes.

In sum, therefore, the question of policy, primarily including economic-aid policy, toward the uncommitted states is not susceptible to an easy answer that permits clear applications. The usual reasons given for aid, namely, that it will make friends, produce political stability, and halt Communism, have little evidence to support them. But, in the end, modernization is probably a good thing. It is doubtful if the demands for modernization can be halted in any event. To the extent that modernization is carried through successfully by non-Communist governments, the expansion of the Communist world system will be halted. Political instability is probably inevitable as rising expectations, new organizations, and political counterelites produce accentuated demands on the governments of the underdeveloped nations. The sooner modernization occurs, the fewer the barriers it must overcome, and the more support the West gives to it, the more successful and the less anti-Western it is likely to be. The more the West attempts either to halt modernization, or use it for ulterior purposes, the more radical and the more susceptible to Communist influence modernization is likely to be. The more disinterested the assistance policy of the West, the greater the control of the West over its allocations of resources and the less susceptible the West is to blackmail in various guises.

Undoubtedly, in nations that lack any democratic experience or tradition, some degree of strong political control—even of authoritarianism—will be needed to handle excessive demands on governmental allocations. In others, such as India, the democratic method may be made to work in modernizing the nation and may serve as a model for other nations, if not in the present, then at least with respect to the future. At present, however, democratic values have no appeal for the poor, the backward, the illiterate. They appear to be luxuries or even undesirable. Our best hope is to produce a period of relative stability during which these values can become appreciated. This will not happen until other and prior—even if less important from our viewpoint—values are first achieved. The present period is a crucial one, and the choices made by the West—and primarily by the United States—will play a critical role in determining the shape of world politics for some time to come.

Although specific choices of aid policy or allocations of funds may be responsive to highly particular circumstances, the philosophy that guides the program will be of major importance in determining its effectiveness and acceptability to the aided nations. This guiding spirit in the intermediate run will have more impact on the consciousness of the leaders and peoples of the developing nations than the details of policy. Mistakes will be made and can be overcome with respect to those details. But the failure of the general outlines of policy to accord disinterestedly with the requirement of modernization eventually will lead to major discord between the aims and accomplishments of policy. The aim of the United States must not be popularity or even instrumental alliances. The major aim of American policy must be a structure of world politics in which the most important Western interests can be protected and the democratic form of government survive. The status quo cannot be preserved. The question concerns the shape of the changes to come. It is here precisely that the West and the United States must take their stand as a matter of principle rather than as a matter of expediency.

IV United States General Alliance Policy

The United States should begin to overhaul its alliance system along with its program of aid. Unfortunately, it is not always wise to scrap alliances that it was initially unwise to form. Withdrawal from an alliance may too easily be interpreted as withdrawal from an obligation to defend and, thus, may set in motion other undesirable events. For instance, withdrawal from SEATO might encourage Chinese aggression and might also encourage political deals favorable to Communism by local political elites. Opportunistic political elites, convinced that withdrawal from the alliances signified withdrawal from an interest in the independence of the area, might then begin to make "hedging" internal political deals. Moreover, some areas literally require an overt United States military guarantee to forestall attack. Taiwan is a case in point.

Except, however, in the NATO area, the system of multilateral military pacts has been a failure. NATO, which so far has been relatively successful, is in serious and, likely, increasing trouble. Many Europeans are afraid of the risk involved in the nuclear age: Some fear that the United States will not risk nuclear war to defend them if they remain in NATO and hope that we will come to their aid anyway, even if they do not contribute to or participate in the nuclear military forces of the free world and desire not to become the locus of nuclear attack. If it is urged that a nuclear-armed NATO is a deterrent to attack, they hope that others will bear the burden of that deterrent. Necessary as a nuclear-armed NATO happens to be, the strains within NATO are bound to increase tremendously as long as it remains a purely military organization.

There is a human tendency to discount risks when the alternatives are especially unpleasant. A Russian military move, therefore, is apt to be discounted if the means of preventing it are nuclear, unless there are incentives additional to military ones for taking risks. If the only incentives are the military, the nation that calls attention to the Russian threat is apt to be disliked; such action forces the attention of other nations on unpleasant things—things they would rather deny or ignore.

It would be much better if NATO were a politically organized community with shared interests and values, and if the problem of shifting risks and responsibilities did not arise in the acute form presently apparent. Nationalism, at least in America and Western European nations, has outlived its usefulness. It is no longer a moral inspiration or a generator of efforts of vast magnitude. Europe has already discovered this in a political and economic sense and is making first efforts to develop larger associations in the form of the Common Market and the various European Communities.

The United States, which has encouraged these efforts so far, has remained aloof. This is unfortunate, for we are no longer viable politically as an independent political entity, though a case might still be made for military viability—at least in the foreseeable future. But even more important, the accession of the United States—and Britain—to the European Community would provide a psychological as well as a material inspiration of the greatest magnitude. A strong case can be made that economic measures, as the least difficult to secure agreement on, should precede political measures in order to prepare the way by establishing practices and habits of joint action. Conceivabl however, the urgency of the situation and the need to capture the imagination of people may require bold political measures, despite the risk that the attempt at this level might forestall action to construct a genuine Atlantic Community. But it is hard to deny the conclusion that the NATO nations soon must face the world as an inseparable unit, dedicated to a common fate, and united by common policies and values.

The building of a viable Atlantic Community is the most important task facing the West. This Community must represent our best hopes and ideals. Present American relationships with Spain and Portugal are inconsistent with these ideals. These nations do not merely lack institutions that would permit them to participate constructively in such a community. The relationship we have with them presently is inconsistent with the appearance we are trying to present to the world.

It might be argued that Portugal is a valuable member of NATO, that the Spanish bases are important to the United States, and that we have cooperated without serious objection with many other authoritarian regimes. There is, however, a fundamental difference between a newly independent nation, such as Pakistan, which is trying to enter the modern world, and old nations, such as Spain and Portugal, whose leaders regard the modern world as evil. Some degree of authoritarianism may be essential in new nations which are desperately trying to modernize and improve the lot of their people. Authoritarianism is much more difficult to justify in old nations that want only to preserve an oligarchic and backward society. The living standards in Spain and Portugal are Asian rather than European. No major efforts are being made to modernize—to improve standards, to educate the people, or to prepare the conditions under which democracy might develop. Instead, Franco and Salazar take pride in their rejection of democracy and have no desire to improve the conditions of their people.

Our bases in these countries may have some importance, but it is quite doubtful that they are worth the political price. Our exhortations to the new nations to choose democracy and our condemnation of totalitarianism in Cuba appear hypocritical. We also make it difficult for ourselves to take our own ideals seriously when we regard them this cheaply. No one desires another prolonged civil war in Spain. But surely Spain and Portugal need not be welcomed as allies and colleagues; surely some pressure can be brought upon the two governments to reform. If they are totally unresponsive, we can support the democrats in exile.

There is a risk that a Castro type of regime might succeed the present regimes if we pursue this course. But a failure to press for democratization and reform may also so discourage the real democrats that the totalitarians have a clear field in advocating change. And, if we oppose the Fascist regimes before they are kicked out, we at least help to legitimize our opposition to a new authoritarianism should such a type of regime succeed the present regimes.

The attempt to institute idealistic principles in the formation of the Atlantic Community undoubtedly will give rise to serious problems: The military services will resist the loss of bases; conservative groups will fear the political effects of the decisions. The alternative political costs, however, would be much greater.

This advice goes against most recognized principles of statecraft. But those principles are designed for stable international systems in which conservative policies are protective of existing interests. We must learn that it is precisely with respect to this issue that the character of our national response must change. We must learn to act in ways that generate support for constructive changes in the shape of world politics in a period when sufficient support cannot be mobilized to preserve the status quo. We must take some of the risks which all revolutionary movements must take or we shall suffer the fate of all systems that fail either to adapt to their environment, or to adapt their environment to them.

V   The United Nations

American policy toward the United Nations also requires drastic revision. American security—and world peace also—undoubtedly rest more on American military power and on the NATO alliance than on the United Nations. If we are ever confronted with a clear-cut, either-or, choice—and, undoubtedly, this would be a tragedy—the United Nations would have to be subordinated to NATO. On the other hand, the United Nations has a real and important role to play in world politics. It would be a serious mistake—unfortunately, we have repeatedly made such mistakes—to attempt to make the United Nations merely an instrument of the Cold War or to attempt to use it to solve problems which it is not and cannot be equipped to solve given the present structure of world politics.

The postwar period has perhaps seen the United Nations misused in two different ways by the United States. The Truman administration attempted to use the United Nations as an instrument of American foreign policy. The Eisenhower administration attempted to use the United Nations as a substitute for American policy. It would be wrong to deny that convincing rationales for either course can be constructed. And, of course, both charges are greatly oversimplified. Yet it is well to weigh the cost both policies have entailed.

It can be pointed out—and rightly so—that the Truman administration faced an intransigent Stalinist regime in Russia which finally supported—and in all probability ordered—the North Korean attempt to unify the Korean peninsula by force. Although an independent American action in Korea probably would have been preferable to the one followed, it was argued with some merit than an American action that bypassed the United Nations would have reduced the organization to impotence. Yet the United Nations' action in Korea did intrude that organization directly into the Cold—and in this case hot—War. The change in the goals of the operation, from defeating aggression to unifying the peninsula by force, clearly placed too great a burden on the organization. It thrust the organization into a war it could not win—at least under the terms the United States was willing to wage it—and made it a direct and continuing party to a dispute rather than a mediatory agency. Moreover, American efforts on many other issues to put the United Nations on record with respect to Cold-War issues alienated many new and uncommitted nations. It again involved the United Nations as a party to Cold-War disputes rather than as a mediator or as an enunciator of universal rules of conduct formulated in advance of and without specific reference to—until application became necessary—specific Cold-War disputes.

General Eisenhower, on the other hand, evidently considered that the United Nations came closer to being a world governmental agency than most other observers of the organization would believe. Even within a national government such as the United States, some have questioned the ability of the government to act effectively in crisis situations without strong leadership from the executive. Nonetheless, General Eisenhower apparently believed that the United Nations was an appropriate deliberative body, with respect to issues involving the use of force, and that support of its decisions by the United States was the method best calculated to build a peaceful world. This, of course, again shifts the function of the United Nations from mediation and places upon it a burden which some may suspect it is ill-prepared to bear. The crisis in the Congo indicated how, despite strong leadership from the Secretary-General, the United Nations can govern only with great difficulty when the interests of the Soviet and American blocs strongly conflict. The present temporary Secretary-General lacks the late Dag Hammarskjold's strength and it is doubtful that any genuinely strong successor can be agreed to.

It is simply a fact of international life that the security of the West—and indeed of much of the uncommitted world—rests upon the military strength of the NATO nations. The United Nations is no substitute for NATO, and primarily military and security problems cannot be relegated now, or in the immediate future, to that organization. It is not prepared to move quickly or strongly where military matters are concerned; consequently, its resolutions, even when not compromises, lack a deterrent effect. It is the threat of American intervention that prevents more direct Soviet intervention in Laos and the Congo, not the possibility of United Nations resolution. Undoubtedly, United Nations actions play a role, indirectly, by creating a political climate in which American intervention becomes politically feasible—because of the reactions of nations whose cooperation is desirable and because of the reactions of the American public. But the two different effects should not be confused.

It is necessary that the United States play a strong leading role in both NATO and the United Nations, but the nature of the leading role ought to differ with the nature and function of the two organizations. The proper function of NATO in a bipolar world is to provide a military deterrent to the Soviet bloc and to present a political image that facilitates unity of action and that at least does not arouse strong opposition from uncommitted nations.

The proper function of the United Nations is to mediate in a way that reduces the possibility of thermonuclear war and that facilitates support for desirable and universal rules of international behavior.

With respect to these functions, there can—and will likely—be conflicts between short-term interests of American policy and the interests of the United Nations organization. Such a conflict occurred at the time of the decision to cross the 38th parallel in Korea. That decision could have been justified from the standpoint of United Nations' interests only had the United States been prepared to carry matters with the Soviet bloc to a military decision at that time.

Another conflict arises with respect to the admission of Red China to the United Nations. Red China is a state within the meaning of the Charter; indeed a very important state. At some point, the United States may have to decide whether keeping Red China out of the United Nations (this is not directly related to American recognition of Red China) is of such overriding importance that it is worth the cost in terms of committing the United Nations organization to universalistic rules of international law. And it must be remembered that it is only on the basis of commitment to such universalistic rules of law that we stand much chance of making effective use of the uncommitted nations in international bargaining procedures.

It is, of course, a grave error to fail to differentiate foreign policies according to the arenas in which they are pursued, for this would assume that the context of a policy decision did not affect the consequences of the policy. If the United Nations plays an important role in American objectives, other objectives—at least when pursued in the United Nations and perhaps also at other times—must be modified to take this objective into account. And as long as the mediatory function of the United Nations is important, or as long as the support of other nations who highly value the United Nations is important, American policies in the organization ought to be related to the nature and functions of the organization and not merely to other objectives of American foreign policy. Much of the opposition to past American policies stemmed from a desire of various nations not to get involved in the Cold War—a not inconsiderable factor to be taken into account—rather than from an understanding of the best way in which the United Nations could execute its functions. But this failure of understanding on the part of other nations does not make less grave the failure of the United States to pursue its own best interests in that organization.

In addition to the mediatory functions of the United Nations, the United States may wish to strengthen functions that isolate some areas or functions from the Cold War in a way that is desirable, or at least acceptable, to both the United States and the Soviet Union. Proposals of this kind ought to be strongly supported and presented in ways appealing to the popular understanding. The present Antarctic treaty, for instance, is not inconsistent with eventual United Nations administration, and such administration might serve as precedent for the moon. Such administration ought to be proposed. The Suez crisis might have been avoided had the Western nations had sufficient foresight to turn international waterways over to international management. It may not be too late for such management, although the issue now would be doubtful at best. It is conceivable that the N-country nuclear problem and arms control may be solved by means of an international agency. In the process, some experience for handling the even more difficult problems that may arise in the future could be gained.

This is a far cry from world government. But there are many disadvantages to world government from the standpoint of human freedom and cultural and social diversity—even were such government feasible. Given the inconsistency of Communist and democratic forms of government and this diversity in cultural and economic standards, clearly such government is not feasible at the present time. To attempt it would be harmful, for such attempts would interfere with support for feasible proposals to control pressing problems.

Even the step toward an international police force, although part of avowed American policy, is unwise at present. *Ad hoc* forces secure, within reasonable limits, cease fires between minor belligerents. But we must assume that the kind of police force advocated as a United Nations police force would be considerable in size and permanent in nature. If roughly equivalent to American or Russian forces, it might only be a source of additional instability. If superior to American or Russian forces, this force might itself engage in military adventures. Moreover, how could it be possible to agree on the composition and control of such a force? United Nations organs are not representative in a consensual sense.

Surely the United States and the Soviet Union would not agree to a United Nations force responsive to United Nations organs, except possibly under conditions of veto. But this condition would undercut an essential function of such a force, namely, to control disputes among the major nations. Moreover, if such a force were controlled by the minor nations, what guarantee— or even reasonable presumption—is there that it would be used responsibly? If strong American or Russian units participated, we could expect resistance, sabotage, or other clandestine measures that would impair actions that displeased either of them. Reliance upon a force that might be crippled by internal strife might subvert the deterrent effect of national armed forces. Such a force under existing world conditions would increase rather than decrease uncertainties and would, thus, raise rather than lower the probability of war. And particularly if the United Nations force controlled atomic weapons, we would have problems arising from the increase in the number of nuclear powers. The world has enough uncertainties without increasing the number. Surely it is not a recent discovery that abstract constitutionalism is no substitute for political analysis.

The United States, however, should support the development and possible expansion of the *ad hoc* police-force procedures of the United Nations. It should attempt to demonstrate how these procedures enter into the stream of world politics in a manner supportive of existing law or even in a manner that leads to the growth of law. The independent functions of the Secretary-General ought to be supported and the civil-service status of the staff protected. There should be less hesitation to demonstrate the destructive consequences of present Soviet proposals to reorganize the United Nations. And, instead of agreeing to a larger Soviet quota of staff employees, the existence of any Soviet quota in the absence of independent recruitment should be attacked. The United States ought not to act defensively under Soviet attack. It ought to counterattack with a program designed to improve the level of the law and orderliness in the world.

The present organization of world politics does not provide a desirable level of security. Attempts either to demonstrate the dangers of the present international organization or the need in at least some respects for new modes of organizing consensus and the institutional means of exercising force are desirable. The belief, however, that radical changes can be implemented at the present time is dangerous, for such belief, unaccompanied by a host of other changes, might produce either an unworkable and dangerous constitutional experiment, or an eroding support for the only measures capable of maintaining even the low level of security we possess under present conditions.

The United Nations is also the forum in which the United States can encourage the new and uncommitted states to support universal principles of law and behavior consistent with the kind of world order we desire to encourage. On specific issues this may involve real costs. For instance, the conflict between American policy on China and universal standards for United Nations representation is one area in which costs may have to be paid. But, in general, the United States desires a world in which overt military intervention in foreign nations is minimized, in which the dangers of nuclear war are reduced, in which new nations are permitted to develop in independence, in which problems of outer space are organized appropriately, and so forth. Within limits too complicated to explain here, the new and uncommitted nations may well support such standards as generally—if not always—consistent with their own interests. As the imperialist or colonial issue vanishes and as political boundaries become more stable in the ex-colonial areas, the coincidence of interest should increase rather than decrease. Support, therefore, may well be won in these areas provided that matters are not confused by attempts to win support on specific issues, as opposed to general policy, and provided that military strength is maintained. If, however, we seek support in the form of generalized alliances, because aid will be withheld if support is not forthcoming, or because we are the "good guys," or if we allow our military strength to dissipate, we shall either frighten off or discourage support, and we shall gain victories on specific individual votes rather than on the issues that count in the long run.

Support for a viable United Nations system may also serve as a positive ideal to disaffected groups in the Western nations; it may also appear as a desirable alternative to those who misunderstand the role and function of NATO. Thus, strong support for an expanded *but realistic* United Nations system may be an important implement in mobilizing the West by appealing to idealism, while many are still wrongly and unfortunately associating NATO only with "power politics."

VI   Policy Toward the Communist Bloc

If the United States desires to encourage political liberalism in the uncommitted nations, it ought also to assert its belief in democracy as the proper way of life for those behind the iron curtain—not merely those in Eastern Europe, but also those in Russia and China. To this end a reasonably democratic China in Taiwan is an important means. Unless we have as much faith in democracy as the Russians have in Communism, Communism will eventually sweep the world. Although we cannot encourage premature uprisings at times when we are unable or unwilling to extend aid, we must not come to terms with the status quo. No status quo ever endures, and if we recognize only one mode of change—toward Communism and totalitarianism —we determine the fate of the future by that decision.

But there are other and stronger reasons why we must oppose not merely Communist expansion, but Communism itself. The world is an unsafe place in which to live and it is becoming increasingly so. The measures required to control or to minimize the nuclear dangers are inconsistent with the organizational structure of Communism. The insulation of the Communist system from the outside world minimizes moderating influences on Communist leadership. It is relatively unresponsive to popular pressures as they arise spontaneously or as they are influenced by trends of opinion elsewhere in the world. High-ranking Russians who reported to outsiders on events in the Soviet Union—perhaps on the secretion of nuclear weapons after an arms control agreement—would lack the sanctuary within the Soviet state that American citizens would have in the American state under analogous conditions. In the Soviet Union governmental leaks occur rarely and then usually as a consequence of a high-level decision to leak. Decisions to hide weapons or to engage in surprise attack can be made secretly by a small group of men who have no need to mobilize public opinion in favor of their move prior to it; neither is there within Soviet society a belief in a norm obligating them to do so or obligating citizens to inform on and oppose the government if it secretly violates solemn agreements, as there is in the West. As long as the Soviet Union remains the kind of nation it is, the dangers of nuclear war may be much higher than many people are willing to accept.

If we cannot induce major changes in the Soviet system, and if we are unwilling to live with the dangers of nuclear war, we have one other alternative:

We can disarm unilaterally—in effect, we can surrender—and pass on to the Soviet Union the task of policing the world. One possible consequence is that the Soviet Union effectively controls the arms race—that it prevents other nations from acquiring nuclear weapons. This contingency cannot be examined in detail, but it is unlikely that Soviet leaders would be able or willing to do this without considerable political interference in other nations. Evasions of Soviet arms regulations would have to be cruelly crushed. And a nation that has transported entire populations within its own territory may exact a tremendous price from other nations in this respect, in addition to exploiting them economically. We would almost surely have to submit to political tyranny. Indeed the immensity of the task would likely insure this. The physical, as well as the political, difficulty of maintaining control might lead to the development and use of behavior-control devices. Even if the worst of these consequences did not occur, life would be difficult and unpleasant.

However, the Soviet Union might not succeed in imposing arms control on the world. We might, as one possibility, enter a world of independent Communist states, many of which controlled effective nuclear systems. This would likely prove a more dangerous world than the present one. Even today there are important strains between Russia and China, for instance. If the threat of the democracies was removed, the strains among the Communists would become much greater. Yet, these would be governments possessing nuclear systems shrouded in secrecy and capable of being employed without advance publicity. (Indeed several hundred millions of excess Chinese might occupy the United States prior to a nuclear war between Red China and Red Russia.) This is a world which might end up both Red and dead.

Moreover, the policy of unilateral disarmament has even graver disadvantages. If implemented, it is, as we saw, bad enough. But there would be much opposition to it. The advocacy of the policy might only produce policy debates, delays, and compromises that weakened the Western posture and encouraged the Soviet Union to take bold steps that only made war more likely. When the West finally resolved to stiffen its position and to make no further concessions, Soviet miscalculations concerning Western intentions might well precipitate a nuclear war. (A strong argument can be made that the peace movement in the 30's made a major contribution to the development of the Second World War.) Thus, surrender to Communism is not likely to constitute an acceptable solution to the grave problems facing the world today. Attempts to change the Soviet system, or at least to mobilize world opinion against that system, would be preferable.

Therefore, the United States must make clear that the great impediment to arms control or disarmament lies in the nature of the Communist political system. So far, most people speak of the concessions that must be made to the Soviet Union because one cannot expect it to change its political system. Unfortunately, the concessions that can be made consistently, with reasonable security, are not sufficient to minimize the present dangers of the nuclear arms race. It has become necessary to emphasize that it is the Soviet system which must change if the world is to have reasonable security in a nuclear age. And it is the Soviet government which must be thrown on the defensive for refusing to make changes consistent with international security. As nuclear technology improves and spreads to other nations, it may become necessary for the powers of the United Nations to be drastically increased. It is important that long before this we have stated the changes necessary in the Soviet system so that everyone will be familiar with the reasons for them.

This cannot be accomplished by shrinking from negotiations with the Russians as we have so often done in the past. It may be that the Russians misuse negotiations in an effort to impede the West from taking needed political measures or in an effort to change the political situation during the course of negotiations. For instance, political negotiations over Berlin might so alarm some people that political events might be set in train to provide the Russians with what they want without the necessity of making counterconcessions.

These possibilities cannot be denied. The Russians are engaged in serious political warfare with us. Khrushchev has stated openly that coexistence means only a willingness to defeat democracy by means other than by military war and not a willingness to live indefinitely in the same world with democracy. Coexistence does not imply the absence of military threats. Khrushchev is a past master at the use of such threats, having learned much from the practices of the late Adolf Hitler. But even if one believes that Khrushchev really will not resort to overt military adventures—and there is no need for him to do so as long as things go well for him—coexistence on his terms means a struggle, without any real community of interest, in which deceit and subversion play major roles. Indeed, a failure to understand this is a failure to take the Russians seriously.

The answer, however, does not lie in a refusal to negotiate with the Russians; neither does it lie in bargaining as the Russians bargain, for those techniques are not appropriate to democracies and free associations of nations. But the United States can debate the issues on its own terms rather than on Russian terms. There is no reason why Russian demands on Berlin should not be countered by demands for UN-supervised elections in all of Germany—or even in the other satellites. There is no reason why the relationship of the totalitarian Russian system to the dangers of the arms race should not become the focus of debate. If these issues are linked to the broader issues of peace and war and disarmament and arms control that worry the peoples of the world, it may be possible to use them effectively against the Soviet Union.

It would be wrong to pretend that Communism alone is responsible for the troubles of our age. Indeed, in part, it is a response to even deeper problems. But it is legitimate to point out that Communist political organization increases existing dangers tremendously. It is the responsibility of the American government to publicize these dangers and how Communism increases them. The political organization of the Communist states is not merely an internal matter beyond the legitimate concern of other nations.

Apart from the fact that the Communist states themselves do not hesitate to interfere in other states and attempt to produce changes in their forms of political organization—itself reason to have interest in the internal organization of the Communist regimes—Communist political organization poses a security problem for other states; it increases tremendously the danger of nuclear war and of partial or total destruction. No nation can remain indifferent to this threat. The United States must call upon the Soviet Union to provide more freedom for its people, to permit political opposition, and to open up the country to inspection. Whatever merit there may have been to the Soviet fear that a freer society would have made the Soviet Union more vulnerable to external attack, that fear no longer can have any validity. The Soviet Union is now one of the two strongest nations on earth. It boasts that it is no longer encircled by capitalism and may soon encircle capitalism. It no longer has a right to behave like a weak nation and to plead fear, whether of attack or of espionage. And, if after forty years of Communist rule, the Russian people are unfit to govern themselves, surely that is an indictment of the regime and an additional reason to advocate change of the form of government.

We should make it quite clear that our objection to Communism lies not in its form of economic organization—although we may prefer a different form or even fear that centralized state control of the economy may make free government more difficult—but in its political organization. We must make clear that we do not desire to impose our own substantive views on Russia but desire a situation in which the peoples of the Soviet Union can influence Soviet policy and decide questions of political leadership—a situation in which differing points of view can be put forward and receive circulation.

We should no longer view the Soviet leaders as supermen in complete control of their internal environment. The Soviet bloc has its own strains and stresses. We should attempt to increase them. Potential conflicts between the members of the bloc should be encouraged by American policies designed to bring them into prominence. Internal stresses within the nations of the bloc should be increased where this can be done responsibly, although obviously we do not desire to encourage another "Hungary" where we are unwilling to come to the aid of the revolutionaries. And, most important, we should throw the Russians on the ideological defensive.

VII   Military Policy

American security must continue to rest upon American and NATO arms, although, of course, a merely military policy is bound to fail. However, combined with a constructive diplomacy, the policy of armed resistance to military attempts to change the political map of the world is a sound one. As we approach a situation, however, in which both East and West possess credible second-strike forces, the policy of massive retaliation loses credibility, although fear of an irrational massive retaliation may still deter military aggression. We might run great risks to deter future aggressions, but massive retaliation under the specified conditions would be suicidal, and, thus, would serve no useful purpose. Moreover, a military machine geared only to massive retaliation would likely grind to a halt if challenged and, thus, might encourage provocatory actions.[6]

The Russians surely would be clever enough in the future, as they have been in the past, to increase the ambiguity of the circumstances in which they acted and to create at least the pretext of legitimacy or legality. We have already seen them maneuver in this fashion in the Congo and Laos in recent years; and they would surely make their demands, each time they made them, relatively moderate. The crisis would be permitted to build slowly, and each time, our allies in Europe and much of the public at home would put pressure on the government to stand firm and inconsistently at the same time to compromise. The Laos incident is a good case in point. The most effective intervention the United States could make would be against North Viet Nam, and for this there is reason in the extent of the Vietminh intervention. There is also strategic reason, for such retaliation would make of intervention something less than a one-way street. Yet clearly, in the present state of opinion, such a measure is not politically feasible.

Unfortunately, despite the inherent incredibility of the policy of massive retaliation, the threat of massive retaliation will have to play a deterrent role in the coming years. However, because of the lessening credibility of the policy, particularly in ambiguous situations, the United States, if it desires an effective foreign policy, will have to be prepared to intervene where necessary with appropriate non-nuclear forces. An inability to so intervene has reduced the bargaining power of the United States in the Laos case. Similar situations may arise elsewhere in Asia or in Africa and Latin America in the future. The lack of trained manpower in Europe, although undesirable, is not quite so dangerous because the tripwire theory, if not the best military doctrine, still possesses considerable deterrent power. Guerrilla warfare and internal subversion are not as effective in industrial Europe as they are in under-developed areas. Therefore, ambiguous measures are more difficult to find. A massive Soviet push across a clearly defined border would confront the United States with a head-on challenge that it could not afford to duck.

Reliance, however, upon local resistance forces is at best an uncertain expedient. Despite assertions about the superiority of defense over offense, with respect to non-nuclear forces, such a policy would probably only slow

---

6. The strategy of using limited strategic nuclear strikes against the Communist bloc probably will be accepted in the heat of war—if there is a war. It seems unlikely to gain sufficient acceptance in time of peace, although it would be most effective in war if adopted during peace. Thus, although the strategy has much to recommend it, discussions are likely to be confined to esoteric circles.

Soviet advances. There have been too many blitzkriegs in modern times to place much reliance in this defensive strategy.[7] The ability of the attacker to choose the place and time of his attack is a considerable advantage. Perhaps, if the policy of non-nuclear defense were combined with a policy of non-nuclear counterattacks at other points of tension, the policy might have more to recommend it. But clearly this combination would meet with more political resistance than any other kind of strategy including limited strategic nuclear reprisals. There is much to be said for building non-nuclear forces that increase the probability that important areas can be held against non-nuclear attacks even without resort to nuclear reprisals, but there is little to be said for a strategy that depends almost entirely upon the workability of this arrangement for its success. It would be as dangerous as a commitment to massive retaliation.

Unfortunately, democracies such as the United States find it politically difficult to develop a coherent and reasonably rational military policy. Regardless of which policy is resorted to, some aspect of it becomes politically infeasible, either through the inability of the United States to carry its allies, or because of domestic opposition within the United States. It is deplorable, not that different strategic doctrines are advocated outside the government, but that various groups place such pressure on government that no coherent doctrine can be adopted. Unfortunately, some vociferous sections of the public cannot distinguish between advice and coercion.

The United States faces one of the most curious and dreadful dilemmas that could be imposed upon a free people. There can be no doubt that democratic political organization is a severe handicap in the kind of world struggle in which the United States finds itself. Yet, the United States cannot win this struggle in a way consonant with its own values without maintaining democratic forms. It, thus, has the problem of presenting its military policy in ways least likely to arouse opposition while at the same time maintaining at least a minimally satisfactory military capability. At best, the means employed will arouse fears and opposition; for this reason it is essential that public attention be directed to non-military policy goals that arouse widespread enthusiasm. Attention must be diverted from risks to prospects.

It is as difficult to defend an adequate military policy as it was to answer the charges of the late Senator McCarthy. Such charges have the element of simplicity—answers that of complexity and subtlety. This is particularly true in the nuclear age when weapons of mass destruction arouse feelings of both horror and fear. It is tempting to the public to believe that there are easy answers to these problems permitting complete avoidance of the dangers. Military strategies immediately frustrate such hopes. Military systems must

---

7. Demonstrations to the contrary do not fully take into account the massing of manpower and armor at the point of the thrust, disruption after the thrust, the response of civilians fleeing the enemy, the ability or lack of ability of defending forces to control these civilians forcibly, fifth-column activities, other political factors, and the character of the threat and promise tactics of the attacking forces.

envisage the possibility of use. It would be useless and wrong to argue that military systems eliminate the possibility of nuclear war. But to demonstrate that appropriate military systems and strategies minimize the probability of nuclear war—and the loss of other values as well—is impracticable, although the argument is correct; understanding the logic of the argument requires considerable knowledge, expertise, and emotional maturity. As is so often the case, the marketplace of ideas does not necessarily make truth popular. And just as Senator McCarthy was finally beaten, not by rational argument but by a change of public sentiment, the case for an adequate military policy rests with the ability of the government to create a climate of opinion in which its proposals will be given the benefit of doubt.

One of the more difficult problems stems from a misguided fear that the military want war or that war is more likely unless civilian authorities have firm control. Undoubtedly, many military men resent the damper which the Kennedy administration has placed on their public utterances. But this new policy is necessary, for, given public stereotypes, the military are their own worst proponents. Confidence is much more important than clarity, and the new administration seems effectively to be restoring a confidence that was badly lacking.

The same reasons arguing for a foreign policy that would direct public attention from military hazards to constructive tasks are also beginning to argue for the removal of overseas nuclear bases. We are reaching the stage at which the major deterrent to the Soviet Union can be based in the United States, the oceans, and perhaps also in the Australian desert. Although there would still be some advantages in having IRBM bases in Europe to insure accuracy in limited strategic retaliation, these reasons probably will be over-balanced by irrational fears that such bases would draw Soviet nuclear fire. A joint NATO deterrent—desirable for still other reasons—could be based in the seas. Thus, Europe would have less reason to fear that American or NATO nuclear bases in Europe would draw Soviet nuclear fire. On the other hand, non-nuclear bases, at least in Europe, would also reassure Europeans that they would not be abandoned by the United States. Although the question is difficult to answer on the basis of public information, serious con-sideration should be given to relinquishing bases entailing more political liability than military advantage. Bases in Spain, Cuba, Japan, and elsewhere may fall into this category. I do not want to argue that military considera-tions are unimportant or should be ignored or to deny that many public reactions to military policy are unwise and unfortunate. But decisions have to be related to the constraints that exist—not to those we would choose.

VIII   Some Specific Trouble Spots

BERLIN

We might take a brief look at a few trouble spots in the world. This will force some qualifications in the more generalized guideposts for policy that have been suggested earlier. However, this is inevitable whenever principles must be applied, and the seemingly anti-climactic nature of the discussion is a necessary price that is paid for greater specificity.

Perhaps the most vulnerable spot lies in Berlin. It is exceedingly unlikely that an airlift would overcome blockade today. Moreover, the Russians or their East German satellites are unlikely to try anything so crude as the blockade, for such a move, although non-military, might permit unified Western resistance. The Communists are much more likely to raise transit costs, to restrict transit routes, and to close off and "repair" facilities in such a way that the city is slowly strangled. There are really no good countermoves available to the West. The suggestion to move Berlin is hardly feasible and in any event would constitute a symbolic capitulation.

The Russians clearly have reasons to apply the squeeze in Berlin. Defeat in Berlin—even by means of a face-saving free-city formula—would constitute a tremendous loss in prestige and would affect the credibility of Western protection elsewhere, including areas where feasible protective measures are available. But even were the Russians forebearing enough not to desire to inflict such a loss of prestige upon the West, they would have reason to apply pressure in Berlin. Berlin is in the heart of East Germany. It not only is an area through which skilled workers and professional people had been able to escape to freedom before the new barriers were imposed, but it also provides a direct contrast for East Germans between democracy and totalitarianism, between a life where joy is possible and a life of Communist drabness and puritanism. Even apart from charges that West Berlin is a spy and propaganda center, the existence of a democratic West Berlin subverts Communist tyranny in East Germany. The East Germans will never accept Communism as a permanent fixture in their lives while they can observe, virtually in their midst, the life of free Germany.

If the issue of Berlin is isolated from other issues, or if the West refuses to consider aggressive action, the trumps are with the Communists. They can choose their moment and need only wait in order not to jeopardize other issues on which they desire negotiation with the West. Their strategic superiority is reinforced by the unwillingness of some Europeans—particularly the British—to take risks for the Germans. Yet, this is an issue on which the West cannot safely concede. It would be morally more indefensible than Munich to sell out the West Berliners, and the political and the military consequences might well be disastrous. If the Communists attempt to strangle Berlin, the West might send an armored column there. Or, alternatively, it might support active paramilitary and subversive actions in East Germany that both threaten the existence of the East German regime and involve a substantial risk of major and nuclear war in central Europe. And the Russians should privately be apprised of a decision to employ such measures before they commit themselves irrevocably with respect to West Berlin. Moreover, we should refuse to treat West Berlin as an isolated issue unrelated to freedom in East Berlin or East Germany. On the other hand, some compromise that genuinely protects the freedom of Berlin ought not to be excluded. However, the sooner the risks on action in Berlin are credibly raised for the Russians, the more likely they are to avoid entrapping themselves, and the less likely they are to confront the West with the alternatives of surrender or of policies involving a high risk of war. The issue here, as in China, should be presented clearly as one of human freedom. We may occasionally have to compromise this principle, but if we betray it, we will destroy the moral basis of our policy. In this present dangerous and unstable bipolar world, we will destroy ourselves unless our policy is based on an idealism that can generate support.

CHINA

Another major American problem is, of course, China, with its attendant problems of Taiwan, Quemoy, and Matsu. There may be indirect reasons in the form of alliance and United Nations relationships to consider Chinese Communist membership in the United Nations, but it is difficult to discover any direct reasons, that is, reasons independent of the interests of third parties, that would establish any American interest in acceding to Chinese Communist representation in the United Nations. There is no substantial evidence that such membership would modify Chinese behavior in any desirable way. It is abundantly clear that such membership would restrict numerous American actions that make life difficult for the Red regime, that bolster non-Communist nations on the periphery, and keep open the possibility of radical change in the regime or of successful revolution.

It is often said that the Communist regime in China is so firmly established that the possibility of successful revolution is, in any event, no longer present. Certainly there is no present reason to predict successful revolution. But it is going much farther than the adequacy of either social science techniques or information warrant categorically to exclude the possibility. On similar grounds, many would have denied the possibility of the Hungarian revolution—certainly successful until the intervention of the Russian army. The Red Chinese regime is indigenous in a sense that the Hungarian regime was not, and this may make difficult a unified national uprising. Moreover, a small nation, with a single major center of national control, is easier to take in revolutionary action. In a large nation, troops can be stationed far from their home area and may not sympathize with revolutionary forces. Such techniques of troop disposition were employed both under the Czars and the dictators in Soviet Russia. And troops can be shifted to trouble spots before the revolution sweeps the entire nation. On the other hand, the Russians could not hope to intervene as they had in Hungary. China is too large. In the last analysis, the possibility of successful revolution cannot be excluded, and if this possibility is less probable than the alternatives, the consequences for the United States would be at least as desirable as the event is improbable.

The supposed changes in Chinese behavior that would accompany Red Chinese representation in the United Nations are as hypothetical as a Chinese revolution, and it is difficult to imagine any changes in behavior that would be strongly supportive of American interests, even though such changes might have some desirability. It is not inconceivable that Communist China in the United Nations would be more intransigent than Communist China outside the United Nations. Whether with American support or against American opposition, whether with an agreement that kept the Nationalist regime in Taiwan in the United Nations or not, the fact of United Nations recognition would confirm to many the Communist Chinese view of the United States as a paper tiger. It is likely that Red Chinese representation would have grave political and military repercussions through Asia.

There are two striking arguments favoring this, however. One concerns the general qualifications of membership which ought to apply universalistically. It is possible that the United States ought to support Red Chinese entry—at least on conditions of representation for the Taiwan regime also—on the grounds that interest in the norms governing membership outweighs other consequences of such representation.

A second consideration is that many other nations—some for reasons that are legitimate—believe such action appropriate or desirable and resent American efforts to prevent such representation. The arguments, however, that one must "recognize" reality or that membership in the United Nations will produce better behavior on the part of the Chinese Communists are not worth serious discussion.

It must be added that United Nations representation for the Chinese need not be determinative of American recognition policy. Of course, United Nations representation would remove a barrier to recognition and make more difficult the policy of non-recognition, but the problems of different forums are themselves different, and the arguments that might weight a decision with respect to the United Nations need not be determinative of the decision in Washington. There is no point to United States recognition until we have more to gain from such recognition than we have to lose. And it is difficult to see what substantial present advantages would flow from such actions. The opportunity to have diplomatic representation, to observe directly, and to influence does not seem of prime importance and has been much exaggerated in discussion. On those issues that require negotiations with the Chinese, appropriate *ad hoc* means can be found in the future as they have in the past. They will be successful or unsuccessful depending upon the incentive for the Chinese to reach agreement. And at least the *ad hoc* means required by non-recognition avoid the infelicities and dangers of negotiations at the level of either chief of state or government or high cabinet.

The problem of recognition of the Chinese Communists also directly involves American policy toward Taiwan. Much misinformation exists about the situation on Taiwan, and it is difficult to resolve it in short space. However, a few remarks are in order. The regime on Taiwan is not Fascist or totalitarian. Neither is it an exemplary democratic regime. The national, as opposed to the provincial, government is supposed to represent all of China, and Taiwan is represented only as one of the provinces of China. Along with other measures, including the control of the army and police, this preserves the control of the Kuomintang and of Chiang Kai-shek over Taiwan. Opposition and dissent are permitted but not to the point at which they would challenge the stability of the regime. Personal freedom is quite satisfactory. Economic conditions are improving rapidly despite one of the world's highest birthrates. The land reform is one of the best in the world and has produced a class of peasant entrepreneurs who are proud of their achievements and determined to defend them. Whether the Chiang regime would win a majority vote after freely conducted elections is difficult to determine, but it has at least the passive support of the immense majority of the population. There is no significant support on Taiwan for revolutionary action against the Chiang regime or for Communism. Any policy that permitted Communist conquest of Taiwan would constitute a betrayal not merely of the Kuomintang, but also of the ten million people on Taiwan who abhor Communism and all it stands for.

On the other hand, the Kuomintang is not the organization best endowed to exploit revolutionary possibilities on the China mainland. Although it has reformed considerably since its loss of the mainland, its reputation both in China and in other countries, without whose support aid to revolutionary forces would be difficult or impossible, is bad. A belief that successful revolution would succeed only in re-establishing the Kuomintang in control, although almost surely incorrect, would nonetheless inhibit successful development of the revolution. There are dangers involved in dissociating the United States from the Taiwan regime that should not be underestimated. Yet, in some fashion, a transition in support attitudes seems necessary.

The Quemoy and Matsu problems are exceptionally difficult. There is little sympathy in other countries for retention of these islands, and there seems little doubt that eventually they must be given up to the mainland regime. On the other hand, they do have considerable strategic importance. They block off the important ports of Amoy and Minhow, interdict coastal shipping, and make most difficult any move toward the Pescadores or Taiwan proper. They are quite defensible militarily and could be taken only at a most severe cost considering the high morale and military ability of the defending forces. Moreover, loss of these islands would bring the active war much closer to Taiwan and have considerable psychological and political consequences on that island. The situation grows progressively more difficult; yet, there seems little reason for a change of policy at this time. Perhaps as part of a deal regularizing many of the problems in Far Asia, return of the islands to the mainland regime should be considered. However, that seems premature presently.

JAPAN

The problem of American policy toward Japan also is quite difficult. We have suffered through a period in which the American Embassy cut itself off from the main currents of Japanese opinion and help to place Japan in a position in which it appeared to have a satellite foreign policy. This has done grave harm to American interests in Japan. American military bases in Japan also do considerable political harm, primarily because their use is misunderstood by most Japanese. Such bases are not designed for offensive operations of either a conventional or nuclear kind. They are important primarily for tactical and logistic reasons. Without these bases, American ability to act rapidly in case of aggression or subversion in important Asian areas would be questionable. The bases also commit America to Japanese defense in a way not possible in their absence. They, thus, deter the use of nuclear threats or blackmail against Japan. There could be no good military reason to use nuclear weapons against these bases without also using them against the United States. Instead, the Japanese wrongly see these bases as increasing the nuclear danger for Japan. It is doubtful, however, whether argument, no matter how correct, will be persuasive on this matter. The United States may have to decide whether the bases are worth the political costs.[8]

Additionally, the United States must encourage Japan to play an independent role in Asia, a difficult proposition because of Japanese unpopularity in much of Asia. But Japanese political frustrations can best be satisfied when Japan has an independent political role that is satisfactory to its dignity as a great and progressive nation. Even though this may mean occasional differences in policy between Japan and the United States, even with respect to a China policy, the improvement of the political situation in Japan ought to be a far more important objective of American foreign policy than the elimination of policy differences. Indeed, it was a fault of American foreign policy under Dulles that we were too fearful of independent foreign policies on the part of associated nations. Since the United States did not have available Communist techniques for coordination of national policies, despite differences in specific interests, this produced dissatisfaction and malaise on the part of governments that felt they were unwisely or inconsistently coerced or on the part of publics that felt their governments lacked the independence of action consonant with pursuit of national interests and dignity.

CUBA

The ill-fated invasion of Cuba in April 1961 compounded military and political errors that need not be detailed here. In brief, however, the United States

---

8. There are vociferous groups opposed to American bases in England also. But even larger segments of the public and leadership understand that the bases constitute a commitment that deters rather than provokes the Russians. Moreover, there is a history of alliance with the United States and some willingness to run joint risks. This is absent in Japan.

moved against Cuba before it moved against Right-Wing dictators; it supported the wrong elements from among the various anti-Castro groupings. These political errors were most serious, for the United States cannot permit itself to appear to oppose Castro only because of his pro-Communism or to support certain Cuban groups because they will re-establish American economic interests in Cuba. Quite apart from the validity of the charges that would arise from such appearances—and I believe them to be false—the fact of the appearances cuts the United States off from the support it needs in a world in which it is not politically feasible to act merely according to the politics of force.

Intervention, as such, was undoubtedly a sound policy, for the present world is not a world in which non-intervention is possible. It is, however, the effectiveness of policy that is important, and it was with respect to this effectiveness that American policy in Cuba failed. Now that intervention has been attempted and has failed, it would be most difficult to resurrect it as a policy in the absence of acute provocation on the part of Cuba. The major American effort must be devoted to reform and modernization in Latin America exclusive of Cuba. This, plus the possible failure of the Cuban revolution to satisfy Cuban expectations concerning modernization, may lead to increased political dissidence and sabotage in Cuba. If the regime can be isolated by the OAS, it may then collapse, or some later intervention may be attempted under more favorable circumstances.

There is another aspect to the problem, however: This concerns the political consequences for the United States of anti-Castro activities on the part of regimes in nations like Mexico and Venezuela which the United States wishes to support. It is possible that too overt an effort by the United States to forge an anti-Castro alignment would produce consequences more undesirable than the ouster of Castro is desirable. Yet, Castro in power does pose a threat to the hemisphere. Moreover, failure to support the anti-Castro forces would constitute betrayal of the best and most democratic elements in Cuba. Thus, it would appear that some form of support for the anti-Castro forces is mandatory. We cannot afford merely to oppose Castro. We must stand for values we can defend to ourselves as well as to others. Otherwise, we shall fail.

ISRAEL

In the dispute between Israel and the Arab states, there is only one honorable course that the United States can take. Contemporary Arab demands on Israel do not have the function of adjusting a wrong; they have the function of destroying Israel. This is particularly true of the repatriation demand. This does not mean that the United States ought not to sympathize with the plight of the Arab refugees, or that it should approve of the more rambunctious actions of the stiff-necked Ben-Gurion. Yet, Israel has a right to exist; the Israelis have as much right to self-government as the Arabs; Israel is a democratic state; and it represents most of the virtues in which America believes. Even if the latter were not true, the United States could hardly connive in efforts to destroy a state that is legitimate according to the standards of international law merely to win the favor of the Arabs.

It is a truism to call the Middle Eastern problem complex. To deny the Arab claims is not to underestimate the depth of Arab feelings or the difficulties Arab politicians would have in trying to make peace with Israel. Neither is it to deny that the existence of Israel imposes costs on the United States that would not exist had there never been an Israel; nor to deny that the venom the Arabs carry toward Israel helps to corrode their own political efforts individually and collectively. But Israel does exist, and one cannot create the conditions that would have existed had there never been an Israel by cooperating in its demise. Arab demands against Israel are of a nature that cannot be compromised and, therefore, they cannot be met in a way satisfactory to the Arabs short of the destruction of Israel. As much as we need to reconcile the uncommitted states, this is an impossible policy for us. This is true not merely for internal political reasons, but primarily because a cold-blooded policy of this nature would corrupt our own decision processes, make the Arabs contemptuous of us rather than friendly to us, increase the demands of those who wish us ill, and destroy and confidence of those who wish us well. We cannot afford a Machiavellian policy. We would only disillusion ourselves if we behaved in that fashion.

The existence of Israel is due primarily to the desires and organizing skills of the Jews of Palestine. United Nations resolutions and American decisions did not create Israel. They only recognized an existing fact which the Arabs did not have the power to change without extensive outside aid. The United States can share neither the credit nor the blame for the existence of the state of Israel, and those in the Department of State who argued "realistically" for a policy opposed to the Israeli state had little genuine understanding of the world in which they lived. If there was any past mistake in American policy, it was in refusing to impose peace while the United States was strong in the Middle East and the Russians weak. Then, compromises of a durable nature might successfully have been imposed on both sides, and sheer duress might have produced adjustment. Clearly, a state of war would have been difficult to re-establish after the formalization of peace treaties. In the meantime, transactions between Israel and the Arab states, beneficial to both and difficult to sever, might have been established. But that opportunity—sacrificed as usual by the "realists"—is past and cannot be recalled. The present situation is most difficult and will remain so almost regardless of what the United States does.

Harsh as it may sound, the United States cannot gain from major efforts to reconcile the Arab states. It must depend upon their self-interest in maintaining independence from the Russians and in continuing the flow of oil. When and if the Arabs ever become ready, the United States ought to cooperate with them in endeavors or projects consonant with American values and Arab interests. Until such time, there is no point in wishing for a world that cannot be.

Conclusion

Any particular policy recommendation may, of course, prove inappropriate on the basis of more careful analysis or more thorough consideration of the relevant factors. But two general considerations emerge from the preceding analysis that, in my opinion, would constitute good guidelines for policy decisions. The United States needs to enunciate foreign-policy goals that are capable of arousing support and enthusiasm both within the United States and among our allies. Indeed, these goals would serve best if they became known behind the iron curtain and had subversive effects there. The status quo will no longer be sufficient for success. We must take our chances with change and attempt to promote those changes harmonious with our own values and with the best interests of peoples everywhere. Time is no longer with us. Holding the line and delaying actions will not do. We are neither rich nor strong enough to be conservative or to ignore or to deny the aspirations of the great masses of mankind. We must choose, and only if we choose rightly can we hope to preserve those values and institutions that we hold dear.

Positive goals must be backed by a sound military and diplomatic posture. Idealism in terms of objectives must not be confused with muddle-headedness in terms of means. We face a strong foe, capable of resorting to military action and willing to employ threats of the most provocative type. This foe will use negotiations and conferences primarily not to reach cooperative agreement but to destroy our institutions and way of life. Unless and until we can force changes in his mode of organization and operation—not necessarily by physical means—we also must regard the situation as a struggle. We must be ceaselessly alert, reasonably confident, and ready to defend what we stand for.

In our relations with our friends and allies, we must recognize that their interests and their goals are not identical with our own. We must expect some disagreements with them and, if we respect their freedom and independence, we shall also respect their right to disagree. Despite the desperate nature of the struggle, we cannot expect to dictate to other nations. We do and ought to expect general support from our friends. But we must earn this support in terms of policies that win their support. Where this is not feasible, and where we are certain that we are right, we must have the courage and moral fortitude to temporarily go it alone, without renouncing our interest in or friendship for other countries.

These are difficult demands to make in a democracy. To repeat what has become trite, but nonetheless remains true, this cannot be accomplished without strong presidential leadership, which takes the people into its confidence and builds the kind of public support, based on trust, that will permit ventures into the untried and the imaginative realms of statecraft. Beneath the layers of selfishness and self-centeredness, the ideals of the United States will still support policies oriented to vision and faith. There is still an American ideal that views democracy and the products of modern civilization as the heritage of all mankind.

10. The Foundations of National Security

J. WILLIAM FULBRIGHT

THERE IS NO LONGER any validity in the Clausewitz doctrine of war as "a carrying out of policy with other means." Nuclear weapons have rendered it totally obsolete because the instrument of policy is now totally disproportionate to the end in view. Nuclear weapons have deprived force of its utility as an instrument of national policy, leaving the nuclear powers with vastly greater but far less useful power than they had before. So long as there is reason—not virtue, but simply reason—in the foreign policy of the great nations, nuclear weapons are not so much an instrument as an inhibition on policy.

By all available evidence, the Russians are no less aware of this than we. The memory of their 20 million dead in World War II is still fresh in the minds of most Russians. In a speech on July 19, 1963, Chairman Khrushchev castigated the Chinese Communists as "those who want to start a war against everybody. . . Do these men know," he asked, "that if all the nuclear warheads were touched off, the world would be in such a state that the survivors would envy the dead?" Or, commenting again in Hungary in April, 1964, on the equanimity with which the Chinese Communists spoke of nuclear war, Khrushchev expressed his opinion that "it is not from an excess of brains but from an absence of them that people say such things."

In the pursuit of its ambitions, whether by militant or peaceful means, the Soviet Union, like any other nation, is subject to the unending pressures for change imposed by time and circumstance. "Man," it has been said, "the supreme pragmatist, is a revisionist by nature."[1] Those who attribute to the Soviet leaders a permanent and unalterable determination to destroy the free societies of the West are crediting the Soviet Union with a strength and constancy of will that, so far as I know, has never been achieved by any nation.

There is, in fact, every reason to anticipate change, both within the Communist nations and in the relations between the Communist and the free nations. If there is any "law" of history, it is the inevitability and continuity of change. It is sometimes for the better, but often for the worse, and we cannot assume that the future evolution of the Communist world will be toward moderate and peaceful policies. But neither are we helpless and passive spectators to the course which the Communist nations follow. We have the means and resources to influence events in the Soviet Union and in other bloc countries. Our ability to put those means to effective use depends in no small measure on our willingness to go beyond a rigidly ideological view of communism and to deal with the Communist countries as the national entities which they are, each with special national interests and aspirations.

If we look at the Communist bloc objectively, and not through the distorting prism of ideological hostility, we can see that important and encouraging changes have already taken place. We perceive that Soviet society and the Soviet economy are becoming highly complex, too complex to be completely and efficiently controlled by a highly centralized dictatorship. We perceive that under the pressures of growing complexity a degree of economic decentralization has taken place, that the police terror of the Stalin era has been abated, that the Central Committee of the Communist Party may even be developing under Khrushchev into a kind of rudimentary parliamentary body. And most important of all, as I pointed out in Chapter I, the unity of the Communist bloc has been disrupted, and we find ourselves confronted with a growing diversity of national outlooks and policies, ranging from the harsh orthodoxy of Communist China to the pragmatism of the Soviet Union, the nationalism of Poland and Hungary, and the astonishing diplomatic independence of Rumania.

There are those who maintain that the only valid test of altered Soviet policies must be the explicit repudiation of those tenets of Marxist ideology that call for world revolution and the universal victory of communism. To ask for overt renunciation of a cherished doctrine is to expect too much of human nature. Men do not repudiate the doctrines and dogmas to which they have sworn their loyalty. Instead they rationalize, revise, and reinterpret them to meet new needs and new circumstances, all the while protesting that their heresy is the purest orthodoxy.

Something of this nature is now occurring in the Soviet Union. Khrushchev has not repudiated Marx and Lenin; on the contrary, he vows his fealty to

---

1. Eric Hansen, "Revisionism: Genesis and Prognosis" (unpublished paper).

their doctrines at every opportunity. But his "orthodoxy" has not deterred him from some striking interpretations of the scriptures. Contrast, for example, the Marxist-Leninist emphasis on discipline and self-sacrifice and revolution with Khrushchev's famous words in Budapest in April, 1964: "The important thing is that we should have more to eat—good goulash—schools, housing, and ballet. How much more do these things give to the enlargement of man's life? It is worth fighting and working for these things." Or contrast the Marxist-Leninist principle of relentless struggle for the universal victory of communism with Khrushchev's answer to his own rhetorical question as to whether the Soviet Union should help the French working class to take over power. "Who asked us to mix in their affairs?" was his reply. "What do we know about them?"

The attribution of an unalterable will and constancy to Soviet policy has been a serious handicap to our own policy. It has restricted our ability to gain insights into the realities of Soviet society and Soviet foreign policy. It has denied us valuable opportunities to take advantage of changing conditions in the Communist world and to encourage changes which would reduce the Communist threat to the free world. We have overestimated the ability of the Soviets to pursue malevolent aims, without regard to time or circumstances, and, in so doing, we have underestimated our own ability to influence Soviet behavior.

A stigma of heresy has been attached to suggestions by American policymakers that Soviet policy can change or that it is sometimes altered in response to our own. But it is a fact that in the wake of the failure of the aggressive policies of the Stalin period, the Soviet leaders have gradually shifted to a policy of peaceful, or competitive, coexistence with the West. This policy confronts us with certain dangers but also with important opportunities if we are wise enough to take advantage of them.

The abrupt change in the Soviet position which made possible the signing of the nuclear test ban treaty in 1963 appears to have been motivated by the general failure of competitive coexistence as practiced in the last few years and by a number of specific problems, both foreign and domestic. The most conspicuous of these is the public eruption of the dispute with Communist China. In addition, the Soviet leaders have been troubled by economic difficulties at home, particularly in agriculture, by the increasingly insistent demands of the Russian people for more and better food, clothing, and housing, and by difficulties between the regime and Soviet intellectuals and artists; by increasing centrifugal tendencies in Eastern Europe, aggravated by the dismaying contrast with an increasingly prosperous and powerful Western Europe; and by the negligible rewards of Soviet diplomacy and economic aid in Asia and Africa.

The most crucial failure of Soviet policy has been in its dealings with the West. Contrary to Soviet expectations of a few years ago, it has proven impossible to extract concessions from the West on Berlin and Central Europe by nuclear diplomacy. Thwarted in Europe, Khrushchev embarked in the fall of 1962 on the extremely dangerous adventure of placing missiles in Cuba, hoping, it would seem, to force a solution in Berlin and an unfreezing of Central Europe. The debacle in Cuba led the Soviet leaders to a major reappraisal of their policies.

That reappraisal has apparently resulted in a decision to seek a relaxation of tensions with the West. The nuclear test ban treaty and subsequent limited agreements with the West were clearly calculated to serve that purpose. In addition, the tone of Soviet diplomacy has changed; in matters ranging from Cuba to Vietnam, vituperation has been muted and the Russians have passed up a number of opportunities to quarrel with the United States.

From the Soviet point of view, a limited *détente* with the West appears to offer certain clear advantages. Three reasons for seeking improved relations with the West seem of major importance. First and foremost is the genuine fear of nuclear war which the Soviets share with the West, all the more since the United States demonstrated in the Cuban crisis that it was prepared to use nuclear weapons to defend its vital interests. Secondly, in the mounting conflict with the Chinese, the Soviet Union can claim a success for its policies of "peaceful coexistence" and, more important, can use the world-wide popularity of the test ban and other arms-control measures to strengthen its position both in the Communist bloc and in the non-Communist underdeveloped countries, thereby further isolating the Chinese. Thirdly, Khrushchev appears to be interested in measures which will permit a leveling off, and perhaps a reduction, of weapons expenditures in order to be able to divert scarce resources for meeting some of the demands of the Russian people for a better life.

In an article written shortly after the signing of the test ban treaty, Professor Zbigniew Brzezinski, Director of Columbia University's Research Institute on Communist Affairs, interpreted the Soviet adherence to the test ban treaty as follows: "Khrushchev's acceptance of an 'atmosphere-only' test ban strongly suggests a major Soviet reassessment of the world situation and an implicit acknowledgment that Soviet policies of the last few years have failed. The Soviet leaders have evidently concluded that the general world situation is again in a 'quiescent' stage. Instead of dissipating Soviet resources in useless revolutionary efforts, or missile adventures of the Cuban variety, they will probably concentrate on consolidating their present position."[2]

If the relaxation of tensions is conceived by the Soviets as an interlude in which to consolidate their position, strengthen their power base, and then renew their aggressive policies against the West, is it wise for us to grant them this interlude? It is indeed wise, for two main reasons: first, because it will provide the West with an identical opportunity to strengthen the power base of the free world; and secondly, because it will generate conditions in

2. Zbigniew Brzezinski, "After the Test Ban," *The New Republic*, August 31, 1963, p. 18.

which the Soviet and Communist bloc peoples will be emboldened to step up their demands for peace and a better life, conditions which the Soviet leadership will find it exceedingly difficult to alter.

From the point of view of the West, an interlude of relaxed world tensions will provide a splendid opportunity to strengthen the foundations of the security of the free world—if only we will use it. First of all, we can use the opportunity to bring greater unity and prosperity to the Atlantic community—by seeking means of resolving our differences over the control of nuclear weapons and by negotiating extensive tariff reductions under the terms of the American Trade Expansion Act of 1962. Secondly, we can re-invigorate our efforts to strengthen the free nations of Asia, Africa, and Latin America by providing a more discriminating and intelligent program of economic assistance and by encouraging co-operative free-world aid programs through such agencies as the International Development Association. Finally, we can use a period of relaxed tensions to focus energy and resources on our long-neglected needs here at home—on the expansion and improvement of our public education, on generating greater economic growth and full employment, on the conservation of our resources and the renewal of our cities.

All of these lines of action have a direct and vital bearing on our national security. If we pursue them with vigor and determination, I think it can be confidently predicted that the free world will be the major beneficiary of a period of relaxed world tension, with a power base so strengthened that the margin of free-world superiority over the Communist bloc will be substantially widened.

The other great advantage to the West of a period of relaxed tensions is that it may release long-suppressed pressures for peace and the satisfaction of civilian needs within the Soviet bloc. Public opinion, even in a dictatorship like the Soviet Union, is an enormously powerful force which no government can safely defy for too long or in too many ways. Russian public opinion is overwhelmingly opposed to war and overwhelmingly in favor of higher wages, of better food, clothing, and housing, and of all the good things of life in a modern industrial society. The Russian *people* may well turn out to be a powerful ally of the free nations, who also want peace and prosperity. It is quite possible that a thaw in Soviet-American relations, even though conceived by the Soviet leadership as a temporary pause, could lead gradually to an entirely new relationship. Motives have a way of becoming lost as the actions to which they give rise generate new attitudes and new and unforeseen motives. Pressed by the demands of an increasingly assertive public opinion, the Soviet leaders may find new reasons to continue a policy of peace and accommodation with the West. Step by step their revolutionary zeal may diminish, as they find that a peaceful and affluent national existence is not really so tragic a fate as they had imagined.

No one knows whether Soviet society will actually evolve along these lines, but the trend of Soviet history suggests that it is by no means impossible.

"Indeed, the most striking characteristic of recent Soviet foreign policy," Professor Shulman has pointed out, "has been the way in which policies undertaken for short-term, expediential purposes have tended to elongate in time, and become embedded in doctrine and political strategy."[3]

It is possible, I believe, for the West to encourage a hopeful direction in Soviet policy. We can seek to strengthen Russian public opinion as a brake against dangerous policies by conveying accurate information about Western life and Western aims, and about the heavy price that both sides are paying for the cold war. We can make it clear to the Russians that they have nothing to fear from the West so long as they respect the rights and independence of other nations. We can suggest to them at every possible opportunity, both by persuasion and by example, that there is no greater human vanity than the assumption that one's own values have universal validity, and no enterprise more certain of failure than the attempt to impose the preferences of a single society on an unwilling world. And finally, we can encourage them to recognize, as we must never fail to recognize ourselves, that adventures born of passion are soon severed from their lofty aims, turning idealism into barbarism and men into demons.

On November 14, 1860, Alexander Hamilton Stephens, who subsequently became Vice-President of the Southern Confederacy, delivered an address to the Georgia Legislature which bears wisdom for our own time. Appealing to his colleagues to delay the withdrawal of Georgia from the Union, Stephens said of the prospective secession: "It may be that out of it we may become greater and more prosperous, but I am candid and sincere in telling you that I fear if we yield to passion, and without sufficient cause shall take that step, that instead of becoming greater or more peaceful, prosperous, and happy—instead of becoming Gods, we will become demons, and at no distant day commence cutting one another's throats. This is my apprehension. Let us, therefore, whatever we do, meet these difficulties, great as they are, like wise and sensible men, and consider them in the light of all the consequences which may attend our action."[4]

The purpose of a realistic foreign policy is not to end the cold war but to modify it, not to resolve the conflict between communism and freedom—a goal which is almost certainly beyond the reach of the present generation—but to remove some of the terror and passion from it. The progress thus far achieved and now in prospect has been small in substance, in the sense that it has brought us scarcely closer to a solution of such great problems as the arms race and the division of Germany. But in another sense—the extremely important psychological sense—it may be that we are doing better than we

3. Statement by Professor Marshall Shulman, August 26, 1963, Hearings before the Committee on Foreign Relations, United States Senate, 88th Congress, First Session, *Nuclear Test Ban Treaty* (Washington, D.C.: U.S. Government Printing Office, 1963), p. 797.

4. Alexander Hamilton Stephens, "Secession," in *Modern Eloquence* (New York: P. F. Collier & Sons, 1928), Vol. II, p. 203.

know. The ultimate criterion of the importance of any issue is its implications for war and peace. The division of Germany is a most important issue in itself, but its global and historical significance, like that of the arms race, is that it has a critical bearing on whether we shall have war or peace. If, by a series of agreements on issues which in substance are much less important than the division of Germany and the arms race—such agreements as the test ban treaty, reductions in the output of fissionable materials, or the opening of consulates and airline connections—we succeed in creating a *state of mind* in which neither side considers war as a likely eventuality or as a real option for itself except under radically changed conditions, then in fact we will have progressed toward precisely the same objective which a German settlement or a general disarmament agreement would help to achieve—a world substantially free of the threat of nuclear incineration.

The point which I am trying, imperfectly, to make is that in our quest for world peace the *alteration of attitudes* is no less important, perhaps more important, than the resolution of issues. It is in the minds of men, after all, that wars are spawned; to act upon the human mind, regardless of the issue or occasion for doing so, is to act upon the source of conflict and the potential source of redemption and reconciliation. It would seem, therefore, that there may be important new things to be learned about international relations through the scholarship of psychologists and psychiatrists.

When all is said and done, when the abstractions and subtleties of political science have been exhausted, there remain the most basic unanswered questions about war and peace and why we contest the issues we contest and why we even care about them. As Aldous Huxley has written: "There may be arguments about the best way of raising wheat in a cold climate or of re-afforesting a denuded mountain. But such arguments never lead to organized slaughter. Organized slaughter is the result of arguments about such questions as the following: Which is the best nation? The best religion? The best political theory? The best form of government? Why are other people so stupid and wicked? Why can't they see how good and intelligent we are? Why do they resist our beneficent efforts to bring them under our control and make them like ourselves?"[5]

In our search for answers to the complex questions of war and peace, we come ultimately to the paradox of man himself, which I have never heard better expressed than in a one-page essay called "Man," written by an American hill-country philosopher whose writings suggest strongly the style and thought of Mark Twain. It reads as follows:

Man is a queer animal, like the beasts of the fields, the fowls of the air, and the fishes of the sea, he came into this world without his consent and is going out the same way.

5. Aldous Huxley, "The Politics of Ecology" (pamphlet, published by The Center for the Study of Democratic Institutions, Santa Barbara, California, 1963), p. 6.

At birth he is one of the most helpless creatures in all existence. He can neither walk, talk, swim nor crawl, and has but two legs while most other animals have four legs. Unlike other animals he has no covering for his body to protect it against the bite or sting of poisonous insects, tooth or claw of ferocious beasts save a little hair which appears about his body only in patches.

With all his limitations he yet has one advantage over animals—the power of reason, but history shows that he often discards that for superstition. Of all the animals on earth, man has shown himself to be the most cruel and brutal. He is the only animal that will create instruments of death for his own destruction.

Man is the only animal on all the earth that has ever been known to burn its young as a sacrifice to appease the wrath of some imaginary deity. He is the only one that will build homes, towns and cities at such a cost in sacrifice and suffering and turn around and destroy them in war.

He is the only animal that will gather his fellows together in creeds, clans, and nations, line them up in companies, regiments, armies, and get glory out of their slaughter. Just because some king or politician told him to.

Man is the only creature in all existence that is not satisfied with the punishment he can inflict on his fellows while here, but had to invent a a hell of fire and brimestone in which to burn them after they are dead.

Where he came from, or when, or how, or where he is going after death he does not know, but he hopes to live again in ease and idleness where he can worship his gods and enjoy himself, watching his fellow creatures wriggle and writhe in eternal flames down in hell.

The root question, for which I must confess I have no answer, is how and why it is that so much of the energy and intelligence that men could use to make life better for themselves is used instead to make life difficult and painful for other men. When the subtleties of strategy and power and diplomatic method have all been explained, we are still left with the seemingly unanswerable question of how and why it is that we *care* about such things, which are so remote from the personal satisfactions that bring pleasure and grace and fulfillment into our lives.

The paradoxes of human nature are eternal and perhaps unanswerable, but I do think we know enough about elemental human needs to be able to apply certain psychological principles in our efforts to alleviate the tensions of the cold war.

In this connection, I would suggest that a great deal—more than one would suspect—depends upon the *manner* in which we seek to negotiate reasonable agreements with the Russians. We must remember that we are not dealing with automatons whose sole function in life is to embody an ideology and a party line, but with human beings—people who, like ourselves, have special areas of pride, prejudice, and sensitivity. I have found, for example, as have others who have discussed current issues with Soviet officials and citizens, that the whole trend of a conversation can be influenced by the way in which you begin it. If you confront them at the outset with an attack on the harshness of their ideology, the shortcomings of their economy, or the excesses of their dictatorship, you are likely to be rewarded with an outburst of chauvinism and vituperation about American policy and practices. There are those who find such encounters emotionally satisfying, but no one can deny that they are singularly barren of productive results.

If, on the other hand, you start out with a compliment about the successes of Soviet society—and there have been a few—or with a candid reference to the shortcomings of our own society—and there have also been a few of these—then it often happens that the response is surprisingly expansive and conciliatory. You are likely to hear an admission that everything, after all, is not perfect in the Soviet Union, and that there are even a few things about America that are admirable and worthy of imitation.

The compliments in themselves are of little importance. But the candor and the cordiality are of great importance. As any good businessman knows, they set a tone and an atmosphere in which emotion gives way to reason and it becomes possible to do business, to move on from cordial generalities to specific negotiations. They generate that minimum of mutual confidence which is absolutely essential for reaching concrete agreements. Under existing circumstances, no one can expect such agreements to be more than modest accommodations which are clearly in the mutual interest; but they are at least a start toward more significant arrangements, and as I have already suggested, the critical question of war and peace may have less to do with the specifications of agreements than with the attitudes they engender and the attitudes they dispel.

"Frightened, hostile individuals tend to behave in ways which aggravate their difficulties instead of resolving them," says the distinguished psychiatrist Dr. Jerome D. Frank, "and frightened, hostile nations seem to behave similarly."[6] A nation, like an individual, Dr. Frank suggests, is likely to respond to a feared rival by breaking off communications, by provocative behavior, or by taking measures which promise immediate relief, regardless of their ultimate consequences.

Among the psychiatrically constructive techniques which might be used to cope with the destructive emotions of the cold war, Dr. Frank suggests the following: that we give Russian views our respectful attention as one way of making the Russians more receptive to ours; that we enormously increase communications between the Communist and the free worlds through cultural, scientific, agricultural, and student exchange programs; that we engage in co-operative activities that will enable both sides to achieve desired goals

6. Letter from Dr. Frank to the author, September 13, 1960.

neither can as readily achieve alone—such activities as joint projects in space exploration or in building health services throughout the world, or such enterprises as the possible Central American canal consortium referred to in Chapter I.

Through such means we may strive to break through the ideological passions and national animosities that fill men's minds with destructive zeal and blind them to what Aldous Huxley called the simple human preference for life and peace. Through such means we may strive to build strong foundations for our national security and, indeed, for the security of all peoples.

We must bring to bear all the resources of human knowledge and invention to build viable foundations of security in the nuclear age—the resources of political science and history, of economics and sociology, of psychology and literature and the arts. It is not enough to seek security through armaments or even through ingenious schemes of disarmament; nor is it enough to seek security through schemes for the transfer of territories or for the deployment and redeployment of forces. Security is a state of mind rather than a set of devices and arrangements. The latter are important because they contribute, but only to the extent that they contribute, to generating a *psychological process* in which peoples and statesmen come increasingly to think of war as undesirable and unfeasible.

It is this *process* that has critical importance for our security. Whether we advance it by seeking a settlement on Berlin or a new disarmament agreement, by the opening of consulates or by a joint enterprise in space, is less important than that the process be advanced. Our emphasis at any one time should be on those issues which seem most likely to be tractable and soluble. As long as we are by one means or another cultivating a world-wide state of mind in which peace is favored over war, we are doing the most effective possible thing to strengthen the foundations of our security. And only when such a state of mind is widely prevalent in the world will the kind of unprecedented political creativity on a global scale which has been made necessary by the invention of nuclear weapons become possible as well.

The cold war and all the other national rivalries of our time are not likely to evaporate in our lifetimes. The major question of our time is not how to end these conflicts but whether we can find some way to conduct them without resorting to weapons that will resolve them once and for all by wiping out the contestants. A generation ago we were speaking of "making the world safe for democracy." Having failed of this in two World Wars, we must now seek ways of making the world reasonably safe for the continuing contest between those who favor democracy and those who oppose it. It is a modest aspiration, but it is a sane and realistic one for a generation which, having failed of grander things, must now look to its own survival.

Extreme nationalism and dogmatic ideology are luxuries that the human race can no longer afford. It must turn its energies now to the politics of survival. If we do so, we may find in time that we can do better than just survive.

We may find that the simple human preference for life and peace has an inspirational force of its own, less intoxicating perhaps than the sacred abstractions of nation and ideology, but far more relevant to the requirements of human life and human happiness.

There are, to be sure, risks in such an approach. There is an element of trust in it, and we can be betrayed. But human life is fraught with risks, and the behavior of the sane man is not the avoidance of all possible danger but the weighing of greater against lesser risks and of risks against opportunities.

We have an opportunity at present to try to build stronger foundations for our national security than armaments alone can ever provide. That opportunity lies in a policy of encouraging the development of a habit of peaceful and civilized contacts between ourselves and the Communist bloc. I believe that this opportunity must be pursued, with reason and restraint, with due regard for the pitfalls involved and for the possibility that our efforts may fail, but with no less regard for the promise of a safer and more civilized world. In the course of this pursuit, both we and our adversaries may find it possible one day to break through the barriers of nationalism and ideology and to approach each other in something of the spirit of Pope John's words to Khrushchev's son-in-law: "They tell me you are an atheist. But you will not refuse an old man's blessing for your children."

11. The Global Crunch

FRANK CHURCH

FOR ALL THEIR immense physical power, the two dominant nations in the world—the United States and the Soviet Union—suffer from a neurotic sense of insecurity, although neither regards itself as being in imminent danger of attack by the other. At tremendous cost, their nuclear armories keep them at bay and, even if each were foolishly to add a new inventory of ABM missiles to the awesome stockpile, the delicate equilibrium will hold, leaving the two rivals in a state of chronic but only low-grade anxiety over the danger of attack by the other. It is a costly and desperately dangerous way of keeping the peace, but it is all we have shown ourselves capable of thus far.

The immediate threat that each superpower perceives from the other is its ideological impact on third countries, most particularly those that it regards as its protective buffers. It is one of the supposed realities of international politics—a kind of higher law transcending such legal documents as the United Nations Charter—that great powers are allowed to have spheres of influence made up of "friendly" neighbors. In the case of maritime powers such as the United States, the neighborhood may extend to the fringes of distant continents; but, whether or not the buffer is contiguous, the principle is the same: In order to guard itself against even the most remote or hypothetical threat to its security, a great power is held entitled to intervene in the affairs of its small neighbors, even to the extent of making the basic decisions

as to how they will organize and run their own societies. This is where ideology comes in. Neither the Soviet Union nor the United States seems to regard
itself as being in danger of *direct* ideological subversion by the other, although there have been times—the period of Stalinism in the Soviet Union
and of McCarthyism in the United States—when they did. In more recent
years, the focus of great-power apprehension has been on their small-power
buffers. Over these, each great power displays frenzied determination to
exert ideological control. Within its sphere, the Soviet Union insists on the
maintenance of Communist governments, inaccurately described, for the
most part, as socialist; the United States, on the other hand, insists on the
maintenance of non-Communist governments that we, for the most part,
incorrectly call free.

Starting with the assumption that ideology is an instrument of foreign
policy through which the rival great power will establish its political domination over others, whenever and wherever the opportunity arises, each great
power seems to look upon its own buffer states as peculiarly susceptible to
ideological subversion by the other great power. It is further assumed that
the ultimate aim of this subversion is to isolate and undermine the great
power itself; that ideology, being contagious, is singularly suited to this purpose; and that, like a disease, it must therefore be isolated and destroyed
before it can spread. These assumptions lead to the conclusion that it is no
more than an act of self-defense for a great power to take such measures as
it judges necessary to preserve the ideological purity of its sphere of
influence.

Seen in this way, the various interventions of the United States and the
Soviet Union are explained not only as legitimate defensive measures but as
positive services. Thus, in the case of the intervention in the Dominican
Republic in 1965, American policy makers were untroubled by the fact that
the U.S. actions violated both the Rio Treaty and the Charter of the Organization of American States and that the revolution the U.S. suppressed was on
behalf of a freely elected government that had been expelled by a coup.
These were judged only superficial considerations when weighed against the
need to defend America from the specter of a "second Cuba" while rescuing
th Dominicans from their foolhardy flirtation with communism. Similarly, in
the case of Vietnam, far from wishing to impose anything on anybody, the
United States, in former Secretary of State Dean Rusk's view during a 1967
press conference, seeks only to save the world from being "cut in two by
Asian communism."

It remained for the Russians to devise a doctrine of ideological justification
for the policy of interventionism. In a document that has come to be known
as the Brezhnev doctrine, published in *Pravda*, the Soviet government
pointed out that, in invading Czechoslovakia, the Soviet Union and its pro-
tégés were doing no more than "discharging their internationalist duty
toward the fraternal peoples of Czechoslovakia" and defending their own

"socialist gains" against "anti-socialist forces" supported by "world imperialism" seeking to "export counterrevolution." Turn this phraseology around, substitute "anti-democratic" for "anti-socialist," "world communism" for "world imperialism," "revolution" for "counterrevolution," and the resultant rationale differs little from the official explanation of our own interventions in recent years.

Whether or not the Russians actually believed their excuse I would not venture to guess. At any rate, I don't believe it; I believe that the Russians—even if they persuaded themselves otherwise—suppressed the liberal government of Czechoslovakia because they feared the contagion of freedom for the rest of their empire and ultimately for the Soviet Union itself. Nor do I believe that, in suppressing revolutions in Latin America and in trying to suppress revolution in Vietnam, the United States is acting legitimately in its own self-defense. There are, God knows, profound differences between the internal orders of the United States and the Soviet Union—ours is a free society and theirs is a totalitarian society whose leaders have shown themselves to be terrified of freedom—but, in their foreign policies, the two superpowers have taken on a remarkable resemblance. Concerned primarily with the preservation of their own vast hegemonies, they have become, in their respective spheres, defenders of the *status quo* against the pressures of revolutionary upheaval in which each perceives little but the secret hand of the other.

The Impotence of Power

Suppressing revolution in its own immediate vicinity is an easy if embarrassing task for a superpower. Suppressing it on a distant continent is more difficult; and, as we have learned in Vietnam, beating down a strongly motivated, capably led and well-organized indigenous force is a virtual impossibility. Confronted with rising nationalistic movements, the superpowers, to their own astonishment, sometimes find themselves muscle-bound. Their nuclear power, though colossal, is so colossal as to be unusable except for keeping *each other* terrified. But in dealing with the unruly third world, as Presidential advisor Henry Kissinger pointed out in a Brookings Institution symposium called *Agenda for the Nation*, "Power no longer translates automatically into influence."

Nor, one might add, does influence translate readily into desirable or usable power. In Europe before World War One, there was a significant relationship between influence and power and between territory and power—though perhaps even then, the correlation was less than it seemed. Yet, by conquering territory or forming alliances, a nation could hope to gain material resources and political predominance. Accordingly, the balance of power was maintained—more or less—by isolating and denying opportunities for territorial expansion to the most powerful or ambitious nation. In our own time, the balance of power is determined far more by economic and technological developments *within* countries than by alliances and territorial acquisition. China, for example, has gained far greater power through the acquisition of nuclear weapons than if it had conquered all of Southeast Asia.

Nonetheless, the great powers struggle to establish their influence in neutral countries. Guided by a ritualized, anachronistic, 19th Century concept of the balance of power, they seek influence for its own sake, as if it were a concrete, negotiable asset. I am thinking not only of Vietnam, but of India, where we worry about Soviet economic aid, and to whom the President once even cut off food supplies because the Indian prime minister had sent birthday greetings to Ho Chi Minh. I am thinking of Laos, where we are not only fighting a proxy war against the Communist Pathet Lao but are engaged in an agitated rivalry with the French for the control of secondary education. And I am thinking of the global propaganda effort of the United States Information Agency, with its festivals and exhibits and libraries carefully pruned of books that seriously criticize America, all aimed at manufacturing a favorable image of the United States.

All this, we are told, is influence, and influence is power. But is it really power? Does it secure something valuable for either the other country or ourselves? If so, I have never heard a satisfactory explanation of what it is; and that, I strongly suspect, is because there is none. The real stake, I apprehend, is not power at all, but a shadow that calls itself power, nourishing an egotism that calls itself self-interest.

Vietnam, in this context, is a showcase of bankruptcy, a hopeless war fought for insubstantial stakes. As a war for high principle, Vietnam simply does not measure up: The Saigon government is neither a democracy warranting our support on ideological grounds nor a victim of *international* aggression warranting our support under the United Nations Charter. As an effort to contain Chinese power, the war in Vietnam is irrelevant as well as unsuccessful; even if a Communist Vietnam were to fall under Chinese control, as I do not think it would, the gains to China would be trivial compared with those accruing from her industrialization and acquisition of nuclear weapons.

The case on which Vietnam must stand or fall—if it has not already fallen— is the theory of an exemplary war, a war fought not so much on its own intrinsic merits as to demonstrate something to the world, such as that America will always live up to its alleged commitments or that "wars of national liberation" cannot succeed. The stake, then, is ultimately a psychological one—influence conceived as power.

Knocking down the case for an exemplary war is at this point very nearly belaboring the obvious. How we can demonstrate faithfulness to our commitments by honoring dubious promises to the Saigon generals while blatantly violating our treaty commitments in the Western Hemisphere—as we did in the covert intervention against the Arbenz government in Guatemala in 1954, the Bay of Pigs in 1961, the Dominican Republic in 1965—is beyond my understanding. As to proving that wars of national liberation cannot succeed, all that we have proved in four years of bitter, inconclusive warfare is that, even with an Army of over 500,000 Americans, we cannot win a victory for an unpopular and incompetent regime against a disciplined, nationalist insurrectionary force. In the harsh but accurate summation of Peregrine Worsthorne, a British conservative who was once a supporter of the war, writing in the *New Republic:*

> Instead of the Americans impressing the world with their strength and virtue, they are making themselves hated by some for what they are doing, and despised by the remainder for not doing it more efficaciously.

At least two prominent members of the Nixon Administration have explicitly recognized the bankruptcy of our Vietnam strategy. Henry Kissinger wrote in *Agenda for the Nation:*

> Whatever the outcome of the war in Vietnam, it is clear that it has greatly diminished American willingness to become involved in this form of warfare elsewhere. Its utility as a precedent has therefore been importantly undermined.

President Nixon's ambassador to the United Nations, Mr. Charles Yost, made the point in *Foreign Affairs* as forcefully as possible:

> The most decisive lesson of Vietnam would seem to be that no matter how much force it may expend, the United States cannot ensure the security of a country whose government is unable to mobilize and maintain sufficient popular support to control domestic insurgency. . . . If indigenous dissidents, whether or not Communist, whether or not supported from outside, are able to mobilize and maintain more effective popular support than the government, they will eventually prevail.

Vietnam is only one—albeit the most striking and costly—instance of a general, if not quite invariable, American policy of opposing revolution in the developing world. In some instances, this policy has been successful, at least for the short term. With our support, repressive governments in Brazil and Greece and a conservative government in the Dominican Republic, to cite but a few examples, have successfully held down popular aspirations for social and economic change. Through our support of reactionary governments in Latin America and elsewhere, we are preserving order in our sphere of influence and momentarily, at least, excluding revolution. But it is order purchased at the price of aligning ourselves with corruption and reaction against aggrieved and indignant indigenous forces that by and large are more responsive to popular aspirations than those that we support.

This policy of preserving the *status quo* is an exceedingly shortsighted one. Sooner or later, there can be little doubt, the rising forces of popular discontent will break through the brittle lid of repression. So, at least, historical experience suggests. We did it ourselves in 1776 and much of the history of 19th Century Europe consists of the successful rebellion of nationalist movements—German, Italian, Belgian, Greek and Slavic—against the powerful European order forged by the Congress of Vienna in 1815. In the 20th Century, we have seen the great European empires—British, French and Dutch—break up in the face of nationalist rebellion in hardly more than a decade after World War Two.

Since then, the revolutionary tide has continued to swell across Asia, Africa and Latin America, and it seems unlikely that even the immense resources of the United States will prove sufficient to contain the tide much longer. We have all but acknowledged our failure in Vietnam. What would we do if Souvanna Phouma's government in Laos should collapse, as it probably would if we terminated our counterinsurgency efforts and as it may, anyway? Or if a popular rebellion should break out against the military dictatorship in Brazil? Or if a Communist-Socialist government should come to power in Chile through a free election, as it could in 1970? Would we send armies to these large countries, as we did to South Vietnam and the small Dominican Republic? With aid and arms, we have helped delay the collapse of regimes whose very existence is an obstacle to social and political justice. Eventually, there seems little doubt, they will collapse, the more violently and with greater upheaval for having been perpetuated beyond their natural life span.

. . .

Thus far, I have been writing of the fragility and shortsightedness of our policy of repressing revolution. Something should be said about its morals as well. "Order" and "stability" are antiseptic words; they do not tell us anything about the way human beings live or the way they die. The diplomatic historians who invoke the model of Metternich's European order in the 19th Century usually neglect to mention that it was an order purchased at the cost of condemning millions of people to live under the tyranny of the Russian czar, the Turkish sultan and other ignorant and reactionary monarchs. The absolute primacy of order over justice was neatly expressed by Metternich in his assertion that "Barbarous as it is, Turkey is a necessary evil." In a similar vein—if not, let us hope, with equal callousness—when we speak of "stability" and "order" in the developing countries, we neglect to note that in more than a few instances, the order purchased by our aid and by our arms is one that binds millions of people to live under a feudalism that fosters ignorance, hunger and disease. It means blighted lives, children with bellies bloated and brains stunted by malnutrition, their parents scavenging food in garbage heaps—a daily occurrence in the omnipresent slums of Asia and Latin America. Only the abstractions of diplomacy take form in high policy councils; to see its flesh and blood, one must go to a Brazilian slum or to a devastated village in Vietnam.

Besides being shortsighted and immoral, our policy of perpetuating the *status quo* has a third fatal defect—a defect that represents our best hope for formulating a new foreign policy: It goes against the American grain. That is the meaning of the dissent against Vietnam and of the deep alienation of so many of our youth. It is their belief in the values they were brought up to believe in—in the idea of their country as a model of decency and democracy—that has confounded the policy makers who only a few years ago were contending that we could fight a limited war for a decade or two without seriously disrupting the internal life of the United States. What they overlooked in their preoccupation with war games and escalation scenarios was the concern of millions of Americans not just with the cost but with the character of wars they fight and their consequent outrage against a war that—even at what the strategists would consider tolerable cost—has made a charnel house of a small and poor Asian country. In this moral sense, there is hope—hope that we will recognize at last that a foreign policy that goes against our national character is untenable.

An Act of Faith

The question to which we come is whether order, in the sense in which we now conceive it, is, indeed, a vital interest of the United States, or whether, in this revolutionary age, we can accommodate ourselves to a great deal of disorder in the world. My answer, as I am sure will be clear by now, is that we must and can learn to live with widespread revolutionary turmoil. We *must* because it is not within our means to stem the tide; we *can* because social revolution is not nearly so menacing to us as we have supposed—or at least it need not be. If we can but liberate ourselves from ideological obsession—from the automatic association of social revolution with communism and of communism with Soviet or Chinese power—we may find it possible to discriminate among disorders in the world and to evaluate them with greater objectivity, which is to say, more on the basis of their own contest and less on the basis of our own fears. We should find, I think, that some revolutionary movements—including even Communist ones—will affect us little, if at all; that others may affect us adversely but not grievously; and that some may even benefit us.

All of which is to say nothing about the *right* of other peoples to settle their own affairs without interference by the great powers. There is, after all, no moral or legal right of a great power to impose its will on a small country, even if the latter does things that affect it adversely. Americans were justly outraged by the Soviet invasion of Czechoslovakia, not primarily because we thought the Russians could have endured Czech democratization without loss to themselves but because we thought the Czechs had a *right* to reform their system, whether it suited the Russians or not. Ought not the same prin-

ciple apply in our relations with Latin America and, indeed, with small
countries all over the world?

I believe that it should. I would go even further and suggest that we re-
dedicate ourselves to the Good Neighbor Policy enunciated by President
Franklin Roosevelt 30 years ago. There is, of course, nothing new about the
principle of non-intervention: We have been preaching it for years. What I
suggest as an innovation is that we now undertake to *practice* it—not only
when we find it perfectly consistent with what we judge to be our interests
but even when it does not suit our own national preferences. I suggest, therefore, as a guiding principle of American foreign policy, that we abstain
hereafter from military intervention in the internal affairs of other countries
under any circumstances short of a clear and certain danger to our national
security—such as that posed by Castro's decision to make Cuba a Soviet missile base—and that we adhere to this principle whether others, including the
Russians and the Chinese, do so or not.

Surely, it will be argued, we cannot be expected to refrain from interference while the Russians hold eastern Europe in thrall and the Chinese foster
wars of national liberation in Asia and both seek opportunities to subvert
non-Communist governments all over the world. Would this not throw open
the floodgates to a torrent of revolutions leading to communism?

Setting aside for the moment the question of whether Communist rule elsewhere is invariably detrimental to the United States, experience suggests a
policy of nonintervention would *not* throw open the floodgates to communism. Communist bids for power have failed more often than they have
succeeded in countries beyond the direct reach of Soviet military power—
Indonesia and Guinea, for example. Of all the scores of countries, old and
new, in Asia, Africa and Latin America, only four are Communist. There is,
of course, no assurance that an American policy of nonintervention would
guarantee against new Communist takeovers—obviously, our abstention from
Cuba in 1959 was a factor in the success of Castro's revolution. But neither
is there a guarantee that military intervention will defeat every Communist
revolution—witness Vietnam. Neither abstention nor military intervention
can be counted on to immunize against communism, for the simple reason
that neither is of ultimate relevance to the conditions that militate for or
against revolution within a country in the first place.

We have, in fact, had positive benefits from pursuing a policy of nonintervention. There is no country in Latin America more friendly to the
United States than Mexico, which expelled American oil interests 40 years
ago, while seemingly enthralled with Marxist doctrines, and which even now
pursues an independent foreign policy, including the maintenance of cordial
relations with Cuba. The thought presents itself that a policy of nonintervention could now serve as well to liberate us from the embrace of incompetent
and reactionary regimes, which ignore popular aspirations at home out of

confidence that, if trouble develops, they can summon the American Marines, while holding us in line by the threat of their own collapse.

The critical factor is nationalism, which, far more than any ideology, has shown itself to be the engine of change in modern history. When an ideology is as strongly identified with nationalism as communism is in Cuba and Vietnam and as democracy is in Czechoslovakia, foreign military intervention must either fail outright or, as the Russians have learned in Czechoslovakia, succeed at such cost in world wide moral opprobrium as to be self-defeating. My own personal feeling is that, in a free market of ideas, communism has no record of achievement to commend itself as a means toward rapid modernization in developing countries. But, be that as it may, it will ultimately succeed or fail for reasons having little to do with the preferences of the superpowers.

We could profitably take a leaf from the Chinese notebook in this respect. The Lin Piao doctrine of "wars of national liberation," often mistaken as a blueprint for world conquest, is, in fact, an explicit acknowledgment of the inability of a foregin power to sustain a revolution without indigenous support. This is what Lin Piao said in the *Peking Review:*

> In order to make a revolution and to fight a people's war and be victorious, it is imperative to adhere to the policy of relf-reliance, rely on the strength of the masses in one's own country and prepare to carry on the fight independently even when all material aid from outside is cut off. If one does not operate by one's own efforts, does not independently ponder and solve the problems of the revolution in one's own country and does not rely on the strength of the masses, but leans wholly on foreign aid—even though this be aid from socialist countries which persist in revolution (i.e., China)—no victory can be won, or be consolidated even if it is won.

One hears in this the echo of President Kennedy, speaking of South Vietnam in 1963: "In the final analysis, it is their war. They are the ones who have to win it or lose it." Or, as Theodore Draper summed it up in *Commentary,* "The crisis in 1965 in South Vietnam was far more intimately related to South Vietnamese disintegration than to North Vietnamese infiltration."

Nationalism is not only the barrier to communism in countries that reject it; it is a modifier and neutralizer of communism in those few small countries that do possess it. As Tito has demonstrated in Europe and as Ho Chi Minh has demonstrated in Asia, a strongly nationalist regime will defend its independence regardless of common ideology; and it will do so with far greater effectiveness than a weak and unpopular regime, also regardless of ideology. It is beyond question that the Tito government has been a vastly more effective barrier to Soviet power in the Balkans than the old pre-War monarchy ever could have been; and, as Edwin O. Reischauer wrote in *Look:*

It seems highly probable that Ho's Communist-dominated regime, if it had been allowed by us to take over all Vietnam at the end of the war, would have moved to a position with relation to China not unlike that of Tito's Yugoslavia toward the Soviet Union.

If freedom is the basic human drive we believe it to be, an act of faith seems warranted—not in its universal triumph, which experience gives us no particular reason to expect, but in its survival and continuing appeal. The root fact of ideology to which we come—perhaps the only tenet that can be called a fact—is that, at some basic level of being, every man and woman alive aspires to freedom and abhors compulsion. It does not follow from this—as, in the rhetorical excess of the Cold War, it is so often said to follow— that communism is doomed to perish from the earth as a distortion of nature, or that democracy, as we know it in America, is predestined to triumph everywhere. Political forms that seem to offend human nature have existed throughout history, and others that have seemed attuned to human needs have been known to perish. All that can be said with confidence is that, whatever is done to suppress them, man's basic aspirations have a way of reasserting themselves and, insofar as our American political forms are attuned to these basic aspirations, they are a long leg ahead in the struggle for survival.

Faith in the viability of freedom will not, in itself, guarantee our national security. But it can and should help allay our extravagant fear of communism. It should enable us to compete with confidence in the market of ideas. It should free us from the fatal temptation to fight fire with fire by imitating the tactics of a rival who can*not* be as sure of the viability of his ideas in an open contest. The Russians, when you come right down to it, have better reason to fear freedom in Czechoslovakia than we have to fear communism in Vietnam. Appealing as it does to basic human aspirations, the contagion of Czech liberty very likely *is* a threat, at least in the long run, to the totalitarian system of the Soviet Union; by no stretch of the imagination can Ho Chi Minh's rule in Vietnam be said to pose a comparable threat to democracy in the United States.

The greatest danger to our democracy, I dare say, is not that the Communists will destroy it, but that we will betray it by the very means chosen to defend it. Foreign policy is not and cannot be permitted to become an end in itself. It is, rather, a means toward an end, which in our case is not only the safety of the United States but the preservation of her democratic values. A foreign policy of intervention must ultimately be subversive of that purpose. Requiring as it does the maintenance of a huge and costly military establishment, it must also entail the neglect of domestic needs, a burgeoning military-industrial-academic complex, chronic crises and marathon wars—all anathema to a democratic society. Every time we suppress a popular revolution abroad, we subvert our own democratic principles at home. In no single instance is the self-inflicted injury likely to be fatal; but with each successive occurrence, the contradiction and hypocrisy become more apparent and more of our people become disillusioned, more become alienated or angry, while a few are simply corrupted.

Being gradual and cumulative, the malady went largely undetected for too long a time. Now, however, a hue and cry has been raised, and for that we may be grateful, because the great debate in which we are engaged can, if we wish, be corrective as well as cathartic, by laying the foundations for a new approach in our foreign relations.

The shape and content of a new foreign policy are still beyond our view. For the moment, all that comes clearly into focus are the contradictions of our present approach and a few basic inferences that can be drawn from recent experience, notably: that we need not rely on military intervention to give freedom a chance of surviving in the world; that, indeed, we cannot do so without compromising our own freedom; and that only by being true to our traditional values and our own best concept of ourselves can we hope to play a decent and constructive role in a revolutionary world.

12. Old Realities and New Myths

MORTON A. KAPLAN

SENATOR FULBRIGHT's recent excursion into the analysis of foreign policy has been hailed as a breath of fresh air that sweeps away the cobwebs of cant and misunderstanding. The history of post-war foreign policy explains why such a study is needed. The inspiring successes and inventive genius of the first Truman Administration—an era unparalleled in American history for resourceful and courageous adaptation to changing circumstances—have been succeeded by disarray and confusion in American foreign policy. Both the early postwar stereotypes and the grand design of policy are breaking down. Thus the Senator's objective—an objective of unmasking old myths and clarifying new realities—is necessary and salutary.

But has the Senator reached his goal or has he rather obscured old realities and created new myths? Has he clarified the failings of our foreign policy since 1950 or is he preparing the way for the mistakes of the late 1960's? Has he analyzed the mistaken assumptions, the lost opportunities, and the changed contours of the problems or has he compounded the set of errors? Has he exorcised true myths or instead ghosts—pale reflections of positions that have been rejected for a decade? Has he correctly outlined the differ-

An early draft of this review article was circulated as a discussion paper at the Hudson Institute. Discussion papers are written at the initiative of the author and are not subject to review. They do not necessarily reflect the views of the Hudson Institute.

ences between the foreign policies of Stalin and Khrushchev or has his analysis falsified both positions? Has Senator Fulbright's use of social science produced deeper understanding of the problems of statecraft or has it produced misleading oversimplifications and erroneous generalizations?

Matters that are very important and also very complex, such as international politics, naturally produce passionate dispute. One therefore often wants to write circumspectly in order to lower the fever of the debaters. There is also a proper role for the deliberately controversial piece. This is sometimes an important means for forcing re-examination of beliefs that are very deeply held. Senator Fulbright's book essays such a role. So does this review article.

I

All political structures require myths in order to operate. These myths provide unity and direction in a disorderly world. Thus the myth of the monolithic nature of the Soviet bloc and of the imminent danger of a premeditated and unprovoked Soviet attack in the West, although factually inaccurate even for the 1947–1950 period, did serve the purpose of mobilizing energies for the Truman Doctrine, the Marshall Plan, and NATO.

No doubt the myth structure had dysfunctional consequences, even during this early period. It fostered a premature effort to achieve German rearmament—an effort that probably delayed German rearmament and that would not in any event have produced German forces during the putative crucial period. It undoubtedly was responsible for other blunders of a more serious nature during the Korean War. Its functional aspects, however, outweighed the dysfunctional in the period up to Korea. The excessive rigidity of the myth and the requirement for policies not completely in harmony with it after this period called for a re-evaluation.

A number of students of international politics were alert to the problem. This reviewer included in his first professional paper in 1952 the caution that more than one interpretation of Soviet policy was possible and that Soviet policy might change in important ways after "an old and sick man dies."[1] But even John Foster Dulles, rigid as he was in his policies, had some understanding of the myth of monolithicity. By 1954 (and in some cases earlier) most officials of the United States government had learned that the Soviet bloc was not monolithic and that the threat of Soviet attack was quite hypothetical. They did not, however, respond appropriately to the recovery of Western Europe, to the growing strains (as opposed to mere lack of monolithicity) in the Soviet bloc and in NATO, and to the consequences of nuclear military weapons, particularly after the Soviet system also had such weapons.

---

1. "An Introduction to the Strategy of Statecraft," *World Politics*, IV (July 1952), 570.

These developments produced alliance difficulties which Senator Fulbright apparently still does not understand and which he attributes to a greater extent than is reasonable to the real—and unfortunate—foibles of General de Gaulle. We will return to this subject, but first we must turn to the analysis which Senator Fulbright makes of the changed Soviet system and of other world problems and to the conclusions he draws.

II

Senator Fulbright states that the Soviet world is hostile to the United States but that the nature of its threat has changed radically: "It has shown a new willingness to enter mutually advantageous arrangements with the West and, thus far at least, to honor them. It has therefore become possible . . . to deal with the Soviet Union, for certain purposes, as a normal state with normal and traditional interest. . . . How the Soviet Union organizes its internal life, the gods and doctrines that it worships, are matters for the Soviet Union to determine. It is not Communist dogma as espoused within Russia but Communist imperialism that threatens us and other peoples of the non-Communist world" (pp. 9–10).

Senator Fulbright here certifies the myth of the contrast between Stalin and Khrushchev (as elsewhere he certifies Khrushchev's myth concerning China). It is true that Stalin had greater control over bloc affairs than Khrushchev had and that this permitted Stalin to follow some lines of policy that were not available to Khrushchev. But it is not true that Stalin's policy was one of utter and implacable hostility to the non-Soviet world or that Khrushchev's policy was one of wholehearted accommodation. Senator Fulbright noted in an earlier book that Stalin was not incautious, as was Hitler.[2] Indeed, one might argue that Stalin showed greater caution in foreign policy than Khrushchev. Stalin rejected the opportunity to support Yugoslavia over Trieste. He was far from enthusiastic about the Greek civil war, which was supported largely by Yugoslavia and Bulgaria. Until the Communists were thrown out of the French and Italian governments in 1947, they were under instructions to hold down strikes in order to facilitate economic recovery. The claims of Soviet support for a Communist takeover in China are apparently mythological. Stalin did support the Korean War and the Communist coup in Czechoslovakia. But these were proxy operations. Khrushchev put down the Hungarian revolution by the direct use of Soviet armed forces and he put Soviet nuclear missiles and Soviet crews into Cuba ninety miles off U.S. shores. Stalin, on the other hand, denounced Yugoslav and Bulgarian plans to recognize the Greek rebels as a Comsomolist preventive war policy. And, as for the keeping of treaties, were any treaties more abjectly kept than

2. J. William Fulbright, *Prospects for the West* (Cambridge, Mass., 1963), 8.

was the Nazi-Soviet Pact by Stalin? As for the support of national democratic revolutions, as opposed to Communist revolutions, had not both Lenin and Stalin supported such revolutions in Asia, particularly in China?

The myth of the contrast between Stalin and Khrushchev with respect to foreign policy is one of the most pervasive in American politics today. And it receives full support from Fulbright. On the other hand, none of the examples of Soviet moderation, either under Stalin or under Khrushchev, establishes the "normality" of the Soviet state. Undoubtedly real states have never conformed exactly to the concept of the normal state. There are too many economic, social, and political organizations or systems that cut across national boundaries. But in a world in which virtually all differences are differences of degree, the number of degrees can assume crucial importance. The difference between the Soviet Union and the "normal" state lies only partly in Communist ideology (which under Stalin, Khrushchev, and Mao did and still does involve the "burial" of democracy). To a greater extent, it lies in the nature of Soviet political organization which provides the means for the implementation of Communist doctrine and Communist state objectives. The Communist parties in other nations have in the past constituted organizations responsive to directives from Moscow in ways that impeded normal diplomatic processes. These organizations made more difficult concerted action against Soviet expansive actions, made easier Soviet pursuit of diplomatic objectives, and provided a cover for intervention in the internal affairs of other states. The existence of this type of apparatus created opportunities that would not otherwise have been present, and confronted "normal" states with weaknesses in their positions that otherwise it would not have been so important to guard against.

The existence of Communist China as an alternative center for communism undoubtedly complicates the picture of an organized bloc directed, if not ordered, from a single center. Even so, world politics today cannot be understood without an understanding of communism and Communist organization. For instance, it is just as wrong to regard the Viet Cong merely as a local uprising—a new myth perhaps—as it is to view the Viet Cong merely as the product of an international Communist conspiracy, whether spawned in North Vietnam, China, or Moscow. To assert that Russia can be treated as a normal state, for the reasons which Senator Fulbright gives, is to obscure important aspects of the nature of current world politics and to sponsor a countermyth.

It is worth remembering that the three great threats to the stability of world order in modern times—Napoleon, Hitler, and communism—have represented revolutionary rejections of the existing state structure and have utilized groups within other nations in support of their objectives. It was not mere expanionism—dangerous as that might have been—but expansionism combined with ideology and, in the case of nazism and communism, party organization that built the threat to its most serious dimensions. Of the three, the Communist threat possesses the best organization and the most attractive ideology. If the Soviet bloc continues to weaken and if communism is transformed, the threat may be mitigated. But it likely will not be eliminated. And present trends may be halted or even reversed.

Despite Senator Fulbright's endorsement, George Kennan's thesis concerning the possibility that United States policy can affect the liberalization of the Soviet bloc is dubious. According to Kennan, "It could well be argued . . . that if the major Western powers had full freedom of movement in devising their own policies, it would be within their power to determine whether the Chinese view, or the Soviet view, or perhaps a view more liberal than either, would ultimately prevail within the Communist camp."[3] This analysis raises more questions than it answers. The lion's share of American aid within the Soviet bloc since 1956—aid that has been justified as a support for liberalization and autonomy—has gone to Poland, which, of all the Russian satellites, has backslid most since 1956 in terms of internal freedoms and autonomy. Hungary and Rumania have been virtually ostracized by the United States until recently. Yet these two nations have made the greatest advances since 1956 in liberalization and autonomy. Perhaps American aid prevented even greater backsliding in Poland. But it seems more likely that the commitment of the United States to the Gomulka regime disarmed the internal opposition and stifled the incentives for changes which, in terms of American values and interests, would have been highly desirable. It is striking that the Senator quotes Mr. Kennan's comment when, to the extent that there is any evidence, it would appear to support the opposite point of view. Here the Senator supports one of the State Department's new myths—a myth that lacks the functional values which the old myths did support.

In principle it would be possible to find a path among the strains of the Communist bloc and to structure a policy that advanced American interests by discriminating among the Communist nations. It is difficult, however, for one who has watched the divagations of the State Department to have any confidence in its attempts to do so. Nor do the leakings of incidental intelligence from the State Department concerning its image of the Communist world lessen the fears of the external observer.

The Department of State and Senator Fulbright have bought Khrushchev's myth of the great changes in Soviet foreign policy since Stalin. This myth invokes a picture of Khrushchev as more moderate and of Stalin as less moderate than either actually was. Khrushchev also sold to the United States his myth concerning the contrast between the peaceful Russians and the war-mongering Chinese. (Undoubtedly it was the boldness of Chinese attacks on Hong Kong, Macao, Quemoy, and Matsu that led us to accept this point of view.) Another aspect of this myth—one to which Senator Fulbright subscribes—is that the Chinese advocate the reckless use of nuclear weapons

3. George Kennan, "Polycentrism and Western Policy," *Foreign Affairs*, XLII (January 1964), 178; quoted in *Old Myths and New Realities*, 13.

(p. 57). Yet, as the Chinese have pointed out, it was Mr. Khrushchev who was reckless. The Chinese have said: "We have always maintained that socialist countries must not use nuclear weapons to support the peoples' wars of national liberation and revolutionary civil wars. . . . A socialist country absolutely must not be the first to use nuclear weapons, nor should it in any circumstances play with them or engage in nuclear blackmail and nuclear gambling. . . ."[4]

At least Senator Fulbright does not seem to subscribe to the emanations from some sources in Foggy Bottom that the United States and the Soviet Union will reach an accommodation that will enable them jointly to stem the aggressive designs of the Communist Chinese. Could any myth be better designed than this one to undermine American interests and values? Russia fronts on an area that is of urgent value to the United States. The skills, resources, and industry of Europe are such that the loss of the area to the Soviet Union would be a disaster. China does not front on any areas of reasonably comparable interest. Moreover, China diverts Russia from Europe. In addition, an alignment of the United States, Western Europe, and the Soviet Union against China would produce a racial confrontation that might undermine the values that characterize our institutions. Even though this notion is still not official policy, it is nonetheless deeply disturbing to hear talk of a U.S.-Russian alignment against China.

Even where Senator Fulbright speaks sensibly of the possibility that the United States and China might eventually cooperate on some issues, he builds into this position the myth that the problems between the two nations stem from China's "implacable hostility toward the United States" (p. 38). Undoubtedly the Kremlin would like us to believe this, but why should we play into his hand? And where is the evidence for this hostility? Korea? We threatened legitimate Chinese national interests when we marched to the Yalu. Our disclaimers that China should not have regarded this as a threat would have been worthless even had our action in marching to the Yalu not repudiated earlier statements by the Secretary of State that our only objective in Korea was to restore the *status quo ante*. There was no excuse for this action on our part unless we intended to have a showdown with one or both of the Communist powers. Taiwan? Undoubtedly we have a moral commitment to the inhabitants of Taiwan not to surrender them to Communist tyranny. But since we cannot expect the Communists to admit that their regime is immoral, our position is weak on the basis of the more traditional criteria. India? The border region is ill-defined. Even where the Indians have a treaty claim, they undermined it themselves by the rationale of their attack on Goa. The Indians consistently refused peaceful negotiations. They en-

4. From *Jenmin Jih Pao*, November 19, 1963, as translated and published by the BBC Monitoring Service in *Summary of World Broadcasts: Part III, The Far East*, 2nd Series (November 20, 1963), C9–C11.

gaged in deep military probes and were preparing an attack when the Chinese beat them to it. The Senator is right that we have nothing to gain now from recognition and much to lose, but why cloak this conclusion in false moralisms? It only confuses the real issue of international politics— namely, that specific interests may be incompatible. And it reinforces the myth that our problems stem from misunderstandings. They may instead stem from proper understanding.

Senator Fulbright thus structures a world in which the Russians show great moderation and the Chinese are reckless. He therefore finds it possible and desirable to achieve a general detente with the Russians, even if he does not advocate an alliance with the Russians against the Chinese. But has he really built his case properly? We have already considered many aspects of that case. We may now consider the final ingredients—ingredients which this time do exist but whose combination in a stew may not produce an edible dish. I agree with the Senator that it is unlikely that we can win the cold war completely or end it immediately and that good and evil are not absolutes. But I do not understand what relevance these comments have. Hitler was good to his dogs. One could even argue for some of his social policies. Genghis Khan undoubtedly had some redeeming features. No doubt St. Francis of Assisi had some very undesirable characteristics. Evil will never be eliminated from the world nor will good ever reign supreme. But not even Barry Goldwater wanted to unleash SAC against Moscow. And if a new Hitler had a big nuclear force, we undoubtedly would think twice about unconditional surrender.

Occasionally one gets a student in the classroom—never one of the best, although rarely one of the worst—who discovers that all nations behave selfishly and who therefore thinks that no interesting or important differences in national behavior can be articulated. On the continuum of national behavior there are significant differences. It makes good sense to recognize the Soviet system as an evil system. This does not mean that we must attempt to suppress the system by force. Even apart from the existence of nuclear forces, such an attempt might only unleash still greater evils. Surely, however, we are and ought to be hostile to the Soviet system and to its existence, just as we should be hostile to the evils of racism within our own system. Would not our policies be better adapted to their proper ends if we did recognize that each agreement with the Soviet system is strictly limited to some specific objective and that no purpose is or could be served by a general spirit of detente?

In addition, there is no significant evidence that a spirit of detente will in fact increase the probability that specific agreements will be reached and maintained in those areas where joint interests outweigh the detestation which the leaders of each system feel for the other. Would not Senator Fulbright's own recognition that American strategic superiority was a necessary element in the partial victory we won in the Cuban missile crisis (p. 5) imply that the Soviets do respond to hard realities and not to expressions of good will? And, although I distrust facile generalizations from history, does not the history of postwar negotiations with the Soviet Union indicate the same?

When Senator Fulbright speaks of the Central Committee of the Soviet Union as developing into a rudimentary parliamentary body (p. 58), he reinforces the new myths in a particularly dangerous way. The development of which he speaks might occur in the Soviet Union. To assert its plausibility on the basis of existing evidence is indefensible. The rarity of genuinely parliamentary regimes in the world, even where conditions are less unfavorable than in the Soviet Union, militates against this hypothesis. The least one would expect is an analysis of the micro-structure of Soviet society and political organs to indicate the factors that give plausibility to this type of development.[5] One would not like to think that major political orientations were based on superficial and fleeting analogies. The Wilsonian myths have long been discredited, and for reasons that are substantial.

Senator Fulbright undoubtedly makes some pertinent specific comments about the nature of the Soviet system, the changes in it, and the implications of these for world politics and American policy. These remarks are surrounded by other less cogent remarks in such a way that in effect a new myth is created—one in which the Soviet system withers away, the bloc disintegrates, the appetite of the Soviet Union diminishes, and it becomes little different from Britain or France. Culturally different perhaps, and a little more boorish, but essentially a member of the club. Although wishful thoughts sometimes come true, wishful thinking is not an adequate guide for policy.

As this review article is going to press, word has just come through of the purging of Khrushchev from the Soviet Russian leadership. This event, which caught official Washington by surprise, underscores the inadvisability of basing American policy upon the supposed attributes of particular Soviet leaders or upon inspired guesses concerning the future transformations that Soviet society and foreign policy are likely to undergo. This is so for three reasons. In the first place, the matter of the particular persons in charge of the Soviet Union may not be critical; that is, Soviet policy may not change in major ways or for the worse under the new leadership. In the second place, our policies may be largely irrelevant in influencing either change or stability in the Russian leadership. In the third place, we may be—and are likely to be—poorly informed concerning the alternatives. Although I do not believe we are likely to be so naïve as to credit information fed to us from Soviet sources as to the nature of internal Soviet quarrels (obviously such accounts

5. For a cogent analysis which indicates the implausibility of this hypothesis, see Allen Kassof, "The Administered Society: Totalitarianism Without Terror," *World Politics*, xvi (July 1964), 558–75.

serve multiple functions), we may become overcommitted to our own Krem-
linological hypotheses.

It is much too early to evaluate the present shift in the Soviet high command. The new leadership is not yet consolidated and the struggle for
control is likely to continue. Although the new leadership may be more
effective in implementing Soviet policy than was the bumbling Khrushchev,
we are less likely to be confronted with the kind of impulsive gambling that
he engaged in. In any event, pragmatic policies based on specific coinci-
dences of American and Soviet interests are likely to serve American interests
better than a general commitment either to detente or to inflexible hostility.
During the succession crisis of 1953, we may have missed an opportunity to
negotiate the German question advantageously because of our commitment
to inflexible hostility. It would be a shame if this time a commitment to
detente made us so unwilling to disturb the new situation that we again
failed to explore the negotiation space available to us.

III

Senator Fulbright attacks several other "myths" of U.S. foreign policy. "We
Americans," the Senator says, "would do well to divest ourselves of the silly
notion that the issue with Panama is a test of our courage and resolve. . . . It
takes stubbornness but not courage to reject the entreaties of the weak"
(pp. 18–19). If the Senator were merely saying that the United States can
afford to be magnanimous in its treatment of Panama, I would not disagree
with him. I favor revision of the treaty, increased benefits for Panama, and
even a different type of regime for the administration of the Canal. Our past
policy has been governed at least by inattention and perhaps also by pettiness
and stupidity.

President Johnson, however, exercised sound judgment when he refused
to "negotiate" a change of the treaty under pressure. For once, in recent
years, the United States refused to quail when subjected to "blackmail" by a
smaller power. And, in this instance, particularly, given the history of our
past attitudes toward the Canal and the irresponsible statements of the
Panamanian representatives, the failure to conform to a "stubborn" line, to
use the Senator's word, probably would have had extremely unfortunate consequences elsewhere in the world.

For years the United States has paid blackmail to petty and unpopular
dictators who have threatened us with the alternative of communism. We
have played with the simple-minded notion that we can "buy off" Nasser
and Sukarno with our largesse, not merely with respect to temporary expedi-
encies, but with respect to long-term goals. Part of this policy has rested on
the liberal myth that the troubles of the world stem not from incompatible
goals but from mutual suspicions. Another part of it rests on characterological

weakness and the inability to take a stand. This weakness was demonstrated for all the world to see when the Secretary-General of the United Nations made the outrageously false charge that we discriminated against Japan in the use of nuclear weapons, as contrasted with Germany, because Japan was a colored nation. The *New York Times* did not record even the weakest kind of official rebuttal, even by a lesser official, let alone by our chief representative to the UN.

On the other hand, I do not understand why we demanded that Bolivia break relations with Castro. I thought that we approved of the present Bolivian government. Since the breaking of relations with Castro by Bolivia does not weaken Castro's regime in any way, but may weaken the Bolivian regime, it would seem to have little to commend it.

Senator Fulbright, however, is dealing with a straw man when he attacks administration policy on Cuba. Of course, it is ridiculous to try to enforce a boycott in ways that we cannot enforce, that only antagonize allies, and that do not do much to hurt Castro. The real alternative, however, is not to remove those measures that do strain his regime and that put an extra burden on the Russians, but to support the exiles in ways that would further harass and weaken the regime.

Since Castro could not have taken over without at least tacit official support from the United States, we do have a moral obligation to the Cuban people to remove his tyrannical regime. The effective arguments against this course lie not in its impossibility in terms of resources but in the demonstrated incompetence of the United States when it comes to implementing programs of this sort. The Bay of Pigs episode demonstrated not only military incompetence and failure of will but also political ineptitude of an egregious nature. We did not have any good idea of what to do with Cuba after Castro was gone or we could not possibly have supported the Cubans we did. We could, if necessary, bring down the Castro regime today, using direct American military force, without risking a nuclear confrontation or political disaster in Latin America, if we possessed the requisite political skills. This undoubtedly would not solve our problems elsewhere in Latin America, but it might give us a respite which we could then utilize. In any event, however, we seem capable only of a policy of pinpricks which seems to satisfy our national ego but which produces little in the way of practical results and at a price which is unnecessarily high. And the opposition party seems only to desire to use the Marines to nursemaid the water taps.

Much the same kind of paralysis affects our Vietnamese policy. It was apparent for years that the Diem regime lacked the political skills to win the war against the guerrillas. It was and is also clear that no other regime can win that war unless the war is extended against the North. Even though much of the Viet Cong support is genuinely indigenous, so that perhaps it could not be halted by simple orders from the North, Viet Cong morale is sustained by the immunity of the Northern bastion. And the morale of the

South is depressed by that same immunity. The present position is completely one-sided.

The fear that extension would merely unleash the North and the Chinese overlooks the difficulty the Chinese would have in intervening, the immense logistic advantages possessed by the United States, and the great reluctance of the North Vietnamese to encourage Chinese intervention. Such intervention would undermine Viet Minh autonomy and create the conditions under which a vigorous guerrilla war against the Viet Minh, utilizing the traditional techniques of such ventures, could be launched. If the United States is unwilling or unable to adopt a winning strategy, which should include the negotiation of definite and moderate political objectives, it might instead cut its losses by withdrawing. This is a less desirable policy, but it is better than the inept policy that is being pursued.

Indeed, one wonders if the present course can be called a policy at all. Whom did the Department of State believe it was fooling by sending General Taylor to Vietnam? Surely the Chinese were not deceived into believing that the sending of General Taylor heralded a potentially tougher policy, when it was transparent that he was sent only because the United States intended nothing that went farther than its current line. One is inclined to believe that the American response in Tonkin Gulf reflected the President's gut reaction, not State Department policy. This is reinforced by the almost unbelievable report in the *New York Times* that some officials recommended that the response be made by the South Vietnamese.[6]

IV

Senator Fulbright fails to understand the legitimate European concern about the nature of the American nuclear commitment. "It is," he says, "clearly understood in the United States that a successful Soviet attack on Europe would almost certainly be followed by an attack on the United States, and that even if it were not, the loss of Europe to the free world would leave the United States so weakened and isolated as to put its security, its economy, and probably its survival as a free society in the gravest jeopardy. Nor is it possible to imagine that the Russians would take the incredible risk of leaving the United States out of the conflict with its forces intact and able to intervene whenever it chose" (p. 99). This position is a ritual incantation in Washington. And among the greatest of myths are ritual incantations.

Possibly if the Soviet Union struck Western Europe in a massive onslaught out of the blue, the American response would approach the certainty of which Senator Fulbright talks. This is perhaps the least plausible way in which a European conflict is likely to begin. Most observers believe it would start slowly, as the consequence of an unplanned incident, in which the

6. James Reston, *New York Times* (August 6, 1964), 8: "One view was that the retaliation should be done by the South Vietnamese to minimize the risk."

equities and objectives of the states involved would be less than clear. We probably would have lots of time to overevaluate the equities on the Russian side and to consider the potential casualties on our own.

The Europeans are most familiar with very interesting public statements by our highest officials. At the hearing to consider his nomination as Secretary of State, Christian Herter said, "I cannot conceive of any President involving us in an all-out nuclear war unless the facts showed clearly we are in danger of all-out devastation ourselves, or that actual moves have been made toward devastating ourselves."[7]

European qualms are increased by comments on the horrors of nuclear war. On July 26, 1963, President Kennedy asserted: "A war today or tomorrow, if it led to nuclear war, would not be like any war in history. A full-scale nuclear exchange, lasting less than 60 minutes, with the weapons now in existence, could wipe out more than 300 million Americans, Europeans, and Russians, as well as untold numbers elsewhere. And the survivors—as Chairman Khrushchev warned the Communist Chinese—'The survivors would envy the dead.' For they would inherit a world so devastated by explosions and poison and fire that today we cannot even conceive of its horrors."[8]

President Kennedy may have overemphasized the likelihood that a nuclear exchange would escalate into a full-scale nuclear war. But if the President makes such a statement, are not Europeans right to fear that Americans may fear nuclear war even more than the loss of Europe? After all, the dangers of nuclear war would be clear and immediate. Those that Senator Fulbright speaks of are indirect and remote. It seems likely that some Americans would be inclined to use the escape clause Senator Fulbright elsewhere invoked: "Our commitment to the defense of Europe is absolute and irrevocable—so long as the critical decisions that led to war or peace are not removed beyond our influence or responsibility."[9] Might we not soon find that that was the case? Moreover, Europeans fear that we might object to military action in a situation that appeared vital to them, and consequently fear that we would then disclaim responsibility for action taken by them.

I do not disagree with Senator Fulbright's analysis of the value of Europe to the United States, although I believe he greatly overestimates the probability that a Soviet attack on Europe would necessarily be part of a plan to attack the United States. The threat to us would likely be indirect and would require great sophistication on the part of the public and high policymakers for its understanding. The Senator is correct when he asserts that that threat would be to our way of life.

Shortly after Sputnik the American guarantee seemed to lose its effectiveness—thus anticipating military developments that had not yet taken place—

7. Committee on Foreign Relations, U.S. Senate, *Hearings on the Nomination of Christian A. Herter to be Secretary of State*, 86th Congress, 1st Session, 1959, 9–10.

8. J. F. Kennedy, "The Nuclear Test Ban Treaty: A Step Toward Peace," *Department of State Bulletin*, XLIX (August 12, 1963), 236.

9. *Prospects for the West*, 60–61.

and the Russian threat also seemed less imminent. Thus the incentives for independence of foreign policy and the development of independent nuclear systems seemed to increase. Many Americans—some of them most influential —began to welcome the latter development in this period. Since this seemed to me to be the wrong policy, I began to circulate in 1958 what I believe to have been the first proposal for a joint NATO nuclear force.[10] The proposal was presented to a conference at Princeton University in 1959. A Bowie-Knorr study group later incisively recommended to the Eisenhower Administration a joint NATO nuclear force based on Polaris submarines. This was followed by a somewhat similar Eisenhower Administration proposal for a NATO Polaris nuclear force which, although inadequate, was nonetheless desirable.

When the Kennedy Administration came into office, it was so thoroughly committed against nuclear diffusion that it pigeonholed the proposal for a NATO force. Only after it became clear that diffusion could not be prevented did it consider an alternative to national diffusion. Unfortunately, when it did consider alternatives, its proposals were gimmicks that attempted more to persuade than to cope with the legitimate problems that the European nations faced. Since the proposals were ineffective in satisfying the needs of the Europeans and were advanced by an administration that had shown hostility to the idea of a real NATO force, most Europeans viewed them as frauds. It is probable that the Germans have backed MLF not because they like it, but because they need American support and hope that present support for the United States may later produce American support for a nuclear force that the Germans can use in their vital interests. In addition, the clearly appropriate technical decision on Skybolt was implemented with peculiar political ineptitude at Nassau. NATO is still paying the penalty for these mistakes. Perhaps even the most sincere, adequate, and judiciously presented proposals would have been scuttled by de Gaulle. But the United States gave de Gaulle every excuse to follow his current policy.

The French force will soon confront the United States with a dilemma. It does not do so yet only because the force does not yet exist. Inspired stories from Washington to the effect that the French force will not be able to penetrate Soviet airspace either are inaccurate or the Soviets have much better low-level radar and anti-aircraft capabilities than we have. The trouble with the French force is that it is a first-strike force highly vulnerable to attack on the ground and therefore provocative. It cannot be integrated into a strategy of limited nuclear strikes. It may deter in all situations except the most provocative. But our nuclear force would be equally deterring for these situations, since the Russians would not run even a small chance of our nuclear intervention unless the provocation were gross. In the most provocative situations, however, the Russians might have to decide whether an attack on the French of such scope that it would eliminate the French force—

10. Subsequently published in revised form under the title, "Problems of Coalition and Deterrence," in Klaus Knorr, ed., *NATO and American Security* (Princeton 1959), 127–50,

an attack that would therefore produce large civilian casualties—would trigger the American force. Although the probability that they would attack the United States as a consequence of such a calculation may not be very high, it nonetheless may be higher than we want to risk. After all, we are building a controlled force because we do not want to run the risks involved in an uncontrolled force—even one that is much better than the French *force de frappe*. It would largely negate this policy for the United States to remain in NATO while the French possess the *force de frappe*. Even those who may think the problem somewhat less drastic must still recognize that it is very serious. The incentive for the United States to remove itself from NATO is reinforced by the fact that even if NATO were dissolved, the existence of an American nuclear force likely would deter the Russians from an attack on Western Europe under all conditions except the most provocative.

We have been much too unwilling as a nation over the last twelve years to recognize that Western Europe has emerged from the period of American tutelage and that it has necessarily become restive about American dominance in the area of foreign policy. We have been unwilling to make concessions when those concessions would have been appreciated and perhaps effective. We have refused to admit that the Europeans have a legitimate problem with respect to our nuclear guarantee, or that those under threat of annihilation have some right to representation in the making of the decisions that might lead to it. We have been unwilling to admit that there are conditions under which it may be legitimate to surrender our nuclear veto or that conditions might develop which would make it desirable for us to leave NATO.

We have been caught within a system of rigid myths. Our paralysis of policy has permitted General de Gaulle to constrain our alternatives for us. We have neglected the opportunities to constrain his alternatives for him. This is demonstrated most clearly by the impotence of our policy with respect to the *force de frappe*. If we had told de Gaulle that if he went ahead with the French force we might leave NATO and drop the American nuclear guarantee, and if we had provided some reasonable alternative for the French, he might have found his alternatives constrained. And there would likely have been political opposition in France to the *force de frappe*, for many Frenchmen have been convinced that the *force de frappe* is a supplement, not an alternative, to American nuclear force—a supplement that increases French independence. If the French had to face the added prospect that the United States might sponsor a German nuclear force if the United States withdrew from NATO, the French might feel even more constrained. If we then suggested, as an alternative, that we would help the Europeans to develop a joint European force, considerable support for it might develop. Although this is less desirable than a joint NATO force, it is better than the likely consequences of the present situation. And this may perhaps be the period in which we have our last opportunity to encourage this development.

The creation of a controllable joint European nuclear force would remove the incentive for American withdrawal from NATO. Thus the United States could maintain its conventional forces in Europe and in this way NATO could retain the conventional superiority that is so important for stability. On the other hand, complete American withdrawal, perhaps coupled with the nuclear offer suggested above, may be the only way to shock Europe into unity—a unity that would have a powerful attractive force for the Soviet satellites. And the existence of such a Europe might clarify for the United States the advantages of a larger Atlantic Union. This plan, however, seems too much to hope for under likely circumstances.

Senator Fulbright, however, believes that NATO is a viable organization. The consultation on nuclear strategy which Senator Fulbright calls for is a requirement for viability, although it is probably too late. But it is not enough. If the reduction of NATO to impotence is to be averted and if we do not desire a joint European nuclear force, actual control of a NATO nuclear system must be devolved from American control under clearly stated conditions. In "Problems of Coalition and Deterrence," the conditions suggested were Russian first use or a massive Russian incursion in Western Europe, followed by a refusal to withdraw upon notice. Given the change in conventional force balances that has recently occurred in Europe, the latter condition may not be so important any more.

Of course, solving the military problem will not solve the real problem of NATO. It could at best provide time for a political solution. Since it may already be too late to form a joint NATO force, serious attention should be given to the alternative of a joint European nuclear force, lest we also be too late in sponsoring this plan.

V

Senator Fulbright is not a social scientist and it is not legitimate to hold him to the standards of social science. It is, however, saddening to see him discard the conventional wisdom of diplomacy, with its virtues as well as its vices, for social science generalizations that come from the bottom of the heap.

"There is," says Senator Fulbright, "perhaps some instruction for us in the experience of Europe before 1914. None of the great powers of that era actually planned a major war, but each of the two major groupings . . . was beset by fears of attack by the other. . . . Mutual fear generated the arms race, which in turn generated greater fear, until almost by accident Europe was plunged into general war" (p. 51). This assertion lacks any kind of historic depth. The system of mobilization of the great powers obtaining at the time may have played a role in the First World War, but not the arms race. The major factors were political; and the fears that existed, both warranted and unwarranted, were not generated by the arms race. The almost insoluble problem of the Austro-Hungarian Empire lay at the center of this problem.

Accidents did play a role, but again not accidents closely connected with an arms race. Moreover, what evidence does the Senator have for his assertion that "a continuing arms race, accompanied by mounting fears and tensions, has frequently led to war in the past" (*ibid.*)?

If one thing is clear about the present, it is that some aspects of the arms race have improved the stability of peace in the world we live in, have diminished the probability that a nuclear accident or a provocative situation will produce war, and have made it possible to control nuclear war, if it occurs. Perhaps much of the "detente" which we perceive can be attributed to this greater military stability. Whether a continued arms race would have similar felicitous consequences or whether these would be overbalanced by unfavorable aspects of the arms race is a matter for sober and cautious analysis.

Matters get even worse when the Senator decides that psychologists have a big contribution to make toward understanding the problems of peace and war. The Senator quotes Gordon Allport to the effect that "The crux of the matter lies in the fact that while most people deplore war, they nonetheless *expect* it to continue. And what people expect determines their behavior. . . .* the indispensable condition of war is that people must expect war, before, under war-minded leadership, they make war."[11] Fulbright says that war is a habit and that one must create the expectation of peace.

It is not possible in this review article to make a full analysis of the kind of muddle-headed thinking that underlies these propositions. The reference terms are completely undefined with respect to their boundary conditions and reflect an ideology rather than intellectual analysis. One might instead argue that if Chamberlain and his group had expected that war was possible, they might have avoided it. The fact is that there is a range of ways in which to settle conflicts; these extend through diplomacy, economic and political moves, armed reprisals, and war. Any intelligent diplomat knows they are all possible, and he attempts to resolve conflict in the least costly way consistent with the set of goals and values that he is trying to implement. The knowledge that a more costly way is possible—that is, that war is possible—reinforces the likelihood of peace. A statesman aware of this is more likely to avoid cornering his opponent or foreclosing all other alternatives than is one who does not believe in the possibility of war.

Some wars may have been started because the rulers of the nations involved believed in war as the most appropriate method of settlement of disputes. Bismarck's small wars in fact did follow this pattern, although, contrary to the expectations of Allport and Fulbright, these wars were expeditious, paid off, and did not produce very large war cycles.[12] The

11. Gordon W. Allport, "The Role of Expectancy," in Hadley Cantril, ed., *Tensions That Cause Wars* (Urbana, Ill., 1950), 43 and 48; quoted in *Old Myths and New Realities*, 144–45 (italics in original).

12. It could be argued that Bismarck's seizure of Alsace-Lorraine did indirectly have the last-named consequence. This does not affect the principle of the discussion, for the issue of the series is too remote to fall within the terms of the generalization.

generalization is an unsatisfactory explanation of the First World War, except in the tautological sense that it is impossible to fight a war without the expectation that war is possible. This is hardly a startling insight. Moreover, it is foolhardy and costly to believe that peace is probable if faced with a revolutionary opponent who believes in war. In this kind of situation, the expectation of war may improve the chances for peace; and the expectation of peace may increase the probability of war. In any event, the proposition that it is the expectation of war that produces war makes central what is at best peripheral and simple what is surely very complex. To borrow a psychological term, it denies the real problems that produce war and maintain peace and runs to a comforting womb in which all will be well when all think good thoughts.

Senator Fulbright quotes a statement in a letter from Dr. Jerome D. Frank to the effect that "Frightened, hostile individuals tend to behave in ways which aggravate their difficulties instead of resolving them, and frightened, hostile nations seem to behave similarly" (pp. 74–75). This generalization is not very helpful with respect to individual behavior, let alone with respect to state behavior. For instance, I have my students read the psychological literature on paranoia, which points out that trying to satisfy the demands of paranoidal individuals does not satisfy them, but may drive them into making even greater demands. According to much of the literature, the only way to handle such people is to keep paranoids closely controlled. The parallel with Hitler—and, some would think, with the Soviet Union—is obvious. My better students, however, recognize that such generalizations can do more harm than good, for they can divert attention from the concrete aspects of the case to abstract theoretical aspects which, even if they were better validated than psychological theory is, would still apply only statistically, and then only to individual behavior. And one would still need to know that the individual really belonged in the category.

Such psychological theories—and one could find a theory that would support any conceivable pattern of response—have value only when they reinforce analyses made on more relevant grounds. That is, an analysis in depth is made of behavior patterns and situational components. Then, if the theory of personality that seems to apply in the individual case supports the conclusion, it tends to reinforce and corroborate judgment. Even so, it probably has only marginal value. Many of the best analysts state privately that the Freudian categories can be used predictively or prescriptively only when the analyst is familiar with the life history and circumstances of the patient in great detail and in context. This is a kind of knowledge we will not have for the relevant political cases.

If prediction, or prescription, is so difficult for individuals, the problem is even worse when we deal with national entities. The individuals who represent these entities are constrained by colleagues, decision-making processes, and role expectations. They respond to regime pressures we know little about; and much of what we know is probably wrong or out of context. We do not understand either the insulating mechanisms or the triggering devices that operate in these circumstances. The psychological generalizations which have at best only minimal utility when dealing with individuals are worse than useless—indeed, are dangerous—when dealing with matters of high international politics.

Moreover, Dr. Frank's generalization would seem to conflict with well-known information about Russian Bolshevik leadership. The Russians—in the past at least—were concerned with concrete results as opposed to "pride." They found it easier to bargain with hostile enemies whose positions they "understood," and with whom they could make limited and temporary agreements that were mutually advantageous, than with opponents who exuded "good will" and whose motives they could neither understand nor trust. Even where the hostility was overwhelming, as in the case of Hitler, Stalin responded by backing down step by step, even to the extent of not mobilizing adequately at the frontier. If I were incautious, I could assert that the way to deal with the Russians is to keep confronting them with threats. This might be true in individual cases; as a generalization, it is dangerous.

It is better to trust the intuition of the experienced participant than vague psychological generalizations. It is, however, true that the intuition of the trained participant may break down when he operates in a different environment. Roosevelt, for instance, did not really recognize that the techniques of persuasion which worked so well in domestic politics were not very useful when dealing with Stalin and de Gaulle. As a consequence, where agreement seemed essential, he may have repressed the evidence that it did not exist—e.g., in the case of Stalin. Where agreement did not seem essential, he likely recognized disagreement and responded with pique, as in the case of de Gaulle. (Is a repetition of history possible?) The psychologist and anthropologist could help by alerting the practitioner to the range of possible variations and the conditions under which the variations are likely to occur. Dr. Frank, however, does not attempt to open the practitioner's mind to the range of variations but to persuade him of the accuracy of a set of dangerously oversimplified generalizations that have only limited applicability at best. This perverts the utility that a knowledge of psychology might have for the practitioner. Unfortunately, Dr. Frank is not merely a bad example. In general, the psychologists who have been talking loudly about international politics make ridiculous and misleading assertions that they attempt to cloak beneath a certificate of professional skill.

If one treated these generalizations with care, it would be apparent that no conclusions could be drawn from them. For instance, Senator Fulbright's quotation from Dr. Frank does not state that friendly behavior on our part would reduce Russian hostility or that Russian hostility would produce difficulties for us. Practitioners would do well to avoid the half-digested contributions of psychologists, anthropologists, and sociologists to the problems of foreign policy. As bad as common sense and conventional wisdom may be, it is much better than what these men have to offer.

VI

There were a number of myths which Senator Fulbright might have dealt with but did not. Why foreign aid, for instance? Except for Marshall Plan aid to Western Europe and for aid to a few selected countries, such as Israel and Taiwan, there is little evidence that our aid has done any good and some that it has done harm. If aid is to be provided primarily as a gesture of sympathy—a not unworthy reason—perhaps we should understand this. If there are other reasons, it is time to discover what they are.

Why support for India? Successful development in democracies in Asia is taking place in Japan and Malaya, but not in India. If we are looking for a counterexample to China, India is the wrong place. Would it really hurt us if India drifted into the Russian orbit in some respects at least? Such a development might support rather than hinder American foreign policy requirements. It might worsen the strains between Russia and China and increase the drain upon Russian resources.

Our relations with Japan are much better now that Ambassador Reischauer has replaced Ambassador MacArthur, but why jeopardize these fine relations by maintaining bases which are an irritant and which probably could not be used in any serious crisis? If the Japanese government is not adding its voice to the attack against the bases, this probably stems more from its fears concerning Congress and trade than from lack of resentment. We conceivably may pay a high penalty for not anticipating this problem and resolving it on our own initiative.

We pay lip service to the problem of German unity. In fact, we do not want such unity any more than the French or the Russians. Yet the division of Germany is by far the most plausible cause of central war or of several other extremely uncomfortable developments. Russia's own interests, if she understood them, would lie in the resolution of the issue as long as the fake government of East Germany could be eliminated in a face-saving way. The failure to understand this and to press the issue may be the neatest ostrich trick of the century.

As for the UN, it undoubtedly is a valuable institution that we would do well to support. However, we overload and overvalue the institution in a whole series of ways that cannot be recounted here. There is more cant than wisdom in our attitudes toward the organization. (This is also true with respect to our position on Russian dues.) And this may in fact help more to undermine the UN than to support it. In the same way, the enormous amount of cant on the subject of disarmament may do more to undermine than to support peace, let alone other values.

Does the United States have the will and the skill to act resourcefully in various areas of the globe? Events in Vietnam, Cuba, Africa, Latin America, and Asia call this into question. We lack the will to act, the coldness to engage in counterterror, and the skill to discriminate among contenders for favor. The Congo is a prime instance of the last-named failing. Perhaps we would be much better advised to cut our commitments—not, as Senator Fulbright contends, because we lack the power, but rather because we lack the will and the skill.

I believed that the development of Atlantic Union was the hope of mankind. I would still believe so if it could be made to work. But is not the evidence now against it and even against smaller designs such as NATO? Perhaps we should still try palliatives like the parliamentary union suggested by Senator Fulbright, but perhaps we should also think seriously about more relevant and feasible objectives. What about union with Australia? The Australians like us; they are far enough away not to fear our embrace, but to fear its lack. If they joined the union as a State, the Canadians might follow suit. We would then unify much of the northern half of the hemisphere and also would have an outpost in Asia which we could use to protect the Philippines and other interests in that part of the world. If the British later joined, we might eventually link up with a Europe that had united in the meantime. This new American union should not be limited to those of white skin and English tongue, but English-speaking white nations are the more likely early entrants.

We can draw one further inference from the disarray of our alliance structure. Our alliances are no longer sufficiently functional for us to worry excessively about the reactions of our alliance partners to our policies. Our concern for Allied reactions serves more to inhibit policy than the existence of the alliance structure serves to support policy. Although we should not be entirely indifferent to the opinions of our allies, it is plausible that our present hobbled policy further undermines our external support and that a more active and determined policy might create new support when its effectiveness has been demonstrated. Perhaps we should allow support to coalesce, as we did at the time of the missile crisis in Cuba, and not worry even about those cases where it is lacking in the immediate event. Just as every case of Soviet economic aid and of revolution somewhere in the world tends to be feared by the United States, we tend to fear any disruption of the existing alliance structure. This may be far too negative a position. And it likely contributes to the existing paralysis of United States foreign policy.

More examples might be given, but they cannot be developed here. Our criticisms of Washington and of Senator Fulbright have been severe. Perhaps to some extent this has been a one-sided account. There are intelligent, dedicated, courageous, and hard-working individuals who have responsibilities for the conduct of U.S. foreign policy and who carry out these responsibilities in the Department of State and in the Executive Office of the President. Still, these organizations do not function well, at least in the top echelons. The contrast with the intellect, sparkle, and skill of the Department of Defense is all too obvious. We have learned the art of war much better than the art of peace. By the most important operational tests, U.S. foreign policy is bankrupt.

At least some of the blame for this bankruptcy of policy can be attributed to the new dysfunctional myths that Senator Fulbright espouses. We do not need these myths. We do need a new analysis that will provide new directions for American foreign policy that are more in harmony with American possibilities, resources, ideals, and will than is present American policy. Undoubtedly it is unpleasant to admit the failures of one's hopes and expectations. But mere denial will not change any of the facts. To succeed in an adverse world, we require the courage to view the world as it is and to mold it, so far as lies within our powers and skills, as we would have it. Now is the time for a real great debate—the debate that Senator Fulbright did not provide for us.

13. Viet Nam and Bureaucracy

ALBERT WOHLSTETTER

I. Of all the disasters of Vietnam, the worst may be the "lessons" that we'll draw from it. The disasters so far are real enough, as is our responsibility in them. I have disagreed with our policy there. But one precedent that should make us thoughtful is the wrong lessons that were drawn in Vietnam from Korea. For example, U.S. advisors expected another conventional invasion across a parallel separating a Communist North from a non-Communist South.[1] To repel it they centered almost all our effort on organizing some 140,000 South Vietnamese in large conventional Army divisions. In the process they created commanders of vast independent political power and so increased the danger of military coups. This reinforced Diem's natural suspiciousness, nepotism and the tendency to avoid any delegation of power; and reduced further the chance that the Vietnamese, in spite of internal attack, would be able to advance in economic and political self-development and to operate under the rule of law. That in turn encouraged subversion, terror and counter-terror and helped make a

1. "Q: With command in your own hands from that point on, what were you trying to achieve?
"A: First of all, to organize the armed forces to repel an invasion coming down from the Communist North." Interview with Former Chief U.S. Military Adviser in South Vietnam from 1955 to 1960, Lieutenant General Samuel T. Williams (Ret.), *U.S. News and World Report*, November 9, 1964.

discriminate response unlikely. Our advisors were responding to a "lesson" of Korea.

Lessons from such complex events require much reflection to be of more than negative worth. But reactions to Vietnam, even more than to Korea, tend to be visceral rather than reflective. We hear now:

That the United States has no valid concern in the physical security or political and economic development of distant peoples. Or of people ethnically distinct from us (that is, those of "us" descended from West Europeans);

That U.S. power is the greatest danger to the world;

That our problem is not to use our power discriminately and for worthy ends but the fact of power itself, that we are better off reducing the choices available to us;

That even the massive retaliation policy which tended to make every confrontation a choice between nuclear war or doing nothing was not so bad after all. (It was and would be fine because we would always do nothing rather than something in between—according to the hopeful left; according to the hopeful right it is fine because our *adversaries* would always do nothing, in order to avoid our massive retaliation, and if not they would be overwhelmed by it.)

That our concerns for security should be limited to direct physical attacks on the continental United States and that we should depend for this purpose on the Navy and an intercontinental nuclear missile force. (There is an odd coalition one might discern forming between the old defenders of Fortress America and the New Left—a kind of SAC-SDS position.)

I think that such cures would be far worse than the disease. In fact they would make likely a sharp deterioration of the international system, including an increased expectation of the spread of nuclear weapons and a greater likelihood of nuclear war. The new isolationism has been justified variously on moral, strategic, economic and ethnic grounds. In my view, none of these grounds can sustain examination.[2]

2. I have not been asked to comment on U.S. policy on Vietnam but on Richard Barnet's diagnosis of what's wrong with that policy and with U.S. foreign policy in general. I have my doubts about Mr. Barnet's diagnosis but that does not imply I believe there is nothing to diagnose. There is. To make that plain, I'll state some of my own views in a very summary way and attach them in an appendix.

3. Mr. Barnet's 39 pages condense a book. The condensation omits perhaps inevitably not only evidence and much qualification but definitions of terms. Many points are asserted without elaboration and sometimes quite ambigu-

2. I examine several of these grounds in "Illusions of Distance," *Foreign Affairs,* January 1968.

ously. And there are many apparent contradictions. Though I have read his paper attentively, I may misunderstand it. The following appears to me to be the main thrust of his argument.

He rejects explanations of Vietnam as a series of mistakes or the fault of individuals like Dean Rusk, Walt Rostow, Maxwell Taylor, William Bundy, and Robert McNamara. There were mistakes and he would have fired all of the individuals listed. But his own thesis is: ". . . the roots of the Vietnam failure lie more in the structure and organization of the national security bureaucracy . . ." which makes the United States ". . . take on revolutionary movements around the world. . ."

The paper doesn't define the U.S. failure in Vietnam. It is not that the United States failed to achieve its goals there. Rather it was intervention itself. Or so it seems. The paper does not make clear whether what is bad is (a) all intervention, or (b) military intervention, or (c) large-scale military intervention, or (d) unilateral military intervention, or (e) intervention by force against any movement that styles itself "revolutionary," or (f) any non-military opposition to any revolution, or (g) any support for any government faced with rebellion, or (h) any opposition to Communist rebellion, or (i) any opposition to rebellions that grounds itself merely on the fact that they are Communist or Communist-leaning.

However the failure is defined, its root is the "national security bureaucracy." While the latter too is undefined, it seems to include all those who manage our foreign or military affairs (p. 12). At least, the State and Defense Departments and the White House staff (p. 12), but also, evidently, the CIA, AEC, NSA, and the international divisions of Commerce, Treasury, Agriculture, etc. And in talking of "roots," most of the time Mr. Barnet appears to mean that such intervention is an unavoidable result of the characteristics of the national security bureaucracy. "Bureaucratic momentum" makes inevitable the escalation of a small use of military force to larger and larger amounts and makes inevitable escalation even from economic aid to military intervention: "The dynamism of the myriad bureaucratic empires dealing in national security assures not only the escalation of U.S. commitments but their progressive militarization as well." And "the progression from aid missions to counter-insurgency 'advisors' to expeditionary forces takes on a kind of Parkinsonian inevitability."

The national security bureaucracy "consistently" exaggerates threats (p. 5). (The supposed missile gap of the late 1950's and the Soviet invasion threat in Western Europe in the 1940's are offered as examples.) This leads to increased military commitments and is indeed a rationalization for them. In fact, the U.S. national security bureaucrats "favor using instruments of violence to solve" political problems (p. 12). American bureaucrats seem worse in this respect than Maoist or Soviet ones. Elsewhere[3] Mr. Barnet has said

---

3. Richard J. Barnet, *Who Wants Disarmament* (p. 76).

that Soviet and Chinese Communists do not scruple at the use of violence but normally prefer other means. American bureaucrats, it seems, *prefer* violence.

Mr. Barnet doesn't deny that the world is "dangerous and anarchic." Other nations are dangerous, too. However, they are less dangerous than the United States (even if they also should prefer violence), because they are less powerful (p. 4).

But the deadly trouble with American national security bureaucracy seems much more general than its American or even its national security character. It has to do with the basic characteristics of bureaucracy. And not simply governmental bureaucracies. Non-governmental ones as well, e.g. commercial bureaucracies. Bureaucracies inevitably must convert means into ends. (Mr. Barnet cites Harold Lasswell, Robert Merton, Robert Presthus as authorities.) For a bureaucrat "to challenge the assumptions behind a policy is to take on the system which is the source of his power and status" (p. 28). Moreover, a particularly important example of this has to do with technology, both military and civilian. So, the supersonic transport in the commercial aviation field. "If the technology to produce a supersonic transport plane becomes available, a new national goal is suddenly discovered and the machine will be built regardless of how dubious its ultimate social utility" (p. 27). And the U-2 in the military field: "a new capability spawned a new requirement and it became necessary to overfly the Soviet Union" (p. 27).

Bureaucrats are conformists. They use unemotional language. This itself makes it easier to commit genocide. In fact, Barnet equates Truman's decision to use the A-bomb to end the war with Japan with Hitler's genocide, the "Final Solution" for the Jews.

Mr. Barnet's paper sweeps over and touches on many other matters. He hints for example that national interests are a function of ethnic ties and a linear function of distance. And he closes with a geo-political view rather like that of Mr. Kennan, who has held that "the effectiveness of power radiated from any national center decreases in proportion to the distance involved." "The global canvas," Mr. Barnet says, is too vast. ". . . making 'grand designs' for other nations when you have neither personal loyalties nor indeed personal relationships of any kind with them puts an unbearable strain on the processes of human judgment. This inherent limitation in the capacity of human organizations to govern at a distance offers a clue as to why empires eventually fail" (pp. 38–39).

4. I hope it will be plain from the views I express in the appendix that I put a great deal of store in reflecting on ends as well as means, and that I feel there was not nearly enough of that in Vietnam. I have frequently written in other connections on the need in systems analysis for searching critiques of the accepted objectives. So I am sympathetic with Mr. Barnet's stress on the dangers of neglecting ends. Moreover, I have spent much of my professional life appraising technologies, several times showing the negative utility

of some major technical innovations—sometimes persuasively. Further I am not at all fond of bureaucracies and I dislike bureaucratic jargon. (Also social science jargon, hippie jargon, and a number of other jargons.) Nonetheless—with all this going for it—Mr. Barnet's paper leaves me unsatisfied. It seems to me to be expressive rather than analytic. It conveys a mood, not an explanation.

And perhaps this is fortunate. Taken literally, Mr. Barnet's main argument seems to leave us almost no hope. If the general characteristics of bureaucracy or any large organization lead us so directly to genocide, nothing remains except a prayer that the world can be broken up into very small self-subsistent units in which contacts are face to face. Perhaps something like the Greek city-states, not counting the slaves. But then they *did* get into quite a few quarrels. And it seems hardly likely that we can manage our foreign and military affairs today in city sizes or in smaller units than commercial enterprises which we are told also have the fatal bureaucratic traits.

But Mr. Barnet's argument cannot be taken literally. It is less downright than it generally sounds. On major points he frequently softens or contradicts it. Thus on "bureaucratic momentum" it seems that the Parkinsonian inevitability is not ineluctable after all. Perhaps "Parkinsonian" should read "Pickwickian." For he follows one such statement immediately with "This is not true everywhere . . . But where the resources of the U.S. appear adequate to suppress insurgent movements, the result is predictable." But even this is not true. The "resources of the U.S." are not that constraining. (See my comments in the appendix.) And the U.S. has plainly not undertaken a good many actions for which it has resources. If one proceeds beyond the very broad constraints of general resources to an analysis showing that a particular military action would have been a *poor* use of our resources, in the sense that it would have meant surrendering something more important, then one says something very uncontroversial: We will act wisely whenever we do not undertake such an action. Almost no one will disagree.

Or take "threats"—an important matter. *Has* the national security bureaucracy consistently exaggerated threats and so led us into intervention? Mr. Barnet qualifies this. The bureaucracy "consistently" exaggerates *"many"* threats. (100% to a certain extent.) And in fact it turns out he doesn't think that having the threat appear *large* always encourages intervention. "Sometimes . . . threats are minimized in order to justify a seemingly rational policy based primarily on the use of military power. Thus North Vietnam can be beaten in a few months, the advocates of military intervention argued" (p. 5). And "The bureaucracy falls prey to the illusion that they are able to control events because they are free of the fear of retaliation" (p. 6).

It is not hard to multiply cases where the military greatly overestimated enemy forces and as a result did not intervene. For example, at the time of our decision not to intervene on behalf of the Chinese Nationalists at the end of the 1940's, General Marshall estimated the number of Russian divisions to be 260.[4] He neglected the considerable Russian demobilization (revealed later by Khrushchev) that had taken place since the war, ignored differences in size, manning and equipment of these divisions (analyzed later by assistants to Robert McNamara, in particular Alain Enthoven), and compared them with categories of U.S. force that were not strictly comparable. And we did not intervene.

That the military nearly always exaggerate enemy capabilities and that this leads to intervention is a cliche; and a vast exaggeration. It isn't so. The truth is that they sometimes overestimate and sometimes underestimate—and sometimes even get it right. And that either sort of mistake may in various circumstances lead toward or away from intervention. Or may be largely irrelevant. It is hard to see what we can conclude—except that it's nice to have better estimates of threats and to consider concretely a good many other things besides threats in deciding on whether, where and when to commit ourselves.

Mr. Barnet's reference to the "missile gap" indicates a very popular misunderstanding. In the first place the "missile gap" was not an issue raised by the *ins*—the top managers of national security under Eisenhower. It was a political gambit of the *outs*—the Democrats. President Eisenhower's top bureaucrats stoutly defended themselves against the charge. (They said we might have fewer missiles but we had and would have more bombers, that in any case there was no deterrent gap.) Second, during the Eisenhower regime the strategic force was genuinely and dangerously vulnerable, but this vulnerability had nothing essential to do with the hypothetical "missile gap." It had to do with the fact that the strategic force in the 1950's had no

---

4. General Marshall told an audience in the Pentagon in November, 1950: ". . . when I was Secretary of State, I was being pressed constantly, . . . by radio message after radio message to give the Russians hell. . . . When I got back I was getting the same appeal in relation to the Far East and China. At that time, my facilities for giving them hell . . . was 1⅓ divisions over the entire United States. This is quite a proposition when you deal with somebody with *over 260* and you have 1⅓rd."

"With reference to the situation in China in 1947 and 1948, General Marshall testified: ". . . There, the issue in my mind, as Secretary of State, was to what extent this government could commit itself to a possible involvement of a very heavy nature in regard to operations in China itself. . .

"We would have to make a very considerable initial contribution and we would be involved in the possibility of very extensive continuing responsibilities in a very large area.

"At that time, our own military position was extraordinarily weak. I think I mentioned the other day that my recollection is . . . we had one and a third divisions in the entire United States.

"As I recall General Wedemeyer's estimates, about 10,000 officers and others would be necessary to oversee and direct those various operations.

"In view of our general world situation, our own military weakness, and the global reaction to this situation, and my own knowledge out of that brief contact of mine in China, we could not afford to commit this government to such a procedure.

"Therefore, I was not in agreement with undertaking that, nor were . . . the chiefs of staff."

Tang Tsou, *America's Failure in China, 1941–1950*. University of Chicago Press, 1963. pp. 366–367.

adequate warning or other protection against even a small manned bomber attack. Moreover, the essential major changes made in the strategic force by President Kennedy and Secretary McNamara had to do with substituting less vulnerable strategic vehicles and a more responsible and protected control of this strategic force. This drastic set of changes was indicated in any case and had been proposed in classified form *before* the Kennedy Administration and *before* a hypothetical "missile gap." The proposed changes had been accumulated by analysts, many of whom took great pains to separate the problems of deterrence, of responsible control against "accidents," and of reducing the vulnerability of strategic forces from the problem of matching forces in number.

The mythology of the "gap" includes not only the potential gap that turned out not to be actual but the myths about the role the gap played. I am quite familiar with them, since I began writing analyses to demonstrate the essential irrelevance of bomber gaps, missile gaps, engineer gaps, and the like beginning in the early 1950's, and as late as 1960 I sent a lengthy explanation to the man who was writing John Kennedy's main campaign speech on defense, specifically to suggest why the "missile gap" was not only a theoretical and operational misunderstanding of the problem, but one that was very likely to kick back politically. It did, but only after the election.[5]

The Russian invasion potential in the late 40's is the other example cited by Mr. Barnet. It would take quite a lot of space to evidence why, but I believe that his judgment about what was wrong on our various estimates at the time and what role our erroneous estimates played in our commitments is itself in error. A study of the quotations from General Marshall suggest why. Let me simply register my disagreement.

On technologies it seems to me Mr. Barnet greatly overstates his case and gets some of the historical record quite wrong. On the historical record the U-2's existence did not create the requirement for overflight. On the contrary, the U-2 was an unusually clear-cut case of a rather precisely defined lack generating a technology. The need at the time for better estimates of Russian forces might be suggested by the troubles I have discussed with early estimates of Russian capabilities. In fact, some of our early knowledge seems to have come from German data and Russian documents captured by the Germans during World War II. These were quite a bit out of date by the early 1950's. And our information then was quite incomplete. In any case, the need for better information was felt in the administration. And according

---

5. Mr. Barnet is in error in suggesting that basic changes in the strategic force made in the early years of the Kennedy Administration depended on the existence of a "missile gap." The gap was strictly inessential. On the other hand, his own comments, in *Twenty Years After*, on the recent state of the missile gap and its future suggest the need for caution about not merely the significance of gaps but their possible future existence and direction. He was confident two or three years ago that the Russians were quite willing to put up with a large gap favoring the Americans. The evidence since suggests they are not.

to public accounts, a variety of government officials and advisors explored the possibilities of gaining reconnaissance at extremely high and hopefully safe altitudes. The crash project at Lockheed to develop the U-2 responded to this perceived need. Quite the reverse of Mr. Barnet's description that overflight of the Soviet Union was decided on because we had the plane. In fact, the desire for information about Soviet military forces appears to have generated not one but several technologically distinct modes of fulfilling the same need.[6] The relationship between technology and aims is usually much more complex. I doubt that there are many examples as clear as this.

Yet Mr. Barnet suggests that the creation of national goals regardless of ultimate social utility is automatic. If this were so, it would be impossible to explain the fact that a great many technological developments have been sharply limited or canceled altogether—military developments such as the Navaho ramjet missile, the B-70 manned bomber, the Skybolt missile, the nuclear propelled aircraft, and a great many others. The world would have been knee-deep long ago in a wide variety of military hardware most of which has never seen the light of day.

The same may be said for civilian technology. Our choices here, as in the military case, are frequently misguided, and often too fascinated by techniques, but it is fortunately not the case that every technology feasible is made actual. There are many in which there is little argument and there are some like the development of the nuclear merchant marine in which arguments against have so far prevailed. And some like Mr. Barnet's own example of the supersonic transport in which there has been a great deal of argument, pro and con, with the pros winning but under much severer restraints than had been proposed. It has not been anything like as automatic as Mr. Barnet suggests. Moreover, the most potent arguments against supersonic transport, perhaps to Mr. Barnet's surprise, have been made by systems analysts borrowed from the Defense Department. (Dr. Stephen Enke, for example—see his paper in the *American Economic Review*, May 1967.)

In fact, Mr. Barnet's description of the automatic coming into operation of any new technologies is excluded by the fact that there are resource constraints. Choice is not only possible, but necessary. To develop one alternative precludes developing some others. Mr. Barnet's nightmare of bureaucracies automatically sponsoring every technology would simply be too crowded. It is a logical impossibility. This does not of course mean that *good* choices will be made. But *choices* will be made. What are we to conclude from this? Only that we should keep working at improving our methods of selection—recalling always that our choice of means is related to our choice of ends.

6. The magazine *Air Force* (March, 1968, p. 53) states that satellites for reconnaissance were studied before as well as after Sputnik. And Soviet accounts report reconnaissance over Russia, not only by the U-2 manned aircraft, but also by balloons. (*New York Times* 2/6/56, 2/12/56, and 10/12/58.)

On the matter of ends and means, once again Mr. Barnet seems to me to have greatly overstated the problem, made it appear in fact insoluble. I quite agree with him that bureaucrats tend to forget about their ends. They frequently, as Santayana remarked about fanatics, redouble their efforts as they lose sight of their goal. On the other hand, as the context of Santayana's remark suggests, this is hardly limited to government bureaucrats, or bureaucrats in commercial enterprise. It can be true in political parties, and had obvious illustrations in the party bureaucracies of the left, which Robert Michels analyzed. But it is also true, sad to say, of violently anti-bureaucratic movements. The anarchists, it is familiar, have frequently taken revolutionary violence as an end in itself. There is a great deal of romanticism current on this subject. And much of the discussion of whether one should support revolution or counter-insurgency proceeds on these sentimental terms. But whether a revolution is worth supporting or opposing surely should depend on what it is a revolution to as well as what it is a revolution from, and what the human costs are of the revolutionary process, and what other alternatives for change there are. Reflection on ends as well as means seems quite as rare among insurgents as among counter-insurgents.

In sum, I do not see that Mr. Barnet shows it to be impossible for men who manage foreign and military affairs to reflect on goals as well as means. And if this is rarer among military men and statesmen than we would like, so is reflective behavior almost any place.

On Mr. Barnet's opposition to intervention, I will not try to select for comment one or two out of the nine or ten possible meanings that I have listed. I will note only that he does relent a little on his indictment of the national security bureaucrats. Although on page 12 he indicates they actually prefer the use of violence, on page 34 he says they prefer non-military to military intervention, but will use force rather than lose control where we have an interest. My own views in this respect are quite close to those of my colleague, Professor Morgenthau:[7] one cannot decide whether it is good or bad to intervene at a given time or place without a great deal of concrete empirical analysis. It is not clear to me that Mr. Barnet agrees.

I will not comment at length here about the bare suggestion in Mr. Barnet's paper of a geo-political view that relates national interests to ethnic ties and linearly to distance. I have written extensively about the limitations of such views elsewhere.[8] On the ethnic argument let me say only that I think it particularly incongruous today when voiced by those who want to turn from

7. "To Intervene or Not To Intervene," *Foreign Affairs*, April 1967.
8. "Technology, Prediction and Disorder," in the *Dispersion of Nuclear Weapons*, edited by Richard Rosecrance, Columbia University Press, 1964. "Illusions of Distance," *Foreign Affairs*, January 1968. "Strength, Interest, and New Technologies," in Adelphi Paper #46, Institute of Strategic Studies, London, 1968. "Theory and Opposed-Systems Design," in *New Approaches to International Relations*, edited by Morton Kaplan, St. Martin's Press, New York and London, 1968; "Distant Wars and Far Out Estimates," written with Richard Rainey.

foreign concerns to the problems of domestic racial, and ethnic inequities. I'm afraid we'll have to deal with both.

Appendix on Mini-Brute Force in Vietnam

A. In Vietnam, I believe the U.S. intervened in a conflict in which the chances were poor to start with for affecting events in the direction of basic U.S. interests and aims for the political and economic self-development of the Third World. The skillful Communist leadership benefitted from its success in the long struggle against the French. They had built up a formidable apparatus of cadres in the South. The heritage of French colonialism left the non-Communist alternatives for leadership weak and badly divided.

B. The nature of the threat, the feasible and worthy objectives of our support, and the main alternatives for achieving such objectives were misconceived. The issues were wrongly defined at each of the major successive stages of decision.

C. They were defined wrongly, moreover, not only by official policy, but also frequently by factions within the Government and by the critics of the Government—and not least by the critics. The question was not whether to "escalate" or "de-escalate". The concept of "escalation", prominent especially in the last few years, merely caps the general confusion. It indicates that we can order and measure the alternatives for choice on a linear scale: Shall we reduce or increase the intensity of the fighting? Or (since the latter is affected by the decisions of the North Vietnamese), should we scale our own effort up or down? How many men should we keep in Vietnam? How much should we spend? How many, and which, target constraints should we remove? These were the wrong questions.

D. If we were to try and help in Vietnam the basic questions concerned not how much, but what for? Such questions were clearly posed at least by 1961—perhaps most clearly by British advisers in Vietnam.[9] Should we concentrate on the slow, persistent attempt to help construct a viable government capable of economic and political self-development, able to protect an increasing proportion of the population from subversion and terror, and so to reduce the local support for guerrillas or infiltrated Northern forces? Or, on the other hand, should we focus our major efforts on trying to hunt down and annihilate guerrillas and the main force units of the DRV? While the level of forces needed is not entirely in the control of one side, the first alternative would have required smaller military forces than the second. It would

9. While I have some differences with them, since the beginning of 1962 I have owed much of my own view of the alternatives to talks with British advisers in Vietnam, in particular Robert Thompson, Dennis Duncanson, and John Barlow.

subordinate conventional military operations, and among other things would aim to prevent the establishment of secure base areas by the Viet Cong and DRV main force units; but it would not expend its efforts to "search and destroy." It would have taken years and may not have been successful at all. The second alternative required the application of brute force massively and at a much greater rate than was politically feasible for the United States and in any case would have destroyed much of the basis for viable government in South Vietnam. On my observation, one of the things that predisposed us to the latter course was impatience and the distaste for any long-term involvement. This explanation runs quite counter to current views that attribute to the U.S. Government the desire to get involved everywhere and specifically to get bases or a "sphere of influence" in South Vietnam.

E. In any event, the U.S. Government tended never to face such basic choices. Instead, it "escalated"—more slowly and less extensively than requested. But it did not change the objectives. In this way, it got the worst of both worlds, what might be called "a mini-brute force policy:" a slow application of brute force in the hope of achieving quickly objectives that could be achieved, if at all, only by a massive and rapid use of force—and the wrong objectives at that. The bombing of North Vietnam, for example, was wrong even in its own terms—it was poorly adapted for reducing the number of North Vietnamese forces in South Vietnam. And the bombing and the artillery in South Vietnam were not for the most part in "close support;" they exacted much too high a toll in bystanders and friendly forces. (This does not, of course, justify the VC's deliberate putting of bystanders in peril.)

Let me elaborate a little on mini-brute force. While a brute force policy was mistaken, it is conceivabe that in its own erroneous terms it could have been successful if it were actually massive enough. And this was *not*, as is usually said, a matter of the absolute limits of U.S. resources. After all, the United States raised armed forces including, in gross, 16,354,000 military personnel in World War II, with over 12,000,000 on duty in 1945 when our population was less than 140,000,000. We have the resources to raise over 20,000,000 men now—more than one for every North Vietnamese man, woman, and child. By brute force we could simply pave North and South Vietnam in concrete. Something less than that undoubtedly would accomplish the "search and destroy" job—however blindly. Of course, even a much less total mobilization of massive force to meet so limited a challenge was not politically feasible. This in itself, quite apart from the more important consideration of what the problems are of a small country under attack by Communist insurgent forces, might have suggested transformation to other objectives. In fact, a change of objectives was never genuinely made. Time and again when requests were made for more resources or the removal of further constraints, the government response was to grant something less than the amount asked in resources or in the removal of constraints; but not to change the objective sought. As a result, we had the wrong objective pursued by a brute force tactic with far less than the amount of force that the objective required: in short a mini-brute force policy.

F. The recent government decision to turn down a request for 206,000 more American ground forces in South Vietnam, courageous though it was, leaves unsettled a basic issue—one that will remain so long as the negotiations drag on in Paris. It does not alter what our forces in Vietnam are doing and for what purpose. They are still chasing Viet Cong. Still forcussing on annihilating elusive DRV main force units. Still largely ignoring the need to establish a politically secure base area relatively free of VC cadres, the need to protect the population, and to have a government that operates under the rule of law.

14. The Viet Nam Negotiations

HENRY A. KISSINGER

A VAST GULF in cultural and bureaucratic style between Hanoi and Washington complicates matters. It would be difficult to imagine two societies less meant to understand each other than the Vietnamese and the American. History and culture combine to produce almost morbid suspiciousness on the part of the Vietnamese. Because survival has depended on a subtle skill in manipulating physically stronger foreigners, the Vietnamese style of communication is indirect and, by American standards, devious—qualities which avoid a total commitment and an overt test of strength. The fear of being made to look foolish seems to transcend most other considerations. Even if the United States accepted Hanoi's maximum program, the result might well be months of haggling whie Hanoi looked for our "angle" and made sure that no other concessions were likely to be forthcoming.

These tendencies are magnified by communist ideology, which defines the United States as inherently hostile, and by Hanoi's experience in previous negotiations with the United States. It may well feel that the Geneva Conferences of 1954 and 1962 (over Laos) deprived it of part of its achievements on the battlefield.

All this produces the particular negotiating style of Hanoi: the careful planning, the subtle, indirect methods, the preference for opaque communications which keep open as many options as possible toward both foe and friend (the latter may seem equally important to Hanoi). North Viet Nam's diplomacy operates in cycles of reconnaissance and withdrawal to give an opportunity to assess the opponent's reaction. This is then followed by another diplomatic sortie to consolidate the achievements of the previous phase or to try another route. In this sense, many contacts with Hanoi which seemed "abortive" to us, probably served (from Hanoi's point of view) the function of defining the terrain. The methods of Hanoi's diplomacy are not very different from Viet Cong military strategy and sometimes appear just as impenetrable to us.

If this analysis is correct, few North Vietnamese moves are accidental; even the most obtuse communication is likely to serve a purpose. On the other hand, it is not a style which easily lends itself to the sort of analysis at which we excel: the pragmatic, legal dissection of individual cases. Where Hanoi makes a fetish of planning, Washington is allergic to it. We prefer to deal with cases as they arise, "on their merits." Pronouncements that the United States is ready to negotiate do not guarantee that a negotiating position exists or that the U.S. Government has articulated its objectives.

Until a conference comes to be scheduled, two groups in the American bureaucracy usually combine to thwart the elaboration of a negotiating position: those who oppose negotiations and those who favor them. The opponents generally equate negotiations with surrender; if they agree to discuss settlement terms at all, it is to define the conditions of the enemy's capitulation. Aware of this tendency and of the reluctance of the top echelon to expend capital on settling disputes which involve no immediate practical consequences, the advocates of negotiations coöperate in avoiding the issue. Moreover, delay serves their own purposes in that it enables them to reserve freedom of action for the conference room.

Pragmatism and bureaucracy thus combine to produce a diplomatic style marked by rigidity in advance of formal negotiations and excessive reliance on tactical considerations once negotiations start. In the preliminary phases, we generally lack a negotiating program; during the conference, bargaining considerations tend to shape internal discussions. In the process, we deprive ourselves of criteria by which to judge progress. The over-concern with tactics suppresses a feeling for nuance and for intangibles.

The incompatibility of the American and North Vietnamese styles of diplomacy produced, for a long time, a massive breakdown of communication—especially in the preliminary phases of negotiation. While Hanoi was feeling its way toward negotiations, it bent all its ingenuity to avoid clear-cut, formal commitments. Ambiguity permitted Hanoi to probe without giving away much in return; Hanoi has no peers in slicing the salami very thin. It wanted the context of events rather than a formal document to define its obligations, lest its relations with Peking or the NLF be compromised.

Washington was unequipped for this mode of communication. To a government which equates commitments with legally enforceable obligations,

Hanoi's subtle changes of tense were literally incomprehensible. In a press conference in February 1968, President Johnson said, "As near as I am able to detect, Hanoi has not changed its course of conduct since the very first response it made. Sometimes they will change 'will' to 'would' or 'shall' to 'should,' or something of the kind. But the answer is all the same." A different kind of analysis might have inquired why Hanoi would open up a channel for a meaningless communication, especially in the light of a record of careful planning which made it extremely unlikely that a change of tense would be inadvertent.

Whatever the might-have-beens, Hanoi appeared to Washington as devious, deceitful and tricky. To Hanoi, Washington must have seemed, if not obtuse, then cannily purposeful. In any event, the deadlock produced by the difference in negotiating style concerned specific clauses less than the philosophical issue of the nature of an international "commitment" or the meaning of "trickery." This problem lay at the heart of the impasse over the bombing halt.

On the face of it, Saigon's reluctance to accept equal status with the NLF is comprehensible for it tends to affect all other issues, from ceasefire to internal structure. The merits of the dispute aside, the public rift between Saigon and Washington compromised what had been achieved. To split Washington and Saigon had been a constant objective of Hanoi; if the Paris talks turn into an instrument to accomplish this, Hanoi will be tempted to use them for political warfare rather than for serious discussions.

Clearly, there is a point beyond which Saigon cannot be given a veto over negotiations. But equally, it is not preposterous for Saigon to insist on a major voice in decisions affecting its own country. And it cannot strengthen our position in Paris to *begin* the substantive discussions with a public row over the status of a government whose constitutionality we have insistently pressed on the world for the past two years. The impasse has demonstrated that to deal with issues on an ad hoc basis is too risky; before we go much further in negotiations, we need an agreed concept of ultimate goals and how to achieve them.

Ceasefire and Coalition Government

Substantive negotiations confront the United States with a major conceptual problem: whether to proceed step by step, discussing each item "on its merits," or whether to begin by attempting to get agreement about some ultimate goals.

The difference is not trivial. If the negotiations proceed step by step through a formal agenda, the danger is great that the bombing halt will turn out to be an admission ticket to another deadlock. The issues are so interrelated that a partial settlement foreshadows the ultimate outcome and therefore contains all of its complexities. Mutual distrust and the absence of clarity as to final goals combine to produce an extraordinary incentive to submit all proposals to the most searching scrutiny and to erect hedges for failure or bad faith.

This is well illustrated by two schemes which public debate has identified as suitable topics for the next stage of negotiations: ceasefire and coalition government.

It has become axiomatic that a bombing halt would lead—almost automatically—to a ceasefire. However, negotiating a ceasefire may well be tantamount to establishing the preconditions of a political settlement. If there existed a front line with unchallenged control behind it, as in Korea, the solution would be traditional and relatively simple: the two sides could stop shooting at each other and the ceasefire line could follow the front line. But there are no front lines in Viet Nam; control is not territorial, it depends on who has forces in a given area and on the time of day. If a ceasefire permits the Government to move without challenge, day or night, it will amount to a Saigon victory. If Saigon is prevented from entering certain areas, it means in effect partition which, as in Laos, tends toward permanency. Unlike Laos, however, the pattern would be a crazy quilt, with enclaves of conflicting loyalties all over the country.

This would involve the following additional problems: (1) It would lead to an intense scramble to establish predominant control before the ceasefire went into effect. (2) It would make next to impossible the verification of any withdrawal of North Vietnamese forces that might be negotiated; the local authorities in areas of preponderant communist control would doubtless certify that no external forces were present and impede any effort at international inspection. (3) It would raise the problem of the applicability of a ceasefire to guerrilla activity in the non-communist part of the country; in other words, how to deal with the asymmetry between the actions of regular and of guerrilla forces. Regular forces operate on a scale which makes possible a relatively precise definition of what is permitted and what is proscribed; guerrilla forces, by contrast, can be effective through isolated acts of terror difficult to distinguish from normal criminal activity.

There would be many other problems: who collects taxes and how, who enforces the ceasefire and by what means. In other words, a tacit de facto ceasefire may prove more attainable than a negotiated one. By the same token, a formal ceasefire is likely to predetermine the ultimate settlement and tend toward partition. Ceasefire is thus not so much a step toward a final settlement as a form of it.

This is even more true of another staple of the Viet Nam debate: the notion of a coalition government. Of course, there are two meanings of the term: as a means of legitimizing partition, indeed as a disguise for continuing the civil war; or as a "true" coalition government attempting to govern the whole country. In the first case, a coalition government would be a façade with non-communist and communist ministries in effect governing their own parts of the country. This is what happened in Laos, where each party in the "coalition government" wound up with its own armed forces and its own territorial administration. The central government did not exercise any truly national functions. Each side carried on its own business—including civil war. But in Laos, each side controlled contiguous territory, not a series of enclaves as in South Viet Nam. Too, of all the ways to bring about partition, negotiations about a coalition government are the most dangerous because the mere participation of the United States in talking about it could change the political landscape of South Viet Nam.

Coalition government is perhaps the most emotionally charged issue in Viet Nam, where it tends to be identified with the second meaning: a joint Saigon-NLF administration of the entire country. There can be no American objection, of course, to direct negotiations between Saigon and the NLF. The issue is whether the United States should be party to an attempt to *impose* a coalition government. We must be clear that our involvement in such an effort may well destroy the existing political structure of South Viet Nam and thus lead to a communist takeover.

Some urge negotiations on a coalition government for precisely this reason: as a face-saving formula for arranging the communist political victory which they consider inevitable. But those who believe that the political evolution of South Viet Nam should not be foreclosed by an American decision must realize that the subject of a coalition government is the most thankless and tricky area for negotiation *by outsiders.*

The notion that a coalition government represents a "compromise" which will permit a new political evolution hardly does justice to Vietnamese conditions. Even the non-communist groups have demonstrated the difficulty Vietnamese have in compromising differences. It is beyond imagination that parties that have been murdering and betraying each other for 25 years could work together as a team giving joint instructions to the entire country. The image of a line of command extending from Saigon into the countryside is hardly true of the non-communist government in Saigon. It would be absurd in the case of a coalition government. Such a government would possess no authority other than that of each minister over the forces he controlled either through personal or party loyalty.

To take just one example of the difficulties: Communist ministers would be foolhardy in the extreme if they entered Saigon without bringing along sufficient military force for their protection. But the introduction of communist military forces into the chief bastion of governmental strength would change the balance of political forces in South Viet Nam. The danger of a coalition government is that it would decouple the non-communist elements from effective control over their armed forces and police, leaving them unable to defend themselves adequately.

In short, negotiations seeking to impose a coalition from the outside are likely to change markedly and irreversibly the political process in South

Viet Nam—as Vietnamese who believe that a coalition government cannot work quickly choose sides. We would, in effect, be settling the war on an issue least amenable to outside influence, with respect to which we have the least grasp of conditions and the long-term implications of which are most problematical.

This is not to say that the United States should resist an outcome freely negotiated among the Vietnamese. It does suggest that any negotiation on this point by the United States is likely to lead either to an impasse or to the collapse of Saigon.

15. An Interview with Ambassador Harriman

HEDRICK SMITH

Governor, you've talked many times about the idea of a Southern solution in Vietnam. Is this just a polite way of saying that in the end we're going to have to settle for a coalition which includes both Saigon elements and the National Liberation Front?

HARRIMAN: I don't know what's going to come out of it. I'd always hoped we could get the people from Saigon together with the N.L.F. and put them in a room and lock the doors and throw away the key until they came out with a decision.

We had arranged—or at least we thought we had, Cy Vance and I—that we would have private talks, the four of us together, right after the first open meeting.

This was last November in Paris?

HARRIMAN: Yes, after the end of the bombing and after we have agreed on the procedures for four-party talks with the South Vietnamese Government represented. In fact, it was so clear that we would have four-party private talks that the North Vietnamese asked if it would be possible for us to continue sometimes to have bilateral talks. I said: "Well, of course it would be, because we must have many subjects of mutual interest."

It hasn't worked out that way; both sides have been rather cautious about being unwilling to talk to each other, and it shows that each side is a bit afraid of the other. But one of the things that's absolutely essential is that the Saigon Government must broaden its base. It's not a very good negotiating team for the future of the South Vietnamese people when it represents such a narrow group.

You mean it should include many other elements, even progressives like the leftist Buddhists?

HARRIMAN: Yes. There are a number of different groups. I'm quite convinced that by far the majority of the people don't want to be taken over by the Vietcong or Hanoi; they want to be independent. The trouble is they're split a dozen different ways, and no one has been able to bring them together.

President Diem was not able to do so. That was the reason for his fall. And he got too arbitrary, put too many people in jail. And this Government is putting a lot of people in jail. I was rather startled when I heard President Thieu, coming back from meeting President Nixon at Midway, announce that he was going to punish severely anyone who suggested a coalition government.

Well, our position has been that we're not opposed to a coalition government. You remember I said in Paris a number of times that we would not impose it. We were against a government's being imposed either by Hanoi or by Washington.

How do you distinguish between broadening the base of the Thieu Government and what Hanoi and the N.L.F. call forming a "peace cabinet"? Are you suggesting we have to dispense with the Thieu regime?

HARRIMAN: No, I'm not. We've been urging Thieu to broaden the base, and he did to some extent when he brought in Tran Van Huong last year as Premier, and then others, but he didn't really bring together a coalition of all the anti-Vietcong forces. There are different groups, different sects, religious groups. There are two techniques, and both should be used. One is to bring in ministers that are representative of different groups, get a coalition that way. Another, possibly better technique, is to have what they once had, which is a council of notables. They could get some fellow who had great popular appeal—Big Minh,[1] for instance—to be chairman, and have it a consultative group, bring in everybody. Now, it couldn't be just a front; it would have to be consulted. Thieu would have to give up some of his arbitrary posi-

1. Maj. Gen. Duong Van Minh, a leader of the 1963 coup that overthrew the regime of President Ngo Dinh Diem. Minh was in exile in Thailand until last fall and since then has been living quietly in Saigon.

tions; he would have to really consult these people as to the kind of settlement they wanted to have.

We've been trying to persuade Thieu to broaden the base, but we've never really put heat on him, and I think that is something that ought to be done; I say put the heat on him and make him understand that this is essential for our support. I think he'd do it then.

I'm afraid that I would disagree with what the Embassy people think is enough. Some people think it's enough that he reshuffle the Cabinet and bring in two or three people who belong to certain different groups. I think he's got to bring them all into something like this council of notables, all the non-Communist groups.

There'd be some very vigorous differences of opinion between these groups, of course. But if Thieu cannot dominate the non-Communist groups, there's not much hope—is there?—for his surviving as a leader in his country, because the other side has no use for him. Thieu has been a very shrewd operator, but he hasn't got the appeal that a fellow like Big Minh has.

Do you think that broadening the base of the Saigon Government would break the present stalemate in the Paris talks, or do you think other steps are necessary?

HARRIMAN: I don't think that we'll ever come to serious negotiations until we're ready to accept the status quo, militarily and politically. The other side made it quite plain to us that they'd continue fighting as long as we continued fighting. This seems rather natural to me. If you're going to try to make a settlement you've got to accept the status quo.

I think that we ought to abandon our efforts to expand the pacification program into new areas. That's an attempt by the Saigon Government, with our support, to improve their position, to get control of more villages which were rather doubtful or were under V.C. control. As I recall it, in December, half of our combat forces were engaged in that operation. So it was a quite important activity.

But the principal object would be for our forces to go into more defensive positions, to be available if the other side attacked, but not to try, at the last minute, either to "win the war" militarily or to pacify the people. You know, there's great hope in the Embassy in Saigon that in a few more months they can do a good deal in pacification. I have grave doubts about the permanent value of this procedure.

What's more important is to consolidate our position in the areas clearly controlled by the Government, and that means getting more of the people back of the Government in the manner that I described. That has to be done or the future elections will be quite unfortunate.

You seem to imply that recognizing the political realities means recognizing that the other side is going to have a share of the political power in the South as part of any settlement. Otherwise, they won't have any interest to stop fighting.

HARRIMAN: That's right. How it can be achieved is very hard. There are certain countries that have survived with an active, vigorous Communist party. In France and Italy, for instance, you have strong Communist parties in opposition to the Government. In Finland, the Communist party is participating in the Government. There are others that were not successful in withstanding this. In the Western European countries, a number of them had Communist participation in government for a short period but the non-Communist forces were strong enough to throw them out.

Let's look at the military side for a moment. We've had 16 months in Paris now, and we've had a battlefield lull this summer, as we had last summer and at other periods. Do you think that the first order of business now should be getting a cease-fire in order to set the conditions for political talks?

HARRIMAN: A cease-fire is a difficult thing. We had hoped in January to— well, as a matter of fact, in November, it was very clear there was not only a lull in the fighting, but there was a disengagement in the northern two provinces of South Vietnam. Ninety per cent of the North Vietnamese troops there were taken out. Half of them went as far north as the 20th Parallel, nearly 200 miles north; the others were kept closer by, either just north of the DMZ or in Laos. There was little or no fighting, and that had been one of the most active battlegrounds. But General Abrams, our commander, was able to take advantage of their pullback to move the First Cavalry Division out of that area, the I Corps, and into the III Corps area to increase our pressure on the enemy there.

Did you feel that Hanoi was ready to proceed with some kind of formal disengagement?

HARRIMAN: We weren't sure what we could do. Our trouble was that we never could talk about military settlements with the North Vietnamese alone because they maintained that they weren't fighting; it was the N.L.F. or the V.C. that was fighting. They wanted to talk to us about a political settlement and we wouldn't talk about a political settlement without the Saigon Government represented.

So we only talked around subjects. But their act of disengagement in the North convinced us in Paris that they were ready to move further in the reduction of the level of violence, working toward a cease-fire.

Now, you have to have a cease-fire if there is to be a political settlement. We thought perhaps we could feel our way into a cease-fire by specific actions; in other words, areas of disengagement—no fighting in the I Corps area, for instance—and see how it worked.

Then we did have a very important negotiating weapon, the B-52 raids. They were extremely unhappy about the B-52 raids. They never told us how effective they were in terms of the damage they did but the effect on the morale of the V.C., N.L.F., North Vietnamese was terrific. Suddenly out of the sky would come the most tremendous explosions, and they wanted to get rid of that.

Now, I think in return for stopping the B-52's we might well have come to an understanding that they would stop a great deal of their violence, or all of their violence in Saigon and the other cities—stop ambushing some of the highways.

This was what we hoped to achieve if the Saigon Government representation had come to Paris and been ready to negotiate. This is what we hoped to achieve right away in November, and I think it would have made a basis for us to withdraw troops even last year because they had taken troops north. This is, after all, one of the ways to come to an understanding. One way is by specific agreement, the other by mutual example. And both are effective.

Now a cease-fire should be our objective, but how we can reach it is a matter that has never been fully worked out. The military have never liked it, you know, because to some extent, what President Nixon said the other day is their view: "We cease and the other side fires." That's a little bit too facetious on a serious subject. And there is a feeling that the conventional armies are at a disadvantage with the guerrillas because you can see an army move, whereas the guerrillas can move around in the jungle without much difficulty.

On the other hand, there are certain things we can tell, such as whether there are terrorist acts in the villages. If they did that sort of thing, we'd know about it.

Did you object last fall to our maintaining unceasing pressure on the enemy—building up the pressure in III Corps, for instance, when the action fell off in I Corps?

HARRIMAN: No. Well, we in Paris were for a change in the orders for all-out pressure, but we were not pressing it because we always thought that the Saigon representatives would appear in Paris and then we would negotiate.

Were there actual proposals being discussed within our Government at that time for a mutual reduction of violence?

HARRIMAN: No—I came back at the end of November, you know, and made our views known here in Washington. But by that time the Saigon Government had agreed to come to Paris. We thought any moment we would start the discussions, so we were going to try to come forward with specific proposals on the mutual reduction of violence. But that never came about because we had this ridiculous performance of Saigon objecting to the shape of the table. I kept telling these Saigon representatives it didn't make the slightest difference what the shape of the table was. We had suggested a round table in October, and the other side had accepted it. The fact the other side accepted it made the Saigon people opposed to it. The round table historically has been a method of ending all dispute as to who has seniority; no one knows where the head of a round table is.

I remember your suggesting—and Secretary of Defense Clifford's suggesting—during this period that if Saigon dragged its feet we'd just go right ahead and talk with the North Vietnamese about this question of military disengagement, de-escalation. Why wasn't that tried?

HARRIMAN: Well, that was not accepted by the President. I was entirely willing to go ahead. I think if we had the Saigon Government would have come along pretty rapidly. But I think that probably our officials in Saigon felt that it would be too much of a blow to the prestige and position of the Saigon Government and would tend to undermine it too much.

On this summer now: Do you think the other side has been trying to signal us with the latest lull that they're willing once again to go into military disengagement?

HARRIMAN: I'm not sufficiently *au courant* with the details. They reduced the fighting, undoubtedly because they ran out of steam. They have these offensives and they carry them on as long as they can. Then they run out of steam and they wait and re-equip and replace their losses and start again. The military are quite right in saying that.

But in almost all the cases in the last year, I think, there was a political intent in connection with it. In fact, they stated it to me once in private talks. They said: "Whenever we attack, you say that this attack is not conducive to an atmosphere which furthers the peace negotiations. But when we stop, Saigon announces we are defeated and forced to end the attack."

They never said—they never will say—"We have stopped for a political purpose." They think that it would be considered by many people in the United States, both the military and other hawks, that they'd been beaten if they were to say, "We've stopped because we wanted to negotiate."

The way to freeze this is to take parallel action, announce that you're taking parallel action; we can afford to announce it. That's one trouble with the present situation. Nobody knows whether we really have stopped offensive action.

Do you take Secretary of Defense Laird's announcement that we're now following a strategy of "protective reaction" as a step in the right direction?

HARRIMAN: I would say it's a step in the right direction, but I don't think it's enough so far because I still see the B-52 raids. Maybe there are discussions going on in Paris that I don't know about. But we have to be very precise about what we're going to do and demand what we expect them to do in return.

I was very much disturbed by these recent terrorist attacks, one at Camranh and one in Saigon. They undoubtedly did this to show that they were not completely impotent, not defeated. They attacked the two supposedly most well-protected areas. Now, this is unfortunate, and one of the things that I certainly would have recommended is that we would make a deal with them that we stop our B-52 raids in return for their agreeing not to take this kind of terrorist action. Unfortunately, fighting has recently increased.

Then you are advocating that we move toward a kind of a territorial accommodation, where they have areas that we really don't go into much, and we have large sanctuaries that they don't hit so forcefully?

HARRIMAN: Well, all I can say is that our program in January was to do what Secretary of Defense Clark Clifford said publicly. "Our first objective should be the reduction of the level of combat," were the words he used. We can't have it both ways—expect the enemy to end their attacks while we keep up a "little" offensive action, "some" B-52 raids and "somewhat fewer" offensive sweeps. There was a plan to avoid contact. In other words, have our probes to avoid contact rather than to get contact. Now Cy Vance, my partner in Paris, has joined the group calling for a cease-fire in place. If the Administration undertook to go that route, I'd support it.

The position I've been taking is for a step-by-step reduction in violence. There may be a more practical way to get at it, but I do feel that one thing is absolutely vital: that the President of the United States take the lead in ending the killing.

So you take issue with the idea that, in offering a mixed election commission and an election open to all, we have gone as far as we can go, to use Nixon's words.

HARRIMAN: I don't understand what's been offered. I don't know why they take this position. It never occurred to me that the Communists would enter an election on the basis of the winner taking all. There has to be some prior understanding on other issues. You've got to go through the N.L.F.'s points.[2]

2. The National Liberation Front put forward in Paris last May a 10-point proposal that is still the basis of its negotiating position. The plan called for the establishment of a provisional coalition government to hold national elections, the implementation of agreements on the withdrawal of U.S. and allied forces, the achievement of "national concord" as the basis for a post-war coalition government, the "step-by-step" reunification of North and South and the payment of war reparations to both North and South Vietnam by the

You can't pick just one aspect of settlement. You've got to go through each one of those 10 points and see how much of it you can give in to and how much you won't. The Saigon Government has its objectives, its eight points; these have to be molded.

I don't think it's a reasonable proposition to just pick one thing in the election, particularly as the Government continues to put people in jail. They give no indication so far that anybody's going to have any freedom in South Vietnam to have a free discussion or free campaigning.

So you have to have some understandings. For instance, you would want to be sure that there would be no reprisals against anyone for their past political actions. If there is to be a political settlement, it must provide for the personal safety of people on both sides. In addition, there might be an understanding about postponing reunification. My own feeling has been that the N.L.F. has been rather keen to see South Vietnam independent of the North for some years. They may want to delay reunification until the South is as strong as the North. I would have thought they'd agree to postponing any merger for a period of five to ten years.

Another point that could be discussed is the character of the postwar society. The N.L.F.'s 1967 program included a provision that the social-economic structure would seem to be a mixed socialist and capitalist society. Peasants would own their own farms. Private capital, both domestic and foreign, would be encouraged in many activities. These are things which might be talked out, and if you could get an arrangement which had some lasting qualities about it, then there'd be a chance for it to succeed.

Doesn't the mixed election commission that Nixon and Thieu have talked about open the way to this sort of thing?

HARRIMAN: It's an important step from Thieu's standpoint, but it isn't enough. What's going to come out of that election? A new constitution isn't provided for—the character of the regime, the manner in which it's to operate.

And, of course, I have the very strong feeling that we have to come to an agreement with Hanoi ourselves—the United States. It's very vivid in my mind that Hanoi didn't abide by the 1962 Laos agreement for a single day. So, no matter what is agreed to in the South, it isn't going to be of any value unless we come to an understanding with Hanoi which makes it in their interest to keep the agreement.

North Vietnam is fiercely nationalistic. It doesn't want to be dominated by China. It doesn't want to be beholden to Moscow. Now, we have every reason to believe that Moscow wants to see Southeast Asia independent, so we have some basis to start to work out some kind of an agreement. This would be of the most vital importance.

United States. The 10 points are considered to be more up to date than a more detailed though generally similar political program published on Sept. 1, 1967.

The North Vietnamese are very anxious, you know, to get economic and technical assistance. Miracle rice is one of the most important things to them. They've had a 300,000-ton food deficit which they're getting from China. They don't like that. If they could get miracle rice and the techniques of growing it from us, I think they would hope to be independent of China.

Do you think that this kind of economic enticement is going to be a sufficient safeguard?

HARRIMAN: Well, there's something to their desire to be independent of China and to have normal relations with us, the desire to have technical assistance, to have loans to buy equipment from us and other ways to rebuild and develop their country. These are all things that are a basis for coming to an agreement.

What other kinds of safeguards ought to be put into an agreement?

HARRIMAN: Of course, we should consider international guarantees and an international police force. They're all very difficult. The International Control Commission set up in '54 has worked badly. The old procedures would not be acceptable; they would have to be improved. But there'd have to be real guarantees that would have a reasonable chance of being effective.

Isn't there going to be inevitable tension after any agreement between the desire of the North Vietnamese—and many other Vietnamese, for that matter—to have the country reunified and our desire that it not be immediately reunified?

HARRIMAN: Actually there's a good deal of evidence to indicate that the N.L.F. want to have independence for South Vietnam for a period of years. That is hinted at in the 10 points and in their program published Sept. 1, 1967. And a number of your reporter friends have reported that they spoke about reunification being a long-delayed matter—10 to 15 years.

These men are Southerners. They don't want to be taken over by the North. My guess is that it would not be too hard to come to an agreement that a merger with the North would be done only after a popular vote in the South, but it would be postponed for several years.

Some people maintain that the other side has sensed the tremendous urge in this country to wind up the war, and that they're content to sit tight and just let American impatience finally drive us and Saigon to accept their terms.

HARRIMAN: It's very hard to tell. They have a very good young researcher. They got the Congressional Record. They could quote speeches of some of our distinguished members of the Senate in detail and sometimes rather embarrassingly to me, but how far they believe that represented the main body of American opinion I don't know.

My own feeling about this is that they want to come to a settlement rather than have a military takeover; there's an advantage to them in having the stability that comes from some sort of a settlement. They had a lot of difficulties from the political opposition when they took over the North. It wasn't an easy thing, and it would be much more difficult to take over the South. I think they'd much rather move into a situation where there's a political agreement.

What has bothered me very much is that very little progress seems to have been made since January. And I'm more concerned about the United States, really, than I am about North Vietnam. The demand for a settlement, the demand for the end of the fighting, may become very real in this country. One hears and talks about student movements next October if there's no settlement by then or if the fighting goes on as it is now.

I'm very much opposed to a cut-and-run strategy, and I'm afraid that if this Administration doesn't make more progress, there will be more and more pressure on the Government.

That can expand, and I would hate to see that. I think it's very important to have an orderly settlement of this, and I believe it can be done if we stick to our limited objectives.

I think we could rally public opinion, world opinion, to us if the President would announce that he was for an end to the fighting, for taking steps for a cease-fire, and that should be the first order of business. I think you'd get a good reaction everywhere. The North Vietnamese pay a lot of attention to world opinion.

What about the Soviet Union, how much can it help achieve a settlement?

HARRIMAN: I want to first say what they won't do. I saw Premier Kosygin just about four years ago and had two long talks with him. He made it very plain that they were going to support Hanoi militarily, both with equipment and with volunteers—any number of volunteers they wished. The great Soviet Union, as leader of the Communist movement, had an obligation to support a "sister Socialist state." I assume the North Vietnamese have some kind of an understanding with China because China has been helping them, too.

But the Russians are not going to come to Washington and say, "What kind of a settlement do you want?" and then try to impose it on Hanoi. They're going to take Hanoi's side in these negotiations. If we can come to some basic agreement with Hanoi, I think they'll be very helpful in smoothing out some of the rough parts of the road. That happened in October and also in January.

They will, I think, add some confidence to Hanoi in its negotiations. Hanoi felt it had an agreement with the French in '46, you remember, and that petered out, and they don't think the '54 agreement worked out as it was intended to. And I think the Soviet Union can be of a good deal of help to them in giving them a sense of confidence and in urging them to give in on some of the less-important details. But they won't take our side in supporting the Thieu Government, for instance.

You mentioned that they had helped before. How did this actually work out before the bombing halt and when you were trying to get four-sided talks started?

HARRIMAN: Well, we made certain progress and then we came to some roadblocks. I kept in touch with the Soviet Embassy in Paris and the State Department kept in touch with the Embassy here. They wouldn't tell us just what they did or how they did it, but in any event, the roadblocks were removed.

Now, in January, the procedures were settled in Paris. A member of the Soviet Embassy talked it over with Hanoi's representatives and persuaded them, I think, that they had more to gain by starting negotiations than they had to lose by this argument over the shape of the table—they were being as stubborn as Saigon, you know.

It's very hard to say just where they would be helpful. We found ourselves in a parallel position with the Soviet Union in India and Pakistan. We supported Mr. Kosygin's initiative in bringing the leaders of the two countries together in Tashkent to arrange for a cease-fire. We are both helping India and Pakistan economically. They are helping them both militarily, and it's quite clear that they want to see a subcontinent strong enough, independent enough, to check China's advance.

You think they have the same common interest with us in Southeast Asia as there?

HARRIMAN: They have parallel interests, not the same, because eventually I think they'd like to see the whole world communized. But in the meantime an immediate objective is to see these countries strong enough to check Chinese expansion. We're not going to come to an agreement, but we will find ourselves in a parallel position. There's no reason to believe they won't act in Southeast Asia as they acted in India.

What sort of things do you think they'll nudge Hanoi on? Are they really going to push Hanoi to do something it wouldn't do anyway?

HARRIMAN: I think they will encourage them to abandon positions which are very difficult for us to accept, and they'll give them a sense of confidence. If they saw us withdrawing and reducing the fighting, I think they'd encourage the other side to agree to stop the fighting and the violence. If we were doing something and expecting Hanoi to take parallel action, I think they'd encourage it.

Some of President Nixon's advisers have spoken rather loosely of the idea that you might be able to link such issues as Vietnam, the Middle East, Berlin, arms talks—this sort of thing—with the Soviet Union. You've been negotiating off and on with the Russians for 40 years. Do you think that this is the way they operate?

HARRIMAN: I would say that this is a most unwise notion. Each situation stands on its own feet. The idea that we could ask the Soviet Union to abandon some of their political positions in one part of the world in order to bribe us to come to an agreement with them about nuclear restraint is just unreal, it isn't so. They have exactly the same interests in nuclear restraint as we have. They want a secure situation; they want to reduce the danger of nuclear war, and we cannot combine these negotiations. This is an absolutely erroneous conception.

Any thought that they will pay us something to come into negotiations for nuclear restraint, I just don't understand. We wouldn't do it. They wouldn't sacrifice their personal security any more than we would, and it only complicates a situation.

Now, the Russians are very much affected by what we do, and I would assume that we are affected by what they do. President Kennedy was successful in the nuclear test ban, which, as you remember, he appointed me to go to Moscow and negotiate, because of his American University speech. It was a conciliatory speech. He didn't give anything away, but it indicated a real desire on his part to come to an understanding. Also, he announced that we would stop testing as long as the other side stopped testing. This persuaded Premier Khrushchev that he was serious and jarred those prolonged negotiations off dead center. When we went to Moscow, we settled it within two weeks.

If today the President would announce that we would not go on testing multiple warheads (we'd of course go ahead with research and development but not test) provided the Soviet Union would abandon any further tests in this field, I think it would expedite the negotiations and carry them forward. One can say that this can't be all one-sided. I'm very much influenced by a conciliatory speech Foreign Minister Gromyko made. I'm affected by the manner in which Mr. Kosygin called in the senior American who happened to be in Moscow at that time, Hubert Humphrey, and spoke very glowingly in congratulating the United States on the moon achievement. That was an unusual thing to do. This must have been particularly difficult because of the failure of their moonshot, whatever it was supposed to do.

These are gestures on their part, in spite of the lack of progress in both the Middle East and Vietnam. Now we want to watch what they do with the greatest of care and see whether the atmosphere is right. But this idea of say-ing, "Well now, you force Hanoi to do thus and so and we'll come to Moscow and trade you," just doesn't work.

In the first place, they can't dominate Hanoi. Number two, they're compet-ing with Peking for the goodwill of Hanoi. They can only go so far.

I gather that Gromyko went to see President Nasser the other day and came back empty-handed. Now, how much pressure the Soviet Union's ready to put on Egypt to get a Middle East settlement I don't know, but it was un-successful. I'm still hopeful that something can be done. Events in the Middle East are heading on a collision course, and the only way we can hope to come to a settlement before that happens again is through the influence of the Soviet Union and ourselves.

They are publicly demanding that Israel accept the Nasser terms, which, of course, Israel isn't going to do and we're not going to ask Israel to do. But it's unrealistic to think that you can link a settlement in Vietnam with a set-tlement in the Middle East. They are not within the Soviet Union's ability to deliver.

You said they would be impressed by what we do. Do you think Moscow and Hanoi were impressed by the theme of President Nixon's trip to Asia, "Asia for the Asians; we're not going to get involved in internal wars in the future"?

HARRIMAN: Well, I would think that they were probably just about as much puzzled as to what President Nixon has in mind as we are puzzled by what Moscow has in mind when they speak about collective security for Asia. If you understand what collective security on the part of Moscow means, why then I think you can explain to me what President Nixon means.

Wasn't that Soviet idea directed primarily against Communist China? What's the possibility of war between the Soviet Union and China in the next few years?

HARRIMAN: I wouldn't want to predict it. We have to remember that the Soviets are used to having minor border conflicts. They had them with Japan before World War II along the Amur River. We may see some minor conflicts.

Something like the Chinese border war against India in 1962?

HARRIMAN: Well, that's a little bit more vigorous than I would think. The Chinese tried to show up the weakness of India. I'm not sure that the Rus-sians will want to go that far; they might. There may be border skirmishes. There may be an attempt by the Soviet Union to teach China a lesson. But I don't think it will develop into a major conflict.

What impact do you think President Nixon's visit to Rumania had on Soviet-American relations?

HARRIMAN: Frankly, I was very glad to see President Nixon go to Rumania. Obviously, the Russians object to it a bit. They don't want to see Rumania become too independent. But it's a move in a healthy direction for the President of the United States to try to develop better relations with the Eastern European countries. And I hope that this Administration explained to the Soviets that this was his objective and in a sense that it will help further some things which the Soviets would like to see accomplished—better trade relations, which they're very much interested in.

And I would hope the talks in Bucharest would lead to President Nixon's recommending legislation to permit us to engage in more trade with Eastern Europe and the Soviet Union. We are denying ourselves of very profitable trade. Western Europe and Japan do about $8-billion in trade with them each year, whereas we have only a few hundred million dollars.

Are you optimistic about the over-all prospects for detente between the United States and the Soviet Union?

HARRIMAN: Not over-all détente. There are still too many subjects on which agreements cannot be reached. They still want to promote Communism to a point where it will dominate the world. We want to see nations of the world free, people free.

There are certain areas, however, in which I think we can come to an agreement. Nuclear restraint is the one which I think is the most important. Despite the discouragement so far, I hope we can work together in finding a solution to the Middle East, and I do expect the Soviets to help us in Vietnam if we can make more progress with Hanoi than we have so far.

You give more over-all importance to the arms talks than the Vietnam negotiations?

HARRIMAN: Yes, Vietnam is the most immediate problem, but—looking at the long term—ending the nuclear arms race is of vital importance. It's important not only to save reckless additional expenditures on both sides but also, as Mr. Kosygin said to me, while the Soviet Union and the United States have the preponderant control of nuclear weapons, it is our obligation to attempt to come to an understanding, which will reduce the risk of nuclear war. I'm satisfied that the Soviets are sincere in that and if we meet them halfway, I think we can come to an understanding.

16. Does The United States Have A "Real" Interest in Supporting Israel?

ALAN DOWTY

PUBLIC SENTIMENT and sympathy have usually ratified American support of Israel, whatever the nature or extent of that support, since the issue of a Jewish national home first became an important foreign policy issue. The extent of this sympathy has, indeed, often created the impression that American policy towards Israel would somehow be less favorable were it not for the "subjective" factors influencing it, in particular the existence of a large bloc of Jewish voters. Given the importance of the Arab world strategically and economically, it has often been felt that a more "objective" policy, reflecting American interests more faithfully, would naturally take a more "neutral" stance in the Arab-Israeli conflict and avoid the close association that has characterized U.S.–Israel relations—at the expense, it is argued, of ties with the Arabs.[1]

Would U.S. policy in the Middle East, if freed of such pressures as domestic electoral considerations, be greatly different, in fact, from that presently pursued? A close look at the Arab-Israel impasse casts doubt upon the overly simple premise that it would be. Though supported—and legitimately so— by public feeling, U.S. policy in the area can also be interpreted in terms of

1. See, for example, the articles by Georgiana Stevens and Richard Nolte in Stevens, ed., *The United States and the Middle East* (Englewood Cliffs, N.J.: Prentice Hall, Inc., 1964).

"realistic" assessments of interests and concrete goals that are independent of, though in consonance with, subjective sympathies.

Let us first of all dispose of the idea that a more "objective" policy would necessarily mean a more neutral policy in the Middle East. If the argument is that American policy must reflect the much greater "objective" importance of Arab states in the world, then the argument is for a policy that likewise would disproportionately favor these states. In fact, there are no clear grounds upon which to base a claim that present American policy toward the Arab-Israeli conflict is in fact "unneutral." The United States has made no formal commitments to Israel's defense that exceed those made to Arab states. Military equipment supplied to Israel has been matched or more than matched by parallel shipments to Arab states. American governmental assistance to Arab states is currently being extended at a rate of about twenty times that of aid given to Israel. American "diplomatic support" of Israel, as it is termed, is in essence a call for compromise between the two sides, which seems pro-Israel only because of the pronounced pro-Arab position of certain other Great Powers. By almost any ordinary measure, then, the American position in the Arab-Israel conflict has been neutral in terms of the issues of the conflict itself.

An American policy toward the Arab-Israel conflict that took as its guideline the strategic and demographic prominence of the respective sides, then, would almost assuredly not be neutral. Neither would it necessarily serve the best interests of the United States. Foreign policy is conducted in an environment much more complex than would be indicated by considerations of physical size alone. There are three aspects to this argument. In the first place, concrete interests are formed by a number of factors, not all of which are proportionate to physical size, and most of which are changeable and difficult to measure. Secondly, given the aim of strengthening U.S.-Arab relations, it is misleading to view these relations as primarily a function of the American position toward the Arab-Israeli conflict. Finally, for reasons of a tactical nature, it is by no means clear that a more pro-Arab stance would be the most effective means of gaining Arab respect for American aims in the Middle East. Let us take these points one by one.

The Canal and Oil: "Objective" Factors

Some observers have pointed out that the overall importance of the Middle East in the world is declining.[2] Dependence on the Suez Canal, as illustrated in the difference between reactions to the 1956 and 1967 closures, has decreased considerably. In any event, American interest in the canal has always been largely a result of European dependence on it for oil deliveries. With the development of oil sources in North Africa and growing *Russian* dependence

2. For example, by Leonard Binder in *The Middle East Crisis: Background and Issues* (University of Chicago Center for Policy Study, 1967).

on the Suez route to the Far East (especially Vietnam, since the China supply routes have been closed), the equation has been changed somewhat. Nor is the question of access to oil as all-decisive as once thought: alternate sources have been developed, and American interests are again either indirect (insurance of European supplies) or private (protection of the oil companies). Moreover, the failure of the Arab oil embargo after the Six-Day War has illustrated that the sale of oil to the West is definitely a two-sided interest, which the oil-producing states in the area (generally states less intimately involved in the conflict with Israel) are less likely to endanger for political reasons than was formerly feared.

And despite its small size, the "objective importance" of Israel is greater than population ratios would indicate. In the light of the Six-Day War it is clear that Israel possesses considerable power over events in the area and must be given the attention due any "local power" in a troubled region. There is little doubt that the relative "weights" have been changing: while the Middle East as a whole has become somewhat less important strategically and economically, Israel's continuing growth has at least begun to put it on the map as a market, as a field for private foreign investments, and as a military power. In any event, neither geography nor demography are by themselves reliable indices of Israel's concrete importance to the United States.

The Many Dimensions of U.S.–Arab Relations

If the Arab-Israeli conflict were the single dominating feature of the Middle Eastern landscape, it might not be too inaccurate to adopt for American policy a one-dimensional model: stronger ties with Israel mean weaker ties with Arab states, and vice versa. In broader terms this is the basis for the overly simple but persistent idea that American ties with Israel are a burden on relations with Arab states and that the latter could be improved if the former were minimized.

But in the light of experience it appears that even if Israel, or at least the Arab-Israel conflict, were to disappear magically, the contours of U.S.–Arab relations would not be greatly changed. Those relations are shaped by a number of forces unrelated to the "Palestine question," and first and foremost by the general drive of anti-Western nationalism, which uses Israel as a symbol but which is actually a part of world-wide pattern of resistance to Western pressures throughout the former colonial areas of the globe. A second force operating independently of the Arab-Israel conflict is the dynamic of inter-Arab rivalry, which again poses an entirely new set of issues—and tactical considerations—for American policy.

The failure to evaluate properly the force of anti-Westernism in the Middle East, and not association with Israel, was at the root of many earlier policy failures in the area. Arab countries had many memories of Western European domination and none of Soviet penetration; in this light the Dulles effort to integrate them totally into the Western camp could not help but be counter-productive. The natural stance of the Arab world in the Cold War is to maneuver between the two blocs, balancing pressure from one with support from the other and in general exploiting a neutral position in order to protect its independence from the greater threat as well as for material gain (at least for the leading Arab states; inter-Arab rivalry might dictate a different strategy for those smaller states, such as Jordan, for whom these leading states are themselves the threat). Thus the "total" goals of American policy were themselves unrealistic, and disassociation from Israel, even total, could not help to attain them. This was abundantly borne out in 1957, when the sharp American pressure for Israeli withdrawal from Sinai and other placatory moves brought no lasting or significant improvement in U.S.-Egyptian relations.

It has become clearer, then, that the best that could be expected for the West in the Arab world, as elsewhere in the "Third World," is a somewhat tenuous but not hostile neutrality. By adopting a more modest set of goals in the area, the United States could learn to live with Arab nationalism and still attain the more important of its aims. Regarding the more important of its concrete goals—the minimization of Soviet influence in the area—the wiser course was obviously not to work against Arab nationalism indiscrimately but even to look upon it, in some cases, as a guarantee against overwhelming *Soviet,* as well as Western, influence. As Deputy Secretary of State U. Alexis Johnson said in 1964, "although Arab nationalism has a large component of neutralism, it is also one of the strongest forces resisting Soviet expansionsim in the area."[3]

The problems posed for American policy by Arab nationalism are, in any event, only partly correlated with the Arab-Israel conflict. The same is true of issues raised by inter-Arab conflict or by domestic problems within the Arab states. Here again there has been a conceptual misunderstanding in analyses of the situation: the tendency to take the ideological content of Arab nationalism, with its uniform and undifferentiated anti-Zionism, at face value. Underneath the verbal mask are hidden a series of specific disputes and problems, and of concrete interests, that reduce the importance of the Palestine issue for most individual Arab states.

In the first place, as Professor Leonard Binder[4] and others have pointed out, the aggressive stance of Arab states on the Palestine question is at least partly a result of internal pressures and domestic problems, particularly in the Egyptian case. The implication for American policy is that, again, attempts to appease Arab states at Israel's expense would not actually touch upon the real sources of the tension and would thus be unproductive.

In addition, for those states furtherest removed from Israel, and for those fearful of the threat of "Nasserism" to their own regimes, the actual strength of anti-Israel ideology is obviously undercut by other strategic or tactical

3. *Department of State Bulletin,* February 10, 1964.
4. Binder, *op. cit.,* pp. 17–19.

considerations. There is reason to believe that Nasser's humiliation in the Six-Day War was a source of comfort to some Arab states, particularly those who benefited from his subsequent withdrawal from the Yemen. For a state such as Saudi Arabia, there is obviously little real incentive to become deeply involved in fighting Israel despite the lip service paid to the "Arab cause"; indeed, there is often an informal complementarity of interests between Israel and other Arab states that remains unenunciated but makes a mockery of the proclaimed ideological unity of the Arab world. The inadequacy of ideological nationalism as an explanation of Arab behavior in all cases and in defiance of all conflicting concrete interests has lately come to the fore in analyses of the Middle East, for example in the report prepared by the Harvard Center for International Affairs for the Senate Committee on Foreign Relations in 1960:

> From the policymaking point of view . . . overt conflicts in the Arab countries with which we have to deal today, involving internal rivalries, dictatorships, military and economic deals with the Soviet Communists, social and economic reforms—and even many aspects of the Arab-Israel conflict itself—are as much the outcome of concrete and pragmatic factors in decision-making as of ideological motivations or collisions.[5]

The Need for Tactical Flexibility

What I have said so far is that American-Arab relations are set by a web of concrete interests on both sides, sometimes conflicting and sometimes not, that are of limited changeability and only slightly responsive to changes in the American position toward Israel—since they are only partly a function of the Arab-Israel conflict. The United States has, in other words, limited leverage in drawing the Arab states to the West, and this leverage is to a great extent unrelated to its policy toward Israel.

But to the extent this leverage exists, its exercise also raises serious tactical questions. Theoretically a state can employ both reward and punishment in order to influence another state, i.e. both the carrot and the stick. But the failure of direct American pressure in the mid-fifties, and particularly the backfire of the clumsily conceived effort to "discipline" Egypt by abruptly withdrawing promised aid for the construction of the Aswan dam, has led to a tendency to rely upon the "soft sell" alone in American policy toward the "revolutionary" Arab states. A reluctance to use punitive measures—what might be termed a lingering "Aswan trauma"—naturally leads to increased reluctance to take any "pro-Israel" step that might "offend" the Arab world. Only slowly does this point of view yield to objective evidence that, just as "pro-Arab" moves have had few magical benefits for relations with Arab

5. *Ideology and Foreign Affairs* (Washington, U.S. Government Printing Office), p. 52.

states, so "pro-Israel" moves (such as the sale of weapons) have not substantially injured these relations. In fact, "pro-Israel" moves, to the extent that they influence Arab relations at all, may have tactical value as a form of pressure on Arab states.

A full tactical view of U.S.-Arab relations would have to take into account the fact that interest in the maintenance of these relations is two-sided. The Arab states can no more "write-off" the West than the United States can "write-off" the Arab world. Given the fact that it cannot organize the Arab world as it would ideally like to do, the United States can seek to make the most of mutual interests in order to stabilize the more modest position it seeks for itself in the area. This means, among other things, a recognition of the limited coincidence of Arab and Soviet interests and a relaxation of the exaggerated concern regarding the likelihood of full integration of Arab states into the Eastern bloc. It also implies a readiness to employ those more limited and measured forms of pressure available to the West in the framework of common interests with the Arab states.

The 1957 debacle created the impression that the United States, out of fear for its position in the Arab world, could be pressured effectively on the Arab-Israel issue. Much of the Arab diplomatic offensive since the Six-Day War has been based on the impression, created in the Suez crisis, of American weakness in the face of threatened Arab defection. But American policy since 1967 has wisely taken the more balanced position that the Arab states must pay a certain price, at least in the initiation of renewed diplomatic ties, before the United States will consider using its influence on Israel (if then). American ties with Israel, in other words, are an important bargaining card in the American hand when dealing with the Arab world.

What this means is that "pro-Arab" or "anti-Israel" moves can bring about no improvement in U.S.-Arab relations *if they can be interpreted as a result of submission to Arab pressure* rather than as a result of mutual bargaining and concessions. Even here all steps must be weighed carefully, for compromise does not always have the same implications in other settings that it has usually had in the genteel and pragmatic diplomatic and political traditions of the West. As Professor George Kirk has expressed it, "Whereas the political behavior of the English-speaking peoples places great store in timely compromise . . . militant Islam views compromise as either a confession of weakness or, at best, a momentary tactical move in a continuing struggle."[6] Unilateral concessions have, indeed, consistently failed to elicit the expected response from Arab states precisely because they were seen as a reward for intransigence, or as simply the triumph of right, rather than as an invitation to a round of "horse-trading."

The disappointing sequel to the 1957 appeasement should have been an eye-opener, and to be sure American charges of "ingratitude" on Nasser's

6. "Even-Handed or Weak-Headed Mideast Policy" (Forum World Features, *Jerusalem Post*, February 25, 1969).

part were frequently heard. The United States had practically destroyed the unity of the Western alliance in order to preserve its position in the Arab world, only to find the Suez episode celebrated in Cairo as a momentous victory over the Western world as a whole—and a "victory" that secured Nasser's psychological hold on Arab masses, leading inexorably to the events of 1957–58 when the victory of Nasserism throughout the area seemed imminent and the position of the United States became more uncomfortable than ever before.

The problem was compounded by a tendency to identify Nasserism with the interests of Arab nationalism in general. Though the stabilization that followed the Lebanonese intervention of 1958, and the eventual collapse of the Egyptian-Syrian union, showed the limits of Nasser's ability to translate his popularity into political dominance, the conclusion reached seemed to be that the key to the future lay in conciliating the Egyptian ruler and coming to terms with his position in the Arab world. Thus the United States embarked in the early 1960's on a "soft sell" approach, resuming large-scale shipments of surplus food and demonstrating at every opportunity a willingness to "live with" Nasser despite evidence of personal ambitions that could not but injure American interests in the area. Wishful thinking often played the part of solid analysis, a tendency skillfully exploited by Nasser in his numerous "moderate" statements to Western newsmen and diplomats who eagerly sought evidence of a mellowing process upon the Nile. Such remains the case even today; the obvious discrepancy between a declared willingness to recognize Israel, reported in American newsmagazines (but not distributed *within* Egypt), and calls for a "no-peace" policy before Arab audiences, is resolved by interpreting the latter as a feigned bellicosity necessary for "internal consumption." Consideration of their own self-esteem apparently deters Westerners admitted to the inner sanctum from considering the possibility that the content of their *tête-à-tête* conference with the Egyptian President might be designed for "external consumption."

In the end the "soft sell" also proved ineffective. Shoring up the Nasser regime brought no apparent profit to the American position and raised continuing apprehension not only in Israel but among the many anti-Nasserist forces in the Arab countries. Coming to terms with Arab nationalism did not necessitate, perhaps, playing the tune that Nasser himself piped. In any event, the grand design that molded Egyptian policy was clearly unresponsive in large part either to sweet overtures of reasonableness or to crude pressure. To the extent that Egyptian policy could be influenced, a patient but firm and unapologetic defense of American interests, where threatened, seemed the logical course of action. Within this framework the United States could—and did—act against Nasserism in such countries as Jordan and sell surface-to-air missiles to Israel. It should have been clear by this time that neither "anti-Israel" or "pro-Israel" moves made much difference in relations with Arab states or with Egypt in particular.[7] The final piece of conclusive evidence in this regard is the fact that the greatest outburst of Arab anti-Westernism in recent years—the charges of air support to Israel and breaking of diplomatic relations in June 1967—bore not the slightest relevance to the actual content of American policy, which at that time was in fact focussed on efforts to avoid a confrontation with Egypt over an issue (Israeli passage in the Straits of Tiran) on which the United States was presumably committed to Israel's support.

A Policy of Stability

Much of the foregoing has been an attempt to show that the disappearance of the Arab-Israel issue in the Middle East would not simplify the problems of American policy in the area. Israel has, in fact, often served as a scapegoat, as a too convenient explanation of the weakness of American ties with Arab states that would, in the best case, remain problematical despite the most arduous placatory moves. But we must also remember that Israel cannot be wished out of existence, even if American policy-making would be simplified thereby, and that policymakers must deal with the "here and now" of day-to-day diplomacy. For the foreseeable future this will include the Arab-Israel conflict.

The many efforts to define U.S. interests in the Middle East—including those of William Polk, U. Alexis Johnson, and other Middle East specialists—revolve around the general aim of stability.[8] All the more immediate aims of U.S. policy—containing Soviet influence, protection of access to oil and strategic routes, maintenance of friendly regimes—are served by the stabilization of conditions and revolutionary forces in the area. The American aim of preventing hostilities in the area is more than a declaration of principle or of general humanitarianism; it is a basic interest connected with the desire of reducing the number of unstable situations that the USSR can exploit or that threaten existing material interests. Thus the United States is committed to a pro-stability, anti-hostilities position by its own basic concerns. This policy may be expressed in various fashions, but one principle that has guided U.S. policy toward the Arab-Israel conflict from its very inception has been the minimization of violent hostilities and the general effort to moderate the entire issue.

A "pro-Arab" neutrality, such as that described at the outset, would only injure American interests if its effects were to encourage a renewal of hos-

7. On the failure of the "soft sell" see Malcolm Kerr, "Coming to terms with Nasser," *International Affairs*, XLIII (Jan. 1967), 65–84. Kerr concludes that Egyptian policy will remain "tiresomely impervious to American wishes," whatever the American policy.

8. Polk, *The United States and the Arab World* (Cambridge: Harvard University Press, 1965), pp. 289–90. Johnson, *op cit.*

tilities. Even a policy of "genuine" neutrality may not completely meet the requirements of a policy of stability when positive moves to keep the peace are required. To the extent that arms shipments to Israel serve to discourage renewal of hostilities by Arab states, for example, they are also contributing to the avoidance of situations—the outbreak of war—that have always proved injurious to American interests in the area.

The United States has an interest both in making war seem an unprofitable proposition from the Arab point of view and in contributing positively to Israel's sense of security. The fact is that Israel possesses the capability, no less than the Arab states, of upsetting the peace and has proved its readiness for action when the feeling of threat becomes unbearable. It is clear that, in view of the declared threat to its existence, Israel cannot tolerate any deterioration, however slight, in its overall security position. American policymakers have every reason, therefore, to take into account the need for a *subjective* feeling of security in Israel, whatever their own objective assessment of the immediate dangers to the state.

Again, remembering that the United States must deal with the situation as it is and not as it might be ideally, the fact that Israel exists and occupies a given position in the Middle East helps to define American interests. Given the present situation, a setback for Israel (say a Four-Power "imposition" of withdrawal from the occupied territories under unacceptable terms) would be a serious blow to the prestige and position of the United States—whatever the merits of the issue. Given the present situation, Arab success in liquidating Israel would be a tremendous setback to the United States because of the impetus it would give to Nasserist Arab nationalism, the destabilizing effect it would have in the more pro-Western Arab countries, the boost it would give to Soviet prestige, and the whole new set of problems that would be created by disputes over the spoils. In other words, even if Israel's presence were, indeed, an embarrassment to the United States, its sudden demise might be infinitely worse.

As a largely *status quo* power the United States cannot outplay the Soviet Union in competition for the favor of Arab extremists. Such a course would contradict many of its own specific interests, would be tactically self-defeating, and would forfeit the real advantages that a *status quo* power in general, and the United States in particular, has at its disposal in the area. Israel seeks from the West primarily two things: the neutralization of the Soviet Union and maintenance of a stable arms balance between herself and neighboring Arab states. Both goals are in fact also in the interest of the United States (and possibly of some Arab states as well), and it would be disastrous for both states were they to be foregone.

PART THREE
Great Issues in Military Policy

Introduction

THE ESSAYS in this section deal with strategy, the arms race, and problems of ballistic missile defense. Arms races and missile defense can be properly understood only in the context of strategy, bargaining, and war. Although nuclear wars are unlikely, they represent the most awesome possibilities and are, therefore, naturally at the center of attention.

Strategic nuclear weapon systems have varying kinds of possible uses. Most obviously, they can be used in the actual conduct of a war. But they can also provide bargaining leverage in an intense international crisis. Thus, for instance, many observers believe that the American bargaining position was greatly strengthened during the Cuban missile crisis by the fact that it had global strategic superiority as well as local conventional superiority. Although the Soviet Union hardly could have responded successfully in Cuba in any event, there were other places where the Soviet Union could have introduced great pressure, such as Berlin or Turkey. Although strategic power is only one of the variables in this process—other variables include national character, political assurance, the characteristics of the leadership, the nature of regime coalition problems—it is probably not an unimportant factor.

Minimum deterrence theorists assume that unless virtually all nuclear weapons can be destroyed in a first strike, deterrence will work. This position is accepted by McGeorge Bundy. In my opinion, Bundy, and those who accept his position, make several basic mistakes. They fail to understand how rapidly military technology changes and how precarious this makes second-strike forces. They also misjudge the importance of the fact that nuclear weapons are useless in most situations (although the recent Russian sabre-rattling against China and the fear this raises among many might indicate that the position is at least overstated). Even if it is true that minimal nuclear forces serve to deter in most situations, even a very small failure rate could prove disastrous. Indeed, one failure of American deterrence in a Russian regime or bloc crisis might produce a catastrophe. Risks that under other circumstances would seem unreasonable might be accepted in such circumstances by the Russian leadership. Moreover, since the Russian threat would not be made against the United States directly, the credibility of a nuclear response by the American strategic force in case of a Soviet attack in Europe might be discounted by a desperate or possibly avaricious Soviet leadership. Even if one does not believe Russian hints of a nuclear strike against China, the fact that such hints stem from the Russian Politburo is not insignificant.

What are the strategic factors that weaken the minimum deterrence theory? Among other things, it assesses much too high the probability that weapons that survive a first-strike will be used against the attacking side. If the attacker in its first-strike reduces its opponent's strategic forces by 90 per cent or more, only a reckless leadership would use that reduced force in an immediate second-strike. In the absence of ballistic missile defense on the other side, it still could do significant damage to it but at the cost of its own obliteration. In the absence of a demand for surrender of one's country, this would hardly be even a semi-reasonable choice. Yet, if high officials are aware in the midst of an intense diplomatic-military crisis that their opponents are capable of launching a first-strike to which they would not respond, their assurance and bargaining position will be eroded even though they may be aware that their opponents cannot be sure they will not respond and even though they expect that more likely than not the opponents will be deterred by the uncertainties.

Although an actual nuclear war is unlikely, if one should unfortunately occur, it is most improbable that one side will launch an all-out attack against the other, hitting both its military installations and its cities. Such a possibility, of course, cannot entirely be excluded, for nations can go crazy. But it is not a likely sequence, for, if this occurred, there would be no hostages, no reason to hold back retaliation with whatever remained of the nucelar force that had been attacked. Although a first-strike is an extremely unlikely event in the nuclear age, if it did occur, it would probably be directed against the strategic forces of the other side. The attacking side would want to keep the cities of the other country as hostages, thinking not of complete victory but of partial victory, of some major gain. Thus, wars of this kind would not end immediately; they would include plausible threats against population and industry—threats that could not be implemented, at least immediately, for fear of reprisal but that could be made psychologically compelling. Such wars would involve complicated intrawar bargaining in which there is a contest of wills.

Alternatively there may not be a large strike against the offensive forces of the other side but instead a limited strategic attack may occur which is designed to test the will of the other side, to force it to stop an attack or to accept some limited objective.

When I first introduced the idea of limited strategic retaliation into the literature, the response to it was quite hostile. Over time this response changed, although many pointed out that the Soviet Union would never accept the doctrine. Khrushchev, after all, had stated that the Western countries were mistaken if they thought that there could be such a thing as a limited nuclear war. If one nuclear weapon exploded, Mr. Khrushchev said, then the entire nuclear arsenal would go off. However, after the Soviet Union shot down the U-2 in 1960, both Khrushchev and Marshal Malinovsky stated that a Russian missile was pointed at the next base from which a U-2 came. This was implicit recognition of a doctrine of limited strategic retaliation and confirmed what some of us had been contending for some time, that statesmen would learn quickly under pressure.

For these reasons, although a nuclear first-strike is an extremely unlikely event because of the vast uncertainties involved, the knowledge that a properly circumscribed nuclear strike probably would not set off a large-scale retaliation might at a time of regime crisis or bloc crisis in the Soviet sphere permit such an attack to be contemplated. This low probability can be reduced significantly if there is an appropriate strategic posture and mix on the part of the United States. If such a posture and mix is not obtained, then the bargaining position of the United States will be greatly reduced in time of crisis. The obtaining of an appropriate deterrent and war-fighting posture is obviously related to arms control agreements and the introduction of new weapons systems. These are complicated issues and are involved in SALT (Strategic Arms Limitation Talks) and the ballistic missile defense issue. The issues, however, have recurred repeatedly and are new only in their details.

The issues raised by arms control are not merely political issues, as Herbert F. York appears to say in his article; they are combined military-strategic-political issues. The central problem is one of independent decision-making in a competitive world.

The Baruch plan for the control of atomic energy foundered on such difficulties. Although the Americans genuinely regarded the Baruch proposals as magnanimous, the stages through which the Baruch plan would have operated would have interfered with Russian development of nuclear weapons. The Russians then would have been dependent upon a continuing decision by the United States to abide by the plan despite changes in the

326 : Great Issues in Military Policy

national executive and in the halls of Congress. Such a risk was clearly in-advisable for the Soviet Union. Yet had the Russian plan for simultaneity in control and turnover of knowledge been accepted, the United States would have turned over its technology without any assurance that the Soviet Union would have remained faithful to the terms of the agreement. This would have seriously reduced the American deterrent capability during a period of several important years in which the Russians held great conventional superiority. Obviously the Russian proposal was not one that commended itself to wise American statesmen.

Arms control agreements are fraught with many difficulties. The naval agreements of the 1920's provide many examples of how such agreements were circumvented by national policies. An agreement, for instance, on bal-listic missile deployment limitations for the United States and the Soviet Union could be circumvented in many different ways. For instance, the Rus-sians could go into cruise (air-breathing) missile development, leading to new offense and defense problems. The Russians could secretly stockpile ballistic missiles or ballistic missile parts, thus permitting a rapid buildup of capability during a slowly developing crisis. It is, for instance, much easier to find construction crews for sites than to expand factories for missile pro-duction rapidly. An agreement not to install MIRV (Multiple Independent Reentry Vehicles) is subject to all sorts of intelligence difficulties. We could not know whether or how many MIRV warheads were installed in particular Russian missiles short of "screwdriver" types of inspection, a kind of in-spection that not even the United States is likely to permit. It is apparently much more difficult to tell whether MIRV has been tested by the Russians than is ordinarily believed. For a long time the United States assumed that the clustered shots fired by the Soviet SS-9's represented warheads that were not independently maneuverable. More recently there has been some evi-dence indicating that the Russians, who have larger and more powerful strategic missile rocketry than the United States, might have been able to put guidance systems into the individual warheads rather than into the busses. If so, the spray pattern that was observed could have been one that was deliberately chosen to test individual warhead guidance for similarly clustered Minutemen sites.

The arms race, at least in a quantitative sense, was self limiting through the early and mid-1960's. For quantitative reasons, the missiles that were then producible would have required extremely large numerical advantages for a first-strike capability; the larger the number of missiles on each side, the geometrically greater the margin would have had to have been. As the accuracy of missiles kept increasing, a phenomenon of the late 1960's, the geometric feature of the quantitative arms race continued but on so reduced a level that the numerical advantage required, even without MIRV, for a first-strike was not beyond contemplation. MIRV, of course, makes the dan-ger enormously greater.

Despite attempts by scientists to dispute his figures, those provided by Secretary of Defense Laird for the dangers of the mid-1970's are, if anything, conservative. The dangers were well known to those who closely followed the arms race and constituted one of the major reasons for my suggestion (in a book review in the *Bulletin of the Atomic Scientists* [December 1967] which did not get published until after his actual resignation) that Secretary McNamara resign. (The other reasons stated in the review dealt with the need for a ballistic missile defense system not primarily with respect to China but with respect to the Soviet Union in the context of the arms race.)

The situation regarding the arms race may be even worse than Secretary Laird indicated. There is strong reason to believe that the Soviet Union may have a complicated but genuine first-strike capability against Minuteman, against SAC, and against the command and control system of Polaris sooner than the 1974 date indicated by Secretary Laird. Despite the arguments of Dr. York in the article contained in this section, it is extremely difficult to maintain an adequate alert system for SAC. The command and control of Polaris is possibly vulnerable.

There have been a number of attempts by scientists to cast doubt upon these facts. Dr. Ralph Lapp made one such attempt which was commented on by Albert Wohlstetter in a statement to the Senate Armed Services Committee.[1]

Finally, Dr. Lapp makes an assumption that is plainly absurd. He supposes that even though such warhead had a very high probability of destroying a single silo, "any military realist" would fire two of his outnumbered attacking reentry vehicles at each silo that is attacked. This would leave three-quarters of the silos untouched. But if each warhead had a 99 per cent probability of destroying a single silo, firing two at one silo would merely increase the probability of destroying that specific silo to 99.99 per cent but would make it quite certain that a silo that could have been destroyed will go unscathed. If a more sensible tactic were followed, namely to fire each of the two missiles at a different silo, there would be a probability of 98 per cent of destroying both silos and a probability of 99.99 per cent that at least one of the two would be destroyed. (This latter is the same probability that Dr. Lapp would have achieved against the specific one that he was aiming at.) In short, Dr. Lapp's tactic would greatly reduce the expected level of destruction achieved by the attack, and it would not increase the probability of achieving some minimum level of destruction. I know of no military realist who would regard Dr. Lapp's tactic as a sensible one for the attacker. I must agree with Dr. Wigner that Dr. Lapp has presumed that his adversary would be unbelievably stupid.

1. *Congressional Record—Senate*, May 27, 1969, F5733 and F5734.

It should be observed that the absurdity of the tactic is not dependent on the roughly 99 per cent single shot kill probability implicit in Dr. Lapp's accuracy, yield and resistance assumptions. If one were to use a 95 per cent single shot destruction probability, the case is equally obvious. In this latter case, an adversary who assigned one missile to each of two targets would have a better than 90 per cent chance of getting them both and a probability of 99¾ per cent of getting one; and he could get no better than a 99¾ per cent probability of at least getting one silo if he sent both missiles against one silo. In the latter case, however, he could destroy at *most* one silo.

Claims almost as ridiculous were made by Dr. Rathjens. Dr. Rathjens admitted that the Soviet Union would develop a first-strike capability by the late 1970's, but he denied that capability for the period projected by Secretary Laird. However, his denial depended upon the assumption of a 500 p.s.i. hardening figure for our Minutemen silos. This figure was based upon a simple misreading of a Pentagon chart. When Dr. Rathjens was challenged and when it was pointed out to him that it was well known that the Pentagon at most claimed a hardening figure that was less than two-thirds of this estimate, Dr. Rathjens instead of admitting his error submitted a classified document to the Committee. Even the figure claimed by the Pentagon is worthy of only low confidence, for it is based upon theoretical calculations that do not square with the small amount of empirical evidence available. When Dr. Rathjens was again challenged publicly on this issue, he wrote a letter to the *New York Times* claiming that the error he made on the subject of hardening would be compensated for by a contrary error with respect to the accuracy of Russian missiles. Yet the accuracy being attributed to the Russian missiles for the 1974 period were those that can be produced today. Thus scientists, who attribute to the Chinese immense capabilities with respect to penetration aids that the United States after many billions of dollars of expenditure and years of experimentation may be just achieving, seem to believe that the Russians are incredibly backward with respect to missile accuracy. Finally this denigration of Russian capabilities by the scientific opposition became so silly that even they could no longer maintain it; so Dr. York held a press conference on the 16th of July 1969 in which he entirely reversed the argument. Now he attributed such great accuracies to the Russians that the Minuteman force was obsolete. Such accuracies may indeed become available but it is improbable that they will be available before the late 1970's. Thus the scientists skip an entire decade during which the United States must and can provide protection for its strategic forces.

Apparently this shifting of arguments does not embarrass the scientists. They remain fixed in one objective: their opposition to ballistic missile defense. Yet, even if the accuracies projected for the late 1970's are obtained, or especially if they are, it may be that ballistic missile defense is the only good answer.

Drs. York and Wiesner who were among the primary proponents of the Sage defense system and who have been opposing ballistic missile defense for nearly a decade, while denying even its possibility at a time in 1963 when the technological breakthroughs making it feasible were occurring, now argue that offense has inherent and permanent advantages over defense. In this respect, they are at odds with the noted physicist, Freeman Dyson, who believes that the defense has an inherent long-term advantage over the offense in the nuclear age. According to Dyson who worked on the Nike-X system and on penetration aid programs, "In the long run the battle between offensive and defensive technology is a battle of information. If the defensive knows where the offensive warheads are, it is not too difficult to destroy them. For the last twenty years the offense has had an overwhelming advantage, but this advantage is being reduced as defensive information-handling capability improves. In the long run, I believe that defense will prevail because the defense will have more accurate and timely information than the offense. Defensive batteries within a hundred miles of the battle should ultimately be able to out-maneuvre incoming offensive vehicles controlled from a command center 5,000 miles away on land or in submarines off-shore. The offensive command will be fighting the battle blind, without any possibility of quick reaction to defensive moves. I consider that it is only a question of time, perhaps ten or twenty years, before these inherent advantages of the defense become actual. The time that it will take to overturn the doctrine of the supremacy of the offensive will of course depend upon political decisions as well as upon technological developments." Dr. Dyson's statement is in part based upon the fact that incoming offensive missiles must carry their computers with them, whereas defensive missiles depend upon huge local computer installations. This is not a subject on which I claim any expertise; but, insofar as a layman can judge the argument, Dr. Dyson appears to have much the better rationale.

Although the arms race is extremely costly and also dangerous, the difficulties of reaching arms control agreements and of policing them may introduce even greater dangers. Although it is extremely important to continue to seek desirable and enforcible arms control agreements, it would be very dangerous to oversimplify the possible pitfalls. Among these are reliance upon intelligence.

Much of the information on enemy strategic forces stems from intelligence sources. There is reason to believe that our information on the numbers of installed weapons the Soviet Union has is very good. We cannot, of course, know how many weapons or weapon parts have been stockpiled. We are also in some trouble when it comes to knowing the characteristics of the weapons. For instance, the Soviet Union has not done any atmospheric testing since the imposition of the test ban in 1963. We cannot know the extent to which they have made increasingly efficient use of fissionable materials. For instance, with respect to one weapons system employed by the Soviet Union, the size and lift capacity of the weapons system could make for a warhead of from x megatons to 4x megatons. According to the National Intelligence Estimates, the missile carries an x megaton warhead. It is difficult to know on what basis the National Intelligence Estimate arrives at its conclusion.

There are various techniques for monitoring the Russian missile tests for accuracy. There are also, however, many techniques for the Russians to provide us with misinformation. For instance, with respect to the placement of a marker in the Pacific Ocean, the Russians could use a randomized computer to aim at some specific spot related to the marker but different from it. Thus we could learn, at best, from this source the outer limit of Russian accuracy. There are other techniques for monitoring Russian tests which the Russians would have to work harder to fool, but this is possible. The Russians, moreover, are culturally a very suspicious and secretive people. Thus the National Intelligence Estimates of Russian warhead capacity and of missile accuracy do not rest on unambiguous hard evidence.

Projections of future Russian procurement pose an even greater problem. The National Intelligence Estimates have been massively and consistently wrong about one particular strategic weapons system each year since 1961. It is obvious that the estimates being made in the Central Intelligence Agency are based partly upon political hypotheses which are shown to be wrong by this degree of consistent inaccuracy, and partly upon strategic theories which the Russians do not accept. (And I happen to agree with the Russians.) Yet the interesting thing is that the Central Intelligence Agency has apparently not become self-conscious about its mistakes.

Attempts to clarify these issues have resulted in charges of demagoguery. Senator Fulbright, for instance, accused Secretary Laird of engaging in a "scare" technique when he detailed the Russian first-strike threat. I do not doubt that one should be scared by the highly conservative information that Secretary Laird presented, but I think this kind of fear is eufunctional. Yet what of the scare techniques employed by the opponents of ballistic missile defense? What of Dr. York's charge before Senator Fulbright's committee that ballistic missile defense systems might take decisions out of the hands of the president and place them in the hands of computers or low-ranking officers? Is this any more true for ballistic missile defense systems than for offensive systems? If the radar shows an incoming attack, a decision must be made whether to launch Minuteman or not. True, the time in the case of the ballistic missile defense system may be shorter, but launching a ballistic missile defense system, unlike the Minuteman, does not automatically start a third world war as a large-scale nuclear war. The range of these weapons is not great enough. A ballistic missile defense system may help to avoid a situation in which the president must either helplessly allow the American strategic force to be knocked out or launch a large-scale nuclear war under conditions of gross uncertainty in response to what may be mistaken radar indications, or an accidental launch, or even an attack from a third source. In any event, the extent to which the thesis would be true depends upon the command and control program adopted.

Dr. Kistiakowsky has said—also before Senator Fulbright's committee—that the explosion of a Spartan missile may blind people. It is true, of course, that if a Spartan missile explodes at a minimum range of 200 miles under perfect atmospheric conditions along one of the less likely but more populated routes an incoming missile might take, someone who is looking directly at the area of explosion might sustain retinal damage. Would Dr. Kistiakowsky really prefer to have the incoming missile land and explode? Would such an explosion produce less retinal damage? Are we really to believe that an illegitimate scare tactic was not being employed against the average citizen of the United States? What of the Sternglass thesis which the last article in this section responds to? According to a full page ad by *Esquire* magazine, the question is: "Will A.B.M. bring death to all children?" Then the advertisement goes on to ask, "Are nuclear weapons the most powerful biological poison that man has yet invented? Would our use of A.B.M. insure that no future generations of children could survive? Now in just-out *Esquire* magazine, noted radiation physicist Ernest Sternglass details the generally unknown facts of the correlation between Strontium 90 and infant mortality. Read scientific evidence detailing how one-third of our infants may have died in the 1960's from peacetime nuclear testing . . . how childhood leukemia doubled in one fallout area. Discover the shocking demonstrated evidence of chromosome damage, fetal and congenital malformations caused by nuclear fallout. Find out why, if successful, the A.B.M. system could cause the extinction of the entire human race." The article by Aranoff and Boylan deals with the Sternglass scare tactic.

Most of the issues of the arms race and of arms control have recently been related to ballistic missile defense. Some of the specific issues—for instance, that of the Russian first-strike threat—have already been covered in passing. Others are covered in the articles by Charles Herzfeld and Herbert York.

According to Dr. York, ballistic missile defense simply cannot work. "This intellectual battle culminated in a meeting that took place in the White House in January, 1967. In addition to President Johnson, Secretary of Defense Robert F. McNamara and the Joint Chiefs of Staff there were present all past and current Special Assistants to the President for Science and Technology (James R. Killian, Jr., George B. Kistiakowsky, Jerome B. Wiesner and Donald F. Hornig) and all past and current Directors of Defense Research and Engineering (Harold Brown, John S. Foster, Jr., and myself). We were asked that simple kind of question which must be answered after all the complicated ifs, ands and buts have been discussed: 'will it work?' The answer was no, and there was no dissent from that answer. The context, of course, was the Russian threat as it was then interpreted and forecast, and the current and projected state of our own ABM technology."

Obviously I was not present at that meeting and there is no public record of it. It is, however, difficult to believe that that simple answer was offered; it is on the public record that John S. Foster does not accept that simple answer. Mr. York must be asking whether the system could work in the same sense against the Russians as against the projected Chinese threat of the 1970's—that is, whether the system could screen out a massive Russian attack—although he fails to give the lay reader a proper indication of this distinction. In this sense, the answer would clearly be that the system does not work, that it cannot do this. The Russians can depend upon either exhaustion or leakage to overcome the system. There are a number of other—and highly important and surely discussed—senses in which it can work, however, as pointed out in Charles Herzfeld's article. The system is cost effective, as against increasing the offensive missile forces; it can prevent the Russians from having a free ride against Minuteman and SAC; it can give sufficient time for warning to either deter a Russian attack or to permit a reprisal if such an attack occurs; it can avoid the dread choice between accepting without immediate retaliation an attack that might destroy the offensive forces and launching on warning in a case in which the attack may be unauthorized or accidental or a chimera stemming from radar failure.

Dr. Herzfeld is one of the more moderate supporters of ballistic missile defense. I believe that he understates the extent to which ballistic missile defense is part of an optimal mix of American strategic systems. Up to some upper limit, available studies show it to be cost effective. It complicates Russian attack plans. Even if the system does not work, the Russians will not have enough information to know that it does not work, and their conservative planners will have to reckon with the possibility that it does work either because of known or of unforeseen effects. Yet most evidence would seem to indicate that it would work. Although some of the computer software needs to be developed—and this cannot be done in the absence of installation—the methods being employed for testing are essentially similar to those which tested part systems of the Apollo system before the unmanned Apollo was sent to the moon. There is, in fact, despite Dr. York's comments to the contrary, a very high expectation that systems tested in this fashion will work. Moreover, they do not even have to work in the Apollo sense, for Apollo was an all-or-nothing system. It was a single vehicle which either went to the moon and returned or did not, in which case in a live run the men would be dead. The ballistic missile defense system need not be completely effective. If it degrades the enemy attacks sufficiently to preserve enough Minutemen for a counter-strike and to provide time within which this attack can be launched, it is an effective deterrent against the Russians. In this sense, it is not at all unlikely that an installed ballistic missile defense system will in fact give a president of the United States an option other than launching a full-scale nuclear war upon radar warning. It is to Dr. York's credit that unlike Senator Fulbright[2] and Dr. Garvin, whom he quotes on another issue, he does not like striking on radar warning. A ballistic missile defense system, however, is the only practicable alternative.

A ballistic missile defense system may give almost perfect defense against the kinds of attacks the Chinese will be capable of launching in the 1970's. It will also provide an effective defense against accidental or unauthorized attack. In these senses also, the system may permit us to avoid nuclear war. Although these examples are not very likely, they are so horrendous in their nature that any normal intelligent person would seek to avoid them.

Dr. York's argument against the possibility of a coordinated attack upon the American deterrent seems to be a little deficient. According to Dr. York, "Since the warning time in the case of an ICBM attack is generally taken as being about thirty minutes, the people who believe the deterrent may be in serious danger usually imagine that the bombers are attacked by missile submarines and therefore have only 15 minutes' warning. This is important because a 30-minute warning gives the bombers ample time to get off the ground. In that case, however, an attack on all three components cannot be made simultaneously; that is, if the attacking weapons are launched simultaneously, they cannot arrive simultaneously, and vice versa."

Of course, Dr. York is correct. If weapons traveling at the same speed are launched simultaneously from different distances, they will not arrive simultaneously. But the 15-minute alert for SAC is purely theoretical and Russian air defense is exceptionally good. Moreover, if enough damage is done to the American strategic force, we will not want to use the few escaping SAC planes against Russian cities for reasons that have already been mentioned. Therefore it is not "incredible that all three of our deterrent systems could become vulnerable in the same period, and it is (not) doubly incredible that we could not know that this would happen without sufficient notice so that we could do something about it." It is, after all, possible to launch different attacking systems at carefully differentiated times. Indeed, I have worked on detailed attack sequences in which exactly such attacks are launched.

Minuteman and SAC are obviously vulnerable. There are some strong reasons to believe that it may be much easier to track and incapacitate Polaris submarines than the Navy, which, after all, is self-interested, admits. Every military system has known vulnerabilities and many have unknown vulnerabilities. Dr. York mentions that military systems are subject to attack by

2. Senator Symington asked, "After PAR finds the incoming missiles, why then couldn't you fire the Minuteman on target instead of the Spartan?" and Senator Fulbright answered, ". . . if the objective is deterrence . . . then . . . this would really concern the Russians to know what you would really do if they sent over a massive attack."
Senator Gore, "Or a light attack."
Senator Fulbright, "Or even a light attack, one that could be detected . . . I would think that is the greatest deterrent you could have, and you are going to release ours before they are destroyed, and you could do it."

opponents and that one cannot be sure that their vulnerabilities will not be exploited. That is precisely why a wise management of the military establishment attempts to maintain a mix of systems so that an unexpected vulnerability of any single system will not leave a nation helpless. Such a mix complicates the enemy's attack and makes it more difficult and expensive for him to acquire the instruments necessary for a successful first-strike. A cardinal rule of defense policy is not to permit the opposition a "free ride." In the absence of ballistic missile defense, the enemy has a free ride against SAC and against Minuteman. If Polaris becomes vulnerable, the United States might have unwisely invited a Russian first-strike. Although Dr. York is right in saying that the ballistic missile defense might fail because the Russians might find an answer to it, this is also true for all our offensive systems. Ballistic missile defense therefore gives the United States a very important additional string to its bow.

Every defense system—offensive and defensive—is subject to uncertainties. Clever enemy "inventions" may immobilize or circumvent them. A carefully chosen mix of weapons systems increases uncertainties for the attack and reduces the damage that can be done by particular technological or strategic "inventions." Although these uncertainties will deter attack in most circumstances—at least for the major nuclear powers—a crisis or especially the combination of a crisis and a strategic or technological breakthrough may permit an attack that could have been avoided. Moreover, reliance upon the kind of minimum deterrence advocated by McGeorge Bundy will decrease one's bargaining strength in a crisis. Bundy has been forced to discount the factor of American strategic superiority in maintaining American strategic resolve in the Cuban missile crisis—a revision of accepted opinion that seems doubtful—to hold his new minimum deterrence theory. Even if the Russian backdown did not result from the combination of American local and strategic superiority—an unprovable speculation that many analysts nonetheless accept—surely there will be some adversary governments that will be influenced adversely by strategic inferiority and some American governments whose bargaining assurance will be increased in crises if they do not have to negotiate from a position of strategic inferiority.

According to Dr. York, "it is now generally agreed that the only ABM system the Russians have deployed is an area defense around Moscow much like our old Nike Zeus system. It appears to have virtually no capability against our offense, and it has been . . . extremely counterproductive insofar as its goal of defending Moscow is concerned." The Galosh system around Moscow is a second-generation ballistic missile defense system. The Russians are now engaged in testing a third-generation system, while we are just beginning to think about the installation of the Safeguard system. Moreover, the Russian Galosh system operates with a much larger warhead than Spartan. Thus the area of intercept is much greater while the channel through which incoming missiles must attack Moscow is relatively small. The Galosh system may not work, but it may work much better than Dr. York, or even the Russian Dr. Sakharov (who is hardly in good standing in Russia and who lacks the most recent information) believes. The extent to which incoming vehicles are genuinely hardened against various emissions from a nuclear burst is subject to engineering calculations in which one cannot have very great confidence. Even with hardening, the area of intercept is believed to be large; it may be extremely large. In any event, many American experts believe that Dr. Sakharov has overestimated the capabilities of actual penetration aids, which are extremely complicated and expensive. In this offensive and defensive race, the defense, as Dr. Dyson points out, may have a genuine long-term advantage. In addition, Dr. York seems to be unaware that the Talinn system may have very real tie-in capabilities with the Galosh system.

The relationship that Dr. York makes between ballistic missile defense and an arms race is questionable. If the United States and the Soviet Union are capable of coming to an arms control agreement (and I would not argue that they are) then each would have its second-strike force best protected with somewhat reduced numbers of offensive missiles and light ballistic missile defense systems. In this sense, a ballistic missile defense system would be an aid to reaching an arms control agreement. If an agreement cannot be reached, then, of course, the arms race will continue, with both ballistic missile defense systems and offensive missile systems. In this case, ballistic missile defense systems will not worsen the arms race but neither are they likely to dampen it. The only advantage of such systems in this case would be that of complicating the job of launching a first-strike. In this sense, BMD increases deterrent capabilities. Long lead times are involved in installing and testing ballistic missile defense systems. If the United States refrains from developing a ballistic missile defense system and if the Soviet Union (which has been greatly increasing its offensive forces—and which, because it has larger warheads than the United States, can more easily achieve a first-strike force if it obtains accuracies comparable to those of the United States—) installs its third-generation ballistic missile defense system as a thick system, it would then be capable of screening out the few live offensive weapons the United States might have left after a Russian first-strike even if the United States had sufficient temerity to desire to use them under these circumstances.

There are several small but important points on which I disagree with Dr. Herzfeld's article. Although I agree that the presence of nth nuclear powers greatly enchances the desirability of a ballistic missile defense system for the Soviet Union and the United States, I would argue that even in the absence of the nth country threat the deterrent situation is much more stable, everything else being equal, if both countries have thin ballistic defense missile systems. Even apart from this consideration, Dr. Herzfeld himself recognizes in a slight inconsistency that the system is protective against accidental or unauthorized launches and that it avoids the terrible choice between premature reprisal and accepting an attack that may destroy the retalitory force. Whether a thick system would be stabilizing or would fuel the arms race is an extremely difficult technical question and one about which I have no firm conclusions. Dr. Donald Brennan, an expert in this area, significantly disagrees with Dr. Herzfeld on this issue, and his views on this matter surely are not simply to be dismissed. Finally Dr. Herzfeld overestimates the survivability of the American strategic forces.

In discussions of national priorities related to the ballistic missile defense controversy, some people argued as if the military had continuously had its way until the recent arguments over ballistic missile defense. This is, of course, a misreading of history. The very low defense budgets of the immediate postwar period—11 to 13 billion dollars—sharply limited American strategic capabilities. It was only after the Korean war that the budget was immensely increased. But even then the military never got their way completely. They did not get the atomic airplane; they did not get the SR-70; and there are numerous other instances where their requests were rejected. A case had to be made for a weapons system; it was not true that every military demand was accepted.

There is undoubtedly much fat in the military budget, and considerable inefficiency. It is surely desirable to reduce the fat, but not at the expense of the sinews. A diplomatic catastrophe that results from inadequate strategic forces will gravely affect the liberal values that some hope to see implemented by cutting away the defense budget. It will also lead to a greatly increased defense budget. Moreover, there is no evidence that the money which is cut back from the defense will go into other worthwhile projects. In 1969 President Nixon proposed not merely the Safeguard system but also aid programs for the impoverished that would add over four billion dollars yearly in expenditures to the welfare programs of the previous administration. Safeguard thus is not fully competitive with this desirable reform. My intuition indicates that most of the money saved from the military by Congress will not go into liberal programs but into tax savings instead. As a taxpayer I welcome this, but as a citizen I do not.

Dr. William Kintner assesses the potentialities for an arms race through the 1970's. It is interesting that his argument seems to suggest joint laboratories in the United States and the Soviet Union—a suggestion I made in an article in 1961. Of course, no one really thinks this suggestion would or could be adopted. However, there would obviously be no incentive to develop a destabilizing weapon system if that meant giving it to the other side.

Mr. Kintner suggests that in the absence of such a development, the exhibition of R and D developments may be useful in decelerating the arms race. This suggestion, though less decisive than the joint laboratory, is much more practicable. One can only hope that Mr. Kintner is correct.

Final mention may be made of the role of many scientists in the weapons debate, for instance, the original decision by the General Advisory Committee of the Atomic Energy Commission on the H-bomb in 1949. Except for the vote of Edward Teller, the GAC unanimously recommended against the project, citing the inefficient use of fissionable materials that would be made by H-bombs using then known construction techniques. Yet the real question was not one of constructing H-bombs on the basis of known technologies but of entering into a project designed to see whether a workable bomb could be constructed. Thus the scientists had managed to ask an elementary wrong question. Both the Russians and the Americans, as might have been expected, made breakthroughs by different methods that permitted the development of H-bombs. If it had not been for the so-called Teller invention—an invention based on a principle that is so simple that grade-school children are familiar with it—and which forced a decision to proceed with the American project, the Russians, who produced a workable H-bomb before the United States did so, might have had a disastrous strategic advantage. Technological breakthroughs are common in areas such as this; the Polaris submarine depended upon four simultaneous technological breakthroughs for success.

However, when scientists did speak out forcefully for a new weapon system, they were often very wrong, as in the case of the Sage Air Defense System advocated by Wiesner and York, among others. Indeed the record of the scientific community is so massively bad that it is simply wondrous that they have any credibility and remarkable that they have any confidence in their own contentions.

17. The Sociology of Strategic Thinking

MORTON A. KAPLAN

THERE IS A growing body of literature in the social sciences by critics of strategic studies in which it is asserted that strategists are constrained in their policy recommendations by the sociological context in which they work and by the nature of strategic thought itself. Thus Herbert Spiro asserts that strategic theorists are mathematicians or physical scientists with little knowledge of the humanities. It is difficult to ascertain the empirical basis for such an assertion. Bernard Brodie, Henry Kissinger, Thomas C. Schelling, and many others received their training in the social sciences and are otherwise indistinguishable from those who make the charges. Albert Wohlstetter, who is now a professional political scientist, began as a specialist in mathematical logic; his core training in philosophy is more centrally humanistic than that of most of the critics. Herman Kahn, it is true, was trained primarily as a mathematician and physicist, but he has probably read more widely and more voraciously in the humanities and social sciences than most who make this charge. Surprisingly for the thesis, most of those who would agree with the strategic preferences of the critics are themselves physical scientists, with little or no background in the humanities. This particular assertion then appears to be more an article of faith, more a means of rallying the true believers, than an empirically meaningful proposition.

There is another thesis that has been widely circulated to account for the behavior of strategists. This thesis is propagated by Anatol Rapoport, whose background is that of a mathematical biologist. Rapoport argues that it is the strategist's reliance on game theory that leads him to make recommendations that increase conflict. This is a strange argument for Rapoport to make, for, although a relatively recent devotee of game theory, he has done more work in the field of game theory than either Schelling or Kaplan, while most of the other strategists have made little or no use of game theory in their strategic calculations. Perhaps, however, he has some personal immunity to the perils of strategic thinking.

According to Rapoport, the strategist believes that both sides must be "entirely and irreparably committed to The System (which must be pictured as utterly evil) and The Game. The essential image is reduced to this: The Game is played exclusively according to strategic considerations, like chess, where it is certain, not merely probable, that whatever can be done to gain an advantage or to harm the opponent will be done by the rational player. The penalty for losing The Game is submission to The System."[1]

It is not clear whether the capital letters used by Rapoport are intended to convey the impression that strategists are paranoid or whether they represent diagnostic indications of a paranoid tendency in Rapoport. Rapoport never cites any empirical evidence for his propositions; this charge also is a metaphysical proposition that represents a Platonically real strategist rather than the work of empirical strategists.

There is a third line of attack to the effect that strategists go crazy as a function of their work. According to Arthur Waskow, strategists cannot carry out experiments, and this failure produces hallucinations. Waskow advocates "the careful observation of a full-scale national campaign of nonlethal offensives with preparations to change tactics if certain techniques did not work. The ability to research nonlethal equivalents of war is no mean advantage over thermonuclear strategy. The hallucinating subject of the sensory-deprivation experiment and the astrologer who never tries to check his predictions are men dangerously adrift in the world. Merely imagining a future is no way to build realistic images; it is those men who shape the future and watch it change *beneath their hands* [italics added] who understand it."[2]

Anatol Rapoport makes a similar charge when he interprets a quotation from a briefing Kahn gave to an air force audience: "You people do not have a war plan. You have a 'war-gasm.'" According to Rapoport, "Who among us is not convinced that this gem was greeted with guffaws and slapping of thighs, an outburst of jolly fellowship among the initiated?"[3] Kahn, of course,

1. *International Conflict and Behavior Science: The Craigville Papers*, Ed. Roger Fisher, New York, Basic Books, 1964, p. 16.
2. *Ibid.*, p. 140.
3. Anatol Rapoport, "Chicken à la Kahn," *The Virginia Quarterly Review*, Summer 1965, Vol. 41, No. 3, p. 389.

employed the term "war-gasm" to embarrass SAC advocates of the strategy of massive retaliation, as the context of the remark makes abundantly clear. Although I do not like the nonintellectual means Kahn employed to accomplish an obviously admirable objective, Rapoport's misinterpretation of his aim as "pornographic" and of him as an "enthusiastic choreographer of the dance of death" raises more questions about Rapoport's ability to perceive the world than it does about Kahn. Although Rapoport undoubtedly wrote these lines from misguided passion, one could with less injustice charge that his attribution of perverse motives to Kahn reflects the projection of suppressed pornographic and destructive impulses than to make the same charges against Herman Kahn.

Similarly, one wonders about a person such as Waskow who feels the need to experiment with the lives and destiny of people and to shape their futures with his own hands. We cannot escape the leap into the unknown, for the future is exactly that, even with respect to nonlethal experiments. One would hope, however, that this leap would be carried out with the hope of improving the lives of people rather than in the form of experiments designed to serve as a crutch for the experimenter's sanity. In any event, since someone must think about weapons systems and their uses, one hopes they will not draw the conclusion that they should carry out a few nuclear wars to avoid hallucinations. A vast amount of speculation may be preferable to one illuminating example.

The attacks on strategists that have been cited are frivolous and, where not merely frivolous, are surely distasteful to decent people. They are also representative and reveal serious deficiences in the understanding of what strategists do and the implications of strategic thinking. The poor quality of the attacks upon strategic thinking does not, however, necessarily invalidate a sociological approach to strategic thinking.

Is there a military-industrial complex and does it influence in subtle and unrecognized ways the thinking of military strategists? Does working in this field predispose one to favor larger and larger arms budgets and destabilizing technological innovations? Does working in the military-strategic area blind one to nonstrategic solutions of various problems? There have been no serious major studies of these problems, although many authors have written upon them. Consequently it may be that the best we can do is to examine a range of eclectically chosen evidence and to estimate the extent to which the evidence supports some of the propositions that have been suggested.

Since President Eisenhower referred to the industrial-military complex, the term has become a cliché. The problem is one that indeed deserves serious study. Many communities in the United States would be seriously affected by a decline in national defense spending; some communities are highly dependent for their prosperity upon production for military purposes. Although the economists may be able to demonstrate that there would be a net economic gain in reducing or eliminating military expenditures, particular localities and businesses would naturally be concerned about both the risks of the transition process and their relative position in the economy after the completion of it. To this extent, there is a built-in lobby that may agitate for unnecessary and even counterproductive military expenditures. The evidence that strategists are influenced by such lobbies is insubstantial. The RAND Corporation, which at the time was entirely supported by the Air Force, spent much of its time lobbying against official Air Force policy, e.g., the strategy of massive retaliation. Most strategists are sufficiently skilled not to need to be concerned about job security.

The military budget is not a small proportion of the national budget; it is capable of shielding wastages of money that in other areas of governmental activity would be regarded as enormous. It would be contrary to our knowledge of American politics, both in terms of pork-barrel politics and in terms of skill of concealment, to think that this problem has been much better handled than that of farm subsidies or of numerous other items. No doubt a lobby, although hardly monolithic, exists and has agitated for unproductive expenditures.

Even so, it is too facile to assume that every external pressure for an increase in the military budget against the position of the Secretary of Defense is a *prima facie* case of military-industrial lobbying against the national interest. Robert McNamara, the former Secretary of Defense, brilliant as he was, was short of infallible. It is, of course, politically legitimate and effective to cite the Secretary of Defense against a military expenditure. But is is sometimes disconcerting to see academics, who reject the arguments of the Secretary of Defense when these arguments run counter to their own positions, claim him as high and infallible authority when his arguments support their positions.

These are very difficult matters to discuss because much of the essential information is highly classified and also because much of the discussion lacks that quality of scrupulous objectivity, both with respect to the information provided to the public and to the information circulated wihin the government itself, that is required for genuine dialogue. For instance, at the time of the test ban negotiations, I mentioned to a high official of the United States government that on balance the test ban was probably a good agreement (a position with which most critics would have agreed) but that certain risks were being run with respect to the development of an effective ABM system. The official turned to me and stated that he had recently been thoroughly briefed on the subject and that there was no possibility of such a development. At the time that this advice was being circulated through the government, the breakthroughs that were necessary for the development of an ABM system had already been made: these included massive improvements in radar, miniaturization of the warhead, and increases in missile accuracy. The use of x-rays, rather than merely of blast, to disarm incoming warheads was already subject to review. The development of effective ABM was highly probable at that time and the reduction of costs to those comparable with offensive missiles was not unlikely, if one made standard projections for cost reductions. This was not an unusual instance, and it should not be thought that I am suggesting that those who take this side are honest and those who take the other side are dishonest. Disingenuous argumentation, although more prevalent among physical scientists than among social scientists, is widely employed as a political device to support positions that are believed thoroughly justifiable on other grounds. In other words, selection and distortion of the evidence is apparently thought to be a legitimate technique in what is viewed as an essentially political process by many advocates on opposing sides of strategic issues.

The current debate over BMD (1967) is misleading. The figures that have been presented to the public are at least doctored to support the policy conclusions the Department of Defense wishes to support. The public does not have access to the range of argumentation and detail that would permit informed judgment.

There is a distinct difference of position between most civilian experts on strategy and most critics on the BMD issue. The experts tend to support the deployment of the thin defense system whereas the critics tend to oppose it. This might seem to support the Rapoport hypothesis that strategists see these issues in terms of a contest with an evil enemy who must be contended with to the nth degree. Before this conclusion is reached, however, it should be noted that most of the civilian experts are opposed to full-scale deployment of BMD at this time and that McNamara by now qualifies as a strategist.

It should also be noted that most of the civilian strategists make fewer assumptions concerning Soviet behavior than those who take the opposite view. Thus those opposed to the thin BMD deployment argue that it will trigger off an arms race with the Soviet Union, that it will be ineffective, and that it will upset the détente. William Foster, the head of ACDA, for instance, would argue that progressive changes are occurring in Soviet society and that it is important to influence these changes in a desired direction. The strategists, on the other hand, would tend to argue that the immediate policies of the Soviet government are much too dependent upon factors that we are not skilled in estimating for us to have confidence in such projections. Although an American deployment of BMD might encourage the Soviet Union to engage in an arms race, it might to the contrary demonstrate to the Soviet Union that further deployment of BMD in the hope of securing a strategic arms advantage is a fruitless business. The strategic experts would further argue that there is little evidence to support the view that agreements with the Soviet Union depend upon refraining from competitiveness; the Soviet Union, for instance, entered a pact with Nazi Germany at a time of exceedingly great mutual hostility and increased shipments of war materials to Nazi Germany as relations between the two states deteriorated. They would argue that the United States had already waited long enough to put up a thin BMD network and that lead times are such that further delay might easily encourage the Soviet Union to pursue an arms race.

With few exceptions, and these would not include any of the leading civilian strategists, the arguments for the thin BMD net would not rest upon an assumption of monolithic Communism, upon an assumption that the Soviet Union was inevitably hostile, or so forth. The arguments would rest mostly upon the assumption that the consequences of American policy could easily be the direct opposite of those predicted by the critics and that at least some prudential considerations give primacy to installing the thin BMD net.

Thus, if it can be argued, as most civilian strategists would argue, that a BMD deployment would make a substantial difference in a nuclear war, then it would also make a substantial difference in a pre-war bargaining situation and might make the difference between stability on the one hand and a provocation, a bargaining loss, or an escalation into nuclear war, on the other. If one important difference could be found between the reasoning of the strategists and the nonstrategists, it would be that the strategists are less confident of predictions concerning Soviet responses to American actions and that they desire a prudential force policy that protects against the worst contingencies should their estimates of Soviet behavior prove wrong. They are not willing to bet too much upon their capacities as political forecasters. They are more aware of the role of contingency in the world. This characteristic probably does distinguish them from other academics, from physical scientists, from politicians and businessmen, and from professional soldiers. This may indeed be a sociological characteristic that is linked to their style of thinking.

It is not surprising that strategic analysts would be less dogmatic than other people with respect to the considerations mentioned. The systems design of strategic systems has as an inbuilt component the requirement that the system be good both against alternative forces and against alternative strategic doctrines of potential opponents. The past history of force design, in which forces were built to cope only with the expected plan, force design, or force usages of the opponent, was replete with too many instances in which these expectations turned out to be erroneous. The system design concept, in which the maximization of a particular variable involves marginal costs for other variables, also alerts the systems analyst to the little known truism that most systems designs and systems use plans can be confronted with alternatives that are better for some objectives and worse for others.

Nothing that has been said so far exempts the strategic analyst from the possibility of blind spots or mistaken perceptions peculiar to his mode of analysis. It would be surprising, indeed unbelievable, were he exempt from this human frailty. It may very well be that when strategic analysts give political, as contrasted with strategic, advice they are more likely than other people to underevaluate the potential for agreement between the Soviet Union and the United States. It may perhaps be the case that thinking in terms of strategic analysis, even though there are cooperative games, leads one to an overly competitive bias. John Foster Dulles, who was not a strategic analyst, seemed to misunderstand the potential for agreement between the United States and the Soviet Union over Germany before the East German uprising of 1953 and the removal of Beria from power in the Soviet Union. We also have the instance of the CIA analysis of the Cuban situation before the Bay of Pigs, in which the projection was made that a spontaneous uprising in Cuba would assist the landings at the Bay of Pigs. It is commonly believed that the CIA underestimated the degree of support that Castro had in Cuba. Although we should be cautious about using the evidence from the abortive invasion, as it is not foreclosed that had the landing been better organized and planned and more successful, an uprising would have occurred that would have received the support of most Cubans, the common belief seems not unreasonable.

On the other hand, most experts on Russian affairs were badly misled with respect to Soviet response patterns during the Cuban missile crisis. To my knowledge only Nathan Leites, among the experts, correctly evaluated the probable Russian response pattern. Most civilian strategic analysts called the terms correctly. I would suggest that the following factors accounted for these differences. Experts on Russian affairs, by and large, used abstract and general social and psychological hypotheses that they adapted to the Russian context. They ignored or were unfamiliar with the evidence that most strategic analysts looked at: past Russian bargaining behavior in crisis negotiations, the conventional force ratios in the Caribbean, and the nuclear strategic capabilities of the two parties, which at that time greatly favored the United States. Moreover, they had an ideological orientation, I suspect, that made them distrustful of military showdowns.[4] Although many unknown factors may in fact have influenced the Russian decisions during the Cuban missile crisis, I should like to suggest tentatively that the superior forecasting ability of the strategic experts in this instance stemmed from two factors: they inferred the probable Russian response from less theoretical or more empirical data, the source for their data was more relevant, i.e., past Russian crisis diplomacy, and they had much better and more detailed knowledge of a major factor in the interchange, the nuclear strategic balance between the contending parties.

The strategists may have a persistent bias toward competitiveness, but the efforts by critics to relate this bias toward the positions they take with respect to specific issues has not been convincing on the merits. It is possible that better informed and better trained critics could sustain their intuition, or their fear, that the strategists are bound within a rigid framework of thought that drives them toward suggesting disequilibrating responses for

---

4. It is worth pointing out that had the Soviet IRBM's remained in Cuba, there is reason to believe that there would likely have been a showdown over Berlin in which the opportunities for miscalculation would have been enormous.

national policy. Characteristically, however, the attack upon strategic thinking does not rest upon an empirical foundation.

As previously mentioned, Anatol Rapoport bases his attack upon the game theoretical style of analysis. Rapoport does not claim, as do some critics, that strategists view international politics as a zero sum game. He uses an example that is non-zero-sum: the prisoners' dilemma. Apart from the fact that most strategists have done almost no work with game theory and that it is therefore difficult to see how game theoretic notions could have influenced them so much, the following objections may briefly be made to the Rapoport thesis. In the first place, the prisoners' dilemma is solvable for the cooperative solution provided there is no finite cutoff point and a time discount. Rapoport contrasts the prisoners' dilemma in the single-shot case with situations of trust and finds the former deficient. It is quite true that if each prisoner were to make the elementary mistake of believing that his decision would govern the decision of the other prisoner, they would both be better off than if both prisoners reason correctly. Thus if a prisoner were presented with a choice as to the world he would live in—a choice between a world in which he and his co-prisoner would reason incorrectly and a world in which they would reason correctly—he would likely opt for stupidity. If, however, he were presented with a third choice, namely a world in which he reasons correctly and his co-prisoner reasons incorrectly, there is little doubt that this would constitute his preference. Since neither prisoner's decision governs the other in the single-shot case, it would be ludicrous to think that national policy would gain by excommunicating the strategists unless one could also excommunicate the Russian strategists at the same time.

If, on the other hand, Rapoport is thinking not of the single-shot case, which is the prototype for the prisoners' dilemma, but of the iterated case without a cutoff and with a time discount, then perhaps he is fearful that the continuity of advice from American strategists might influence the Soviet Union to think strategically, whereas in the absence of the evil influence of strategists the Soviet leaders would be revealed as trusting souls who wish nothing better than to enter cooperative arrangements with the United States.

Unfortunately, the Soviet Union does not need to be taught about conflict theory or competitiveness by American strategists. Marxist theory is explicitly based upon the struggle between thesis and antithesis which then moves the system to a higher synthesis. Russian leaders have stated repeatedly and publicly their belief in conflict between Communism and capitalism and have emphasized that their recognition of the horrors of nuclear war does not imply their renunciation of the struggle at other levels. One might argue with at least as much justification that the way to move the Soviet Union from competitive thinking is to behave with sufficient vigor to demonstrate to Russian leaders that they cannot succeed in their objectives by that method and that to obtain any reasonable set of goals they would have to reduce their competitiveness in arms races with the United States. Generalizations of this kind are always dangerous unless they are adapted to specific circumstances of place, person, and organization; nonetheless at the level of generalization employed, I would prefer the latter hypothesis. It is not insignificant that McNamara's effort to convince the Soviet Union not to enter a BMD arms race apparently was based on the beliefs of at least some strategists that the USSR could be moved to a decision by a rational demonstration of the strategic advantages of cooperation. The USSR apparently was less interested in words; we will see whether it is more interested in deeds.

If one were to analyze the arms race in game theoretic terms, which no strategic analyst does to my knowledge, it would probably turn out that the prisoners' dilemma is, in any event, a bad model. The strict solution associated with the writings of Luce and Raiffa, in which cooperation is the solution, would probably come closer to a correct metaphor. There were at least two instances, before the installation of numerous American missiles, when, under standard SAC operating procedures, radar blips would have called for sending SAC aloft in accordance with the fail-safe procedures. In both cases, General Powers, the SAC commander, decided to keep SAC grounded. This gives rise to the inference that SAC leadership, intemperately hawkish though some believe it to be, nonetheless viewed the situation as one that could be interpreted by a strict solution metaphor, and that the system, even before the installation of missiles, was much more stable during non-crisis situations than many of the critics, who themselves seem to possess a Strangelove point of view, seemed willing to believe.

One way to make the military situation more stable is to change the system itself through technology. Thus as the deterrent system changed from a SAC system to a ballistic missile system, the potential stability of the system increased greatly. This is no longer true as MIRV comes into play. The system is clearly becoming less stable. Many of the critics are suspicious of the strategists for urging development of such weapons systems. They feel that such recommendations reflect the competitive bias of strategists, their fear of the future, and their assumption concerning the hostility of Russia. They fear that commitments by the United States to the development of such systems only spur the Soviet Union to maintain the competitive arms race.

To some extent Secretary McNamara may have accepted these arguments, for he deliberately refrained from deploying BMD in the United States; for a considerable period of time after the Russians began to deploy their own BMD system, he tried to reach agreement with the Russians to remove their system. The trouble with even small gestures of this kind is that the lead time for the deployment of such systems, even if development has been carried on, may be quite long—five to seven years in the case of BMD. One runs the risk, particularly when facing a country, many of whose developments are secret, that the strategic balance may be gravely upset by one of these gestures. The Russian breaking of the test moratorium, the BMD deployment, and the testing of a Fractional Orbital Ballistic System do not lend credence to the supposition that the Soviet Union is unwilling to attempt a strategic breakthrough.

It might be argued, as the mathematician Jeremy Stone does, that the Soviet Union is merely trying to make up for the previous advantage attained by the United States during its rapid missile buildup in the early 1960's. This explanation is possibly correct, but several qualifications must be noted: the Soviet Union allowed the United States to obtain this early advantage by deliberately holding back for third-generation systems; the Soviet Union was aware of the McNamara policy of slowing down the arms race and of allowing the Soviet Union to achieve practical parity; and, whatever the Soviet motivation, the opportunity for a breakthrough, once apparent, might prove politically irresistible. The facts as noted are at least as consistent with the hypothesis that it is the McNamara policy of permitting the Soviet Union to "catch up" that has encouraged the Soviet Union to believe that it has an opportunity to make a breakthrough. This inference seems to be supported by the most recent (1969–1970) Soviet strategic missile developments, which far surpass those of the United States and which run well beyond Mc-Namara's (or even Laird's) predictions.

Differences between strategists and critics seem to involve differences as to which risks are to be run, but it is not genuinely clear that the different options of the strategists and critics really do involve different risks. The prudential policy advocated by the strategists protects better against a strategic breakthrough while encouraging an arms race that is destabilizing on one assumption of Russian motivation and reducing it on another. On the other hand, the policy of the critics risks security while reducing the probability of a destabilizing arms race upon one hypothesis as to Russian motivation and increasing the probability of an unstable arms race upon the other hypothesis. In any event, the economy probably places limits on the arms race in both the United States and the Soviet Union, and, for most arms races, although not for all, competition dampens the race by decreasing marginal dollar effectiveness.

How consistently this difference in orientation would distinguish civilian strategists from social scientists who are not strategists or from physical scientists is difficult to answer. The extent to which it involves a difference of perspective or a difference of information is also difficult to answer. Most civilian strategists would argue that the critics misunderstand the complexities of the strategic issues, are relatively uninformed concerning past Russian crisis behavior, and operate in these unknown areas upon the basis of abstract generalizations that they would take much less seriously in areas where they do substantive work. If these arguments are correct, the differences in perception would involve differences of role only insofar as the role differences permitted access to more information and forced the users of that information to consider it both more systematically and more professionally.

One can nonetheless perhaps detect a greater willingness on the part of the civilian critics to run major risks on the basis of infirm hypotheses in order to avoid what they regard as the dangers that an arms race will bring. One may detect on the part of the strategists an unwillingness to run genuinely major risks on the basis of such infirm hypotheses and a greater confidence in the ability of defense management to avoid the dangers stressed by the critics. There is still insufficient evidence to demonstrate the existence of these differences, let alone to imply whether such differences involve either the selection of different types of people by the strategic profession, the shaping of the people who enter the profession by the style of thinking that is part of it, or access to better information more perceptively utilized. That the distinction is not a thoroughly clear one is suggested by the fact that most strategists would approve General Powers' position not to send SAC up despite SAC standard operating procedures to the contrary, and, for example, by the fact that strategists would differ among themselves as to whether an air warning system should lay greater stress on detecting attacks at the risk of triggering a response on a false signal or run the greater risk that an actual attack will not be detected in order to avoid false alarms.

We do not desire to brush these issues away. They deserve responsible study from the standpoint of a sociology of knowledge. But we do wish to insist that the debate carried on by the critics is one that confuses rather than clarifies the issues. Strategists do not employ game theory. They do not assume the rationality of their opponents, although they search for strategies that enhance the motives of an opponent to be rational. They do not ignore cooperative solutions; indeed some of the more practicable proposals for cooperative solutions between the Russians and Americans have come from strategists. The strategists do not ignore long-term rationality and are concerned to support military procurement programs that enhance such long-term rationality. In this respect, they are quite willing to run risks; but they may be unwilling to run risks as large as those the critics are willing to run. This is the core area in which analysis might be helpful. This subject can become the focus of proper academic study only when it is divorced from the realm of political propaganda and moral hysteria.

18. To Cap the Volcano

McGEORGE BUNDY

I

THE NEGLECTED TRUTH about the present strategic arms race between the United States and the Soviet Union is that in terms of international political behavior that race has now become almost completely irrelevant. The new weapons systems which are being developed by each of the two great powers will provide neither protection nor opportunity in any serious political sense. Politically the strategic nuclear arms race is in a stalemate. It has been this way since the first deliverable hydrogen weapons were exploded, and it will be this way for as far ahead as we can see, even if future developments should be much more heavily one-sided than anything now in prospect. This proposition does not square with the complex measurements of comparative advantage which dominated the ABM debate, but I think it can be supported both by logic and by history.

In light of the certain prospect of retaliation there has been literally no chance at all that any sane political authority, in either the United States or the Soviet Union, would consciously choose to start a nuclear war. This proposition is true for the past, the present and the foreseeable future. For sane men on both sides the balance of terror is overwhelmingly persuasive. Given the worst calculations of the most pessimistic American advocate of new weapons systems, there is no prospect at all that the Soviet Government could attack the United States without incurring an overwhelming risk of

349

destruction vastly greater than anyone but a madman would choose to accept. Conversely, even the most cold-blooded of American planners has always understood, at least since 1954, that the concept of a strategic first strike by the United States is wholly unacceptable because of the prospect of Soviet retaliation.

There is an enormous gulf between what political leaders really think about nuclear weapons and what is assumed in complex calculations of relative "advantage" in simulated strategic warfare. Think-tank analysts can set levels of "unacceptable" damage well up in the tens of millions of lives. They can assume that the loss of dozens of great cities is somehow a real choice for sane men. They are in an unreal world. In the real world of real political leaders—whether here or in the Soviet Union—a decision that would bring even one hydrogen bomb on one city of one's own country would be recognized in advance as a catastrophic blunder; ten bombs on ten cities would be a disaster beyond history; and a hundred bombs on a hundred cities are unthinkable. Yet this unthinkable level of human incineration is the least that could be expected by either side in response to any first strike in the next ten years, *no matter what happens to weapons systems in the meantime.* Even the worst case hypothesized in the ABM debate leaves at least this much room for reply. In sane politics, therefore, there is no level of superiority which will make a strategic first strike between the two great states anything but an act of utter folly.

My argument evidently rests upon an assumption of sanity. It does not protect against madness. But neither is there any protection against the madman in close calculations of "assured survivable destruction capability." Indeed it may be easier for a madman to understand the simple horror of *any* exchange between the superpowers than to be persuaded by intricate calculations of residual "advantage" after the world as we know it is destroyed.

What we have somehow forgotten, in the expanding megatonage of the age of missiles, is that already fifteen years ago we were scorpions in a bottle, able to sting each other only at the price of death. Yet what either side had then was insignificant in comparison to what both sides have now. Moreover, we have somehow let the necessary comparisons of one weapons system with another delude us into a belief that these calculations of cost-effectiveness are also calculations of real advantage. Certainly when we determine that a certain level of deterrent strength is needed (a calculation which has always been generous in both our countries), it makes very good sense to do our best to pick the systems that will do the job most economically, and it follows that close comparative analysis is well worthwhile. But the fact that Minuteman is better in these terms than the B-70—or Poseidon better than Polaris—does not tell us anything about the real value, politically, of any one system, or of all our systems together. Their one purpose is deterrence. They must not do less, and they cannot do more.

Thus the basic consequence of considering this matter politically and not technically is the conclusion that beyond a point long since passed the escalation of the strategic nuclear race makes no sense for either the Soviet Union or the United States. Nothing in the national interest, the ideology or the personal political position of any leader in either country can be advanced by any strategic nuclear exchange. No weapons systems now in sight for either side can change that fact. It follows that in political, as distinct from technical, terms we have all been wrong to talk of nuclear superiority. President Nixon was surely right when he changed the terms of the discussion from "superiority" to "sufficiency." Sufficiency is what we both have now, in ample measure, and no superiority worth having can be achieved. It is sometimes argued that in the past nuclear superiority—ours over the Soviet Union or that of the Soviet Union over Western Europe—has had a decisive influence on events. I find this a very doubtful proposition. This is not the place for a close reexamination of relevant crises like Suez, Berlin and Cuba, but my own belief is that in none of the three has the nuclear "superiority" of any major power been decisive. In all three cases the risk of escalation has certainly been an element in the problem, and in all three, in different ways, that risk has been a deterrent to action. But in all three cases, questions of will and purpose have been more important than questions of nuclear numbers. In none of the three cases, I feel confident, would the final result have been different if the relative strategic positions of the Soviet Union and the United States had been reversed. A stalemate is a stalemate either way around.

Since it is vital to avoid misunderstanding, let me emphasize here that in asserting the preëminence of the political judgment on the use and non-use of nuclear weapons I am not at all downgrading the importance of technical proficiency in the deterrent forces we do decide to maintain. It seems to me wholly plain that a credible strategic nuclear deterrent is indispensable to the peace, and for that reason no task is more clearly indispensable than that of maintaining and protecting such a force. There is a great distance between a belief in strategic stalemate and any suggestion that we should proceed to unilateral disarmament. We have bought and paid for parity, and we must not lose it. So it will be as true in a future of stable balance as it has been in the past of presumed supremacy that the men who stand guard over our strategic forces are men who place us all in their debt.

But it is one thing for military men to maintain our deterrent force with vigilant skill, and it quite another for anyone to assume that their necessary contingency plans have any serious interest for political leaders. The object of political men—quite rightly—is that these weapons should never be used. I have watched two Presidents working on strategic contingency plans, and what interested them most was simply to make sure that none of these awful events would occur. Political leaders, whether here or in Russia, are cut from a very different mold than strategic planners. They see cities and people as part of what they are trying to help—not as targets. They live with the daily struggle to make a little progress—to build things—to grow things—to lift the quality of life a little—and to win honor, and even popularity, by such achievements. The deterrent that might not please a planner is more than deterrent enough for them. And that is why the deterrent does work, even at a distance, as in Berlin. *Maybe* the American nuclear commitment is not as firm as it seems—but what sane Soviet leader wants to put the whole Soviet society in the scales to find out?

It is also important to distinguish the nuclear sufficiency of the super-powers from the very different level of deterrent strength which has been sought by such a leader as General de Gaulle. French theorists have some-times argued as if a very small number of thermonuclear weapons would be a sure and permanent deterrent. Most American analysts, in my view cor-rectly, have been skeptical of this thesis. The armaments of the middle-level nuclear powers are indeed vulnerable to an obliterating first strike, and that situation may not entirely disappear even if they shift to seaborne missiles. But several orders of magnitude, and as many orders of complexity, separate the difficulties of an attack on such a force from those of a preëmptive attack on either the Soviet Union or the United States. The nuclear sufficiency of the superpowers is as far removed from the deterrent capacity of the *force de frappe* as the Great Pyramid from a molehill.

II

At this point in the analysis our effort to move from technology to politics may seem encouraging, but now we must take account of a much less cheer-ful aspect of the matter. The politics of the analysis so far is the politics of international relations—of what one state or another will actually do on the world stage. This analysis points plainly to the advantages of limiting the strategic arms race, since it tells us that the existing parity between the super-powers is all that they can hope to use internationally, and since no one in any society wants to pay tens of billions for nothing.

Unfortunately we have not exhausted the politics of strategic weapons. Along with this crude but powerful international politics of common sense goes the politics of consensus and consent within each superpower. Presi-dents and Politburos may know in their hearts that the only thing they want from strategic weapons is never to have to use them; in their public postures they have felt it necessary to claim more. They may not themselves be per-suaded by the refined calculations of the nuclear gamesmen—but they do not find it prudent to expose them for the political irrelevance they are. The public in both countries has been allowed by its leaders to believe that some-where in ever-growing strength there is safety, and that it still means something to be "ahead." The politics of internal decision-making has not been squared with the reality of international stalemate.

In consequence, the internal politics of the strategic arms race has remained the prisoner of its technology. The ABM debate showed a shift from an earlier emphasis on American "superiority" toward the question whether somehow now the Russians might move "ahead"—but there were only a few voices raised to support the notion that within very broad limits no one now can have a lead worth having. That may be the necessary premise of international political behavior; it is not yet the possible premise of national political debate. Internally, in both countries, the present premise of the debate leads remorselessly toward escalation. In both countries, moreover, this framework of argument is powerfully sustained by the force which Americans have been taught to call "the military-industrial complex." Since the opponents of escalation refuse to contest the basic political premise, they are driven back to technology; those who oppose the ABM tend to argue that it may not work technically—not that it is irrelevant politically. And while excellent answers were made to the Pentagon suggestion that the Russians might be "going for a first strike," there were few to suggest that the necssary assumption of any such scenario must be that the Soviet Government had gone suicidally mad.

What appears in our ABM debate appears also in Soviet behavior. The Russians continue to spend much too much money on large weapons which do them no good and whose only real effect is to frighten us into further efforts of our own. We can afford it better than they can, of course, and in terms of economic cold warfare there has always been a certain spurious attractiveness about trapping the Russians into a constantly accelerating competition. Fortunately, that particular brand of nonsense has never been anyone's official policy, and the tenor of the ABM debate suggests that it may be permanently out of fashion. But the fact that we are not trying to induce this sort of Soviet folly does not make it less real, or less foolish. In every international crisis of the last fifteen years Soviet leaders have shown their understanding that the strategic balance requires mutual restraint between the superpowers. But in their weapons decisions they have been as heedlessly and unproductively excessive as we.

There is a curious and distressing paradox in all this. The same political leaders who know these terrible weapons must never be used and who do not run the foolish risks of nuclear gamesmanship abroad still do not hesitate to authorize system after system. The usual resolution of the paradox is to describe the decision to build as an "insurance policy." But the argument is unsatisfying; the gap between what the political leader orders and what he can do with it is too great. I know of no escape from the conclusion that both in his sensible abhorrence of nuclear conflict and his persistent attachment to still more weapons systems the political leader is reflecting his constituency. The fault is less in our leaders than in ourselves.

19. The Uncertain Strategic Balance in the 1970's

WILLIAM R. KINTNER[*]

Strategic Posture and Perceptions

Any strategic arms control agreement must be founded upon an analysis of strategic arms balance and the nature of security within that relationship. Although strategic conceptions of security in the nuclear age have evolved from "The Balance of Terror" and "Superiority" to "sufficiency" and "parity," these phrases are worth re-examining in the light of The Deterrence of Uncertainty. The Balance of Terror, for instance, an illustrious memoir of Sir Winston Churchill, expressed the essence of nuclear deterrence. Neither hand will squeeze the trigger because of *fear*, the *fear* of retaliatory consequences. What sustains this fear? First, the known destructive efficiency of the hydrogen bomb; second, the uncertainty inherent in the technology of strategic systems. This uncertainty has two edges: first, the uncertain reliability of one's own delivery system and that of the enemy; second, the possibility that sudden innovation might render one's current weapon systems obsolete.

Since 1945, the development of explosives has gone through one "revolution" of efficiency: first fission weapons, then fusion weapons. Each successive step has been accompanied by increased efficiencies that have resulted in improved yield to weight ratio, reduced size, increase in enhanced ra-

*I am indebted to Harvey Sicherman for his assistance in the preparation of this paper.

diation effects, i.e., EMP. Delivery systems have evolved in efficiency and sophistication as well: just as the long-range, intercontinental jet bomber became available in 1954–58, the intercontinental rocket appeared. The ICBM and its shorter range cousins, the IRBM/MRBM/SLBM, have, over the years, become more accurate, reliable, survivable, and complex. The use of solid fuel has made the booster much simpler, but the need for decoys, electronic hardening, MIRVS, chaff, etc., has made the front end more complicated. Manned aircraft have also become more complex, i.e. V/STOL requirements, heavier payload, ECM–ECCM equipment, avionic requirements, lower flight profile requirements, speed, and swing-wing. Despite the improvement in delivery systems, they are very complicated systems requiring high degrees of maintenance, are susceptible to component reliability problems, and can be affected many ways by the environment they operate in or may have to operate in. At the time of the Cuban missile crisis, for instance, Minutemen vehicles supposedly capable of launching despite the debris created by a first-strike against their emplacements, were hampered by snow on silo covers.[1] More recently, during the course of the ABM dispute, Congress was astonished when various analysts stood forth to decry the incapacity and erratic action of various components, *especially the key electronic guidance systems,* in order to demonstrate that the ABM system could not work or could not work reliably.[2]

For these reasons, the arms race may be seen as a constant attempt to research and deploy the possibly unreliable to meet the probably uncertain. In reviewing this cycle, Dr. Herbert F. York, one of President Eisenhower's scientific advisors, expressed the practical sentiment: "We err on safety's side."[3] Thus, if one side or the other sees an innovation or numerical increase on the part of the other, it responds in the form of an imitation, some novel development, or offers to discuss arms limitations because: "What *if* their system really *does* work?"

This interchange has become inextricably mixed with the "targeting" and "rate of fire" controversy. Targeting is essentially the question: shall we hit enemy cities (countervalue) or enemy weaponry (counterforce)? Simple logic reveals that an aggressor, if he seeks to secure his victory, will aim to destroy his victim's retaliatory capacity: counterforce. The victim or "defender," in turn, must retaliate upon his assailant's cities, since there is no point in blasting empty silos. "Rate of fire" implies either "massive retaliation," firing the entire arsenal nearly at once, or selective release of salvos. The game theorists, as you might expect, have had a field day here.[4] But no satisfactory

1. *Science and Technology,* October 1968.
2. Cf. Congressional Record, February 7, 1969, S.1450. A report by the Budget Bureau. See also Dr. Wohlstetter's testimony and the articles by Licklider and Rodberg in *ABM: An Evaluation,* by Chayes and Wiesner, 1969.
3. *Scientific American,* August 1969.
4. "Debate over Missile Strategy," *ORBIS,* Winter 1968.

strategic doctrine and corresponding command and control system for an optimally mixed strategy have been devised.

The crunch in these disputes lies in perceptions of the opposing strategic "posture." Because of the doubts we have explored before, to "err on safety's side" in maintaining a countercity, second-strike capacity might appear to one's opponent a counterforce, first-strike capability. A first-strike posture really means ability to survive a nuclear exchange, either because you can "limit damage" by civil defense or by smashing most of your enemy's weapons. Herman Kahn argues such a posture is necessary to make even a second-strike capacity credible.[5] Otherwise, the aggressive party can operate freely on bluster, since governments are usually rather adept at discovering reasons not to commit suicide.

The McNamara Parity Gamble

What we have then, is an arms race inspired by the uncertain delivery of efficient weapons, whose postures designed on safety's side resemble first-strike capacity. This "rhythm" or "cycle" appalled Mr. Robert McNamara, who thereupon embarked on the boldest arms control path hitherto devised. He sought to reach some "balance" of security, that is, some point where both powers would not feel anxious about the other's posture with a *minimum* of inspection or artificial tinkering. By erecting two concepts, Assured Destruction Capacity and Damage Limitation, McNamara sought to establish some *certainty* as a foundation for security. Assured Destruction Capacity merely means a countercity force comprising "the small, absolute number of unsophisticated (but hardened or mobile) missiles"[6] necessary to destroy that level of population and industrial percentage deemed fatal to modern society.[7] McNamara defined "an unacceptable degree of damage" in rough percentages:

> In the case of the Soviet Union, I would judge that a capability on our part to destroy, say one fifth to one fourth of her population [i.e., about 50 million Russians] and one half of her industrial capacity would serve as an effective deterrent.

Damage Limiting Capacity is that mixture of civil or missile defense and first-strike capacity that enables a modern society to survive a nuclear war. If both sides possessed the "minimum deterrent," that is, if they developed an unmistakable second-strike capacity, why seek damage-limiting "overkill" postures that sustain the arms race? Thus, tacit arms control could be achieved on the basis of "parity" or "equality."

5. See Herman Kahn, *On Thermonuclear War*, which makes this central point: of the two first-strike postures, civil defense is less provocative than massed weaponry.
6. *ORBIS*, Winter 1968, p. 1145.
7. See McNamara's Posture Statement, FY1968.

Four developments undermined Mr. McNamara's plan. First, and almost inescapably, no artificial technological plateau could be created. Thus, defensive measures (like an ABM) could introduce uncertainty into Assured Destruction and "look like" a key part of first-strike capacity.

Second, various electronic components continued their sporadic performance. For example, on the three occasions when Congressmen came to see Minutemen perform, our chief deterrent rockets malfunctioned.[8] Further, perhaps because of this failure, no precise warhead figure ever emerged as the destructive minimum. Dr. Fink, former Deputy Director of Defense Research and Engineering, wrote an article in which he frankly discussed a number of estimates (with the usual show of statistical wizardry) and spoke about 150 megaton bombs "optimally" delivered, destroying two thirds of Soviet industry—but 400 bombs required for a population fatality of 30 percent.[9] According to Dr. Fink's calculation of wastage rates, between 1,100 and 2,200 weapons and their delivery vehicles should be required to assure the 150 to 400 megatons of minimal deterrence. The rub in this reasoning may be seen if we imagine both powers scaled to the magic figure of 1,100. Supposing one side then begins deploying new vehicles. The other side should sit supinely until the number approached 2,200. But might not an offensive missile deployment program portend a first-strike capacity, since the long lead-time required for the more passive competitor to reach 2,200 could give crucial advantage to the opponent? In other words, the spread of 100 percent is so broad, first-strike posturing is not eliminated. Yet it might be argued that the 1,100 to 2,200 range is really unimportant since the key quantity is 150 to 400 *deliverable* megatons—and vehicles can be built to ensure their delivery despite a competitor's program. Yet, how do these approaches differ from the arms race which "minimum deterrence" was supposed to curtail? Thus, the notion of a destructive minimum is prey to the very psychological uncertainty it supposedly replaces.

Third, the doctrine of "superiority" remained potent if unproved.[10] "Superiority" has two facets. First, there is physical superiority: more weapons or higher quality. Second, there is psychological superiority. One can feel morally superior in a second-strike capacity. One can also feel superior in virtue at not exercising a first-strike capacity. (The United States probably had one during the Cuban affair.) For the Western powers, who find "aggression" or "first-strike" strategies unethical, this moral superiority is most important. But if the most secure physical and psychological superiority re-

8. *Op. cit.* See Licklider. Missiles through testing exhibit a 50–70 percent reliability; site installation and time lessen this further.

9. Cf. *Science and Technology*, October 1968, p. 63.

10. Arguments over our superiority in the Cuban Missile Crisis continue. See *War/Peace Report*, December 1968. Robert F. Kennedy's *Thirteen Days* mentions no "superiority" discussions at all. In 1964, McGeorge Bundy was sure "nuclear superiority" had made the difference. In 1969, McGeorge Bundy reversed himself: superiority meant nothing. *Foreign Affairs* is to be commended for printing self-contradictory authors.

sides in first-strike capacity, *even if never exercised,* no statesman—whatever his views concerning the likelihood of nuclear war—can be expected to ignore the possibility of a sudden superiority, especially since everyone's faith, hope, and money is tied up in the "miraculous breakthroughs" we have come to expect from R&D.

When we speak of "sudden," "momentary" or "miraculous" regarding superiority and R&D, we exaggerate for educational purposes. The momentary advantage, in a planner's mind, may be no more than a projection based on a forecast based on an assumption of a possible or probable threat some years hence. A recent article (September 25) in the Soviet Defense Ministry newspaper expressed the same thought:

> Special attention here should be given to [Vladimir Lenin's] words "may possess." These mean that an estimation of the military, economic and scientific potential of a probable enemy must be made after close examination of both the situation that exists and the real prospects that shape up.[11]

The "real prospects" are always over five or ten years. These "posture analyses" or "threat forecasts" and the impressions they produce on both sides concern us primarily.

The arms race at its core is really a lead-time race: the installation and perfection of the possibly unreliable innovation before the other chap does the same. Superiority has become a function of momentary advantage. "Parity" has become a function of oscillating estimates.

Fourth, for McNamara's "parity" concept to work, both American and Soviet planners should have to agree that this "momentary advantage" is either impossible to attain or too momentary for first-strike considerations. As Harold Brown, former Secretary of the Air Force and a leading member of the U.S. Arms Control delegation has noted, parity as an idea fixée requires (in the words of the *New York Times,* October 27, 1969): "a conscious rejection by both sides of any appetite for a first strike." If "superiority" in the arms race is impossible physically or psychologically, the armed racers must recognize the futility of it all.

There is no evidence now that Soviet strategists believe in either physical or psychological "parity." Mr. William Lee (Program Manager of the Threat Analysis Studies of the Strategic Studies Center, Stanford Research Institute), summarized the trend in June 1969:

> The Soviets . . . have continued to stress the role of defense and damage limiting rather than moving toward the assured destruction strategy.[12]

11. The *New York Times,* Monday, October 27, 1969, p. 18.
12. William R. Kintner (ed.) *Safeguard: Why the ABM Makes Sense* (New York: Hawthorn Press, 1969), p. 177.

As we said before: while damage limiting capacity through defensive posture need not indicate a first-strike *intention*, it can confer a first-strike capability. American planning, therefore, on "safety's side," projects from capability rather than intention. The Soviet ABM, strenuously emphasized by Mr. Kosygin as a defensive measure, is a case in point.

This disturbing feature of the technological competition between the superpowers cannot be wished away, even if one agrees with McGeorge Bundy's assertion:

> In sane politics, therefore, there is no level of superiority which will make a strategic first strike between the two great states anything but an act of utter folly.[13]

There is inconclusive evidence, however, that the Soviet political leadership fully agrees with McGeorge Bundy. If we think about the Soviet experience of surprise attack from Germany in 1941, their oft-proclaimed fear of NATO as a vehicle for "German Revanchism," and whatever malice they believe animates "capitalism's" foreign policy,[14] we can understand recent Soviet articles on strategic doctrine that exalt the defense and survival capacity of the country and neglect or refute the "perceptions" McNamara's doctrine requires. As Marshall Sokolovskii wrote:

> Present means of reconnaissance, detection, and surveillance can opportunely disclose a significant portion of the measures of direct preparation of a nuclear attack by the enemy and in the very first minutes locate a mass launch of missiles and takeoff of aircraft of the aggressor . . . plus the *possibilities exist not to allow a surprise attack of an aggressor; to deliver nuclear strikes on him at the right time. . . .*[15]

According to the Commander in Chief of the Navy, Admiral S. G. Gorchov:

> . . . great attention in the theory of waging contemporary war is now being given to the timely and reliable detection of signs of nuclear attack and one's own combat readiness to seize the strategic initiative.[16]

In short, the Soviets appear to believe that the incipient appearance of a first-strike intention can be throttled by a "preventive" strike and survival measures, which, in their turn, look to us like first-strike capabilities, if not intentions.

13. McGeorge Bundy, "To Cap the Volcano," *Foreign Affairs,* October 1969, p. 10.
14. Urie Bonfenbrenner's extremely interesting "pseudo-experiment," *Allowing for Soviet Perceptions,* sustains an ancient axiom: "Man uses his past to interpret his future."
15. Quoted in William R. Kintner (ed.) *Safeguard: Why the ABM Makes Sense* (New York: Hawthorn Press, 1969), p. 397.
16. *Op. cit., Safeguard,* p. 398.

This is precisely the situation Mr. McNamara aimed to alter. The epilogue to his efforts is the ABM and MIRV.

Technological Forecast and Arms Control Proposals

If an arms control agreement is to govern the arms race in this climate, it must inspire a sentiment of security, secure not only in a resolute second-strike capacity but also secure in elimination of first strike postures inspired by "safety's side" planning, thereby removing the R&D joker-of-the-pack, the lead-time superiority possibility.[17]

Let us now consider a prospectus of varied and interesting armaments innovations for the next decade. We can then evaluate arms control proposals in a proper context, the arms race potential through 1980.

Our forecast has been developed from various trade magazines and commentaries. Its forecasting method resembles the so-called Delphi technique, essentially a sampling of "expert" opinion. Since the experts are frequently self-proclaimed, and even more frequently Delphic in their conclusions, opinion often resembles the speech Julian Sorel perfected in Stendhal's *The Red and the Black:* "Remarks from which everything could be drawn, but nothing in particular."

The devices discussed are divided into four parts: (1) Warning and Surveillance, (2) Defense, (3) Offensive Strike, and (4) New Bombs, Et cetera. Although the curious logic of nuclear strategy often renders the defensive offensive, nonetheless the Oracles think at the moment that these particular devices can be clearly classified.

Lastly, we emphasize the belief of our sources in the practicality of the list for construction in the next decade. Indeed, the forecasting in the journals represents merely current "applied science" projects mixed with an engineer's imagination. We have therefore attached commentary on the political prospects, distinguishing between opinions gathered from the trade journals and our own opinions, deriving from a layman's puckish intuition.

I. WARNING AND SURVEILLANCE

Because of the great speed characterizing nuclear delivery systems, Warning and Surveillance remains a crucial area. Improvements loom in three directions:

1. SAMOS-type or all-purpose reconnaissance satellites. Satellites can now provide telephotos and "real-time" communications.[18] The SAMOS system, already operational, requires a minimum of nine units in orbit, or a dozen launches yearly, a reasonably expensive proposition. Better real-time devices are perfected which permit the units to remain useful for longer

17. This paper eschews discussion of the relationship between "war-winning" strategy and first-strike posture.
18. *Aviation Week and Space Technology,* September 16, 1969.

periods. One can anticipate a satellite system similar to this, but capable of seeing ICBM launches, test explosions, or even troop concentrations.[19]

2. To solve low-level penetration, presently so troublesome to radar units, an airborne collection of sensors, also capable of ocean surveys. New and much longer lived power units are already available (e.g., nuclear) but cost is still prohibitive.[20]

3. Laser rangefinders and satellite-coordinated early-warning systems essentially grafted upon the present hodge-podge arrangements, along with radar (multiphase) improvements necessary to make ABM work.[21]

Commentary. Educated opinion foresees items 1 and 2 as deployments towards the end of this period, with "technical grafts" (number 3) serving as interim substitutes. If, however, a serious arms control discussion occurs, our research establishment should fall heavily upon 1, which is a prerequisite to any reliable arms control agreement not providing local inspection. We must also stress that these devices are ever so much better at surveillance than warning. The great breakthrough to be expected is surveillance of current nuclear submarines.

II. DEFENSE

Defense developments fall into two types: passive (resistance to blasts, etc.) and active (missile interception). The devices below are already on the horizon.

1. ABM: A new computer, part of whose capacity must be used for self-checking, and phased-array radars resisting "black-out" by ionization from nuclear explosions remain chief items. Both of these improvements require engineering, not breakthroughs. If the test ban continues, the blast problem will probably not be solved with full confidence for either the defense or the offense.

2. BAMBI program and anti-satellite launch is essentially a space-launched ABM. But the satellites must make low orbits to be accurate, and that means—like SAMOS—a great number of them. This attractive approach is tremendously expensive, especially since the early-warning capacity vital to its operation as a primary defense does not appear possible.[22]

3. SABMIS or ABMIS: The Navy and Air Force ABM proposals have one tremendous advantage. They would intercept missiles *before* they reached our mainland, and *before* the missiles separated into penetration tactics or MIRV. These deployments, needing much less complicated computer work than the ABM, also have one tremendous disadvantage. For the Navy: the Soviet "threat tube" (most advantageous missile route) lies over the Polar

19. *Space/Aeronautics*, January 1969.
20. *Aviation Week and Space Technology*, June 2, July 7, 1969.
21. *Ibid.*, July 7, 1969.
22. *Space/Aeronautics*, January 1969.

icecaps or land areas, not the ocean. For the Air Force: maintenance cost for a useful system is incredible. The Navy may be permitted some SAMBIS deployment towards the end of the decade, when the Soviet "Polaris" fleet warrants some defense.[23]

III. STRIKE

Many new developments are within easy deployment possibility by 1980, most of them offensive responses to defense improvements.

1. Minuteman III, with MIRV (three warheads) attachment, features a greater payload than its predecessors. The present silos will require modification. Minuteman III deployment by 1975–1978 may be confidently expected.[24]

2. Sea-based missiles: the Poseidon, with twice the payload, up to 10 MIRV and 3000-mile range, is already being deployed. No new improvements in command/control are foreseen but a counter-surveillance breakthrough, in the form of eliminating all mechanical noise, is eagerly being sought by the Navy.[25]

There is some discussion of sea-bottom missiles, as a cost-effective addition for replacement, but the technical problems remain too formidable as yet. It should be noted that neither the Poseidon missiles nor any sea-based launcher have much capacity against "hard" ICBM sites. They are mostly "soft" (city) weapons.

3. SRAM project, a plane-launched rocket, primarily aimed at well-defended targets (hard) with a short range.[26]

4. Fluidics and the Ovshinsky device, both intended to replace transistors and thus make the guidance systems impervious to ionization. The fluidics can now be considered although they are applicable to very few missiles as yet. By using pneumatic or gaseous inertial guidance, missiles can be rid of their electrical components. Fluidics have been tested (spring 1967) but it should take until the end of the decade for them to be widely employed on present equipment—unless new equipment is designed around them.[27]

The experimental Ovshinsky device, substituting glass conductors for transistors, offers a similar advantage. The "glassy state" stands at a threshold: Ovshinsky's conductor, however, has defied quality control. Reliable development cannot be predicted by the experts. A reasonable gamble would be that either fluidics or glass will eliminate the ionization problem for guidance systems by 1980.[28]

23. *Ibid.* The Sentinel/Safeguard command is currently letting a contract to study and develop possibilities. See *Commerce Business Daily*, R&D Sources Sought, September 17, 1969.
24. *Aviation Week and Space Technology*, May 12, 1969.
25. *Undersea Technology*, November–December, 1968.
26. *Space/Aeronautics*, September/October 1968.
27. *Ibid.*, July 1969.
28. *New Scientist*, November 21, 1968.

5. Common computer for guidance and control, a digital computer break-through expected by middle 1970's, "will reduce by as much as 16 percent" the probable launch failures, according to *Space/Aeronautics* (July 1968). Combined with cybernetic work at equipping these missiles with some self-adaptive capacity ("artificial neurons" patterned after the human brain and designed to respond to program impulses previously simulated), the ICBM of 1980 will be a much more reliable and flexible unit *compared to what we have now.* If the computer/cybernetic improvements occur, an ICBM could double as an ABM interceptor, which would upset considerably all previous offense/defense calculations. This is likely, and a good example of what the forecasters call "synergy," a coalescing of advances into a revolutionary combination.

6. AMSA, the Air Force's new bomber, features a nuclear SRAM capacity or carriage of 100,000 lbs. conventional iron. Designed for swing-wing take-off in less than 6,000 feet, with a Mach 2.5 capacity, the AMSA would be ready by 1978. The Air Force and the aeronautics industry have mustered enough persuasion to get this plane and its SST relative financed, but by the time it flies defensive counters will render it extremely expensive for the additional strike capacity AMSA offers.[29]

7. Multi- or fractional-orbit bombardment systems (FOBS) are chiefly surprise vehicles whose control and accuracy improvement will not be worth-while during the next decade. The Soviet FOBS, though probably in deployment, is more the joker-in-the-pack than an accurate payload; the BMEW, in conjunction with surveillance satellites, locates them rather easily (John Foster, *DDR&E*, February 1968).[30]

8. Various improvements to jet interceptor capacity include laser range-finders (already on the French navy version of the British-French Jaguar) and new, composite material combinations.[31] Materials science is another area about to burst with possibilities. Most promising is the carbon-boron fibre series, whose most advanced form remains a British (Rolls Royce) property. By the decade's conclusion, these fibres should realize projections like those made, for instance, on a Convair F-106; a weight savings of nearly a ton over past materials. War planes by 1980 should be substantially lighter and therefore more potent.[32]

IV. NEW BOMBS AND OTHER WEAPONS

Since 1960, when ICBM's full of H-bombs became the chief deterrent, various new or improved bombs have been discussed as successors to hydrogen weapons.

1. The neutron bomb, or clean bomb, setting off a fusion explosion without a fission reaction to start it, has long been under consideration. There is little

29. *Aviation Week and Space Technology*, May 12, 1969.
30. *Astronautics/Aeronautics*, February 1968.
31. *Aviation Week and Space Technology*, June 2, 1969.
32. *Ibid.*, mid-December 1968; *Space/Aeronautics*, July 1969.

support, however, for a "crash program" that could probably produce a neutron bomb by 1980.[33]

2. A more likely prospect is use of the laser for a fusion reaction, particularly for nuclear power. The laser apparatus as yet remains too heavy and cumbersome and the laser itself is not now sufficiently powerful for weapons.[34]

3. Chemical-biological warfare is little discussed in the trade literature despite a growing public flap. These weapons have a dark and mysterious history; poisons and antidotes seem to be without number. But they all lack proper testing, safe control after release, and a clear purpose. They have been developed since the end of World War I "because others have them"; they are still the darlings of some chemists and biochemists. They will remain highly dubious, except for "defoliation" and low-level violence situations. By 1980, one can expect more of the same, a curious case where the development of the unknown produces more of the unknown.

In summary, then, over the next decade both the offense and the defense will remain subjected to complicated uncertainty in both reliability and innovation. Will this uncertainty syndrome permit the creation of a second-strike capability without the appearance of first-strike posture? How will uncertainty affect the various proposals being suggested for negotiations at the forthcoming SALT talks?

One such proposal, and a popular one, is the "freeze": an agreement to cease deployment of a specific weapon or a category of weapons. This arrangement boasts the virtue of minimal inspection; presumably the same spy devices and satellites currently gathering intelligence would continue their clever surveillance. Let us consider three cases of freeze.

1. Both parties merely agree to halt construction of silo-ICBMs. This could certainly fulfill the concept of an artificial, mutually agreed upon, assured destruction countercity capacity. If both sides deployed MIRVs they should merely maintain their capacities on a higher numerical level of deliverable weapons. Differing nose cone capacity might favor the side possessing the bigger rockets when the agreement went into effect, but presumably some balance could be struck.

Would this agreement forestall the first-strike counterforce race deriving from uncertain innovation? Obviously not. The full weight of R&D might then fall profitably upon some of the devices sketched in the technical prospectus. We discount the "miracle weapon"—a single discovery or development conferring decisive advantage, but a combination of related improvements could be easily conceived. Missile defense and detection—

33. *New Scientist*, November 21, 1968; *Foreign Affairs*, January 1960.
34. *New Scientist*, November 21 & 28; *Foreign Affairs*, April 1960. See the *New York Times*, Friday, September 19, 1969, for latest developments; the French are especially interested.

SABMIS, ABMIS, and location of submarines before "silent" engines are perfected—would provide one side or the other with a significant, even if transient, advantage so that the enemy's countercity weapons might then be largely negated. Thus, defensive and detection measures, on the *short* term, with a single extra silo ICBM or even a single extra Polaris, can develop a first-strike posture.

2. In a more comprehensive "freeze" no MIRVs, new silos, ABM improvements, or "silent" submarines would be permitted. Let us also assume that both sides keep their bargain, even though MIRVs cannot be checked by satellite.

Both sides will still retain formidable strategic forces. Under the circumstances, suppose the guidance systems of the re-entry vehicles could be made impervious to radiation disturbance. A counterforce strike following a precursor attack on the opponent's defense radars might then become feasible enough to destabilize the agreement.

COUNTERFORCE: UNTHINKABLE BUT UNSINKABLE

There is an obvious anomaly in insisting upon an arms control whose basis is a security of countercity (assured destruction) capacity when technical advances *not* violating such an agreement might still create a momentary, and perhaps politically exploitable, first-strike (counterforce) superiority. Could either power resist attempting the surprise demoralization of its enemy in a contrived, or even unanticipated, test of strength? This is not to suggest that either power will be confident or certain enough to risk such maneuvers. But the fear arising from this possibility is real and this fear fuels feverish competition. Thus, an arms agreement fixing countercity ratios will not necessarily eliminate either the dangers or the expense of an arms race.

The written "freeze" type arms control although not justifiable on technical grounds alone may be rationalized differently. There are more ways to security than the securing of arms. Could not a written agreement to "cease and desist" be regarded as an indication of lessened suspicion between the great powers? In short, a treaty symbolizing their willingness to risk some security at each other's hands would support an entire subsequent series of discussions whose linkage might then spin an international web of reconciliation.[35] This thesis, which we may call "the demonstration theory" from an arms control angle, and "the linkage theory" from a diplomatic angle, has considerable support. The theory is no youngster: the Franck Report of 1945 opined that control of nuclear weapons was the chief obstacle to world cooperation and reconciliation. The theory is also no neophyte: the Baruch proposal and American arms control and disarmament policy have frequently reflected the premise. Indeed, one can view Mr. McNamara's parity defense plans as a "demonstration theory" without a treaty.

35. See, for example, Jeremy J. Stone, *Containing the Arms Race, Some Specific Proposals*. Foreword by Jerome B. Wiesner, MIT Press, 1966.

We have a partial nuclear test ban treaty, a treaty banning nuclear weapons from outer space, a nuclear Non-Proliferation Treaty awaiting ratification, a new proposal to ban nuclear weapons from the sea bed, and extremely patient negotiators at Geneva. We are told a bilateral nuclear "SALT" (Strategic Arms Limitations Talks) conference is "forthcoming." These treaties and proposals can or should reduce atmospheric pollution while engendering a certain air of political expectancy. But a very elaborate chain of cause and effect should have to be forged before anyone could produce proof that these "demonstration" nuclear security treaties have had "reconciling security linkages." Mr. Laurence W. Beilenson, a prominent lawyer, summarized international experience since 1661 with security treaties:

A nation should give little or no weight to the expectation of performance. . . .[36]

Apparently, the Soviet Union and the Western states do have an easy parity here:

In observance and breach . . . the USSR has merely equalled the pattern of the West.[37]

In fact, treaty observance has followed individual interest rather than mutual obligation.

These rude facts apply equally to various schemes like "war control" with the United Nations as monitor of arms races, or international scientific education as the required mental change preceding physical change. The United Nations cannot act if the superpowers will not agree beforehand; the superpowers then hardly need the complications of the United Nations. "International science" as a political agency has produced Pugwash; otherwise, the astonishing fact of the Atomic Age is the "nationalization" of science and the scientists.

If the strategic arms race and its modernization has become the premier world political problem, then it must be solved by a supreme act of political reconciliation. Otherwise, arms control remains problematical because any "frozen plateau" may be undone by technological innovations; and with it the whole train of subsequent agreements. What then, are the prospects for arms control?

ARMED COMPETITION, ARMS CONTROL, AND INTERNATIONAL POLITICS

In an article in *Foreign Affairs*,[38] McGeorge Bundy denounces the arms race as "irrelevant." He maintains that "superiority" postures are too temporary

36. Laurence W. Beilenson, *The Treaty Trap*, (Public Affairs Press, 1969), p. 212.
37. *Ibid.*, p. 190.
38. McGeorge Bundy, "To Cap the Volcano, *Foreign Affairs*, October 1969.

for action, and that deterrence through the next decade may be assumed. Believing that superiority is both wrong and meaningless, Mr. Bundy, like many commentators, would like to ignore the technological component of the race. Deterrence arising from uncertainty and efficiency has as its price an enormous and expensive research and development competition. If the motivational engine of the race is possible "superiority," the physical engine of the race is dynamic technology. If we are to abandon the Deterrence of Uncertainty to gain Deterrence of Certainty, we must understand both aspects.

Let us jettison momentarily both "freeze" and "treaty" notions, and omit the premise that nuclear arms control "demonstrates" favorable "linkages" for non-nuclear problems. How can we assure security without technological competition? Liddell-Hart wrote:

To sterilize offensive potency is to sterilize war itself.[39]

Both the posture and the capacity inspiring that offensive posture are products of research and development. This process has essentially three parts: (1) pure research, (2) applied research, and (3) development. Development includes testing of prototypes, which involves pilot plants but is shy of mass replication or deployment.

Mr. Bundy tells us "the slim progress we have made in the last twenty years has been possible only when we have skirted the issue of agreed international inspection."[40] Inspection is only a means of "knowing." If knowledge is the antidote to uncertainty and consequently the prerequisite for security, how much of each other's research and development must the competitors know to suspend their competition? A good case can be made that knowledge of pure science and deployment is possible through scientific exchange and satellites, without "agreed international inspection." But the crucial intermediate stages, applied research (research undertaken to solve a specific problem) and development (a workable prototype of the applied solution of the problem) are perforce state secrets. If these stages were inspected the uncertainty and postures problem would be resolved decisively. Then the "race" could cease at an agreed parity, in tacit or written form.

Such an agreement might become the linkage auguring a new era of international harmony. But the knowledge sustaining that agreement requires at least two states (the United States and the USSR) initially, and at least three states (the United Kingdom, France, and China) later on to renounce whatever advantages they imagine their sovereign strategic military establishments can supply besides "deterrence." In other words, the nuclear powers would have to embrace general nuclear "parity" as a political—not only a military—concept and ratify it openly.

39. B.H. Liddell-Hart, *The Defense of the West* (New York: Wm. Morrow & Co., 1950), p. 307.
40. *Ibid.*

The requisite inspection and knowledge is unlikely, probably because no competitor ever dismisses a chance for advantage, especially a military advantage that can be "linked" to a political advantage. Further, given the "spin-off" connections between military and commercial enterprise, inspection involves more than mere military consequence. In absence of effective treaty or technological freezes, the decade ahead resembles the decade past; an arms race sustained by "safety's side" research and development, strengthened by ignorance and suspicion.

We have sketched a gloomy portrait. The strategic balance depends upon the terrible efficiency of the atomic weapon and the uncertainty of innovation and performance of its delivery systems. Arms control or disarmament arrangements can be effective only if they replace the Balance of Uncertainty, whose price is an arms race, with the Balance of Certainty, whose price is secure knowledge of another power's research and development programs. Short of this antidote, none of the nuclear powers can be expected to complement a numerical freeze with a research freeze as an act of faith that the others will also "cease and desist." To do so alone would lay a strategic arsenal open to obsolescence. By the time one government discovered or assured itself that its quantitative and qualitative freeze had *not* been reciprocated qualitatively, it should be too laggard in lead-time to recoup previous parity.

If the arguments be accurate that a numerical freeze alone would *not* eliminate the R&D inspired arms race, and a unilateral numerical and research freeze would mean inferiority, not parity, has the taxpayer any hope of respite? The economics of strategic arms offer prospects of tacit moderation in arsenal innovations. Research, development, and deployment have become so complicated, so extensive, and so expensive that even the United States with its gigantic economy finds future strategic choices seriously foreclosed. Since deployment is by far the most costly part of the process,[41] we can expect a more judicious and cautious willingness to buy the operational gadgets of the future. An arms control agreement, again either tacit or written, far from being either demonstration or linkage, may be thought of as merely mutual recognition of technological rapacity. To guard interests, planners seek options; their range of options in the future will keep flexible only if deployment follows less hastily from development projections. This should also reduce "uncertain" performance while maintaining the uncertainty of innovations supporting deterrence.

Hesitant deployment bred by financial stringency finds good company in the confused advice now being lavished upon governments. Strategic bewilderment, evident in attempts to halt an arms race, essentially counterforce, by arranging a "parity," essentially countercity, has a valuable quality

---

41. We speak of the United States and the USSR, who benefit from economics of scale. For the British or French—and the Chinese—the R&D is by far the more expensive part of the process because of the few units finally deployed.

frequently overlooked. For the problems have so many sides, and compre-hending the sides requires such an open mind, that the analyst lays himself open to the inspired remark of Mr. George Bernard Shaw: "The open mind never acts." Perhaps world peace depends upon the minimum deterrence provided by the paralyzing advice of a few, open-minded, many-sided counsellors: arms control will thus depend upon the strategic placement of key intellectuals in the high council of both sides, personages the universi-ties are doubtless both willing and able to supply. The basic or minimum number is two advisors; that is, three opinions: "yes," "no," and, "well, there are advantages to both sides and I'll tell the best choice in a lengthy report next month!" Thus, "overkill" may evaporate through "overtalk."

If we alone, however, decide to 'complement a numerical weapons freeze with a research and development freeze, the arms race sustaining the balance will end in short order as our forces become obsolete—specifically when some of the technical developments we have previously sketched are de-ployed by the Soviet Union. While nervous or "anxious" parity deters uncertainty, supine technical inferiority deters only the inferior. We should then be in dire straits, unless the Soviet government fails to capitalize upon its technical advantage. There is no reason why the Soviet government should be so helpful unless a radical change in the behavior of nations has stolen upon us unnoticed. It would be tantamount to faith without knowledge if one side announced a numerical and qualitative freeze without reciprocity.

The strategic arms situation for the next decade can now be summarized. Strategic arms competition between the United States and the Soviet Union will continue unless strategic arms become superfluous because the super-powers accept a system of mutual inspection for verifying an agreement to end secret R&D of strategic weapons. This blessed situation is unlikely of attainment during the next decade.

We cannot imagine a unilateral U.S. withdrawal from R&D competition as either a prudent or profitable course, for if the United States freezes its nuclear forces to a static technology, their political utility will disappear. NATO's military strategy, for instance, relying upon obsolete nuclear forces to redress a conventional disadvantage, will open the Alliance to strategic paralysis. As Professor Blackett remarked about massive retaliation after Sputnik: "When official policy is to do the impossible, then nothing is done."

A technological research and development competition in strategic arms, with lessened operational deployment, will sustain "an anxious strategic parity" between the superpowers. Barring an unexpected, mutually inspected arms control agreement, this condition is likely to provide the safest path toward an ultimate future in which nuclear weapons will become com-pletely irrelevant to global politics.

Although the most likely situation is continued competition in strategic arms, it is possible to visualize a different form of competition than in the past. Given the financial burdens of deployment, the "anxious parity" we have detailed might be maintained by aggressive research and development strategies, one of whose purposes would be to decrease any gain from extensive deployments on both sides.

At the prototype stage, where a workable device virtually ready for mass replication *exists demonstrably*, testing could be used as a political demonstration, something like the old-time naval exercises with foreign observers invited. By revealing both technical and manufacturing capacity, one side might convince its competitors of the futility or obsolescence of their own striving for superiority.

In short, the uncertainty of innovation and operation could be diminished by knowledge, thus combating the insecure sentiments beneath "posture" analysis and long-range "threat" projections.

This approach has two great advantages. First, by exposing prototypes, both sides should have to exchange important information. Such an exchange represents a goodly step towards that mutual knowledge of R&D that constitutes a secure basis for general arms control agreements. The "prototype strategy" does this without requiring an unlikely trust to develop between the United States and the USSR, a trust at the heart of present approaches as characterized by the question: "Can the other side afford to halt its weapons development or deployment without running unacceptable risks?"[42]

In our scheme, each side can afford to halt its deployment by demonstrating that its developments can always maintain parity. And each side can do this without a roving corps of inspectors or lengthy interpretation of satellite observations.

Second, fully competitive military research and development has been a potent source of beneficial "spin-off" to industry in the United States and presumably also in the Soviet Union. Under the "prototype strategy" these benefits could continue unabated without the major construction and financial drain production entails.

In promoting this strategy, we speak only of the next decade. Ten years may be ample time for the superpowers to achieve the political reconciliation needed to end strategic arms competition. If not, revolutionary replacements for present strategic arms might be adopted by the same kind of necessity that forced navies to abandon wooden ships. Perhaps the treaty banning nuclear weapons from outer space will prevent this unwanted prospect.

Barring such extraordinary developments and an unexpected, mutually inspected arms control agreement, adoption by both sides of the "prototype strategy" may create conditions leading toward the eventual "quarantine" of nuclear weapons from international politics. In this circumstance, the influence of "the Bomb" upon the conventional courses of diplomacy will be greatly reduced.

42. The *New York Times*, October 26, 1969, p. 1.

20. Military Technology and National Security

HERBERT F. YORK

THE RECENT public hearings in the Senate and the House of Representatives on anti-ballistic-missile (ABM) systems have provided an unprecedented opportunity to expose to the people of this country and the world the inner workings of one of the dominant features of our time: the strategic arms race. Testimony has been given by a wide range of witnesses concerning the development and deployment of all kinds of offensive and defensive nuclear weapons; particular attention has been paid to the interaction between decisions in these matters and the dynamics of the arms race as a whole.

In my view the ABM issue is only a detail in a much larger problem: the feasibility of a purely technological approach to national security. What makes the ABM debate so important is that for the first time it has been possible to discuss a major aspect of this larger problem entirely in public. The reason for this is that nearly all the relevant facts about the proposed ABM systems either are already declassified or can easily be deduced from logical concepts that have never been classified. Thus it has been possible to consider in a particular case such questions as the following:

1. To what extent is the increasing complexity of modern weapons systems and the need for instant response causing strategic decision-making authority to pass from high political levels to low military-command levels, and from human beings to machines?

2. To what extent is the factor of secrecy combined with complexity leading to a steadily increasing dominance of military-oriented technicians in some vital areas of decision-making?

3. To what extent do increasing numbers of weapons and increasing complexity—in and of themselves—complicate and accelerate the arms race?

My own conclusion is that the ABM issue constitutes a particularly clear example of the futility of searching for technical solutions to what is essentially a political problem, namely the problem of national security. In support of this conclusion I propose in this article to review the recent history of the strategic arms race, to evaluate what the recent hearings and other public discussions have revealed about its present status and future prospects, and then to suggest what might be done now to deal with the problem of national security in a more rational manner.

The strategic arms race in its present form is a comparatively recent phenomenon. It began in the early 1950's, when it became evident that the state of the art in nuclear weaponry, rocket propulsion and missile guidance and control had reached the point in the U.S. where a strategically useful intercontinental ballistic missile (ICBM) could be built. At about the same time the fact that a major long-range-missile development program was in progress in the U.S.S.R. was confirmed. As a result of the confluence of these two events the tremendous U.S. long-range-missile program, which dominated the technological scene for more than a decade, was undertaken. The Air Force's Thor, Atlas and Titan programs and the Army's Jupiter program were started almost simultaneously; the Navy's Polaris program and the Air Force's Minuteman program were phased in just a few years later.

More or less at the same time the Army, which had had the responsibility for ground-based air defense (including the Nike Ajax and Nike Hercules surface-to-air missiles, or SAM's), began to study the problem of how to intercept ICBM's, and soon afterward initiated the Nike Zeus program. This program was a straightforward attempt to use existing technology in the design of a nuclear-armed rocket for the purpose of intercepting an uncomplicated incoming warhead. The Air Force proposed more exotic solutions to the missile-defense problem, but these were subsequently absorbed into the Defender Program of the Department of Defense's Advanced Research Projects Agency (ARPA). The Defender Program included the study of designs more advanced than Nike Zeus, and it also incorporated a program of down-range measurements designed to find out what did in fact go on during the terminal phases of missile flight.

By 1960 indications that the Russians were taking the ABM prospect seriously, in addition to progress in our own Nike Zeus program, stimulated our offensive-missile designers into seriously studying the problem of how to penetrate missile defenses. Very quickly a host of "penetration aid" concepts came to light: light and heavy decoys, including balloons, tank fragments and objects resembling children's jacks; electronic countermeasures, including radar-reflecting clouds of the small wires called chaff; radar blackout by means of high-altitude nuclear explosions; tactics such as barrage, local exhaustion and "rollback" of the defense, and, most important insofar as the then unforeseen consequences were concerned, the notion of putting more than one warhead on one launch vehicle. At first this notion simply involved a "shotgun" technique, good only against large-area targets (cities), but it soon developed into what we now call MIRV's (multiple independently targeted reentry vehicles), which can in principle (and soon in practice) be used against smaller, harder targets such as missile silos, radars and command centers.

This avalanche of concepts forced the ABM designers to go back to the drawing board, and as a result the Nike-X concept was born in 1962. The Nike-X designers attempted to make use of more sophisticated and up-to-date technology in the design of a system that they hoped might be able to cope with a large, sophisticated attack. All through the mid-1960's a vigorous battle of defensive concepts and designs versus offensive concepts and designs took place. This battle was waged partly on the Pacific Missile Range but mostly on paper and in committee meetings. It took place generally in secret, although parts of it have been discussed in earlier articles in this magazine [see "National Security and the Nuclear-Test Ban," by Jerome B. Wiesner and Herbert F. York, October, 1964; "Anti-Ballistic-Missile Systems," by Richard L. Garwin and Hans A. Bethe, March, 1968; "The Dynamics of the Arms Race," by George W. Rathjens, April, 1969].

This intellectual battle culminated in a meeting that took place in the White House in January, 1967. In addition to President Johnson, Secretary of Defense Robert S. McNamara and the Joint Chiefs of Staff there were present all past and current Special Assistants to the President for Science and Technology (James R. Killian, Jr., George B. Kistiakowsky, Jerome B. Wiesner and Donald F. Hornig) and all past and current Directors of Defense Research and Engineering (Harold Brown, John S. Foster, Jr., and myself). We were asked that simple kind of question which must be answered after all the complicated ifs, ands and buts have been discussed: "Will it work?" The answer was no, and there was no dissent from that answer. The context, of course, was the Russian threat as it was then interpreted and forecast, and the current and projected state of our own ABM technology.

Later that year Secretary McNamara gave his famous San Francisco speech in which he reiterated his belief that we could not build an ABM system capable of protecting us from destruction in the event of a Russian attack. For the first time, however, he stated that he did believe we could build an ABM system able to cope with a hypothetical Chinese missile attack, which by definition would be "light" and uncomplicated. In recommending that we go ahead with a program to build what came to be known as the Sentinel system, he said that "there are *marginal* grounds for concluding that a light

deployment of U.S. ABM's against this possibility is prudent." A few sen-
tences later, however, he warned: "The danger in deploying this relatively
light and reliable Chinese-oriented ABM system is going to be that pressures
will develop to expand it into a heavy Soviet-oriented ABM system." The
record makes it clear that he was quite right in this prediction.

Meanwhile the U.S.S.R. was going ahead with its own ABM program. The
Russian program proceeded by fits and starts, and our understanding of it
was, as might be supposed in such a situation, even more erratic. It is now
generally agreed that the only ABM system the Russians have deployed is
an area defense around Moscow much like our old Nike Zeus system. It appears to have virtually no capability against our offense, and it has been, as
we shall see below, extremely counterproductive insofar as its goal of defending Moscow is concerned.

Development and deployment of offensive-weapons systems on both sides
progressed rapidly during the 1960's, but rather than discuss these historically
I shall go directly to the picture that the Administration has given of the
present status and future projection of such forces.

Data recently presented by the Department of Defense show that the U.S.
and the U.S.S.R. are about even in numbers of intercontinental missiles, and
that the U.S. is ahead in both long-range aircraft and submarines of the
Polaris type (*see illustration on page 375*). The small Russian missiles are
mostly what we call SS-11's, which were described in the hearings as being
roughly the equivalent of our Minutemen. The large Russian missile is what
we call the SS-9. Deputy Secretary of Defense David Packard characterized
its capability as one 20-megaton warhead or three five-megaton warheads.
Our own missiles are almost entirely the smaller Minutemen. There currently
remian only 54 of the larger Titans in our strategic forces. Not covered in the
table are "extras" such as the U.S.S.R.'s FOBS (fractional orbital bombardment system) and IRBM's (intermediate-range ballistic missiles), nor the
U.S.'s bombardment aircraft deployed on carriers and overseas bases in
Europe and elsewhere. There are, of course, many important details that do
not come out clearly in such a simple tabular presentation; these include
payload capacity, warhead yield, number of warheads per missile and, often
the most important, warhead accuracy.

In the area of defensive systems designed to cope with the offensive systems outlined above, both the U.S. and the U.S.S.R. have defenses against
bombers that would probably be adequate against a prolonged attack using
chemical explosives (where 10 percent attrition is enough) and almost certainly inadequate against a nuclear attack (where 10 percent penetration is
enough). In addition the U.S.S.R. has its ineffective ABM deployment around
Moscow, usually estimated as consisting of fewer than 100 antimissile
missiles.

What all these complicated details add up to can be expressed in a single
word: parity. This is clearly not numerical equality in the number of war-

heads or in the number of megatons or in the total "throw weight"; in fact, given different design approaches on the two sides, simultaneous equality in these three figures is entirely impossible. It is, rather, parity with respect to strategic objectives; that is, in each case these forces are easily sufficient for deterrence and entirely insufficient for a successful preemptive strike. In the jargon of strategic studies either side would retain, after a massive "first strike" by the other, a sufficiently large "assured destruction capability" against the other in order to deter such a first strike from being made.

There is much argument about exactly what it takes in the way of "assured destruction capability" in order to deter, but even the most conservative strategic planners conclude that the threat of only a few hundred warheads exploding over population and industrial centers would be sufficient for the purpose. The large growing disparity between the number of warheads needed for the purpose and the number actually possessed by each side is what leads to the concept of "overkill." If present trends continue, in the future all or most missiles will be MIRVed, and so this overkill will be increased by perhaps another order of magnitude.

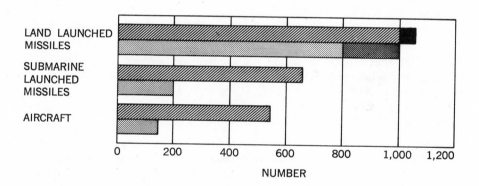

Figure 20.1. Present status of the deployment of strategic offensive forces by the U.S. (▨■) and the U.S.S.R. (▨▩) shows that the two superpowers are about even in numbers of intercontinental ballistic missiles (ICBM's), and that the U.S. is ahead in both long-range aircraft and submarine-launched ballistic missiles (SLBM's) of the Polaris type. The U.S. ICBM's consist almost entirely of Minutemen (▨▨▨), which carry a nuclear warhead with an explosive yield in the megaton range; there currently remain only 54 of the larger Titans (■■■) in our strategic forces. The smaller Russian missiles (▨▨▨) are mostly SS-11's, which are roughly equivalent in size to our Minutemen. The larger Russian missiles (▨▨▨) are SS-9's, which are comparable in size to our Titans. The figures used are from a speech given by Secretary of Defense Melvin R. Laird on March 25.

Here let me note that it is sometimes argued that there is a disparity in the present situation because Russian missile warheads are said to be bigger than U.S. warheads, both in weight and megatonnage; similarly, it is argued that MIRVing does not increase overkill because total yield is reduced in going from single to multiple warheads. This argument is based on the false notion that the individual MIRV warheads of the future will be "small" when measured against the purpose assigned to them. Against large, "soft" targets such as cities bombs *very much* smaller than those that could be used as components of MIRV's are (and in the case of Hiroshima were proved to be) entirely adequate for destroying the heart of a city and killing hundreds of thousands of people. Furthermore, in the case of small, "hard" targets such as missile silos, command posts and other military installations, having explosions bigger than those for which the "kill," or crater, radius slightly exceeds "circular error probable" (CEP) adds little to the probability of destroying such targets. Crater radius depends roughly on the cube root of the explosive power; consequently, if during the period when technology allows us to go from one to 10 warheads per missile it also allows us to improve accuracy by a little more than twofold, the "kill" per warhead will remain nearly the same in most cases, whereas the number of warheads increases tenfold.

In any case, it is fair to say that in spite of a number of such arguments about details, nearly everyone who testified at the ABM hearings agreed that the present situation is one in which each side possesses forces adequate to deter the other. In short, we now have parity in the only sense that ultimately counts.

Several forecasts have been made of what the strategic-weapons situation will be in the mid-1970's. In most respects here again there is quite general agreement. Part of the presentation by Deputy Secretary Packard to the Senate Foreign Relations Committee on March 26 were two graphs showing the trends in numbers of deployed offensive missiles beginning in 1965 and extending to 1975 [*see illustrations on page 377*]. There is no serious debate about the basic features of these graphs. It is agreed by all that in the recent past the U.S. has been far ahead of the U.S.S.R. in all areas, and that the Russians began a rapid deployment program a few years ago that will bring them even with us in ICBM's quite soon and that, if extended ahead without any slowdown, would bring them even in submarine-launched ballistic missiles (SLBM's) sometime between 1971 and 1977.

One important factor that the Department of Defense omitted from its graphs is MIRV. Deployment plans for MIRV's have not been released by either the U.S. or the U.S.S.R., although various rough projections were made at the hearings about numbers of warheads per vehicle (three to ten), about accuracies (figures around half a mile were often mentioned, and it was implied that U.S. accuracies were better than Russian ones) and about development status (the U.S. was said to be ahead in developments in this

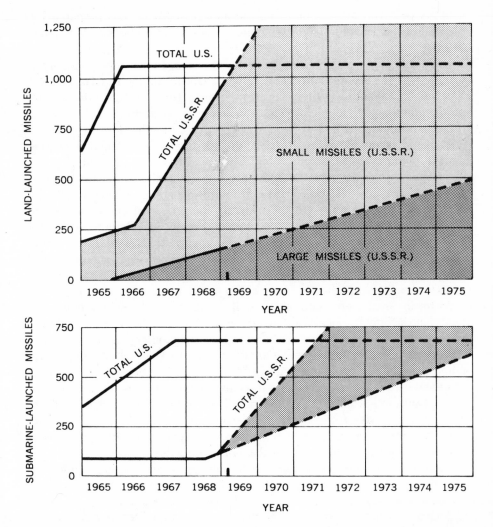

Figure 20.2. Extrapolated trends in the deployment of strategic offensive missiles by the U.S. and the U.S.S.R. are indicated by the broken lines in this pair of charts, which are based on a presentation by Deputy Secretary of Defense David Packard to the Senate Foreign Relations Committee on March 26. The chart at top shows the numbers of deployed ICBM's for both sides during the period 1965–1975. The Russian total is broken down into "small" missiles (the one-megaton SS-11's) and "large" missiles (the multimegaton SS-9's). The chart at bottom shows the deployed SLBM's during the same period. The extrapolations suggest that the Russians will be even with us in ICBM's quite soon and will catch up in SLBM's sometime between 1971 and 1977. One important factor omitted from the charts is the imminent deployment by both sides of MIRV's (multiple independently targetable reentry vehicles).

field). A pair of charts emphasizing the impact of MIRV was prepared by the staff of the Senate Foreign Relations Committee (*see illustration on page 379*).

One could argue with both of these sets of charts. For example, one might wonder why the Senate charts show so few warheads on the Russian Polaris-type submarine and why they show only three MIRV's on U.S. Minutemen; on the other hand, one might wonder whether the Department of Defense's projected buildup of the Russian Polaris fleet could be that fast, or whether one should count the older Russian missile submarines. Nonetheless, the general picture presented cannot be far wrong. Moreover, the central arguments pursued throughout the ABM hearings (in both the Senate Foreign Relations Committee hearings in March and the Senate Armed Services Committee hearings in April) were not primarily concerned with these numerical matters. Rather, they were concerned with (1) Secretary of Defense Melvin R. Laird's interpretation of these numbers insofar as Russian *intentions* were concerned, (2) the validity of the Safeguard ABM system as a response to the purported strategic problems of the 1970's and (3) the arms-race implications of Safeguard.

As for the matter of intentions, those favoring the ABM concept generally held that the only "rational" explanation of the Russians' recent SS-9 buildup, coupled with their multiple-warhead development program and the Moscow ABM system, was that they were aiming for a first-strike capability. One must admit that almost anything is conceivable as far as intentions are concerned, but there certainly are simpler, and it seems to me much more likely, explanations. The simplest of all is contained in Deputy Secretary Packard's chart. The most surprising feature of this chart is the fact that the Russians were evidently satisfied with being such a poor second for such a long time. This is made more puzzling by the fact that all during this period U.S. defense officials found it necessary to boast about how far ahead we were in order to be able to resist internal pressures for still greater expansion of our offensive forces.

Another possible reason, and one that I believe added to the other in the minds of the Russian planners, was that their strategists concluded in the mid-1960's that, whatever the top officials here might say, certain elements would eventually succeed in getting a large-scale ABM system built, and that penetration-aid devices, including multiple warheads, would be needed to meet the challenge. Whether or not they were correct in this latter hypothetical analysis is still uncertain at this writing. Let us, however, pass on from this question of someone else's intentions and consider whether or not the proposed Safeguard ABM system is a valid, rational and necessary response to the Russian deployments and developments outlined above.

To many of those who have recently written favorably about ABM defenses or who have testified in their favor before the Congressional committees, Safeguard is supported mainly as a prototype of something else: a

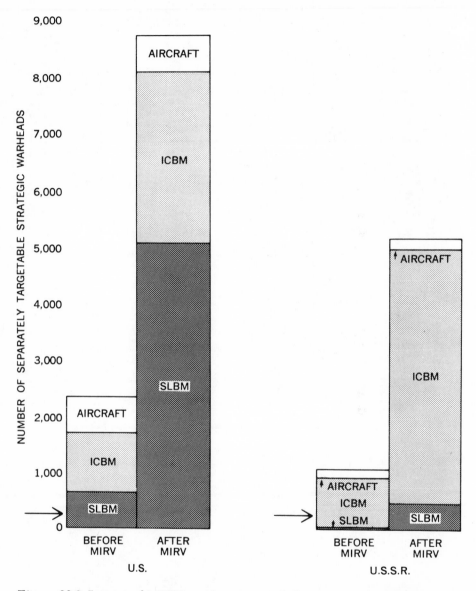

Figure 20.3. Impact of MIRV on the strategic balance is emphasized in this chart, which is based on one prepared by the staff of the Senate Foreign Relations Committee and presented by Senator Albert Gore of Tennessee on March 26. The chart depicts the strategic balance in terms of separately targetable strategic warheads before and after MIRVing, which is expected to take place in the next five years. The two black arrows near the bottom indicate the number of warheads that could devastate the 50 largest cities on each side.

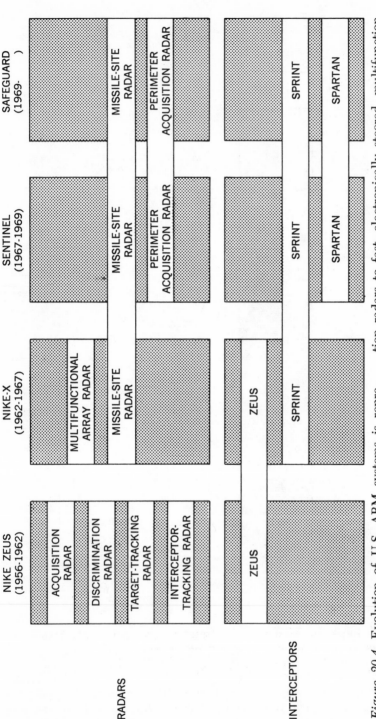

Figure 20.4. Evolution of U.S. ABM systems is represented in this illustration, which is adapted from a chart introduced by Daniel J. Fink in his testimony before the Senate Foreign Relations Committee on March 6. In general the radar components of the successive designs have progressed from slow, mechanically steered, single-function radars to fast, electronically steered, multifunction radars. The slow Zeus ABM missile has been superseded by the short-range Sprint (for terminal defense) and the long-range Spartan (for area defense). The components of the Safeguard system are the same as those that were originally intended for the earlier Sentinel system.

"thick" defense of the U.S. against a massive Russian missile attack. This is clearly not at all the rationale for the Safeguard decision as presented by President Nixon in his press conference of March 14, nor is it implied as more than a dividend in the defense secretaries' testimony. The President said that he wanted a system that would protect a *part* of our Minuteman force in order to increase the credibility of our deterrent, and that he had overruled moving in the direction of a massive city defense because "even starting with a thin system and then going to a heavy system tends to be more provocative in terms of making credible a first-strike capability against the Soviet Union. I want no provocation which might deter arms talks." The top civilian defense officials give this same rationale, although they put a little more emphasis on the "prototype" and "growth potential" aspects of the system. For simplicity and clarity I shall focus on the Administration's proposal, as stated in open session by responsible officials.

From a technical point of view and as far as components are concerned, President Nixon's Safeguard system of today is very little different from President Johnson's Sentinel system (*see pages 382 and 383*). There are only minor changes in the location of certain components (away from cities), and elements have been added to some of the radars so that they can now observe submarine-launched missiles coming from directions other than directly from the U.S.S.R. and China. As before, the system consists of a long-range interceptor carrying a large nuclear weapon (Spartan), a fast short-range interceptor carrying a small nuclear weapon (Sprint), two types of radar (perimeter acquisition radar, or PAR, and missile-site radar, or MSR), a computer for directing the battle, and a command and control system for integrating Safeguard with the national command. I shall not describe the equipment in detail at this point but pass on directly to what I believe can be concluded from the hearings and other public sources about each of the following four major questions: (1) Assuming that Safeguard could protect Minuteman, is it needed to protect our deterrent? (2) Assuming that Safeguard "works," can it in fact safeguard Minuteman? (3) Will it work? (4) Anyway, what harm can it do?

First: Assuming that Safeguard could protect Minuteman, is it needed to protect our deterrent?

Perhaps the clearest explanation of why the answer to this first question is "no" was given by Wolfgang K. H. Panofsky before the Senate Armed Services Committee on April 22. He described how the deterrent consists of three main components: Polaris submarines, bombers and land-based ICBM's. Each of these components alone is capable of delivering far more warheads than is actually needed for deterrence, and each is currently defended against surprise destruction in a quite different way. ICBM's are in hard silos and are numerous. Polarises are hidden in the seas. Bombers can be placed on various levels of alert and can be dispersed.

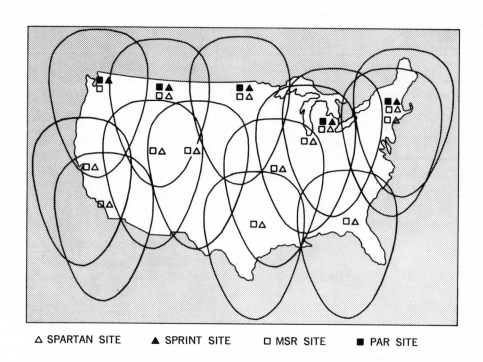

△ SPARTAN SITE   ▲ SPRINT SITE   □ MSR SITE   ■ PAR SITE

Figure 20.5. Sentinel system was described by the Johnson Administration as a "thin" ABM system designed to defend the U.S. against a hypothetical Chinese missile attack in the 1970's. The main defense was to be provided by long-range Spartan missiles. The Spartans would be deployed at about 14 locations in order to provide an area defense of the whole country. The range of each "farm" of Spartans is indicated by the egg-shaped area around it; for missiles attacking over the northern horizon the intercept range of the Spartan is elongated somewhat to the south. The Sentinel system would also include some short-range Sprint missiles, which were originally to be deployed to defend the five or six perimeter acquisition radars, or PAR's, which were to be deployed at five sites located across the northern part of the country. Missile-site radars, or MSR's, were to be deployed at every ABM site.

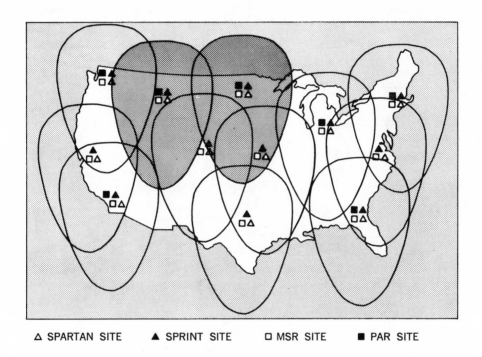

△ SPARTAN SITE   ▲ SPRINT SITE   □ MSR SITE   ■ PAR SITE

Figure 20.6. Safeguard system, President Nixon's proposed modification of the Sentinel scheme, uses essentially the same components in a slightly different array to accomplish an entirely different primary purpose: the defense of a part of our Minuteman force against a hypothetical surprise attack by the Russians. Phase I of Safeguard covers the construction of ABM sites at two Minuteman "fields": one near Malmstrom Air Force Base in Montana and the other near Grand Forks Air Force Base in North Dakota (■■■■). The completed system would have a total of 12 sites, each with Sprint and Spartan coverage, located somewhat farther away from the cities. In addition two new PAR sites would be included in order to observe submarine-launched missiles coming from directions other than due north.

384 : *Great Issues in Military Policy*

Since the warning time in the case of an ICBM attack is generally taken as being about 30 minutes, the people who believe the deterrent may be in serious danger usually imagine that the bombers are attacked by missile submarines, and therefore have only a 15-minute warning. This is important because a 30-minute warning gives the bombers ample time to get off the ground. In that case, however, an attack on all three components cannot be made simultaneously; that is, if the attack weapons are launched simultaneously, they cannot arrive simultaneously, and vice versa.

Thus it is incredible that all three of our deterrent systems could become vulnerable in the same time period, and it is doubly incredible that we could not know that this would happen without sufficient notice so that we could do something about it. There is, therefore, no basis for a frantic reaction to the hypothetical Russian threat to Minuteman. Still, it is sensible and prudent to begin thinking about the problem, and so we turn to the other questions. We must consider these questions in the technological framework of the mid-1970's, and we shall do this now in the way defense officials currently seem to favor: by assuming that this is the best of all possible technological worlds, that everything works as intended and that direct extrapolations of current capabilities are valid.

Second: Assuming that Safeguard "works," can it in fact safeguard Minuteman?

One good approach to this problem is the one used by George W. Rathjens in his testimony before the Senate Armed Services Committee on April 23. His analysis took as a basis of calculation the implication in Secretary Laird's testimony that the Minuteman force may become seriously imperiled in the mid-1970's. Rathjens then estimated how many SS-9's would have to be deployed at that time in order to achieve this result. From this number, and the estimate of the current number of SS-9's deployed, he got a rate of deployment. He also had to make an assumption about how many Sprints and Spartans would be deployed at that time, and his estimates were based on the first phase of Safeguard deployment. These last numbers have not been released, but a range of reasonable values can be guessed from the cost estimates given. Assuming that the SS-9's would have four or five MIRV warheads each by that time, Rathjens found that by prolonging the SS-9 production program by a few months the Russians would be able to cope with Safeguard by simply exhausting it and would still have enough warheads left to imperil Minuteman, if that is indeed their intention (*see illustration on page 396*).

The length of this short safe period does depend on the numbers used in the calculations, and they of course can be disputed to a degree. Thus if one assumes that it takes fewer Russian warheads to imperil Minuteman (it can't be less than one for one!), then the assumed deployment rate is lower and the safe period is lengthened; on the other hand, if one notes that the missile-site radars in our system are much softer than even today's silos, then the first attacking warheads, fired directly at the radars, can be smaller and less accurate, so that a higher degree of MIRVing can be used for attacking these radars and a shorter safe period results. To go further, it was suggested that the accuracy/yield combination of the more numerous SS-11's might be sufficient for attacking the missile-site radars, and therefore, if the Russians were to elect such an option, there would be no safe period at all. In short, the most that Safeguard can do is either delay somewhat the date when Minuteman would be imperiled or cause the attacker to build up his forces at a somewhat higher rate if indeed imperiling Minuteman by a fixed date is his purpose.

In the more general case this problem is often discussed in budgetary terms, and the "cost-exchange ratio" between offense and defense is computed for a wide variety of specific types of weapon. Such calculations give a wide variety of results, and there is much argument about them. However, even using current offense designs (that is, without MIRV), such calculations usually strongly favor the offense. This exchange ratio varies almost linearly with the degree of MIRVing of the offensive missiles, and therefore it seems to me that in the ideal technological future we have taken as our context this exchange ratio will still more strongly favor the offense.

Third: Will it work? By this question I mean: Will operational units be able to intercept enemy warheads accompanied by enemy penetration aids in an atmosphere of total astonishment and uncertainty? I do not mean: Will test equipment and test crews intercept U.S. warheads accompanied by U.S. penetration aids in a contrived atmosphere? A positive answer to the latter question is a necessary condition for obtaining a positive answer to the former, but it is by no stretch of the imagination a sufficient condition.

This basic question has been attacked from two quite different angles: by examining historical analogies and by examining the technical elements of the problem in detail. I shall touch on both here. Design-oriented people who consider this a purely technical question emphasize the second approach. I believe the question is by no means a purely technical question, and I suggest that the historical-analogy approach is more promising, albeit much more difficult to use correctly.

False analogies are common in this argument. We find that some say: "You can't tell me that if we can put a man on the moon we can't build an ABM." Others say: "That's what Oppenheimer told us about the hydrogen bomb." These two statements contain the same basic error. They are examples of successes in a contest between technology and nature, whereas the ABM issue involves a contest between two technologies: offensive weapons and penetration aids versus defensive weapons and discrimination techniques. These analogies would be more pertinent if, in the first case, someone were to jerk the moon away just before the astronauts landed, or if, in the second case, nature were to keep changing the nuclear-reaction probabilities all during the development of the hydrogen bomb and once again after it was deployed.

Proper historical analogies should involve modern high-technology defense systems that have actually been installed and used in combat. If one examines the record of such systems, one finds that they do often produce some attrition of the offense, but not nearly enough to be of use against a nuclear attack. The most up-to-date example is provided by the Russian SAM's and other air-defense equipment deployed in North Vietnam. This system "works" after a fashion because both the equipment designers and the operating crews have had plenty of opportunities to practice against real U.S. targets equipped with real U.S. countermeasures and employing real U.S. tactics.

The best example of a U.S. system is somewhat older, but I believe it is still relevant. It is the SAGE system, a complex air-defense system designed in the early 1950's. All the components worked on the test range, but by 1960 we came to realize, even without combat testing, that SAGE could not really cope with the offense that was then coming into being. We thereupon greatly curtailed and modified our plans, although we did continue with some parts of the system. To quote from the recent report on the ABM decision prepared by Wiesner, Abram Chayes and others: "Still, after fifteen years, and the expenditure of more than $20 billion, it is generally conceded that we do not have a significant capability to defend ourselves against a well-planned air attack. The Soviet Union, after even greater effort, has probably not done much better."

So much for analogies; let us turn to the Safeguard system itself. Doubts about its being able to work were raised during the public hearings on a variety of grounds, some of which are as follows:

First, and perhaps foremost, there is the remarkable fact that the new Safeguard system and the old Sentinel system use virtually the same hardware deployed in a very similar manner, and yet they have entirely different primary purposes. Sentinel had as its purpose defending large soft targets against the so-called Chinese threat. The Chinese threat by definition involved virtually no sophisticated penetration aids and no possibilities of exhausting the defense; thus were "solved" two of the most difficult problems that had eliminated Nike Zeus and Nike-X.

Safeguard has as its primary purpose defending a part of the Minuteman force against a Russian attack. It is not credible that a Russian attack against the part of the Minuteman force so defended would be other than massive and sophisticated, so that we are virtually right back to trying to do what in 1967 we said we could not do, and we are trying to do it with no real change in the missiles or the radars. It is true that defending hard points is to a degree easier than defending cities because interception can be accomplished later and at lower altitudes, thus giving discrimination techniques more time to work. Moreover, only those objects headed for specific small areas must be intercepted. These factors do make the problem somewhat easier, but they do not ensure its solution, and plenty of room for doubt remains.

Second, there is the contest between penetration aids and discrimination techniques. This was discussed at length by Garwin and Bethe in their March 1968 article in *Scientific American* and mentioned also in varying degrees of detail by many of those who testified recently concerning the ABM issue. The Russian physicist Andrei D. Sakharov, in his essay "Thoughts on Progress, Coexistence and Intellectual Freedom," put the issue this way: "Improvements in the resistance of warheads to shock waves and the radiation effects of neutron and X-ray exposure, the possibility of mass use of relatively light and inexpensive decoys that are virtually indistinguishable from warheads and exhaust the capabilities of an antimissile defense system, a perfection of tactics of massed and concentrated attacks, in time and space, that overstrain the defense detection centers, the use of orbital and fractional-orbital attacks, the use of active and passive jamming and other methods not disclosed in the press—all of this has created technical and economic obstacles to an effective missile defense that, at the present time, are virtually insurmountable."

I would add only MIRV to Sakharov's list. Pitted against this plethora of penetration aids are various observational methods designed to discriminate the real warheads. Some of the penetration devices obviously work only at high altitudes, but even these make it necessary for the final "sorting" to be delayed, and thus they still contribute to making the defense problem harder. Other devices can continue to confuse the defense even down to low altitudes. Some of the problems the offense presents to the defense can no doubt be solved (and have been solved) when considered separately and in isolation. That is, they can be solved for a time, until the offense designers react. One must have serious reservations, however, whether these problems can ever be solved for any long period in the complex combinations that even a modestly sophisticated attacker can present. Further, such a contest *could* result in a catastrophic failure of the system in which all or nearly all interceptions fail.

Third, there is the unquantifiable difference between the test range and the real world. The extraordinary efforts of the Air Force to test operationally deployed Minutemen show that it too regards this as an important problem. Moreover, the tests to date do seem to have revealed important weaknesses in the deployed forces. The problem has many aspects: the possible differences between test equipment and deployed equipment; the certain differences between the offensive warheads and penetration aids supplied by us as test targets and the corresponding equipment and tactics the defense must ultimately be prepared to face; the differences between the installation crews at a test site and at a deployment site; the differences in attitudes and motivation between a test crew and an operational crew (even if it is composed of the same men); the differences between men and equipment that have recently been made ready and whom everyone is watching and men and equipment that have been standing ready for years during which nothing happened; the differences between the emotional atmosphere where everyone knows it is not "for real" and the emotional atmosphere where no one can believe what he has just been told. It may be that all that enormously complex equipment will be ready to work the very first time it must "for real," and it may be that all those thousands of human beings have performed all their interlocking assignments correctly, but I have very substantial doubts about it.

Fourth, there is the closely related "hair-trigger/stiff-trigger" contradiction. Any active defense system such as Safeguard must sit in readiness for two or four or eight years and then fire at precisely the correct second following a warning time of only minutes. Furthermore, the precision needed for the firing time is so fine that machines must be used to choose the exact instant of firing no matter how the decision to fire is made. In the case of offensive missiles the situation is different in an essential way: Although maintaining readiness throughout a long, indefinite period is necessary, the moment of firing is not so precisely controlled in general and hence human decision-makers, including even those at high levels, may readily be permitted to play a part in the decision-making process. Thus if we wish to be certain that the defense will respond under conditions of surprise, the trigger of the ABM system, unlike the triggers of the ICBM's and Polarises, must be continuously sensitive and ready—in short, a hair trigger—for indefinitely long periods of time.

On the other hand, it is obvious that we cannot afford to have an ABM missile fire by mistake or in response to a false alarm. Indeed, the Army went to some pains to assure residents of areas near proposed Sentinel sites that it was imposing requirements to ensure against the accidental launching of the missile and the subsequent detonation of the nuclear warhead it carries. Moreover, Army officials have assured the public that no ABM missile would ever be launched without the specific approval of "very high authorities."

These two requirements—a hair trigger so that the system can cope with a surprise attack and a stiff trigger so that it will never go off accidentally or without proper authorization—are, I believe, contradictory requirements. In saying this I am not expressing doubt about the stated intentions of the present Army leaders, and I strongly endorse the restrictions implied in their statements. I am saying, however, that if the system cannot be fired without approval of "the highest authorities," then the probability of its being fired under conditions of surprise is less than it would be otherwise. This probability depends to a degree on the highly classified technical details of the Command and Control System, but in the last analysis it depends more on the fact that "the highest authority" is a human being and therefore subject to all the failures and foibles pertaining thereto.

This brings us to our fourth principal question: Anyway, what harm can it do?

We have just found that the total deterrent is very probably not in peril, that the Safeguard system probably cannot safeguard Minuteman even if it "works," that there is, to say the least, considerable uncertainty whether or not it will "work." Nonetheless, if there were no harm in it, we might be prudent and follow the basic motto of the arms race: "Let us err on the side of military safety." There seem to be many answers to the question of what harm building an ABM system would do. First of all, such a system would cost large sums of money needed for nondefense purposes. Second, it would divert money and attention from what may be better military solutions to the strategic problems posed by the Administration. Third, it would intensify the arms race. All these considerations were discussed at the hearings; I shall comment here only on the third, the arms-race implications of the ABM decision.

It is often said that an ABM system is not an accelerating element in the arms race because it is intrinsically defensive. For example, during the hearings Senator Henry M. Jackson of Washington, surely one of the best-informed senators in this field, said essentially that, and he quoted Premier Kosygin as having said the same thing. I believe such a notion is in error and is based on what we may call "the fallacy of the last move." I believe that in the real world of constant change in both the technology and the deployed

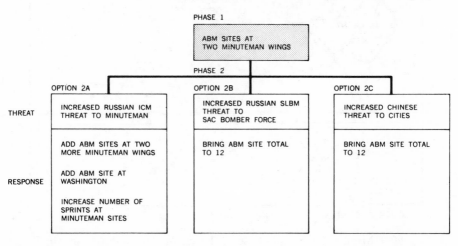

Figure 20.7. Safeguard Phase II provides for three different optional responses to various potential threats in the 1970's. A possible further addition would be sites in Alaska and Hawaii. This chart is also adapted from Deputy Secretary Packard's testimony on March 26.

numbers of all kinds of strategic-weapons systems, ABM systems are accelerating elements in the arms race. In support of this view let us recall one of the features of the history recited at the start of this article.

At the beginning of this decade we began to hear about a possible Russian ABM system, and we became concerned about its potential effects on our ICBM and Polaris systems. In response the MIRV concept was invented. Today there are additional justifications for MIRV besides penetration, but that is how it started. Now, the possibility of a Russian MIRV is used as one of the main arguments in support of the Safeguard system. Thus we have come one full turn around the arms-race spiral. No one in 1960 and 1961 thought through the potential destabilizing effects of multiple warheads, and certainly no one predicted, or even could have predicted, that the inexorable logic of the arms race would carry us directly from Russian talk in 1960 about defending Moscow against missiles to a requirement for hard-point defense of offensive-missile sites in the U.S. in 1969.

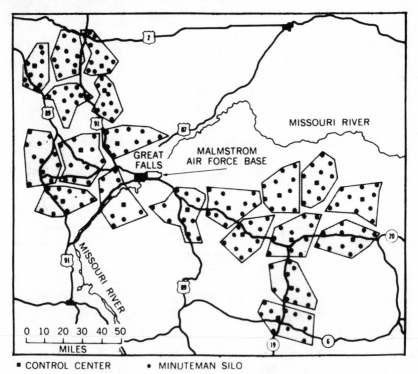

● CONTROL CENTER   • MINUTEMAN SILO

Figure 20.8. Minuteman missile base in the vicinity of Malmstrom Air Force Base is shown on this map, which is based on information released by the Department of the Air Force. The Minuteman missiles are grouped in 20 flights of 10 missiles each for a total of 200 missiles. Every flight has its own control center, each of which is capable of launching an entire squadron of 50 missiles.

By the same token I am sure the Russians did not foresee the large increase in deployed U.S. warheads that will ultimately result from their ABM deployment and that made it so counterproductive. Similarly, no one today can describe in detail the chain reaction the Safeguard deployment would lead to, but it is easy to see the seeds of a future acceleration of the arms race in the Nixon Administration's Safeguard proposal. Soon after Safeguard is started (let us assume for now that it will be) Russian offense planners are going to say something such as: "It may not work, but we must be prudent and assume it will." They may then plan further deployments, or more complex penetration systems, or maybe they will go to more dangerous systems such as bombs in orbit. A little later, when some of our optimistic statements about how "it will do the job it is supposed to do" have become part of history, our strategic planners are going to look at Safeguard and say something such as: "Maybe it will work as they said, but we must be prudent and assume it will not and besides, *now* look at what the Russians are doing."

This approach to strategic thinking, known in the trade as "worst-case analysis," leads to a completely hopeless situation in which there is no possibility of achieving a state of affairs that both sides would consider as constituting parity. Unless the arms race is stopped by political action outside the two defense establishments, I feel reasonably sure there will be another "crash program" response analogous to what we had in the days of the "missile gap"—a situation some would like to see repeated.

I also mentioned in my own testimony at the ABM hearings that "we may further expect deployment of these ABM systems to lead to the persistent query, 'But how do you know it *really* works?' and thus to increase the pressures against the current limited nuclear-test ban as well as to work against amplifying it." I mentioned this then, and I mention it again now, in the hope that it will become a self-defeating prediction. It is also important to note that the response of our own defense establishment to the Russian ABM deployment, which I have outlined above, was not the result of our being "provoked," and I emphasize this because we hear so much discussion about what is a "provocative" move and what is not. Rather, our response was motivated by a deep-seated belief that the only appropriate response to any new technical development on the other side is further technical complexity of our own. The arms race is not so much a series of political provocations followed by hot emotional reactions as it is a series of technical challenges followed by cool, calculated responses in the form of ever more costly, more complex and more fully automatic devices. I believe this endless, seemingly uncontrollable process was one of the principal factors President Eisenhower had in mind when he made his other (usually forgotten) warning: "We must be alert to the . . . danger that public policy could itself become the captive of a scientific-technological elite." He placed this other warning, also from his farewell address, on the same level as the much more familiar comment about the military-industrial complex.

Several alternative approaches to Safeguard for protecting Minuteman have been discussed recently. These include superhardening, proliferation, a "shell game" in which there are more silos than missiles, and land-mobile missiles. Although I was personally hopeful before the hearings that at least one of these approaches would maintain its invulnerability, a review of the recent debates leaves me now with the pessimistic view that none of them holds much promise beyond the next 10 years.

Silo-hardening most probably does work now, in the sense that the combination of SS-11 accuracy and yield and Minuteman silo-hardening works out in such a way that one incoming warhead (and hence one SS-11 missile) has less than a 50-50 chance of destroying a Minuteman. If one considers the technological trends in hardening, yield per unit weight, MIRVing and accuracy, however, it does seem convincing that this is a game in which the offense eventually will win. Albert Wohlstetter, testifying in favor of the Safeguard system before the Senate Armed Services Committee, quoted a paper he wrote with Fred Hoffman in 1954 (long before any ICBM's were actually in place anywhere) predicting that the ability of silo-hardening to protect offensive missiles would run out by the end of the 1960's. That was a remarkably prescient study and is wrong only in numerical detail.

If we take the same rosy view of technology that was taken in almost all the pro-ABM arguments, then hardening will not work for more than another five years. My own view of the technological future is clearly much less rosy, but I do believe that the situation in which hardening is no longer the answer could come by, say, 1980 or, more appropriately, 1984.

Proliferation of Minuteman would have worked in the absence of MIRV. Now, however, it would seem that the ability to MIRV, which no doubt can eventually be carried much further than the fewfold MIRV we see for the immediate future, clearly makes proliferation a losing game as well as the dangerous one it always was.

The "shell game" has not in my view been analyzed in satisfactory detail, but it would appear to have a serious destabilizing effect on the arms race. Schemes have been suggested for verifying that a certain fraction of the missile holes are in fact empty, but one can foresee a growing and persistent belief on each side that the "other missiles" must be hidden somewhere.

Road-mobile and rail-mobile versions of Minuteman have been seriously studied for well over a decade. These ideas have always foundered on two basic difficulties: (1) Such systems are inherently soft and hence can be attacked by large warheads without precise knowledge of where they are, and (2) railroads and highways all pass through population centers, and large political and social problems seem unavoidable.

Where does all this leave us insofar as finding a technical solution for protecting Minuteman is concerned? One and only one technically viable solution seems to have emerged for the long run: Launch on warning. Such an idea has been considered seriously by some politicians, some technical

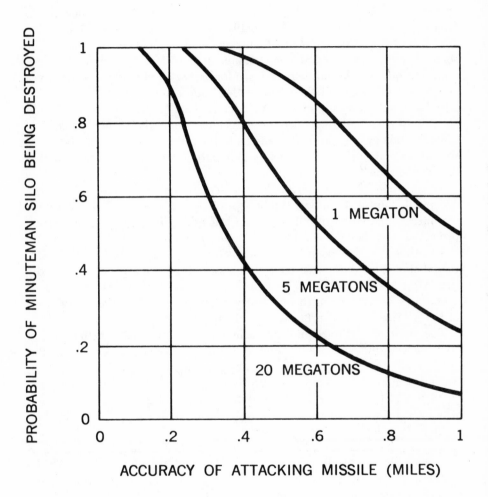

Figure 20.9. Vulnerability of Minuteman is revealed in this graph, which relates probability of destruction of a hardened Minuteman silo to accuracy for three different sizes of attacking warhead. This graph was interpreted by Deputy Secretary Packard as demonstrating the seriousness of the threat to Minuteman posed by the large Russian SS-9 missile, which he said is capable of carrying either one 20-megaton warhead or three five-megaton warheads.

men and some military officers. Launch on warning could either be managed entirely by automatic devices, or the command and control system could be such as to require authorization to launch by some very high human authority.

In the case of the first alternative, people who think about such things envision a system consisting of probably two types of detection device that could, in principle, determine that a massive launch had been made and then somewhat later determine that such a launch consisted of multiple warheads aimed at our missile-silo fields. This information would be processed by a computer, which would then launch the Minutemen so that the incoming missiles would find only empty holes; consequently the Minutemen would be able to carry out their mission of revenge. Thus the steady advance of arms technology may not be leading us to the ultimate weapon but rather to the ultimate absurdity: a completely automatic system for deciding whether or not doomsday has arrived.

To me such an approach to the problem is politically and morally unacceptable, and if it really is the only approach, then clearly we have been considering the wrong problem. Instead of asking how Minuteman can be protected, we should be asking what the alternatives to Minuteman are. Evidently most other people also find such an idea unacceptable. As I mentioned above, the Army has found it necessary to reassure people repeatedly that ABM missiles would not be launched without approval by "the highest authorities," even though this is clearly a far less serious matter in the case of the ABM missiles than in the case of Minuteman.

The alternative is to require that a human decision-maker, at the level of "the highest authorities," be introduced into the decision-making loop. But is this really satisfactory? We would be asking that a human being make, in just a few minutes, a decision to utterly destroy another country. (After all, there would be no point in firing at *their* empty silos.) If, for any reason whatever, he was responding to a false alarm, or to some kind of smaller, perhaps "accidental," attack, he would be ensuring that a massive deliberate attack on us would take place moments later. Considering the shortness of the time, the complexity of the information and the awesomeness of the moment, the President would himself have to be properly preprogrammed in order to make such a decision.

Those who argue that the Command and Control System is perfect or perfectable forget that human beings are not. If forced to choose, I would prefer a preprogrammed President to a computer when it came to deciding whether or not doomsday had arrived, but again I feel that this solution too is really unacceptable, and that once again, in attempting to defend Minuteman, we are simply dealing with the wrong problem. For the present it would seem the Polarises and the bombers are not, as systems, subject to the same objections, since there are now enough other approaches to the problem of ensuring their invulnerability to sudden massive destruction.

In my view, all the above once again confirms the utter futility of attempting to achieve national security through military technology alone. We must look elsewhere. Fortunately an opportunity does seem to be in the offing. There appears to be real promise that serious strategic-arms-limitation talks will begin soon. The time is propitious. There is in the land a fairly widespread doubt about the strictly military approach to security problems, and even military-minded politicians are genuinely interested in exploring other possibilities. The essay by Academician Sakharov, as well as the statements of Russian officials, indicate genuine interest on the other side. The time is propitious in another sense: both sides will be discussing the matter from a position of parity. Moreover, this parity seems reasonably stable and likely to endure for several years.

Later, however, major deployments of sophisticated ABM systems and, even more important, widespread conversion of present single-warhead systems to MIRV will be strongly destabilizing and will at least give the impression that parity is about to be upset. If so, the motto of the arms race, "Let us err on the side of military safety," will come to dominate the scene on both sides and the present opportunity will be lost. Therefore in the short run we must do everything possible to ensure that the talks not only start but also succeed. Although the ABM decision may not forestall the talks, it would seem that success will be more likely if we avoid starting things that history has shown are difficult to stop once they are started.

Such things surely include deployment of ABM missiles and MIRV's. There have been successes in stopping programs while they were in the development phase, but seldom has anything been stopped after deployment had started. The idea of a freeze on deployment of new weapons systems at this time and for these reasons is fairly widespread already, but achieving it will require concerted action by those believing strongly in the validity and necessity of arms limitations as a means of increasing national security. Thus the principal result of the recent national debate over the ABM issue has been to make it clear that Safeguard will safeguard nothing, and that the right step for the immediate future is doing whatever is necessary (such as freezing present deployments and developments) to ensure the success of the coming strategic-arms-limitation talks.

In addition, the ABM debate has served to highlight more serious issues (for example the implications of MIRV for the arms race) and to raise serious questions about other weapons systems. For instance, I suggest that we have also found that silo-based missiles will become obsolete. The only sure method for defense of Minuteman beyond, say, the mid-1970's seems to be the unacceptable launch on warning. As long as we must have a strategic deterrent, we must find one that does not force us to turn the final decision over to either a computer or a preprogrammed President. Minuteman was conceived in the 1950's and served its purpose as a deterrent through the 1960's, but it appears that in the 1970's its threat to us will exceed its value,

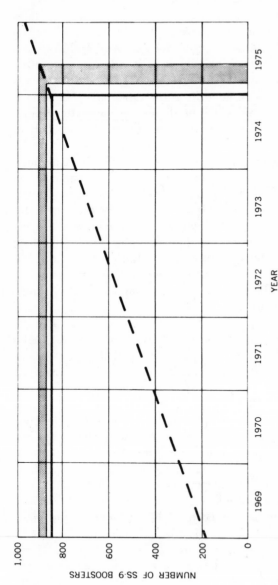

1,000

800

600

400

200

0

NUMBER OF SS-9 BOOSTERS

1969   1970   1971   1972   1973   1974   1975

YEAR

Figure 20.10. Safeguard could be nullified within a few months after its Phase I deployment, according to this graph, which is based on calculations presented by George W. Rathjens in his testimony before the Senate Armed Services Committee on April 23. His analysis took as a basis of calculation the implication in Secretary Laird's testimony that the Minuteman force may become seriously imperiled in the mid-1970's. Assuming that the Russian SS-9's would have four or five MIRV warheads each by that time, Rathjens then estimated that approximately 850 SS-9's would have to be deployed in order to achieve this result. From this number, and the estimate of the current number of SS-9's deployed (about 200), he got a rate of deployment (about 100 per year). Making certain assumptions about the numbers and effectiveness of the Spartan and Sprint ABM missiles that would be deployed at that time, Rathjens found that by prolonging the SS-9 production program by two to five months the Russians would be able to cope with Safeguard by simply exhausting it and would still have enough warheads to imperil Minuteman. Recently different numerical assumptions have been made, but they do not change the general conclusion that the proposed Safeguard system is much too thin to safeguard Minuteman.

and that it and other silo-based missiles will have to go. The deterrent must have alternatives other than "go/no-go," and for the 1970's at least it would now appear that other strategic weapons (Polaris/Poseidon and bombers) could provide them. I expect, however, that as the continuing national debate subjects the whole matter of strategic arms to further public scrutiny we shall learn that these other alternatives also have dangerous flaws, and we shall see confirmed the idea that there is no technical solution to the dilemma of the steady decrease in our national security that has for more than 20 years accompanied the steady increase in our military power.

21. Missile Defense: Can It Work?

CHARLES M. HERZFELD

Introduction

A comparison of offense and defense effectiveness involves facts, judgments, and (very importantly) the logical structure of the arguments used. For the last ten years or so, there have been public and private disagreements about the facts. Though there are now far fewer such disagreements, some remain. Differences in judgments have existed and some persist. But perhaps most importantly, some flaws in the logical structure of the arguments seem to have gone largely unnoticed. These flaws are basic. They involve the use of grossly asymmetric logic, which largely begs the questions supposed to be resolved. The use of asymmetric logic has been aggravated by the fact that the majority of Defense technologists and analysts have concentrated professionally on either the offense or on the defense alone.

In this chapter we try to sort out the issues in ABM effectiveness by trying to clarify the facts, by isolating the crucial judgments, and by resolving the logical asymmetries.

Much of the discussion is relevant to general offense-defense interactions, and the analysis of logical asymmetries should be a useful tool for the construction or critique of a wide class of arguments in the field. The main thrust of the chapter is devoted to the examination of ABM systems in general, and of the Safeguard system in particular. Portions of this analysis have appeared elsewhere.[1]

What Is the Job of ABM?

SOME GENERAL REFLECTIONS ON OFFENSE AND DEFENSE

To understand clearly the role of ABM, a short discussion of the general role of defense in warfare is perhaps indicated. There are basically two missions for any defense.

First, the defense should exact a price from the offense of the other side, and

Second, it should complicate the attacker's job, and deny him a "free ride."

Only very rarely in history can a defense provide real security, or immunity. It can do so only when the defense is far ahead of the offense technologically, as the English defense was at the battle of Crecy and as the technology of castle-building was "ahead" before the systematic use of gunpowder.

In the field of air defense and offense, the offense has been said to be ahead of the defense technologically for a long time. Attrition rates of attacking aircraft of three to five per cent have been quoted widely as being representative of the relative state of the art of air defense and offense. This argument is often used to depreciate the value of any kind of defense, especially ABM.

The numbers are correct, but *only* on the *average*. What really happens is more complicated, and also more significant: The defense can and should defend some targets, those of higher value, more heavily than the rest of the targets. When the offense attacks these well defended targets it loses quite heavily, losses of twenty-five to thirty percent of attacking aircraft are possible, together with only moderate damage to their target. But the offense cannot sustain such losses for long, goes off after less well defended (and less important) targets, and in these attacks loses much less. This occurred in World War II, and in the North Vietnam bombing campaign. Thus, in any analysis of the relative effectiveness of offense and defense, one must know the defensive goals and strategy, the offensive goals and strategy, and assess the actual damage involved. Gross averages can divert too easily from the mainpoint.

We conclude: A defense which frightens the attacker away from heavily defended targets has done the first part of its job, and is a major military asset.

1. C. M. Herzfeld, Ballistic Missile Defence—This Time for Real, *Nature.* Vol. 219, 1315–17, September 28, 1969; Ballistic Missile Defense, Center for the Study of Democratic Institutions, 1968, unpublished; Hearings before the Subcommittee on National Security Policy and Scientific Developments, Committee on Foreign Affairs, House of Representatives, April 1969.

Another often-used argument against ABM is also fallacious. It runs like this: Because any defense can be countered by some reaction to it which can be imagined, no defense should be built at all. The argument is irrelevant and it misleads. All defense systems of whatever kind can eventually be countered, but this, by itself, does not reduce the value of the defense system to zero. To argue against anti-tank systems by saying that tanks can be built to supersede a given anti-tank technology is about as sensible an argument against anti-tank systems as saying that because safes can be cracked there is no point to having safes.

Any defensive system that diverts resources of the offense, either by forcing a building up of the offense qualitatively or quantitatively, or by "absorbing" part of the offense in an attack has done a major portion of its second task stated above.

The real issues of offense vs. defense are different. They have to do with two questions:

1. does having the defense solve problems worth solving?
2. what other consequences (good or bad) does installing the defense have?

Both questions will be discussed below in some detail.

THE TECHNICAL FUNCTIONS AND THE JOBS ABM CAN DO

The technical functions of an ABM system are these: The target, that is, the attacking missile, has to be acquired. This is customarily done with a radar, and can usually be done at very great distances, though at these distances the defense may not know the details of what is coming, because the attacker can deny this detailed information by hiding the attacking objects in chaff. Next, the defense must discriminate the real targets, the re-entry vehicles carrying nuclear warheads, from false ones, i.e., the decoys, the chaff, and others. Discrimination is the most difficult part of the defense problem, and hundreds of millions of dollars of R&D have been expended towards its solution. No easy foolproof discrimination methods have been found so far, but much has been learned, especially about what *cannot* be done to decoy the threat, a most important thing to understand well.[2] Finally, interceptors must be launched against the threatening objects. The interceptors are likely to be large and fast rockets, carrying nuclear warheads.

The choice of interceptor warheads is a subtle matter. Nuclear warheads are the most effective, because they have the largest lethal radius. But when they explode, they also create interference for the defense's radars, the so-called "radar black-out," which is a serious problem for the defense.[3] (It is

2. It turns out that there are no *foolproof, cheap, simple* and *high confidence* ways to decoy the threat. The best *high confidence* methods are not cheap, nor are they simple to execute. These methods are however quite feasible, but at a considerable price in the effort required to install them and, particularly, to verify their effectiveness.
3. This blackout is taken into account when calculating the expected effectiveness of a missile defense. See note at end of the present chapter.

not true, by the way, that the explosion of a defensive warhead, when used according to plan, produces damage in the defended area. Nor would such an explosion produce radioactive fall-out locally.) Non-nuclear warheads for interceptors produce no black-out, but because of their much smaller lethal radius they would require vastly better (and much more complicated and costly) guidance for the interceptor. As a consequence, nuclear warheads are preferred at this time.

Ballistic missile defense systems can be characterized by the portion of the missile trajectory in which intercept is to take place and by the military problem to be solved by the defense. It is possible to contemplate a defense system which attacks enemy ICBM's during their launch phase. The principal advantage of such a defensive system, should it be feasible, would be to catch the enemy over his own territory, to fight "over there," rather than closer to home. Another advantage would lie in the fact that a real defense in depth would become feasible, by combining a launch defense system with other systems described below. The BAMBI system was a launch defense system where all functions such as detection of launches, discrimination of real from false targets, and launching interceptors, were to be carried out from satellites. A reasonably effective system would have involved thousands of satellites. After several years of intensive studies, it was concluded that such a system would cost between ten and a hundred billion dollars per year to maintain. Further work on the system was, therefore, abandoned. (In the event of future radical improvements in reliability and reductions in launch cost, such a system may become reasonable from a purely technical point of view.) Other launch defense systems can perhaps be built, but this is not certain.

Other defensive systems attack the enemy missiles in the mid-course phase of flight, while the enemy missiles float through space on a ballistic trajectory. (Such a defensive system would be similar technically to an anti-satellite defense system.) The chief advantage of such a system would be its long reach, again providing the possibility of defense in depth. Its chief problem would be discrimination of the warhead from chaff and balloon decoys. It is possible to design a defense system for "late mid-course" interception, when the effects of the atmosphere on the reentry vehicle are still slight, while retaining the advantageous long reach of the mid-course system. The proposed Safeguard system includes such a defense. It is discussed again below.

The U.S. Navy has been studying a shipborne ABM system called SABMIS. This would involve putting radars and interceptors on ships. It would be basically a mid-course defense. Because it would be movable it could be used to defend allies from off-shore positions. This system is still in the paper-study phase.

The terminal defense system is designed to intercept in the atmosphere. Its chief advantage is the feature that much of the air battle occurs in the atmosphere, which makes certain kinds of discrimination methods feasible,

Another way to categorize ABM systems is by the military problem to be solved by the defense. One type of system is geared to defend cities which are targets of moderate size (two to ten miles in diameter) and which are rather soft, i.e., vulnerable to attack. Cities must be defensible for a long time, and casualties should be held to low levels. Airfields and major troop concentrations are also soft targets. Airfields need to be protected only long enough for the aircraft required to retaliate to take off. To protect these soft targets requires that attacking warheads of large yield be intercepted at large distances. This is difficult for a terminal defense, and one of the arguments for a late mid-course defense.

A still different type of defense is designed for the protection of "hard points," such as hardened missile silos, hardened command posts, and the like. These targets are small, and highly resistant to the effects of nuclear explosions. As a consequence, the defense can let the attacker come close, and be satisfied with a very late terminal interception system. This is turn makes atmospheric discrimination more effective, and, hence, the defense relatively more effective. It is sufficient that some fraction of these targets survives for retaliation purposes.

Another system which needs some protection is the National Command and Control System. It consists of command posts (some of which are hardened) and an elaborate warning and communications network. This latter is not particularly hard but survives through much redundancy. This Command and Control system must be defended long enough for the President to authorize retaliation.

Finally, there is the area defense. Here, using mid-course or late mid-course defense methods, large areas are defended. This is made possible by the use of powerful long-range radars, together with large interceptor missiles carrying large warheads and having a long reach. Such a system can be easily supplemented by terminal defense. In fact, it is wise to defend the principal radars of an area defense system by a special terminal defense, because these radars (usually fairly few in numbers) make attractive targets for the offense, since their destruction would eliminate the fighting capability of the defense. The Safeguard system is a combination of a thin area defense, together with some terminal defense for the added protection of particularly important targets.[4]

As is indicated in our last example, defensive capability is to some degree an additive matter. The defense can be designed for a certain "thickness," which requires the offense to pay a certain "entrance price" in missiles to

4. Thin area defenses have been studied for some time, though this is not appreciated outside of the ABM field. Early studies by the Rand Corporation on this subject were carried out for ARPA in 1962 and 1963. At the direction of the Secretary of Defense, a number of detailed, parallel studies of such systems were carried out from 1963 to 1966. The tentative results of these studies were reported by this writer to the New York Academy of Sciences in 1965, 119, Vol. 34, 1965; reprinted in *Survival*, March 1966.

overwhelm the defense. The cost of a defense increases with the entrance price it wishes to exact from the offense.

THE TASKS OF SENTINEL AND SAFEGUARD

Both Sentinel and Safeguard were designed to cope with only some of the problems discussed above. Both are basically an area defense, augmented by a terminal defense. The purpose of the Safeguard System was defined by President Nixon as follows:[5]

1. Protection of our land-based retaliatory forces against a direct attack by the Soviet Union.

2. Defense of the American people against the kind of nuclear attack which Communist China is likely to be able to mount within the decade.

3. Protection against the possibility of accidental attacks from any source.

The emphasis is different from the original Sentinel purpose, but only by modifying the relative priorities of the tasks.

The Safeguard system is to consist of large PAR's, perimeter acquisition radars, of smaller MSR's, missile site radars, of large Spartan missiles, and smaller Sprint missiles.

The "phase I deployment" will be designed to provide some protection for Minuteman; the later phases will address tasks 2 and 3, and strengthen the protection for Minuteman, if this becomes desirable.

In addition, Safeguard will provide for some protection from sea-launched ballistic missiles, and also includes some other improvements.

It is important to be quite explicit about what Safeguard does not intend to provide. It does not intend to provide significant protection against a large, all-out first strike of Soviet ICBM's against U.S. cities. It does not intend to provide fool-proof protection against a future large Soviet attack launched from submarines against U.S. cities. Nor does it intend to provide full protection against a *large* and *sophisticated* attack such as Communist China might be able to launch in the 1980's. Its goals are quite modest, relatively speaking, and I believe it can meet these goals.

Let me address briefly here the question whether ABM is needed for the goals cited, or whether alternative methods might be preferable.

Task 1. Protection of our land-based retaliatory forces. At this time (May 1969) I believe that our Minuteman force could not be easily wiped out by a surprise attack from the Soviet Union, and that, should such an attack occur, a substantial portion of Minuteman would be available for a retaliatory strike, together with a significant portion of the SAC bomber force and of the Navy Polaris force.

There are some disturbing signs on the horizon, however, that this will not always be so, and that in a relatively few years, perhaps three to five, the Soviet Union may have the capability to destroy essentially all of the Minute-

5. March 14, 1969.

man force in a first-strike. These new developments are chiefly the rapid buildup in the Soviet missile inventory and Soviet experiments in multiple warhead technology.

In the light of these developments, the U.S. must respond. It does not seem wise to rely in the future only on bombers and Polaris/Poseidon for deterrence. Soviet activity in submarine-launched ballistic missiles will degrade the effectiveness of bombers, and Soviet ABM could degrade the effectiveness of Polaris/Poseidon, as could improvements in Soviet ASW.

A proper U.S. response must, it seems to be, cover several approaches simultaneously. First, and in my view most importantly, we must try to negotiate with the Soviet Union a leveling off of strategic arms. Such discussions may achieve important results. On the other hand such talks may fail, and fail after prolonged negotiations. Therefore, some additional steps should be taken now. These should include R&D on harder missile silos (such a program is under way) and also some protection of Minuteman by deployment of some form of hard point ABM such as Phase I of Safeguard. Past ARPA R&D programs have shown how to build an optimal hard point defense, using many small radars and many short range interceptors. Sprint is quite a good hard point defense interceptor, but smaller radars than the MSR may be desirable. However, *Safeguard technology* is the *only technology which is ready for deployment now*, and hence can reach operational status roughly at the same time at which the threat becomes most serious.

Some opponents of the Safeguard System now go so far as to urge a national policy of launching Minuteman on early warning of a Soviet attack on the U.S. Quite apart from the considerable technical problems involved in achieving such a posture, it seems that such a posture would represent the ultimate in world-wide *in*stability, and that such a posture would make accidental and undesired war much more likely than it is now. The many implications of such a drastic proposal should be studied carefully, but until such studies are completed, it does not seem wise to actively pursue this policy.

Task 2. Protection of the population against Chinese Communist and other "Third Country" attacks. Sometime in the 70's Communist China (CPR) is very likely to have a capability to launch small ICBM and submarine-launched ballistic missile (SLBM) attacks against the U.S., as well as against the USSR and other countries. I believe that it is a sensible precaution for the U.S. (and also for the USSR) to deploy a thin area ABM system of such size that it would reduce greatly the damage which the Chinese could do with such an attack.

Let me be very clear here. I do not desire or expect war with the CPR. I think it is highly desirable, and possibly even feasible, for the U.S. to establish meaningful relations with the Communist Chinese in the future. But should such moves fail, crises more serious than any we have known can arise, during which threats and counter threats may be common occurrences. It is not at all clear that the CPR can be deterred by U.S. missiles and bombers alone. Relatively few of their population live in cities (a much smaller percentage than in the U.S. and the USSR), where they would be threatened by retaliation. Further, so called "irrational" attacks occur all the time; ships are hijacked on the open sea, aircraft shot down over international waters, countries are suddenly invaded, and so on. It is not far-fetched to suppose that such provocations as recently carried out by North Korea and others could reach nuclear proportions, given the means.

It is my conviction that a system like Safeguard could defend the population of the U.S. against attacks from the CPR for many years. Critics of Safeguard claim that countermeasures can be cheaply and quickly devised which would largely negate the effectiveness of such a system. It is not correct that a well designed thin area defense can be easily countered by a third country such as Communist China. This matter will be discussed in more detail below.

Another problem which Safeguard could solve is countering the following threat. In the not-too-distant future, several technologically sophisticated "third powers" may have submarine-launched ballistic missiles. Britain and France already are procuring such forces, and others may follow. This means that there may arise the danger of small attacks, *whose country of origin is unknown,* carried out, perhaps, for catalytic purposes, to stimulate war between various nuclear powers. A thin defense would deny such attacks any large measure of confidence, hence reduce tension levels in large, thinly defended countries such as the U.S. and the Soviet Union during intense crises involving such "third countries."

Safeguard, together with improved Early Warning of SLBM attacks will go far to reduce the importance of such threats.

Task 3. Protection against accidental attacks, and the ability to manage intense crises. We must begin this discussion by considering how war between the U.S. and the USSR might break out. Most people talk and worry about an all-out surprise attack by either the USSR or the U.S. on the other. This surprise attack is said to occur without any warning, without a crisis, without any hint. While this is certainly a conceivable event, it seems a very unlikely way for major war to start. Rather, several of the following ways seem more plausible:

1. An accidental or unauthorized launch of a few ICBM's by one country, which is interpreted as an all out attack by the other country. Then the other country ties to pre-empt with an all out strike against the first.

2. In a very serious crisis between the USSR and the U.S., the USSR threatens to attack a few targets in the U.S. to demonstrate its seriousness.

3. A nuclear attack by a third country on either the U.S. or the USSR, in the hope of catalyzing war between the U.S. and the USSR.

A thin ABM defense system can be extremely useful in the above types of crises, and would enable the U.S. to view such events with a measure of confidence and restraint.

Penetration Aids and Tactics

THE MAGNITUDE OF THE PENETRATION TASK

A variety of penetration aids and tactics are available for the offense. In fact the profusion of *possible* penetration aids clouds the present ABM debate. Various myths have arisen in the public discussions of penetration aids (pen aids) and ABM. Among these myths are these: any pen aid will work, pen aids are cheap, they are quickly procured and easily installed, a few pounds of decoys uses up a multimillion dollar interceptor, and so on.

The real story is more complex, more interesting, and more relevant.

The facts are that *real* pen aids (as opposed to pen aids on paper) are not cheap, are not easily developed, are not quickly procured and installed. Most importantly, not all pen aids work.

The U.S. has been fortunate in its approach to ABM and pen aids. It has had large R&D programs working on both sides of this question: the Army Nike program on ABM, the Air Force and Navy programs on pen aids, and ARPA's Defender program (until recently) working on both ABM and pen aids. As a consequence of the size and kind of these programs, a degree of knowledge, valid competition and cross fertilization exist in these two fields which are unequalled in recent Defense R&D history.

It is perhaps of interest to summarize the sheer magnitude of the U.S. R&D effort which has been carried on over the last ten years in this area. The grand total of R&D expended on ABM so far is approximately four billion dollars. This includes about ten years of Sentinel, Nike X and Nike Zeus funding, and about nine years of Project Defender effort. This is a larger, and more thorough, R&D effort than has been expended on any other single military problem. The magnitude of the U.S. effort on penetration is comparable and ranges, depending on how one allocates costs, from one to two billion dollars. Also, a large fraction of the information obtained from ABM R&D has contributed directly to improving U.S. penetration capability and, in fact, was required for pen aids research and development.

These costs have gone to support relevant laboratory work, very extensive flight programs and field measurement programs, as well as radar and missile development. Also, a comparatively very large effort has gone into detailed system studies. It is hard for the outsider to imagine how detailed these system studies were, and how many of them were carried out and indeed still are carried out. The total effort has been large. More importantly, the effort has been of very high quality. Some of the best technical talents of universities, of industry, and the government were devoted to this effort.

Several important insights have come out of all this effort. The most important one is, perhaps, that there is a *relatively wide gap between being conservative in designing a defense, and being conservative in designing an attack.* Let me explain. When designing a defense one must take into account the number of attackers and their technological sophistication, the quality of their pen aids and tactics. The number of attackers comes either from intelligence projections, or from assumptions designed to be reasonable or interesting. The estimate of the attacker's pen aids technology, and also of one's defense technology, comes from estimates of what will be in operation on both sides at the time the study applies to, say X years from now.

When making this technology estimate in designing a defense, it is proper and wise to be "defense conservative." This means that one takes all the known or possible ways for the offense to penetrate the defense and estimates how many enemy missiles it will take to penetrate the defense. While doing this, one tries to make the *defense* "look bad," that is, one shades the technological uncertainties (and there are always some) in the direction that favors the offense, and counts heavily those things that may go poorly for the defense and well for the offense. In this way one arrives at an estimate of the *minimum* effectiveness of the defense, one gets a *minimum* price that the defense can exact from the offense. Being "offense-conservative" when designing the offense, means, on the other hand, that one shades all the technological uncertainties (just as many) against the offense. In this way one gets the maximum penetration price, the *maximum* price the defense can exact from the offense. Each conservatism is appropriate for its task, and most people who look at only offense or only defense are not confused by this. But if one wishes to strike a net balance between offense and defense, the matter becomes more subtle. Then one must be consistent, and one must take into account a balanced estimate for the attackers and defenders of *both* sides. It is, of course, true that propagandists for weapons systems rarely make or use conservative estimates, but I am talking here of serious analysis, not propaganda.

NET COMPARISON OF OFFENSE AND DEFENSE

Three basic logical errors must be avoided in making net comparisons of offense and defense. These are: comparing effectiveness of technologies of different vintage (errors of type I), ascribing grossly different technological sophistication to offense and defense of one country at one time (errors of type II), and using only offense-conservative or defense-conservative estimates for the net comparison (errors of type III). The errors are obvious, and they vitiate any argument in which they occur.

Let me explain in more detail what these errors are, and how they compound confusion in complicated analyses.

The first (type I) error is to set up a straw man by pitting a technologically old system against a technologically new system when both sides have comparable technical capabilities and comparable resources. Of course, such an asymmetric situation could develop (by good luck or bad, as the case may be) but no one should count on it, nor is there anything inexorable about such an asymmetry developing, or remaining.

Examples of such errors are:

1. Old Soviet ICBM's vs. new U.S. ABM. Clearly the U.S. defense wins. This was a popular fallacy in the early 60's.

2. New Soviet ICBM's vs. old U.S. ABM. This is the argument often used to prove that "no" U.S. defense can cope with "any" Soviet attack.

3. Old Soviet ABM vs. new U.S. ICBM's. This is the proper argument to prove that the U.S. has "gone too far," has "over-reacted," in improving its missile force.

Such arguments are actually used by some advocates. Clearly more logical symmetry is required.

When comparing net offense-defense effectiveness of countries that have greatly different technical resources such asymmetries can occur, and can to some extent be relied on existing. Thus, the CPR is not likely to *overtake* U.S. ABM discrimination know-how, and it is unlikely that it will match it.

Another error (type II) occasionally committed is to suppose that a country would let a great imbalance in sophistication between different important military systems technologies happen in similar time frames. Yet, some opponents of ABM are logically comfortable predicting a Soviet defense posture that has:

1. Soviet ICBM's modern, hence U.S. ABM is useless, and

2. Soviet ABM outmoded, hence U.S. ICBM assured penetration techniques (MIRV's) not needed.

(And all this for the Soviets, who are well-known to believe in having strong defensive systems!)

The third, and most serious error of logic (type III) is to consider only the defense-conservative calculations for both sides, which results in the answer that all defense is useless, or else to consider only the offense-conservative calculations for both sides, which yields the answer that defense is "very good." Clearly both approaches are wrong. The problem is exhibited in Table 1. (All entries are calculated in a conservative way, thus the U.S. estimate of U.S. offensive technology from the offense's point of view, done in an offense-conservative way says: U.S. offensive technology is weak; the Soviet estimate of U.S. offensive technology, done in a defense-conservative way says: U.S. offensive technology is strong.) The solution to the problem is this: Each technology is in fact either weak or strong, or in between, no matter that each side assesses it differently. What has to be done is to look at a balance between offense-conservative and defense-conservative estimates. The defense is not likely to be as bad as the defense-conservative calculation indicates, nor as good as the offense-conservative calculation indicates. Conversely, the offense is never as bad as the offense-conservative calculation

Table 21.1

U.S. estimate	Soviet estimate
U.S. offense technology is weak (offense-conservative)	U.S. offense technology is strong (defense-conservative)
U.S. defense technology is weak (defense-conservative)	U.S. defense technology is strong (offense-conservative)
Soviet offense technology is strong (defense-conservative)	Soviet offense technology is weak (offense-conservative)
Soviet defense technology is strong (offense-conservative)	Soviet defense technology is weak (defense-conservative)

indicates, nor as good as the defense-conservative calculation indicates. This is summarized in Table 2. The point is basic and simple, but is often lost sight of, when advocacy rather than analysis is the objective. Most arguments about ABM involve some degree of violation of this logical point.

In addition to logic, facts are needed for the comparison. It is possible that gaps in technology do exist. Some are obvious, such as the gap in ICBM technology between the CPR and the U.S. Others may be less obvious. When real technology gaps exist, they are important, at least for a time. Technology comparisons are important for estimating capabilities in the future, because the technology of today fundamentally determines the quality of the forces in being five to ten years from now. In the short run, however, forces in being (which were determined by the technology and the deployment decisions of five years or more ago) determine net comparisons.

OFFENSE CONSERVATIVE (HIGH CONFIDENCE) PENETRATION METHODS

The methods most certain to penetrate a defense are two: interceptor exhaustion, and leakage. Interceptor exhaustion is simply the tactic of attacking with more warheads than the defense has interceptors, and to do this in such a way that the defense must expend at least one interceptor per warhead, that is, to deny the defense multiple kill of warheads. This is, on principle, an absolutely sure method, and it is the most expensive method. It

Table 21.2

Defense-conservative calculation:	*Offense-conservative calculation:*
overestimates offense capability	underestimates offense capability
underestimates defense capabilities	overestimates defense capability

is absolutely sure (at least on principle) because once the defense has run out of interceptors, the defense is finished, and the offense can attack where it will. It is the most expensive, because it matches offense warheads with interceptor warheads and, roughly, offense payload with defense payload. The most serious difficulty with the method is that the number of interceptors available to the defense is not known with certainty.

Leakage works differently. It counts on the fact that the defense is not perfect at any time of the engagement, but can only intercept and kill some fraction of attacking warheads. What this fraction is, whether twenty or ninety-five percent, or in between, is an important question. It will be discussed below. But whatever it is (unless it be one hundred percent which no one believes to be correct) there will be some level of attack which will let a certain number of attacking warheads slip through. Those that slip through hit targets. *How much this matters depends on the job of the defense.* If the job is defense of cities, then this slipping through is serious. If the job is to defend missile silos it is serious only if the warheads that slip through damage or destroy the radars of the hardpoint defense.

One way to reduce the effectiveness of leakage penetration is to put in several layers of defense, as in Safeguard. Here, those warheads which leaked through the first layer are attacked by the second layer of defense.

A disadvantage (or confidence reducing factor) of a leakage attack is the fact that the attacker must estimate the kill probability of the defense. It makes an enormous difference to the leakage rate whether the kill probability is twenty or ninety-five percent. There is not much likelihood that the Soviets, or Chinese Communists, will find it easy to measure the kill probability of Safeguard. They will have to estimate it.

Another high confidence penetration method against an area defense is the FOBS (fractional orbital bombardment system). Because it comes over the horizon in a very shallow trajectory, it reduces the area which can be covered by the area defense. Again the importance of this effect depends on the job of the defense. If the job is to protect hard points, or a few large population centers, a protection against FOBS is feasible.

PENETRATION METHODS OF LOW CONFIDENCE

There exists a whole host of penetration methods of lesser confidence than those discussed above. They include decoys, chaff, jammers, nuclear blackout, and others. These methods must be considered seriously when making the defense-conservative estimate. These methods *might* work, and so the *defense calculation must* take them into account. On the other hand, they *might not* work, and so an offense-conservative *offense calculation* must *not* take them into account.

The effectiveness of these types of methods can be estimated only if certain crucial properties of the defense are known, particularly how much knowledge the defense has of discrimination technology, and the extent to which this discrimination technology is implemented in the defense system. The offense can make some estimate of the defense's *knowledge* of discrimination technology, by estimating the capability of the ABM research radars of the defense, but the offense does *not* know with *high reliability* how much of this discrimination knowledge has been *implemented.* The effectiveness of the "low confidence" pen aids depends crucially on the quality of discrimination technology implemented by the defense, and may range from total and complete effectiveness to total lack of effectiveness. In fact, the chief purpose of low confidence pen aids is to force the defense to become more sophisticated, to deny *it* a "free ride."

The pen aids of lower confidence listed above have always been favorites of opponents of ABM. Such pen aids are always easily invented, usually "on the back of an envelope," and they "always work." As part of the large U.S. Pen Aids R&D effort mentioned above, an enormous variety of decoys, chaff and of other pen aids has been built and flown for years against an extremely well instrumented R&D facility in the Kwajalein Atoll. The overwhelming majority of these pen aids tested have been ineffective. The few that have survived this screening and that can be usefully introduced into the inventory have taken many years (and the expensive Kwajalein facility) to develop. It was neither cheap nor simple nor fast. In addition, this research has provided an impressive catalog of discrimination methods effective against many of these penetration aids.

Low confidence penetration methods are only useful if they are the outcome of a large R&D effort. The purchase price of these items finally put on missiles may be low, but the R&D price to get them was very high, and so was the time it took to get them.

One of the arguments much heard against Safeguard deployment is that the CPR could easily and quickly provide its missiles with pen aids which would make Safeguard useless. This argument completely ignores the difficulties of getting such pen aids, and of getting them to be effective. Any country that wishes to design and build high confidence penetration aids must have research radars of sophistication and complexity comparable to the radars of the defense which the missile with its penetration aids is supposed to go against. If the defense radars are sufficiently sophisticated and complex, then the penetration aid research radars must be of comparable sophistication and complexity to yield a penetration aid of reasonable performance. It is absurd to suppose that Communist China or any other third country can quickly or cheaply develop a radar capability comparable to that of the U.S. in this field. On the other hand, if this type of pen aids R&D effort has not gone on, the penetration aids cannot be of a high quality, and *we* and *everyone else would know* this fact. Therefore, such penetration aids would not provide a credible threat.

POSSIBLE CATASTROPHIC FAILURES

It is perhaps useful to make a few remarks about possible catastrophic failure modes of the defense. These are things that might happen and that would make the defense totally ineffective. A significant catastrophic failure mode might be that the authorization to fire "never comes." Others can be imagined. They all have several things in common. First of all, they are real threats, and a conscientious defense builder will examine each of them and will "fix" them as well as possible. Second, the attacker cannot count on any of them. While they have the highest effect when they work, they are also the least reliable.

The Capabilities of Safeguard

SOME "GROUND RULES"

Let us limit our attention to hard point defense, to area defense against attacks of moderate size and sophistication, and to defense against an attack of very few (accidental) launches of high sophistication. I believe that the defense of cities against a large, sophisticated, well-designed and executed attack is not really worthwhile. (For a different estimate, see Chapter 5). Another "ground rule" that we have invoked is to insist on logical symmetry in our viewpoint, and to avoid basing our final conclusions only on one-sidedly conservative estimates.

Whenever anyone assesses the probable performance of any complex type of hardware, he needs to know three things:

1. How similar is the hardware to its predecessors, that is, how big a step was taken in developing the hardware to be evaluated;

2. What do test data show so far, and how far "up the learning curve" are they, that is, how much improvement can be expected; and

3. What technological growth is possible for the hardware, to overcome difficulties encountered during its service life, or to counter enemy counters to the equipment.

The risk in developing a complex hardware item for actual deployment depends greatly on the first and last of the three factors just mentioned. If the new hardware is too similar to its predecessor, then the risk is low, to be sure, but then there is also no point in developing the new hardware. If the new hardware is too far ahead of its predecessor, if the step to be taken is too great, then the risk is too high. The wise choice lies in between. The new hardware to be deployed should be an improvement over existing types, but should not go all the way to the most advanced concepts and techniques which are being studied.

New hardware should, at the time of a deployment decision, have some growth potential, so that the new system can evolve to keep pace with a changing threat, and does not get frozen into an ineffective posture.

A comment is required here about the usefulness of test data. It is often alleged that an ABM system is, by its very nature, untestable, and can therefore be expected to fail catastrophically from any one of many causes. This argument is basically incorrect (type III error) and is fundamentally irrelevant. *No strategic weapon system can be tested realistically in a nuclear war environment whether the system is defensive or offensive. Just as the ABM cannot be tested with full realism, so neither can the offense which must penetrate the ABM be tested with full realism.* It may be said that ABM is peculiarly vulnerable, much more so than the offense. Those who have to concern themselves professionally with the hardness of the offense against attack would probably not agree. We have here another example of the unbalanced judgment which can be obtained by looking only at a defense-conservative estimate. In fact, there are serious uncertainties on both sides, and both sides must constantly concern themselves with reducing the gap of uncertainty in the performance of their systems.

In what follows below we will examine each subsystem of Safeguard with respect to its technological ancestors, its test status, and its growth potential. In addition, we will examine very briefly some of the arguments that have been made throwing doubt on the ability of the subsystems to function properly. We will close with an equivalent discussion of the system as a whole.

THE PAR

At present the PAR is being brass boarded, that is, a fully functioning model is being built that will, however, not use the final packaging of the parts. Components have been tested. The technological ancestors are many and illustrious: Phased array radars have been studied in the U.S. in detail since the work at Lincoln Laboratory, MIT, (approximately 1958 onward), and several advanced types have been built, e.g., ESAR, Typhon, ADAR, the now operational FPS-85 (which is in important ways similar to the PAR), and the Nike X MAR radar. The degree of risk in building PAR is very slight. The radar has considerable growth potential. Its power can be increased, and more sophisticated ways to transmit and process radar signals (now in R&D) can be installed.

Critics have claimed that some penetration aids are easily employed to make the PAR useless. They overestimate the ease with which such pen aids are developed and deployed, and give the PAR no growth potential at all (Type III error). Others have estimated that the average availability of PAR would be poor. Yet experience has shown that a system as complex as the DEW line had 99.8 percent of its equipment available between 1959 and 1964, except for a few months, when overall equipment availability was lower, but never below 99.6 percent.[6] Present performance is comparable.

6. W.G. Donaldson, 8th MIL E Con., Washington, D.C. Sept. 14, 1964. Publ. in *Electrical Communications*, 40, 369, 1965.

THE MSR

Because its functions are more complex than the PAR, to reduce risk, an early MSR was tested in White Sands. Another is being tested in Kwajalein. Otherwise, the MSR has the same general ancestry as PAR, and similar growth potential.

SPARTAN

The Spartan missile is a moderately scaled-up version of the Nike Zeus missile, but improved in several ways. A successful test-firing program has been going on for over a year, which will be continued. A number of growth-directions are available for Spartan, especially a longer range. Development risk is small. Some critics have claimed availability factors of thirty-five to sixty percent, and on this basis have assumed that three to ten interceptors have to be allocated per attacking warhead to have a high probability of interception. These assumptions are wrong in two important ways. First of all, interceptor availability can be counted on to be higher than what they assume. Second, most failures of interceptors occur at launch or in the early parts of the trajectory. Therefore, should an interceptor fail at launch or early in flight, another interceptor can be launched to take its place. Hence, in normal operation, between one and two interceptors per warhead are required. This makes a dramatic difference in the defense of hard points against large attacks, or in the area defense against unsophisticated attacks.

SPRINT

Sprint has been in a very good test program since 1965. These tests will continue at Kwajalein. Growth potential is excellent. A "hotter" interceptor technology, Hibex, is now available, should it become required. The risk of development is minimal.

THE COMPUTER, COMMAND AND CONTROL SYSTEM

This is the heart of the whole system which integrates all the rest. Much has been made by ABM opponents of the difficulties of making this part of the system work effectively. But Safeguard does not start from scratch. The Kwajalein complex once had a completely integrated piece of Nike Zeus, which was functionally practically equivalent to a Nike Zeus battery, complete with Zeus missiles, with four types of radars, one ZAR (Zeus acquisition radar), two TTR's (target track radars), one DR (discrimination radar) and several MTR's (missile track radars), all tied together by a computer, which did all the things such computers need to do. The U.S. will have a similarly complete complex at Kwajalein for checking out any bugs in the computer which is now being built. Opponents of ABM seem to confuse the problem of building an ABM battery with its computing center, which is not so terribly hard but is essential, with the problem of netting all the batteries together, which is harder, but not essential. This degree of netting is, in fact, one of the important possible growth areas for the system. Another confusion about risks concerns the use of time-sharing in the ABM computers. There is a wide range of possible degrees of time-sharing and while it is true that some of the extreme forms of time-sharing are still research problems, other, lesser forms of time sharing are commercially available now, earlier difficulties notwithstanding. The early forms of ABM computing will, no doubt, be comparatively simple. But as time goes on, better and more sophisticated computing will become feasible, and could be installed if required. This form of soft-ware growth of an ABM system implies considerable growth potential in performance, and is one of the most important advantages of the defense.

THE OVER-ALL SYSTEM AND ITS CAPABILITIES

As the component subsystems discussed above go through their test phases, more attention will properly focus on overall system integration and its many problems. The Phase I deployment will offer an excellent opportunity to work out the various problems which will arise. There is no real reason to suppose that a system will be fielded that will not be effective in doing the jobs assigned to it. Virtually all objections of informed critics seem to have erred either in fact or in logic or both. I believe that the verdict on their charges must be "not proven".

Does Safeguard Solve Problems Worth Solving?

In the section above entitled What Is the Job of ABM?, we posed the real issue of defense deployment as:

1. does having the defense solve problems that are worth solving?, and
2. what other consequences (good or bad) does installing the defense have?

We now return briefly to these two most important questions.

It is clear that any serious approach to the issues of national security is one in which arms control must play a large role. We have all learned in the recent past the need to control, limit and, if possible, reduce the burdens which an arms race would put on the peoples of the world. We need to reduce the likelihood of war, and we need to try to reduce the destructiveness of war if it should break out. At the same time we must preserve U.S. military strength commensurate with the requirements of U.S. foreign policy.

Therefore, weapons systems should be designed to avoid accelerating the arms race, to avoid increasing the fears of war, and to reduce the likelihood of war.

Beginning in the late 50's and early 60's we learned that in a bipolar nuclear world, a secure deterrent was the key factor providing stability. We learned that offensive weapons systems should be able to survive a surprise attack by an enemy, and that therefore ICBM's should be in hard silos, that bombers should have the ability to take off in time to avoid being hit on the ground, and that submarines with ballistic missiles should be able to hide in the oceans of the world. This approach has worked well so far.

We are now, however, moving into an era which differs from the early and middle 60's in several important ways. First of all, there has been an unfortunate diffusion of nuclear weapons. Second, the Soviet Union has begun to deploy ballistic missile defense, and the U.S. has decided to do so also. Third, the Soviet Union has approached parity with the U.S. in the number of ICBM's, and has probably more payload in these ICBM's than the U.S. Fourth, the U.S. has begun development of the MIRV, and will probably deploy this.

These and other changes affect in a significant way the national security problem and hence the problem of defense and of arms control.

Many arms controllers still say that "the only good ABM is no ABM". This was probably true in the early 60's when there were only two large nuclear missile powers, the U.S. and the Soviet Union. At that time a posture without missile defense deployed by either had some advantages. But this seems no longer correct. In fact, I am convinced that the most weighty reasons in favor of the deployment of an ABM of a certain type are arms control reasons.

To keep the tone of the discussion neutral, I propose to talk about two countries, A and B, with large missile forces and several countries, C, D, etc., with small missiles forces. What are some of the large concerns country A, say, should have? Country A would surely be concerned about some of the following dangers:

1. An accidental or unauthorized launch of a few ICBM's by country A, which is interpreted as an all-out attack by country B. Then country B tries to pre-empt with an all-out strike against A; or,

2. In a very serious crisis between A and B, B threatens to attack a few targets in A, to demonstrate B's seriousness, or, finally,

3. A third nuclear power, C threatens either A or B, to force A or B to comply with some desire of C.

Any posture designed to handle the above three threat situations should also have the feature that it not accelerate the arms race between A and B, and in particular that it give neither A nor B a credible first-strike capability against the other.

One should therefore devise a defense system which has the following properties:

1. The defense should be good enough to take care of a few attacking missiles from anywhere. This would take care of an accidental or unauthorized launch, and would thus reduce the danger of an accidental war very substantially. *Both* A and B would find such a system useful to have.

2. The defense should be good enough to make incredible a threat by A to attack B in a small way, as a "demonstration of seriousness." Such a defense would have the effect of raising the stakes in such a situation. The "demon-

stration" would either fail or would have to be a large attack. Therefore such a defense system would act as a "fire break" in an extremely serious crisis, and would give both sides a chance to cool off, and to negotiate their way out of the crisis. *Both* A and B would find such a defense useful to have.

3. The system should be good enough to reduce the credibility of a nuclear threat by a third party C against A or B. *Both* A and B should find such a defense useful to have.

4. The system should not be good enough to stop a second strike by either A or B, hence it would not imperil mutual deterrence. *Neither* A nor B should feel threatened by such a system, and hence the system should not accelerate the arms race.

It seems that a thin area defense like Safeguard would satisfy these requirements, and thus help solve some significant problems of national security.

Let me recapitulate here briefly why a "thick city" defense is not attractive compared to the "thin area" defense.

The "thin area" defense, such as Safeguard and the "thick city" defense are really limiting cases of ABM. They provide significant benchmarks of real systems. Each of these systems is rated in Table 3 in terms of several sets of standards. Consider some of the entries of Table 3 briefly. The thin system is *no* help in confrontation with a large sophisticated attack, and the thick system, *not much* help. The thin system is quite effective against an unsophisticated attack, the thick system is more effective than is necessary. Both systems provide marginal, though possibly important, advantages in times of serious crisis, accident, etc. Both systems provide fire breaks in very serious crises, because they make small token attacks, made for bargaining purposes, ineffective and not credible. Finally, the thin system is much less likely than the thick system to exacerbate the arms race with the Soviet Union, or to induce miscalculations in the U.S. or the Soviet Union concerning its effectiveness. A "thick" defense buys too little for the probable cost, and would exacerbate the arms race with the Soviet Union. A thick system also could mislead a future U.S. leadership into thinking that the defense system was really better than was supposed, and hence encourage more risk-taking than is desirable.

Finally a remark about other consequences of deployment of a thin area defense. These are treated extensively in other chapters of this volume. I would like to comment only on one aspect. One of the standard arguments against a thin defense system is that deployment of the system will ruin the chances of serious arms limitation discussions with the Soviet Union. There is no evidence available that such a deployment would jeopardize these talks. Furthermore, Soviet military thought and Soviet weapon system implementation are well known to be heavily oriented in favor of defense systems. There seems to be no reason to suppose that the Soviets would consider a thin ABM system as any kind of threat to them. In fact, I think it is likely that they will consider a thin ABM system desirable for them for the reasons mentioned

Table 21.3. Effectiveness of Thin Area Defense (TAD) and Thick City Defense (TCD)

	TAD	TCD
Against Sophisticated Attack (by Soviet Union)		
effect on Soviet war planning	small effect.	increases Soviet planning problem.
effect on deterrence of Soviets	no effect.	some effect.
effect on war outcome	no effect.	small to medium effect.
Against Unsophisticated Attack (e.g., CPR)		
effect on war planning by CPR	strong effect.	very strong effect.
effect on deterrence of CPR by U.S.	makes threats by CPR not credible.	unnecessarily good.
effect on war fighting by CPR	very good defense.	unnecessarily good.
Other Aspects		
effect on large irrational attacks	provides poor defense.	provides good defense.
effect on small irrational attacks	provides good defense.	provides too good defense.
effect on accidents	provides good defense.	provides too good defense.
stimulation of arms race with Soviet Union	small or zero.	large.
fire break in large crises	yes.	yes.
danger of miscalculation by U.S.	small.	large.

above, and that they would find it possible to understand our reasons for deploying Safeguard.

Note on "Blackout"

It may be useful to say a word about "blackout." A nuclear explosion above the ground produces a "cloud" consisting of fragments of the nuclear weapon and ionized air. This cloud may absorb, reflect, or deflect radar waves, making it difficult or impossible for the radar to see behind the cloud. The area coverage and duration of the cloud depends on the altitude of the nuclear burst, its yield, the radar operating frequency (and related technical characteristics), and the object observed.

How much these clouds interfere with the defense depends on their timing and spacing in relation to the location of the defense, and the timing and spacing of the attack. The attack levels at which blackout is a problem can be estimated reasonably well (based on pre-1963 atmosphere tests and later related experiments) to assess the minimum defense capability. A blackout penetration is, however, fraught with major uncertainties about both the timing of the attack, and defense radar design and tactics.

22. ABM Won't Kill Kids

SANFORD ARANOFF and
EDWARD S. BOYLAN

IN LIGHT OF Ernest Sternglass' warning that such action would result in "The Death of All Children" (*Esquire*, September 1969), there are only two reasons why *Esquire* readers should not view the recent vote in the Senate, supporting deployment of ABM, with dismay: a) there is no reason to believe Sr-90 from radioactive fallout has resulted in the death of any children; b) in any case, the presence of ABM would tend to reduce the total amount of radiation resulting from a nuclear attack.

Such statements may seem hard to believe in view of the seemingly convincing evidence Professor Sternglass offered supporting his thesis that Sr-90 from atmospheric nuclear testing has resulted in the death of one child per hundred infants born. If one turns to other sources besides Dr. Sternglass, however, it soon becomes clear that his "evidence" consists mostly of inaccurate quotations and rather misleading statistics. Perhaps the clearest way of illustrating this is to contrast Dr. Sternglass' claims with the findings of other experts in other sources.

Sternglass

1. "There was no change in the infant death rate in 1946—the year after the Trinity test—but by 1950 the rate in Texas, Arkansas, Louisiana, Mississippi, Alabama, Georgia and both Carolinas deviated upward from normal expectancy. Increases in excess of infant mortality of some twenty to thirty percent occurred . . . in Arkansas, Louisiana and Alabama."

2. "The infant mortality rate began to level off sharply in the Eastern, Midwestern and Southern states within two years after the onset of atomic testing in Nevada in 1951, while it continued steadily downward in the dry Western states."

3. "In contrast to New York, the fetal death rate for California—upwind of the Nevada test site, and therefore not affected by it—continued its steady decline in line with the 1935–50 figures."

4. "by 1950 a clear change toward excess infant mortality appeared in the states over which the fallout cloud had drifted, and only in those states."

5. "K. G. Luning . . . [injected] small amounts of Sr-90 . . . into male mice . . . [which] produced an in-

Other Sources

1. White infant mortality rates continued to decline, at the same rate through 1956, in Texas, Alabama and Mississippi. In Louisiana and North Carolina white infant mortality rates leveled off after 1950. "Recent Change in Infant Mortality Trend" by Dr. I. Moriyama (*Public Health Rep.* 75:391–405, May 1960).[1]

2. As given in 1. above, white infant mortality rates in the South continued declining steadily through 1956. The white rates in Maine and nonwhite rates in Massachusetts also showed no leveling off. In the West, Oklahoma's infant mortality rates, white and nonwhite, leveled off in 1945. Utah and Colorado leveled off after 1950, while Montana leveled off after 1951. (Dr. Moriyama, *ibid.*)

3. The infant mortality rate for California leveled off after 1950 for whites, after 1951 for nonwhites. Oregon's infant mortality rate leveled off after 1950. (Dr. Moriyama, *ibid.*)

4. Dr. Sternglass' own reference, *Day of Trinity* by L. Lamont (Atheneum, New York, 1965) indicates the radioactive cloud went in a northerly, not an easterly direction. The state receiving the bulk of the fallout was New Mexico, where infant mortality rates declined almost 40% below expected value.

5. The "small" amount of Sr-90 was 18 microcuries, roughly a million times as much Sr-90 as was

1. Dr. Moriyama estimated when a change in trend occurred only by eye. This gives a feel, however, when significant changes did, or did not, occur. Results were presented mainly in tables, making direct quotations impossible.

Sternglass	Other Sources
crease in fetal deaths among their offspring."	found per liter of milk in 1961–64. The effect of the Sr-90 on the mice wore off in about 6 weeks.
6. "fetal deaths and congenital malformations [were caused] in the offspring of female mice injected with Sr-90 before and during pregnancy."	6. Regardless of its effect on mice, Sr-90 has caused little change in infant deaths due to congenital malformations. The rate of infant deaths due to congenital malformations "has changed little in almost a quarter of a century." (P.H.S. Pub. #1000, Ser. 3, No. 4, p. 10.)
7. "an international conference devoted entirely to infant mortality in 1965 [observed that] none of the factors so far considered—medical care, population movement, new drugs, pesticides, smoking or epidemics of infectious disease— suffices to explain the observed facts."	7. The international conference, which lasted only two days, did not consider what effect, if any, drugs, pesticides, smoking or epidemics had on infant mortality rates. The following quotation from the summary report of the conference (P.H.S. #1000, Ser. 4, No. 3) reveals how restricted were their conclusions. "In some areas, especially those associated with medical aspects, data were not available for the evaluation of their impact on infant and perinatal rates."
8. "direct quantitative correlations between Sr-90 and infant mortality . . . will be published . . . in the Proceedings of the 9th Annual Hanford Biology Symposium."	8. Dr. Sternglass' paper to the Hanford Symposium offers *no* quantitative correlations between Sr-90 and infant mortality.
9. ". . . the U.S. must be prepared to launch some 5,000 to 15,000 ABM's . . . [and since] each Spartan missile [has] a warhead of at least 2 megatons . . . use of this system . . . would require the detonation of some 10,000 to 30,000 megatons into the stratosphere . . ."	9. The total number of defensive missiles scheduled to be deployed is approximately 1,000, the bulk of which are Sprint missiles, having a warhead in the kiloton range. (See any *New York Times* article describing the proposed Safeguard ABM system.)

Points 1, 2, and 3 illustrate how misleading Dr. Sternglass' "results" are. Infant mortality rates in the South did level off after the Trinity blast. However, it was only non-white infant mortality rates which changed. For the most part white infant mortality rates continued to decline as if they had

granting that "excess" mortality occurred, it is improper to disregard
ctors, such as insecticides, smoking, new (more resistant) germs, etc.,
nay also affect infant mortality rates. It is true, as Dr. Sternglass is
observing (though, as we have seen in point 7 above, he does over-
e case) that none of these factors is believed to entirely account for
r performance of the United States (vis-a-vis other countries) in lower-
nt mortality rates. This does not mean they can be disregarded, how-
nless the effects of smoking, insecticides, etc. can be filtered out, it is
to measure the influence Sr-90 has on infant mortality rates.

over, certain causes of death, such as birth injuries and accidents are
ly unconnected with Sr-90. Congenital malformations is another
f death whose rate of occurrence has remained remarkably constant
)40 (there are minor changes when incidence in white or nonwhites
e considered, but they balance each other out). In his appearance on
ay show on NBC-TV, Dr. Sternglass claimed that one mechanism by
ir-90 "killed" infants was through congenital malformations. Why
sn't the rate climbed sharply since 1945? On the other hand, if Sr-90
t cause congenital malformations, then this factor too must be dis-
before examining what effect, if any, Sr-90 has an infant mortality
Congenital malformations, birth injuries and accidents together cause
25% of all infant deaths.)

cientific evidence Dr. Sternglass offers in support of his thesis that
uses genetic damage actually, as we have seen in points 5 and 6
asts doubt on his thesis. Mice given dosages of Sr-90 roughly a miles as large as Americans drank in a liter of milk had the fetal death
heir offspring rise to 12.25 per cent, as compared to rates of 7.82 and
cent for control groups. How great an effect could a dose only one
h the size have? Moreover, the reproductive organs of mice are closer
bone structure than is the case in man. This means that the Sr-90,
ould stay mostly in the bone structure, would tend to cause much
netic damage in mice. The offspring of female mice injected with
d show a rise in fetal deaths and congenital malformations but, in
the fact that the death rate from congenital malformations has re-
essentially constant for 25 years, this indicates Sr-90 has not had an
infant mortality rates.

possibility remains to be discussed, however. Small continuous
of Sr-90, as would be received by a person drinking milk, might
mulative damage where a single large dose might not. Two distinct
nts, performed independently and separately of one another investi-
is question. In one experiment, described in *Nature* (Vol. 137, pp.
February 16, 1963), female miniature swine were given feed con-
arying dosages of Sr-90 daily, including dosages high enough to kill
the swine. No significant effect was found in the offspring of these
wine, neither a marked change in birth weight nor in the number of

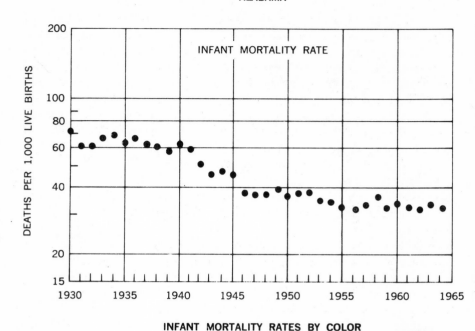

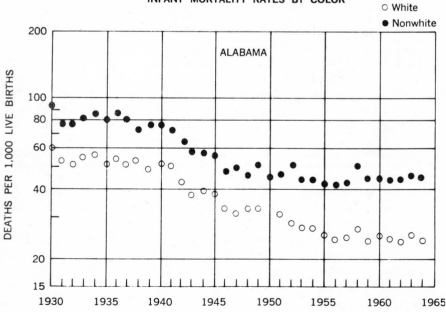

never heard of Sr-90 or Ernest Sternglass. (We reproduced the behavior of Alabama as an example.)

Unless Dr. Sternglass has data that shows Negroes in the South drink much more milk than whites, or are more susceptible to genetic damage from Sr-90, it is clear that causes other than Sr-90 affected nonwhite infant mortality rates. In the opposite direction, states which by Dr. Sternglass' own admission did not experience significant amounts of fallout, such as California, had their infant mortality rates level off sharply by 1951.

This data above indicates how doubtful it is that Sr-90 is the villain causing the leveling off of infant mortality rates. It is important, however, that numerous other flaws in Dr. Sternglass' method be pointed out, if only that other men at other times do not err in the same manner.

Perhaps the most important point to emphasize is that there is no correlation between increases in Sr-90 levels and increases in infant mortality. Infant mortality rates have risen only twice since 1950 while Sr-90 levels have increased in far more years. What Dr. Sternglass attempts to connect is Sr-90 levels and "excess" infant mortalities. By "excess" deaths is meant the difference between a computer predicted infant mortality rate and the actual mortality rate. Moreover, Dr. Sternglass looks at the percent excess infant mortality, which makes comparisons between states and between predicted and experienced rates somewhat difficult. If the predicted rate is 20 and 22 deaths per thousand actually occur there is a 10% excess infant mortality. If the predicted rate is 10 and 12 deaths per thousand occurs, there is a 20% excess mortality. In either case, however, the most deaths Sr-90 could have "caused" would be 2 per thousand.

Even neglecting Dr. Sternglass' use of per cent excess mortality, perhaps the most striking aspect of Dr. Sternglass' efforts is that he presents no statistical data correlating infant mortality and Sr-90 levels (in milk, on the ground, etc.). Contrary to his promise, Dr. Sternglass' paper to the Hanford Symposium contains no correlations, no statistics, no concrete quantitative examination of the relationship between Sr-90 levels and changes in infant mortality. He only presents charts reflecting the behavior over time of Sr-90 levels and percentage excess infant mortality for a few selected states. There is no attempt to examine what relationship, in different states, there is between Sr-90 levels and excess infant mortality. He does provide a table giving, among other things, average Sr-90 levels in milk and excess infant mortality rates for 12 states. An examination of the table showed that there was no simple, strong correlation between Sr-90 levels and excess infant mortality. New York, with a Sr-90 level of 16, had 82.1% excess infant mortality. Massachusetts, with a Sr-90 level of 22, had 50.3% excess infant mortality. Georgia, with a Sr-90 level of 24, had 103.9% excess infant mortality. Louisiana, with a Sr-90 level of 33, had 90% excess infant mortality.

We reproduced an abridged version of Dr. Sternglass' table:

	Sr-90 In Milk (pc/L)	Percen
Massachusetts	22	
Pennsylvania	18	
Illinois	14	
New York	16	
Georgia	24	
Mississippi	26	
Missouri	17	
Louisiana	33	
Wyoming	14	
New Mexico	7	
Idaho	16	
Colorado	13	

There was, to a certain extent, a weak correlation bet excess mortality. Roughly speaking, a state with a "lo have "low" excess infant mortality. As the examination ever, it is far from a linear or a simple relationship. M the actual infant mortality rates instead of the artific infant mortality, a negative correlation holds, i.e. gene with "high" Sr-90 levels had "low" infant mortality ra clude from this that Sr-90 causes low infant mortality last example illustrates the hazards of drawing strong tive or negative correlations, especially when the total is small.

It must be made clear, before leaving the topic of that the entire method of "predicting" what infant mo be and declaring deviations from these predictions highly questionable. There is no rule of nature which mortality rates must forever decline at a constant or Dr. Sternglass' own efforts illustrates the hazards of su attempt to dramatize the "effect" of the Trinity test, basis of rates from 1940–45, what infant mortality rates 1950, and then computed what excess infant mortality 1950. He secondly noted that the only states having sig mortality were those "downwind" of Alamogordo. (To b other states, but he can explain their behavior as we observe, however, is that in over 20 states his calcu what the infant mortality rate "should" have been by 1 words, in states where Sr-90 was not a factor the "pre more than 10% in approximately half the states. How place in a prediction that isn't valid as often as it is val "predictor" of what the rates "should" be, deviations unreliable as well. Correlations based upon them, questionable.

Ev other whicl fond state the p ing in ever. difficu

Mo obvio cause since alone the Te which then h does counte rates. rough

The Sr-90 above, lion ti rate of 9.05 p million to thei which more g Sr-90 view o maine effect

One dosage cause experi gated 670–67 taining some o female

aborted fetuses occurred. In *Nuclear Science Abstracts,* November 15, 1968, abstract #45457 reports of an experiment where mice were fed water containing .001 microcuries of Sr-90 per milliliter of water (an amount much higher than that contained in cow's milk in 1958). The results, following such a diet, included "lengthening of life-span, superiority of total numbers of litters" (as compared to a control group). It is true that large doses of Sr-90 (.01 or .1 microcures of Sr-90 per milliliter) did cause considerable genetic damage. The main point, however, is that mice being given continuous concentrations of Sr-90 at levels much above those experienced by Americans through drinking milk, and above levels one might expect even from a massive nuclear war, caused no harm, indeed *improved* the breed. We are not advocating Sr-90 be added to the diet, only noting that life is more complex than Dr. Sternglass would like it to be.

Well then, we can imagine Dr. Sternglass asking, why hasn't the U.S. mortality rate continued to decline from 1950 onward, as it did previously? Why did the mortality rates continue to decline in other West European countries? These are difficult questions, and the authors of this article do not claim to know the answers to them. Because we do not have a good answer, however, does not mean we must accept Dr. Sternglass' solution. There may not be one single simple reason why the United States has done so poorly, recently, in lowering infant mortality rates. Smoking, pesticides, resistant strains of germs, poor health conditions in the ghettoes, all of these factors cause infant mortality rates in the U.S. to be (relatively) poor. Other, less obvious, factors also have an effect. Children born to young, teenage women have poorer mortality rates than those born to older women. Can we blame an increase in the number of teenage mothers on Sr-90?

We do not claim that the evidence we have presented proves that Sr-90 does not have any adverse effect on infant mortality. Such a conclusion would require much experimentation and careful evaluation of test results. What does seem clear, however, is that there is no reasons at the present time to believe that Sr-90 has been harmful to infants or adults.

So far we have considered the "evidence" Dr. Sternglass has offered to substantiate his claim that Sr-90 has caused one infant death per hundred infants born. As we have seen, Dr. Sternglass has neglected to explain why white infant mortality rates have not been so badly affected and neglected to assess the effects of other causes of infant mortality, such as smoking and pesticides. Let us now turn to Dr. Sternglass' analysis of the genetic effect a large scale nuclear exchange would have.

Sr-90 to date, claims Dr. Sternglass, has caused one infant death per hundred infants born. A nuclear war would create at least one hundred times as much Sr-90, which would cause at least one hundred times the genetic damage, i.e., one hundred deaths per hundred infants born, the dreaded "death of all children." Such a conclusion, however, is based on a belief that the genetic damage done by Sr-90 is related in a linear fashion to the amount of Sr-90. One simply does not know if this is so. There may well be a "law of diminishing returns." For example, a 10 megaton hydrogen bomb will destroy less than twice the area destroyed by a 5 megaton bomb. The scientific experiments discussed above, where mice were given quantities of Sr-90 even higher than one would expect to result from a nuclear war did not cause such severe damage. This is not to say that the damage resulting from a massive nuclear exchange will not be considerable, or can be viewed as anything less than a catastrophe. However, Dr. Sternglass must produce much more evidence before he is justified in claiming that a nuclear war will result in genetic genocide.

Moreover, while spending much effort contemplating the damage Sr-90 may inflict, Dr. Sternglass spends little time considering how the effects of radioactivity might be avoided or overcome. The chief villain, apparently, is Sr-90 in milk. Adults of childbearing age might simplify stop or cut down on drinking milk until Sr-90 levels in milk decline declined. (This seems a rather cheap price to insure the future of humanity.) Fruits and vegetables can be washed. Cow's milk itself can be treated to reduce its radioactivity. One need not act like the residents of Nevil Shute's *On the Beach*, passively awaiting radioactive doom.

Finally, how is ABM related to Dr. Sternglass' thesis? Will the presence of ABM raise or reduce the total amount of Sr-90 produced by a nuclear exchange? As should come as no surprise, in view of the numerous flaws in his presentation of statistical and scientific facts, Dr. Sternglass' discussion of strategic matters contains many errors.

Dr. Sternglass' major strategic error is his assumption that the only value of ABM is to defend U.S. missile silos from a massive U.S.S.R. attack. It has other roles as well: to *deter* the Soviets from launching such an attack; to provide a framework for meaningful arms control agreements; to defend against unauthorized or accidental launches of Soviet ICBM's at American cities; to deter and defend against a Chinese ICBM attack. The amount of damage, genetic and otherwise, caused by a massive nuclear exchange between American and Russia will be enormous with or without ABM. The key question is—will ABM make such an exchange more or less likely? Opponents of ABM claim the Soviet Union will never launch a massive first strike because, following Dr. Sternglass' arguments, such an attack would result in the death of millions of unborn Russians as well. However, what if, for the reasons outlined above, the Russians do not accept the Sternglass thesis? In this case, even if Sternglass is correct, the Russians will not be deterred. The presence of an ABM system defending our Minuteman missile force would make a successful Soviet first strike more uncertain, and hence reduce the chances of the Soviets pursuing such a course. If the Russians do accept the Sternglass thesis, then they may well be reluctant to markedly increase their offensive forces, which would be necessary, in the presence of ABM, to insure a successful first strike. Thus, whether the Russians accept

the Sternglass thesis or not, an American ABM acts to reduce the likelihood
of a Soviet first strike.

Dr. Sternglass does not consider the possible consequences of an accidental or unauthorized launch of a Soviet ICBM aimed at a major American
city. Without ABM millions of Americans—children and adults—will lose
their lives immediately and violently. The political repercussions of such an
event might lead to further, perhaps massive nuclear exchanges. Thus, ABM
would be saving millions of lives and preventing or reducing the likelihood
of a massive nuclear war. (Those who doubt the likelihood of "accidents" are
advised to read "The Failure of Fail-Safe" by John Raser in *Trans-Action,*
January, 1969.) A deliberate Chinese attack may seem irrational, but when
one considers the "human wave" attacks in Korea, where men were squandered in attempts to gain military objectives, can one be sure that the Chinese
will not risk 100 million of their own to kill (say) 10 million Americans?

Will an American ABM system help or harm the forthcoming arms control talks? When one considers that the Russians have built their own ABM
system around Moscow, are continuing to test an advanced ABM missile and
have never objected to America deploying its own ABM (indeed, there have
been occasions where the Soviets *defended* the U.S. decision), it should be
obvious that ABM is unlikely to be a bar to meaningful arms control agreements. In fact, considering the traditional Soviet emphasis on defense, U.S.
insistence that neither side have ABM would be much more damaging to
the success of the talks. Moreover, by providing protection against "cheating,"
with ABM each side may be more willing to limit deployment of offensive
missiles. It should be noted that all these points argue in favor of deploying
Safeguard, regardless of the validity of Dr. Sternglass' thesis.

Would the presence of ABM mean that the radioactivity released in a
"first strike" would increase considerably? As we have seen in point 9 above,
Dr. Sternglass either is completely ignorant or completely misleading regarding the scope of the proposed Safeguard ABM system. Dr. Sternglass pictures
a system of some 5,000 to 15,000 interceptors each having a two megaton
warhead. The total number of missiles scheduled to be deployed is much
smaller than 5,000, nearer 1,000. The Spartan missile, which is one of the
two interceptors in the Safeguard system, does indeed have a large warhead.
The bulk of the interceptors, however, are Sprint missiles, which have low
yield warheads in the kiloton (1/1,000 of a megaton) range. If, say, a 50
kiloton ABM prevents a 10-megaton warhead from exploding then the total
radiation produced has decreased, not increased. Moreover, Dr. Sternglass
errs in only considering the megatonnage produced with and without ABM.
What is important, so far as production of Sr-90, is the fission component of
the explosion. Without much greater knowledge than we presently have regarding how "clean" or "dirty" the Soviet ICBM's are, it is far from certain
that ABM will cause more Sr-90 to be produced. Dr. Sternglass dismisses
the distinction between "clean" and "dirty" weapons by noting that radio-

active carbon 14 would be produced by clean weapons. Carbon 14 is very weakly radioactive and even Dr. Sternglass does not claim to have evidence linking carbon 14 with changes in infant mortality. Thus it is not at all clear as Dr. Sternglass would have us believe that ABM would increase the genetic damage caused as an aftereffect of a Russian first strike.

There may be some who feel that by making the public more aware of the hazards of nuclear war and by creating great public interest in the whole question of how dangerous is radioactive fallout, Dr. Sternglass has performed a useful public service, regardless of whether his thesis is correct or not. We cannot agree with this view. In arguing in favor of his thesis we believe Dr. Sternglass has resorted to means which must be repudiated by all responsible scientists, regardless of how praiseworthy are his ends. He has misrepresented the findings of an international conference, he has described scientific experiments in a misleading manner, he has neglected data which did not support his thesis.

Finally, even less defensible is Dr. Sternglass' attempt to influence the ABM decision. Issues of gravest national security should be resolved with as much reason and as little emotion as possible. In trying to panic the Senate and the American people by warning that ABM would cause "The Death of All Children" Dr. Sternglass was misusing his position and results in an attempt to influence one of the most important political decisions of recent years. Scientists have both the right and responsibility to speak out on crucial political questions, but they also have the responsibility to adhere to the high professional standards the public expects in their words as well as their work.

Index of Major Concepts

Various subjects, for instance, U.S. or Soviet policies, that are discussed throughout the volume are indexed only where such entries are likely to be of particular assistance to the reader.